LITERARY CULTURE AND U.S. IMPERIALISM

LITERARY CULTURE
AND U.S. IMPERIALISM

From the Revolution to World War II

JOHN CARLOS ROWE

OXFORD
UNIVERSITY PRESS

2000

OXFORD
UNIVERSITY PRESS

Oxford   New York
Athens   Auckland   Bangkok   Bogota   Bombay
Buenos Aires   Calcutta   Cape Town   Dar es Salaam
Delhi   Florence   Hong Kong   Istanbul   Karachi
Kuala Lumpur   Madras   Madrid   Melbourne
Mexico City   Nairobi   Paris   Singapore
Taipei   Tokyo   Toronto

and associated companies in
Berlin   Ibadan

Copyright © 2000 by John C. Rowe

Published by Oxford University Press, Inc.
198 Madison Avenue, New York, New York 10016

Oxford is a registered trademark of Oxford University Press

Library of Congress Cataloging-in-Publication Data
Rowe, John Carlos.
Literary culture and U.S. imperialism:
from the Revolution to World War II/John C. Rowe.
p. cm.
Includes bibliographical references and index.
ISBN 0-19-513150-9; ISBN 0-19-513151-7 (pbk.)
1. American literature—History and criticism.   2. Imperialism in literature.
3. Politics and literature—United States—History.   4. Literature and history—
United States—History.   5. United States—Foreign relations.   I. Title.
PS169.I45 R69   2000
810.9'358—dc21   00-025620

9 8 7 6 5 4 3 2 1

Printed in the United States of America
on acid-free paper

For my students

When we had looked well at all of this, we went to
the orchard and garden, which was such a wonderful
thing to see and walk in, that I was never tired of
looking at the diversity of the trees, and noting the
scent which each one had, and the paths full of roses
and flowers, and many fruit trees and native roses,
and the pond of fresh water. . . . Then the birds of
many kinds and breeds which came into the pond. I
say again that I stood looking at it and thought that
never in the world would there be discovered other
lands such as these, for at the time there was no
Peru, nor any thought of it. Of all these wonders that
I then beheld to-day all is overthrown and lost,
nothing left standing.

Bernal Díaz del Castillo,
The Discovery and Conquest of Mexico: 1517–1521,
trans. A. P. Maudslay

The Person Sitting in Darkness is almost sure to
say: "There is something curious about this—
curious and unaccountable. There must be two
Americas: one that sets the captive free, and one
that takes a once-captive's new freedom away from
him, and picks a quarrel with him with nothing to
found it on; then kills him to get his land."

Mark Twain,
"To the Person Sitting in Darkness" (1901)

Preface

This book grew out of my research on the special part played by U.S. culture in the conduct of, political protest against, and historical representation of the Vietnam War. In my efforts to understand the historical backgrounds of our foreign policies in Southeast Asia, I studied earlier examples of U.S. conduct toward peoples and territories considered "foreign," as well as the responses by writers and artists to formal U.S. policies. What began simply as the consideration of historical examples to test various claims to the unique or traditional aspects of our foreign policies in Southeast Asia eventually became a subject in its own right. This book is, then, an extended introduction to my next book, which will focus centrally on U.S. neoimperialism in the post–World War II period and deal with the many different media—film, television, music, literature, and computer technology—that have contributed to and at times challenged the global authority of the United States.

Much is written today about culture's role in imperialism both as it was practiced in the era of the great territorial empires controlled by European nation-states and as it has been redefined in our nominally "postcolonial" epoch, but there have been surprisingly few studies of how U.S. culture has contributed centrally to both kinds of imperialism. Of course, influential works on how the "internal colonization" of ethnic minorities and native peoples contributed to our quest for national identity have been fundamental to American Studies since the 1950s. Roy Harvey Pearce, Robert Berkhofer, Richard Drinnon, Richard Slotkin, Annette Kolodny, Reginald Horsman, and Jane Tompkins, among others, have argued convincingly that Manifest Destiny was an imperialist project that relied on hierarchies of race, class, and gender as arbitrary, rigorous, and inherently violent as those employed by the British, French, Dutch, Belgians, Spanish, Portuguese, Germans, and Italians in their colonial ventures around the globe. Yet little has been written to connect Manifest Destiny, antebellum slavery, and the economic racism and sexism in the industrialized Northeast, for example, with our foreign ventures in the South Pacific, the Philippines, China, Japan, Korea, Southeast Asia, the Caribbean and Latin America, and Africa.

This book examines the relationship between our "internal colonialism" and our more recognizably colonial ventures in foreign countries from the end of the eighteenth century to the 1940s. I do not conclude that there is a single connection between internal and external versions of U.S. colonial domination in this very large historical period. What justifies the length of this book and its many historical and textual examples is the variety of ways in which the United States has exercised and justified its imperial ambitions in the modern period. The same may be said for the cultural responses by U.S. writers and intellectuals to the idea of the United States as an imperial power. Some of the figures treated in the following chapters contribute directly, if not always self-consciously, to those imperial ambitions, as I try to show Charles Brockden Brown, Edgar Allan Poe, and Henry Adams do. Some of these authors aggressively criticize the United States for its imperialist policies and their impact on subjugated peoples and individual lives, as I claim for such recognized anti-imperialists as Herman Melville, Mark Twain, and W. E. B. Du Bois. Still other writers find themselves deeply divided between obligations to a certain national consensus and their outrage at specific failures of U.S. democracy, as I suggest John Rollin Ridge, Stephen Crane, Nick Black Elk and John Neihardt, and Zora Neale Hurston demonstrate. Stated abstractly, these judgments may sound reductive and categorical, but the following chapters reach such conclusions by way of interpretations focused on the historical and textual complexities of representative works by these authors. My critical judgments are certainly open to debate, but my purpose is to demonstrate the range of literary responses to ideological constraints within concrete historical circumstances.

Recognizing these three different modalities for the cultural response to U.S. imperialism, I also find a common concern in all these writers with the cultural means by which the United States has conducted very concrete colonial ventures both at home and abroad. From mere political rhetoric, such as was used to boost "free trade," "open doors," and "fair competition" to the violent imposition of lifestyles on unwilling people, as the United States did to Native Americans in the reservation period, U.S. imperialism has traditionally manipulated cultural and social psychological territories. Reginald Horsman observes that many nineteenth-century Americans "believed that the trappings of colonialism would ruin the republic" and also thought "non-Anglo-Saxon peoples" were "inferior peoples" who would also "ruin the republic."[1] Opposed both to territorial domination outside U.S. borders and to the admission into the United States of immigrants and their cultures, these nineteenth-century citizens, whose values would often be represented in various phases of our isolationist policies in this period, helped shape the ideology of cultural assimilation and adaptation to a mythical

"American" identity that distinguishes our entrance into global politics as a major power at the turn of the century.

Crucial to that American myth—composed of many different mythemes, including self-reliant individualism, masculine potency, technical ingenuity, and perseverance—were economic ideals of "free-enterprise" capitalism as the proper "test" of individual and national mettle. Under the banner of free trade, the United States developed a powerful and complicated ideology of "free-trade imperialism" that relied crucially upon the exportation of American culture, often in the form of democratic institutions and values. From the beads, medals, and certificates Lewis and Clark liberally bestowed on Native Americans, often bewildered or angered by such insubstantial gifts, to the consumer commodities and heavy industrial equipment we shipped to South Vietnam in a futile effort to "modernize" and "industrialize" President Diem's doomed regime, the United States has traditionally understood its foreign policies to be functions of its commercial ambitions. Even if we do not consider the conquest of foreign territory by the United States in the period of so-called Manifest Destiny or in this century, its ideological rationalization has always been to "encourage free trade" and "economic competition"—to export, in other words, the practices and values of laissez-faire capitalism to convert people into consumers and thereby expand markets.

Among other cultural products of modern capitalism, literature has been especially important in representing such powerful economic and political interests as the "nation," "people," "government," or "way of life." This is not to say, of course, that literature is always an *effect* of economic and ideological forces. One of my points in this book is to show how U.S. writers have relied on literary discourse, especially in a period dominated by print technology, to challenge and criticize our imperial ambitions and practices. In the following chapters, I try to show how from the late eighteenth century to the middle of the twentieth century literature in some cases performed ideological work and in other cases profoundly criticized such ideological formations. In every textual situation, however, I try to show the historical limitations constraining each writer and limiting his or her understanding of U.S. imperialism. The historical "horizon" I identify in each writer's work is not intended to trivialize that author's work by dismissing it as "unsuccessful," but rather to remind us how historically bound every act of social criticism is—and to encourage us thereby to offer our own historically specific criticisms of U.S. foreign policies. As many of these writers demonstrate, the "civic virtue" of good citizens in a democratic society is sustained by such critical acts and by the cultural traditions of social critique they continue.

In the following chapters, I treat race, class, gender, and sexuality as common terms for U.S. authors addressing U.S. nationality, especially as the nation was justified by territorial and economic expansion. There are inevitably gaps in my account, other forms of imperialism treated cursorily in my survey, and theoretical frameworks that would supplement and enrich my critical approach. As I argue specifically in seven of the following chapters, the histories of Asian-American and other Pacific-Rim cultures are profoundly involved in the development of U.S. imperialism. Yet this book does not treat centrally literary and cultural work by authors representing these groups, so my own study must be supplemented by such specialists in these fields as Ronald Takaki, whose relevant works are cited in the following chapters.

Insofar as my interpretation of U.S. imperialism focuses on the intersection of territorial, commerical, and social psychological methods of domination, then the ideological construction of public and private spheres, especially as they were gendered in the nineteenth and early twentieth centuries, must be counted an important aspect of this study. Six of the following chapters treat gender hierarchies and roles, as well as the different discourses of the marketplace and the home, as central to the modes of domination and control analyzed, but I do not focus on sentimental and domestic fiction, particularly popular in the nineteenth-century United States, even though they are obviously literary genres that deserve special consideration in our understanding of U.S. expansionism. What Amy Kaplan has aptly termed "manifest domesticity" is an important consideration in this book, but it is more centrally treated by her, Jane Tompkins, Julia Stern, Ann Douglas, Lauren Berlant, Gillian Brown, and the other scholars whose specific works are cited gratefully in the following chapters.[2]

Queer theory and gay studies have added much to our understanding of the social psychologies of domination, and the ideological construction of the homosexual "other" in the latter part of the nineteenth century shares certain structural resemblances with territorial and commercial modes of colonization in both the United States and Great Britain, among the several imperial powers of the period. Although this study deals only peripherally with same-sex relations, my general approach is compatible with work by Eve Sedgwick, Michael Moon, Scott Derrick, Eric Haralson, Terry Castle, Lauren Berlant, and Robert Martin in this area. While openly acknowledging the omissions and relative backgrounding of some of these topics for our understanding of the development of U.S. imperialism, I want to suggest the complementarity of these other approaches with the imperial imaginary I interpret critically in this book.

I have learned a great deal from other scholars in the course of writing this book, and that learning has ranged from the extraordinary books and articles that inform the following chapters to the casual conversations I have had with some of their authors. All of this scholarship belongs properly, of course, to the social criticism I consider essential to democratic civic virtue. In particular, I want to thank Marilyn Young for urging me to think about U.S. involvement in the colonial wars in Southeast Asia as part of a much longer history of U.S. imperialism. I owe a profound debt to Edward Said, whose career as a rigorous scholar and public intellectual has inspired many others, as well as me. Although he never taught me in my undergraduate, graduate, or postgraduate work, I still consider him an important teacher. My idea for this book owes much to Said's work in general and in particular to his remarks in *Culture and Imperialism* that "so influential has been the discourse insisting upon American specialness, altruism, and opportunity that 'imperialism' as a word or ideology has turned up only rarely and recently in accounts of United States culture, politics, history. But the connection between imperial politics and culture is astonishingly direct."[3] Indeed, for the majority of the time I was writing this book, I referred to it simply as *"Culture and U.S. Imperialism."*

I have a wide circle of brilliant and generous friends, each of whom has contributed to this book and deserves mention here: Nancy Armstrong and Len Tennenhouse, Lindon Barrett, Alfred Bendixen, Rick Berg, Homer Brown, Eduardo Cadava, Bill Cain, Rey Chow, Michael Cowan, Gabrielle Daniels, Emory Elliott, Thelma Foote, Giles and Deborah Gunn, Robin Harders, Abdul JanMohamed, Susan Jeffords, Amy Kaplan, Jerry Kennedy, Paul and Annie Lauter, Frank Lentricchia, Günter and Ruth Lenz, David Lloyd, Kevin McNamara, Liisa Malkki and Jim Ferguson, Wendy Martin, J. Hillis Miller, Mark Mullen, Chris Newfield, Pat O'Donnell, John Orr, Don Pease, Mark Poster, Leslie Rabine, Russ Reising, Gaby Schwab and Paul Harris, Eric Sundquist, Cheryl Walker, and Robyn Wiegman. Another group of good friends deserves special mention, because they were members of the research group on "Post-Nationalist American Studies" that I convened at the University of California's Humanities Research Institute in 1996–1997. They read, wrote comments on, and discussed helpfully several portions of this manuscript: Barbara Brinson-Curiel, David Kazanjian, Katherine Kinney, Steven Mailloux, Jay Mechling, George Sánchez, Shelley Streeby, and Henry Yu.

Some of these chapters were first presented as papers at colleges, universities, and scholarly conferences. As always, I am grateful to my hosts and audiences for their invitations and the valuable discussion of these ideas at the 1994 Modern Language Association Convention in San Diego, the 1996 American Literature Association in San Diego, the 1991 "Cultures of U.S. Imperialism" conference at Dartmouth College, the 1995 "Red Badges of Courage: Wars and Conflicts in American Culture" conference organized by Associazione Italiana di Studi Nord-Americani in Rome, the Claremont Graduate School and Huntington Library, the 1988 Modern Language Association Convention in New Orleans, the Department of English at Rice University, and the 1996 conference on "Empire" organized by the Swiss and Austrian North American Studies Associations in Salzburg. The special seminar of California Americanists that Alfred Bendixen organized for the American Literature Association, which met in Puerto Vallarta in February 1996, brought this project together in ways I had not previously recognized; I thank Alfred and the small group of scholars at that meeting for an intellectually transformative experience.

I wish to thank the following presses for permission to publish substantially revised versions of work that first appeared as chapters in books or essays in journals they published: Duke University Press for portions of Chapter 4 that first appeared in *National Identities and Post-Americanist Narratives*, ed. Donald Pease; *Novel: A Forum on Fiction* for portions of Chapter 5 that first appeared in volume 30, no. 2 (Spring 1998); Cambridge University Press for portions of Chapter 6 that first appeared in *The Cambridge Companion to Twain*, ed. Forrest Robinson, and for portions of Chapter 8 that first appeared in *New Essays on "The Education of Henry Adams,"* ed. John Carlos Rowe; Rivista di Studi Anglo-Americani for portions of Chapter 7 that first appeared in *Red Badges of Courage: Wars and Conflicts in American Literature*, ed. Rosella Mamoli Zorzi; and Gunter Narr Verlag, publisher of *Swiss Papers in English Language and Literature*, for portions of Chapter 9 that first appeared in the "Empire" special issue, vol. 10 (1997).

My wife, Kristin, and I have three sons, who have grown up to be wonderful readers and observers of life. Sean and his partner, Katherine Syroboyarsky, gave me Sherman Alexie's *The Lone Ranger and Tonto Fistfight in Heaven* for my fiftieth birthday and thus one of my epigraphs for Chapter 5. Kevin read carefully *At Emerson's Tomb: The Politics of Classic American Literature* and urged me to apply those ideas to more general problems of U.S. life and history. Mark is studying nineteenth-century American literature in the eleventh grade. On my recommendation, he is reading *Typee* and wondering where the "adventure" went; every night we discuss his other assigned texts, *The Scarlet Letter* and *The Crucible*. Life is sweet.

Newport Beach, California   J. C. R.
September 1999

Contents

1. Literary Culture and U.S. Imperialism   3

2. The Dream of Enlightenment and the Nightmare of Imperialism:
Charles Brockden Brown's *Wieland* and *Edgar Huntly*   25

3. Edgar Allan Poe's Imperial Fantasy and the American Frontier   53

4. Melville's *Typee*: U.S. Imperialism at Home and Abroad   77

5. Highway Robbery: "Indian Removal," the Mexican-American War,
and American Identity in John Rollin Ridge's (Yellow Bird)
The Life and Adventures of Joaquín Murieta   97

6. Mark Twain's Rediscovery of America in
A Connecticut Yankee in King Arthur's Court   121

7. Race, Gender, and Imperialism in Stephen Crane:
A Monstrous Case   141

8. *The Education of Henry Adams* and the American Empire   165

9. W. E. B. Du Bois's Tropical Critique of U.S. Imperialism   195

10. The View from Rock Writing Bluff:
The Nick Black Elk Narratives and U.S. Cultural Imperialism   217

11. Opening the Gate to the Other America:
The Afro-Caribbean Politics of Hurston's *Mules and Men*
and *Tell My Horse*   253

12. After America   293

Notes   299

Index   367

LITERARY CULTURE AND U.S. IMPERIALISM

1

Literary Culture and U.S. Imperialism

Author derives from *auctor*, he who augments. It
was the title Rome bestowed upon her generals
when they had conquered new territory for the City.
> José Ortega y Gasset,
> "The Dehumanization of Art" (1925)

Culture is one of the two or three most complicated
words in the English language. . . . *Colere* had a
range of meanings: inhabit, cultivate, protect,
honour with worship. Some of these meanings
eventually separated, though still with occasional
overlapping, in the derived nouns. Thus "inhabit"
developed through *colonus*, L[atin] to *colony*.
> Raymond Williams, *Keywords*, rev. ed. (1983)

Americans' interpretations of themselves as a people are shaped
by a powerful imperial desire and a profound anti-colonial
temper. This book deals with these contradictory self-conceptions and the
ways American writers have represented them. Sometimes canny legitimists
of American empire, sometimes vigorous critics of our colonial impulses,
U.S. writers from the early days of the republic to the present testify diversely
to the imperial heritage of the United States and to a strong intellectual tradition of challenging the imperialism of the United States along with other
global powers. There is nothing exceptional about the imperial aura in U.S.
culture from the late eighteenth century to the first half of the twentieth
century; it is the consequence of political, economic, and social expansion
by U.S. and European powers that was central to social experience in the
modern period. After observing that "nearly everywhere in nineteenth- and

3

early-twentieth-century British and French culture we find allusions to the facts of empire," Edward Said adds, "There is also a dense body of American writing, contemporary with this British and French work, which shows a peculiarly acute imperial cast, even though paradoxically its ferocious anti-colonialism, directed at the Old World, is central to it."[1] As Said suggests, what often distinguishes U.S. cultural responses from British and French views in the same period is the tendency of U.S. writers and intellectuals to be stridently anti-colonial with respect to other imperial powers while endorsing, sometimes even helping to formulate, U.S. imperialist policies.

Richard Van Alstyne has observed that "American foreign policy has a vocabulary all its own, consciously—even ostentatiously—side-stepping the use of terms that would hint at aggression or imperial domination." Van Alstyne has in mind such "abstract formulae, stereotyped phrases, and idealistic clichés that really explain nothing" as the "'Monroe Doctrine,' 'no entangling alliances,' 'freedom of the seas,' 'open door,' 'good neighbour policy,'" which he claims "strew the pages of American history but throw little light on the dynamics of American foreign policy."[2] Specialists in American Studies have long understood that the archetypes of "American self-reliance," "radical individualism," "transcendental soul," "isolato," as well as "errand into the wilderness," "city on a hill," "virgin land," "westward expansion," "noble savage," and "free-enterprise" complement this foreign policy rhetoric. Not only does this more general cultural symbology for American character and identity complement key terms of our foreign policy, but it also suggests a profound interrelation of our very conceptions of what constitutes "domestic" and "foreign" affairs. Van Alstyne explains the "heretical phrase" he uses for the title of his book, "The American Empire," by arguing that "this approach gives precedence to foreign affairs over domestic affairs, reversing the customary practice of treating national history from the standpoint of the nation preoccupied with its own internal affairs and only incidentally looking beyond its borders."[3]

Of course, every major imperial power in the modern period developed its military, political, economic, and cultural means of colonial expansion by consolidating different territories, peoples, languages, and currencies into a "nation." We can trace Western "national consciousness" back to the print revolution of the late fifteenth and early sixteenth centuries, as Benedict Anderson has done, or to the somewhat later, albeit different, periods in which European monarchies consolidated their respective principalities and kingdoms into nation-states, often in formal acts, such as the Act of Union of 1707, whereby "Great Britain" was defined by the incorporation of England, Wales, and Scotland.[4] In either chronology, imperial attitudes and rhetoric with regard to extraterritorial regions often serve the purpose of bolstering national policies, laws, and behaviors. In modern Europe, the relation between "nation" and "empire" is consistently dialectical.

The same general pattern certainly describes the relation between domestic and foreign policies and their cultural representation in the United States, except for the rhetoric of anti-colonial revolution that is considered fundamental to the American symbology.[5] As a *national* liberation movement, the American Revolution successfully identified imperialist injustices with Great Britain and justified the expansion of U.S. territory in North America as part of national "consolidation," a necessary defense against the imperial ambitions of Spain, France, and Great Britain in the Western Hemisphere that continued throughout the nineteenth century. By a similar rhetorical legerdemain, the United States in the nineteenth century employed the rhetoric of "emancipation" derived from the American Revolution to promise, often falsely, various subaltern groups—African Americans, Native Americans, Chinese Americans, Latin Americans, European Americans, and women—the hope of eventual social justice tied inextricably to national progress and American individualism. Thus the representation of the Civil War and abolition as part of a "second" or "unfinished" American Revolution could be understood as part of the national mission of anti-colonial struggle against lingering European feudalism in the South, rather than as a rebellion against the class and racial hierarchies integral to the enlightenment principles of the original Revolution.[6] In a similar sense, the Mexican-American War was promoted by some in the United States as an effort to extend to the Mexican people the democratic ideals of liberty and justice of which they had been deprived under Spanish, French, and Mexican rule. In effect, that expansionist war was rationalized in some quarters in the United States as an "anti-colonial" struggle, in keeping with our best revolutionary principles.[7]

Thus Van Alstyne's effort to shift the historical focus from domestic affairs to foreign affairs in the study of the United States—radical as this gesture was in 1960—misses the complex relation between U.S. imperialism as it worked to expand national territory and functioned within its territory to consolidate the idea of the nation. This dialectical process is complicated further by the important work of American Studies scholars who have focused on "internal colonialism" in U.S. history, including slavery, criminalization, and racism as modes of colonizing African Americans; conventional and germ warfare, "removal" and deterritorialization, the various "reservation" systems, and assimilation as means of colonizing Native Americans; taxation without representation, vigilante violence, "exclusion laws" forbidding or strictly limiting immigration, criminalization, and racism as means of colonizing Chinese, Mexican, Latin-American, and other immigrant populations; gender hierarchies, the fetishism and commodification of the feminine body, and the exploitation of feminine sexual reproduction, as well as the exclusion of women from a wide range of civil and economic rights as part of the colonial domination of women; and the construction of strict sexual mores for the definition and regulation of "proper" sexual "morality," in order to police lesbians and gays and/or "purge" the nation of their "deviance." The "internal colonization" thesis has been developed by a long list of distinguished scholars in books and articles that are fundamental to American Studies as a discipline. Among the most influential for the following chapters are Robert Berkhofer's *The White Man's Indian: Images of the American Indian from Columbus to the Present* (1978), Richard Drinnon's *Facing West: The Metaphysics of Indian-Hating and Empire-Building* (1980), Reginald Horsman's *Race and Manifest Destiny: The Origins of American Racial Anglo-Saxonism* (1981), Annette Kolodny's *The Lay of the Land: Metaphor as Experience and History in American Life and Letters* (1975) and *The Land before Her: Fantasy and Experience of the American Frontiers, 1630–1860* (1984), Patricia Nelson Limerick's *The Legacy of Conquest: The Unbroken Past of the American West* (1988), Michael Paul Rogin's *Fathers and Children: Andrew Jackson and the Subjugation of the American Indian* (1975), Richard Slotkin's trilogy—*Regeneration through Violence: The Myth of the American Frontier, 1600–1860* (1973), *The Fatal Environment: The Myth of the Frontier in the Age of Industrialization, 1800–1890* (1985), and *Gunfighter Nation: The Myth of the Frontier in Twentieth-Century America* (1992), and Ronald Takaki's *Iron Cages: Race and Culture in Nineteenth-Century America* (1979) and *A Different Mirror: A History of Multicultural America* (1993).[8]

Indispensable as the historical critique of U.S. "internal colonialism" is, however, it tends to focus on domestic policies and to interpret foreign policies, when it does, as self-evident extensions of domestic affairs. There are important exceptions, of course, including Drinnon, Horsman, Slotkin (especially in *Gunfighter Nation*), and Takaki, but most scholars follow an argument that reinforces theories of "American Exceptionalism" by distinguishing U.S. imperialism from the history of other imperial projects in this same period of modern nation and empire building.[9] Assuming too often that the "real" colonialism is being done at home, scholars of the "internal colonialism" thesis also tend to accept the traditional view that the United States does not emerge as an imperial power until the Spanish-American (1898) and Philippine-American wars (1899–1901), the same period in which "imperialism" is used popularly as a pejorative term and directed against the United States, along with the more recognizable European imperial powers, by organized anti-imperialists, like members of the politically conservative Anti-Imperialist League. Yet this latter argument is based on a restricted definition of imperialism as the conquest and domination of foreign territory, which theorists of the "internal colonization" thesis should reject from the outset. For although "internal colonization" depends significantly on the territorial acquisitions of the Louisiana Purchase, the Treaty of Guadalupe Hidalgo, other territories settled during westward expansion, as well as the purchase of Alaska and annexation of Hawaii, the national myths and political rhetoric justifying such expansionism were also developed in the colonization of peoples and their folkways living within the United States prior to or apart from these acquisitions.

The metropolitan centers of European imperialism were certainly transformed by the appearance of peoples, goods, and cultural practices from colonized lands, but London, Paris, Madrid, Lisbon, and Amsterdam were not *directly* affected or structurally transformed by the different stages of European and Asian immigration, importation of slaves, and displacement of native peoples that were integral to the economies, politics, and cultural practices of settlers in American colonies and their subsequent nation-states. Well before the United States emerged as a global player in the late nineteenth-century struggles for imperial influence and power, it developed techniques of colonization in the course of breaking the colonial rule of Great Britain and establishing its own national identity. Such colonial practices emphasized the control of different peoples, their labor, and their means of communal identification. Whether encouraged to assimilate to U.S. culture or racially targeted for exclusion, people and their social behaviors, as much as territory and markets, were the focuses of U.S. colonization.

The internal colonization of different peoples depended centrally on hierarchies of race, class, and gender to do the work of subjugation and domination. Although every imperial system relies on socially constructed categories distinguishing the colonized "native" from the metropolitan "subject," in which elements of the imperial power's hierarchies of race, gender, sexuality, and class are usually reflected, these social and economic distinctions are often easily maintained by the geographical and cultural distances separating the "home country" from its colonies.[10] In the United States, social distinctions between "citizens" and "foreigners" were from the very beginning confused both by the relative novelty of the idea of the nation and the presence of culturally and ethnically diverse peoples with various claims to civil liberties and property rights at least abstractly upheld by the Constitution and other founding documents. Virtually from the moment the original colonies defined themselves as a nation, there was an imperial project to restrict the meaning of the American by demonizing foreigners, in part by identifying them with the "savagery" ascribed to Native and African Americans.

Reginald Horsman contends that the mythology of Anglo-Saxon racial identity was often used in nineteenth-century America by anti-expansionists and isolationists, who feared "contamination" by "inferior" or "mongrel" peoples: "In the mid-nineteenth-century opponents of aggressive expansionism for the most part did not object when other races were condemned to permanent inferiority. They were far more concerned with what was to happen to the United States than with what was to happen to the rest of the world. Those who expressed a faith in the innate capacity of other peoples were overwhelmed by a surging tide of arrogant racial theory."[11] Implicit in Horsman's analysis of the history of racial theory in the United States is the conclusion that anti-expansionism and isolationism in the United States often explicitly relied on internal colonial hierarchies of race, gender, and class established in the process of nation-formation. The apparent paradox that many groups were anti-imperialist precisely because they feared the collapse of the imperium at home helps explain, I think, why so many organized anti-imperialist movements, like the Anti-Imperialist League, were politically conservative and often overtly racist.[12] Rather than defending the rights of foreigners against imperial aggression, most nineteenth-century Americans upheld ideals of "American" racial purity against the "inferiority" of such foreigners: "Rarest in the opposition to the expansionism of the mid-nineteenth-century were those who combined a dislike of military aggression with disbelief in the current racial assumptions."[13]

What is striking, however, in the history of racial hierarchies in the United States is the degree to which such otherness is imagined both inside and outside the nation to have an isomorphic resemblance that contradicts the most obvious social, cultural, and regional or geographical differences. In the following chapters, literary authors and popular culture draw analogies between the Lenni-Lenape (the Delaware) and Irish peasantry, African Americans and Lakota Sioux, African Americans and South Asians, Mexicans and Cherokee, South Sea islanders and African Americans, feudal English serfs and southern slaves or northern industrial workers, northern urban African Americans and Mexican rural peasants, Euro-American women and African-American men, Lakota Sioux and the urban proletariat, northern urban African Americans and Haitian rural peasants. This double narrative of an emerging imperialist ideology has certain troubling consequences for both existing hierarchies of race, gender, and class within the United States and changing conceptions of foreign cultures, especially those designated as subaltern to U.S. domination. Rather than exposing the utter fictionality of racial and gender hierarchies, these shifting analogies among peoples of color, women, and workers consistently colonized *within* the United States with a variety of "foreign" peoples successively colonized by the United States *outside* its territorial borders provided an adaptable and yet surprisingly stable racist, sexist, and classist rhetoric that could be deployed for new foreign ventures even as it was required to maintain the old systems of controlling familiar groups within the United States.

The human "territories" colonized by the United States are often linked with what defines their productive capacities: commerce and technology. Thus I do not think that Edward Said's introductory generalization in *Culture and Imperialism* applies exactly to the entanglement of U.S. nationalism and imperialism: "The main battle in imperialism is over land, of course, but when it came to who owned the land, who had the right to settle and work on it, who kept it going, who won it back, and who now plans its future—these issues were reflected, contested, and even for a time decided in narrative."[14] Said is considering in this passage the general relationship between territorial conquest and its narrative representation—"what explorers and novelists say about strange regions of the world"—and his model is primarily that of European powers, especially in the historically different stages of their conquests of foreign countries.[15] Understanding as he does in the remainder of this passage that territorial colonization *always* involves human access to that land as both economically productive and politically symbolic, Said does provide an approach relevant to U.S. imperialism, but his insistence on the materiality of "land" or "territory" as crucial to imperialism should be revised. To be sure, all of our early colonial ventures are primarily struggles to control the land, whether it is the territory of eighteenth-century Pennsylvania stolen from the Lenni-Lenape in the infamous Walking Purchase or that of the Louisiana Purchase and lands still further west. Nevertheless, it is extraordinary how many of our imperial ventures had more to do with controlling trade routes and markets than with the inherent value of the land that happened to lie along the way. From Captain David Porter's effort to annex the Marquesas Islands for the United States in 1812, arguably the first formal act of U.S. imperialism, to the "spheres of influence" the United States attempted to develop in the Caribbean and the Philippines in the wake of the Spanish-American and Philippine-American wars and the avowedly commercial interests of John Hay's foreign policies, U.S. imperialism has primarily been as intent on commercial, technological, and human as on territorial control. Particularly interesting to the cultural historian are the ways these different aspects of colonization have worked together not only to do the usual imperial work of domination but also to disguise the imperial mission itself.

Writing these pages in the year of Ken Burns's celebrated PBS docudrama, *Lewis and Clark*, which follows the success of Stephen Ambrose's 1996 bestseller, *Undaunted Courage*, I am reminded how central commercial development was in Thomas Jefferson's conception of the expedition and in his instructions to Meriwether Lewis of June 1803.[16] Not only did Jefferson order exploration that would result in "the most direct and practicable water-communication across the continent," he also charged Captain Lewis with developing "commerce . . . with the people inhabiting the line you will pursue."[17] Reading the original *History of the Lewis and Clark* amid the current media-induced patriotism inspired by this early U.S. colonial venture, I am struck by how Lewis and Clark record in tedious detail possible water routes crossing their travel along the Missouri and the Columbia rivers to the Pacific. Otherwise haphazard both in the collection of natural specimens requested by Jefferson and the identification of likely sites for agricultural and urban development, the explorers are virtually river mad, identifying minor tributaries and impassable feeder-streams in anticipation of commercial opportunities.[18]

This commercial imagination is complemented by Lewis and Clark's interference in tribal politics by offering to settle disputes the explorers did not understand and distributing with ludicrous solemnity symbolic regalia—a military dress-coat, cockaded hat, and a federal certificate declaring Washington's federal authority—to baffled Native Americans. To their credit, many tribal leaders and warriors rejected these "presents," often complaining that they were useless, although several leaders did pledge allegiance to their "Great Father," President Jefferson, probably without understanding the full implications of the political shift of power from France to the

United States resulting from the Louisiana Purchase. As far as "trade" with Native Americans was concerned, Lewis and Clark quickly discovered that the majority of native peoples they met along their route were destitute by Euroamerican standards and had little of value to trade, much less the means to purchase commodities that might be of use to them. *Access* to the land on which they hunted and gathered was about the only capital commanded by Native Americans at the beginning of the nineteenth century, at least when measured by Euro-American standards.[19] Of course, safe passage *across* that land would help develop commercial opportunities in the West and eventually in Asia, realizing the original dream of "a passage to India."

The Lewis and Clark expedition suggests that westward expansion across the North American continent was driven both by the needs to "open the West" for settlers who would cultivate the land and then develop and try out transportation and communications technologies, such as steamship, railroad, and telegraph, that in reaching the Pacific demonstrated the efficacy of industrialization and its complement, intensive investment in technological research. Indeed, most family farms on the frontier failed; the large agribusinesses and western ranches that took over failed settlers' farms, often converting them to other purposes, depended on the latest technologies of farming, ranching, communication, and transportation.[20] And, of course, Manifest Destiny proved to be our own "Final Solution" to the "problem" of native peoples, which is also relatively unique in modern imperialisms: that the purpose of territorial expansion is not to subjugate native peoples for the purposes of exploiting their labor but simply to remove them from useful colonial territory with the ultimate purpose of eliminating them and their lifeways altogether. In the wake of the Dawes Act (1887), federal policies of "allotment and assimilation" urged not only the appropriation of Native American lands, but also the legitimation of settlers' colonization by virtue of Native Americans following their example by adopting the lifestyles dictated by private property and its economy.[21]

Commerce and technology were, of course, original motives for the voyages of exploration that initiated the Spanish, Portuguese, English, French, and Dutch imperial systems. J. H. Parry's classic 1963 study, *The Age of Reconnaissance*, focuses on the technological developments in shipbuilding, navigation, astronomy, cartography, and communications and the economic developments in financial backing and venture capital that made the "discovery" of "new worlds" possible between 1450 and 1650.[22] More recent studies of the discursive and rhetorical features of the earliest efforts to colonize other lands, especially the Western Hemisphere, such as Tzvetan Todorov's *The Conquest of America*, Eric Cheyfitz's *The Poetics of Imperialism*, Stephen Greenblatt's *Marvelous Possessions*, and Mary Louise Pratt's *Imperial Eyes: Travel Writing and Transculturation*, argue that these technological and commercial purposes were complemented by the narrative, symbolic, and rhetorical media necessary for imperial control.[23] On the evidence of such important studies of colonialism and imperialism, especially those influenced by Michel Foucault's methods of interpreting cultural forces, it is fair to conclude that U.S. imperialism extends the established practices of European exploration, conquest, and colonization against which the United States struggled in its own anti-colonial revolution.

Even as it pursued traditional imperial ends of territorial acquisition, however, the United States developed *non-territorial* forms of colonial domination, ultimately systematized in an "imperial" system that in the nineteenth century complemented American nationalism and in the twentieth century grew to encompass "spheres of influence" ranging from the Western Hemisphere to the farthest corners of the earth and by the last three decades of this century to include outer-space travel routes, especially those traversed by satellites for communications and military defense, and scientific research with technological applications.[24] There is, then, an imperial heritage—a repertoire of methods for domination—on which the United States drew in the nineteenth century as it expanded westward; considered publicly and secretly specific extraterritorial ventures in the Caribbean, Central America, the South Pacific, and Asia; and formulated influential foreign policies, such as the Monroe Doctrine and Open Door Policy, that are still invoked today. Yet the United States added new means of displacing people, defining "territory," and pursuing its "national interests" that anticipate the more commercial, technological, and *cultural* systems of control characteristic of twentieth-century imperialisms, especially those that emerged in the course of overt *decolonization* following World War II. From its very beginnings, U.S. imperialism employs the rhetorical and cultural means other colonial powers used to legitimate their claims to foreign territories to "win hearts and minds," in the infamous slogan of the Vietnam War, and more prosaically to control trade routes, corner markets, and manipulate consumers' desires. Such *neoimperialism* has been traditionally associated with late modernity and postindustrialism, but in the following chapters I argue that it is recognizable in U.S. culture of the late eighteenth and nineteenth centuries.

There are good reasons to extend the history of U.S. imperialism beyond the Revolution to the colonial period, including thereby its narratives of Indian captivity, travel and natural description, as well as religious and historical writings. In *Regeneration through Violence*, for example, Slotkin defines the historical period as "1600–1860" precisely because it straddles the colonial and national periods in which the original myths of the "American Frontier" were formulated. Slotkin refers to the "first two hundred and fifty years of American history" as a period in which "the problems and preoccupations of the colonists became transformed into 'visions which compel belief' in a civilization called American."[25] My general approach in this book welcomes such a longer historical view and assumes that the sources of U.S. nationalism are traceable in part to this colonial culture, just as they derive in part from the post-Renaissance intellectual, social, and economic traditions in Europe. Although I begin with Charles Brockden Brown's "early

[handwritten margin note: Connection of US nationalism to colonial culture]

American" Gothic romances for the sake of focusing on the ways U.S. and extraterritorial expansions are linked together by self-conscious ideas of U.S. nationalism after the Revolution, I do not want to distinguish sharply "national" from "colonial" cultural attitudes.

The history of literary culture in North America suggests an important continuity between colonial America and U.S. nationalism. As Benedict Anderson has shown, the development of print-capitalism was crucial to the transformation from religious and dynastic empires to nation-states in Europe, and the Protestant Reformation played a key role in this history:

> The coalition between Protestantism and print-capitalism, exploiting cheap popular editions, quickly created large new reading publics—not least among merchants and women, who typically knew little or no Latin—and simultaneously mobilized them for politico-religious purposes. Inevitably, it was not merely the Church that was shaken to its core. The same earthquake produced Europe's first important non-dynastic, non-city states in the Dutch Republic and the Commonwealth of the Puritans.[26]

This "coalition between Protestantism and print-capitalism" is also evident in the same period in the development of "literary culture" in the American colonies, establishing foundations for a "reading public" composed of individual readers, each of whom has confidence in the existence of others "of whose identity" such readers have not the "slightest notion." Anderson exemplifies this process through which readers interpellate their identities as "citizens" in the "mass ceremony" of reading the daily newspaper, in which the reader "is continually reassured that the imagined world is visibly rooted in everyday life."[27] Certainly the sources of this literary culture can be found in part in the Puritan theocracy and its imbrication of textuality, spirituality, and economy, but it is also fair to conclude that the *secularization* of Puritan hermeneutics in the "national" narrative involves important differences between religious and national imperialisms that are manifest only after the United States establishes itself formally as a nation-state.

Nevertheless, the Puritan effort to colonize the soul and its body along with specific territory survives in the central role literary culture plays in U.S. imperialism from the earliest years of the new republic. Literary culture legitimates the ideological aims of print-capitalism and its residual Protestantism by invading the mind and psyche and transforming the body into a representation of the former, often thereby legitimating prevailing hierarchies of race, class, and gender. Romantic idealism and American Transcendentalism typify the process through which an external, resistant physicality is historically metamorphosed into a representation of inner being, whether the latter be named "free rationality" or "Spirit." When this process of internalization is played out in global and historical terms, as it is in Hegel's philosophy, it describes a "civilizing" process in which literary culture is both the means to and goal of spiritual self-consciousness. It seems nearly impossible today to read Hegel and the other idealist philosophers in Europe and the United States without recognizing the profoundly imperialist character of their philosophy.[28] The historical process of "spiritualization" Hegel traces from ancient China and India through Egypt to Greece and Rome as preparatory stages in the rise of the West from medieval Christendom to the great bourgeois revolutions is also an imperial map.[29] Hegel not only colonizes world history with his philosophy, but he also contributes to an intellectual tradition of cultural colonization by means of writing and reading.

Raymond Williams is right that "culture" is "one of the two or three most complicated words in the English language," and the competitive definitions of culture have grown even more diverse as scholars and critics recognize the constitutive powers of culture in social, political, and economic formations.[30] With the advent of "cultural studies," the term "culture" has become a theoretical football, whose possession is the key to the game. But abstract theorization of "culture" or alternatively a strict philological account of the word's semiotic migrations should not be considered indispensable tasks before we can do the work of cultural interpretation. Cultural critics aren't as interested in providing a categorical and totalized definition of "culture" as they are in understanding how this term designates certain practices and values for a specific society. Citizens of a historically specific society tacitly agree upon what constitutes "culture" for them, even when this term is used in such a society in exclusive and hierarchical ways. The cultural critic wants to look primarily at the social, human, and natural consequences of that assumption, avoiding totalizing assumptions in his or her own work. Defining the term "culture" is beside the point; "culture" is whatever people happen to take it to be at a particular time and in a particular place. What matters is how that term works to organize diverse experiences and information. In the following chapters, I take this historically pragmatic approach to the otherwise vexed term and concept "culture."

In his introduction to *Culture and Imperialism*, Said explains his use of the term "culture" in both this book and his earlier *Orientalism* in a similarly pragmatic manner:

> First of all it means all those practices, like the arts of description, communication, and representation, that have relative autonomy from the economic, social, and political realms and that often exist in aesthetic forms. . . . Second, . . . culture is a concept that includes a refining and elevating element. . . . In time, culture comes to be associated, often aggressively, with the nation or the state; this differentiates "us" from "them," almost always with some degree of xenophobia. Culture in this sense is a source of identity, and a rather combative one at that.[31]

Although my emphasis on literary culture in the following chapters is influenced by Said's two definitions, I want to suggest that U.S. imperialism challenges the "relative autonomy" of literary culture and often employs it directly to achieve economic, social, and political ends. Yet just as literary culture may be viewed in this book as fundamental to the colonial practices of the United States both inside its borders and in its increasingly global ambitions, it may also be used to "write back," making visible its own potential complicity in such ideological work and sometimes subverting the very rhetoric of colonization and expansion. My own use of the term "literary culture" thus revises Said's first definition, follows the second definition, and adds a third definition in which the very flexibility and adaptability of literary discourse can be used to challenge the ideological purposes served by the first two definitions. Although my interest in this revised definition is its relevance to U.S. literary culture, I do not want to argue that it is uniquely applicable to the United States.

Said stresses "cultural forms like the novel," because his "exclusive focus" in *Culture and Imperialism* "is on the modern Western empires of the nineteenth and twentieth centuries."[32] My own historical focus is nearly identical, although I have restricted my attention to U.S. imperialism, but my examples of literary culture are not exclusively novels, although they are primarily prose writings. The novel is certainly an important genre in the culture of print-capitalism and for nationalism generally, and it is thus one of the chief cultural means of legitimating imperial practices. Yet in the history of modern U.S. culture, a wide variety of prose genres are used both to justify and challenge the dominant hierarchies of the national mythology. In the following chapters, I treat Gothic romances, narratives of discovery and exploration, ethnographic travel and autobiography, popular thrillers, historical romances, autobiographies, novellas, short fiction, and scholarly treatises. Although I refer at times to many of these works as "novels," most of the narratives interpreted in this book are *not* technically novels. There are three reasons for the generic diversity in this study, each of which has important relevance for my argument regarding U.S. imperialism.

First, I have selected cultural works in which there is some explicit engagement of internal and extraterritorial forms of U.S. colonialism as they were understood in a particular historical moment. After all, the geopolitical map of the United States changes dramatically in the 150 years framing this study. Elsewhere I have discussed the importance of Mary Louise Pratt's notion of the "contact zone," where different cultures meet and negotiate their different social realities, for the comparative study of American cultures and as a social theory in which literature plays an important role.[33] The contact zone in the case of each literary narrative treated in this book suggests how the boundaries of U.S. national identity have changed historically while maintaining certain hierarchies of race, class, and gender as constants. Thus the frontiers separating settlers and Native Americans in Charles Brockden Brown's Pennsylvania and Edgar Allan Poe's South and Midwest are today contained within the continental United States, just as John Rollin Ridge's frontier California in the decade following the Mexican-American War is now the most populous and politically influential state in the Union. Our new global "frontiers" or "contact zones" appear more recognizably in the Black Atlantic that links African Americans (in both the United States and the Caribbean) with West Africans in W. E. B. Du Bois's and Zora Neale Hurston's twentieth-century narratives and yet still suggests the boundaries separating Euro-American from African-American cultural traditions in the United States. As the boundaries distinguishing national and foreign have shifted historically, certain constants of racial, gender, and class division persist that can be understood better in terms of U.S. imperial ambitions than by considering only domestic circumstances. By studying comparatively not only the different cultures represented in these literary works but also their historical periods, often separated into discrete scholarly specializations, this book attempts to represent those constants of U.S. imperialism while respecting the diversity of its historical development. By concentrating on the shifting boundary between internal and external forms of imperialism, I hope to avoid the limitations of earlier studies of "internal colonization" I have discussed above and to go beyond the traditional Marxist critique of U.S. capitalism as inherently expansionist.

In this latter approach, literary texts and cultural works are often treated as explicitly anti-imperialist or as imperialist propaganda, following a crude classification that implies the superstructural function of cultural work.[34] With their reliance on an aesthetics of pleasure and their address to relatively stable middle-class audiences, novels tend to reinforce the notion that culture contributes to imperialism primarily by mystifying the otherwise ugly practices of the military conquest of foreign lands. To be sure, Gothic and historical romances, like those by Brown and Mark Twain discussed; popular thrillers, like Ridge's *Joaquín Murieta*; and shorter fiction, like Stephen Crane's *Red Badge of Courage* and "The Monster," are evaluated in part by their contribution to or departure from the cultural work of ideological legitimation. But scholarly narratives like Du Bois's *The Souls of Black Folk*, literary ethnographies like Herman Melville's *Typee* and Hurston's *Mules and Men* and *Tell My Horse*, and literary "translations" of Native American oral storytelling like the various Nick Black Elk narratives make special claims for social and political activism that are distinct from the moral conclusions and aesthetic pleasures of the middle-class novel. Thus my second reason for focusing on a variety of cultural narratives in which internal and external modes of U.S. imperialism are represented is to suggest both the scope of U.S. ideological manipulation of "cultural work" *and* the range of possible reactions to and subversions of such uses of culture.

The third important reason for selecting such a variety of genres from the period of print-capitalism is to give prominence to "literary culture" as a constitutive force in U.S. imperialism while avoiding the impression that this study is merely practical literary criticism. In this final regard, I am struggling with a problem addressed previously by Slotkin and Said, each of whom understands how influential literature was in forming and maintaining national myths and "imperial attitudes, references, and experiences" but also knows that traditional literary criticism, with its emphasis on formal and technical questions, is often part of the problem rather than the solution.[35] Any cultural critic whose purpose is to sharpen the critical faculties of his or her readers to the discursive and rhetorical powers of imperialism wants to avoid interpreting literary texts in such a way that those "readings" will merely be "added" to the plurality of available interpretations. The aim of the present study is not to refine interpretations of the specific literary works treated, but instead to shift our literary attention from literary texts, whose aesthetic values are often commodified, to discursive forces that contribute to larger social, political, economic, and psychological narratives. Having done that, we must then *evaluate* the consequences of those literary contributions or challenges to this cultural narrative.[36]

Despite my reservations about traditional literary criticism's ability to interpret the relation between literary culture and U.S. imperialism, I still rely on techniques of close reading in the following chapters. Although some chapters deal with several texts, each chapter situates a single author within cultural and historical "contact zones" by way of interpretations of specific texts. The goal of such readings, however, is not the same as many formalist interpretations, which often work to establish the discreteness and uniqueness of the literary work apart from sociohistorical circumstances. My interpretations locate the texts historically and culturally as contributions to the public debates that have motivated these texts. In this context, literary explication respects the complexity of ideological discursive formation, which includes the roles played by literary texts and culture in general. Such attention to the text also has the advantage of demonstrating how cultural studies can follow the logic of a text without lapsing into trivial formalism or celebration of literary ambiguity or linguistic undecidability. These anti-formal close readings are designed to use the text to gain access to a wider historical and cultural field of debate and inquiry. Each text thematizes a cultural contact zone that has a specific historical reference; taken together, these interpretations offer a "cultural history," with noticeable gaps to be sure, but nonetheless a history of literary culture's role in the development and criticism of U.S. imperialism from the Revolution to World War II.

Charles Brockden Brown's Gothic romances *Wieland* and *Edgar Huntly* represent literature's contribution to the invention of national consciousness by defining the "alien" in the 1790s. Like the Alien and Sedition Acts, Brown's romances demonize the Irish, European Free Masons, the French, and the Lenni-Lenape people as threats to national stability. Racially marking these dangerous aliens, Brown also ritually internalizes their presumed powers both in the thematics of these two romances and in his own imaginative process. Brown's fame as the founder of the American novel has often been challenged, but in ideological terms he certainly inaugurates an American literary tradition that has been preoccupied with imaginatively incorporating foreign cultures while symbolically exorcising racially imagined "aliens." Behind this fictional dreamwork, the cultural historian often finds specific events motivating these literary defenses; in this regard, Brown goes to considerable lengths to allegorize the infamous Walking Purchase of 1737, whereby Thomas Penn and John Penn cheated the Lenni-Lenape of their ancestral lands in Pennsylvania.

Poe's frontier fantasy, "The Journal of Julius Rodman," may be merely a pastiche of other frontier narratives, including *The History of the Lewis and Clark Expedition* and Washington Irving's *Astoria* and *Adventures of Captain Bonneville, U.S.A.*, but it continues Brown's work of racializing the "alien" and interprets the western frontier of the United States as part of a larger global struggle by rational Europeans to control "savagery." Not surprisingly, the distinguishing characteristic of enlightenment rationality is its command of language, and Poe imagines the standard for such literacy to be maintained by poets and other imaginative writers, who help us distinguish between mere savage mimicry and the authentic communication of rational discourse. The political struggle between the United States and Great Britain over the Oregon Territory and the political transition from French to U.S. rule in the territory of the Louisiana Purchase are incorporated in the character of Julius Rodman and his leadership skills. Poe's otherwise minor and unfinished frontier narrative helps us reinterpret the colonial subtext in his more famous tales, such as "A Tale of the Ragged Mountains," "Hop-Frog," and "The Murders in the Rue Morgue." In Poe's short fiction of the 1830s and early 1840s, U.S. Manifest Destiny is already understood to be part of the West's inevitable domination of the globe. Poe not only envisions the future of the United States in such imperial terms but also the central roles "the power of words" and the poet will play in this historical process.

In *Typee*, Melville registers the first major literary resistance to an emerging imperial imagination in the United States by calling attention to U.S. involvement in various European colonial ventures in the South Pacific. Reminding readers of the 1840s of the history of Captain David Porter's bid to annex the Marquesas Islands to the United States, Melville also reflects upon the general ethnographic problem of interpreting a culture, like that of the Marquesan Typee, that differs significantly from our own. Melville's interpretations of incipient U.S. colonialism in the South Pacific leads him to make specific connections between extraterritorial colonialism and the racial, gender, and class hierarchies within the United States. Melville certainly betrays many of the contradictory impulses of the liberal intellectual of the 1840s in *Typee*, but he recognizes the difficulty of combating forms of cultural imperialism at home and abroad that rely on the very rhetorical powers that are the resources of the imaginative writer. If only for that recognition, then, Melville represents an important turning point in literary culture's response to U.S. imperialism, insofar as *Typee* argues that the critique of such imperialism must be directed both at the hermeneutics as well as the politics of our foreign and domestic policies.

The incipient extraterritorial U.S. imperialism criticized by Melville is actually well under way in this same period in Texas, the Southwest, and California, and the Treaty of Guadalupe Hidalgo concluding the Mexican-American War increased U.S. territory by *one-third*. Nevertheless, the cultural impact of this war and annexation of territory is significantly absent from most accounts of nineteenth-century U.S. literature, even though the political debates surrounding the war are unavoidable anticipations of the racial conflicts that would result in the Civil War. In this regard, however, the treatment of the Mexican-American War as a "prelude" to the Civil War typifies our dangerous tendency to interpret racial conflicts in U.S. history according to the black-white binary. In reading John Rollin Ridge's popular thriller, *The Life and Adventures of Joaquín Murieta*, as an account of the racialization and criminalization of "foreigners" in postwar California, I am able to consider racial categories invented to exclude Mexican, Californio, Chilean, Peruvian, Chinese, and Native Americans from the civil liberties and property rights guaranteed U.S. citizens by law. This particular text by the Cherokee Ridge (Yellow Bird) also enables me to consider the appeal of nineteenth-century theories of assimilation to many members of minority cultures. Ridge's advocacy of assimilation, his endorsement of progressive individualism, and his consistent defense of southern slaveholding economies suggest just some of the internal conflicts dividing those groups dominated by U.S. imperial ideology in the nineteenth century.

Mark Twain's *A Connecticut Yankee in King Arthur's Court* brings this study to the verge of the historical period in which anti-imperialists, like Twain and William Dean Howells, would publicly condemn our imperial ambitions. Nevertheless, *A Connecticut Yankee* precedes by nearly a decade the Spanish-American and Philippine-American wars, as well as Twain's overtly anti-imperialist politics and satires. By interpreting *A Connecticut Yankee* as a fantasy of nineteenth-century U.S. imperialism in sixth-century Arthurian England, I argue that Twain's anti-imperialism is integral to his entire literary career, rather than restricted to a particular period in it. Twain uses the historical romance of *A Connecticut Yankee* to indict the technological and economic means the United States employed to pursue its global ambitions; in this manner, Twain understands the nonterritorial character of U.S. expansionism and its special reliance on racial and class hierarchies for conquest and domination. By the same token, Twain's return to the English "origins" of U.S. nationalism allows him to trace the etiology of modern U.S. racial ideology to the class hierarchies of the European dynastic empires. Twain's tendency to universalize such anti-imperialist targets as tyranny and slavery, as well as to treat reductively complex modern economic and technological issues, results in his endorsement of a reformed democratic ideal as a model for republican revolutions around the world and throughout history. One result of Twain's anti-imperialist critique, then, is his affirmation of U.S. democracy, purified of its feudal corruptions, as a model for worldwide emancipation, unwittingly anticipating the neoimperialist practice of exporting U.S. lifestyles, political institutions, and economic infrastructure to societies where they may not be appropriate or even possible.[37]

Twain's commitment to criticize imperialism and renew democratic idealism is shared by a number of other modern U.S. intellectuals known for their anti-imperialist writings. Yet the political consequences of their arguments are often quite different, as are their attitudes toward the continuing national problems occasioned by the racial, gender, and class inequalities in modern America. Often celebrated for his anti-imperialist journalism and nonfiction, Stephen Crane is strangely ambivalent, at times contradictory, in his representations of peoples of color and women both in the United States and in the foreign countries he visited as a journalist. As the author of one of the most celebrated literary works about the Civil War, *The Red Badge of Courage*, Crane is difficult to evaluate in terms of such important issues in that war as the abolition of slavery, racial discrimination, and socioeconomic sectional differences between the North and South. In an effort to bring these concerns together, I turn to "The Monster," the only work in which Crane foregrounds racial differences as central to the dramatic action. Written on the verge of the Spanish-American War and in the midst of those global upheavals occasioned by imperial destabilizations of global politics, "The Monster" deals ostensibly with racial relations in upstate New York and more subtly with the relation between national and international politics, especially as determined by processes of modernization.

My approach to Stephen Crane is a test case for the arguments in this book, as well as its method of literary and historical interpretation, because I try to show how careful attention to the literary text and its historical contexts enables us to make more precise judgments of what hitherto have been rather general claims for a writer's anti-imperialist politics. By arguing that Crane criticized vigorously European imperialism, in part to bolster an American Exceptionalism that was notably racist and sexist, I argue that we must evaluate not only the overt political position of important writers and intellectuals but also the implicit *utopian* aims of their social criticisms. In more general terms, I make explicit in this chapter the evaluative purposes of my critical approach to literature and culture in this book. Like it or not, we are always making judgments in the course of interpretation; whereas literary criticism has very often focused on a text's aesthetic value, my approach in this book is to assess the literary work's relative contributions to social consensus and social reform.

We must also be attentive to the ways sophisticated intellectuals design their rhetoric for several different audiences, as I argue Henry Adams does in his *Education*. Representing himself as an ironic, skeptical, and often world-weary modern, Adams has given us one of the archetypes of modernist selfhood. By the same token, he was a willing, albeit informal, advisor to his close friend and Washington neighbor, John Hay, while the latter served as secretary of state in the period U.S. foreign policy assumed its modern and decidedly neoimperialist design. Often distancing himself from Hay, Adams nonetheless mythologizes Hay in *The Education of Henry Adams* as modern successor to the traditional American statesman and thus American *self*, whose type Adams claims was defined by such distinguished forebears as John Adams and John Quincy Adams. Henry Adams's ambivalence, at times downright diffidence, about international politics disguises a much more serious interest and involvement in the global politics of his times, ranging from international relations between Great Britain and the United States during the Civil War to the U.S. role in the Caribbean and South Pacific at the turn-of-the-century.

The rhetorical subtlety of Stephen Crane and Henry Adams, each ostensibly advocating liberal and anti-imperialist politics while often reaffirming racial, gender, and class hierarchies in U.S. society, is some measure of the problem confronting those intellectuals who attempted to "write back" against the continuing marginalization of minorities and women within U.S. society and the growing neoimperialist ambitions of the United States in the first half of the twentieth century. W. E. B. Du Bois's early writings criticize U.S. domestic policies, especially as they disadvantaged African Americans, in terms of Du Bois's wider critique of global imperialism. What has not been sufficiently recognized in Du Bois's writings from *The Souls of Black Folk* (1903) to *Black Reconstruction in America* (1935) is the degree to which his critique of "inner" and "outer" imperialism includes a searching consideration of gender hierarchies. This relative neglect may well be a result of the central importance placed on *The Souls of Black Folk* in Du Bois's reputation among scholars of American literature—a work in which Du Bois only begins to reflect upon the related consequences of racial and gender inequities in the United States and abroad. By considering less frequently interpreted literary works, like *Darkwater*, I argue that Du Bois's criticism of gender and racial hierarchies is central to his thought and politics in the first four decades of his career.

Du Bois's subsequent rage regarding U.S. neoimperialism, motivated in part by the U.S. government's harassment of him and in part by the relative neglect of U.S. global ambitions by other intellectuals, drove him into the politically unacceptable (and uncritical) Stalinism that informs his later writings. To be sure, Du Bois's double-standard in criticizing U.S. neoimperialism while ignoring Soviet global ambitions has led to the neglect of his political thinking, especially as it was expressed in his later writings. Insofar as he imagined literary and scholarly writing to be partial means both of calling attention to and potentially *changing* inequitable social practices, however, Du Bois deserves greater scholarly attention as a model for the ways writers and intellectuals may challenge the dominant values of a powerful society, like the United States. By the same token, Du Bois represents the limited choices available to the modern intellectual struggling to criticize U.S. neoimperialism at a time when such foreign policies were as inadequately recognized by the general public for their inequities as were our domestic policies with respect to minorities, women, and the economically disadvantaged.

One of my conclusions in this book is that many anti-imperialist writers and intellectuals recognized how profoundly rhetorical practices, literary forms, and related behavioral identities and roles help perpetuate systems of domination and mask them from critical view. Yet, this insight also requires the development of critical strategies for unmasking such imperialist practices *and* new forms of representing communities that will avoid the limitations and universalizing tendencies of conventional American types, ideals, rhetorical strategies, and narratives. There is, then, a deliberate effort to try out alternative, avant-garde modes of representation in the very period when such experimentalism seems identified principally with the cosmopolitanism of the high-modernist tradition. My aim in this book is to reassess by *broadening* literary "modernism" to include a variety of alternative narrative strategies and forms intended to challenge the dominance of Euro-American cultural forms.[38]

These formal and narratological problems are epitomized by the various published accounts of Lakota culture associated with the Medicine Man, Hehaka Sapa, or Nicholas Black Elk, whose oral storytelling was variously transcribed, translated, edited, and published by John Neihardt, Joseph Epes Brown, and Raymond J. DeMallie. Taken together, the Nick Black Elk narratives employ multiple authors, incorporate diverse and often incompatible cultures, rely on allusive styles, and criticize urban capitalism in ways that resemble more celebrated modernist classics as Ezra Pound's *Hugh Selwyn Mauberley* (1920), T. S. Eliot's *The Waste Land* (1925), John Dos Passos's *Manhattan Transfer* (1925), and Walker Evans and James Agee's *Let Us Now Praise Famous Men* (1941). By the same token, the Black Elk narratives address very specific historical events and federal policies with direct impact on the lives of Native American peoples. Like Du Bois's political novels, the Black Elk narratives are designed to contribute to the public policy discussions in hopes of alleviating the suffering of an oppressed minority people. However, the complex narrative invention of "Nick Black Elk" in U.S. literature, anthropology, and history as one of the most famous "Indians" of the twentieth century raises a wide range of questions about U.S. culture's central role in the colonization of other peoples and their cultures. There is no simple conclusion to be drawn from this history, which entangles literature, anthropology, historiography, religion, and public policy in a social and political narrative of how we mistreated native peoples from the Dawes Act (1887) to the so-called Indian "New Deal" of the 1930s and 1940s.

The study of this narrative invention of "Nick Black Elk" is also a reminder of how centrally the scholar can participate in U.S. neoimperialism, which is one reason I conclude this book with Zora Neale Hurston's efforts to develop an alternative anthropology in her study of rural African-American folklore and hoodoo, *Mules and Men*, and Caribbean politics and religion, *Tell My Horse*. What is sometimes considered the anticipation of more contemporary "literary anthropology" in these two books also poses questions about our tendency to forget or ignore significant historical differences between modern and postmodern intellectuals. Hurston's criticism of the continuing racism and sexism in domestic society does not prevent her from endorsing the sort of "Good Neighbor" posture the United States would adopt increasingly in Latin American and Caribbean politics in the 1940s and 1950s. *Tell My Horse* criticizes Euro-American colonialism in the Caribbean, for example, but it is ambivalent about the U.S. occupation of Haiti (1915–1934) and ends up supporting the ideology of Pan-Americanism, sustained by U.S. economic assistance, that would help rationalize U.S. interference in the politics of other nations in the Western Hemisphere during this century.

There are, of course, a wide range of other literary, historical, scholarly, and popular texts that might have been selected to develop this thesis about U.S. imperialism at home and abroad. Concerned as I am to explain my selection of authors and works, I do not wish to exaggerate their claims to privilege in the history and interpretation of culture's role in U.S. imperialism. In short, there is no canon of works that ought to be studied; in a certain sense, almost any aspect of cultural production might be interpreted to reveal the system of and the possibilities for challenging the ideology of U.S. imperialism. Nevertheless, the works discussed in the following chapters have enabled me to discuss an extraordinarily wide range of explicitly colonial ventures pursued by the American colonial and U.S. governments since the eighteenth century. When recounted solely in terms of recognizable military and political conflicts, the cultural history of U.S. imperialism these texts make available is far-reaching and diverse, including the French and Indian War, the American Revolution, and the XYZ Affair (Chapter 2); conflict between the United States and Great Britain over the Oregon Territory and the Louisiana Purchase (Chapter 3); the War of 1812 (Chapter 4); the Mexican-American War and the Trail of Tears (Chapter 5); the Civil War and U.S. involvement in the Taiping Rebellion (Chapter 6); the Spanish-American and Philippine-American wars (Chapters 7 and 8); racially motivated riots in Atlanta and St. Louis and World War I (Chapter 9); George Armstrong Custer's defeat and the Massacre at Wounded Knee (Chapter 10); and the U.S. military occupation of Haiti (Chapter 11). Add to this list the many different congressional acts, constitutional amendments, new and revised laws, and federal and state policies that we must understand in order to read these literary texts, and you have a syllabus that is as historical as it is literary. Although I claim no canonical status for these texts, I do argue that the historical understanding they help organize gives them special *educational* and thus *pedagogical* values. When interpreted in terms of their different genres and cultural purposes, these texts do not constitute an aesthetic or political tradition. What connects them is their contribution, by complicity, equivocation, or protest, to the genealogy of U.S. imperialism.

We often organize and debate the meaning of "American Literature" in terms of canonical values based on aesthetic criteria, which lend themselves to evaluations of discrete works. Although debates about literary canons in the U.S. and other societies still have great importance, there are other ways to judge the "value" of literary and cultural works. My method in this book is to establish relationships among texts that are historically determined, so that I can investigate the scope and variety of U.S. colonial ventures from the Revolution to World War II while remaining attentive to possible critical responses to such colonialism. I have selected works according to what I term a *curricular*, rather than *canonical*, standard, by which I mean that the works function together by virtue of their representation of a common historical subject. Judged according to conventional aesthetic standards, these works would not ordinarily be considered together and thus would not do the cultural work I have attempted in the following pages.

I use this term "curricular standard" to emphasize the importance of our pedagogical purposes in the selection and organization of cultural texts in scholarship. After all, *teaching* should be one of the primary tests of the validity of our scholarship in many of the humanities and social sciences. How does this scholarly argument help me educate students about the meanings, values, and uses of "American Literature"? Most canonical approaches, including those designed to revise the literary canon, are limited to teaching the "best that has been thought and written" and substituting thereby a history of "genius" (or "history of ideas") for a more nuanced cultural and political history. By the same token, I do not want to insist that the selection of works and authors, even of historical events and policies, constitutes *the* curriculum for the study of cultural responses to U.S. imperialism. Scholarship informs course design and actual classroom teaching in complex, often indirect, ways, in part because our acts of teaching are so performatively diverse, thanks to different teachers, students, and levels of education. The texts discussed in the following chapters should be suggestive for teachers interested in treating topics relevant to U.S. nationalism and expansionism. These teachers should always take responsibility for developing their own courses and curricula, but the combination of canonical and non-canonical works and authors in the following chapters might provide some guidance about how to address the particularly complex intersection of literary culture and U.S. imperialism.

In its effort to suggest the range and variety of U.S. cultural responses to the emerging imperialist policies of the United States from the earliest days of the republic to the 1940s, this book also attempts to historicize carefully the ideological limitations of each writer considered. None is free of intellectual limitations occasioned by the specific historical and political situation in which that intellectual worked; none solves the problem, then, of how to criticize and thus overcome neoimperialist tendencies of the United States, although many of those considered offer specific alternatives to the racial, gender, and class hierarchies that U.S. democracy is supposed to reject. It is just this variety of approaches and common historical and ideological limitation that justifies the scope of this study, because the conclusion to be drawn from the following chapters is that there is no comprehensive theory of how U.S. culture has contributed to or vigorously criticized U.S. imperialism both at home and abroad. In a similar sense, there is no simple solution to the problem of U.S. neoimperialism. The different historical *practices* of intellectuals who have been willing to risk political mistakes, suffer persecution for their social criticism, and endure often equivocal assessments by subsequent scholars require careful study that respects the historical conditions in which such writings and ideas were produced. After all, such predecessors are our best teachers. In regard to artists and intellectuals like Melville, Twain, Du Bois, Black Elk and Neihardt, and Hurston, who risked their careers and reputations to challenge U.S. democracy for failing to realize its promise of liberty, equality, and justice for all, my study attempts to continue their work in the spirit of respectful criticism.

2

The Dream of Enlightenment
and the Nightmare of Imperialism

Charles Brockden Brown's Wieland *and* Edgar Huntly

Wishanem	Frightened,
Tulpewi pataman	The Turtles prayed;
Tulpewi paniton	The Turtles saved [some earth
Wuliton	And restored [the world].

Wallam Olum (*The Red Record*), Book II, verse 15,
trans. David McCutchen (1993)[1]

And after *Mikwon* came the children of *Dolojo Sakima*
(King George) who said more landmore land we
must have, and no limits could be put to their steps
and increase.

"Fragment: On the History of the Linapis
since abt. 1600, when the Wallamolum closes,"
trans. from Linapi by John Burns,
Rafinesque ms., *Wallam Olum* (*The Red Record*) (1833)[2]

"He had a dream," I says, "and it shot him."
Huck about Tom, *Adventures of
Huckleberry Finn* (1885)

Charles Brockden Brown's Gothic romances draw much of their interest and power from their settings in the unstable political landscapes of eighteenth-century Europe and North America. How is it possible, then, that readers for so long have ignored or accepted as mere Gothic mechanics the colonial disturbances and anxieties so fundamental to his narratives? Behind this rhetorical question is another, more profound one: how have Americans managed to ignore the inherently colonial and imperial character of eighteenth-century American society, even as they have criticized vigorously the colonialism of other nations in this same period? There is no simple answer to this question, but at least one compelling answer is that many Americans have been willfully deceived by political, social, and cultural rhetoric that has disguised U.S. colonialism while exposing and condemning its practice by other nations. This general discourse of displacement will recur frequently in the following chapters, and it is well illustrated both by the formal devices of Brown's fiction and the curious history of our reception of his romances as allegories of U.S. nationalism.

Written in the wake of revolutionary violence and amid the ongoing conflicts of frontier life in eighteenth-century Pennsylvania, Brown's romances consistently condemn violence caused by "foreign" or "savage" immorality that Americans must purge by way of a rational social order that would justify the new nation's domestic and foreign policies. In a revolutionary era plagued by potentially anarchic violence on both sides of the Atlantic, Brown's distinctions between "good" and "bad" violence have special appeal to readers confused by warring political factions and uncertain of their own identities and personal safety in the new nation. Brown's Gothics dramatize, then, the defensive anxieties of the new nation and thereby produce an "author," Charles Brockden Brown, whose reputation has ever since been wedded to the ideal of American literary nationality.[3] This intersection of literary authority with national authority is what makes Brown such an appropriate beginning for this study of U.S. imperialism, both because his romances return us to the seminal events of the new republic and because the mythology of the "author" is entangled so often with the expansive and defensive qualities of the typological "American self."

Jay Fliegelman, Robert Levine, and Jared Gardner stress the ways in which Brown's fiction plays upon the contemporary fears of political subversion that led to the passage of the Alien and Sedition Acts of 1798.[4] Engineered by Federalists in hopes of gaining political advantage over the Republicans in response to the XYZ Affair, the Alien and Sedition Acts were directed overtly at the French, whose harassment of U.S. shipping and U.S. retaliation from 1798 to 1800 constituted our first "undeclared war." Indeed, popular fears of Jacobin subversives or wandering Bavarian Illuminati in North America disguised the more practical commercial and mercantile conflicts the United States had with France and England in this period. But the Alien and Sedition Acts also represented popular resentments toward a wide variety of social and political groups. Gardner points out that it was "the Irish, . . . a highly politicized republican community, who came to epitomize the alien for the Federalists. Many of those active in the 1798 Irish Rebellion were believed to be in exile in the U.S., and the professed affinities between the United Irishmen in this country and the pro-French revolutionaries in Ireland sparked widespread hostility towards this immigrant population."[5] Both Carwin in *Wieland* and Clithero Edny in *Edgar Huntly* are associated with Ireland, the American "wilderness," and the "savagery" of the Native American.

Entangled in this historical web of European and American commercial, territorial, and ethnic conflicts, native peoples were renarrativized as "savages" and "Indians," thereby serving as convenient substitutes for political, social, and economic issues utterly alien to them and their cultural realities. In *Wieland* and *Edgar Huntly*, the violence of the frontier may thus be rationalized as simply one more example of the profound corruption and moral contradiction that haunts the European imagination and can be identified with various (and often contradictory) signifiers: Catholic, tyrant, anarchic mob, the working or serving class, the "Indian," the uncivilized frontiersman, and the Irish immigrant.

As Michael Gilmore points out, Brown's fiction also reflects postrevolutionary anxieties about the shift from predominantly oral to print cultures and related fears of democratic rule:

> The consolidation of established authority in the postrevolutionary era amounted to a print "counterrevolution." It was aimed against those persons in American society who inhabited an oral subculture where books other than the Bible and the almanac were practically unknown. These groups, which included disaffected farmers in the North and evangelicals in all regions of the country, found expression in popular verbal forms like extempore preaching and political oratory; they were people of the spoken, not the written, word.[6]

But the conflict in Brown's novels cannot be treated exclusively as an opposition between aristocratic writing and republican speech. Changing social and economic factors put both modes of cultural representation and self-representation in jeopardy of moral corruption; both oral and written eloquence had to be "saved" from degradation by the mob.

The early republic of letters thus performed the task of creating a vague consensus about the civic virtues and identifying qualities of the American by demonizing other peoples and cultures. In so doing, it established provisional boundaries distinguishing U.S. citizens from noncitizens. As Cathy Davidson shows, the early American novel was part of a wider cultural and political crisis of authority, in which "nearly every American leader saw the nation at risk unless the majority could be educated to the 'right' principles" and accordingly worried about "how . . . that worthy end" was to be achieved, "given the rudimentary system of schooling of the time."[7] In such a cultural context, the novel played a crucial pedagogical role. As Scott Bradfield has argued: "In the late eighteenth and early nineteenth centuries, revolutionary Western bourgeois culture instituted the idea that acts of transgression generate social order, both in terms of political reform and imperial expansion; in other words, transgression began to be conceived of as a disciplinary activity."[8] This idea of a revolutionary society, however, encouraged the first citizens to distinguish their morally righteous transgressions against the British and the French from a long list of immoral violations of social order, including Indian savagery, aristocratic tyranny, and democratic anarchy, such as in the Reign of Terror. One such discipline was literature, itself involving different disciplines, of course, in Enlightenment culture.

The metafictional aspects of Brown's fiction reflect not only the ambitions of this early U.S. writer but also the legitimation crisis of the new nation. As he works out his own rationale for literary authority, Brown borrows the terms used to justify national authority and its incorporation of new lands, peoples, and customs. What remains so compelling about Brown's fiction is its representation in microcosm of the ideology of the new nation, especially as it would justify the violence against others required for its founding. The new nation emerged from its own anti-colonial struggle against Great Britain, but it achieved its authority as the "United States" also by justifying its own colonization of the lands and peoples of North America, as well as of people violently imported from Africa for the southern slave economy. Brown's obsessive concern with literary authority does not simply mirror the new nation's struggle for political authority; it also helps distort and disguise the colonial aspects of that bid for national identity, implicating literature as an institution in the new nation's colonial imaginary.

The overt moral imperative of Brown's fiction is for the reader to distinguish between true and false representations by reconnecting a voice with its proper body. Amid all the usual distractions of Gothic technology, Brown's anxieties persist regarding the ethical consequences of a literary author *impersonating* someone else in the fictional body of a "character" or the "authority" of an allusion, to mention only two of the many different kinds of impersonation that literature employs. Characters like the ventriloquist, Francis Carwin, in *Wieland* (1798) and the unfinished sequel, *Memoirs of Carwin, the Biloquist*, and such doppelgänger as Clithero Edny in *Edgar Huntly* (1799) act out Brown's anxieties, often transforming them from the mere neuroses of the aspiring writer—again, celebrated as the *first* American who tried to make a "literary career"—to the insecurities of the new republic, lacking as it did the symbolic means to "represent" itself as such.

In *Wieland*, the evil genius Carwin uses his powers to mimic and redirect his voice to wield power over Theodore Wieland, the dedicated religious scholar, and his brother-in-law, Henry Pleyel, the rational skeptic, as well as Wieland's sister, Clara, and his wife (Pleyel's sister), Catharine. Deceived by Carwin's appearances, Henry imagines Clara to be Carwin's dishonored mistress; mistaking Carwin's calls for divine authority, Wieland murders his family and commits suicide when he learns of his mistake. Jay Fliegelman interprets *Wieland* as responding to the crisis of social, political, familial, and epistemological authority attending the democratic revolutions of the period: "Brown's novel of authority misrepresented and authority imagined is a terrifying post–French Revolutionary account of the fallibility of the human mind and, by extension, of democracy itself. Ventriloquism and religious enthusiasm . . . seem with a sardonic literalness to call into question all possible faith in the republican formula *vox populi, vox Dei*. In the year of the Alien and Sedition Acts here were embodied the larger fears that informed the Jacobin anxiety."[9]

Fliegelman implies that Carwin's evil has its roots in postrevolutionary anxieties regarding the mob as the demonic version of democratic consensus. Henry Pleyel first meets Carwin in Spain, where the latter has converted to Catholicism and declares his intention of living the rest of his days, but the association of this very modern villain with older Gothic anxieties about Catholicism and the aristocracy is a mere disguise. Rumored to have escaped an Irish prison, where he was being held for theft and murder, Carwin comes originally from the American colonies. His rhetorical skills and wide learning seem contradicted by his rude dress and the rough appearance of a common man, indicating in his person the contradictions between Enlightenment ideals of the "representative man," whose education entitles him to "represent" others, and the new democratic ethos, in which the terms for political and cultural representation are in doubt.

Henry Pleyel first meets Carwin in "the theatre of old Saguntum," the site of a Greek and then Roman colony in ancient Iberia.[10] Classical scholars like Wieland and Pleyel would know the ancient city for its valiant but unsuccessful resistance to Hannibal's siege in 219 BCE and its fall as one cause of the Second Punic War. Carwin first appears in a location full of reminders of Greek and Roman colonialism, but he also appears in a theater, where Greeks and Romans legitimated their religious and cultural traditions. It is, of course, Carwin's role as a "clown," in its now archaic connotation of performer, that Brown uses to identify his evil, because the parts Carwin plays are intended merely to increase his personal power at the expense of others. Unlike the Wielands and Pleyels, who study and debate together as one way of constituting their happy little community, a microcosm of an ideal commonwealth, Carwin uses his considerable learning to divide and dominate others. As Julia Stern has argued, Brown refers to drama at key moments in the narrative to question "the morality of spectacles," in keeping with Enlightenment debates about the proper use and potential abuse of theater as a didactic medium.[11]

Carwin's misuse of learning obviously serves Brown's didactic and self-promotional purpose of establishing the *novel* as the genre for sorting out true from false representations. Carwin not only throws his voice around in the most destructive manner, but he frequently shows up as other characters are writing—Clara in her bedroom writing in her private diary—or in some mysterious conjunction with manuscripts—hidden in Clara's closet, he again has access to her locked (he has found the key) and shorthand (a "system" he "had learned from a Jesuit") diary (W, 205). This persistent motif of *textuality* in Brown's novels has caused many twentieth-century scholars to find in him anticipations of the modern novel and its self-reflexivity, but Brown's allusive, often convoluted, prose style appeals to the past for a literate, often classical tradition.[12]

Even before Carwin arrives at their estate, the Wielands and Pleyel revere the rhetorical tradition of "the Latin writers," chief among them, Cicero, whose bust is placed at the center of their summerhouse, and their classical interests appear to parallel Brown's own (W, 24).[13] Brown's invocation of classical rhetoric as one of the binding forces of this little community of colonial gentry—*Wieland* is set "between the conclusion of the French [French and Indian Wars] and the beginning of the Revolutionary War"—connects the Wielands and Pleyels with neoclassical aesthetics and social values (W, 3). The family name Wieland probably alludes to Christoph Martin Wieland (1733–1813), the German poet and prose writer whose work developed from an early Christian idealism, like Theodore Wieland's, to the preromantic sensibility of the French Enlightenment. As a translator of Horace, Cicero, and Lucian, the German Wieland shares the classicism and cultural cosmopolitanism of his American namesakes. Yet whereas Christoph Martin had written a great variety of literary works by the end of the eighteenth century, Theodore Wieland leaves no literary legacy other than his sister's sensational account of his murders and suicide. Imaginably measuring himself against the German Wieland, who is still considered a founder of German fiction, Charles Brockden Brown implies that the American environment may not be conducive to a truly cosmopolitan culture.

However, Europe no longer seems the best place to carry on the classical tradition. Theodore Wieland refuses to return to Saxony to claim the "large domains in Lusatia" that he inherits, citing his obligations to his wife and children and "the ambiguous advantages which overgrown wealth and flagitious tyranny have to bestow" (W, 39). Wieland's democratic sentiments are those of the landed gentry in colonial America, whose education imposes on them moral and political responsibilities that entitle them to "represent" their society. Carwin's evil is an uncanny combination of old European and new American corruptions. In the former case, Carwin imitates the "degenerate" authorities of the political "tyrant and voluptuary" and the Catholic church. Condemnation of Catholic mystery is conventional in the Gothic novel, but Brown appears to have Frederick the Great (Frederick II, 1712–1786), king of Prussia, in mind as his model for the European tyrant whom Carwin emulates in America. The Seven Years' War (1756–1763), whose American phase is the French and Indian War of 1754–1763, was the dynastic struggle between Frederick the Great and Maria Theresa of Austria for control of territory now comprising Germany and Poland.[14] Indeed, Carwin is introduced to the Wielands by Henry Pleyel, who is engaged to the Saxon baroness Theresa de Stolberg, and Carwin commits his first evil act against the families while Henry is trying to convince Wieland to return to Saxony to claim his vast inheritance.

Wieland refuses to claim his inheritance in part because he condemns the "recent devastations committed by the Prussians" as evidence that the "horrors of war would always impend over" Germany until it "were seized and divided by Austrian and Prussian tyrants; an event which he strongly suspected was at no great distance" (W, 38). Wieland's choice of family and social obligations over unnecessary wealth aligns him with William Godwin's moral utopia in Godwin's *Enquiry Concerning Political Justice* (1793), as well as Godwin's Enlightenment opposition to kings, nobles, and priests.[15] Brown is especially critical of Frederick the Great, because he encourages and epitomizes Enlightenment reason on the one hand and yet continues to behave as a dynastic monarch in the territorial wars he wages. It is just this perversity of knowledge that Carwin embodies—using reason for personal power—to illustrate Brown's moral didacticism in *Wieland*.

In both Europe and North America, social problems seem to originate in the contradiction between man's disinterested commitment to rational principles and the lure of personal self-interest. Brown's concerns in both *Wieland* and *Edgar Huntly* are for the future of American democracy, which seems to him to lack the traditions and institutions of learning needed to prevent democratic anarchy. Clara's servant, Judith, represents the decadence of the democratic mob, and how it might be made to serve the purposes of a leader like Carwin (or Frederick the Great), whose main purpose is to use knowledge to achieve personal ends. Clara's honor is apparently ruined when Carwin convinces her servant, Judith, to impersonate Clara in a manner suggestive to Henry Pleyel of her sexual license with Carwin. Like later figurative equations of the lewd woman and the crowd, this one plays upon the opposition between sexuality and reason and tacitly reinforces patriarchal hierarchy at levels of both the family and the state.[16] Indeed, Carwin makes it clear that Judith has prostituted herself to him: "Your servant is not destitute of feminine and virtuous qualities; but she was taught that the best use of her charms consists in the sale of them" (W, 201).

Wieland and *Edgar Huntly* fascinate modern readers in part because the narratives employ erotic imagery and plots that often depend on conflicting sexual desires. Brown generally identifies uncontrolled sexuality with the breakdown of personal, familial, and social structures, and he rhetorically associates ordinary sexual desire with a wide range of deviant behaviors, including incest, rape, and madness. The licentiousness of Judith seems to contaminate Clara as well, not only in the "misunderstandings" of characters, like Pleyel, who have mistaken Judith for Clara, but also in Brown's moral universe. "Irregular sexual desires," Shirley Samuels argues, are "the direct result of excessive styles of belief," as Theodore Wieland exhibits in the novel, and the hint of an incestuous desire between Clara and Theodore seems directly related to some breakdown in the controlling mechanisms of faith and reason.[17] As Julia Stern observes of the common theme of incest in the early American novel: "The eruption of such interdicted desire in novels exploring questions of identity and legitimation in the post-Revolutionary period points to the epistemological contradictions that underlie the grounding of selfhood and nationhood in a dialectic of exclusion."[18]

So is reason degraded when made to serve simply the purposes of personal power or pleasure, Brown seems to argue in such contexts, warning his readers against a utilitarianism exclusively tied to personal self-interest. In this regard, Brown again follows Godwin's ideal of "true virtue" as a consequence of a disinterested and thus "benevolent intention" that "cannot be personalized, but must rather always apply to what benefits another human being."[19] Yet as Pamela Clemit has argued, Brown's interpretation of Godwin remains fundamentally conservative, subordinating as it does Godwin's "faith in the individual's development of his or her own rational capacity" to "inherited values and sources of external authority and control."[20]

When false moral authorities are followed, not only terror, chaos, and uncontrolled sexuality result, but so does a particular form of *savagery* that Brown often exemplifies with the Native American.[21] When Wieland follows Carwin's ventriloquized commandments in the mistaken belief that they are in fact Antinomian revelations of God, he murders his wife and children and then tries to murder his sister, Clara, in an act that Brown can describe only as "in the highest degree inhuman. It was worthy of savages trained to murder and exulting in agonies" (W, 174). Not only does Brown equate diabolism and savagery in this passage—an established convention of colonial North America—but he virtually defines the "savage" as one "trained" to perform immoral acts. In sum, the worst "savage" is not a product of Nature but the result of contradictions within its social system, so that we might imply from the earlier passages that Brown would consider Frederick the Great's troops to be "savages" in their mindless pursuit of *his* personal ends as they pillage villages and occupy territory in Saxony and Austria during the Seven Years' War. *Ormond; or, The Secret Witness* (1799) offers many examples of the barbarity of European warfare, although Brown associates the worst "savagery" with Russians and Turks in the two Russo-Turkish wars of 1768–1774 and 1787–1792, in keeping with contemporary Orientalist caricatures of bloodthirsty "Cossacks," "Turks," and "Mongols."[22]

The same logic would apply, of course, to the Native Americans fighting for the French during the French and Indian War, and Brown seems concerned in *Wieland* to distinguish the American Revolution from the "savagery" of other colonial wars in North America, in which political and military affiliations were often motivated by local and transitory interests. In *Wieland*, Clara describes the French and Indian War as a distant, curiously pleasurable phenomenon:

> The sound of war had been heard, but it was at such a distance as to enhance our enjoyment by affording objects of comparison. The Indians were repulsed on the one side, and Canada was conquered on the other. Revolutions and battles, however calamitous to those who occupied the scene, contributed in some sort to our happiness, by agitating our minds with curiosity and furnishing causes of patriotic exultation. (W, 26)

Brown is in part commenting on the innocence of those, like the Wielands and Pleyel, who imagine they can remain aloof from such political crises. Wieland's murder of his wife and children may be nominally based on the sensational story of James Yates, the Tomhannock, New York, farmer who believed he had been commanded by angels to kill his family, but it also evokes "Indian massacres" of English settlers during the French and Indian War, especially after the defeat of General Edward Braddock's force near Fort Duquesne on July 9, 1755. In fact, James Yates's first thought after having murdered his wife and four children was to set his house on fire and blame everything on the Indians.[23] After Braddock's defeat, "the western frontier" of the Ohio Valley and eastern Pennsylvania were "wide open to France's Indian allies, whose angry raids forced settlers to withdraw hurriedly to the east as much as a hundred miles."[24] Brown is also suggesting that the ideal, Godwinian community of intellectual exchange, mutual regard, and independence of the Wielands and Pleyel prior to the arrival of Carwin is in fact the political opposite of the colonial wars that rage around them.

Whereas the French actively recruited Delaware, Shawnee, Ottawa, and other tribes in the Ohio River Valley to fight the English, Theodore Wieland's father had sought to "disseminate the truths of the gospel among . . . North-American Indians," but "a nearer survey of savage manners once more shook his resolution" to such a degree that "he relinquished his purpose" and farms instead, growing rich thanks to "the cheapness of land, and the service of African slaves" (W, 10).[25] Having gained wealth and leisure, the father turns these assets to good spiritual use, reading "the Scriptures, and other religious books" and reviving thereby "his ancient belief relative to the conversion of the savage tribes" (W, 10). Once again his efforts end in failure, despite the "sometimes . . . temporary power" of his "exhortations," because of the "license of savage passion, and the artifice of his depraved countrymen" (W, 11). Withdrawing into "solitude," he adopts a "sadness . . . unmingled with sternness or discontent," but it does seem directly connected with his mysterious death in his summerhouse, where he is fatally wounded by a strange explosive light that burns the clothes from his body, scorching and bruising his body (W, 17).

Whether the elder Wieland's death is some Antinomian miracle, divine punishment, or natural accident is deliberately left unanswered by Brown, but there is an explicit connection between his disillusionment with reforming the corrupt American environment and his stoic anticipation of a "strange and terrible" death (W, 13). What he takes upon himself in an *imitatio Christi* is represented in the novel as his reaction to the unreformed savagery of colonists, Europeans, and Native Americans that will return to wreak its ultimate vengeance on his heirs. Although *Wieland* appears to make these brief introductory references to Native Americans in a conventional manner—to confront the father's Godwinian civilization with his corrupt and savage environment—the novel condenses colonial anxieties about Indian raids during the French and Indian War *and* displaces British colonial massacres of *Native Americans* in the more recent history of the Pennsylvania and Ohio frontier during the American Revolution.

Such narrative condensation and displacement are used much more pervasively to deal with Native Americans in *Edgar Huntly*, but before turning to that novel I want to show that these psychopoetic techniques are also operative in a text as overtly unconcerned with local colonial history, especially colonists' relations with Native Americans, as *Wieland*. Although the elder Wieland "allied himself with no sect, because he perfectly agreed with none," his wife worships "after the manner of the disciples of Zinzendorf," the eighteenth-century follower of Jan Hus and reputed founder of the "renewed" (or modern) Moravian church, the Protestant sect that placed great importance on its missionary efforts in colonial New York and Pennsylvania (W, 12). James Fenimore Cooper's Natty Bumppo is raised by the Moravians, whose legacy he credits with his spiritual leanings and "sensitivity" to native peoples, such as Chingachgook, or "John Mohegan," named and converted by Moravians, who thereby console him for the "death of all his tribe and his son."[26]

In the last half of the eighteenth century, several settlements of "Christian" or "praying" Indians were established in eastern Pennsylvania, western Ohio, and New York. Many of these settlements were sponsored by the Moravians, such as the community of Wyalusing, founded outside Philadelphia in 1765, and Gnadenhütten, Ohio, founded in 1772 by Christianized Indians from Pennsylvania.[27] Such settlements were efforts to solve the problem of the displacement of Native American peoples by European settlers and the colonial wars of the period, but these settlements were often prey to white marauders and their inhabitants liable to be blamed by Europeans for attacks by other Native Americans.[28] Colonists also thought that Christianizing Native Americans was a means of pacifying them. By adopting the economic, social, and religious organization of European settlers, such Native Americans might peacefully coexist with colonists in an early version of "separate-but-equal" ideology.

During the American Revolution, most Christianized Indians, including many Delaware, made treaties of neutrality with the Continental Congress and remained peacefully in their villages. Throughout the Revolution, however, Native Americans, especially those tribes belonging to the Six Nations' League, divided their loyalties between the British and U.S. forces or remained neutral. The war was marked by British-inspired Indian raids against colonists and attacks by troops of the Continental Congress and by colonial settlers against Native Americans.[29] Particularly noteworthy for my purposes are the several incidents of unjustified violence by European settlers against Christianized Indians during the American Revolution—episodes that may be strangely allegorized and thereby *rationalized* in Brown's *Wieland* and *Edgar Huntly*. Such incidents represent the general suspicion colonial settlers felt toward "Praying Indians," who were frequently suspected of masking their hostility and savagery behind their Christian pacifism.

The massacre of "peaceful, unarmed Conestoga Indians" in Lancaster, Pennsylvania, by the "so-called Paxton Boys" in December 1763 epitomizes the sort of colonial violence experienced by neutral Native Americans in this period.[30] Such events were sensational news in the colonies and new republic in the latter half of the eighteenth century, in part because they created such moral divisions in the European population. The Paxton men also "threatened to kill a group of about 140 peaceful Moravian Delawares, averse to war, whom Governor John Penn housed in the military barracks in Philadelphia for safety."[31] Debates in the Pennsylvania legislature about the Paxton Boys' massacres indicate concern that "Indian-hating" militia and other frontier bands might well jeopardize the colonial governments' authority. Such concerns were well warranted and anticipated the European settlers' inconsistent behavior toward Native Americans, especially in areas of what are now West Virginia, Kentucky, Pennsylvania, and New York during the American Revolution.[32]

In his pamphlet *Narrative of the Late Massacres* (Philadelphia, 1764) Benjamin Franklin "reverses the traditional roles of Indians and whites in recounting the massacre by the Paxton Boys," describing "the white frontiersmen" as behaving "like fiends" and representing the Indians "in terms usually reserved for the good Quakers of Enlightenment mythology."[33] Conflicts between native and European populations throughout this period often involved basic questions regarding just who represented "civilization" and who epitomized "savagery." In March 1782 Colonel David Williamson took 100 militiamen from Fort Pitt to remove Moravian Indians from the settlement of Gnadenhütten, Ohio, to the fort and destroy the town after warriors accompanying these pacifist Indians had attacked white settlers in Washington County, Pennsylvania. The Indians did not resist and were imprisoned by the militia prior to transport to the fort. When militiamen saw an Indian woman wearing the dress of a European woman captured in Washington County, however, they were so angered that they voted to kill the entire group of Moravian Indians, dismembering and scalping 96 residents of Gnadenhütten on March 8, 1782.[34]

Such questions about the savagery or civilization of European and Native American inhabitants were also entangled with anxieties about citizenship in the new republic. Wieland's insane violence is directed toward his own family and ultimately himself. However critics decide Brown's moral didacticism, they agree that this symbolic action represents the potential (or actual) self-destructiveness of colonial society on the verge of the Revolutionary War. Brown might well be addressing very specific political concerns, such as the concern on the part of Governor Penn and other statesmen in colonial Pennsylvania that they might lose control of militias (as had happened in the case of the Paxton Boys' massacre) that had specifically been created to control Indian attacks on settlers. When Carwin leaves the estate of Mettingen shortly after Wieland has committed his violent acts, he heads for the frontier of western Pennsylvania, where his brother is reputed to have a farm in the wilderness. Most militias had been formed in remote areas of the frontier in the absence of more formal military defenses, and during the Revolution these same militias, albeit recruited by the Continental Congress for the war effort, prized their independence and often struck out on unauthorized military adventures, many of which resulted in the kinds of atrocities against native peoples as had occurred at Wyalusing (site of the Paxton Boys' massacre) and Gnadenhütten.[35] Brown not only relies on conventional class distinctions when he identifies Carwin and the servant, Judith, with the potential "anarchy" of the mob, but he also creates regional distinctions between the lawlessness of the frontier and the moral and intellectual order of Philadelphia and its suburban estates, like the Wielands' Mettingen.

It may appear from these analogies between Brown's narrative and the history of colonists' relations with Native Americans that I am interpreting Brown as warning colonists that moral "savagery" may result from their cruel treatment of Native Americans. Were this the case in *Wieland*, then Brown might be expected to make more frequent and different reference to Native Americans than he does. Brown is by no means pursuing a liberal argument, even by eighteenth-century standards of political liberalism, in the connections he makes among violence, moral contradiction, savagery, and Native Americans in *Wieland*.[36] These four categories are exchangeable with each other throughout the narrative, and it is Brown's purpose to threaten his cultivated reader with the *danger* that he or she will come to *resemble* the self-evident "savagery" of local Native Americans should that reader fail to solve the moral puzzles at the heart of the novel's narrative action. Such solutions are in most cases in keeping with Godwinian ethics—the general ethos of Enlightenment rationality and the appeal to individual responsibility based on education and the common good of humanity.

Brown was as aware as other Pennsylvanians of the savagery frontier militias had directed at native populations, but these atrocities do not inspire in Brown the sort of sympathy for native peoples that one finds in Franklin's *Narrative of the Late Massacres*. Instead, Brown appropriates such frontier violence for the purpose of a Gothic and thus very urban romance, the reception of which is part of the European settlers' effort to "civilize" the "wilderness" of Pennsylvania. The rhetorical procedures through which Brown's *Wieland* causes native peoples to become "Indians" exclusively identified with their "training" in "savagery" is a subtler version of the ideology that substitutes European place names for traditional Native American sites. In the perverse logic of Brown's Enlightenment rationality, the "praying Indians" are themselves conceptual contradictions—thus the elder Wieland's fatal mistake in trying to convert natives—that only betoken trouble for the colonists. The Indian might be capable of miming the conventions of civilized man, including his religious devotions; but the Indian is not susceptible to the sort of self-governing moral consciousness (and *conscience*) that Brown urges Clara Wieland, Thomas Pleyel, and Theodore and Catharine Wieland to emulate. And because the Indians can represent either pure "savagery" or the moral contradictoriness of a religious "conversion" that will always subordinate them to the missionary's authority, then their destruction and the march of civilization seem to be ineluctably linked.

The mysterious death of Theodore and Clara Wieland's father may also be reinterpreted as a singular instance of European culture's sublimation of its anxieties regarding *its own violence* toward Native Americans. However stoically he appears to accept the corruption of both Indians and colonists, he actually despairs of the human improvement on which his philosophy is based and thus expects some "terrible" death. The supernatural "cloud impregnated with light" that strikes him in his "summer-house"—his special place of daily communion with Nature and God—stages the "savagery" of frontier attacks either by Native Americans or Europeans on settled people. The elder Wieland's body virtually displays such violence in the manner of a religious monstrance:

> My father, when he left the house, besides a loose upper vest and slippers, wore a shirt and drawers. Now he was naked; his skin throughout the greater part of his body was scorched and bruised. His right arm exhibited marks as of having been struck by some heavy body. His clothes had been removed, and it was not immediately perceived that they were reduced to ashes. His slippers and his hair were untouched. . . . A mortification speedily showed itself in the arm, which had been most hurt. Soon after, the other wounded parts exhibited the like appearance. (W, 18)

In his own "imperfect account" before he dies, Clara's father personifies what otherwise seems naturally explicable as a lightning strike—his summer-house is perfectly located for such a natural accident: "His fancy immediately pictured to itself a person bearing a lamp. It seemed to come from behind. He was in the act of turning to examine the visitant, when his right arm received a blow from a heavy club. At the same instant, a very bright spark was seen to light upon his clothes. In a moment, the whole was reduced to ashes" (W, 18).

Brown conscientiously discounts this possibility by insisting that "the purity and cloudlessness of the atmosphere . . . rendered it impossible that lightning was the cause," in an apparent effort to represent the divine destruction or spontaneous combustion of the elder Wieland as a mysteriously significant event. The scene is a condensed, even surreal embodiment of frontier violence, in which attacker and victim are strangely bound up in the same action and agency is rendered natural or divine. Jane Tompkins argues that the elder Wieland's life and death refer allegorically to "the first

Puritan settlers": "Like the Puritans, he makes an unsuccessful attempt to convert the Indians, and, as he grows more prosperous materially, like them falls prey to spasms of religious anxiety."[37] Brown has more local experiences of the frontier in mind, even if the Puritans' responses have certain similarities with those of settlers in Pennsylvania, especially as far as native peoples are concerned. Like the clubs and axes used by the Paxton Boys' militia at Wyalusing or the Iroquois warclubs used on settlers, the "heavy club" represents the violence of the surprise attack. Like the fires often set by militias or warriors to frontier habitations, the spark that turns the father's clothes to "ashes" eradicates the signs of civilization in an effort to prevent the enemy from returning. Even the father's "naked" body, its "skin . . . scorched and bruised," with only his "slippers and his hair untouched," suggests the cultivated Euro-American gentleman reduced to a state of primitivism with his skin darkened and thus racialized by such primitive violence (W, 18).[38]

Yet, the mysterious death of the elder Wieland condenses a variety of late eighteenth-century American fears, not just those associated with violence between European and native peoples. Robert Levine has effectively argued that *Wieland* allegorizes "the preposterous Illuminati fear of 1798–9" in America.[39] More than just "provincial paranoia," the popular fantasy that the defunct Bavarian Order of Illuminati, an anti-Jesuit and anti-national group often confused with anti-clerical and anti-monarchical French Jacobins, was working to subvert the new American republic reflects wider fears in the United States of the anarchy reported during the French Reign of Terror.[40] The mysterious light that attacks the elder Wieland may be in part a literalization of the Illuminati and thus an anticipation of the evils that will arrive with Carwin, a character who embodies much of the popular fear that radical ideas will lead to social anarchy and violence. Ormond, the villain of Brown's *Ormond*, is explicitly identified as "a utopian schemer and Bavarian Illuminatus."[41] Amid the many possible allusions for the elder Wieland's strange death, the frontier violence associated with the U.S. colonization of Native American lands and peoples, as well as the various wars among the European colonial powers in North America during the eighteenth century, is sublimated, if not fully repressed. The "mystery" of the father's end is vaguely identified with a wide range of possible "threats" posed to citizens in the early republic.

Scott Bradfield argues that in *Edgar Huntly*, Brown disciplines a wild and threatening "nature" whose transgression by narrative is "colonized" conceptually and thus made part of "geopolitical integrity."[42] In *Regeneration through Violence*, Slotkin argues that the Gothic fantasies of murder and revenge in the novel are enacted on the stage of the American wilderness for just such an ideological purpose: "Huntly's quest is a hunt for his identity among the choices offered him by the American wilderness—that symbolic equivalent of the tangled mind of man. His adventure is psychological as much as physical."[43] The absolute, threatening otherness of the wilderness can be tamed only by projecting upon it some recognizable narrative derived from European history. For Bradfield, this narrative is explicitly the class conflict between aristocracy and bourgeoisie acted out in the European Gothic; for Slotkin, it is the myth of heroic quest acted out now in a modernizing process that ritually purges "savagery," in order to constitute civic identity. For Levine and Gardner, the cultural narrative tells of the territorial and commercial conflicts by which nations compete with each other to establish their respective national identities. All of these interpretations build upon Roy Harvey Pearce's insight that "in our earliest fiction the image of the ignoble savage, like that of the novel, has no meaning intrinsic to itself."[44]

Ironically, all such interpretations of Brown's fiction repeat the intentions of the text to render both the American wilderness and its native inhabitants predicates of the European narrative and its moral didacticism, even as they attempt to deconstruct that master narrative. In the preceding reading of *Wieland*, I have followed that narrative logic and reproduced just what Brown's Gothic secretly desires: the subordination of the Native American as a mere fictive device, part of the regionalism of the text and "a means to literary terror."[45] Such a dynamic of reading fulfills the literary text's purpose of cultural imperialism, whether or not Brown is consciously working out such a destiny in the deliberately ambiguous rhetorical games he plays with his reader for the sake either of Gothic suspense or moral education. Yet this game of reading is also a trap from which the twentieth-century reader can escape only by restoring to Brown's "Indians" their historical integrity as specific native peoples with traditions, languages, histories, and cultures of their own. In reconstructing such Native American traditions, the modern reader also must recognize the secret complicity between the mystifying, but apparently innocent, game of Brown's early American novels and the deceptive and finally genocidal discourses of the treaties, laws, and political policies adopted by Europeans in regard to native peoples.

In *Wieland*, the "Indian" is completely marginalized, not only in the spare references made to native peoples but also in Brown's lack of specificity with regard to which "Indians" he means. As I have suggested above, the history of Pennsylvania from the earliest of the French and Indian Wars to the American Revolution made it imperative for settlers to distinguish among the tribes who were variously enemies, allies, or neutral. In *Edgar Huntly*, Native Americans not only play much more central roles in the dramatic action and receive thereby far more narrative discussion, but they are also specified as the *Delaware*—or Lenni-Lenape, in their own proper name and language (Linapi). Brown still renders the Lenni-Lenape as mere ghosts or phantoms in a fantastic and nightmarish narrative of Euro-American anxieties concerning the ethics distinguishing insane murder from justifiable homicide, anarchy from just revolution. In the social psychology of *Edgar Huntly*, ethical, legal, and genealogical questions in the novel already constitute the "inside," which situates the Delaware in a cultural topography that is identified as an "outside," defined as unchecked savagery and wildness.

The modern critical fascination with this novel has often focused on the modernity of the psychological states described and as a consequence has helped reinforce the ideological transposition of both the "wilderness" and its "savages" into categories of the Euro-American unconscious, rather than referents for specific locales and peoples. Norman Grabo, for example, blithely turns the narrative into an Oedipal romance, which is "so basic . . . to our nature" as to define the very different histories and lives of Huntly, Clithero, Sarsefield, the "captive girl," and even the Native Americans.[46] To play this game of reading, then, is to do the work of cultural colonization, even when the attentive reader analyzes this transformation of the historical Lenni-Lenape into the "Delaware renegades" ordered to enact "Queen Mab's" revenge upon the settlers in *Edgar Huntly* or reveals Indian "savagery" as the mere horizon for Brown's ethics in *Wieland*. In sum, the customary readings of the Native American subplot of *Edgar Huntly*, no matter how attentive they may be to this commodification of the "Indian," reproduce it as they retrace the complex lines of the Gothic plot.[47]

Jared Gardner's "Alien Nation: Edgar Huntly's Savage Awakening" and Sydney J. Krause's "Penn's Elm and *Edgar Huntly*: Dark 'Instruction to the Heart'" help us escape this narrative of European cultural colonialism.[48] Both scholars achieve critical distance by means of rigorous historical reconstruction of the events in colonial and early republican Pennsylvania. Krause focuses on colonial treaties that deprived the Lenni-Lenape of their lands in and around the "Forks of the Delaware," in Solesbury Township, where Huntly lives in the novel. Gardner concentrates on the Alien and Sedition Acts as legal and political referents for the popular demand in the new republic for terms to distinguish the "American" from others, the citizen from the "alien," and the civilized from the "savage." Such historical reconstruction, however, leads each scholar to a different conclusion regarding Brown's political and historical aims.

For Krause, Brown's fictional treatment of the unhappy history of relations between the Lenni-Lenape and settlers expresses Brown's consciousness of the sins of colonialism. Krause rereads *Edgar Huntly* as the allegorization of the history of colonial relations with the Delaware. Krause traces this history to William Penn's legendary "Elm Treaty" of 1682, in which everlasting peace and cooperation between the Quakers and the Lenni-Lenape was sworn, and suggests that subsequent violations of this treaty are what Brown symbolically "mourns" in Clithero Edny's nightly visitations to the elm in *Edgar Huntly*: "But as historical commentary, the applicability of Brown's Elm rests on a pointed distinction: under Penn's tree the transaction was for peace and friendship, under Brown's for vengeance and murder. On the one hand, Penn's tree memorializes a founding Quaker desire for amity between the races; on the other, it testifies to an eventual erosion of that policy—predictably, the triumph in time of racial enmity over amity."[49] Krause traces the violation of William Penn's founding dream of harmony between Europeans and native peoples to the infamous Walking Purchase of 1737, whereby John and Thomas Penn, wastrel sons of William Penn, cheated the Lenni-Lenape of their land and helped incite frontier violence between settlers and Native Americans in colonial Pennsylvania for the remainder of the eighteenth century. Allying themselves with the French in the French and Indian War, in part because of their anger toward the English settlers for the Walking Purchase cheat, the Lenni-Lenape were defeated along with the French at Fort Duquesne in 1758 and had to accept English domination.[50]

Krause reads this history in relation to *Edgar Huntly* as Brown would have probably wanted him to: as evidence that "fiction is a perfected form of history, best told as the autobiography of a character worthy of interest and attention," and this "fictitious history is thus moral, elevating, and even openly didactic," as Norman Grabo interprets the aesthetic Brown presented in his 1799 *Monthly Magazine* article, "Walstein's School of History: From the German of Krants of Gotha."[51] Krause's conclusion is that Brown was fictionally rethinking the moral implications of our colonization and destruction of Native American peoples and cultures. The Gothic nightmare in *Edgar Huntly* can thus be read as a kind of displaced narrative of guilt, of the "sins" of the sons of more noble and idealistic fathers, such as William Penn, being visited and revisited upon the young republic.

Krause cites one of the "Memorandums" that Brown published in his *Literary Magazine* in August 1801, after Brown had given up his own career as novelist, to support the claim that he consciously shares the guilt with his fellow citizens for having supplanted the Lenni-Lenape (and other Native Americans) "in their native possessions" and having "root[ed] out their posterity from the country, and [trampled] down the graves of their fathers."[52] Such evidence can also be found in *Edgar Huntly*, in which Brown notes that "a long course of injuries and encroachments had lately exasperated the Indian tribes," but Huntly's conclusion is practical, rather than moral: "An implacable and exterminating war was generally expected."[53] Preceded by Huntly's description of his parents and their infant child "murdered in their beds; the house . . . pillaged, and . . . burnt to the ground," the sympathy for the injustices suffered by local tribes is insufficient to dispel the way memories of Indian violence structure Huntly's attitudes: "I never looked upon, or called up the image of a savage without shuddering" (EH, 173). Acknowledging that Brown was "of two minds about the Indian over a span of four years"—from the writing of *Edgar Huntly* to the "Memorandums" in his *Literary Magazine*—Krause finds the same contradictory attitudes organizing Huntly's demonization of the Native American and his emulation of him.[54] Such contradictoriness is characteristic of the psychology of the nineteenth-century "Indian-hater" and its less obvious epiphenomena from the development of "Indian ethnology" to our contemporary fascination with Native American arts, crafts, and decorative styles.

Krause's historical reconstruction is illuminating, but it is used to reaffirm the traditional purposes of Brown's Gothic fiction, rather than to interpret the part his literary work continues to play in the mystification of the historical relations between the Lenni-Lenape and colonial settlers of Pennsylvania.[55] The history Krause recounts is actually so fantastic, so full of fictional devices and shadowy contrivances, as to make even a Gothic story as improbable as *Edgar Huntly* begin to seem realistic. The infamous Walking Purchase, for example, was based on an entirely imaginary "treaty" of 1686, in which Thomas and John Penn claimed their father's agents had paid "for an unspecified tract of Forks land to be measured as far as a man could walk in a day and a half, or roughly forty miles." That preposterous proposal was made even more improbable when the Penns hired "trained runners . . . to do the 'walking,' which yielded over twice the area that they thought they had bargained for."[56]

Brown's fictitious history in *Edgar Huntly* compounds and elaborates, rather than exposes, the colonists' treachery toward the Lenni-Lenape. Reputed himself to be a "famous walker," Brown incorporates into his novel the theme of walking that allows his own narrative to reproduce, sometimes in precisely the same historical locales and sometimes strategically displaced sites, the original Walking Purchase of those cheating Penns. The special irony of the Walking Purchase is that the term refers to one of the few ways in which the Algonquin conceived of land-measures— that is, in terms of the distance a man could walk in a certain time. The questionable "deed of 1686," for example, which Thomas Penn produced in an effort to convince Lenni-Lenape leaders to grant the colonists the new territory, referred to "a strip some thirty miles long and a few miles deep, and the measurement descriptions were cast in [Delaware] language since they did not compute, at the time, in English miles. Neither party anticipated the distance would ever be walked off."[57]

The Lenni-Lenape's own history, the *Wallam Olum*, is the pictographic record of the wanderings of the tribe from Asia across the land-bridge of the Bering Strait and then across North America to the Great Lakes and East Coast.[58] In effect, the history of the Lenni-Lenape is one of diaspora, which may well be why the idea of a walking contest or measure had some appeal to tribal leaders. In effect, the sons of Penn cheated the tribe by manipulating its own legends and practices, equating the tribal concept of land—what can be traversed by the migratory hunter—with the European notion of land as property established by purchase, deed, and enclosure. In his account of the agreement reached between the colonial proprietors of Pennsylvania and the Lenni-Lenape, Joseph J. Kelley, Jr., represents how the tribal leaders were cheated:

> Several meetings were held between Thomas Penn and the chiefs, at which an earlier deed of 1682 to Penn was quickly recognized and authenticated. But the 1686 deed gave them pause. As he pressed for its acceptance, Thomas Penn determined that once it was acknowledged, he would ask for the boundaries to be actually walked, and he undertook a

scheme to mark a course that would enable strong walkers to traverse ground far in excess of thirty miles. . . . The walk was fixed for September 19, 1737, at a time when days and nights were of equal length. Expecting the white walkers to move at the same pace as their own, the Delaware were stunned to see three specially selected athletes move off so briskly from the landmark chestnut tree near Wrightstown Friends Meeting House, totally unaware their route had been prearranged and a party with provisions sent ahead on horseback. . . . At two o'clock the next afternoon, the agreed termination time, [the white walkers] had gone beyond the Blue Mountains and reached the north side of Pocono Mountain. . . . Edward Marshall, the last of the three walkers, had covered some sixty-six and a half miles.[59]

The Lenni-Lenape leaders were surprised and outraged: "They killed [Edward Marshall's] wife and son and wounded his daughter" in what would be only the first of many acts of violence between the Lenni-Lenape and English colonists directly traceable to the injustice of the Walking Purchase.[60]

This method of narratively appropriating the native people's homes by manipulating their own stories and cultural practices is repeatedly enacted in the shabby history of U.S. colonialism at work in Manifest Destiny. It follows the curious logic of the "Indian-hater," whom Slotkin identifies as "he who becomes one with the thing he wishes to kill."[61] Huntly becomes the "savage" in the course of his Gothic nightmare, in part by "knowing" how to speak the "Delaware language," even though the "Delawares" in the romance do not utter a single intelligible word, as Leslie Fiedler long ago pointed out.[62] Nevertheless, Huntly already has the means of "becoming one" with what he hunts and wishes to kill; he knows how to "translate" Lenni-Lenape into "Delaware."

Fiedler is right that the Lenni-Lenape do not speak in *Edgar Huntly*, but Brown goes to considerable lengths to discuss Old Deb's special discourse and Huntly's ability to understand it. Having parted "about thirty years ago" from the main tribe of "Delawares or Lennilennapee," who "in a general council of the tribe" decided to move westward "in consequence of perpetual encroachments of the English colonists," Old Deb remains "to maintain possession of the land which her countrymen should impiously abandon" (EH, 207). Once the rest of the tribe moved westward, Old Deb "burnt the empty wigwams" on the spot now occupied by Huntly's "uncle's barn yard and orchard" (EH, 207). Moving to a hut abandoned by "a Scottish emigrant," who has "disappeared" and was probably "murdered by the Indians," she lives with "three dogs, of the Indian or wolf species," who serve as "her servants and protectors" (EH, 210). As Krause points out, Old Deb's hut and other frontier sites in *Edgar Huntly* are located squarely in the land appropriated in the Walking Purchase.[63] Amid her everyday tasks of weeding her cornfield, preparing food, and trapping small animals, her "chief employment . . . was to talk," emulating thereby the oral traditions of Lenni-

Lenape culture. Her "conversation was merely addressed to her dogs," and Huntly understands that "she was merely giving them directions," because he "had taken some pains to study her jargon, and could make out to discourse with her on the few ideas which she possessed" (EH, 209). Commenting explicitly on how he has come to name this old Lenni Lenape woman after English folkloric and poetic sources, Edgar notes that "her pretensions to royalty" and "her romantic solitude and mountainous haunts suggested to my fancy the appellation of *Queen Mab*. There appeared to me some rude analogy between this personage and her whom the poets of old-time have delighted to celebrate: thou perhaps wilt discover nothing but incongruities between them, but, be that as it may, Old Deb and Queen Mab soon came into indiscriminate and general use" (EH, 209).

Such cultural work is, of course, self-evidently achieved in the Euro-American naming of the Delaware in the novel even before the Lenni-Lenape are blamed for the murders and inexplicable acts of violence in the narrative. "Queen Mab" or "Old Deb" both are names invoking European traditions. The authoritative, nearly "legendary" Queen of the Delaware, who sends her "renegades" to take "revenge" on the settlers for their ancestors' theft of the Indians' lands, is merely a character of Anglo-Welsh folklore ("mab" in Welsh, probably "baby"), given special cultural authority by Shakespeare as "the fairies' midwife" in *Romeo and Juliet*.[64] To be able to name and narrate the Other in this manner, especially if the manner derives from or at least finds some affinity with the legends of that other culture, is one powerful mode of colonization. This is Tzvetan Todorov's thesis in *The Conquest of America*—that European rhetoric had the power to appropriate Nahautl.[65] Whether or not this was true of Cortés's military defeat of the Aztecs, it is surely the case that some such rhetorical colonization was well under way in eighteenth-century confrontations between European settlers and native peoples in North America.

More systematically and explicitly than *Wieland*, *Edgar Huntly* rationalizes the colonial displacement of and violence toward native peoples. Pressured by colonial settlements, the Lenni-Lenape decide formally to move westward, turning those like Old Deb, who refuse the "council's" decision, into renegades from their own people. Old Deb, not settlers, burns the abandoned wigwams of the Lenni-Lenape village, effectively clearing the space for what would become Edgar's uncle's farm and orchard. In place of habitation with her own kind, Old Deb usurps the abandoned Scottish immigrant's "hut, his implements of tillage, and his corn-field," substituting her own savage ways, including the hint of the Scot's murder by *her* Indians, for the progressive "civilization" of the colonial settler.[66] In Brown's fictional topography, the distant Native American exhibits some modicum of reason, but the few Native Americans still neighboring colonial settlements are savage, murderous, and rebellious, thus justifying their violent removal. This particular hut figures in the novel as the boundary between civilization and savagery, and it is where Huntly seeks "shelter and relief" after his ordeal in the wilderness fighting Indian warriors and rescuing a captive white woman from them. It is also the psychic site of the return of the repressed, because in it he remembers how his parents were murdered. Leaving the hut to find food, Huntly discovers that the rifle he has taken from the hut "is his very own piece, a weapon bearing unmistakable devices to identify it. He concludes that the Indians have massacred" his adoptive family, thus repeating "the memory of his natural parents' murder by Indians" and reaffirming "the aversion to savages which he developed after the discovery of that crime."[67]

As the subsequent plot reveals, Huntly's uncle and adopted father has died courageously *battling* the Indians, and the captive white woman Huntly saved from the Indians has been rescued by settlers looking for Huntly. Although repeatedly mistaking colonists for Indians and being in turn misidentified by colonists as himself a "savage," Huntly undergoes this confusion of realms and identities to purge colonial anxieties not so much regarding settlers' treatment of native peoples, but about their own insecurities regarding the "civilization" of their colonial enterprise. The hints of murder on all sides, especially as it may have been committed involuntarily in the somnambulistic trances of Edgar Huntly or his Irish double, Clithero Edny, reflect settlers' concerns about the self-destructive potential of the colonies. Remote from traditional sources of Western civilization and as yet uncertain about the terms of their own political and social authority, American colonists anxiously cast about for cultural means to justify themselves. As Slotkin puts it: "The Puritan captivity narrative had developed largely as a device for dealing with the anxiety of the Puritan emigrants, an anxiety that expressed itself as a feeling of guilt for having separated themselves from the parental household."[68]

Edgar Huntly's narrativization of relations between the Lenni-Lenape and colonists in Pennsylvania as part of a Gothic novel thus extends and elaborates the rhetoric of the "stories" told by early settlers from William Penn through his sons, John and Thomas Penn, to the agents of the colonial proprietary who "compensated" the "Delaware" for the southern portion of what is roughly Pennsylvania today with "a payment of 400 pounds." Virtually every reader captivated by this text has been so in large part by Huntly and Edny's "wanderings," asleep or awake, in the wilderness. Krause points out that the "sterile and uncultivated" qualities of the wilderness of Norwalk, where so much of the confrontation between Edgar and the "Delaware" occurs, is a landscape of the soul, "suggestive of the blighted relations with Native Americans."[69]

Yet, Brown's topography is actually quite fertile and cultivated when judged in terms of the erotic and libidinal passions it contains once these Euro-Americans begin wandering about in it. It has often been noted that the curious sublimity of this landscape is one of gorges and depths, rather than the usual heights and vistas, in part to suggest the depths of the psychic unconscious Brown promises to reveal in his narrative.[70] In *Wieland*, despite its reliance on hidden spaces, the views from the summerhouse where the elder Wieland is mysteriously wounded or the garden retreat where Clara meditates are vast and expansive and thus more conventionally sublime. The landscape of the unconscious in *Edgar Huntly* relies on the sublimity of secret caverns, chasms, and abysses. Brown takes possession of this geography by way of a narrative that is entirely cultivated in its European Gothic and romantic conventions, right down to the suspenseful entertainment provided by a plot full of perverse murders, insane violence, desperate circumstances, and twisted passions. Erotic desire is sublimated into the horrors of a guilty conscience: incest, rape, matricide, parricide, fratricide, and suicide.

The topography through which Huntly travels as he identifies and then fights with the Lenni-Lenape is curiously feminized, even in an era in which the feminization of Nature was commonplace.[71] At the mouths of dark caves, Huntly encounters threatening Indians, savage beasts, or the insane Clithero Edny sleepwalking. As so many critics have noted, the term "savage" effectively links the other terms in a sort of metonymic chain: Indian, panther, Clithero are all predicates of the inchoate "savagery" discussed earlier in this chapter as the horizon of the Godwinian morality Brown revises in *Wieland*. In both Gothic novels, savage passion includes uncontrolled sexuality, and it is just this that is hinted throughout *Edgar Huntly* as what is most "threatening" in the figures of Queen Mab/Old Deb, her "renegades," and Clithero Edny. The sexualized and feminized landscape "materializes"—as so many psychic phenomena in the novel do—in the figure of the captive white maiden who must be saved from the Indians by Huntly. Organizing the narrative, such "transformations" reinforce the reader's sense that the "empty" territory of the American wilderness is being rendered significant by way of these psychic projections. In a rhetorically more sophisticated but ideologically similar manner, Brown's narrative of cultural colonization recalls James Yates's decision to set his house on fire, run to his sister's house, and blame the murder of his wife and children, as well as the destruction of his property, on the Indians.[72]

Control of this "savage" and "feminine" wilderness is what Brown's narrative attempts to achieve, not what it criticizes. Those readers caught up in the literal or psychological plot pay far too much attention to Huntly's struggle with the savagery Clithero Edny is presumed to represent. The two characters are doubles according to the psychic logic of the uncanny, and thus their difference is their resemblance: they depend upon each other. In the course of the narrative, they sleep in each other's beds, trade places countless times, re-enact the other's actions, and are confused by or for the other. What Edny and Huntly find in the midst of this sterile, uncultivated "wilderness" are constant reflections of each other, in keeping with the way each character respectively finds doubles in the Lenni-Lenape.

Huntly's pursuit of Edny throughout the narrative in hopes of finding the murderer of Waldegrave is rhetorically figured as both a hunt and a seduction. The homoerotic aura of their secret relationship adds not only to the conventional excitement of the Gothic, in which fear and eroticism are complementary, but to the narrative's sense of forbidden and thus primitive passions. In his effort to maximize the strangeness of their psychological entanglement, Brown represents each character as variously masculine and feminine. Nightly weeping beneath the tree where he does penance for what he imagines was his murder of Mrs. Lorimer, Clithero Edny typifies an eighteenth-century feminine sensibility.[73] Threatened by wild beasts and Indians, cowering in the caves of Norwalk, and acting in a dream rather than by conscious decision, Huntly resembles the white maiden he rescues from Indians and then loses. But the transgression of gender boundaries does not mean that Brown rejects the sexual hierarchies of the late eighteenth century and endorses radical changes in gender roles. The confusion of gender and sexuality is always an indication of madness and disempowerment, the point at which "savagery" overtakes "reason." In every case, such liminal moments require narrative violence to reassert the "control" of civilization, subtly justifying more tangible acts of colonial and early republican violence against Native Americans, "aliens," and women.

The "savagery" that Huntly finds within the holes, chasms, and caves of Norwalk's landscape is by all means his own, but in Brown's fictional history it is a reassuring and decidedly masculine face that finally emerges. It is the look of reason that appears out of all the insanity, savagery, and psychic repetition. Its psychic opposite is the face of Clithero Edny, which undergoes a seemingly unending series of transformations that at their furthest point render him as a "gray panther" that fantastically takes his place in a cave and the "Indian savage" for whom he and Huntly are so frequently mistaken. In the secret recesses of Brown's narrative, much like the chests with secret openings that play their parts in the plot, the interior of Nature is relentlessly refigured according to the intellectual and rhetorical categories of European civilization.

Pursuing the sleepwalking Clithero Edny into the wilderness, Huntly faces and kills a "gray panther" with his "tom-hawk," and in so doing shifts the historical conflicts between the Lenni-Lenape and settlers into the universal conflicts of good and evil, reason and madness, within the hearts of men. Huntly is suddenly transported by virtue of his "sleepwalking" from home and bed to wilderness cave and deprivation. In quick succession, he fears death, meditates suicide, is driven to atavistic cruelty, kills the panther, ferociously devours the raw flesh and blood of the "beast," is physically revolted by his "detestable" banquet, and yet awakens refreshed and restored by its nourishment.[74] This scene of savage instruction is in fact one of colonial investiture, insofar as the internalization of the "savage" simultaneously identified as panther, Indian, and Edny is now also Huntly himself. When he drinks his own perspiration to quench his thirst, Huntly is for the reader part of the metonymic chain of a narrative of civilization that stretches from this wilderness to Old Deb's hut and finally back to colonial settlement (EH, 169).

Slotkin reads the many different allusions Brown makes in these wilderness scenes to colonial captivity narratives, most of which in turn alluded to sensational events of conflict between settlers and Native Americans, including Mary Rowlandson's *Narrative* and the "Abraham Panther captivity," which is a "brief narrative first advertised in a Connecticut journal, *The Middlesex Gazetteer* for May 18, 1787" and "pseudonymously signed 'Abraham Panther.'"[75] This captivity narrative draws upon the death during the Revolutionary War of Jane McCrea, a British partisan who was mistakenly killed and scalped by Wyandot Indians paid by the British: "The leader of the Indian troop, known as Panther, received the honor of strapping Jane's luxuriant chestnut locks to his belt. When Panther returned with his prize, the scalp was immediately recognized and the tragic error discovered."[76] In Fliegelman's analysis, the "death of Jane McCrea" had tremendous propaganda value for the revolutionary forces, because it identified the "savagery" of the Native American with the British enemy. In the "Abraham Panther" narrative of 1787, the Wyandot warrior, Panther, is replaced by a "giant (in one edition an Indian, in another a black man)" who holds the maiden captive "in a cave whose four apartments, containing weapons and dead bodies, give it the appearance of a charnel house." This racialized giant makes "sexual demands" of the maiden, who "in the middle of the night . . . mutilates and quarters her captor," avenging thereby the earlier murder and mutilation of her fiancé by Indians.[77]

The pro-American propaganda of Jane McCrea's accidental murder by Wyandot mercenaries fighting for the British and the more general colonial anxieties about the wilderness as a place of violation in the "Abraham Panther" narrative seem condensed in Edgar Huntly's battles with "panthers" that have now become the very wild beasts for which the Wyandot warrior and the pseudonymous author of the 1787 narrative have been named. Yet, rather than these allusions giving a regional specificity to Brown's novel that would locate it in the conflicts between European settlers and native peoples, they merely contribute to a metonymic chain of semiotic equivalents that allow Brown to universalize the historically and geographically specific events on which he draws. The equation between "beast" and "Indian" already informs the news story about Jane McCrea's death in the name of the warrior who wears her scalp, but the 1787 narrative allows "black" to be added to the list of equivalents for "beast" and "Indian," at least in the variant to which Fliegelman refers, and Brown's introduction of Clithero Edny, the outcast, half-insane "Irishman" adds a fourth term to this rhetorical chain. Although finally revealed to have been born in colonial America, Carwin's roots are Irish in *Wieland*, and the linkage of the colonized European Irish with the African-American slave, Native American, and the threatening wilderness seems to be Brown's means of constituting the vital "center" of cultivation and social order for the symbolically reborn Edgar Huntly. The racialization of the Irish was characteristic of English discourse in both popular and high culture from the eighteenth century throughout the Victorian period.[78] And the association of the Irish with wildness and primitivism often draws on rhetoric that is uncannily similar to the language Brown uses to represent the Native Americans and wilderness of Pennsylvania, as the following passage from a seventeenth-century narrative of travel in Ireland suggests: "These wild Irish are not much unlike wild beasts, in whose caves a beast passing that way might perhaps find meate, but not without danger to be ill entertained, perhaps devoured of his insatiable Host."[79]

From chapter 17 on, *Edgar Huntly* enacts the process of acculturation in miniature, and Huntly emerges from the wilderness as an individual who has been "nourished" by it or has somehow made it "fertile." Steven Watts concludes that Brown uses "a crude anthropology of juxtaposed 'Civilization' and 'Savagery'" in his fictional "descriptions of the steadily more sophisticated dwellings Edgar" encounters "as he made his way from the Indian wilderness to the Anglo settlements," a kind of cultural version of ontogeny recapitulating phylogeny.[80] At a certain level, all of the early European discoverers' fantastic anxieties about "cannibalism" are re-enacted by Edgar Huntly, who now acts out these fears in a manner meant to control the real threat through fictive play. But what has in fiction been enacted is just the "cannibalizing" of the native peoples that the Walking Purchase achieved in the theft of the Lenni-Lenape's land, their only means of survival. In Huntly's Gothic fantasy, the "need" of the native peoples becomes that of the settler, and the act of colonization, which may be figured both as cannibalism (ferociously devouring the panther, a version of natural self) and narcissism (drinking one's own fluids), is projected onto the colonized as just what the colonizer seeks to overcome.[81]

To be sure, the long Western tradition of symbolically ingesting the Self as Other, suggested in the traditions of Catholic communion, is connected with the desire to figure the Self through the Other in the act of telling either fiction or history. Jared Gardner interprets Brown's fiction as anticipating his subsequent political pamphlets endorsing an early nineteenth-century U.S. imperialism, specifically his Federalist call for the United States to move against the French and Spanish in the western territory. Brown's proposal that we take the Louisiana Territory by military force rather than purchase is for Gardner perfectly compatible with the American identity Brown develops in the characters in *Edgar Huntly*:

> Deriving its terms from the debates surrounding the Alien and Sedition Acts, *Edgar Huntly* describes how the act of exorcising from the land the alien (be she or he Indian or, as we shall see, Irish) allows American identity to come into existence. In staging an Indian war thirty miles outside the nation's capital, Brown leaves his young hero, unguided by family,

religion, or any authority higher than his own self-conceived notion of benevolence, to meet single-handedly the crisis of identity facing the nation as a whole.[82]

Gardner's argument suggests that Brown's work of early imperialism in his fictitious histories is one of exclusion and even exorcism, as Edny's death in the wilderness, rather than face incarceration in the "insanity ward of the Pennsylvania Hospital," seems to confirm.[83]

Gardner's conclusions suggest that Brown's Gothic novels offer subtle endorsements of the imperial policies of the young republic as it expanded westward, relying on territorial possession and Indian removal to secure its physical advance. By the same token, Brown's literary contributions to the formation of "American identity" complemented the Alien and Sedition Acts' goal of defending U.S. mercantile interests against French and British competition. The cultural work of the early American novel did not pave the way for the more recognizable territorial and economic aspects of imperial domination; it *accompanied* and complemented such imperialist practices. Indeed, rhetorical legerdemain is as fundamental to the texts of the Walking Purchase and the Alien and Sedition Acts as it is to *Wieland* and *Edgar Huntly*.

Whatever passion, savagery, insanity, and finally even imagination the alien Irishman, Clithero Edny, represents in *Edgar Huntly* is "consumed" and internalized by Huntly in the dreamwork of his first-person narration.[84] Francis Carwin is exiled at the end of *Wieland* to the savage frontier, where both white settler and native people are outside of Brown's ideal of Enlightenment reason. In *Edgar Huntly*, however, this threatening *outside* is psychically colonized as the work of culture matches that of negotiators like Thomas Penn, politicians like John Penn, and the surveyors and walkers who carried out their cheat of the Lenni-Lenape. In a similar manner, the cultural difference of the Lenni-Lenape is transformed from a society and economy that challenge the key terms of European individualism and property into a shadowy reflection of the settler's own savagery.

In the next chapter, I will show how Poe's fantastic narratives contribute to this sort of cultural colonialism in even more explicitly racialized terms. Often considered the direct heir of Charles Brockden Brown's adaptation of the European Gothic to the American scene, Poe willingly inherits much more than Brown's literary forms and styles. Poe finds in Brown a sympathetic conservative, whose ability to mime the liberal rhetoric of the Enlightenment is a feat of ventriloquism worthy of Brown's Carwin and will eventually find its way into the character of M. Dupin. Dupin is a counter-revolutionary who detests the crowd and a poet who holds his readers in silken bonds. In Brown's eighteenth century, the literary author is only one small player in the larger political and economic struggles for dynastic or national authority that literate Europeans and Americans knew were fought as much through texts as on fields of battle. Poe has the vision to anticipate a gradual historical shift in this balance of imperial powers. Although he failed as profoundly as Charles Brockden Brown to make his living from letters, he foresaw the power of words and of the author in an age like ours where the territory to be conquered and the commodities to be exchanged are already effects of discursive production.

3

Edgar Allan Poe's Imperial Fantasy and the American Frontier

Such are the fluctuating fortunes of these savage
nations. War, famine, pestilence, together or singly,
bring down their strength and thin their
numbers. . . . There appears to be a tendency to
extinction among all the savage nations; and this
tendency would seem to have been in operation
among the aboriginals of this country long before the
advent of the white men.

Washington Irving, *Astoria* (1836)

Poe's fictional representations of racialized "savages" as threatening figures, often associated by Poe with mass murder and
mob rule, are not only evidence of his identity as a southern regionalist.
Poe's rhetorical uses of non-European peoples should also be interpreted in
relation to late eighteenth- and nineteenth-century imperialism and the discursive practices employed by the imperial powers to rationalize their subjugation and, in many cases, destruction of native peoples. In making this
argument, I do not wish to distract scholars from the important work of
reinterpreting Poe's writings in relation to the ideology of the antebellum
southern slavocracy. We must never forget that slavery is an instance of the
fundamental violence of colonialism: the conscious effort to take from others their very means of survival. Southern slavery and westward expansion
in the United States have often been treated differently from the colonial
institutions of other nations, because the former are assumed to be acts of
"internal colonization." Yet, the slave trade in the United States caused
political, social, and economic instabilities in Africa and the Caribbean that
should be understood as "colonial," and the domination of African Ameri-

cans in the antebellum South was accomplished with the familiar colonial instruments of economic, political, legal, and psychological control.[1]

In the reassessment of how U.S. imperialism took shape in the eighteenth and nineteenth centuries, providing in many cases foundations for twentieth-century foreign policies and cultural attitudes toward other nations and peoples, we should consider the similarities between the southern colonization of Africans and more general U.S. efforts to colonize the frontier by subjugating its native peoples. The cultural histories of southern slavery and westward expansion are complicated by the tendency of U.S. politicians and intellectuals to emulate the authority and cultural superiority of Great Britain, in whose vast imperial shadow the United States continued to live as its leaders developed its imperial "destiny." Not only was the culture of the antebellum South notable for its imitation of English culture, but westward expansion was often rationalized as a continuation of the migratory and conquering nature of the "Anglo-Saxon." Such Anglophilia in the United States was complicated in the nineteenth century by the general U.S. effort to achieve economic, political, and cultural independence from its former colonial ruler and by the mounting anti-English feelings of the southern slavocracy in response to the effective antislavery movement in Great Britain.

Reginald Horsman neatly sorts out U.S. Anglophilia and Anglophobia in the 1840s by observing how frequently in public discourse the "English people" were "respected as fellow Anglo-Saxons," whereas the British government was typically condemned for its interference with U.S. expansionist aims, notably in this period in the Oregon Territory.[2] Popular contempt for British economic, territorial, and military meddling in North America did not disturb the strong identification so many citizens felt with the English, in part because many Americans still believed that the British government represented older aristocratic powers that had been eliminated in the United States. Horsman cites Missouri representative James B. Bowlin, who argued in 1845 that "destiny had arranged for Americans to check in Oregon England's drive for universal dominion" and that the "English were in trouble in Oregon . . . , because they were meeting free representatives of the same Anglo-Saxon race."[3] Matching his own rhetoric to this popular discourse in the 1840s, Poe imaginatively re-travels English routes of trade and colonial expansion with American characters, and he appropriates for these characters what he judges to be the best qualities of British culture and imperial power.

Cultural apologists for southern slavery and westward expansion worked diversely in the first half of the nineteenth century to develop what might be termed homegrown defenses of our colonial practices, even if the sources in English policies were often still readable. In this chapter, I interpret the ways Edgar Allan Poe developed an "American" rhetoric of imperial power that reinstates many of the racial hierarchies recognizable in nineteenth-century British imperialism. Shifting the racial hierarchies from the "peoples of color" in British India, Africa, and the Pacific to African Americans and

Native Americans, Poe ostensibly rejects the hereditary class-system of the English aristocracy for a meritocracy that still relies on racial hierarchies and frequent appeals to the tests of reason and its complement, rhetoric. In this regard, too, he differs little from the prevailing public discourse in the United States in the 1840s regarding Anglo-Saxon racial "purity," especially as it was invented to contrast with the *mestizos* of Mexico and thereby provide legitimacy for our aggression toward Mexico in the Mexican-American War (1846–1848).[4]

In "The Journal of Julius Rodman" and "A Tale of the Ragged Mountains," Poe's model for imperial power in North America and India, respectively, is Great Britain, but there is a strange doubling of Great Britain and the United States in these two narratives that works out what I will call Poe's *imperial fantasy*. What Poe imagines in these two fantastic travel narratives is achievable only in and through his own poetic authority; it is a fantasy of imperial power and authority vested in the literary author and by no means realizable in what Poe considers the increasingly decadent politics of democracy. Fantastic as such poetic authority may thus remain, it is by no means harmless or trivial; it remains very much a part of the neocolonial practices that can be traced from the late eighteenth century to the present and are uniquely influential in the development of U.S. imperialism in this same modern period.

Poe's unfinished "Journal of Julius Rodman," which was published anonymously in *Burton's Gentleman's Magazine* from January to June 1840, when Poe left the editorial staff of the magazine, has justifiably received little attention.[5] As previous scholars have pointed out, much of the narrative is paraphrased or directly plagiarized from actual frontier narratives, including his major sources—Washington Irving's *Astoria* (1836) and its sequel, *The Adventures of Captain Bonneville* (1837), and Nicholas Biddle's *The History of the Expedition under the Command of Lewis and Clark* (1814)—and lesser borrowings from John K. Townsend's *Narrative of a Journey across the Rocky Mountains to the Columbia River* (1839), the journals of Sir Alexander Mackenzie, and "other accounts of American exploration" by "Flagg, . . . Samuel Parker, and others."[6] Grandly subtitled, "Being an Account of the First Passage across the Rocky Mountains of North America ever achieved by Civilized Man," and beginning with the sort of hyperbole that typifies Poe's parody of other travel narratives and affirmation of his own poetic ambitions in *Narrative of Arthur Gordon Pym* (1838), the six chapters published in *Burton's Gentleman's Magazine* never make it across the Rocky Mountains, leaving the reader hanging at the end of the frontier party's conventionally sensational combat with two hostile brown bears.

Left unfinished by Poe, never published by him in book form, and not even acknowledged by him as his own work, "The Journal of Julius Rodman" has rarely been interpreted in relation to the chief themes of Poe's other writings, with the exception of the evidence it gives of Poe's interest in grounding such "imaginary voyages" as *Pym* in the facts of actual narratives of exploration.[7] To be sure, there is virtually nothing of aesthetic value in "Julius Rodman," but there is much political relevance for the current re-valuation of Poe as a southern writer, including my own interest in expanding Poe's southern regionalism to include his contributions to the culture of U.S. imperialism. In his biography of Poe, Kenneth Silverman comments on the "manumitted black servant Jupiter" in "The Gold-Bug" and the slave, Toby, in "Julius Rodman" as evidence that "Poe opposed abolition, and identified with slaveholding interests in the South, whom he felt Northern writers misrepresented."[8] In his brief but perceptive remarks on "Julius Rodman" in "The Literature of Expansion and Race," Eric Sundquist takes seriously what other critics have considered the hoax of Poe's invention of a character, Julius Rodman, who crossed the Rocky Mountains *before* any other European:

> Poe's temporal dislocation of the narrative of Julius Rodman into the past has a multiple significance. . . . It corresponded to contemporary efforts by Parkman and others to displace the conquest of the continent and the "doom" of the American Indian into an earlier century. At the same time, it accentuated Poe's own obsession with America's futurity as expressed in his short science fiction tales or in the philosophical dream tract *Eureka* (1848), in which boundless cosmic space appears in part as a figure for the unfolding destiny of the nation.[9]

Sundquist's discussion of Poe's unfinished "imaginary voyage" is included in a section of the new *Cambridge History of American Literature* entitled "Exploration and Empire," in which he focuses on the ideological function of frontier narratives in the racialization of Native Americans that served the emerging myth of the Vanishing American and the larger imperial ambitions of the United States in the era of Manifest Destiny. The ideological purposes of "The Journal of Julius Rodman" may appear unexceptional when understood in the context of other frontier writings, full of the same ethnocentrism and racial demonization of Native Americans abundantly evident in the work, but it is finally the significance of this conventional ideology of Manifest Destiny for the otherwise uniquely elite Edgar Allan Poe that deserves critical attention.

Julius Rodman is introduced as a native of England, from a good family and well educated, who immigrated to the United States in 1784 at the age of eighteen with "his father, and two maiden sisters."[10] From New York City, the family traveled to Kentucky, then to Missouri, where they "established themselves, almost in hermit fashion, on the banks of the Mississippi, near where Mills' Point now makes into the river" (JR, 1188). After his father and sisters conveniently die, Rodman sells the family's "plantation" and sets out on a fur-trapping expedition in the spring of 1791, returning in 1794 to take up residence in Abingdon, Virginia, where he "married, and had three children, and where most of his descendants now live" (JR, 1188). Burton Pollin points out that Kentucky in 1784 was a rough frontier region, where most settlers lived on small farms, lived in fear of Indian raids, and sought protection in military stockades: "In short, Poe's use of the term 'plantation' is anachronistic for 1792, but not for 1840."[11] The anachronism that troubles Pollin, however, is easy to explain: Poe imagines the expansion of the slave economy into the frontier territories, citing Kentucky as one historical example. In a period when public debate revolved around how the question of slavery would be decided in the new territories, Poe follows typically southern leads in extending the plantation system and slaveholding to the new frontier.

The direct line connecting the southern and obviously aristocratic Rodmans with their good family in England is typical of Poe's southern pretensions. The region that Rodman proposes to explore in the course of his fur-trapping expedition is in 1791 "the *only* unexplored region within the limits of the continent of North America," and it seems to encompass basically the same route as Lewis and Clark's—up the Missouri River from St. Louis through the Midwest, then across the Rocky Mountains eventually to reach the Columbia River and the Pacific Coast. Poe's unfinished narrative stops at the Rocky Mountains, but the completed story would have represented two regions crucially contested by the European colonial powers: the French territory between the Mississippi and Missouri rivers sold to the United States as the Louisiana Purchase and the Oregon Territory.[12] Thomas Jefferson arranged for Meriwether Lewis to explore the territory up the Missouri River and as far as the Pacific in hopes not only of finding a water-route across the continent "for the purposes of commerce" but also to discover what "commerce . . . may be carried on with the people inhabiting" the regions explored.[13] Although formal disputes between the United States and Great Britain over the Oregon Territory would not become public issues until 1811, Jefferson probably had in mind as early as 1803 the idea of a U.S. expedition from St. Louis to the Pacific Ocean as a means of establishing a commercial and then political claim to these two frontier territories.[14]

Under the French, the territory of what became the Louisiana Purchase (1803) had been open to French trappers and traders throughout the eighteenth century, even though at the end of the French and Indian War France ceded Louisiana, west of the Mississippi, to Spain by the terms of the Treaty of Fontainebleau (1762). Lewis and Clark encounter several trading posts operated by venturesome French traders along the Missouri, as well as ruins of previous sites of early commerce with native peoples. With some regularity, they pass French traders' rafts carrying furs acquired from Native Americans farther up the river. Some of this French trade in the area of Louisiana Purchase is, of course, a consequence of the relatively recent retrocession of the territory from Spain to France, under the terms of the secret treaty of San Ildefonso (1800) that Napoleon signed with the Spanish. But much of the French influence in the Louisiana Territory traveled by Lewis and Clark, then by Poe's Rodman, represents the continuous presence of French trappers, *voyageurs*, and small entrepreneurs who succeeded under either French or Spanish colonial rule. Both the Oregon Territory and Louisiana from the 1790s (the time of Rodman's travels) to 1840 (publication of the "Journal") are areas of intense international political and commercial competition and are marked accordingly with the influences of the several different Euro-American powers trying to take permanent possession of them.[15]

As Poe knew from Irving's *Astoria*, the public relations book that John Jacob Astor had commissioned Irving to write about the failed settlement of Fort Astor at the mouth of the Columbia River, the Oregon Territory was between 1811 and 1846 a special region of "free-trade imperialism," in which commercial ventures of the Canadian North West Company, the British Hudson's Bay Company, U.S. merchants like Astor, and Russian commercial interests virtually governed their respective and often conflicting trade territories. Like British India under the East India Company, the disputed Oregon Territory was a colonial territory ruled primarily by commercial rather than governmental masters. This confusion of private commercial ventures and U.S. government efforts to foster commerce is typical of these early ventures into territory west of the Mississippi. The rugged individualism of the frontiersman often thinly disguised a governmental plan, as Lewis and Clark's expedition demonstrates, and the "entrepreneurial spirit" of early capitalists, like John Jacob Astor, often succeeded thanks to generous political, military, and financial support from the government.

After the death of his father and sisters, Rodman "took no further interest in our plantation" and sells it "at a complete sacrifice," choosing instead to go "trapping up the Missouri . . . and try to procure peltries. I believe that much more property might be acquired in this way" (JR, 1196). Like so many of Poe's poetic characters, particularly Roderick Usher, Rodman suffers from romantic melancholia, in this case named "hereditary hypochondria," of which he hopes to find some cure on his expedition. Burton Pollin suggests that Poe draws on Meriwether Lewis's well-publicized hypochondria, especially as recounted by Jefferson in his "Memoir of Meriwether Lewis," as the basis for Rodman's *melancholia*.[16] Given Poe's heavy reliance on Jefferson's memoir and the 1814 *History* of the Lewis and Clark expedition, as well as public fascination with Meriwether Lewis's mysterious death or suicide in 1809, this is a reasonable speculation. But Rodman's hypochondria and *melancholia* are also typical qualities of many other characters in Poe. When these characters head into the natural world to discover some cure, they find instead the unconscious causes of their illnesses exposed. Bored, distracted, and mournful in his Missouri home, Rodman becomes vital, energetic, and interested on his frontier journey. For Poe, Rodman's unconscious poetic and romantic inclinations reveal themselves to the reader on the frontier. For us, the civilization of Rodman's settled life on his Missouri plantation is exposed as another version of the trapper's savage and violent life on the frontier: both are versions of Rodman's colonial will-to-power.

In his account of the settlement at Astoria, Irving makes clear how Astor imagined his American Fur Company and its post at Astoria as a commercial "empire" within the democratic United States:

> He was already wealthy beyond the ordinary desires of man, but he now aspired to that honorable fame which is awarded to men of similar scope of mind, who by their great commercial enterprises have enriched nations, peopled wildernesses, and extended the bounds of empire. He considered his projected establishment at the mouth of the Columbia as the emporium to an immense commerce; as a colony that would form the germ of a wide civilization; that would, in fact, carry the American population across the Rocky Mountains and spread it along the shores of the Pacific, as it already animated the shores of the Atlantic.[17]

The complicity of the U.S. government with large U.S. corporations in the work of what some have termed "free-trade imperialism" is recounted by Irving[18]: "[Astor] was aware of the wish of the American government . . . that the fur trade within its boundaries should be in the hands of American citizens, and of the ineffectual measures it had taken to accomplish that object. He now offered, if aided and protected by the government, to turn the whole of that trade into American channels" (A, 15–16). Astor's commercial ambitions are not surprisingly international, stretching beyond the continental United States and disputed Oregon Territory to encompass what he envisioned as a chain of islands across the Pacific controlled by the American Fur Company to secure the route to China, the largest buyer of North American furs.[19]

Unlike Astor, Rodman receives no offers of help from the U.S. government for his 1791–1794 expedition, but Poe makes it clear that the earliest explorations of this region were motivated by commercial interests with international ambitions. Referring to Jonathan Carver's (1710–1780) exploration of the Northwest Territory in search of the elusive Northwest Passage, Poe summarizes Carver's ambitions: "A settlement in this neighborhood would disclose new sources of trade, and open a more direct communication with China, and the British possessions in the East Indies, than the old route afforded, by the Cape of Good Hope. He was baffled, however, in his attempt to cross the mountains" (JR, 1192). In many respects, Jefferson imagined Lewis and Clark's expedition as the ultimately successful effort to find such a water-passage west to the Pacific, but within territory Jefferson expected the United States would soon control. After he returns from his travels, Rodman is contacted by André Michaux (1746–1802), the French botanist whom Thomas Jefferson had asked in 1792 to explore the territory subsequently charted by Lewis and Clark; Michaux urges Rodman to write out in detail an account of the expedition, which Rodman originally recorded as "an outline diary." In this regard, Rodman's diary seems modeled on Meriwether Lewis's diary of the 1804–1806 expedition and William Clark's copy of it (together with Clark's additional comments), both of which were sources used by Nicholas Biddle for the 1814 *History* and subsequently revised by Elliott Coues in a four-volume edition published in 1893 and considered the authoritative nineteenth-century account of the Lewis and Clark expedition.[20] Indeed, Poe's fictional use of Michaux is a thin paraphrase of what Jefferson himself recounts in his August 18, 1813, "Memoir of Meriwether Lewis" of Michaux and Lewis's early plans to "explore [the] region . . . by ascending the Stony [Rocky] mountains, and descending the nearest river to the Pacific."[21] In keeping with the usual Poe complications regarding missing, misplaced, and mis-sent manuscripts, Rodman's revised "MS. when completed, however, never reached M. Michau [*sic*], for whose inspection it had been drawn up; and was always supposed to have been lost on the road by the young man to whom it was entrusted for delivery at M. M[ichaux]'s temporary residence, near Monticello" (JR, 1189).[22]

Poe quickly abandons any pretense of describing an actual commercial expedition, however, in his account of the travels of Julius Rodman. Except for some early descriptions of beaver and techniques of beaver trapping, reminiscent of the technical digressions on the "drying" of *biche de mer* in *Pym*, Poe's narrative quickly swerves in the direction of a loosely constructed ode to the sublimity of Nature that Rodman encounters and as a thinly disguised metaphor for a *supernatural* dimension that Poe likely would have added to the finished narrative. Yet what assures us that this narrative belongs with those "free-trade imperial" narratives of commercial expansion West are the unmistakable class and racial hierarchies that Rodman's journal so clearly establishes.

Leaving the slave economy of the Missouri plantation behind, Rodman is nonetheless accompanied by a representative slave, "a negro belonging to Pierre Junôt, named Toby." Toby is probably based on the "black servant," York, "belonging to Captain Clark," who joined the Lewis and Clark expedition and is the only member of the expedition *not* granted a military title as part of his service (Coues, 1:2). Poe characterizes Toby as "a faithful negro" who "was rather too old to accompany such an expedition as ours; but Pierre was not willing to leave him. He was an able-bodied man, however, and still capable of enduring great fatigue" (JR, 1199–1200). In respect to age and physical abilities, Toby differs markedly from Captain Clark's servant, York, who is described as "a remarkably stout, strong negro," who will entertain the Arikaras with "feats of strength" and who will find special sexual favor with the Arikara women (Coues, 1:159, 164). Was Poe afraid to attribute sexual powers to an African American, as Lewis and Clark quite openly do, in keeping with Poe's southern fears of miscegenation? Whatever the reason, Poe's change of York from the physically able and youthful man to the aged and dependent Toby seems curious, given Poe's heavy reliance on Lewis and Clark's York as a model for Toby. One possible explanation is in the name "Toby," which Poe may have borrowed from the name Lewis and Clark give to the Shoshone, "our old guide Toby and his son," who leads them over the Rocky Mountains (Coues, 2:1008).[23] In conflating the Shoshone guide and African-American servant, Poe departs from Lewis and Clark's tendencies in their diaries to distinguish between Native American and African-American racial characteristics and thus conforms to the popular discourse of the period that deliberately combined and confused Native American, African American, and Mexican.

Poe must have had greater plans for Toby in the extended narrative, because he claims that "he was not the least important personage of our party," even though Toby will play only one part in the subsequent six chapters—a stereotyped performance of exotic Negritude for a band of Assiniboins who venture upon the expedition and with whom Rodman makes friends by virtue of Toby's display. "Struck with sudden amazement at the sooty appearance of our negro, Toby," the Assiniboins request "a good look at Toby," and Rodman agrees to let them examine Toby in exchange for a boat they have seized. He thus sends the old slave ashore "*in naturalibus*, that the inquisitive savages might observe the whole extent of the question." Toby's nakedness recalls the slave auction, as does his body as an item of exchange, even though in this case it is merely his display that is exchanged for the pirogue. What *is* displayed is Poe's racism, as the Assiniboins express their astonishment at the features of Toby, which Poe describes according to the pseudoscientific racism of the early nineteenth century: "Toby . . . was as ugly an old gentleman as ever spoke—having all the peculiar features of his race; the swollen lips, large white protruding eyes, flat nose, long ears, double head, pot-belly, and bow legs" (JR, 1242).

Toby's racialized physical characteristics are an amalgam of those Poe used for Dirk Peters and Nu-Nu in *Narrative of Arthur Gordon Pym*, serialized only three years (1837) and published in book form two years earlier (1838). The physically powerful Peters, who will survive the tale to live out his days in Illinois, is introduced as a "half-breed"—"son of an Indian woman of the tribe of Upsarokas [Absarokas]" and "a fur-trader . . . connected in some manner with the Indian trading-posts on the Lewis river"—and physically described as having "arms, as well as legs, . . . *bowed* in the most singular manner" and a "head . . . equally deformed, being of immense size, with an indentation on the crown (like that on the head of most negroes)."[24] Late in the *Narrative*, only paragraphs before he expires, Nu-Nu displays his "black" teeth, prompting Pym to reflect: "We had never before seen the teeth of an inhabitant of Tsalal" (*Pym*, 1178). These and other racialized descriptions of the Tsalalian natives in *Pym* suggest affinities with the "swollen lips" of Toby. In contrast, Peters's "lips were thin" and "the teeth . . . exceedingly long and protruding, and never even partially covered, in any instance, by the lips," giving him the look of "a demon" (*Pym*, 1043–44). The African-American York on the Lewis and Clark expedition seems a possible model for the *Pym*'s Dirk Peters, whereas Nu-Nu's physical deterioration, admittedly in response to the tabooed "white," seems to anticipate the physical decrepitude of Toby in "Julius Rodman." And yet Dirk Peters shares physical characteristics with Poe's black characters, such as the "bowed" legs and "deformed" head.

Poe's confusion of different racial characteristics is not unusual in this period. Pseudo-ethnographies, legal judgments, publications in the natural sciences, and many other discourses confirm the prevailing U.S. ideology of "white" as designating the U.S. "citizen" and a wide range of peoples of color constituting "the opposite of 'white.'" The preceding quotation is from the 1854 Supreme Court of California decision in the case of *The People v. George W. Hall*, who had appealed his murder conviction to the Supreme Court on the grounds that "the testimony of Chinese witnesses" should not have been allowed.[25] Citing such odd and contrary evidence as Columbus's confusion of Native Americans and Chinese ("Mongolians," in the language of the court) and Baron Georges Cuvier's "scientific" classification of "the human species" into "three distinct types," the court not only "excludes black, yellow, and all other colors" from the "citizenship" available to "Caucasians," but treats peoples of color as "a distinct people, . . . recognizing no laws of this State, . . . a race of people whom nature has marked as inferior, and who are incapable of progress of intellectual development beyond a certain point."[26] Thus when Poe mixes and matches characteristics of Teton Sioux, Tsalalian islanders, and African Americans to suit his fictional purposes, he merely follows the prevailing racial ideology in the nineteenth-century United States.

Poe's account of Toby's antics follows in many respects Lewis and Clark's diary entries about York's performances for the Arikaras (the "Ricaras" in the diaries). Lewis and Clark's accounts represent unmistakably early nineteenth-century U.S. racism regarding both Native Americans and African Americans, but with important differences from Poe's racism in "The Journal of Julius Rodman." Unlike Poe, Lewis and Clark do not stress York's ugliness, focusing instead on his color as the source of the Arikaras' fascination:

> The object which appeared to astonish the Indians most was Captain Clark's servant York, a remarkably stout, strong negro. They had never seen a being of that color, and therefore flocked round him to examine the extraordinary monster. By way of amusement he told them that he had once been a wild animal, and caught and tamed by his master; and to convince them showed them feats of strength which, added to his looks, made him more terrible than we wished him to be. (Coues, 1:159)

What attracts the Arikaras to York is precisely his difference from their own appearance, and York's novelty is what Lewis and Clark conclude cause the Arikaras to encourage him to engage in sexual intercourse with their women: "Two very handsome young squaws were sent on board this evening, and persecuted us with civilities. The black man York participated largely in these favors; for, instead of inspiring any prejudice, his color seemed to procure him additional advantages from the Indians, who desired to preserve among them some memorial of this wonderful stranger" (Coues, 1:164).[27]

Toby's physiological markers of race are accompanied for Poe by the behavioral qualities familiarly identified with African Americans in proslavery propaganda of the period. Once he has been examined by the Native Americans, Toby performs "a jig dance" for them, and Rodman notes that "had Toby but possessed a single spark of ambition he might then have made his fortune for ever by ascending the throne of the Assiniboins, and reigning as King Toby the First" (JR, 1243). Pollin points out that "jig" dances in the United States probably originate with late eighteenth-century Irish immigrants and that the "earliest dated references to Negro jigs that I have found are to blackface impersonators doing 'jigs and clogs of English and Irish origin' on the American stage in 1810."[28] In other words, Poe is once again conflating 1840, when African-American jigs were popular entertainments, with his imaginary "1791–1794," when Rodman pursues his explorations of the West. Lewis and Clark pause to comment on York's importance among the Arikaras, especially as a figure of sexual interest, and the Native Americans' relative lack of racial prejudice. However, Poe repeats racist clichés about African-American "laziness" in close conjunction with his accounts of Native Americans elsewhere described in "The Journal of Julius Rodman" as similarly lacking in industry and prone to theft. Whereas the white southern aristocrat Rodman diligently finds more beaver than he had expected on this voyage, so that he may devote extended periods to mere contemplation of Nature to the neglect of trapping, Toby is associated with the racial stereotypes of "laziness," good humor at his own humiliation, and entertainment.

The final connection made in the narrative between the Assiniboins and Toby, between Native Americans and African Americans, is by no means a casual identification. Different as Toby may appear to these Native Americans, he shares with them the racial degradation that Poe has elsewhere identified with the hostile and "thieving" "rascals," the Lakota Sioux. From the beginning of his journal, Rodman claims to know little about Native Americans. Nevertheless, before having encountered *any* tribal peoples on his journey, Rodman judges the Sioux "as, in the main, a treacherous race, not to be dealt with safely in so small a party as ours" (JR, 1204).[29] Indeed, Rodman's obsession with the Sioux is such that even the "editor" of the journal feels compelled to comment: "The Sioux, indeed, appear to have been Mr. Rodman's bugbears *par excellence*, and he dwells upon them and their exploits with peculiar emphasis" (JR, 1221). Among the "warlike" Sioux, Rodman (by way of the editor's summary) distinguishes the Teton as "most renowned for their violence." One tribe of the Tetons, the Bois-Brulé, turn out to be lying in ambush for Rodman's expedition as it passes "near the White and Teton" rivers' confluence with the Missouri (JR, 1221). Not surprisingly, then, when Rodman finally does encounter these fierce Bois-Brulé, he "discovers" the physiological markers of racial inferiority he also finds in old Toby; the Sioux are described as "an ugly ill-made race, their limbs being much too small for the trunk, according to our ideas of the human form—their cheek bones are high and their eyes protruding and dull" (JR, 1222).

Poe's language in this passage is a paraphrase of Lewis's diary entry for September 26, 1804 (Coues, 1:138). This rhetoric of racial classification is, of course, typical of frontier writing published in the first half of the nineteenth century. Nevertheless, there are important differences between Lewis and Clark's and Poe's descriptions of these "Indians." Lewis and Clark distrust the Teton Sioux, whom they initially feared and with whom they have an encounter that nearly deteriorates into a violent confrontation that threatened to end prematurely the expedition. Although Lewis and Clark comment on various aspects of Teton Sioux tribal life they obviously consider primitive, such as dancing and music they do not understand, they also note social practices, such as policing tribal behavior, that they consider equivalent to their own state of civilization (Coues, 1:136–37, 141). For Poe, however, the physical ugliness of the Sioux is matched by their stupidity, and Rodman easily convinces them that the expedition's deck cannon is a "Great Spirit" who is "displeased" with the Sioux warriors who have insulted it by misnaming it "a great green grasshopper." Justifying his act of firing this cannon into a crowd of 100 Sioux warriors, killing six men and seriously wounding eighteen more, Rodman goes among the wounded, giving them small presents, only to spend a sleepless night and part of a paragraph reflecting how: "Human blood had never, before this epoch, been shed at my hands; and although reason urged that I had taken the wisest, and what would no doubt prove in the end the most merciful course, still conscience, refusing to hearken even to reason herself, whispered pertinaciously within my ear—'it is human blood which thou hast shed'" (JR, 1229–30). The next morning Rodman has recovered fully, his thoughts of charity and morality apparently sufficient to justify such murder. In contrast, Lewis and Clark's diaries make much of the explorers' good fortune in being able to avoid firing the "swivel-gun" mounted on the bow of their keelboat, not out of any regard for their Teton antagonists but for the sake of continuing their journey without fear of reprisals and attacks from local inhabitants (Coues, 1:133 and 133n.1).

Both Poe's literary and Lewis and Clark's historical accounts stress the warlike qualities of the Native American tribes they encounter for the sake of justifying U.S. removal and destruction of native peoples. In the epigraph to this chapter, I quote Washington Irving's sentiments regarding the "tendency to extinction" of native peoples that Irving is convinced antedates the arrival of Euro-American colonists. In a similar manner, Lewis and Clark describe their own "peacemaking" efforts with the perpetually "warring" tribes of Native Americans to be part of the process of civilization and progress over the inherent violence of supposedly less "civilized" peoples. Never does it occur to Lewis and Clark that the consequence of Euro-American colonization has been the displacement of native peoples that has directly resulted in conflicts among different tribes over basic resources. In sum, both Poe and Lewis and Clark shape the myth of the Vanishing American by means of historical revisionism: displacing the violence of Euro-American colonization into the "inherent" tribal violence of "primitive" native peoples.

What is unique in Poe's racially constructed narrative of the frontier is his insistence that African Americans and Native Americans are "unnatural" presences in a landscape that meets all his requirements for aesthetic sublimity. When the Bois-Brulé first appear, they do so in a "landscape of the soul" reminiscent of the ravines in which the "treacherous" natives ambush Pym and Dirk Peters on the island of Tsalal in *Pym*: "The region infested by the tribe in question" is "deeply cut by gorges or ravines, which in the middle of summer are dry, but form the channels of muddy and impetuous torrents during the season of rain. Their edges are fringed with thick woods, as well at top, as at bottom; but the prevalent aspect of the country is that of a bleak low land, with rank herbage, and without trees. The soil is strongly impregnated with mineral substances in great variety . . . which tinge the water of the river and impart to it a nauseous odor and taste" (JR, 1223).

In contrast, Rodman contemplates vast prospects and Edenic delights on his journey that are deliberately, if conventionally, literary. It is sublimity for which Rodman yearns and which the narrative suggests may be the proper "cure" for his "hereditary hypochondria." He is "possessed with a burning love of Nature; and worshiped her, perhaps, more in her dreary and savage aspects, than in her manifestations of placidity and joy" (JR, 1190). These are typical Poe sentiments, as are Rodman's descriptions of this Nature in its cultivated, often Asiatic aspects: "The prairies exceeded in beauty any thing told in the tales of the Arabian Nights. On the edges of the creeks there was a wild mass of flowers which looked more like Art than Nature" (JR, 1211). The aura of romance in the Nature Rodman encounters is elsewhere described as a landscape that "rather resembled what I had dreamed of when a boy, than an actual reality" (JR, 1212). And of an island in the Platte River, Rodman writes: "The whole bore a wonderful resemblance to an artificial flower garden, but was infinitely more beautiful—looking rather like some of those scenes of enchantment which we read of in old books" (JR, 1213). Such romantic passages depart notably from the plain style of Lewis and Clark, as well as that of their sergeant, Gass, in their descriptions of the country traversed on the expedition.[30] Lewis and Clark comment repeatedly on the "vanishing" Native American, usually attributing the diminution of certain tribes and disappearance of others to warfare among tribal peoples, rather than to the effects of French, British, and U.S. colonialism disrupting Native Americans and provoking warfare. But Lewis and Clark's early version of the myth of the Vanishing American never suggests that the Native American's "savagery" is "unnatural" within the paradise of North American wilderness. Poe's romanticism adds another dimension to an ideology that had developed perverse nuances in the thirty-five years separating these historic and fictive expeditions.

Like Patrick Quinn's reading of *Pym* as an "imaginary voyage" and Jean Ricardou's reading of it as a *textual voyage*, so "The Journal of Julius Rodman" appears to be headed in the direction of some unrealized poetic displacement of the "factual" voyage. In the course of this displacement, Rodman must pass *through* the primitive "nature" represented by Toby and the Sioux, as well as the treacherous landscapes with which the latter are identified, in order to reach the poetic domain that would be fully under his control (and the poetic authority of his true master, Edgar Allan Poe). Such a poetic will-to-power is very much the equivalent of an emerging commercial power over new territories, such as John Jacob Astor's, which Poe clearly admires both for its progressive qualities and for its refunctioning of an older, feudal hierarchy. The happy jig danced by the guileless and powerless Toby is matched by the inability of the Teton Sioux to read properly signs, like that of the bronze deck cannon that destroys one quarter of their number in punishment for their ignorance. The enforced illiteracy of the African American and the predominantly oral cultures of Native Americans exclude them from the appreciation of that higher Nature only available to Poe and his educated readers.

Some evidence of this narrative intention to move from a treacherous, primitive nature toward a poetic, transcendental Nature is provided by the "remarkable cliffs" Rodman encounters in the last chapter of the unfinished "Journal." Like the chasms on the island of Tsalal, these western cliffs are "of the most singular appearance" and possess "a very regular artificial character." Composed of "very white soft sandstone, which readily receives the impression of the water," the face of these cliffs "is chequered with a variety of lines formed by the trickling of the rains upon the soft material, so that a fertile fancy might easily imagine them to be gigantic monuments reared by human art, and carved over with hieroglyphical devices" (JR, 1246–47). For Rodman, they "had all the air of enchanted structures, (such as I have dreamed of,) and the twittering of myriads of martins, which have built their nests in the holes . . . aided this conception not a little" (JR, 1247). Not surprisingly, these cliffs affect Rodman with emotions of sublimity: "It left upon my mind an impression of novelty—of singularity, which can never be effaced" (JR, 1248). The projection of romantic fantasies on the actual landscape of the West is typical of frontier writing from the earliest explorers to the present day, so I do not wish to single out Poe as unique in this regard.[31] Nevertheless, Poe's romantic extremity, especially as it manifests itself in exotic Middle Eastern and Asiatic imagery and settings, contributes to the tendencies of explorers, frontier writers, and natural scientists to exoticize, romanticize, and Orientalize the West.

These dreamlike, psychic topographies are familiar in Poe's writings, of course, but they have rarely been connected with what I have termed Poe's *fantastic imperialism*. When reread in terms of the colonial and racial rhetoric in "The Journal of Julius Rodman," these features become far more visible in Poe's poetic landscapes. In "A Tale of the Ragged Mountains," which Poe published in *Godey's Magazine* in April 1844, the narrator sets Bedloe's experience of the transubstantiation of souls in the hills southwest of Charlottesville, Virginia—in the region "where [Poe] had lived as a student at the University of Virginia"—and uses rhetoric remarkably similar to that in "The Journal of Julius Rodman."[32] Loaded up with his morning dose of morphine, still under the hypnotic suggestion of his physician, Dr. Templeton, Augustus Bedloe strolls into the "chain of wild and dreary hills . . . dignified by the title of the Ragged Mountains," which legend associates with "the uncouth and fierce races of men who tenanted their groves and caverns."[33] Like Julius Rodman, Bedloe is a wealthy young southerner, who betrays all the personality traits of the imaginative and poetic character. Like Pym and Rodman, Bedloe enters a dreamlike region where he is "the very first and sole adventurer who had ever penetrated its recesses" (RM, 658). What Bedloe discovers in this "singular" and "novel" place is a spiritual and temporal passage from Virginia to the mysterious Orient. Stumbling on a "wild man" pursued by "a huge beast . . . a hyena," Bedloe next finds himself looking down upon "an Eastern-looking city, such as we read of in the Arabian Tales, but of a character even more singular than any there described" (RM, 659). The city turns out to be the holy Indian city of Benares (the modern city of Varanasi) on the Ganges, and Bedloe has been transubstantiated into the spiritual place of a British officer, Oldeb, who fought on the side of Warren Hastings, the East India Company's governor of Bengal from 1771–1784, against Cheyte Singh, the raja of Benares.

Poe's description of the dreamscape of Benares is a conventional Orientalist fantasy in nineteenth-century Western literature, including "wildly picturesque" houses, "millions of black and yellow men," a "wilderness of balconies, of verandahs, of minarets," abundant "bazaars," turbans, beards, graceful maidens, "idols," and "elephants gorgeously caparisoned" (RM, 660). The fantastic appearance of Benares in the hills southwest of Charlottesville condenses the "wildness" of primitive peoples of the North American continent, including Native Americans and African Americans, with the European fantasy of the "sensuous riot" of the "mysterious" East.[34] The coincidences between this Orientalism and Rodman's "first" expedition across the Rocky Mountains are instructive, because they involve the connection between colonial and racial issues. Bedloe's South, like Rodman's West, is contaminated by people of color—red, yellow, and black—who are immediately recognized as natural enemies by both characters. Just as Rodman fires on the Sioux without any real provocation (they have demanded his stores of whiskey and tobacco, but they are waving spears at Rodman and his men, who are floating in the middle of the Missouri River), so Bedloe finds himself magically transported into the combat of British officers and sepoys against a "rabble pressed impetuously upon us, harassing us with their spears, and overwhelming us with flights of arrows" (RM, 662).[35]

Bedloe's soulmate, Oldeb, whose name the narrator will learn is the mirror-image of Bedloe's (without the "e"), dies fighting in a remote and apparently obscure Indian colonial skirmish that nonetheless has considerable significance for the United States, in which Poe has fantastically resituated this battle. When France allied itself with the colonies in the American Revolution against Great Britain, there were global consequences. In India, Warren Hastings took over the direction of military affairs in Bengal and virtually eliminated French influence in India by consolidating British holdings. In order to finance what amounted to a series of local wars, Hastings demanded contributions from Bengali rajas, especially Chait Singh, the raja of Benares, who was deposed by Hastings when the raja resisted such colonial extortion. In his dream, Bedloe finds himself with the British troops and sepoys "driven to seek refuge in a species of kiosk," from which he "perceived a vast crowd, in furious agitation, surrounding and assaulting a gay palace that overhung the river. Presently, from an upper window of this palace, there descended an effeminate-looking person, by means of a string made of the turbans of his attendants" (RM, 661). This episode is described in the manner of a story out of the "Arabian Nights," the source both for Bedloe's vision of the Eastern-looking city in the Ragged Mountains and Rodman's sublime vision of the western prairies along the upper reaches of the Missouri. Bedloe's personal physician, Dr. Templeton, will soberly explain to him that his dream has its solid basis in historical fact and that his double, Oldeb, was in fact Dr. Templeton's dear friend, killed in "1780 . . . during the administration of Warren Hastings." As Dr. Templeton reconstructs the history of that battle in which Bedloe "dies" again:

> You have described . . . the Indian city of Benares, upon the Holy River. The riots, the combats, the massacre, were the actual events of the insurrection of Cheyte Sing, which took place in 1780, when Hastings was put in imminent peril of his life. The man escaping by the string of turbans, was Cheyte Sing himself. The party in the kiosk were sepoys and British officers, headed by Hastings. Of this party I was one, and did all I could to prevent the rash and fatal sally of the officer who fell, in the crowded alleys, by the poisoned arrow of a Bengalee. (RM, 663–64)

The "poisoned arrow" of the East Indian is doubled by the "poisonous sangsue" that Dr. Templeton mistakenly applies as a "medicinal leech" in his effort to cure Bedloe of the illness induced apparently by his dreamy struggles in Benares of 1780. In typically pseudoscientific manner, Poe provides us with a "Nota Bene," in which he explains: "The poisonous sangsue of Charlottesville may always be distinguished from the medicinal leech by its blackness, and especially by its writhing or vermicular motions, which very nearly resemble those of snake" (RM, 664). Apparently playing upon the Hindu belief that to die in Benares assures a Hindu release from endless rebirths, Poe has Bedloe and Oldeb "die" two deaths, one in Benares and the other in Charlottesville, that apparently close the cycle of this very Western version of the Hindu transubstantiation of souls.

Poisoned arrows and poisonous snakes, "millions of black and yellow men," beards, turbans, temples, and colonial skirmishes fill out Poe's Orientalist fantasy, but the precision of his historical events are unusual amid the huge volume of xenophobic Western writings about the exotic and mysterious Orient. Like the counterrevolution I have argued elsewhere Dupin stages in "The Purloined Letter," so the dramatic action of "Ragged Mountains" revolves around the very precise efforts of Warren Hastings to secure British colonial mastery in India over France in the period of the French alliance with the American revolutionaries, offering a further explanation for why Poe substitutes the Anglo-American Rodman for the more characteristic French trappers of the 1790s in the region of North America described in "The Journal of Julius Rodman."[36] Poe clearly represents Hastings as a heroic figure, victimized by the "insurrection" of the raja of Benares, when in fact Hastings's effort to extort financial support from the Bengali rajas for his colonial ventures in India would be a major cause of his impeachment by the House of Commons in May 1787 on charges of oppression, cruelty, bribery, and fraud while he was the governor of Bengal.[37] Just as Rodman identifies himself with the commercial or "free-trade imperialism" of John Jacob Astor and the American Fur Company, so Hastings is associated with the East India Company's rule of India. Whether or not Poe connects consciously the colonialism of Rodman and Astor with that of Bedloe/Oldeb and Hastings, there are clear thematic connections that establish what I would term an *imperialist unconscious* in Poe's writings. Horsman points out that despite the anti-British sentiments in the United States of the 1840s, fueled in part by conflict over the Oregon Territory, British imperialism *outside* North America was often viewed favorably in U.S. popular culture. In such contexts, "British imperial power could be viewed" not as "resistance to American desires but a general triumph of the Anglo-Saxon race."[38]

Two other significant details link "A Tale of the Ragged Mountains" with the unfinished "Journal of Julius Rodman." First, the near "hieroglyphic" markings in the cliffs toward the end of the "Journal" suggest the usual poetic transubstantiation Poe typically effects in his pseudo-factual narratives, such as the *Narrative of Arthur Gordon Pym*. In a similar fashion, the mirror-image of the two names, "Bedloe" and "Oldeb," suggests that the *real* transubstantiation of souls is effected by means of the *poetic journey* that the "educated" author, always from a "good family" and properly descended from his European (usually English) forebears, directs for his grateful readers. Second, not only is the name "Bedloe" significant for its reversal of "Oldeb," but it is also the name of the island in New York Harbor where Fort Wood was established in 1841, only three years before Poe published "A Tale of the Ragged Mountains."[39] The fortifications of the British East India Company and those of an ideal United States are rhetorically linked in the name, suggesting a "destiny" for an American imperium that would follow the racist and aristocratic values represented by Rodman and Bedloe. Hindu reincarnation and the migration of souls are mere superstitions typical of "primitive" peoples of color, whether red or yellow or black. Poe's repeated judgment that these peoples are variously deformed, ignorant, or effeminate is obviously part of the racial and gender hierarchies of nineteenth-century Western culture, typified in its extreme form by the proslavery rationalizations and xenophobia of white southerners. History "repeats itself" only by that appeal to "tradition" that is best achieved by the "culture" sustained by those authors who represent such ruling-class values. In such contexts, it is difficult, if not impossible, to distinguish Poe's verbal plays, his literary hoaxes, his outright plagiarisms, and his unreliable narrations from the sorts of mystification and rationalization of the racial and imperial ideologies of the period.[40]

It is not just the conventionality of Poe's racist and imperialist fantasies that we should condemn, but also the extent to which Poe has employed his undisputed powers as a creative writer to weave such fantasies into what has for so long been appreciated for its aesthetic qualities. To be sure, "The Journal of Julius Rodman" has never been judged as "great art," even by Poe's most dedicated readers, but "A Tale of the Ragged Mountains" enjoys a modest reputation as a "realistic treatment of the supernatural [that] was rarely done better by Poe."[41] What should interest us are the ways in which Poe's enthusiasm for racism and imperialism, especially as he finds his own poetic way to participate in their new forms, infects even his most famous tales. In "Poe, Antebellum Slavery, and Modern Criticism," I suggested how the racism and colonialism in *Pym* might be read as well in "The Purloined Letter" and "The Man of the Crowd." I will conclude this chapter by suggesting that the same rhetoric may be found in "The Murders in the Rue Morgue," which appeared just a year after "The Journal of Julius Rodman," in April 1841 in *Graham's Magazine*, and "Hop-Frog" (1849).

Kim Hall has shown how seventeenth-century European narratives of travel to Africa frequently identify African peoples with apes and both people and apes with their predilections for theft and mimicry. In works like Edward Topsell's *The Historie of Foure-footed Beastes and Serpents* and Thomas Herbert's *Account of the Cape of Good Hope*, we find early formulations of "racial traits" based on fantasies of the identification of humans with animals that would be elaborated in the pre-Darwinian evolutionary theories proposed by Baron Georges Cuvier in the first two decades of the nineteenth century.[42] Hall points out that these identifications are by no means exclusively *African*, although they are all linked in her argument with an incipient European colonial ideology; Herbert, for example, compares Africans "both with Apes and the already colonized Irish."[43] Topsell also describes human features that resemble those of apes in terms that reflect moral and behavioral qualities: "Men that have low and flat Nostrils are Libidinous as Apes that attempt Women, and having thicke lippes the upper hanging over the neather, they are deemed fooles, like the lips of Asses and Apes."[44] Topsell calls particular attention to the "lustfull disposition" of the various kinds of apes and monkeys he includes in his seventeenth-century "history."[45] Topsell interestingly attributes the power of speech to apes, even though it appears to be merely linguistic imitation without rational understanding:

> And as the body of an Ape is ridiculous by reason of an indecent likeness and imitation of man, so is his soule or spirit; . . . A certaine Ape after a shipwracke swimming to lande, was seene by a Countrey man, and thinking him to be a man in the water, gave him his hand to save him, yet in the meane time asked him what Countrey man he was, who answered he was an *Athenian*: well, saide the man, Doost thou know *Piraeus* (which was a Port in *Athens*) very well saide the Ape, and his wife, friends and children, whereat the man being moved did what he could to drowne him.[46]

In her discussion of the racial implications of the orangutan in "The Murders in the Rue Morgue," Loisa Nygaard points out that the ape is not only "the perfect suspect, the ultimate 'foreigner' with whom no one need identify," she also suggests "distant echoes of the slave trade," insofar as the orangutan was "then believed to be one of the closest relatives of the human race."[47] As Nygaard points out, Dupin's "role in this story is not to bring a criminal to justice, . . . but instead to restore the runaway ape to its proper owner, who promptly sells it for a large sum just as he had planned. Poe, himself a Southerner and a supporter of slavery, defended it on the basis of the private individual's right to undisturbed enjoyment of his property."[48] Although he draws no conclusions regarding the ideological consequences of Poe's use of the orangutan in "The Murders in the Rue Morgue," Shawn Rosenheim interprets the ape as Poe's "own myth of human origins, which condenses within itself both individual and evolutionary history."[49] Combining Nygaard and Rosenheim's observations, I would conclude that Poe enacts in "Murders in the Rue Morgue" his own myth of human, linguistic, and social origins by *distancing* himself, his art, and his fictional double, Dupin, from the racialized savagery and animality of the orangutan.[50]

Dupin's solution of the mystery depends crucially on his ability to resolve the disagreement among those overhearing voices in the hall at the time of the crime about the language spoken by the party responsible for the "shrill voice." As it turns out, those overhearing the voices of the French sailor and his orangutan are respectively English, Dutch, French, German, Spanish, and Italian, suggesting the cosmopolitanism of Paris as a new global capital, and they variously identify the language of the "shrill voice" in terms of languages with which they are respectively unfamiliar. Dupin himself entertains the possibility that the "foreign languages" misidentified by these witnesses might in fact be a non-European language, "the voice of an Asiatic—of an African."[51] But Dupin quickly sidesteps this reasonable possibility by claiming: "Neither Asiatics nor Africans abound in Paris; but, without denying the inference, I will now merely call your attention to three points. The voice is termed by one witness 'harsh rather than shrill.' It is represented by two others to have been 'quick and *unequal*.' No words—no sounds resembling words—were by any witness mentioned as distinguishable" (M, 416).

Once again, the "solution" to a Poe mystery revolves around language use, and the specific solution begins with Dupin commanding the narrator: "Read now . . . this passage from Cuvier," in which a "minute anatomical and generally descriptive account of the large fulvous Ourang-Outang of the East Indian Islands" is given, including the animal's "gigantic stature, . . . prodigious strength and activity, . . . wild ferocity, and . . . imitative propensities" (M, 424). Nygaard contends that neither Cuvier nor the American translation of Cuvier by Thomas Wyatt that Poe most likely used mentions the "orangutan's alleged 'ferocity' or 'prodigious strength.'"[52] Rosenheim argues that "in Poe's version the description of the orangutan virtually reverses Cuvier's actual claims," concluding from this that "Poe's intellectual allegiance to Cuvier was subservient to his need to magnify the melodramatic and gothic aspects of the murders."[53] In McMurtrie's abridgment and translation of Cuvier, the orangutan "when young, and such as he appears to us in his captivity, . . . is a mild and gentle animal, easily rendered tame and affectionate."[54] Despite Poe's liberties with Cuvier, however, the latter provides plenty of pseudoscientific "evidence" to suggest superficial affinities between the orangutans and human beings: "Of all animals, this Ourang is considered as approaching most nearly to Man in the form of his head, height of forehead, and volume of brain."[55] Unlike earlier naturalists, Cuvier makes no claim for the orangutan's powers of speech, but he does stress the orangutan's propensity to imitate human behavior: "He is enabled by his conformation [to human physical characteristics] to imitate many of our actions, but his intelligence does not appear to be so great as is reported, not much surpassing that of the Dog."[56] What Poe borrows from Cuvier are just those "primitive" and "savage" qualities that he would attribute to the Teton Sioux and to the "millions of black and yellow men" in his fictional India. Rosenheim concludes that "Poe finds in [Cuvier's] mode of analysis an analogue to his own technique of detection," establishing thereby a connection between Poe's verbal and Cuvier's zoological analyses.[57] What links Cuvier's natural and Poe's semiotic sciences is finally their shared commitment to Enlightenment rationality and its inherently imperialist imaginary.[58] What appeals to Poe is Baron Cuvier's pseudo-evolutionary classification of human types in the manner of animal species, as well as the flagrant Eurocentrism of his taxonomies of the human.[59]

With remarkable frequency, Poe racializes masters and servants, even when there is no strictly regional or realistic purpose served. In "Hop-Frog" (1849) Poe appears to identify with the dwarf, Hop-Frog, who rebels against the tyrannical king and his ministers after the king abuses Trippetta, a female dwarf and Hop-Frog's "sworn friend." Hop-Frog's ingenious and apparently just rebellion involves disguising the king and his seven ministers as "eight chained ourang-outangs," in part by covering them with tar and simulating fur with flax.[60] Although Poe normally associates mob actions, such as tar-and-feathering, with the breakdown of reason and thus proper class hierarchies, in "Hop-Frog" he justifies rebellion by means of a fictional masquerade, in which false rulers are made to reveal their true natures—dark beasts—and suffer appropriate punishment. By the same token, Poe compares Hop-Frog with a monkey on several occasions and announces the climax of the dramatic action with the grinding noises made by his "fang-like teeth" (HF, 900, 907).

The secret savagery of illegitimate rulers differs, however, from the monkey-like mimicry of their fool, Hop-Frog. Identifying his own poetic wit with the dwarf's ingenious and implacable revenge, Poe *appropriates* anti-monarchical sentiments and open rebellion to serve his own profoundly authoritarian values. Like Dupin in open competition with Minister D———, Poe usurps another's formal power by turning his own trickery against him. In the end, the king and his ministers have been doubly blackened, both by the tar and the fire Hop-Frog sets to them, leaving "eight corpses" swinging in "their chains, a fetid, blackened, hideous, and indistinguishable mass" (HF, 908). What Hop-Frog has properly "mimicked" in his monkey-like fashion is just the "hideous" moral "blackness" and "savagery" of the tyrannical king. The "masquerade" staged to testify to the king's authority—for "some grand state occasion—I forget what"—becomes instead testimony to the power of artistic disguise, thus rendering the nominal ruler "savage" in comparison with the artist and his delegates, Hop-Frog and Trippetta. Yet, for such an imaginary usurpation to occur, Poe must "blacken" his antagonist, as well as disguise him as an orangutan, whose figurative significance for Poe is worked out in even greater detail in "The Murders in the Rue Morgue."

The razor-wielding, imitative, ferocious, and prodigiously strong orangutan of "The Murders in the Rue Morgue" acts out a racist fantasy regarding civilized women—Mme and Mlle L'Espanaye—brutalized by "savages" incapable of "proper speech," lacking the linguistic competency of those "Caucasians" classified by Cuvier as the group that "has the most highly civilised nations."[61] At the end of his classification of the orangutan, Cuvier distinguishes the "*Simia troglodytes*" of Linnaeus, or "The Chimpasé," to which Cuvier attributes very human social organization and behavior: "It inhabits Guinea and Congo, lives in troops, constructs huts of leaves and sticks, arms itself with clubs and stones, and thus repulses men and elephants; pursues and abducts, it is said, negro women, etc."[62] Like the Black

Cook in the mutiny in *Pym*, the orangutan in "The Murders in the Rue Morgue" enacts a fantasy of slave insurrection loosely tied to southern white hysteria regarding Nat Turner's Southampton insurrection in 1831 and the more general anxiety of antebellum southerners that the immoral system of slavery might well provoke bloody revolution.[63] In "Hop-Frog," this overt racism is more subtly shifted to include false authority, such as the tyrannical king represents, and in Poe's imitations of frontier narratives, such as "The Journal of Julius Rodman," such poetic racism includes Native Americans who "contaminate" the otherwise romantic moonscape of the West.

The racial connotations of Poe's rhetoric are today perfectly readable, despite the neglect of them by several schools of previous scholarship, and they have cultural significance not only for Poe's southernness but also for the emerging imperial ambitions of the young nation, which frequently imitated the British imperium even as the United States was already trying out variations of its own "free-trade imperialism." Poe's writings do not restrict racial hierarchies to the antebellum South or to class and caste systems of nineteenth-century British imperialism. Poe's nominally fantastic, Gothic narratives actually help destabilize racial categories, even as these narratives rely upon many conventional pseudoscientific accounts of racial identity. Yet by confusing the customary referents for racial superiority and inferiority on the American frontier, in the British Empire, and the slaveholding South, Poe helped popularize the sort of ambiguity of racial difference that would enable new hierarchies to emerge in the aftermath of slavery as complements in the "conquest" of the West, U.S. imperial ventures in the Caribbean and Philippines, and even the assimilative work of modern immigration. Of course, racism does not in and of itself constitute imperialism, even if the latter term is broadly interpreted as it is in this book. Poe's representations of racial differences generally refer to specific hierarchies of peoples and cultures that help legitimate historically specific ventures of U.S. territorial expansion and cultural appropriation or removal.

Many frontier writers commonly relied on racial hierarchies, as well as flexible racial stereotypes, to rationalize U.S. imperialism, but Poe more ingeniously dramatizes in his aesthetic practice the rhetorical superiority that allows his concept of the modern author to be prototypical of Euro-American superiority over "savage" mimicry. Lacanian and other post-structuralist interpretations of Poe's writings have explained them ingeniously as narratives that anticipate modern psychoanalytic accounts of the linguistic differences essential to psychic experience. Yet, these same post-structuralist critics miss the ideological consequences of the psychic and linguistic origins Poe has offered us. Long before the modern psychiatrist promised to cure patients by understanding the psychic logics of their stories, Poe played with the gendered and racialized "bodies" he believed confidently were effects of the language of which he was master. Crucial for any imperial authority was the establishment of racial and gender hierarchies that increasingly would be judged by one's relative command of a "linguistic competency," whose arbitrary standard and curious genealogies were maintained by such heralds of the American Empire as Edgar Allan Poe.[64]

4

Melville's *Typee*

U.S. Imperialism at Home and Abroad

[The Polynesians] have been civilized into draught
horses, and evangelized into beasts of burden.
                                        Melville, *Typee*

As I shall not visit Nukuheva, where I had hoped to
sketch for you the scenes of Melville's book, I send
you a photograph of a Marquesan house to paste into
your copy of Typee [*sic*]. I suppose Stevenson must
have described the valley, which is said to be now
abandoned to a sand-fly worse than the mosquito.
. . . We have heard so much and talked so much of
the Marquesas . . . that I seem almost at home
there, and have the less curiosity to go.
             Henry Adams to Elizabeth Sherman Cameron,
                                            May 3, 1891

The ugliest beast on earth is the white man, says
Melville.
       Lawrence, *Studies in Class American Literature*
                                                (1923)

Herman Melville's *Typee* is one of the first U.S. literary texts to
establish a connection between the institutions of slavery in
the United States and Euro-American colonialism in Polynesia. Like other
travelers to Polynesia in the first half of the nineteenth century, Melville
reserves most of his criticism for the British and the French. In at least two
significant ways, however, Melville turns the familiar nineteenth-century
criticism of the British and the French into a critique more specifically

relevant to his white U.S. readers in the 1840s and 1850s. First, his references to Captain David Porter (1780–1843), the U.S. naval commander who claimed the Marquesas Islands for the United States, and his general invocation of this little South Seas episode of the War of 1812 suggest that Melville wanted to use his experiences in the Marquesas for purposes that went well beyond the merely autobiographical or purely literary. Second, his emplotment of his own experience has uncanny resemblances with two important and characteristically American narrative forms in Melville's time: the Puritan captivity narrative and the fugitive slave narrative.

Melville analyzes in *Typee* the relationship between domestic policies of southern slaveholding and the extraterritorial policies of U.S. colonization that began as early as the War of 1812. By "extraterritorial," I mean "outside the North American continent," and I realize that the term is itself something of a contradiction, since the "territory" of the North American continent was from the very outset of European exploration and settlement an extraterritorial region of European colonization. But this great paradox of U.S. history remains as difficult to communicate today as it must have been in Melville's nineteenth century. Our revolution against English rule not only ignored deliberately the continuing domestic colonization of African Americans under the perverse laws and practices of North American slavery, but it also led to a series of acts on the part of the new United States by which we consolidated our national identity by exercising political power in a colonial manner.

Two formal ways in which Melville makes the connection between domestic and foreign policies are his adaptations in *Typee* of well-established conventions of the Puritan captivity narrative and the fugitive slave narrative, in order to put his primarily white reader in the position of the victim. By using the "imaginative experience" fundamental to the nineteenth-century travel narrative form, Melville hoped to transform the affections, as well as the intellectual attitudes, of his readers with respect to domestic slavery, Euro-American colonialism in Polynesia, and the reader's understanding of different cultures.

This is an odd thesis to offer in view of the prevailing criticism of Melville's ideological blindness, if not complicity, in the propagation of the myth of the imperial self. In 1980 Carolyn Karcher argued in *Shadow over the Promised Land: Slavery, Race, and Violence in Melville's America* that Melville was a vigorous critic of slavery but was ambivalent about the best political solution: "Melville betrays the same qualms about endorsing violent rebellion in all his works, be the rebels black or white. At the same time, he consistently exhibits tyranny as unbearable and resistance to it as essential if the victim of oppression is to preserve his manhood. The conflict between these two positions . . . is central not only to Melville's art, but to his life as well. By temperament, Melville seems to have been at once a refractory conformist and a reluctant rebel."[1] At the end of the 1980s Wai-Chee Dimock argued that "Melville dramatizes the very juncture where the logic of freedom dovetails into the logic of empire, or (which is the same thing) where the imperial self of Jacksonian individualism recapitulates the logic of Jacksonian imperialism."[2]

From Karcher's politically conflicted Melville to Dimock's Melville, whose "authorial practices" are "ultimately analogous to the terms of America's national sovereignty," we can chart the transformation in recent critical judgments of Melville.[3] We have gained a great deal in the revaluation of U.S. literature by paying more attention to the ideological functions of culture. Yet, in our haste to acknowledge aesthetic culture's contributions to ideology, we may also have neglected the ways in which artistic representation can serve emancipatory and progressive purposes. If we are truly interested in *historicizing* the literature we teach, then we must develop subtler means of assessing the historical and political functions of literature in its own and for our times. We need more varied standards of political and thus aesthetic judgment if we are to respect the complexity of literature's "action" in a historical moment, especially when such a moment is defined by crisis and conflict. As I argue throughout this book, none of the literary critiques of U.S. imperialism would be judged today adequate to the complexity and range of U.S. global influence in the last half of the twentieth century. Even in their own times, such critiques always suffer from fundamental limitations—Twain's ahistoricism, Du Bois's uncritical Communism, Nick Black Elk's Catholicism, for example—that reveal the complicity of their authors with the very ideology they wish to transform. Such limitations do not necessarily negate the political effectivity of the critiques in which they appear. There are important differences between the ideological legitimation served by Brown, Poe, Ridge, Crane, and Adams's writings and the political consequences of the social criticisms offered by Melville, Twain, Du Bois, Nick Black Elk and John Neihardt, and Zora Neale Hurston. One of the purposes of this book is to learn how to tell the difference between literary practices that serve or challenge the dominant ideology while recognizing how all cultural acts remain to some degree captives of their historical and thus ideological situations.

The historical crises and conflicts of the 1840s included not just the issues of domestic slavery, westward expansion, and the treatment of native peoples and the theft of their lands, but also the widening horizon of European and a burgeoning U.S. colonialism in the Pacific. *Typee* addresses the complication of domestic and foreign policy issues by way of what T. Walter Herbert considers its anthropological dimension:

> *Typee* moves along a course that remains perilously close to the brink of sheer confusion. We have found Melville working with contradictory points of view, discontinuous states of mind, resounding moral declarations crosscut by equivocal disclaimers, and moments of hapless incomprehension. It is now time to recognize that Melville's skillful flirting with

such vexations has the effect of rendering tolerable the conflicts which it provokes.[4]

Herbert's argument in *Marquesan Encounters: Melville and the Meaning of Civilization*, which appeared in the same year as Karcher's study, suggests that somewhere between literature's contribution to ideology and its contribution to social reform there remains the possibility of literature as the experience of the instability and contradictoriness of ideological categories. Herbert does not conclude that the subversion of nineteenth-century U.S. ideology regarding the Marquesans and, by extension, other "primitive" peoples, is simply the effect of Melville's "genius" or conscious artistry. Instead, Herbert argues that *Typee* generates out of the "fusion of fact and meaning" a resulting "verbal texture that has a life of its own."[5]

Just what distinguishes this "life of its own" is too often for literary critics the intrinsic literariness of the text, but in the case of *Typee* this "life" must be understood as the vicarious experience of the reader, who lives through wage-slavery, captivity, colonial subjugation, and several modes of ideological commodification in the course of reading *Typee*. Unlike the nineteenth-century U.S. accounts of the Marquesans discussed by Herbert in *Marquesan Encounters*—ranging from Captain David Porter's plans for a private colony to the proselytizing efforts by the Reverend Charles Stewart (chaplain for the American sloop of war *Vincennes*) described in his *A Visit to the South Seas* (1831)—Melville's anthropological gesture in *Typee* destabilizes our very processes of understanding other peoples. In that regard, *Typee* rejects the prevailing ethnographic models of its time and anticipates the more literary anthropologies of our own age.[6]

Because *Typee* is based so firmly on Melville's experiences on the island of Nuku Hiva in the summer of 1842, few scholars of the narrative pay much attention to why Melville might have considered the Marquesas to have been the appropriate setting for a critique of burgeoning U.S. imperialism. Ever since Harper and Brothers rejected Melville's manuscript "on the grounds that 'it was impossible that it could be true and therefore was without real value,'" the realism of *Typee* has been a central concern of readers. Most arguments supporting Melville's fictional techniques in his first book-length narrative tend to reinforce the assumption that *Typee* is primarily an autobiographical account of Melville's youthful experiences. Melville may thus vary narrative perspective by playing upon the "I" recounting his experiences and the more youthful "Tommo," who is the dramatic agent (or character) of those experiences. In a similar manner, Melville may draw upon previously published "accounts by travelers like Langsdorff, Porter and Stewart" either to give his own account greater historical credibility or to trivialize their versions for the sake of his own authority for this "peep" at "Polynesian life." But in these and other instances of literary liberties taken with such autobiographical materials, Melville is operating very much within the accepted terms of literary autobiography.[7]

The insistence upon *Typee*'s autobiographical realism has caused many literary critics to neglect what historians of the Marquesas in the nineteenth century have simply taken for granted: that the discovery, exploration, and exploitation of the Marquesas by various European powers and the United States presented a microcosm of modern imperialism at its worst. Herbert points out that "the destruction of the Marquesan way of life" was "one of the principal horrors of Pacific history"; the population of the islands declined in the nineteenth century from an estimated 100,000 in the early 1800s to "4,865 in 1882."[8] Beyond this depressingly familiar pattern of Euro-American imperialism eradicating the native population, there is the equally relevant subject of how colonial competition for the Marquesas reflects the larger competition among European, Asian, and U.S. powers in other areas of the Pacific for colonies and commercial dominance. David Long, the biographer of Commodore Porter, contends that by the time a Russian expedition "led by Captain Ivan Federovich Krusenstern" visited the Marquesas in 1803, a decade before Captain Porter arrived in Taiohae Bay, "Great Britain, the United States, France, and Russia, the nations which led in opening East Asia and the Pacific to Western influence during the nineteenth century, had presented in this minuscule archipelago a preview of the development of part of a continent and most of an island world."[9]

The "preview" to which Long refers is the race among these and other European nations and the United States to increase trade with China and Japan by way of sea routes across the Pacific. What would lead to John Hay's famous "Open Door Policy" and his apparently democratic call for "free competition," rather than colonial warfare, among the European nations vying for influence in the Far East had its origins in the early part of the nineteenth century as various nations sought to control the Pacific islands that would be virtual "stepping stones" to the lucrative trade with Asian markets. As early as Porter's visits to the Marquesas in 1813, it was clear that these and other Pacific islands were of little commercial value in their own right. As whaling stations, safe harbors, and later in the century as coaling stations, these islands were thought to provide the necessary "stages" in a commercial bridge between the West and the East.

Such economic imperialism has characterized U.S. foreign policies from the Revolution to the present, and our conduct in the Marquesas makes this continuity strikingly clear. As many have pointed out, Melville repeatedly criticizes U.S. society for having failed to "complete" its revolution against colonial rule by ignoring the issue of slavery and its own colonial policies with respect to native peoples. Whereas Melville endorses the democratic idealism of the Revolution, he understands quite well the economic realities behind our failure to realize such ideals. Washington Irving may have represented the old Dutch patroons of New York as part of a vanishing world, but Melville considers them mere prototypes of the new ruling elite in the United States.[10] Melville criticizes the unrecognized and thus especially powerful social and racial hierarchies of U.S. democracy later in *Pierre* and

Benito Cereno, and he anticipates that cultural critique with his consideration in *Typee* of U.S. colonial projects in the Marquesas by Captain Joseph Ingraham of Boston in his visit of April–May 1791 and Captain David Porter in his quixotic plan for a "private" colony under the sponsorship of the U.S. government in 1813.[11] Ingraham arrived only eight years after the formal end of the Revolutionary War; Porter attempted to annex the Marquesas during his efforts to interrupt British shipping in the Pacific during the War of 1812 (1812–1814). In short, while the United States was struggling to establish its own fragile independence in the last decade of the eighteenth and first decades of the nineteenth century, it was also actively competing for its own colonial territory in the Marquesas.

Until Herbert's *Marquesan Encounters* appeared in 1980, most efforts to link Melville with Captain Porter circled around Melville's explicit denial of any knowledge of Porter's account of his visit to the Marquesas and Melville's apparent reliance on specific details of Porter's published *Journal of the Cruise of the U.S. Frigate* Essex. In *Melville in the South Seas* (1939), Charles Anderson made a convincing case for Melville's familiarity not only with the history of Porter's visit to the Marquesas but also with the actual text of his *Journal* of 1815.[12] But few scholars until Herbert had paid much attention to the fact that Porter's efforts to annex the Marquesas were connected with the earlier visit by Captain Ingraham and thus with what might be termed our first imperial venture outside North America.

Anderson does not mention Captain Ingraham in *Melville in the South Seas*, but Melville pays special attention to Ingraham's discovery of the northern islands, in what Ingraham named the "Washington group," including Nuku Hiva, which: "Although generally called one of the Marquesas, is by some navigators considered as forming one of a distinct cluster, comprising the islands of Ruhooka, Ropo, and Nukuheva; upon which three the appellation of the Washington Group has been bestowed. . . . Their existence was altogether unknown until . . . 1791, when they were discovered by Captain Ingraham, of Boston, Massachusetts, nearly two centuries after the discovery of the islands by the agent of the Spanish Viceroy."[13] Although Melville goes on to say that he "shall follow the example of most voyagers, and treat them as forming part and parcel of the Marquesas," he has gone to considerable lengths in the preceding quotation to insist upon their separate discovery by the American captain.[14]

Melville's reference to Captain Ingraham and "the agent of the Spanish Viceroy," Alvaro de Mendaña y Castro, who first discovered and named the southern islands "Marquesas," anticipates in certain ways Melville's doubling of Captain Amasa Delano and Don Benito Cereno in *Benito Cereno* (1855), published less than a decade after *Typee*. In James Kavanagh's reading, *Benito Cereno* explicitly indicts the United States in its colonial and revolutionary origins, as well as its nineteenth-century practices, for complicity in the European imperialism in the New World that relied so fundamentally on the economy of slavery.[15] Brook Thomas directly relates *Typee* to Melville's more obvious indictment of New World slavery in *Benito Cereno*: "In *Typee* Melville lays bare the imperialistic motives behind the introduction of Christianity to non-Western cultures, the savagery it causes rather than eliminates. Most important, if opponents of slavery think the eradication of slavery from America's shores will finally make America the land of the free, Melville's works offer example after example demonstrating exploitation in the 'free' states."[16]

In *Benito Cereno*, Captain Delano orders his men to attack the rebellious slaves on board the *San Dominick* and return the survivors to bondage. Captain Ingraham did not explicitly enslave the native peoples of the "Washington" group, but he did rename the islands, "commemorating John Adams, Benjamin Franklin, John Hancock, and Henry Knox by giving their surnames to individual islands. Nukahiva, where Porter later resided, was named 'Federal Island.'"[17] And Ingraham *did* claim the islands for the United States, to the cheers of those on board his small ship, the *Hope*, thus giving him the dubious claim of being the first agent of U.S. imperialism outside North America.

Only three weeks after Ingraham sailed from the Washington group, Captain Etienne Marchant in the *Solide* claimed them as part of the "Îles des Marquises" in the name of French colonial power in Polynesia. But it was Captain (later Commodore) David Porter whose annexation of the island of Nuku Hiva on November 19, 1813, likely had the most relevance for Melville and has, according to Porter's biographer, earned him "title as the first American imperialist."[18] Were it not for Captain Porter's vigorous military campaign against the Taipi during his occupation of Nuku Hiva, his "annexation" of the island as U.S. territory would be as nominal as Ingraham's in 1791. Less imaginatively than Ingraham, albeit in a more obvious entrepreneurial spirit, Porter "prepared for his spate of expansionism by providing a brand-new nomenclature: he christened Nukahiva 'Madison's Island,' the American settlement 'Madisonville,' his defensive position there 'Fort Madison,' and, afraid perhaps of too much of a good thing, contented himself with calling Taiohae Bay 'Massachusetts Bay.'"[19]

Porter had sailed to the Marquesas from the Galapagos, having spent the first year of the War of 1812 interrupting British shipping and whaling in the Pacific. He sailed toward the Washington group for three reasons: to find a safe haven to refurbish his ships, to scout possible British targets in the South Pacific, and to provide his men "relaxation and amusement after being so long at sea," by which he clearly meant sexual intercourse with young Marquesan women, renowned since Mendaña y Castro's visit for both their beauty and reputed sexual compliance.[20] Although Porter immediately notified President Madison of his unauthorized annexation of Nuku Hiva, neither Madison nor Secretary of State James Monroe even acknowledged Porter's messages and letters. As Long points out, "the main reason for executive inaction was that the intelligence of Nukahiva's entry into the Union arrived just about the time the British were invading Chesapeake Bay, burning public buildings in Washington, and driving the President [Madison] into humiliating flight."[21]

Such an irony would not have been lost on Melville were he aware of these consequences of Porter's annexation of the island. The War of 1812 was, after all, ostensibly fought to protect U.S. sailors from impressment by the Royal Navy, although it was more likely fought to protect U.S. commercial interests and shipping rights during the Napoleonic War. But it was not simply these historical ironies that interested Melville in Porter's annexation of the Marquesas. The portion of *Typee* that Charles Anderson identifies as convincing evidence that Melville not only knew Porter's *Journal* of his visit to the Marquesas but also relied on it, "together with Stewart's two volumes," as "the chief source of his information for his own narrative of Marquesan life," is Melville's description of "Porter's invasion of Typee Valley."[22] In four compact paragraphs in chapter 4, Melville recounts how Porter, having been caught up in the intertribal rivalries on Nuku Hiva, marched against the Typee with a "considerable detachment of sailors and marines from the frigate Essex, accompanied by at least two thousand warriors of Happar and Nuku Hiva" (T, 26). Although the modern biographer of Porter, David Long, entitles his chapter of Porter's curious annexation of the Marquesas, "Imperialism in the Marquesas, 1813," he sidesteps what Melville makes explicit about this punitive military expedition against the Typee:

> Valiantly, although with much loss, the Typees disputed every inch of ground, and after some hard fighting obliged their assailants to retreat and abandon their design of conquest. The invaders, on their march back to the sea, consoled themselves for their repulse by setting fire to every house and temple in their route; and a long line of smoking ruins defaced the once-smiling bosom of the valley, and proclaimed to its pagan inhabitants the spirit that reigned in the breasts of Christian soldiers. Who can wonder at the deadly hatred of the Typees to all foreigners after such unprovoked atrocities? (T, 26)

We should remember that this description of Porter's "unprovoked atrocities" is occasioned by Melville's recollection of witnessing the military annexation of the Marquesas in 1842 by French admiral Dupetit-Thouars. In fact, as Melville entered Taiohae Bay (which Porter had renamed "Massachusetts Bay"), the French were launching an expedition against the hostile Taioas, as if to repeat the expedition of Porter against the Typee nearly three decades earlier.

Melville's conclusions regarding Porter's imperialist adventure in the Marquesas are interesting for yet another reason. Easy as it would have been for him simply to equate Porter's attack on the Typee with the larger-scale efforts of the French and British to colonize the peoples and islands in the

South Pacific, Melville makes the following observation at the end of his indictment of Porter:

> The enormities perpetrated in the South Seas upon some of the inoffensive islanders wellnigh pass belief. These things are seldom proclaimed at home; they happen at the very ends of the earth; they are done in a corner, and there are none to reveal them. But there is, nevertheless, many a petty trader that has navigated the Pacific whose course from island to island might be traced by a series of cold-blooded robberies, kidnappings, and murders, the iniquity of which might be considered almost sufficient to sink her guilty timbers to the bottom of the sea. (T, 26–27)

Of course, French and British navies might be charged with the same crimes, but it is significant that Melville's account of Porter's actions in the Marquesas should conclude with his indictment of the crimes that follow from *trade*. What Melville anticipates here and elsewhere in *Typee* is the extent to which U.S. imperialism would be predicated on commercial, rather than territorial, control of other cultures and peoples. Porter's interest in the Marquesas as islands where he might find a temporary safe harbor, refit his ships, and entertain himself and his crew very much fits the pattern of U.S. imperialism in the South Pacific throughout the rest of the nineteenth century. Captain Ingraham himself discovered the Washington group while on a voyage from Boston to Canton, like so many other whalers and traders who brought the Marquesas to public attention in the period from 1790 to 1850. Captain Fanning, who visited the Marquesas in 1798, was also on his way to China. The Marquesas fit ideally into the navigational plans of ships traveling from the west coast of South America to China.

Just how much Melville knew of Porter's specific plans to develop the Marquesas is not known, but Melville's comment in *Typee* about the sins of western traders in the region seems to comment directly on Porter's formal proposal in 1815 to President Madison "that he be placed in charge of a voyage of exploration into the Pacific," specifically for purposes of commercial and military colonization. Herbert summarizes Porter's larger ambitions in this post–War of 1812 proposal to Madison: "Porter argues that his voyage might open trade relations with Japan, which was then closed to all Western nations except the Dutch. He further argues that great improvements could be made in the American relation to China. While the American national territory extended scarcely west of the Appalachians, in short, Porter had a vision of Pacific empire. He conceived a dominant international position for America as a leader in the advance of civilized achievement."[23]

In this regard, Herbert's interpretation of the larger significance of Porter's otherwise quixotic effort to annex the Marquesas is especially relevant to any rereading of *Typee* as a commentary on U.S. imperialism:

Porter's voyage of discovery was never sponsored by the United States government, and his taking possession of the Marquesas Islands was never ratified. But his imperial conception of America has had a long train of successors that have provided a series of corresponding definitions of the meaning of America's relationship to nations conceived not to be civilized. During his stay at the Marquesas he sought to embody his idea of America as a great nation in a form that would bring the blessings of America's superior position to a people he thought well fitted to benefit from them. Porter "took possession" of the Marquesas in the name of the United States because he considered this an appropriate display of the greatness of America; but his definition of civilization also led him to believe that this action was suited to the character of the Marquesans, which he very sincerely admired.[24]

Just how much Porter admired the Marquesans is debatable, despite the paternal rhetoric in his *Journal* regarding their social coherence and technical and technological ingenuity. But what Herbert treats at the level of Porter's Enlightenment values, I understand more practically and materially in terms of those commercial motives that link the Southern slave economy with the Northern industrial economy and its growing demand in the nineteenth century for global markets. Of course, Porter's ideas could be read in terms of the paternal rhetoric characteristic not only of the pro-slavery legitimist in the antebellum period but also more benign proponents of Enlightenment notions of "representative man"—that paradigm of a ruling elite that would stake its claim to speaking for (as well as creating jobs for) the rest of society.

To be sure, Porter did not enslave the Marquesans; instead, he involved himself from the outset in their intertribal conflicts, much in the manner that the United States in the early modern period, in its access to global power, would offer to negotiate conflicts in the West (Manifest Destiny), Central America and the Caribbean (the Spanish-American War and the Canal treaties), the Philippines (the Spanish-American and Philippine-American wars), China (the Taiping Rebellion, the Boxer Rebellion, and the "Open Door Policy" of John Hay), and the Russo-Japanese War (the Portsmouth Treaty of 1905). His motives prefigure the general U.S. role of global policeman—the legitimation of U.S. authority for the sake of winning hearts and minds, and thus the attainment of both material and immaterial ends. In the former sense, Porter, like U.S. secretaries of state John Hay and Henry Kissinger, wanted to establish trade routes and commercial spheres of influence, recognizing that the future of global domination depended as much on markets, trade routes, and commercial opportunities as on forts, settlements, and the exploitation of raw materials. In the latter sense, he and his more powerful successors in the nineteenth and twentieth centuries recognized that such markets would have to be *made*, in part by converting other peoples not to religious ideals but to the political and social programs of liberal democracy.

What, then, is Melville's role in the historical narrative of emerging U.S. colonialism and its complicity with domestic slavery? Following Dimock, we might argue that the "author as monarch" she finds first developed in Melville's *Mardi* has certain affinities with Captain Porter's behavior toward the Marquesans. Interestingly, Dimock excludes *Typee* and *Omoo* from her critical reading of Melville, on the grounds that the historical and autobiographical constraints of both works prevented Melville from exercising the poetic "freedom and invention" so essential to his "empire for liberty."[25] In this respect, Herbert may be read as extending Dimock's argument to include *Typee*, because he finds much in Melville's views of the Typee to compare with the Enlightenment thinking of Porter: "Melville enunciates the Romantic moral outlook that governs the second phase of Tommo's sojourn among the Typees; it is an outlook analogous to the view of David Porter, holding that man has an innate knowledge of good and evil."[26] Still acknowledging Melville's artistic ability to represent his inner conflicts, Herbert nonetheless concludes that *Typee* typifies the inner contradictoriness of the liberal romantic in this period: "Instead of applying a coherent interpretive framework to Marquesan society, Melville struggles with passionate impulses and moral convictions that refuse to be ordered in a general design. . . . In *Typee* the crisis of meaning is located within Melville himself: he finds his mind radically divided between horror and profound admiration for the islanders, as it is also divided between hatred for civilization and a frantic desire to return to it."[27]

Without wishing to dismiss or resolve entirely the question of Melville's conflicted identity as a white, male, New England writer in Jacksonian America, I want to propose that his inner contradictoriness does progressive work in the narrative of *Typee* both for the American 1840s and for our own times. What is significantly missing from most accounts of Melville as critic of imperialism or as critic of U.S. slavery is the relation between the two practices and their discourses of legitimation. In *Typee*, the narrative connects slavery and colonialism from the moment that Toby and Tommo flee the wage-slavery on board the *Dolly* to their hysterical efforts to escape what they fear is the cannibalism for which the Typee are preparing them.

There were two popular narrative forms available to Melville as possible models for dramatic situations in which the protagonist's confusion and doubt might serve advantageously the aims of the narrative: the captivity narrative and fugitive slave narrative. Like other literate New Englanders, Melville did know Cotton Mather's *Magnalia Christi Americana*, which includes the famous narrative of Hannah Dustan's captivity. Melville refers to *Magnalia* as a "mouldy book," and Mather's highly conventionalized treatment of colonial captivity as a form of Puritan conversion would likely have made a negative impression on him.[28] But less conventional versions, like Mary Rowlandson's *The Sovereignty and Goodness of God, Together with the Faithfulness of His Promises Displayed; Being a Narrative of the*

Captivity and Restauration of Mrs. Mary Rowlandson (1682), in which she narrates her captivity by Narragansetts in 1676 during King Philip's War, is full of uncanny moments in which Rowlandson is simply unable to reconcile her admiration for the Narragansetts with what she believes should be her religious and moral *contempt* for her captors.[29]

In a rather different manner, the fugitive slave narrative (perhaps the most famous example of which is Frederick Douglass's 1845 *Narrative*, published a year before *Typee*) often plays upon the fundamental social and ethical problem that "freedom" for the fugitive slave means adaptation to a system of laws and culture (especially reading and writing) that has played a central role in the maintenance of the slave system itself.[30] Although the geopolitical distinction between North and South always defines the map of the fugitive slave narrative, many express ambivalence about the otherwise strict boundary of the Mason-Dixon Line—that is, the distinction between chattel-slavery and freedom. Harriet Wilson's *Our Nig* (1859) and Harriet Jacobs's *Incidents in the Life of a Slave Girl* (1861) are published too late to have any immediate relevance for *Typee*, but both narratives expose how profoundly racist the nominally "free" North is, both in terms of social practices of racial segregation and discrimination and an urban economy designed to deepen such racial divisions.[31]

A simple allegorization of slavery in *Typee* would, of course, lead us to one of the racialist assumptions so prevalent in the travel writings of nineteenth-century Westerners—that peoples of color are related, especially in the imagination of the Western and colonial observer. Even an argument working by way of the common fates of enslaved African Americans, displaced and murdered Native Americans, and colonized Polynesians risks equating very different peoples, as well as different historical circumstances. But if we understand the relation of colonialism and slavery in *Typee* to be exemplified by Tommo and Toby, rather than the Typee, then we get some very different results. First, the bond between the commercial working class and subjugated peoples under colonialism and slavery is foregrounded, especially with regard to the issue of who controls the labor-power of the body itself. Second, the experience of the commodified subject under chattel-slavery is simulated by Tommo and Toby by virtue of the roles they play in the contest between the French and Typee. However well they are treated, they are still hostages held by the Typee most likely for the purposes of commercial or military exchange. Powerless to control their own self-representations for each other, the Typee, or the competing Euro-American powers, they fall prey to the most fantastic imaginings and paranoia.

Tommo and Toby's flight from the *Dolly* follows the familiar theme in Melville's subsequent works from *Omoo* to *Billy Budd* that life on board a ship is a microcosm of the tyranny exercised in most nineteenth-century societies. It is the brutality of their captain that drives Tommo and Toby into the interior of Nuku Hiva in the beginning of *Typee*; it is the weakness of the captain of the *Julia* in *Omoo* that provokes the mutiny. As

Carolyn Karcher puts the matter: "Almost equally relevant to the issues raised in these later confrontations is the ambivalent attitude toward authority figures that Melville evinces in *Typee* and *Omoo*, on the one hand through his nostalgic characterizations of the Typee chieftains who befriended him, and on the other hand through his overwhelmingly negative portrayals of the captains whose tyranny and meanness drove him to desertion and mutiny. . . . The gallery of sea captains Melville displays in his subsequent fiction contains a preponderance of petty despots and weaklings."[32]

Tommo and Toby's escape from the *Dolly* and headlong plunge through the Marquesan wilderness in chapters 5 through 9 have the most immediate affinities with the fugitive slave narrative. Rather than welcoming and nurturing Tommo and Toby, the interior of this natural paradise is the site of psychological terror and genuine physical suffering. In these chapters, Melville shares the fugitive slave's sense that the natural wilderness can be a very real threat to freedom. Both the fact and metaphor of Tommo's wounded leg, as well as the general rhetoric of "rebirth" in these chapters, have received considerable comment from previous critics.[33] But the rhetoric of rebirth, especially as difficult and perilous, is common to the accounts of flight in slave narratives, for reasons that are perfectly obvious: after all, successful flight *was* an instance of rebirth from legally defined "property" to freedom and self-possession.

The rhetoric of the colonial captivity narrative, admittedly without the Puritan theology, appears primarily in the chapters (10–33) describing Tommo's acculturation to Typee society. Where both of these conventions come together is in Tommo's discovery that as a captive he has a distinct political value for the Typee and that their interests in him are considerably less flattering to his person than he initially suspected. Whether or not Tommo ever recognizes that he is protected and even pampered primarily for his future worth in ransom or other forms of political barter, Melville makes it clear to the reader that Tommo is "property" both for the captain of the *Dolly* and for the Typee. Of the two forms of social life he experiences, Tommo clearly would prefer life with the Typee to the drudgery of the ordinary seaman's life aboard a ship like the *Dolly* were it not that Tommo begins to fear for his life among the Typee. But what becomes Tommo's obsession with cannibalism—the common phobia, if not fetish, of Western imperialists—is for Melville more reasonably understood as the commodification of the body by forces over which the subject has little control.

Such an interpretation of Tommo's experience of what is the subject's schizophrenia under slavery or colonialism—"I am this body that does not belong to me"—must take into account his daily relations with Kory-Kory and his family, including Fayaway. To be sure, Kory-Kory's role as Tommo's "savage valet" suggests nothing so much as some colonial fantasy of the exotic leisure to be found by Westerners in the paradise of the South Seas, most often at the cost of the native's labor. Carrying Tommo about on his back, Kory-Kory daily enacts that grotesque colonial romance, which in the antebellum South had its equivalent in the clichés of the plantation romance. Even the more benign interpretation of Kory-Kory's relation to his nominal master, Tommo, that suggests the mutual dependence of master and servant in the manner of Hegel's romantic paradigm is subject to criticism for its liberal idealization of the otherwise drudging labor of the colonial subject.

In his final escape from the Typee, Tommo narrates how Kory-Kory, his father, Marheyo, and Fayaway mourn his departure and yet facilitate it. But Tommo's perception of Kory-Kory as the faithful servant, who eventually grows attached by bonds of sentiment to his master, ignores substantial evidence that Kory-Kory acts merely in the interests of the community and in obedience to the order of King Mehevi. Tommo and Toby both imagine that they are being well cared for in anticipation of a cannibal feast, but the more likely explanation is that both have a different value for the Typee. Throughout the narrative, Tommo is asked for information about French troop movements (about which he knows nothing), how to repair an old musket (for which he does "not possess the accomplishments of a gunsmith, and was likewise destitute of the necessary tools" [T, 185]), and other practical and cultural matters that might be of use in Typee military conflicts with the Western colonial forces.

Like the vast majority of European colonists taken hostage by Native Americans in the seventeenth and eighteenth centuries, Tommo is a hostage worth healing and feeding for his value in future exchanges for goods, prisoners, or the information he has of the enemy. He is an exchangeable commodity for the Typee, rather than a worker to be exploited for his physical labor power. Although it seems typical Melvillean irony for the reader to discover that Tommo has virtually no value other than his physical labor power, it is also one of the serious points of the narrative: that the system of slavery in the so-called "civilized" West manipulates far more crudely the value of human beings than what the Typee think they see in Tommo and Toby. Observing King Mehevi's disdain after telling the king that he cannot repair the musket, Tommo reflects: "At this unexpected communication Mehevi regarded me, for the moment, as if he half suspected I was some inferior sort of white man, who after all did not know much more than a Typee" (T, 185).

Tommo's liaison with Fayaway seems to argue against the interpretation that the Typee merely indulge Tommo's fantasies of leisure-class authority for the sake of maintaining his hostage value. No other parts of the narrative seem so clearly to reveal the contradictoriness of Melville's liberal sympathies with the Marquesans and his longing to preserve the authority of the white, male, New England visitor. Like Captain Porter and his men, Tommo and Toby are familiar with and perfectly willing to exploit the legends of Marquesan women's sexual openness. The voyeurism of Tommo's narration is common enough in nineteenth-century travel narratives, especially when non-Western cultures are described. Prurient interest in the native woman's body is often disguised by romantic sentiments regarding feminine naturalness, as when Tommo notes the relative lack of feminine tattooing among the Typee. Yet these conventions are often undercut by other analogies that relate Marquesan and Western women. In particular, Tommo compares Fayaway's leisure with that of aristocratic Western women: "The hands of Fayaway were as soft and delicate as those of any countess; for an entire exemption from rude labour marks the girlhood and even prime of a Typee woman's life. Her feet, though wholly exposed, were as diminutive and fairly shaped as those which peep from beneath the skirts of a Lima lady's dress" (T, 86).

Insofar as Fayaway's leisure is analogous to that of women in Euro-American societies, then it may be said to do ideological work. In effect, this is what Fayaway's relationship with Tommo accomplishes, along with Kory-Kory's work as personal "servant" to him. Only Tommo's naïveté prevents him from understanding that the servitude of a native like Kory-Kory or the sexual favors of Fayaway may well be staged in the interests of the community. Such awareness, of course, would require Tommo to acknowledge a bond between himself and Kory-Kory or Fayaway that is based on their shared condition as those required to work for others. It is a connection that Tommo never makes, but that Melville's narrative repeatedly emphasizes.

Typee society is patriarchal in governance, but domestic polygamy seems to grant women special authority as a consequence of the custom that "no man has more than one wife, and no wife of mature years has less than two husbands" (T, 191). The practical purpose of such polygamy is to deal with the fact that "males considerably outnumber females" among the Typee, and this anthropological observation gives Tommo the opportunity to suggest various reforms of Western monogamy. Yet women do remain subordinate to Typee men, in large part because the women lack the religious and thus social authority displayed by the men in the tattooed bodies that signify specific ranks. The tattooing of women, like the "skirts of a Lima lady's dress," represents quite clearly patriarchal authority. As Tommo learns from Kory-Kory, women are tattooed when married and then not on the faces, as men are, but on "the right hand and the left foot," which are "most elaborately tattooed; while the rest of the body was wholly free from the operation of the art." As if to make the analogy with Western marriage practices unavoidable, Tommo adds: "It answers, indeed, the same purpose as the plain gold ring worn by our fairer spouses" (T, 190).[34]

Horrified by the Typee custom of tattooing men's faces, Tommo recognizes a new danger of his captivity: "That in some luckless hour I should be disfigured in such a manner as never more to have the *face* to return to my countrymen" (T, 219). By contrast, the marriage bond is tattooed on the woman's "hand and foot," the means but not the objects of self-representation. Indeed, the tattoo artist whose "painter's enthusiasm" Tommo "narrowly escapes" rejects "indignantly" Tommo's "compromise" of "my arm" (T, 220). Whatever horror Tommo expresses at having his face tattooed, he knows well enough the custom among seamen to tattoo their torsos and limbs. *Typee* begins with a risqué anecdote of tattooing that equates the subordination of seamen in the Western navies with that of women in Marquesan society. Melville tells us that this event occurred "between two and three years after the adventures" of *Typee*, but he chooses it as the reader's passage into Tommo's experiences with another culture. Receiving King Mowanna and his queen on board an American man-of-war, the U.S. commodore and a French officer representing French colonial authority in the Marquesas witness the King arrayed "in a magnificent uniform, stiff with gold lace and embroidery," itself the "tattooing" of the French colonial powers. The queen is similarly marked by colonial rule, "habited in a gaudy tissue of scarlet cloth, trimmed with yellow silk, which, descending a little below the knees, exposed to view her bare legs, embellished with spiral tattooing, and somewhat resembling two miniature Trajan's columns" (T, 7–8). There is a continuity in this description that links the "gaudy tissue" of traders' cloth with those tattoos on the legs; it is a rhetorical continuity reinforced by the classical analogy Melville makes between her bare legs, their spiral tattoos, and "Trajan's columns."

Like many of the classical allusions in *Typee*, this reference to Trajan reminds the reader of the colonial histories of Europe and the Americas.[35] Melville does more than simply warn us that we are repeating in the South Seas the colonial projects of the Romans in Europe and Europeans in the Americas. By rhetorical contiguity, Melville dramatizes just who these new colonial subjects are. Mowanna's queen singles out from the ship's company "an old *salt*, whose bare arms and feet, and exposed breast were covered with as many inscriptions in India ink as the lid of an Egyptian sarcophagus. Notwithstanding all the sly hints and remonstrances of the French officers, she immediately approached the man, and pulling further open the bosom of his duck frock, and rolling up the leg of his wide trowsers, she gazed with admiration at the bright blue and vermilion pricking, thus disclosed to view" (T, 8). The scene enacts at once the Westerner's expectation of the Polynesian woman's licentiousness and *her* recognition that she shares this sailor's marked body. In the "India ink" of his tattooed body, he shares with this woman and the New World slave the "mark" that is variously figured by the colonizer as race, class, or gender.

Amid the bawdy sentiments of the queen rolling up this salt's trousers, "caressing him, and expressing her delight in a variety of wild exclamations and gestures," Melville also dramatizes a serious recognition between these two actors in the drama of colonization. Inverting the classic scene of recognition, Melville concludes by exposing the licentiousness of the colonial imagination, rather than the two characters in this figurative passage. It is a display that produces an actual retreat, momentary though it may be, of the colonial forces:

> The embarrassment of the polite Gauls at such an unlooked-for occurrence may be easily imagined; but picture their consternation, when all at once the royal lady, eager to display the hieroglyphics on her own sweet form, bent forward for a moment, and turning sharply round, threw up the skirts of her mantle, and revealed a sight from which the aghast Frenchmen retreated precipitately, and tumbling into their boat, fled the scene of so shocking a catastrophe. (T, 8)

The last word of this chapter is, of course, a reference to the Fall, and it is for Melville a re-enactment of that Original Sin that is under way in the colonial ventures in the South Pacific.

The "hieroglyphics" that must be read are not so much secret signs as the different modes of historical and cultural domination that Melville's anthropology in *Typee* attempts to comprehend. Is it merely the bawdy gesture of the queen that sends the "aghast Frenchmen" into retreat, or is it the exposure of the unconscious of colonial domination that causes them to flee the scene? In his romance with Fayaway, Tommo substitutes his own version of woman, tattooing her hand and foot in this way as decisively as the Marquesan marriage ceremony. When the Typee taboo against women entering boats interferes with Tommo's ludicrous desire to float with Fayaway on the village lake in imitation of some moonstruck youth from an illustrated magazine, Tommo convinces Kory-Kory to argue with the Typee priests for Fayaway's "dispensation from this portion of the taboo" (T, 133). Unable to explain his success in achieving Fayaway's emancipation, Tommo nonetheless insists that "for the life of me I could not understand why a woman should not have as much right to enter a canoe as a man" (T, 133).

There is a symbiotic relation between the "ludicrous behavior of the queen" revealing her tattoos to the old salt and Tommo's similarly absurd "emancipation" of Fayaway. Both actions hint at the possible effectiveness of political coalitions among those traditionally exploited, but both episodes end with merely symbolic victories. The retreat of the French is achieved only by indulging the reader's desire to witness savage lewdness, and the emancipation of Fayaway from the unreasonable taboo only by entertaining Tommo's desire to act out the patriarchal fantasy of romantic courtship. Yet just such missed recognition by Melville's characters may be Melville's way of awakening the consciousness of his readers.

Tommo himself hardly ever recognizes how his own captivity by the Typee parallels the bondage that he experienced on board the *Dolly*. By the same token, he never acknowledges the degree to which his own actions among the Typee often reproduce those of the Euro-American masters he fled and the Typee rulers he soon desires to escape. In this regard, *Typee* refuses the enlightenment of conversion in the captivity narrative and ironizes the emancipation of the fugitive slave narrative. When his opportunity to escape the Typee arrives, Tommo seizes it with all the military zeal of the colonial masters criticized by Melville. The sentimental scene of parting with his adoptive family and lover, Fayaway, is replaced soon enough with Tommo's murder of the pursuing Mow-Mow. Dashing the boat hook at Mow-Mow's throat, Tommo "felt horror at the act" but claims "no time for pity or compunction" (T, 252). Even in this unreflective action, however, Melville pauses to comment, because this "strong excitement" causes Tommo to fall "back fainting into the arms of Karakoee," who represents clearly the colonized Marquesan (T, 252).

Tommo's escape is as equivocal as many of the passages of African-American slaves to Northern freedom, for what he soon discovers is that he has been "saved" by the "captain of an Australian vessel, being in distress for men in these remote seas" (T, 252). There is a special irony in the fact of Tommo's deliverance back into the seaman's servitude by a ship flying the colors of a British colony (and one begun as a penal colony), but it is an irony lost to Tommo in his transport from strange to familiar captivity. Tommo has learned relatively little of his own complicity in the colonization of workers, women, and peoples of color, but Melville's narration of *Typee* has uncovered the shared system of colonial domination in those moments otherwise identified as ludicrous, horrifying, or fantastic.

Melville understands how the act of narration can itself be part of the colonial project. Euro-American colonization depends crucially on distinctions between the apparent naturalness of the colonizers' cultural symbolism and that of the colonized. Melville attempts to counter this process of colonial subordination by frequently drawing analogies between the contrived practices of Europeans, Americans, and Marquesans. In many eighteenth- and nineteenth-century European narratives of contact with native peoples, classical references are used to assert tacitly the superiority of the European heritage and often offer it as an ideal for native culture.[36] Melville finds more than an ironic connection between the Marquesan tattoo artist and the Euro-American portrait artist; both remind him that the body is always framed and thus marked by cultural codes that are the prerequisites for the colonial projects of military conquest and economic exploitation. In *Marvelous Possessions*, Stephen Greenblatt argues that "everything in the European dream of possession rests on witnessing, a witnessing understood as a form of significant and representative seeing. To see is to secure the truth of what might otherwise be deemed incredible."[37] Tommo is the site of just such witnessing in *Typee*, but Melville repeatedly ironizes Tommo's ability to be such a significant representative. Even as he returns to the unfolding narrative of Western colonialism, Tommo has assumed for the other seamen a "strange appearance." In Melville's very literary treatment of his own experiences, he holds before the reader what Greenblatt finds only fleetingly hinted in Renaissance narratives of New World conquest but elaborated and sustained in such literary meditations as Montaigne's "Of Cannibals": "Where we expect to find two terms in Montaigne—subject and object—we find a third: subject, object, and go-between. And if in the history we have been examining the go-between has served often as the agent of betrayal, Montaigne's essay suggests that the go-between can also serve as the agent for a marvelous dispossession, a loss of the fiercely intolerant certainty that licensed unbearable cruelty."[38]

The very act of narrating his experiences in the Marquesas through the character of Tommo seems to be one way Melville performed his own "dispossession" in *Typee* as a direct response to what he recognized as every human's proclivity for the complex modes of domination explored in this uncanny text. Understanding as he does just how deeply entangled the will to possession and the powers to represent are in human beings, Melville may have understandably wondered at the most effective means to defeat the imperial imaginary as it told its story on the bodies of workers, women, and peoples of color. If Dimock is right that Melville's works after *Typee* and *Omoo* enact the narrative of Jacksonian individualism as a prelude to the new empires claimed by the United States in the West and the Pacific, then the dispossession of that authorial self is what distinguishes these two "travel narratives" from Melville's more literary productions. However, it may be that what Dimock uncovers as a "poetics of individualism" is less the territory of Melville than the horizon of our own deep-seated habits of reading, which would account well for our relative neglect of *Typee* as that autobiographical narrative the more "literary" Melville would seek to transcend. My argument in this chapter interprets *Typee* as an anticipation of Melville's social criticism in his subsequent works, such as *Pierre* (1852) and "Bartleby, the Scrivener" (1853) and *Benito Cereno* (1855), of the forms of imperial domination employed by the United States from its earliest years.

In this context, Melville incorporates in many of his narratives a searching critique of the very "individualism" that Dimock finds integral to his aesthetic practice. Like Greenblatt's Montaigne, this Melville "peeps" at a strange New World only "as a means of articulating the horror at home."[39] The literariness of this gesture is not so much Melville's ability to sustain the manifold cultural contradictions of the colonial experience, but his refusal to represent that experience as a simple or singular narrative. It is a literary function that is by no means intransitive or apolitical; indeed, it depends on its profound implication in the ideologies that it seeks to represent. And it is a literariness that depends on an author radically different from Poe's masterful Dupin (or Kant's genius); Melville's author is a participant in the very historical events he represents, often confused and baffled by them. The full significance of his experience *escapes* him, just as we are to be dispossessed in the act of reading, in the hope (desperate though it may be) of offering another way of seeing than that of the explorer, conqueror, trader, and scientific recorder, whose confidence goes without saying.

5

Highway Robbery

"Indian Removal," the Mexican-American War, and American Identity in John Rollin Ridge's (Yellow Bird) The Life and Adventures of Joaquín Murieta

Representatives of their nation these gold-seeking
Californian Americans were; yet it remains true, and
is, under the circumstances, a very natural result,
that the American had nowhere else, save perhaps as
conqueror in Mexico itself, shown so blindly and
brutally as he often showed in early California, his
innate intolerance for whatever is stubbornly
foreign.

Josiah Royce, *California from the Conquest in 1846 to the
Second Vigilance Committee in San Francisco: A Study of
American Character* (1886)

Remember Custer's saying? The only good Indian is
a dead Indian? Well from my dealings with whites I
would add to that quote: "The only interesting
Indian is dead, or dying by falling backwards off a
horse."

Nector Kashpaw in Louise Erdrich,
Love Medicine (1993)

"Listen," Samuel said. "Coyote, who is the creator of
all of us, was sitting on his cloud the day after he
created the Indians. Now, he liked the Indians, liked
what they were doing. *This is good*, he kept saying to
himself. But he was bored. . . . So he decided to clip
his toenails. . . . He looked around and around his
cloud for somewhere to throw away his
clippings. . . . Then he accidentally dropped his
toenail clippings over the side of the cloud and they
fell to the earth. The clippings burrowed into the

ground like seeds and grew up to be the white man. Coyote, he looked down at his newest creation and said, *Oh, shit.*"

"The whites are crazy, the whites are crazy," the children would chant and dance around Samuel in circles.

"And sometimes so are the Indians," Samuel would whisper to himself.

Sherman Alexie, *The Lone Ranger and Tonto Fistfight in Heaven* (1993)

John Rollin Ridge's 1854 thriller, *The Life and Adventures of Joaquín Murieta*, is an extraordinary example of how literary texts condense the contradictory political, social, legal, cultural, and psychological effects of colonial conquest. Indeed, literature's ability to incorporate conflicting social experiences is one of my reasons for focusing this study of U.S. imperialism primarily in terms of literary narratives, whose interpretations are often occasions for exploring larger social and political events associated with U.S. colonial ventures at home and abroad. Yet just what I mean by literature's *condensation* of the historical consequences of colonialism requires a diverse account of the many ways literature distorts, displaces, and incorporates these materials, as well as an equally nuanced treatment of how such literary varieties have been understood by readers. The weird reception-history of Ridge's novel and the even stranger history of the U.S. conquest of California teach us the futility of ever *theorizing* how literature functions in relation to ideology. Instead, we should begin with specific cases of ideological instability and use theory to help us *select* literary or other kinds of texts that respond to such a historical crisis, in order to assess the roles played by culture in ideological normalization. Although theory, especially critical social theory, can be of immense help in this work, there can be no *general rule* that covers the many possible roles of literary and cultural texts in this process.

I argue in this chapter that Ridge's novel resolves the conflicting and traumatic experiences of his personal history as a Cherokee, of the U.S. conquest of California in the Mexican-American War, and of the social disorder in California during the Gold Rush in a narrative organized around the myth of progressive individualism, a crucial part of dominant cultural values in the United States in the 1850s. In short, I contend that Ridge's *Joaquín Murieta* fits most definitions of the category of "mass culture" in its resolution of social and political problems by recourse to established cultural conventions. Yet, we should be especially interested in the ways in which Ridge's narrative does this work of cultural normalization, including the formal and technical aspects of the novel, keeping in mind that the *value* of

Joaquín Murieta resides primarily in the *history* it requires for its comprehension. A new category of literary value is required, I think, to account for works of little intrinsic aesthetic interest that nevertheless bring into sharp relief historical and ideological issues crucial to the formation of dominant cultural values.

Shelley Streeby has argued that the Mexican-American War of 1846–1848 has been largely forgotten as an important U.S. colonial venture, in part because its history challenges our understanding of American national identity.[1] The Treaty of Guadalupe-Hidalgo not only increased the territory of the United States by one third, but it also guaranteed under U.S. law the civil and property rights of those people living and working in this territory before the war. These peoples included native-born Californios, many of whom owned the large cattle and sheep *ranchos* on which the agrarian economy of California under Mexican rule depended; working-class Mexicans and Latin Americans; Native Americans representing more than 100 different tribes; Chinese laborers; and U.S. settlers, who first came to California as illegal aliens after the U.S. annexation of Texas in 1836.[2] The discovery of gold at Sutter's Mill on January 22, 1848, barely antedates the signing of the Treaty of Guadalupe-Hidalgo on February 2, 1848, and the great influx of "Forty Niners" would arrive after the conclusion of the war. These miners included at various times representatives of all the prewar groups living in California, as well as foreigners from Peru, Chile, Australia, England, Ireland, Germany, France, Holland, and a host of other countries.[3] By 1850 California was both an extraordinarily diverse and violent society. The legal protections of property and civil rights provided by the treaty were generally ignored, and new territorial laws were adopted, like the Land Act of 1851, that violated specific provisions of the treaty.[4] To justify claims to the mineral resources and productive land of California, interested and powerful groups quickly established social binaries between "foreigners" and "U.S. citizens" that drew upon the prevailing racial, class, and gender hierarchies of U.S. culture at midcentury.

The U.S. colonization of California was the result of the economic and military struggle with Spanish colonialism in the region and, to a lesser extent, with continuing British efforts to control territory on the Pacific Coast.[5] Mexican *rancheros* who were victimized by new Yankee laws had themselves displaced Native Americans from their ancestral lands, systematically destroyed Native Americans' food sources, and employed Native Americans under conditions of virtual serfdom. Defined as *"sin razón"* by the Franciscans, Native Americans in California were the first group to be constructed ideologically as "alien" by Eurocolonial forces, and they constituted thereby the cultural horizon of civilized "identity" and "selfhood" well in advance of U.S. conquest.[6] In mid-nineteenth-century California, they were collectively named "Diggers," a derogatory term referring to their hunting-and-gathering societies and homophonically linked with the racist epithet "nigger."

By the 1850s public policy favored reservations for the "protection" of Native Americans in California, legitimating both U.S. governmental paternalism toward the Indian and tacitly acknowledging the continuing genocide of Native Americans. With the passage in April 1850 of the "Act for the Government and Protection of the Indians," Native Americans were legally defined as subalterns, prevented from testifying against "a white person," and made virtual slaves to the capitalist economy advocated by Yankee settlers.[7] The displacement and murder of Native Americans increased dramatically during the Gold Rush as prospectors poured into the remote Sierra foothills and mountains that under the Mexican rule of California had been left largely to Native Americans.[8] Driven out of the mining areas, often unemployed as a consequence of the part-time hiring policies of most *rancheros*, and increasingly desperate for food and clothing, Native Americans in California often appeared as vagrants, by necessity committed petty thefts, and in such ways increasingly fulfilled the prophecies of those advocating laws to "govern" Native Americans—laws that actually hastened their extermination.[9]

After the war, the Californio landowners, who had traditionally emulated the aristocratic cultivation of Spanish Hidalgos, found themselves lumped together in the U.S. cultural imaginary with Mexican and Latin American immigrants. Whereas many *rancheros* in California had grown weary of Mexican rule in the 1840s and distanced themselves from the central government, they were identified in postwar California with the losing side and with those *mestizos*, who were racially denigrated by U.S. troops as a "'mongrel,' largely Indian race."[10] The derogatory term "greaser" was not just reserved for working-class Mexican and Latin American immigrants; it was increasingly used in reference to the *rancheros*, who were often imagined to be in conspiratorial league against U.S. law and economic "free-enterprise" in the California of the 1850s. Such U.S. cultural anxieties were inflamed by envy of the sudden profits the *rancheros* made from the Gold Rush as beef and sheep prices soared, along with land prices, and organized mining efforts by Californios resulted in conspicuous successes.[11] Australian, Irish, European, and other foreigners, as well as Texans and proslavery Southerners, brought their own racial and cultural prejudices along with them to California during the Gold Rush and quickly adapted them to any individual or group likely to get the better of them in the increasingly crowded gold fields.

This was the sort of adversarial and extremely dangerous cultural, political, and economic context in California that John Rollin Ridge encountered when he arrived in 1850 as one of the many young Cherokee joining the Gold Rush.[12] Given the degraded status of the California Native Americans, Ridge and other Cherokee must have taken special pains to avoid identification with the demonized "Diggers," anticipating the distinction Ridge would make in his journalism between Native Americans "west of the Rocky Mountains—the Utah, Oregon and California Indians"—and those tribes east of the Rockies, who "have manifested the traits upon which the immemorial ideas of Indian heroism, nobility of character and dignity of thought are founded."[13] Handsome and cultivated in his speech, elegantly dressed even in the rough mining towns of California, Ridge apparently did not experience racial discrimination or exclusion during the few months in 1850 he worked in the gold fields, but he must have known how important his education, speech, and dress were in protecting him from the violent, racist xenophobia experienced by so many other "foreigners" in the mines.

The son of the successful Cherokee lawyer and landowner John Ridge and grandson of Major Ridge (The Ridge), who "got his name from fighting for the Americans in the Creek War," John Rollin Ridge had been raised and educated to inherit the wealth and political power of his family in the Cherokee nation.[14] Advocates of Cherokee assimilation to the dominant culture, politics, and economy of the United States, the Ridges and Boudinots, especially Major Ridge's influential nephew, Elias Boudinot (1803–1839), a founding editor of the *Cherokee Phoenix*, and his younger brother, Stand Watie (1806–1871), were signatories of the New Echota Treaty of 1835, "agreeing to the imperialistic demands of the state of Georgia that insisted upon the removal of the indigenous people west to Indian Territory."[15] Under the terms of this treaty, the Cherokee were moved from their homes in Georgia to Oklahoma Territory in two stages, the first involving the voluntary move in 1836 by those Cherokee able to afford their own transport and "sixteen thousand . . . removed by force in 1838 and marched at bayonet point" on the infamous "Trail of Tears," during which as many as 8,000, or *one-half*, died.[16] Their political opponents in the Cherokee leadership, John Ross and John Howard Payne, condemned not only the New Echota Treaty but also the authority by which the Ridges and Boudinots had signed it, and the Ross faction accused the Ridges and Boudinots of treason.

The Ridges and Boudinots moved to Oklahoma Territory in the first phase and used their capital to establish stores that would cater to the newly arrived Cherokee immigrants. The two political factions continued their rivalry for control of the Cherokee nation in Oklahoma, and the Ross faction met secretly to condemn John Ridge, Major Ridge, and Elias Boudinot to death, under the "provision of Cherokee law—one John Ridge helped frame in 1829—that anyone involved in the sale of Cherokee land without the sanction of the people would be put to death."[17] On June 22, 1839, John Ridge, Major Ridge, and Elias Boudinot were separately ambushed and assassinated by three "execution squads," and Stand Watie, also targeted for execution, escaped only because he was forewarned. Dragged from his bed at dawn, John Ridge was stabbed repeatedly ("twenty-nine times" in the son's account) by one man as two others held him and twenty-two more surrounded the house while the whole family, including the twelve-year-old John, watched. As Ridge's biographer, James Parins, puts it, "John Rollin Ridge was to carry that image in his mind for the rest of his life."[18]

Hostility between the Ross faction and those Cherokee who advocated assimilation to U.S. culture continued unabated, even though the Ridge family moved to Fayetteville, Arkansas. Educated in Fayetteville and later at the Great Barrington Academy in Great Barrington, Massachusetts (1843–1845), where W. E. B. Du Bois would be born a quarter of a century later (1868), married in 1847 to a white woman, Elizabeth ("Lizzie") Wilson, and interested in poetry, the arts, and the law, Ridge exemplified the cultivation and cosmopolitanism he argued Native Americans could achieve within Euro-American society. He also typified everything that was abhorrent to the Ross faction, and when he participated in the 1845–1846 treaty negotiations between the Cherokee Nation and the U.S. government he renewed the deep enmity between the Ross and Ridge factions.[19] In 1849 that old dispute again involved the Ridges in violence, and this time it was John Rollin Ridge who killed his neighbor, "a pro-Ross man named David Kell." According to Parins, the dispute that resulted in Ridge shooting Kell was superficially about "Ridge's missing stallion" and more likely a plan by the Ross faction "to provoke a fight with young Ridge in order to have an excuse to kill him."[20]

John Rollin Ridge's decision in 1850 to join a party heading west to the California gold fields was motivated in part by his desire to avoid prosecution for this event and his fear that his trial, especially if influenced by pro-Ross supporters, might be unfair. In California, Ridge quickly learned that gold mining in 1850 was drudging physical labor that exposed miners to constant, unpredictable dangers and rarely resulted in profits, much less fortunes. Abandoning gold mining after little more than two months and turning to a career in journalism, Ridge followed his background and education to pursue a professional, urban career for which he was suited.

Most of the scholars who have interpreted Ridge's *Life and Adventures of Joaquín Murieta* have interpreted it as a complex sublimation, if not explicit allegory, of the violence his family experienced in the stormy politics of Cherokee removal and the establishment of a government for the Cherokee Nation in Oklahoma Territory. In his seminal reading of Ridge's novel, Louis Owens argues that "Ridge transforms himself and his bitterness against the oppression and displacement of Indians" into his Mexican character, Joaquín Murieta, using the novel as "a disguised act of appropriation, an aggressive and subversive masquerade."[21] In his brief account of Ridge's novel in *The Cambridge History of American Literature*, Eric Sundquist characterizes it as a "double-edged" narrative that "may be understood to be Yellow Bird's own indirect statement about the justification for revenge against whites felt by American Indians, whether in California, Georgia, or Oklahoma."[22] But when read as the novel of an educated, cosmopolitan, urban professional, who repeatedly endorsed the values of progressive individualism, *Joaquín Murieta* appears to be a reasonable indictment of violence unchecked by law, whether such anarchic violence was experienced personally amid the political upheavals of Cherokee removal or in the gold fields of California.

In many respects, then, Ridge's *Joaquín Murieta* belongs with the countless popular adventure stories of frontier life that exploit citizens' fears of lawless anarchy, barbarism, and other threats to civilized life resulting from westward expansion. Thus Ridge's novel does ideological work similar to Brockden Brown's Gothic romances, and it achieves these ends in ways thoroughly compatible with the Native American politics of the wealthy, slave-owning, assimilationist Ridges and their Treaty party in the Cherokee Nation. To be sure, anxieties in the United States about the effects of frontier anarchy and "savagery" "contaminating" the rest of the nation have different connotations in the aftermath of the Mexican-American War from those prompting the Alien and Sedition Acts of 1790, but there are considerable similarities in crises separated historically by more than half a century and geographically by a continent. In both cases, the "purity" of "American identity" is threatened by "foreigners" coming from all corners of the globe, whose dangerous conduct is nevertheless judged by a standard of "savagery" defined by Native Americans. "American identity" is an unstable category in both postrevolutionary Philadelphia and in California, where the Yankee settlers before the Mexican-American War were perceived by Californios as "foreign" by the cultural and economic standards of California under Mexican rule. In both historical cases, the ideological construction of "foreigners" was crucial to legitimate an American identity threatened by specific historical crises and its own internal contradictions.

Ridge uses the crisis of the U.S. conquest of California (and, of course, the rest of the Mexican Southwest) and the accompanying social disorder, exacerbated by the arrival of foreigners during the Gold Rush, to develop his position on the assimilation of "foreigners" into the United States as part of a rational legal and cultural process guided by the prevailing myth of "American individualism" and its economic complement, free-enterprise capitalism. His position in no way contradicts the class and racial hierarchies the Ridge family and Treaty party members would endorse in Cherokee politics and in their support of the Confederacy—and extension of slavery to new territories—during the Civil War. In his journalism during the Civil War, Ridge was a staunch anti-abolitionist, who was frequently attacked for his anti-Lincoln editorials and Copperhead affiliations.[23] In this same period, Ridge wrote the three articles intended to be the first parts of a long, scholarly series on "the North American Indians for *Hesperian* magazine," which reflect not only his knowledge of Native American cultural and tribal histories but also his commitments to Native American rights and politics.[24] Ridge's interests in Native American history in these three articles focus on their potential for gradual and successful adaptation to Euro-American social and economic practices, thus complementing rather than contradicting the assimilationist argument of *Joaquín Murieta* and his proslavery, anti-abolitionist journalism of the Civil War period.

Despite John Rollin Ridge's complaints that he had earned no money from the first edition of *The Life and Adventures of Joaquín Murieta, the Cele-*

brated California Bandit, published by W. B. Cooke of San Francisco, it does seem that the ninety-page pamphlet circulated rather widely among the reading public of California in the mid-1850s.[25] Whether or not Ridge was right that the publisher had gone bankrupt and "left me, along with a hundred others, to whistle for our money," the pamphlet was "widely read and reviewed and, eventually, frequently plagiarized."[26] One reason for the popularity of Ridge's fictional account of the exploits, final capture, and beheading of the legendary bandit, Joaquín Murieta, was public anxiety in California regarding several groups of bandits operating there in the early 1850s. The legend of the Mexican *bandido* is traceable to the political divisions of the anticolonial forces in Mexico from the 1820s, when strong military leaders, *caudillos*, like Santa Anna supported various regimes according to their preferences and special interests.[27] The Mexican-American War added to these legends of *caudillos* with powerful organizational skills. Many of the popular novelettes about the war not only celebrate U.S. heroes who are "thinly disguised Natty Bumppos," but demonize the enemy as ruthless Mexican *bandidos* or *caudillos*, who stand in the way of the Mexican people's desire for liberty. In these formula texts, the U.S. military helps the Mexican people achieve the full revolution against colonial and tyrannical rule they have been unable to accomplish on their own.[28]

Reginald Horsman has argued that "the overt adoption of racial Anglo-Saxonism" that "became commonplace by the mid-1840s" was driven in large part by "the meeting of Americans and Mexicans in the Southwest, the Texas revolution, and the war with Mexico."[29] Americans associated Mexican peasants with "Indians," both of whom were imagined to be "unable to make proper use of the land." In the U.S. imaginary in 1850, this was specifically attributed to the large *mestizo* population in Mexico: "Since the time of the Texas Revolution the Mexicans had been repeatedly attacked in the United States as a degenerate, largely Indian race unable to control or improve the territories they owned."[30] Unable to govern themselves, as shown by their constant internal warfare, these imagined "Mexicans" also exemplified the dangers of unchecked miscegenation that southern, proslavery interests argued would result from the abolition of slavery and the open transgression of racial and class boundaries.

In the California gold fields following the Mexican-American War, the racialization and "mongrelization" of Mexicans was used to exclude them from overcrowded mining regions and to justify Yankee claims to mineral wealth, land, and political power. This stereotype of the Mexican also served the convenient purpose of lumping together thoroughly different peoples and cultures for the purposes of economic and political exclusion. The passage of the Foreign Miners' Tax in 1850, authored by Thomas Jefferson Green, a Texan émigré well known for his proslavery and anti-Mexican views, was nominally directed against all non–U.S. citizens, but the monthly tax was levied primarily against Mexicans, Californios, Chileans, Peruvians, and Chinese.[31] Often collected by unauthorized individuals, the tax was widely viewed as unjust in conception and practice. At one point in Ridge's novel, Joaquín saves a group of Germans from the bloodthirsty Three-Fingered Jack by "remarking that it was better to let them live as he might wish to collect taxes off of them for 'Foreign Miners' Licenses,' at some other time" (JM, 130).[32] Joaquín's comments are meant, of course, to be ironic, suggesting both how the tax was often collected illegally and yet rarely levied against Europeans, like these Germans. In his history of California, Josiah Royce sarcastically condemns that tax as an attempt "to exclude foreigners from these mines, the God-given property of the American people," and describes in detail American mob violence against Mexicans and Latin Americans protesting the tax.[33] Vigorous opposition by Mexican miners to the tax resulted in the formation of local militias to respond to what many imagined might be a recommencement of the Mexican-American War. Such militias often included substantial numbers of veterans, decked out in their old uniforms. The tax also resulted in countless foreigners abandoning their claims as too expensive and too dangerous to mine, thus leaving boomtowns that had grown up to provide supplies and services to the miners. Although merchants in these towns recognized the economic crisis produced by the tax and had it repealed in 1851, the "ultimate result . . . was the expulsion of non-Americans—Mexicans and Chinese especially were singled out—from the mining opportunities of California through apparently state-sanctioned mass violence against people of color."[34]

The Foreign Miners' Tax was simply one highly visible example of American animosity toward racially and linguistically identifiable "foreigners" competing with them in the gold fields and more generally for economic power in California. Shortly after gold was discovered, Californios began well-organized mining operations. Pitt estimates that "1,300 native Californians mined gold in 1848" versus 4,000 Yankees, and that the Californios' greater organizational skills and experience enabled them to extract as much gold as the Yankees in that year. Yankee miners began to harass Californios soon after, and by 1849 few Californios returned to mining.[35] Replacing them were experienced miners from the Mexican state of Sonora, who were also well organized in their mining operations, albeit more recognizably *mestizo* than the more Spanish Californios, and they were joined by Chilean and Peruvian miners. Lumping together Latin Americans, northern Mexicans, and Californios, the Yankee miners helped create the very social disorder they feared. Driven from the gold fields either by overtly unfair laws, like the Foreign Miners' Tax, or by mob violence and racially driven vigilantism, some recent immigrants did begin robbing gold dust from traveling miners, horses from *rancheros*, and food and supplies from small farmers and merchants. By the same token, white gangs preyed upon displaced Latin American, Mexican, and Chinese miners: "The notorious San Francisco gang, the 'Hounds,' for example, which was staffed by former New York Volunteers and Australians, took particular delight in attacking the Chileans who came to San Francisco after fleeing enemies in the mountains."[36] In the Los Angeles area, Texans who settled in El Monte formed vigilante groups called "Monte boys," who would lynch Mexicans suspected of robbery and murder.[37] It was common practice for these white vigilantes to cut off the heads or mutilate the bodies of their victims as visible warnings to others.

Ridge's *Joaquín Murieta* plays upon these social upheavals, paranoias, and the history of racial and national conflict in the competition for gold between 1848 and 1853. By tracing the origins of Joaquín's banditry to the injustice he and his wife, Rosita, experience repeatedly at the hands of lawless Yankees, Ridge appeals to the reader's sympathy for a man whose forbearance is almost saintly and whose eventual vows of revenge seem more than justified. Yet it is neither as a Sonoran nor as a disguised "Cherokee" that Joaquín gains the reader's sympathy, but as a man who has left Sonora in order to become an *American*:

> At an early age of his manhood . . . he became tired of the uncertain state of affairs in his own country, the usurpations and revolutions which were of such common occurrence, and resolved to try his fortunes among the American people, of whom he had formed the most favorable opinion from an acquaintance with the few whom he had met in his own native land. The war with Mexico had been fought, and California belonged to the United States. Disgusted with the conduct of his degenerate countrymen and fired with enthusiastic admiration of the American character, the youthful Joaquín left his home with a buoyant heart and full of the exhilarating spirit of adventure. (JM, 8)

In this introduction of Joaquín, Ridge replays popular stereotypes of Mexican degeneracy, our military heroism in the war, and the consequent legitimacy of our colonization of California and implicitly the rest of the Southwest.

"Born in the province of Sonora of respectable parents," Joaquín is *mestizo* but has the physical characteristics and character of a Californio of the *ranchero* class: "[T]he proud blood of the Castilians mounted to the cheek of a partial descendant of the Mexiques, showing that he had inherited the old chivalrous spirit of his Spanish ancestry" (JM, 9). Ridge also gives Joaquín just the physical qualities necessary for him to be able to "pass" in Californian society as a Yankee, an ability he will use on the several occasions he disguises himself to spy and avoid capture: "He was then eighteen years of age, a little over the medium height, slenderly but gracefully built, and active as a young tiger. His complexion was neither very dark or very light, but clear and brilliant, and his countenance is pronounced to have been, at that time, exceedingly handsome and attractive" (JM, 8–9). Several times in the novel, Ridge moralizes about the evils of the "prejudice of color, the antipathy of races" and how such prejudices are used by "the ignorant and unlettered" to "excuse" "their unmanly cruelty and oppression" (JM, 9–10). Yet Ridge's didactic aim will be to appeal for justice "*to individuals*" as the best possible defense against "prejudice of color or from any other source" (JM, 158).

Joaquín's "rich mining claim" is stolen from him by "lawless and desperate men, who bore the name of Americans but failed to support the honor and dignity of that title," and thus the reader is not surprised when they not only steal his claim, but also beat him and rape his wife (JM, 9–10). Abandoning the gold fields for "a little farm on the banks of a beautiful stream that watered a fertile valley, far out in the seclusion of the mountains," Joaquín and Rosita are again attacked by a "company of unprincipled Americans—shame that there should be such bearing the name!"—who "coveted his little home surrounded by its fertile tract of land, and drove him from it" (JM, 10). Although he is "twice broken up in his honest pursuit of fortune," Joaquín's "spirit was still unbroken," a determination indicating that his very *soul* is defined by the "honest pursuit of fortune," a typical predicate of progressive individualism in 1850s America.

Joaquín's subsequent experiences of Yankee xenophobia merely confirm Ridge's claim that the lawlessness in California discourages the honest pursuit of the basic ideals of American individualism, especially when the immigrant is racially identified with a debased group. Unsuccessful mining in Calaveras County, Joaquín turns to "dealing 'monte,'" and Ridge is careful to point out that this is "in no manner a disreputable employment" either in Mexico or frontier California (JM, 11). Despite his apparent success as a monte dealer, however, he ends up victimized again, this time accused of stealing a horse, which his "half-brother" has lent him. Tying Joaquín to a tree, an angry mob whips him, then "proceeded to the house of his half-brother and hung him without judge or jury" (JM, 12). "Then it was," Ridge writes, "that he declared to a friend that he would live henceforth for revenge and that his path should be marked with blood" (JM, 12–13).[38]

Raping Rosita and lynching Joaquín's half-brother, the Americans violate his family and privacy; whipping him without due process, they violate his legal and civil rights. Jumping his mining claim and driving him from his farm, they violate his property rights. In all three cases, the dishonor Joaquín Murieta experiences is not so much that of the Spanish Hidalgo—although many Californios were similarly abused by ruthless and greedy Yankee interlopers in this same period—but that of his *American* identity. What Joaquín Murieta had expected in the United States was protection of his individual and familial rights—rights by no means guaranteed in his native Mexico, as Ridge represents the postwar nation, in keeping with anti-Mexican stereotypes of the period.[39] What Joaquín had also expected was "liberty" to pursue his own fortune in a laissez-faire capitalist system unaffected by considerations of race and class; what he discovers in California is a society that fails to realize the democratic (and progressive) promise of individual liberty. The failure of democratic idealism in postwar California is a social problem that Ridge's narrative proposes both to analyze and solve, but it does so not by staging a well-justified rebellion, engineered by the heroic Joaquín and his loyal followers, but by demonstrating the anarchic consequences of this failure. Appealing for the law to suppress such anarchy and restore the democratic promise that first drew Joaquín and Rosita to California from Sonora, Ridge sounds much like law-and-order politicians of the late twentieth century.

Cheryl Walker has analyzed at length how Ridge's novel appeals repeatedly to the sort of sublime and absolute "law" that would adjudicate the social, political, and psychological contradictions of mid-nineteenth-century California. Paying special attention to Ridge's 1852 poem, "Mount Shasta, Seen from a Distance," which Ridge includes early in *Joaquín Murieta*, Walker interprets the poem as representing the desire of humans amid the social anarchy of the period for the "sovereign law" Ridge allegorizes in the natural sublimity of Mount Shasta's transcendental power—a law, whose "pure administration shall be like / The snow, immaculate upon that mountain's brow" (JM, 25). Nevertheless, Walker views this ideal of natural law as so inapplicable to the socially constructed and transient circumstances of the characters in Ridge's novel and California in the 1850s that she concludes the novel contradicts Ridge's effort to find some "absolute"—"Nature, Law, and Nation"—"by means of" which these contradictions might be resolved or adjudicated.[40]

Ridge's novel is, I think, more consistent than Walker suggests in its appeal to the law; what it demands is a legal system that ignores different classes, races, and political or economic interests for the sake of judging the individual alone according to his deficiencies or merits. The poem opens with a view of the mountain as a sublime representation of just such individualism:

> Behold the dread Mount Shasta, where it stands,
> Imperial midst the lesser hight, and like
> Some mighty, unimpassioned mind, companionless
> And cold. (JM, 23)

The mountain's allegorical sublimity is that of "genius," itself an idealization of human individuality, a category crucial to romantic idealism.[41]

> We may not grow familiar with the secrets
> Of its hoary top, whereon the Genius
> Of that mountain builds his glorious throne!
> Far-lifted in the boundless blue, he doth
> Encircle, with his gaze supreme, the broad
> Dominions of the West, that lie beneath
> His feet, in pictures of sublime repose
> No artist ever drew. (JM, 24)

The personification of genius as a divine power, predictably masculine, is typical of romantic idealizations of human rationality as the "divine mind," and it is the utopian goal of realizing such genius that justifies Manifest Destiny and transposes colonial tyranny into a metaphysical (and thus less obviously politicized) "imperial" power. Without forgetting the sufferings of his own family and the Cherokee people in the course of their removal from Georgia to Oklahoma, keeping before him the racial prejudice and social violence in California in the aftermath of the Mexican-American War, Ridge argues that such history can be redeemed only by a rule of law that will allow each citizen to be judged as a free individual and, of course, a system of immigration that will permit "foreigners" to be admitted to such a legal and ethical utopia.

Walker reads Ridge's novel as divided between his commitments to the American national culture such individualism supports and his nostalgia for the Cherokee community that was the source of his tribal identity as a member of the powerful Ridge family and the Treaty party.[42] But most of the violence in Ridge's novel focuses on the group action by Joaquín's "well-organized" gang, which has several branches with different leaders, coordinated masterfully by the elusive Joaquín. Frustrated in his efforts to realize his identity as an individual, who governs his family and his personal fortunes, Joaquín becomes a tyrant. Ridge represents him as admirable in many respects, still displaying the personal qualities that should have served him so well as a democratic citizen of the United States, but Joaquín's tragedy is that his talents for civic virtue can swerve so easily into criminality.

It is, I think, difficult for readers today to understand how Ridge could so thoroughly condemn cooperative labor and its communal ideals as he seems to do in *The Life and Adventures of Joaquín Murieta*. There are, however, specific ideological reasons for doing so in postwar California. In the gold fields, *rancheros* used ranch workers, including Native Americans, to mine gold far more efficiently than Yankee miners, who worked primarily alone or in pairs. Although the Treaty of Guadalupe-Hidalgo guaranteed prewar California land titles, the end of the war initiated a period in which Yankee settlers manipulated existing laws and passed new ones and used overtly illegal means to alienate the land of the Californios and break up the large *ranchos*, generally under the banner of "free-enterprise capitalism." By driving Californio, Chilean, Peruvian, and Sonoran miners out of the gold fields, Yankees had also provoked incidents of retaliation by these groups, often working together. These incidents fueled paranoia regarding "conspiracies" by Spanish-speaking "foreigners" to retake California from the U.S. Militias and "vigilance committees" were often formed quickly in response to real and imagined threats from ousted foreigners, with such groups usually including veterans of the Mexican-American War.[43]

Ridge's Joaquín is no Robin Hood, who robs from the corrupt rich to save the victimized poor. Despite episodes in which he displays his honor and respect for others, Joaquín is ruthlessly violent, even if he is not as thoroughly bloodthirsty as his henchman, Three-Fingered Jack. Many critics point to the grisly beheading of Joaquín by Captain Harry Love and his rangers at the end of the novel as evidence that Ridge criticizes the brutality of a society that claims to be "civilized," just as Ridge elsewhere condemns the barbarism of the lynchings, ear-croppings, and whippings by which

Americans enforced their authority over "foreigners" in the gold fields (JM, 138). Unquestionably, Ridge intends for the reader to share his criticism of a society that fails to rule by laws to which all members have equal access, but he also intends for Joaquín's gang to represent the violent anarchy that will result when the rule of law is ignored or unequally applied. Joaquín's decapitation is foreshadowed several times by the violence of gang members, especially Three-Fingered Jack, who cuts off an "American's" head early in the novel, shouting with murderous exultation as he tosses the head into the rocks (JM, 59).[44] Despite the common practice by militias and vigilantes of decapitating and disfiguring bodies of their victims, usually Mexicans, Ridge stresses the practical necessity behind Captain Harry Love's order that the bodies of Joaquín and Three-Fingered Jack be decapitated: "It was important to prove, to the satisfaction of the public, that the famous and bloody bandit was actually killed, else the fact would be eternally doubted, and many unworthy suspicions would attach to Capt. Love. He, accordingly, acted as he would not otherwise have done" (JM, 155).[45]

Three-Fingered Jack's violence is reflected on a grander scale by Joaquín's plan to cut off southern from northern California in a revolt that would divide California and avenge "'our wrongs and . . . the wrongs of our poor, bleeding country'" (JM, 75). Joaquín does not clarify what the goal of this revolt would be, and his outraged honor regarding Mexico seems to contradict his earlier contempt for a country so corrupt as to be defeated easily by nobler Americans. Nevertheless, the purpose of his elaborate organization of different bands operating throughout California is conspiratorial and political. One gang leader, Joaquín Valenzuela, a historical figure often confused with the historical Murieta, "had acted for many years in Mexico as a bandit under the famous guerilla chief, Padre Jurata [sic]" (JM, 18). As Americo Paredes points out, Father Jarauta was "the fighting priest who was a guerilla against [Winfield] Scott's forces" in Mexico during the war "and was executed because he refused to recognize the Treaty of Guadalupe."[46] Ridge follows his description of the legislative action authorizing Captain Harry Love to organize his "rangers" to capture Joaquín with an account of the larger political dangers these *bandidos* posed to U.S. territorial rule: "[Joaquín's] correspondence was large with many wealthy and influential Mexicans residing in the state of California, and he had received assurances of their earnest co-operation in the movement which he contemplated. A shell was about to burst which was little dreamed of by the mass of the people, who merely looked upon Joaquín as a petty leader of a band of cutthroats!" (JM, 147–48). Although class distinctions kept Californio *rancheros* from associating with Sonoran, Chilean, and Peruvian immigrants to the gold fields, even after the latter groups had been forced into the urban areas of Los Angeles and San Francisco, Ridge identifies the Sonoran Joaquín with the Hidalgo Californios by stressing his noble appearance, cultivation, honor, and preference for elegant clothing.[47]

Ridge seems careful to discriminate between the "evil" of Joaquín's conspiratorial and revolutionary designs and the residual "good" of his individualism. When Joaquín and some of his men lure a group of hunters into their camp with promises of hospitality, only to surround them and threaten them with murder, a young Arkansan "bravely" steps forward and swears to the bandit: "'I stake my honor, not as an American citizen, but as a man, who is simply bound by justice to himself, under circumstances in which no other considerations can prevail, that you shall not be betrayed. If you say you will spare us, we thank you. If you say no, we can only fight till we die, and you must lose some of your lives in the conflict'" (JM, 78). Ridge, who grew up in Arkansas before the family moved to Oklahoma and returned there after the murder of his father and grandfather by the Ross party, invests his own sense of manly honor in this character, distinguishing such courage from mere patriotism and stressing that it always has its roots in a certain pragmatism. Yet the split between the Arkansan's manhood and American citizenship reflects the social disorder in postwar California and the failure of U.S. law to support and protect such a worthy individual.[48]

Such individualism is bound up with nineteenth-century U.S. stereotypes of manhood, and it is thus inevitably connected with the bandit's protection of the sexual honor of women. While considering the Arkansan's proposal, for example, "Joaquín drew his hand across his brow, and looked thoughtful and undecided. A beautiful female approached him from the tent near by and touched him on the shoulder. 'Spare them, Joaquín,' she tremulously whispered, and, looking at him with pleading eyes, retired softly to her seat again" (JM, 78–79). In another episode, just twenty pages later, Joaquín's lieutenant, Reis, who abducts the beautiful Rosalie from her mother and her fiancé, is "stung with her voluptuous beauty" and thus protects her from his men, who are intent on raping her. Even though he risks "a mutiny" among his own men over this blonde, blue-eyed woman, Reis fears even more "Joaquín's opinion of his conduct in this specific matter"; when Joaquín does show up, he curses and threatens Reis on the suspicion the latter has "done her any injury" or "taken any advantage of that girl" (JM, 104–5). Such displays of honor may seem perfectly conventional in patriarchal U.S. culture in this period, but they are by no means typical of prevailing U.S. attitudes toward Mexican men and their treatment of women. In his study of U.S. literary and cultural responses to the Mexican-American War, Robert Johannsen points out that:

Soldiers' perceptions of the role of women in Mexico mirrored the culture in which they had grown up. They regarded Mexico's women as superior to the men, more industrious, more humane, and more keenly sensitive to human needs. At the same time, they were indignant at the attitude of contempt in which the women seemed to be held by the men, and they charged Mexican males with treating their women as little more than slaves or beasts of burden.[49]

Joaquín's fierce respect for women's honor combines the Hidalgo culture of the Californios and the prevailing paternalism of U.S. culture at mid-century, suggesting that he has just the personal qualities needed to incorporate the best of Hidalgo California into the recently admitted state (1850) of California.

On the other hand, several of the women accompanying Joaquín's gang fit the equally prevalent "stereotype of exotic, receptive Mexican women," including a certain savagery they share with men like Three-Fingered Jack.[50] Margarita, widowed when her husband, Pedro Gonzales, is killed by Harry Love, quickly takes up with another gang member, the rough Guerra, who beats her. Plotting her revenge as calmly as Joaquín plans his, but now acting against her "family" (and her gender), Margarita waits until Guerra is asleep, then tips "from a ladle" "just one drop of hot lead into his ear" (JM, 81). Mourning loudly and long over the husband she "had made a corpse," Margarita promptly takes up with yet another gang member, Isidora Conejo, "who loved her much more tenderly than did the brutal Guerra" (JM, 81–82). Quoting Byron on the deviousness of women, Ridge hardly intends Margarita to represent a positive example of just revenge, but much rather the dangerous unruliness of women when the regulation of patriarchal society fails. Margarita fits the type of the femme fatale: "Twice widowed, her sorrows had not dimmed the lustre of her eyes, or taken the gloss from her rich dark hair, or the rose from her cheeks. Her step was buoyant as ever, the play of her limbs as graceful, the heave of her impulsive bosom as entrancing, and her voice as full of music as if she had never lost Gonzalez or murdered Guerra" (JM, 82). On the other hand, Joaquín's wife, Rosita, and Reyes Féliz's "devoted Carmelita" are both faithful to their husbands even after these two gang members are killed; Rosita returns to Sonora, where she "silently and sadly work[ed] out the slow task of a life forever blighted," and Carmelita commits suicide to be "buried . . . by the side of her well-beloved" (JM, 159, 54). Like heroines in Victorian novels, Rosita and Carmelita sacrifice themselves for their lovers, who earn such worship by protecting fiercely their feminine dependents. Reyes Féliz is also Rosita's brother and thus Joaquín's brother-in-law, so these bonds of fidelity are strengthened by *family* ties (JM, 17). Such men, Ridge suggests, are natural leaders, both of the family and in the state, even if their abilities are misused in organizing the gang's violent raids.

The bloodthirsty and utterly lawless behavior of Joaquín's gang is tempered only by occasional glimpses of the heroic individual, distinguished by manly virtue and a nearly transcendentalist self-reliance. Reflecting on the hanging of Reyes Féliz and Carmelita's suicide, Ridge echoes the romantic sublimity of Mount Shasta in his celebration of the immortal soul: "We may go down to our graves with the scorn of an indignant world upon us, which hurls us from its presence—but the eternal God allows no fragment of our souls, no atom of our dust, to be lost from his universe. Poised on our own immortality, we may defy the human race and all that exists beneath the throne of God!" (*JM*, 55). The Christian sentiments here seem to support primarily the romantic individualism Ridge affirms. Although in this passage Ridge pits the transcendental self against "the scorn of an indignant world," as if echoing the iconoclasm of Emersonian man, he clearly favors a social order designed principally to protect the rights to such individualism, which is an equally transcendentalist position.[51]

Ridge's advocacy of liberal individualism as part of the politics of assimilation helps explain his otherwise inexplicable prejudices toward other ethnic minorities in the novel, especially the Chinese. Even for the reader of the 1990s, accustomed to the lurid and accelerated violence of films starring Steven Seagal and Arnold Schwarzenegger, among others, *Joaquín Murieta* is often shockingly violent. Gang members, including Joaquín, kill travelers without a moment's hesitation and on the flimsiest pretexts of self-defense or to avoid identification by distant pursuers. Joaquín's occasional acts of mercy occur so unpredictably as to make the overall conduct of the gang appear even more nightmarish. Nowhere is this violence more terrible than in the gang's robberies of Chinese miners, and none more horrible than Three-Fingered Jack's torture and murder of the defenseless Chinese: "'I love to smell the blood of a Chinaman. . . . It's such easy work to kill them. It's a kind of luxury to cut their throats'" (*JM*, 64). Although Joaquín applies his erratic mercy in several cases of Chinese threatened by Three-Fingered Jack, he defends them as "pitiful," sometimes entertaining, "creatures," whose uncivilized qualities are reinforced by animal imagery (*JM*, 64).

As Ronald Takaki has shown, the ideological representation of the Chinese as the "'new barbarians'" in the nineteenth century linked them with African Americans and with Native Americans, in keeping with the prevailing racial binaries of white versus non-white, American versus foreign.[52] One of the larger purposes of this monologic racism was to rationalize the much larger project of Manifest Destiny to extend U.S. authority across the continent and the Pacific. As Takaki points out, "The war against Mexico reflected America's quest for a passage to India."[53] California was the point of intersection of internal and external forms of nineteenth-century U.S. imperialism.

As an anti-abolitionist, Ridge undoubtedly hoped to distance himself and his distinguished family from those African Americans, Native Americans, and Chinese Americans ideologically treated as a single racialized "other."[54] Whereas Ridge's rhetorical tirades against the racial discrimination experienced by Joaquín and his wife at the hands of Americans ought to lead him to condemn *all* discrimination based on race, ethnicity, or class, Ridge is actually quite selective and treats both the Chinese and California Native Americans with a mixture of amused paternalism and contempt. Although the gang at various times murders German, French, Dutch, Native American, and Mexican travelers, its greatest cruelty seems reserved for Chinese miners. To be sure, newspaper accounts of the gang's crimes stressed its robbery and murder of Chinese, but Ridge uses these rumors to support his own assimilationist and hierarchical social values.[55]

At one point, Ridge offers a simple explanation for why one gang leader prefers to kill Chinese victims: "It was a politic stroke in Reis to kill Chinamen in preference to Americans, for no one cared for so alien a class, and they were left to shift for themselves" (JM, 97). Yet such sentiments do not lead Ridge to identify with the Chinese; instead, he appears to use them as subjects of the gang's worst violence, as if to indulge white readers' fantasies of punishing the alien Chinese. In Ridge's account, the Chinese are always cowardly and abject, indistinguishable from each other, compared with sheep or ants following a herd mentality.[56] In one robbery, the gang surprises "two helpless Chinamen," who "were sleeping off their fatigue and the effects of their luxurious pipes of opium" (JM, 47). In the most violent scene in the novel, Joaquín allows Three-Fingered Jack to murder six Chinese miners, who "made no effort to defend themselves," even though "each had a double-barreled shot-gun," but instead "begged for their lives" (JM, 133). Dragging each into a line by "his long tail of hair," Jack "tied their tails securely together," robs them, and murders them all. Although the scene is intended to reinforce the Satanic qualities of Three-Fingered Jack, it also emphasizes the extent to which the group psychology of the Chinese contrasts with the radical individualism of the American that both Ridge and his character, Joaquín, emulate.

In one of his 1858 articles for the Marysville, California, newspaper, the *Daily National Democrat*, which he was editing at the time, Ridge refers to some Chinese participants in a parade, who "'finding themselves in the rear—(a very unenviable position to occupy in a retreating army, but a very appropriate one in this case)— . . . *bolted* from the ranks of the main procession . . . , and they slunk off to their own more congenial hovels, muttering curses loud and deep on "Melican men" generally.'"[57] Like the "Digger Indians" of California, the Chinese are used by Ridge to establish a horizon of civilization, according to which others are judged. Just as he mocks in this newspaper column the imperfect English of the Chinese, so he satirizes in *Joaquín Murieta* the illiteracy of the Euro-American mining population, implicitly contrasting the latter's phonetically spelled, garbled written messages with the elegance and correctness of his narrative, with its allusions to Byron and inclusion of his own verse.[58]

The "Digger Indians" are similarly used by Ridge to establish his cultivated distance from their savagery and to criticize the failure of Americans to live up to their social ideals in California. Several critics have commented on Ridge's characterization of the chief of the Tejon tribe, who is introduced "seated upon his haunches in all the grandeur of 'naked majesty,' enjoying a very luxurious repast of roasted acorns and dried angle worms" while his "swarthy subjects were scattered in various directions around him, engaged for the most part in the very arduous task of doing nothing" (JM, 36). Reinforcing prevalent stereotypes of California tribes as primitive and "lazy"—

often the result of their displacement from native hunting grounds by white settlers—Ridge adopts a consistently mock heroic style to refer to Chief Sapatarra's "Nation," "capital," "majesty," "council of state," and "dominions" (JM, 36). Louis Owens argues that Ridge's representation of the Tejon people lacks "any sense of irony," suggesting that "Ridge thought primarily and perhaps almost exclusively of his own people when he addressed the concern of racial injustice through the example of Joaquin Murieta."[59] Cheryl Walker, on the other hand, considers Ridge's treatment of both the Chinese and the Digger Indians to be ironic, even dismissive, in part because both groups are "fundamentally nonaggressive," "cowardly," and "are therefore not to be taken seriously."[60]

Both Owens and Walker interpret Ridge's treatment of the Tejon as evidence of what Owens terms his "internal conflict," divided between his passionate condemnation of racial injustice toward Joaquín and Rosita (and his own Cherokee people) and his endorsement of the racial ideology of his times in regard to Chinese and Californian Native Americans. In his journalism, Ridge condemned strongly Euro-American violence against the "Digger Indians" as "inhuman acts" caused by "civilized ignorance," but he also describes California tribal peoples as "a poor, humble, degraded, and cowardly race."[61] However conflicted Ridge was in these respects, he is quite consistent in working out the explicit moral of his story "that there is nothing so dangerous in its consequences as *injustice to individuals*—whether it arise from prejudice of color or from any other source; that a wrong done to one man is a wrong to society and to the world" (JM, 158). The Chinese and Tejons, even when they are named, as "Woh Le" and "Chief Sapatarra" are, lack the crucial qualities of romantic individuation: self-consciousness, control over one's representation of self, manly assertiveness, a distinct power over signs, and the desire of higher civilization.[62] In short, they lack those qualities that in the highest degree constitute romantic *genius*, the *soul* (or "spirit") of radical individualism.

Joaquín Murieta has all of these qualities in abundance, but lacks a social order in which they could be protected and developed. His innate sense of honor, as well as his fierce dedication to avenging dishonor, are complemented by a courage that often verges on the reckless and by abilities to disguise himself that indicate how well he understands the social construction of the self by way of fashion, rhetoric, and general deportment. Able to slip in and out of towns in various disguises, Joaquín encourages the late twentieth-century reader to interpret him, as well as John Rollin Ridge, as precursors of the postmodern subject.[63] Certainly the elements of the socially constructed, multicultural, and multiregional subjectivity often identified with postcolonial metropolitan societies may be found in nineteenth-century texts and characters, but it is probably more historically accurate to understand Ridge's Joaquín Murieta as the embodiment of a liberal individualism Ridge imagined would "solve" the problem of racial discrimination and, more specifically, of the violent political struggles within the Cherokee Nation by being made available through education and cultural imitation to "aliens" desiring a place within the encompassing nationality of the United States.

The romantic sublimity of Ridge's "Mount Shasta" is emulated, albeit never achieved, by Joaquín Murieta on several occasions in the novel, but never as explicitly as when he adopts the fictional pose on which the illustrator of the third edition of *Joaquín Murieta* (1874), Charles C. Nahl, would base his famous 1868 painting, *Joaquín Murieta*, which is reproduced on the cover of the University of Oklahoma Press's paperback edition of the novel. Having just tricked twenty-five miners by speaking "very good English," so that "they could scarcely make out whether he was a Mexican or an American," Joaquín is identified by Jim Boyce, who knows him by sight, and is forced to flee by way of "a narrow digger-trail which led along the side of a huge mountain, directly over a ledge of rocks a hundred yards in length, which hung beatling over the rushing stream beneath in a direct line with the hill upon which the miners had pitched their tents, and not more than forty yards distant (JM, 86–7)." Shouting to his pursuers, Joaquín identifies himself with the "monarch-mountain" of Ridge's poem and defies the "inferior minds" below (JM, 24):

> Knowing that his only chance lay in the swiftness of his sure-footed animal, he drew his keenly polished bowie-knife in proud defiance of the danger and waved it in scorn as he rode on. It was perfectly sublime to see such super-human daring and recklessness. At each report, which came fast and thick, he kissed the flashing blade and waved it at his foes. He passed the ordeal, as awful and harrowing to a man's nerves as can be conceived, untouched by a ball and otherwise unharmed. In a few moments, a loud whoop rang out in the woods a quarter of a mile distant, and the bold rider was safe! (JM, 87).

Joaquín's triumphal "whoop" echoes that of "the genuine North American red" men, whom Ridge celebrates in his journalism as "brave, subtle, and terrible in their destruction" during the "bloody frontier wars of the United States," but they are not to be confused with the "poor and imbecile" California "Diggers," whom Ridge believes should be moved to reservations and thus "protected by the General Government."[64] Embodying the residual qualities of the "noble savage," a figure rapidly giving way at mid-century to the myth of the degraded and unregenerate "Indian," in the hybrid form of a Sonoran with Hidalgo traits and democratic aspirations, Ridge's Joaquín is literally *incorporated* in a landscape borrowed from the Euro-American romantics.

And the figure *works*, because the ideology of assimilation allows such hybridities to cohere, shedding those dangerous or incongruous elements that mark the boundaries of Ridge's verbal painting. Nahl's 1868 portrait accurately follows several details of Ridge's prose, including the hat shot from Joaquín's head to let his "long black hair" stream "behind him" and the wild look of horse and rider that express a natural sublimity (JM, 87). But in his dress, face, and his horse's equipage, Nahl's *Joaquín Murieta* is decisively *Mexican*, from the fringed serape, scarlet waistband, and silver buttons dotting the seams of his breeches to the tooled leather saddle, boots, and stirrup guards. In Nahl's iconography, the figure is the prototype of the demonic, exotic, and often strangely honorable Western *bandido*, whose image would migrate from Mexico to Texas, California, and the Southwest in risktaking outlaws like O. Henry's "The Cisco Kid" and Johnston McCulley's Zorro.[65] In his poem, "Joaquin Murietta" (1869), Joaquin Miller represents the dangerous and Mexican qualities of a romantic figure, who can at the same time be used to affirm U.S. imperial ambitions in the West. Effectively stripped of his political qualities, Miller's *bandido* is part of the general California legend, a reminder of:

> What wondrous marvels might be told!
> Enough, to know that empire here
> Shall burn her loftiest, brightest star;
> Here art and eloquence shall reign,
> As o'er the wolf-rear'd realm of old. . . . [66]

In Miller's mythic landscape, the U.S. aspires to ancient Roman authority in part because of its ability to sustain "legends" as dramatic (*melodramatic?*) as the story of Joaquín Murieta. Miller's poetical figure, however, is stripped of the threatening anarchy and rebellion with which Ridge invests his *bandido*, and it is proportionately more conventional.

For Ridge, Joaquín's sublimity embodies the identity that U.S. culture ought to cultivate in a democratic society: self-reliance based on an ability to harness natural power and to defy social conventionality. In Ridge's portrait, Joaquín is decisively *American*, far more so even at his most rebellious and criminal than those "lawless and desperate men, who bore the name of Americans but failed to support the honor and dignity of that title" by first attacking Joaquín and his wife (JM, 9). Ridge by no means endorses Joaquín's specific plot to rebel against the United States and return the southern counties of California to Mexico, but he invests Joaquín's rebellious spirit with the zeal of revolution that Ridge identifies with the democratic aspirations of romantic individualism. Walker concludes that "liberty as individualism, as Ridge himself seems to know at some level, undermines the force of nation in which Indian life was traditionally rooted."[67] If so, then Ridge is the deeply conflicted, postmodern metropolitan that both Louis Owens and Cheryl Walker represent in their readings of this novel. But there is little evidence that Ridge endorses the more communal or collective values of the Cherokee in preference to the prevailing individualism of mid-century U.S. culture.

In his articles on North American Indians for *The Hesperian*, for example, Ridge makes virtually no comment on how Native American social organizations differ from Euro-American, looking instead for points of connection and comparison. Even when such opportunities present themselves, as when Ridge discusses the special stoicism and fortitude of Native Americans, he does not explain such cultural differences as the result of the Native American's greater sense of social obligation or the imbrication of religious, legal, and personal ethics in Lakota society, for example (*Trumpet*, 79–80). In the few places he does comment on Native American political organization, he notes how the Iroquois confederation of "The Six Nations" was a "confederated system" that "was the most remarkable example of native political sagacity and *untaught savage forecast* that occurs in all history," referring thereby to the Iroquois's anticipation of U.S. nationality (*Trumpet*, 71; my italics). Throughout these articles, he refers to tribal organizations as "nations," in keeping with the prevailing and quite unreflective nationalism of nineteenth-century U.S. culture.

A good deal has been written about the wayward historical reputation of Joaquín Murieta, whose name dots the California countryside and is still considered the state's most popular legend.[68] Beyond California, the story has been revised in Spanish-language versions of "nationalistic narratives in Chile, Spain, and Mexico," which have drawn upon Joaquín's rebellion against the U.S. conquest of California for nationalistic or anti-colonial purposes of their own.[69] The most celebrated of these revisionary accounts of Joaquín's legend is Pablo Neruda's *Fulgor y Muerta de Joaquín Murieta* (Splendour and death of Joaquín Murieta, 1967), the five-act musical drama in which Neruda claims Joaquín was a Chilean, following the Chilean legend that he was born in Quillota.[70] Neruda's Joaquín predictably defends the working classes against Yankee imperialism, and he is martyred by "a man wearing Uncle Sam's tall hat and striped trousers."[71] Connecting Joaquín's banditry in California of the 1850s with the Vietnamese struggle against U.S. imperialism in the 1960s, Neruda plays upon a potential within Joaquín's legend that Ridge clearly does not intend.

The postcolonial refunctioning of colonial narratives is often a self-conscious way of establishing counter-discursive authority amid a history saturated with colonial cultural traces. Something of this sort seems to motivate Neruda's revision of the legend of Joaquín Murieta, a modern interpretation complemented by nineteenth-century appropriations of the story designed to indulge Chilean miners' fantasies of revenge against their American persecutors. In this case, however, the counter-discursive, often anti-colonial Chilean and Mexican versions of the legend are themselves matched by the persistence of the story in the popular literature, folklore, and even placenames of modern California. From the 1859 *California Police Gazette* version of Ridge's novel to Walter Noble Burns's *The Robin Hood of El Dorado* (1932), the Hollywood script based on that book, and even James Varley's recent *The Legend of Joaquín Murrieta: California's Gold Rush Bandit* (1995), the myth of Joaquín Murieta has bolstered U.S. ideology. The legend has done this work by maintaining Joaquín as the criminal "outsider," whose romance depends crucially on his ritual exorcism by means of literary denouement; laws "regulating" foreign immigration, from the Chinese Exclusion Acts to California's recently adopted propositions 187 and 209; and physical violence of real and imaginary sorts.

Scholars are fond of pointing out how Ridge's novel originated a legend that came to be taken for historical fact, gaining for Ridge a reputation for literary verisimilitude capable of fooling such nineteenth-century historians of California as Hubert Howe Bancroft and Theodore Hitell.[72] But the realism with which Ridge's version of Joaquín has been invested is more likely the result of the adaptability of Ridge's character to the ideology of American individualism, which is itself crucial to late nineteenth- and early twentieth-century U.S. historiography, than Ridge's technical skills as a novelist. This is not to diminish in any way his accomplishment in *The Life and Adventures of Joaquín Murieta*, which ought to be measured both by its successful incorporation of romantic idealist concepts and by its help in establishing the pulp literature and dime-novel industry that would shape so profoundly U.S. cultural attitudes from 1840 to 1940.[73] Both the high and low cultural traditions did real and enduring violence to native peoples, racialized "foreigners," and ethnic minorities while waving banners of liberty, justice, and economic opportunity, not simply by stereotyping and caricaturing such marginal groups but by colonizing in advance many of the counter-discursive practices available to them. In the long and still-to-be-determined history of multiculturalism in California, this ideological co-optation of the right to speak out, to rebel, to conspire against injustice may be the ultimate, and finally postmodern, highway robbery.

6

Mark Twain's Rediscovery of America in *A Connecticut Yankee in King Arthur's Court*

We had a steamboat or two on the Thames, we had
steam war-ships, and the beginnings of a steam
commercial marine; I was getting ready to send out
an expedition to discover America.

Hank Morgan in *A Connecticut Yankee
in King Arthur's Court* (1889)

Shall we bang right ahead in our old-time, loud,
pious way, and commit the new century to the
game; or shall we sober up and sit down and think it
over first? Would it not be prudent to get our
Civilization-tools together, and see how much stock
is left on hand in the way of Glass Beads and
Theology, and Maxim Guns and Hymn Books, and
Trade Gin and Torches of Progress and
Enlightenment (patent adjustable ones, good to fire
villages with, upon occasion), and balance the books,
and arrive at the profit and loss, so that we may
intelligently decide whether to continue the business
or sell out the property and start a new Civilization
Scheme on the proceeds?

Mark Twain, "To the Person Sitting in Darkness,"
North American Review, February 1901.

Twain is famous for his jeremiads against European imperialism and the United States' fledgling efforts at colonial expansion in the Philippines; Twain's name is frequently mentioned in discussions
of anti-imperialism as both a political movement and cultural ethos in the

turn-of-the-century United States. As scholars have pointed out, most of Twain's anti-colonial zeal dates from the late 1890s and early 1900s, provoked by such international crises as the Spanish-American War (1898), the Boxer Rebellion in China (1900), and the Boer War in South Africa (1899–1902). Twain's rage over U.S. annexation of the Philippines in "To the Person Sitting in Darkness" (1901) and "A Defense of General Funston" (1902), the cruel despotism of Belgium's Leopold II in the Congo Free State in "King Leopold's Soliloquy" (1905), and Czar Nicholas II's exploitation of Russians, Poles, and Finns in "The Czar's Soliloquy" (1905) belongs to the historical period in which "imperialism" had entered the popular vocabulary as a term of opprobrium.[1]

Powerful as Twain's anti-colonial writings from this period are, they seem to differ from the more ambivalent sentiments regarding the uses and abuses of "civilization" he had expressed as late as 1897 in *Following the Equator*. Despite frequently expressed sympathies with native peoples throughout his travels on his global lecturing tour, Twain also appears to acknowledge the inevitability of Euro-American hegemony over the modern world. Richard Bridgman concludes in *Traveling in Mark Twain* that such a destiny did not in 1897 disappoint Twain: "For all the abuses of conquest that Twain had documented and lamented, his conclusive feeling was that 'all the savage lands in the world are going to be brought under the subjection of the Christian governments of Europe. I am not sorry, but glad.' He was not being ironic. He believed, he wrote, that India demonstrated that after much bloodshed the result would be 'peace and order and the reign of law.'"[2]

Twain was impressed powerfully by historical events from the Spanish-American War to the Russo-Japanese War that underscored the brutality of Euro-American colonialism and foreshadowed the violence of the First World War. Yet these historical events alone cannot be cited as the primary reasons for changes in Twain's views on colonialism from *Following the Equator* to the anti-imperialist tracts Twain wrote between 1898 and 1905. What Bridgman confidently decides is that Twain's preference for imperial order, British India over the "misrule" of the Thugs, for example, by no means applies generally to Twain's often contradictory attitudes in this travel narrative regarding the uses and abuses of Western civilization both at home and abroad. Forrest Robinson concludes that "its humorous interludes notwithstanding, the book is first and foremost a troubled, often angry report on the misery wrought by Western imperialism along the equatorial black belt."[3] The strict periodization of the "anti-imperialist" Mark Twain of the fin de siècle, as distinct from the apparently patriotic and nationalist Twain of the 1870s and 1880s, has prevented us from recognizing how anti-colonial and anti-imperialist attitudes inflect virtually all of Twain's writings.[4]

In Twain's earlier writings that focus on the sins of territorial conquest and the domination of other peoples, his potentially anti-imperialist argument is often neutralized by a pervasive cynicism and world-weary fatalism that, his rational arguments notwithstanding, human folly triumphs over all. In *Roughing It* (1872), for example, Twain lampoons westward expansion as itself a "tall tale" disguising the actual anarchy, physical violence, and naked will to power of miners and other frontiersmen, but in so doing he satirizes the colonized as well as the colonizers.[5] As Eric Sundquist points out, "Twain's vicious portrait of the 'Goshoots Indians,' for example, is meant to trash the comforting liberal myth of the Noble Savage and elicit the reader's 'Christian sympathy and compassion,' but by depicting the Indians as little more than dirty, village-less beggars, whose Great Spirit is whiskey, Twain altogether loses control of his morality play."[6] Creating a series of odious comparisons in his treatment of the "Goshoots Indians," Twain also manages to condemn "the despised Digger Indians of California," "the ordinary American negro," and "the Bosjesmans [Bushmen] of South Africa."[7] Echoing the pseudoscientific racism of contemporary ethnographers in his own parodic "classification" of native peoples, Twain claims: "The Bushmen and our Goshoots are manifestly descended from the self-same gorilla, or kangaroo, or Norway rat, whichever animal-Adam the Darwinians trace them to."[8] A similar pattern of social criticism turning into universal parody, often playing to the audience for comedy that runs counter to Twain's larger political purposes, flaws many of his writings, especially those about the frontier. Even so, *Roughing It* raises troubling questions about U.S. imperialism twenty-five years before the Spanish-American War, simply by treating in a single work the violence of U.S. expansion that stretches across the continent and the Pacific, encompassing in the American West areas as geopolitically different as Nevada, California, and Hawaii.

One of Twain's most obvious literary treatments of imperialism, indeed one of the most obvious in nineteenth-century literature in general, is *A Connecticut Yankee in King Arthur's Court*, but it is not customarily treated in terms of its serious reflections on imperialism. In part this historical romance also relies on cynicism and fatality regarding the inevitability of colonialism, in this case displacing it to a distant past that effectively universalizes the human susceptibility to conquest and the equally powerful will to conquer. Another reason for this neglect is that *Connecticut Yankee*, published in 1889, belongs to the decade preceding Twain's overt "change of mind" about the dangers of colonialism and imperialism. Of course, the setting of the romance itself is a formal distraction; Arthurian England "invaded" by a nineteenth-century Yankee does not seem to be a fictive *donnée* likely to encourage discussion of the dangers of Euro-American colonialism in the modern period. Yet, more familiar literary indictments of Western imperialism, such as Joseph Conrad's *Heart of Darkness* (1899), often recall the colonial origins of the European colonizers, as Marlow does at the beginning of his tale: "'Imagine the feelings of a commander of a fine—what d'ye call 'em—trireme in the Mediterranean, ordered suddenly to the north. . . . Imagine him here—the very end of the world, a sea the colour of lead, a sky the colour of smoke. . . . Sandbanks, marshes, forests, savages— precious little to eat fit for a civilised man, nothing but Thames water. No Falernian wine here, no going ashore.'"[9] At times, such invocations of Roman conquerors work to rationalize European or American ventures abroad, either by connecting the modern nations with a great tradition or by encouraging resignation to the "inevitability" of man's will to conquest and expansion.[10] In other cases, previous colonial projects are recalled to remind us that history repeats itself primarily when humans refuse to acknowledge the fundamental theft involved in colonization, as Melville recalls the Roman generals and legions in Europe in *Typee* (1846) and the decadence of Charles V, Holy Roman Emperor, in *Benito Cereno* (1855).[11]

The most convincing argument for excluding *Connecticut Yankee* from a consideration of Twain's anti-imperialism is the relative novelty of the terms "imperialism" and "anti-imperialism" in the United States at the end of the 1890s, primarily as a result of public debates over the Spanish-American and Philippine-American wars. Rudyard Kipling's poem "The White Man's Burden" (1899), in which Kipling specifically urges the United States to assume its "responsibilities" in the Philippines as the European powers had done elsewhere, is often considered a sort of historical marker for the infection of public discourse in the United States with the jingoism of conservative European imperialists.[12] In the 1896 presidential campaign, William Jennings Bryan ran on a free-silver platform and, after being defeated by William McKinley, served as colonel of a Nebraska regiment of volunteers in the Spanish-American War. In the 1900 campaign, however, Bryan combined free silver with anti-imperialism to challenge McKinley once again, recognizing that the incumbent president was closely associated with expansionist foreign policies.[13]

This sort of historical specificity regarding the popular use of the terms "imperialism" and "anti-imperialism" in political debates in the United States seems to be reinforced by Twain's own statements regarding the "change" in his position on our foreign policies between 1898 and 1902. In his 1947 essay, "Mark Twain and Howells: Anti-Imperialists," William Gibson restricts his consideration of Twain's anti-imperialism to this period in large part because of Twain's public declarations that he has changed his mind about American expansionism after our betrayal of Aguinaldo and the Philippine people's revolution. Responding to a Chicago *Tribune* reporter's statement in 1900, "'You've been quoted here as an anti-imperialist,'" Twain replied, "'Well, I am. A year ago I wasn't. I thought it would be a great thing to give a whole lot of freedom to the Filipinos, but I guess now that it's better to let them give it to themselves."[14] Gibson and others have pointed out that Twain, like Henry Adams, supported our foreign policy in the nominal "liberation" of Cuba from Spain, but changed his mind about U.S. foreign policy when it shifted from one of aiding republican movements to annexing foreign territory, as it did however "accidentally" at the end of the Philippine-American war.[15]

Twain's public statements about his "change of mind" belie, however, the continuity of his thinking about imperialism from *Connecticut Yankee* to his overtly anti-imperialist satires of the period 1898–1905. His ambivalence regarding Euro-American imperialism is also quite consistent throughout his career, as is his tendency to conclude cynically that the colonial conquerors in one era are likely to be different, but no less brutal, in the next. Robinson points out that in *Following the Equator*, Twain "casts a grateful eye on the results of colonialism," even as "he takes aim at Western hypocrisy."[16] Robinson interprets these contradictions in Twain's thinking about imperialism to express his guilt about his family's ownership of slaves and thus his understanding of slavery in the United States as part of global imperialism.[17] If Robinson is right, this may also explain why Twain often rationalizes European imperialism by arguing that *all* people throughout history contemplate the conquest and colonization of their neighbors, as in this passage from *Following the Equator*:

> All the territorial possessions of all the political establishments in the earth—including America, of course, consist of pilferings from other people's wash. No tribe, however insignificant, and no nation, howsoever mighty, occupies a foot of land that was not stolen. When the English, the French, and the Spaniards reached America, the Indian tribes had been raiding each other's territorial clothes-lines for ages, and every acre of ground in the continent had been stolen and restolen five hundred times.[18]

The only solution to this vicious historical cycle of conquest and exploitation seems to be the emancipation that Twain identifies with the American and French Revolutions, both of which used war and conquest in the interests of the people's rule. Twain's problem throughout his writings, whether he is questioning domestic politics or foreign policies, is to find a standard for judging correctly the degree to which republican aims and their emancipatory struggles can be distinguished from the tiresome business of conquest by kings, priests, and tycoons.

It is just this division between the republican sentiments of Hank Morgan and his bid for despotic power in sixth-century England that organizes the dramatic action and social criticism of *Connecticut Yankee*. In the course of negotiating this fundamental division in his protagonist's character, Twain anticipates most of the explicitly anti-imperialist views in his satires between 1898 and 1905. In exposing the ways that the usual tyrants would learn to disguise themselves as bearers of enlightenment and thus emancipation both from despotic rule and the drudgery of everyday labor, Twain anticipates the more modern critique of neoimperialist strategies of "winning hearts and minds" in the course of shaping consumers—

the sort of neoimperialism we associate with today's multinational corporations, heirs both of Hank Morgan's late nineteenth-century capitalist feudalism and the Euro-American colonial "missions" into the earth's "hearts of darkness."

For all its modernity, however, Twain's anti-imperialism remains fully grounded in older definitions of imperialism as "the personal sovereignty of a powerful ruler over numerous territories, whether in Europe or overseas."[19] What Twain likes to call the "game" in his anti-imperialist writings remains much the same as it has been for centuries. In "To the Person Sitting in Darkness," Twain writes: "The Blessings-of-Civilization Trust, wisely and curiously administered is a Daisy. There is more money in it, more territory, more sovereignty, and other kinds of emolument, than there is in any other game that is played. But Christendom has been playing it badly of late years."[20] In *Following the Equator*, his metaphor for the masquerade of colonial exploitation as enlightenment is clothing, both in terms of what has been hung out to dry on the clothesline, stolen wash, and "fashionable" dress of the day, with its hints of the Emperor's New Clothes:

> In one hundred and fifty years England has beneficently retired garment after garment from the Indian lines, until there is hardly a rag of the original wash left dangling anywhere. In eight hundred years an obscure tribe of Muscovite savages has risen to the dazzling position of Land-Robber-in-Chief; she found a quarter of the world hanging out to dry on a hundred parallels of latitude, and she scooped in the whole wash.[21]

In his attacks on Chamberlain's conduct in the Boer War and McKinley's annexation of the Philippines, Twain equates these democratic leaders with the German kaiser and Russian czar in their willing deception of the people they represent and conquer: "We all know the Business is being ruined. The reason is not far to seek. It is because our Mr. McKinley, and Mr. Chamberlain, and the Kaiser, and the Tsar and the French have been exporting the Actual Thing *with the outside cover left off.* This is bad for the Game. It shows that these new players of it are not sufficiently acquainted with it" ("Person," 295). In *Connecticut Yankee*, he anticipates this indictment of imperialism by showing how despotism secures its power by controlling people's attitudes and values, either by encouraging their superstitions, as the church and Merlin do, or by manipulating public opinion, as Hank and Clarence do with their weekly newspaper. When Twain writes in 1901 that "Mr. Chamberlain manufactures a war out of materials so inadequate and so fanciful that they make the boxes grieve and the gallery laugh" ("Person," 295), we are reminded that the theatrical publicity used by Chamberlain to disguise the real motives of the Boer War is anticipated in the theatricality of Hank Morgan's republican postures in *Connecticut Yankee*.

There are numerous scenes of such political theater enacted by the Boss from the Eclipse and the restoration of the Holy-Well to his penultimate duel with the Knights of the Round Table. I want to focus now on that duel both to exemplify Twain's treatment of political theatricality in *Connecticut Yankee* and to connect it with one of the most legendary events of nineteenth-century British colonialism: Charles "Chinese" Gordon's death at the hands of the Mahdi and his "dervishes" in Khartoum. My purpose here is not to challenge in any way interpretations of this scene as a parody of the "Western," either in the dime novel or the Wild West show. Walter Blair, Ronald Takaki, and Richard Slotkin have shown how Twain has refashioned western motifs in many of his writings, including *Connecticut Yankee*, both to criticize and draw upon the popularity of such mythologized events as "Custer's Last Stand."[22] Yet Twain's burlesque of frontier myths is entangled with his satire of other scenes of mythic heroism with which international narratives of travel, exploration, and conquest are replete in the late nineteenth century. What Slotkin understands so well in his reading of our myth of the frontier is that the West is another version of the colonial and imperialist ventures of the European powers.[23]

In chapter 39 Twain deliberately confuses the contemporary western street-fight, the "last-stand" of the heroic frontier officer overwhelmed by "Indians" or "natives," the southern duel of honor, and the chivalric jousting tournament. Calmly standing before the charge of a mounted knight in full armor, Hank uses his Colt "Dragoon" revolvers to demonstrate his military power. Shooting Sir Sagramour out of his saddle, he calmly fires nine more shots and kills nine more of the 500 knights massed against him. This scene in chapter 39 obviously anticipates the genocide at the very end of the narrative, as well as the failure of Hank's revolution, doomed by its own fortifications and by its own perverse logic. Hank's "bluff" in facing down 500 knights with two Colt revolvers holding twelve cartridges is the sort of scene repeated countless times in the dime novels of western adventure and in the heroic exploits of British and European adventurers in exotic colonial sites.[24] Not only is the legendary stand of General George Armstrong Custer at the Little Big Horn in 1876 recalled ironically here, but so are such feats of European colonial heroism as "Chinese" Gordon's tragic bravura in Victorian Khartoum. Morgan's exploits often allude simultaneously to the histories of U.S. Manifest Destiny and European colonialism, thereby linking U.S. policies, especially toward Native and African Americans, with the imperial practices of the European powers.

Twain "conceived, composed, and finally revised *Yankee* during five years of intermittent work between December 1884 and September 1889."[25] One of the most celebrated events of European colonialism in that period was the death on January 26, 1885, of Charles George Gordon, "Chinese Gordon," in Khartoum, Sudan, where he had returned in February 1884 to put down the rebellion led by the Moslem leader Mohammed Ahmed (the Mahdi), whose forces had destroyed British general William Hicks's Egyptian force of 10,000. Like the final battle between the Church's knights and the Boss's boys, the fabled end of Chinese Gordon, besieged by the rebels at

Khartoum, was the result of a religious "revolt." Like Hank Morgan, Chinese Gordon's "progressive reforms" in Egypt and North Africa had helped "precipitate the inevitable disaster," as Lytton Strachey would put it in his apt conclusion to *Eminent Victorians* (1918), "The End of General Gordon."[26] Among the reforms Gordon had accomplished while serving as governor of the equatorial provinces of Central Africa (1873–1880) was the "suppression of the slave trade," which is the first reform Hank Morgan makes after he has made public his revolution against knight-errantry, following his shooting of ten knights out of their saddles in chapter 39.

The legend of Chinese Gordon as imperialist hero begins with his appointment in 1863 as military commander of the forces organized by the United States and Great Britain to quell the Taiping Rebellion (1850–1864) and to prop up the tottering Manchu dynasty in China. Led by the Christian mystic Hung Hisu-ch'üan (1812 or 1813—1864), the Taiping Rebellion combined religious zeal to convert peasants to Pai Shang-ti Hui (Association of God Worshippers) and to open rebellion against the ruling Manchus for failing to protect the Chinese from Western imperialists. In 1853 Hung captured Nanking, which became his capital until Gordon retook the city in 1864, wiping out Hung's followers. The United States and Britain provided both arms and infantry in response to the Manchu appeal for foreign aid in suppressing the rebellion, and it was Gordon's modern artillery that was principally responsible for recapturing Nanking and ending the rebellion.[27] Anticipating the vainglory he would exhibit in the Sudan, Gordon refused any financial reward from the emperor for his military services, but he accepted the title "mandarin of the first class," thereby returning to England celebrated with the informal title of "Chinese" Gordon.[28] One advantage, then, of connecting Hank Morgan with Chinese Gordon is to remind the reader of U.S. participation in Western imperial ventures that antedate the Spanish-American and Philippine-American wars. It is particularly appropriate that Chinese Gordon's exploits in China involve the sort of "mercantile" imperialism that is the nineteenth-century origin of the "free-trade imperialism" that would become characteristic of twentieth-century ventures by the United States in foreign lands.

Contemporary accounts of Chinese Gordon's death at Khartoum are typically legendary; not surprisingly, they display the proper range from saintly forbearance to martial valor. Strachey's account captures just this legendary quality of the progressive European colonizer sacrificing himself in the cause of Civilization:

> Another spear transfixed him; he fell, and the swords of the three other Dervishes instantly hacked him to death. Thus, if we are to believe the official chroniclers, in the dignity of unresisting disdain, General Gordon met his end. . . . Other witnesses told a very different story. The man whom they saw die was not a saint but a warrior. With intrepidity, with skill, with desperation, he flew at his enemies. When his pistol was ex-

hausted, he fought on with his sword; he forced his way to the bottom of the staircase; and, among a heap of corpses, only succumbed at length to the sheer weight of the multitudes against him. (EV, 190)

Strachey concludes that these contradictory accounts of Chinese Gordon's end typify just what he represents in the European imperial project at the end of the Victorian age: "But General Gordon had always been a contradictious person—even a little off his head, perhaps, though a hero; . . . At any rate, it had all ended very happily—in a glorious slaughter of 20,000 Arabs, a vast addition to the British Empire" (EV, 192).

Chinese Gordon's contradictions are, of course, just what subsequent literary representations of the Eurocolonial adventurer would stress, even romanticize, as Joseph Conrad's Kurtz and his biographer, Marlow, attest. In a similar manner, Hank Morgan combines contradictory impulses favoring emancipation of the people from their slavery and the conventional conqueror's desire for absolute power.[29] Interpreted in this way, the Yankee "Boss"—Gordon assumed the title, "Gordon Pasha"—can be linked with the imperialist projects of European monarchs and the church's missionaries, but in a manner that is at once notably farsighted for 1889 and curiously archaic.[30] Interpreting the Yankee entrepreneur and his alter-ego, the Barnum-like promoter, as a version of the frontier military or political representative of imperial power—Custer or Gordon—Twain makes the equation between capitalist expansion and Euro-American imperialism that does not enter the public debate until several decades later.[31] But Twain's apparent equation of the frontier hero, colonial adventurer, and capitalist entrepreneur with the feudal despot seems to ignore the important changes that have occurred in the intervening thirteen centuries, especially in terms of how these different fictions are marketed and consumed.

In connecting Morgan with Gordon, capitalism with political imperialism, I may seem to imply that Twain was a forerunner of such early modern critics of capitalism as Lenin, who in *Imperialism, the Highest Stage of Capitalism* (1916) argued that capitalism had entered its "last" phase in the imperial expansion that had temporarily saved the industrial nations, only to plunge them into the sort of world conflict (World War I) that would assure their final collapse.[32] There is little evidence in *Connecticut Yankee*, however, that Twain fully comprehends what the shift from the older forms of political imperialism to the newer modes of economic domination involves. All the evidence works in the contrary direction to argue that Twain hopes to show that the Yankee capitalist is simply a revival of the feudal monarch, who claims his power either by force of arms or theatrical display of "divine right." Rather than viewing the new modes of economic and political power—what Lenin considered the inevitable expansion of capitalism by whatever means—as significant transformations of such older modes of domination as hereditary wealth and title, Twain treats capitalism as simply a repetition in different dress of the same old story of the will to power of the "damned human race." Despite much attention to economics in *Connecticut Yankee*, the actual theory of political economy is quite simple and involves little transformation of economic conditions from Arthur's sixth-century Britain to Morgan's nineteenth-century America. Hank does attempt to "enlighten" the feudal peasantry regarding their rights to their own labor-power and how wages for such labor must be determined in relation to prices, endorsing a "free-trade" economic philosophy that, while lost on the serfs he lectures, appears to be Twain's answer to imbalances of international power occasioned by older forms of political imperialism.

In chapter 33, "Sixth Century Political Economy," Hank uses the differences of wage-price ratios in the several different tributary kingdoms of Arthur's disunited England to condemn protected trade and endorse free-trade economies in ways unmistakably relevant to the late nineteenth century and the increasingly global economy stimulated in large part by imperialism. At the end of the elaborate banquet he has staged to boost Marco's status with his neighbors, but which has the actual effect of glorifying the disguised Boss as a kind of demigod, Hank assumes his willful place as ruler by lecturing the peasants while Arthur "went off to take a nap." The substance of his lesson is the promise of free trade: "At a first glance, things appeared to be exceeding prosperous in this little tributary kingdom—whose lord was King Bagdemagus—as compared with the state of things in my own region. They had the 'protection' system in full force here, whereas we were working along down towards free trade"[33] Morgan's endorsement of free trade is preparatory to his pitch for trade unions and the rights of the worker to "take a hand in fixing his wages himself"—the familiar late nineteenth-century bid for "free labor" (CY, 190). Whatever doubts we may have about Morgan representing Twain's views elsewhere, there can be no such doubt here. In his March 22, 1886, address to the Monday Evening Club of Hartford, Connecticut, "The New Dynasty," Twain powerfully supports the cause of organized labor, attacks the protective tariffs of the Republicans, and links exploited workers with such "victims" as "the nations of the earth":

> Now so far as we know or may guess, this has been going on for a million years. Who are the oppressors? The few: the king, the capitalist, and a handful of other overseers and superintendents. Who the oppressed? The many: The nations of the earth; the valuable personages; the workers; they that MAKE the bread that the soft-handed and the idle eat.[34]

Henry Nash Smith argued many years ago that Twain's analysis of economics in *Connecticut Yankee* is one of the several failures of the book, attributable to Twain's inability to provide the "concrete detail" for a "complex of institutions that had previously been little more than a vague abstraction for him."[35] Twain's problem in representing modern economic theories is not, however, his confusion over the "concrete detail," but his endorsement of a "progressive" free-trade theory that was already showing in the 1880s its adaptability to the new modes of imperial domination. Since the seventeenth century, free trade advocates had argued that tariffs and economic parochialism only wasted economic energies that should be used to increase the world's wealth. "Free-trade" theory is central to Enlightenment political economies, and Adam Smith's *Inquiry into the Nature and Causes of the Wealth of Nations* (1776) is the classic text, especially in its advocacy of the coordination of free trade with what might be termed a global "division of labor," or specialization by region or nation in modes of production best suited to it.[36] Hank Morgan and Twain clearly agree that free trade will help maximize the wealth of a united England, bring an end to its sixth-century division into many different "tributary kingdoms" (i.e., "colonies"), and do so by awakening serfs (i.e., workers) to their rights over their own labor and thus to their roles in negotiating appropriate wages for that labor.

If this is the "enlightenment" that Hank Morgan brings to the "colony" of sixth-century England, it is nonetheless a wisdom that did not prevail in the course of early modern imperial expansion. Insofar as Twain links "free trade" and "trade unionism" in chapter 33, we may conclude that *Connecticut Yankee* deals with the important relationship between domestic and international economies, between the rights of labor in the United States and the rights of colonized peoples in the various Euro-American empires Twain would satirize so explicitly between 1898 and 1905. As I argue in Chapter 9, it is a coalition that Du Bois also attempts to build from *The Souls of Black Folk* (1903) to *Black Reconstruction in America* (1935), but with racial oppression added to economic exploitation as one of the rallying points for such political organization.

Slotkin points out that Twain "shared [William Dean] Howells's concern about the apparent spread of anarchism among the laboring classes and a spirit of oppression among the masters of capital."[37] Both were attracted to Edward Bellamy's socialism in *Looking Backward* (1888) as a possible solution, because both thought that labor's domination by capital in Europe and the United States anticipated the "scramble" for colonies and even more easily exploitable labor in the early twentieth century. For both Howells and Twain, the critiques of capitalism and of imperialism were interrelated.[38] Yet what Twain does not take adequately into account in *Connecticut Yankee* or in his later anti-imperialist writings is what subsequently came to be termed "free-trade imperialism," which explains how neoimperialist practices can flourish under the banner of "free trade." That is, the very economic principle that Howells and Twain imagined might liberate the industrial worker from the exploitation of capital and eventually free the colonial subject from imperial domination in many cases turned out to be the basis for a *new* imperialism.

Mommsen traces "free-trade imperialism" to a "pioneer study" in 1953 by Ronald Robinson and John Gallagher, "The Imperialism of Free Trade":[39]

By developing the theory of "informal empire" Robinson and Gallagher broke decisively with the tradition which defined imperialism exclusively in terms of formal territorial colonial rule, and instead emphasized the importance of imperialist factors of a non-governmental character. The true motive force of Victorian expansion was economic, and the imperialists were at first content to exercise informal control from a few coastal stations. Political methods were in the main used only to open up previously closed markets to the ostensibly free operation of Western competitive capitalism. . . . "The usual summing up of the policy of the free trade empire as 'trade, not rule' should read 'trade with informal control if possible; trade with rule when necessary.'"[40]

Robinson and Gallagher's theory of "free-trade imperialism" was developed in the period of decolonization that took place in the years following the Second World War, but their primary focus is on nineteenth-century European, with special emphasis on British, imperialisms, as the title of their influential book, *Africa and the Victorians: The Official Mind of Imperialism*, suggests.[41] Arguing effectively that British imperialism developed primarily in the interests of establishing trade and controlling markets, rather than to control physical territory, Robinson and Gallagher conclude that the development of colonial administrations, especially in Africa, resulted from the inability of the European powers to work cooperatively in an increasingly global economy.[42] The expense and trouble of territorial colonies, then, was the unfortunate result of the failure of "free-trade imperialism."[43] Although elsewhere in this chapter I argue that Twain could not be expected to have foreseen scholarly arguments about Euro-American imperialism developed seventy-five years later, there is considerable evidence that Twain *does* interpret the etiology of imperialism as beginning in greed, developing by the desire for commercial advantage, and concluding with the theft of land and murder. Such is the course of empire charted, for example, in "The Fable of the Yellow Terror," one of Twain's manuscripts posthumously published.[44]

Ronald Robinson places great importance on the Berlin Conference of 1884–1885, attended by representatives of European powers, the Ottoman Empire, and the United States who "met in the Reich Chancellery . . . to decide the future in . . . tropical Africa," which was convened at precisely the time Twain was writing *Connecticut Yankee*.[45] Among the many weighty reasons the conference was convened were growing European disagreements over commercial jurisdiction in Africa, including the sort of quarrels, such as those between France and England, that resulted in General Gordon's widely publicized theatrics in Khartoum. Less conspicuous perhaps, but no less notable in international affairs, the Berlin Conference began with the German chancellor proposing that "a congress should guarantee free trade 'in all the unoccupied parts of the world not yet legally occupied by a recognized Power,'" but his immediate goal was to get France to "join Germany and her allies in a maritime league against English pretensions to 'informal empire' and break down the chief obstacle to German commercial overseas expansion."[46] The details worked out by the great imperial powers regarding what would become the eventual territorial partition of Africa among them is beyond my scope in this chapter and not entirely relevant to Twain's critique of U.S. imperialism, although Twain's subsequent satire, "King Leopold's Soliloquy," certainly recognizes how capitalism and imperialism collaborated to produce African misery.[47]

Robinson and Gallagher do not develop an argument regarding "cultural imperialism" or even the work of culture in the spread or critique of imperialist policies and attitudes. Their thesis focuses on the economic motives for modern imperialisms and how the military and political forces required for territorial occupation and control follow from the failure of "free-trade" practices that they nonetheless recognize to be means of colonial domination. For my purposes, Robinson and Gallagher's theory of "free-trade imperialism" implicitly challenges later theories of U.S. neoimperialism as primarily a *postmodern* phenomenon and thus radically distinct from its European forebears.[48] One conclusion is that the development of global markets and manipulation of consumers' desires often criticized as part of contemporary neoimperialism may well be a revival or refunctioning of modern colonial practices. Twain can hardly have been expected to be farsighted enough to have predicted the neocolonial dangers that could be seen as still operative even as former colonies were being granted their nominal independence in the subsequent history of decolonization, but he does seem to understand the motivated relationship between commercial and political forms of Euro-American imperialism at the turn of the last century.

What Twain does anticipate, even as he relies on an older theory of imperialism, is the degree to which science and technology will contribute to the economic and political forms of human exploitation and territorial conquest that he believes have always plagued the "damned human race." When Hank Morgan begins to play the "Game" on his own, making public his revolution against knight-errantry and the church, his admirable social reforms are explicitly linked with his own colonial practices:

> Slavery was dead and gone; all men were equal before the law; taxation had been equalized. The telegraph, the telephone, the phonograph, the type-writer, the sewing machine, and all the thousand and handy servants of steam and electricity were working their way into favor. We had a steamboat or two on the Thames, we had steam war-ships, and the beginnings of a steam commercial marine; I was getting ready to send out an expedition to discover America. (CY, 228)

Twain makes sure the reader knows how false Hank's claims for progress in sixth-century Britain are. His "thousand and handy servants of steam and electricity" are complemented by the "boys" he turns out in his "factories."[49]

Whether they follow the church and king or "the Boss," the medieval peasantry is still systematically exploited. Hank's theatrical displays and deadly force differ little from the church's enactment of miracles and terror: both are intended to control the workers.

In short, "slavery" is hardly "dead and gone," just as Twain argues in so many of his writings that slavery in the United States has survived, too often unrecognized, the Civil War and Emancipation, thanks to capitalism, its new technologies, and its zeal for imperial expansion. Slotkin and others have shown how Twain organizes *Connecticut Yankee* around a general critique of slavery's historical persistence from feudalism to capitalism.[50] When the disguised Hank and Arthur are sold as slaves in chapter 34, they experience both the physical brutality and the social psychology of slavery from inside its bonds. Some readers might complain that the white man's imagination of slavery tends to sentimentalize the experiences of African-American slaves, just as Twain's generalization of slavery across the ages risks trivializing its modern consequences. But Twain is able in this way to expose the arbitrariness of race as the basis for modern slavery. Obviously transposing the rhetoric of slave narratives to the adventures of Hank and the king under sixth-century slavery, Twain universalizes the slave's experience in order to diminish the significance of race both as a motive for slavery and for subsequent forms of social discrimination.

Susan Gillman argues that one of Twain's achievements in *Following the Equator* is to demystify the racial binaries in the United States by emphasizing the rich variety of racial hybridities in the equatorial regions he visits: "The logic of U.S. racial division, based on the 'one-drop rule' and therefore assuming degrees of blackness only—white is a 'pure' category—is exploded within the context of colonial race relations, where nation competes and blurs with race, and whiteness is made to appear alien, defamiliarized by the 'massed dark complexion of the public.'"[51] Twain's critique of the racial basis for slavery in *Connecticut Yankee* is motivated in large part by his eagerness to stress the economic motives for slavery. One disadvantage to such a strategy, however, is that it tends to ignore the historically different economic factors involved in the various ways people have had their labor stolen from them. One reason Marxists have often praised Twain's writings is his straightforward and consistent exposure of the exploitation of labor as one root of evil. And it is just Twain's conviction that feudalism, capitalism, and imperialism are commonly related by their economic exploitation of powerless serfs, workers, and native peoples that makes my case for *Connecticut Yankee* as an important early text in Twain's anti-imperialism. There is nevertheless a certain fatal oversimplification in Twain's interpretation of slavery's historical persistence that also affects his understanding of modern imperialism and prevents him from recognizing the full implications of the new forms of domination employed by modern capitalism, including the racism Du Bois identifies explicitly with modern forms of slavery.[52]

Given the unbroken history of the powerful exploiting the weak, Twain seems only able to offer violent revolution as a way to break this pattern. Yet, his advocacy of revolution forces him to confront his own abhorrence of the violence required, so that Twain often concludes his satires with *false* revolutions or, in less extreme cases, subversions of the social order. The infamous "Evasion" at the end of *Adventures of Huckleberry Finn* (1884) is often read as a parody of sentimental abolitionists (and the Underground Railroad), even though Twain has convinced the reader by this point in his narrative that the racism of the society he depicts is so profound as to require very extreme social reforms. In *Pudd'nhead Wilson* (1894), Roxy's "rebellion" against the corrupt society of Dawson's Landing is the "burglary plot" she masterminds for Tom, rather than the Fanon-like insurrection by victimized slaves that seems required for social change. Too often Twain calls passionately for apocalyptic tongues of fire to purge a corrupt world, only to conclude with a joke or parody. The same may be said about the Battle of the Sand Belt, in which Hank tries desperately to purge history of those powerful forces—church, monarchy, capital—that have otherwise doomed us to vicious struggles between masters and servants.

The Boss's ultimate revolution, "a rounded and complete governmental revolution without bloodshed . . . a republic," to be declared "upon Arthur's death," seems to accord well with Twain's advocacy in his anti-imperialist satires of republican revolutions in colonized countries like Cuba and the Philippines (CY, 229). But the failure of the Boss's project—a failure that in the context of the historical romance occasions thirteen centuries' more of despotism, slavery, and suffering—is already inscribed in the reforms of which he is so proud.[53] Once again, Twain offers us a potential social revolution that merely allows him to extend his social criticism. There is, however, some sense that Hank's failed revolution achieves more than the usual joke that ends Twain's serious texts. By stressing Hank's use of modern technology in the Battle of the Sand Belt, Twain begins to reflect on the concrete differences between the sixth and nineteenth centuries and thus of their modes of human exploitation. In short, modern imperialism may be traceable back to feudal Britain, but Twain suggests that the practices of the former are considerably different. At first, the difference seems to Twain merely one of *scale*: everything in Hank Morgan's world is done in the vast terms made possible by mechanization and industrialization. But in the very composition of his conclusion to *Connecticut Yankee*, Twain begins to understand the categorical difference between feudal monarchy and global imperialism.

Cataloguing the weaknesses of *Connecticut Yankee*, Henry Nash Smith adds Twain's "meager" development of the "theme of technological advance": "Despite Mark Twain's occasional efforts to give fictional substance to the Yankee's mechanical prowess, he actually performs no constructive feat except the restoration of the holy well; and it will be recalled that the technology of this episode does not go into repairing the well, but into the fraudulent display of fireworks with which he awes the populace" (Smith, 86). Actually, Twain provides considerable details about the technologies he considers basic to Morgan's capitalist and free-trade economy. Morgan's initial "miracle" depends on his knowledge of astronomy to predict the life-saving solar eclipse. It is just the sort of scientific knowledge early European explorers used to gain authority over local, less technologically advanced peoples. In addition to Hank's talents with munitions and astronomy, he is adept at the new modes of transportation and communication he introduces into sixth-century England, ostensibly to end feudal provincialism and encourage national unity, but secretly to secure his power and influence. What his various mines and factories serve are, after all, the development of the telegraph lines, newspaper and publishing enterprises, and steam-powered transport that enable him to "unite" and, of course, thereby *rule* an "England" soon to become the "British Empire," as Hank prepares to "send out an expedition to discover America."

I cannot review here all that has been written about Twain's own contradictory attitudes toward the new technologies, except to point out how perfectly *Connecticut Yankee* expresses those contradictions. This is not to claim that Twain took no intellectual position on the new technologies of "electricity and steam," or that he condemned them in print while hypocritically trying to develop and market the Paige typesetter and other inventions in which he invested. Twain's views in *Connecticut Yankee* about the role of capitalism in the old styles of political imperialism may be somewhat archaic, but he understands quite clearly how *control* not only of the means of communication but also of the *technology* of such communicative instruments would become increasingly crucial factors in determining social, political, and economic power in the modern age. More farsighted in this regard than Robinson and Gallagher, Twain understands the importance not only of scientific research and the development of new technologies in free-trade imperialism but also the specific role *communications* technologies would play in the economic as well as the political and military imperialisms of the twentieth century.[54]

If the republican revolutions he supported in his anti-imperialist writings were to succeed, then they would have to take into account the new modes of communication and transport—modes of "colonization" that extended from everyday life at home and in the workplace to the most distant and exotic "foreign territory." Yet, just how people were to control these means of communication eludes Twain in *Connecticut Yankee*, as well as in his anti-imperialist satires. The Boss's vocational training schools (Boy and Man factories) and his normal schools ("Teacher-Factories") are unsatisfactory solutions in two respects. First, he provides little insight into the curricula and pedagogy of these "schools"—that is, of their basic modes of production. Second, Warner and Twain had already exposed in *The Gilded Age* the vulnerability of such educational institutions to control by the usual political despots and confidence men.[55] Among those educated by the Boss and his new social system, only Clarence displays the sort of independence of mind, healthy disrespect for authority, and creative imagination requisite to control the new technologies rather than simply operate the machines. Clarence's qualifications for such authority are already in evidence when Hank Morgan first meets him. With the exception of his quick aptitude for technical training, Clarence gains little from the modern education provided by the Boss. There is little evidence that the boys and teachers "trained" under the new educational regime have learned anything beyond the mere manufacture and operation of the new technologies; they are still profoundly dependent on the ruler, who has simply exchanged his crown or miter for the scientist's laboratory coat. As Takaki points out, Hank Morgan is a "scientific manager," whose aim "is not production or profits but control for the sake of control."[56]

The failure of conventional education often signals in Twain's writings the alternative of Twain's special brand of satiric instruction. Twain's subtle, artistic solution to the despair his own social criticism encourages is to teach the reader how to expose truth behind the ceaseless lies of those in power. In his anti-imperialist writings, he teaches us to recognize the "Actual Thing" those in power have for millennia tried to "sell" to "the Customer Sitting in Darkness" as "Civilization." In place of that false "enlightenment," Twain offers the "many" who are "oppressed" the means to bring their own light into the shadowy game played by those in power ("Person," 295). Twain also struggles in these writings to distinguish between "good *intentions*, and evil ones" in global history, knowing that the "*results* are not foreseeable. They are of both kinds, in all cases."[57] This conclusion need not reduce all intentions to the same historical result, but merely call our attention to the need to interpret history and model future conduct according to the demonstrable *contingencies* of history. He knew quite well how to subvert the pretensions of language and other signs of power that allow kings to assume their arbitrary powers. In short, Twain teaches us that there are possibilities for resisting, even occasionally overturning, the chances and weird determinisms of history.

Yet, the new technologies of communication that were already replacing the dominant medium of print and the new modes of transportation that were drastically changing global geography and commerce in the 1880s were far more difficult to comprehend and control than even the infamously deceptive language of power and pretense that Twain had learned to subvert with such genius. At the end of *Connecticut Yankee*, Hank Morgan is trapped within Merlin's Cave by the very military technology he has employed to defend his forces and annihilate knight-errantry. Electrocuting, drowning, and machine-gunning "twenty-five thousand men," the Boss enacts in the sixth century the special horrors of modern, mechanized warfare as they were revealed in the unequal battles between European imperial powers and preindustrial peoples: "Within ten short minutes after we had opened fire, armed resistance was totally annihilated, the campaign was ended, we fifty-four were masters of England! Twenty-five thousand men lay dead around us" (CY, 255). Terrible as the cost of this imbalance of power between colonizers and colonized would be throughout the Victorian period, Twain's criticism hardly begins to address what were already becoming the new means of economic imperialism that would employ in far subtler and more pervasive ways the new technologies Twain treats here as mere instruments of military conquest.

Twain is nevertheless curiously "sensitive"—I mean in a nearly extrasensory way—to the larger consequences of the new technologies in *Connecticut Yankee*. During the week of waiting for the Battle of the Sand Belt to begin and then as he convalesces from his wound, Hank Morgan "was writing all the time . . . turning my old diary into this narrative form," writing letters to Sandy, and later bringing the story we are reading to the abrupt end requiring Clarence's "P.S." (chapter 44) and Twain's "Final P.S." (formally beyond the "End of the Manuscript") (CY, 246). From the site of feudal superstition and tyranny to the site of modern technological terror, the Cave continues to function as it had in *Adventures of Tom Sawyer* as Twain's metaphor for the cultural unconscious. Throughout his career, Twain was himself always trying to write himself *out* of that Cave, but something always seems to block the entrance. In *Tom Sawyer*, it is the corpse of Injun' Joe; in *Connecticut Yankee*, it is the disease-breeding mass of rotting corpses that hang from or float in the Boss's fortifications.

Twain imagines at the very end that he *has* escaped the Cave, insofar as the Boss's manuscript is both protected and "post-scripted" by Clarence, then "framed" by the modern storyteller, "M.T.," who in turn leaves this fictive history to the reader. Such literary circulation is often Twain's answer to the determining power structures he so abhorred, and the collaborative project of "writing" our own history offers a charming, if sentimental, answer to the question of how the true Republic should employ technology in the interests of democratic representation. Yet even as Twain wrote *Connecticut Yankee*, the neoimperialist policies that would lead the United States from the Philippines to Vietnam and the Persian Gulf were already being developed in the marketing strategies of global capitalism and the technologies of the telegraph and steamship.

The formal political empires of the nineteenth-century European powers metamorphosed at the turn of the century into the "informal imperialism" that combines "commercial penetration and political influence" so characteristic of the First World's global power in our own age.[58] Crucial to what some have termed the contemporary process of *recolonization* under the conditions of "informal" or "new" imperialism is control of the means of communication and thus representation.[59] Twain imagines in *Connecticut Yankee* that the bodies heaped at the mouth of the Cave, like the colonial atrocities exposed by "that trivial little kodak" in King Leopold's Congo Free State, will at last become visible as the "Actual Thing."[60] Only a year after the publication of *Connecticut Yankee*, Big Foot's band of Lakota would be massacred by the U.S. Army at Wounded Knee. In our own age, Third and Fourth-World peoples and countries are increasingly rendered "invisible," even as their everyday fields of vision are saturated by the consumer products and media technologies of the First World.[61] This commercial and technological penetration of every corner of the globe, which at the same time works to render invisible the peoples so dominated, begins with the well-intentioned republican and progressive rhetoric epitomized by Hank Morgan and historically performed by turn-of-the-century diplomats, like Secretary of State John Hay, then complicated by more contemporary figures, like Henry Kissinger and Oliver North, who seem as fantastic as Twain's Morgan.

In *Connecticut Yankee*, Twain warns the reader that the United States is already following the lead of the European imperial powers, a message he would repeat with growing volubility in his anti-imperialist writings from 1898 to 1905, most of which require little interpretation. Twain did not understand, however, what he had himself written, or perhaps what had been telegraphed by the cultural unconscious that worked so fantastically through him: that the very medium which he had protected so jealously for its ability to resist tyranny and build republican consensus had already been invaded, if not conquered.[62] Unable to explain how the nineteenth-century "man of letters" might leap into the communications expert—both spin-doctor and computer scientist—of our postmodern age, Twain could only condemn the instrumentality of the new technologies and the repetition of the older forms of despotism under the conditions of modernity.[63] In this respect, his critique of Euro-American imperialism failed to account for the transformation of nineteenth-century modes of political domination into twentieth-century modes of commercial and technological domination. The scholarly identification of Twain's ideological limitations, at least by today's standards, should in no way trivialize the great achievement of his critique of European and emerging U.S. imperialisms. Both Twain and Howells spoke out against U.S. imperialism in Cuba and the Philippines, for example, on the bases of flawed social utopias, but they spoke out at a time when few were able to understand and even fewer were willing to challenge the emergent imperium of the United States. Had they waited for "purer theories," Twain and Howells would have missed the time in which their criticism of imperialism could have its effect. My effort to understand the roots of Twain's anti-imperialism in an earlier period and works, like *Connecticut Yankee*, attempts to detail the long study that enabled him to comprehend what few others did about the direction of U.S. foreign policy and national identity. By imagining in *Connecticut Yankee* the curious intersection of feudal modes of domination with the progressive claims of nineteenth-century capitalism—the uncanny resemblance of Merlin and Morgan—Twain sent yet another of his prophetic warnings from the mouth of the Cave.

7

Race, Gender, and Imperialism in Stephen Crane

A Monstrous Case

To put it drastically, if war, as Clausewitz insisted, is
the continuation of politics by other means, it
requires little imagination to see American life since
the abandonment of the Reconstruction as an abrupt
reversal of that formula: the continuation of the Civil
War by means other than arms.

Ralph Ellison, "Stephen Crane and the Mainstream
of American Fiction," *Shadow and Act* (1964)

Only four paragraphs into the first chapter of Stephen Crane's
The Red Badge of Courage, the reader encounters "A negro
teamster who had been dancing upon a cracker box with the hilarious en-
couragement of twoscore soldiers." "Deserted" suddenly by the soldiers who
"scattered into small arguing groups" to debate the news that they are about
to move into battle positions, the "negro teamster" "sat mournfully down."[1]
As several critics have pointed out, notably Ralph Ellison in his 1960 introduction to the novel, this is the only African American who appears in *The
Red Badge of Courage*, despite the centrality of the issue of slavery in the Civil
War and the presence of African-American Union soldiers fighting that
war.[2] It is indeed one of the strangest features of an American novel notable
for its curious twists that Crane selected the Civil War as the setting for an
otherwise dehistoricized and overtly depoliticized account of the social psychology of war.

After all, Crane knew well his famous battles of the world, and many of
them are better settings than the Civil War for the sort of distant, ironic, often
mock-epic treatment Crane accords Henry Fleming's little drama of manhood in *The Red Badge of Courage*. From his education at the "semi-military"

Claverack College and Hudson River Institute through his years as war correspondent in the Greco-Turkish War of 1897 and the Spanish-American War of 1898 to his last book, the potboiler *Great Battles of the World*, Crane gained considerable knowledge of military history.[3] In the latter work, Crane described two historic battles that would have served his purposes better than the Civil War: the Battle of Plevna, in which the Turkish commander Osman Pasha "lost" to the Russians but nonetheless kept them from advancing on Constantinople, and the Battle of New Orleans, the "real battle" of which was fought on January 8, 1815, two weeks after the Treaty of Ghent had been signed, concluding the War of 1812.[4] Of all the modern wars Crane might have selected, the Civil War least met his purpose of demonstrating the inherent injustice of war and exposing the propaganda that convinced soldiers to risk their lives for an abstract ideal. When considered in terms of the long political and legal struggles for the abolition of slavery against the stubborn resistance of the proslavery South, the Civil War seems in retrospect a horrible and bloody necessity. After the Compromise of 1850, passing the Fugitive Slave Law, even northern moderates like Ralph Waldo Emerson passionately called for war.[5]

Why, then, did Crane choose the Civil War to argue the vainglory of war at its best and the waste and futility of war at its worst? The positive answer to that question is that Crane, like his contemporary Mark Twain, wanted to demonstrate how little had changed in America since the Civil War, especially in regard to the treatment of African Americans. The standard explanation of why Twain would choose to set *Adventures of Huckleberry Finn* in the antebellum, slaveholding South is that Twain wanted readers of the 1880s to recognize the persistence of the social psychology of slavery in the social behaviors and specific laws that by the 1896 decision *Plessy v. Ferguson* would constitute the "separate-but-equal" racism of modern America.[6] According to such a reading, the single "negro teamster" appearing on the first page of *The Red Badge of Courage* would be at once a reminder of the real political and human issues in the Civil War as well as of the systematic forgetting of this truth by the Union soldiers in the remainder of the narrative.

"Dancing upon a cracker box," the African-American teamster entertains the Union soldiers in a way that suggests that this war has changed nothing in the social psychology of racism that would be exemplified throughout the nineteenth and early twentieth centuries by minstrel shows, black-face caricatures of African-Americans performed by whites, and other cultural forms through which a white ruling class asserted its authority by humiliating people of color. Read in this way, the African-American teamster's sole appearance in the narrative is full of symbolic significance about just what Americans *failed* to achieve in the Civil War; already northern whites have adapted to the southern entertainments by which African Americans were kept in subaltern positions. In this sense, Henry Fleming's studied innocence in the face of the terrible machinery of war is part of the larger cultural repression at work in the conduct of all the Union troops, who when they are the most obedient to their commanders' orders ironically end up reproducing just the sorts of hierarchies that would defeat the emancipatory purposes of the Civil War.

There is, however, another interpretation of this teamster's appearance that conflicts with what appears to be Crane's sympathy with oppressed African Americans both in antebellum and postbellum America. Two paragraphs before the teamster is described, "a certain tall soldier developed virtues and went resolutely to wash a shirt. He came flying back from a brook waving his garment bannerlike. He was swelled with a tale he had heard from a reliable friend, who had heard it from a truthful cavalryman, who had heard it from his trustworthy brother." The news this soldier brings with "the important air of a herald in red and gold" is: "'W're goin' t' move t' morrah—sure'" (RBC, 5). This is a familiar example of Crane's use of the mock-epic both to distinguish his own narrative authority from the vulgarity of the common people he describes (and often displays contempt for) and to introduce us to one of his chief arguments about the psychology of war: that heroism and authority in war are often absurd self-delusions of individuals desperate to defend themselves psychically against the unpredictable events of war. In this context, the dancing teamster seems merely a *fictional device* to emphasize the entertainment value of the "tall soldier's" report: what he tells his fellow soldiers is of no more value than the antics of a "negro teamster . . . dancing upon a cracker box." In such a reading, Crane rhetorically uses this African-American character as American ideology used African Americans both before and after slavery: as servants to perform physical or cultural work *for* the white majority.

How we decide just which reading applies to Crane's meaning in *The Red Badge of Courage* has considerably greater significance than settling a critical dispute over the proper interpretation of a single passage in the novel. The larger stakes include not only the important issue of Crane's attitude toward race in the late nineteenth century, but also his view of the United States as a democratic society committed uniquely to the goal of equal rights and social justice. This latter topic was almost always framed in the 1890s by some judgment of a nation's role in the growing imperialist ventures of the great European powers in Africa, Asia, the South Pacific, the Middle East, and South America. Thus I shall inflate this very brief opening scene from *The Red Badge of Courage* to assume significance in the important judgment of whether Crane endorsed equal rights or subscribed to the racial attitudes of his time and whether or not Crane connected racism in the United States with the more evident racism of the European powers in their zeal to expand their empires. At stake in this argument will also be the interpretation of *The Red Badge of Courage* as: an antiwar protest that merely uses the most recent American war (the Civil War) to portray the general absurdity and futility of war; a narrative of education adapted to the ideological purposes of indoctrinating young men to the "heroism" of war; an existentialist trivialization of war, politics, and social relations for the sake of the high and bitter truth of man's fundamental alienation in the universe.

I propose to return to these questions not by way of a close reading of *The Red Badge of Courage*, but by looking at Crane's more extended treatment of race relations in his story "The Monster," written in 1897 and published in *The Monster and Other Stories* in 1899.[7] Set in Whilomville, New York, Crane's fictional version of his hometown, Port Jervis, New York, and focusing on the transformation of the town to a modern city, "The Monster" gives prominence to race relations in the North, connects these relations with the changing economy of the late nineteenth-century United States, and quite unpredictably makes certain links between these important domestic issues and current foreign policy issues regularly in the news of the late 1890s.

Henry Johnson, the African-American hero of "The Monster," is also a teamster, but he does not drive supplies to the Union troops; instead, he drives the carriages and cares for the horses of Dr. Trescott, a prominent doctor in Whilomville. Crane based Johnson on Levi Hume, a white man "who hauled ashes in Port Jervis." Stallman notes that Levi Hume's "face had been eaten by cancer" and was thus "an object of horror to the children" in the town.[8] Crane obviously elevates the cancer-stricken trash collector Levi Hume in his characterization of Henry Johnson, especially before the bizarre injury to his face that occurs in Dr. Trescott's home laboratory while Henry is saving Dr. Trescott's son, Jimmie, from the burning house. Henry Johnson is introduced to the reader as "a very handsome negro, . . . known to be a light, a weight, and an eminence in the suburb of the town, where lived the larger number of the negroes."[9] Like so many of Crane's introductions, this one is filled with stylistic ironies and doubles entendres. The apparent oxymoron, "known to be a light, a weight," with its hint of "lightweight," actually puns on Henry's importance in the African-American community of Whilomville based in part on the suggestion he is light in color, a distinction in the African-American community that followed racist stereotypes prevalent in the nineteenth-century United States and in part on the complex figuration of Henry as a "shining light" for both his wit and his kindness.

The rhetorical introduction of Henry as "a light" is especially complex, because his disfigurement by the fire will "blacken" him to such a degree that it is impossible for the reader to determine with any certainty after the fire whether Henry's "color" is a consequence of biological pigmentation or the social accident of the fire.[10] And Henry's "blackness" after the fire is also an effect of the scopic occlusion, the specific "blindness" of those townspeople who *refuse to look* at his disfigurement, a refusal to look that as much as the fire itself *disfigures* by *effacing* Henry Johnson. Thus his introduction as "a light" is especially interesting as an anticipation of the dramatic action, and it is made more interesting by the clear competition Crane establishes between Henry as "a light" and Dr. Trescott as "the moon." We must recall here that Henry is introduced to us when Dr. Trescott's son, Jimmie, "went down to the stable" for comfort following his father's gentle rebuke of him for having broken a flower ("a wheel of his cart destroyed a peony" [M, 9]) in the garden: "Obviously this glory was over Jimmie's horizon; but he vaguely appreciated it and paid deference to Henry for it. . . . However, on all points of conduct as related to the doctor, who was the moon, they were in complete but unexpressed understanding" (M, 11). Crane does not quite say that Henry Johnson is the "sun" either to Jimmie Trescott or to the African-American community in the suburbs of Whilomville, but his description as "a light" assumes this connotation when Dr. Trescott is called "the moon."

The contrast between this "sun" and "moon" is also full of Crane's irony. The fiery "light" of Henry's wit and good humor is associated with the more elemental world in which he and other African Americans live in Crane's Whilomville. The stable is Henry's domain, and it is a place of physical power and substantial reality, which Crane reinforces with sensuously evocative descriptions: "Sometimes the horses in the stalls stamped thunderingly on the pine floor. There was an atmosphere of hay and of harness. . . . It was not until he began to spin a wheel on the tree, and the sprinkling water flew everywhere, that the boy was visibly moved" (M, 12). The scene in the stable is in direct contrast with the opening scene of "The Monster," in which little Jimmie plays in the garden by pretending to be a railroad engineer and his cart "engine Number 36" while his father mows the lawn with "the whir-ring machine," "shaving this lawn as if it were a priest's chin" (M, 9). These opening references to the machinery of urban society—the child's cart and the father's lawnmower—will gather with many others by story's end to sug-gest how mechanization has transformed the natural world into a surreal urban landscape in which human beings have been thoroughly mechanized.

In *Bodies and Machines*, Mark Seltzer has interpreted Crane's use of metaphors of mechanization as part of the general modern fascination with the "body-machine" complex that was part of the ideological work of industrial capitalism. Although he does not treat "The Monster," Selt-zer focuses on *The Red Badge of Courage* and its "two stories," the first a psychological "'inside' story" of "male hysteria, registering fears of unman-ning and infantilization in the face of threats of bodily dismemberment" and the second a sociological "'outside' story of social discipline, mecha-nization, body counts, and the industrial and *corporate* disarticulation of natural bodies."[11] That "inside story," essentially a "love story," that Selt-zer reads in Henry Fleming's hopes and fears before going to the war, compli-cated as these emotions are by his absent father and his all-too-present mother, enables Seltzer to interpret the ideological gendering of "nature" and "culture" in early modern industrial societies as respectively "feminine" and "mascu-line." Interpreting a typical passage from *The Red Badge of Courage* that de-scribes the dehumanization and mechanization of soldiers in battle, Seltzer concludes: "The becoming-artifactual of persons, in these descriptions, is perfectly compatible with the substitution of the regimental and regimented body for the natural body—the military 'making of men.'"[12]

This masculine-mechanical complex is not a simple version of an older Marxian concept of the *naturalization* of the artificial practices of industrial production and its mechanics, Seltzer rightly warns us, because far more than mere "masking" or "mystification" is involved in this process. As Seltzer points out, what was once described as "naturalization" is in effect a suite of actions "which are at once identified with *and realized through* the reworking of natural processes and landscapes." Seltzer connects this cultural work to the emphasis in this period on "the culture-work of channeling, bridge-building, and canalization," such that "the civil engineer" becomes "a culture hero in the literature of the 1890s (in the novels of Richard Harding Davis, for instance)," or I might add like Ames, the electrical engineer in Theodore Dreiser's *Sister Carrie*. Following the theoretical model of Klaus Theweleit in *Male Fantasies*, Seltzer wants to show how such a new idealization of the "body-machine" complex occurs strategically by demonizing the natural body as "feminine" and "weak," because in large part uncontrollable: "Put simply, to the extent that the anti-biological and anti-natural biases of naturalism involve . . . the transcendence of 'the natural' and 'the female' both, they involve the transcendence of a female/nature, identified with liquid interiors and flows."[13] What must be added to Seltzer's equation, however, on the "natural" side of this new binary of "machine culture" is the racially marked other, which sometimes is infantilized, sometimes feminized and subject to still other figurations associating racial otherness with the natural, wild, and primitive. Although "primitivism" and "savagism" are old terms by which the racially marked other has been subordinated to the culture of colonial domination, I would argue that Seltzer and Theweleit help us specify the mutual signification of race, gender, and nature in modern Western cultures.[14]

The obvious importance of the battle scenes and their mechanization of humans in *The Red Badge of Courage* makes my emphasis on the quotidian opening scenes of "The Monster" appear somewhat exaggerated, but these scenes may be all the more important for their very ordinariness. Lawnmowing and child's play are now deeply invested in the "machine culture" that manifests itself so graphically in the combat of the Civil War, and the exclusion of the African American from the scenes of war in *The Red Badge of Courage* becomes in "The Monster" an "effacement" or "invisibility" incorporated into the structural oppositions of "nature" and "culture" in this social world. Even Henry Johnson's literal effacement as a consequence of the acid that spills from that "exploding" jar in Dr. Trescott's fiery laboratory is not his exclusive property. If it were, then Henry's monstrosity, like the threatening figure of the feminine other in many modern narratives, might truly threaten and challenge this culture. But even before we are introduced to Henry Johnson, we are told: "It was apparent from Jimmie's manner that he felt some kind of desire to efface himself. He went down to the stable. Henry Johnson, the negro who cared for the doctor's horses, was sponging the buggy" (M, 11). The "effacement" of Henry Johnson, like the "invisibility" of Ralph Ellison's narrator in *Invisible Man* (1952) half a century later, is the effect of a certain mode of vision, including what it does *not see*, that is characteristic of modern U.S. culture as it legalized separate-but-equal racism in *Plessy v. Ferguson* and embarked on its own ventures in the domination of other cultures and peoples in the Philippines, Cuba, and Central America.[15]

The idea that Henry Johnson's "effacement" is actually the result of someone else's "desire to efface himself," in this case the young son of a prominent white citizen, gives new interest to John Berryman's psychobiographical reading of "The Monster" in his 1950 biography, *Stephen Crane*. Berryman treats the narrative as organized around the theme of "rescue-and-punishment," allegorizing the narrative events as versions of Crane's own need to redeem himself in the eyes of his father, the Reverend Jonathan Townley Crane. Recalling Crane's troubles in New York when he testified on behalf of the prostitute, Dora Clark, against a New York police detective, resulting in Crane's expulsion from New York City, and Crane's relationship with Cora Taylor Crane, former madam of the Hotel de Dream in Jacksonville, Florida, Berryman concludes:

> For trying to rescue the boy, the Negro is punished with mutilation and idiocy, he becomes a "monster" and has to hide his no-face. For rescuing the Negro, the doctor is ostracized. For trying to rescue Dora Clark, Stephen Crane had been beaten out of New York, and he was now making up his mind to do the same thing again, to "rescue" Cora Taylor by (as it were) marrying her. . . . The story essentially *confesses* and *reassures*. As a confession, it is a propitiation of the spirit of the Reverend Jonathan Townley Crane (on page one occurs the image: "The doctor was shaving his lawn as if it were a priest's chin") for the crime done against the family by his son's resolve to rescue a "broken flower."[16]

In itself a quaint reminder of the Freudian literary criticism of the 1940s and 1950s, Berryman's reading does suggest that Crane may be using Henry Johnson for his own purposes as crudely as the community "uses" Henry Johnson as ritual scapegoat for its anxieties. Like the dancing teamster in *The Red Badge of Courage* as an ironic foil for the soldier who adopts "the important air of a herald in red and gold" to bring his gossipy news of troop movements, so Henry Johnson may serve only the purpose of allowing Crane to investigate group psychology and even mob hysteria in the face of anything that challenges social conventions. If this is the case, then Crane's accurate and complex literary representation of the new agency of the "machine-body" of early modern urban America might help to legitimate its set of cultural values by marginalizing viable alternatives, such as the "light" and "weight" of Henry Johnson in his own African-American identity.

We ought to know well enough by this date the dangers of certain kinds of sympathetic identifications with the racially, sexually, or gendered other as being ways of appropriating another's power. Norman Mailer might have claimed for the hipster the "cool" and "jive" of African-American culture in his infamous essay of the 1950s, "The White Negro," but he overlooked the possibility that such identification might also be a means of *displacing* and thereby *effacing* the African American.[17] Berryman finds psychobiographical traces of Crane in Jimmie, Henry, and Dr. Trescott, but the more frequent critical tendency is to identify Crane primarily with Henry Johnson. Thus Christopher Benfey points out that "The Monster" "is about a doctor and a patient, and how illness alienates its victims, a theme increasingly close to Crane's obsessions."[18] Like Berryman, Benfey understands Crane's use of familiar themes in "The Monster"—rescue, fire, social ostracism—as ways Crane worked out his private demons in fiction.[19] Such psychobiographical readings of Crane are undoubtedly valid—authors generally work out personal concerns in their fictional characters and situations; there is a certain self-evidence in claiming that a character is a "double" for the author. It is thus easy to forget how identification across social divisions like race, gender, sexuality, and class can have two very different consequences: first, the author can subvert such false divisions by establishing a commonality with the imagined other; second, the author can submerge the difference of the other by claiming it as the author's own. It is the second tendency that seems most marked in Crane's use of Henry Johnson to represent Crane's personal and social concerns.

Henry Johnson's greatest sin in the cruel judgment of Whilomville is his ability to act, his *heroism* in saving Jimmie from the fire, and his general sense of his own human agency. From the beginning, Jimmie admires Henry's skills as a teamster: "Henry could drive a horse, and Jimmie had a full sense of this sublimity. Henry personally conducted the moon during the splendid journeys through the country roads, where farms spread on all sides, with sheep, cows, and other marvels abounding" (M, 12). Such childlike wonder is replaced by a near frenzy of envy and finally rage on the part of townspeople who have themselves been stripped of any effective agency by the machinery of urban society and its technologies. "Whilomville" means "former town," and like Fort Romper, Nebraska, in "The Blue Hotel" or Yellow Sky, Texas, in "The Bride Comes to Yellow Sky," this town is rapidly becoming a city thanks to problematic progress. Electric arc lights cast fantastic shadows on the main street and in the town park while gaslights continue to illuminate the interiors of Reifsnyder's barbershop, stores, and private homes. The "shrill electric street-car, the motor singing like a cageful of grasshoppers" is another visible and audible feature of modernization, and its "great gong" clanging "forth both warnings and simple noise" matches the "great hoarse roar of" the factory "whistle," which will also announce the fire at Dr. Trescott's house on that fateful Saturday night (M, 13, 17–18). While young people listen to "the band" that "played until ten o'clock in the little park"—a clichéd image of small-town America—one young man "said that the music reminded him of the new engines on the hill pumping water into the reservoir. . . . The young man did not say it because he disliked the band's playing. He said it because it was fashionable to say that manner of thing concerning the band" (M, 17).

Such imagery may appear to be the representation of urban alienation and dehumanization that is commonplace in literary naturalism; more witty and ironic than Dreiser or Norris's accounts of modernization in Chicago or San Francisco, Crane's style here seems to be making an utterly conventional point. Yet it is the ways in which the people of Whilomville are stripped of individual agency by the new industrialization and mechanization of urban space that makes Crane's account worth our attention. Otherwise realistic descriptions of crowds take on new meaning when read in this larger context. Let me quote three examples in succession to suggest how pervasively Crane fills "The Monster" with this new sociology of the crowd:

> Through this radiant lane moved a crowd, which culminated in a throng before the post-office, awaiting the distribution of the evening mails. (M, 13)

> The younger lads . . . were careering madly through the crowd, precipitating minor accidents from time to time, but usually fleeing like mist swept by the wind before retribution could lay hands upon them. (M, 17)

> In the shivering light, which gave to the park an effect like a great vaulted hall, the throng swarmed, with a gentle murmur of dresses switching the turf, and with a steady hum of voices. (M, 17)

These urban crowds anticipate by only a few paragraphs the presumably "organized" crowd of the volunteer fire company, "Tuscarora Hose Company Number Six," that races to Dr. Trescott's burning house in response to the factory whistle's "great hoarse roar." Critics have often praised Crane for the sheer tour de force of this description of "the black crowd that poured after the machine": "The cart seemed to be the apex of a dark wave that was whirling as if it had been a broken dam. Behind the lad were stretches of lawn, and in that direction front doors were banged by men who hoarsely shouted out into the clamorous avenue, 'What district?'" (M, 19).

The "lawn," the "cart," and even the imaginary "engine" of Jimmie Trescott's child's play on the front lawn of his house in the opening scene are strangely condensed in this description of the fire company heading to the fire at Dr. Trescott's house. Indeed, the opening scene of child's play seems here reenacted but not by way of contrast with the more important and serious work of firefighting. It is as if Crane wishes us to understand the work of firefighting itself as a kind of children's game. This is part of Crane's characteristic and unique adaptation of the mock-heroic to literary naturalism, of course, but the larger purpose may be to suggest how individuals are *infantilized* by the machinery that strips them of individual agency for the sake of coordinated action. It is also a "crowd" marked by its "blackness" in three quick references to "the black crowd," "a dark wave," and "a kind of black torrent" (M, 19). Critics have also been quick to observe that this crowd culminates in a kind of mad frenzy when it reaches Dr. Trescott's house. Only Chief Hannigan, Henry Johnson, and "a young man who was a brakeman on the railway, and lived in one of the rear streets near the Trescotts,"[20] acting clearly as individual agents, manage to save Mrs. Trescott, Jimmie, and Henry Johnson, respectively (M, 26). Otherwise, the crowd seems to be represented aptly by the actions of one of its unnamed members: "As they swung into the open air a man ran across the lawn and, seizing a shutter, pulled it from its hinges and flung it far out upon the grass. Then he frantically attacked the other shutters one by one. It was a kind of temporary insanity" (M, 21–22).

This impression of people as extensions of machines is reinforced by the general level of conversation in Whilomville. Crane was a master of capturing the bathos of everyday conversation, and he used this technique to particularly nasty effect in his tales of lower-class life in the Bowery, "Maggie: A Girl of the Streets" and "George's Mother." Maggie's brother, Jimmie Johnson, whose common name actually anticipates Jimmie Trescott and Henry Johnson, typifies the mock eloquence Crane attributes to his lower-class urban characters: "Nevertheless, he had, on a certain star-lit evening, said wonderingly and quite reverently, 'Deh moon looks like hell, don't it?'"[21] Such accidental poetry is more than matched by the "hully gees!" and "outa sites!" with which Crane has his lower-class characters respond to their circumstances. In "The Monster" characters speak frequently in unfinished phrases, successive statements that contradict preceding sentences, and clichés. Like Jimmie Trescott initially responding to the broken peony by uttering the same word, "There!," over and over again, many adults in Whilomville seem incapable of using language beyond its most elementary denotative functions. As the Tuscarora Hose Company Number Six races toward the Trescotts' house, the call-and-response "What district?" and "Second" syncopates the mechanical movement, as if language itself has been reduced to a mere effect of technology, rather than of the human voice. In many ways, Crane suggests that the machine has replaced nature as the chief force subordinating people to some higher, mysterious law. Crane generally represents such a transformation in ironic terms, as he does by naming one of the fire companies for the Tuscarora tribe and suggesting thereby a new "primitivism" in man's obedience to the machine.[22]

Thus it is especially unusual when anyone acts independently of the existing systems of social and economic life in Whilomville. Henry Johnson's appearance at the Trescotts' house is described as a surreal, miraculous event: "There was one man who ran with an almost fabulous speed. He wore lavender trousers. A straw hat with a bright silk band was held half crumpled in his hand. As Henry reached the front door, Hannigan had just broken the lock with a kick" (M, 21). Stallman observes that "No white American author had pictured a Negro performing a truly heroic act before Crane did in 'The Monster.'"[23] Jim's many courageous acts (often to protect Huck) in Twain's *Huckleberry Finn*, the heroism of many African-American characters Harriet Beecher Stowe's *Uncle Tom's Cabin* (1852) and *Dred: A Tale of the Great Dismal Swamp* (1856) belie this claim to Crane's originality.[24] Nevertheless, Stallman's statement still expresses a horrible truth about the subordination of African-American agency to white authority in the vast majority of white American literature—a point made in more sophisticated terms by Toni Morrison in *Playing in the Dark*: "Autonomy, authority, newness and difference, absolute power . . . not only become the major themes and presumptions of American literature, but . . . each one is made possible by, shaped by, activated by a complex awareness and employment of a constituted Africanism. It was this Africanism, deployed as rawness and savagery, that provided the staging ground and arena for the elaboration of the quintessential identity."[25] This complex ideological work of creating an "Africanism" that both enables white identity and is thereby marginalized describes accurately what Crane does by transforming the heroism of Henry Johnson into his social monstrosity. It may also explain Stallman's neglect of the heroism of Twain's Jim and Stowe's Eliza, Celia, and Dred, among others.

Henry's "fabulous speed" and the brilliant colors of his splendid clothes set him off from the "black torrent" and "dark wave" and "black wave" that is the mob, and his ability to act in an emergency is just what morally distinguishes him from the passive crowd following the fire companies to the Trescotts' burning house. What Henry Johnson does inside the Trescotts' burning house has been read many times before, often with special emphasis on Crane's stylistic skill in transforming the fire into a metaphor for the revolution against slavery left unfinished by both the Revolutionary War (and its founding documents) and the Civil War. As the windows burst from the internal heat, Crane compares the house to "a haunted house" and the firestorm as an "outbreak" that "had been well planned, as if by professional revolutionists." The ghosts of the unfinished revolutions against American slavery return, much as Toni Morrison's "Beloved" does much later in literary history. If we want to give Crane the fullest possible reading of this scene as one of insurrection against slavery and racism in America, then we must consider the scene to recall the millennial aims of Nat Turner's Southampton Insurrection in 1831 or the earlier rebellions of Denmark Vesey and Gabriel Prosser.[26] Despite Crane's virtual neglect of race in his previous works, this scene seems charged with just such revolutionary significance in response to the persistence of American racism. As he heads up the stairs, Henry "turned blue with horror," and "in the hall a lick of flame had found the cord that supported 'Signing the Declaration,'" which "slumped suddenly down at one end, and then dropped to the floor, where it burst with the sound of a bomb" (M, 21).[27] The deliberate omission of slavery as an issue from the U.S. Constitution made in retrospect the Declaration of Independence, that great Enlightenment document, seem even more a mockery to antebellum slaves and nineteenth-century abolitionists. William Lloyd Garrison burned a copy of the Constitution on July 4, 1854, during a dramatic abolitionist speech at Framingham, Massachusetts, to illustrate his repudiation of what he considered a "pro-slavery" document.

Such an interpretation is tempting for many reasons, but it unfortunately will not hold up in the face of the explicit referents for "revolution" and for "salvation" enacted in the scene of the fire. It is the threatening *fire* that is associated with revolutionists, insurrection, and the "burning" of "Signing the Declaration"; Henry Johnson works cooperatively with Chief Hannigan, who "followed him up the stairs, and grappled the arm of the maniacal" Mrs. Trescott, "screaming for Henry to save her son Jimmie."[28] Hannigan's "face was black with rage," as he "bellowed" to Mrs. Trescott, "You must come down" (M, 21). Most critics overlook the fact that Hannigan saves Mrs. Trescott as Henry Johnson saves Jimmie, so that as heroes of the fire they share a common purpose. What they do together is what the crowd outside cannot do: defeat this natural threat to social order and human life. Two others characters help save Jimmie and Henry, respectively: Dr. Trescott, who finds his son wrapped in a blanket near a window, and a young railway brakeman who lives near the Trescotts and arrives on the scene separately from the mob.[29] In Crane's thematics, as well as the general rhetoric of literary naturalism, it is just such natural force that usually provokes instincts for social cooperation that at their best renew the social bond and result in heroic acts.

Yet in describing Henry's heroism, Crane qualifies and subordinates it, preparing us for the ways such heroism will be variously interpreted by the community as either "monstrosity" or "injustice" but never properly the strong and willful act of an individual. The scene in Jimmie's bedroom where Henry takes the child up in his arms is by no means a scene of even disguised rebellion against American racism; it is, in fact, nothing other than a revised version of countless scenes from nineteenth-century sentimental romances, in which the angelic child is helped tenderly by his childlike and brutish African-American friend:

> The little chamber . . . was faintly illuminated by a beautiful rosy light reflected circuitously from the flames that were consuming the house. The boy . . . sat in his bed, his lips apart, his eyes wide, while upon his little white-robed figure played caressingly the light from the fire. As the door flew open he had before him this apparition of his pal, a terror-stricken negro, all tousled and with wool scorching, who leaped upon him and bore him up in a blanket as if the whole affair were a case of kidnapping by a dreadful robber chief. (M, 22)

From the "little white-robed figure" of Jimmie to his "pal," Henry, as "terror-stricken negro . . . with wool scorching" and as "a dreadful robber chief," we recognize immediately the racial stereotypes of nineteenth-century white American writing. The scene not only links Jimmie's childishness with Henry, but Henry is also predictably feminized: "As Johnson, bearing him, reeled into the smoke of the hall, he flung his arms about his neck and buried his face in the blanket. He called twice in muffled tones: 'Ma-ma! Ma-ma!'" (M, 23). Although ostensibly calling out for his mother, Jimmie is also acknowledging Henry's posture and action as expressing maternal safety. Infantilized and feminized even as he acts heroically, Henry is in the very next paragraph figuratively enslaved by the power of the fire: "He was submitting, submitting because of his fathers, bending his mind in a most perfect slavery to this conflagration" (M, 23). Crane's suggestion that Henry is still determined by the fate of his slave ancestry will be developed further in the descriptions of Henry when he is finally overcome by the fire in Dr. Trescott's laboratory. This fictional enactment of Henry Johnson's abjection is necessary for Crane to allow Dr. Trescott, not Henry, *really* to save his son. It serves the larger symbolic purpose of transferring the heroic powers of Henry Johnson to his white "protector" for the remainder of the narrative.

The actual disfigurement of Henry Johnson in Dr. Trescott's laboratory seems to offer possible evidence to refute Crane's reliance on African-American stereotypes in his representation of Henry's heroism. The home laboratory itself is not unusual for even a small-town doctor nor is Dr. Trescott's interest in "devoting himself to experiments which came in the way of his study."[30] The poisonous atmosphere in the laboratory as the chemicals combine with the fire suggests, like Dr. Rappaccini's poisoned garden, some perversion of nature. The infernal "garden" of "burning flowers," with "flames of violet, crimson, green, blue, orange, and purple . . . blooming everywhere," is compatible with Crane's critique of urban industrial societies as "unnatural" in most of his writings (M, 24). But the temptation to read Dr. Trescott's laboratory as the site of experiments in the new eugenics established by Francis Galton and his followers in 1883 does not seem warranted. What Galton termed "the study of the agencies under social control that may improve or impair the racial qualities of future generations either mentally or physically" may be ironically suggested by the *disfigurement* Henry experiences in Dr. Trescott's laboratory. But it is more likely that Crane's irony in this regard is directed more at modern science with its pretensions to improve and even master nature than it is concerned with the inherent racism of the pseudo-science of eugenics.

Overcome by the flames and smoke, Henry on the verge of collapse is represented by various caricatures of nineteenth-century African Americans: the terrified fugitive slave—"He cried out again in the negro wail that had in it the sadness of the swamps"; the cowardly and abject slave—"Johnson shrieked, and then ducked in the manner of his race in fights"; the exoticized primitive living in wild places—"An orange-colored flame leaped like a panther at the lavender trousers. This animal bit deeply into Johnson," and "suddenly the glass splintered, and a ruby-red snake-like thing poured its thick length out upon the top of the old desk . . . and then . . . flowed directly down into Johnson's upturned face" (M, 24). Whereas there is some reason for Crane to connect the otherwise dedicated and honest Dr. Trescott with the problems of modern society represented by Whilomville, there is virtually no reason to turn the only person who remains faithful to Henry Johnson and his heroism into the "evil genius" of eugenics and its theories of racial engineering. Dr. Trescott must in fact "save" Jimmie from the fire, confirming the ultimate inability of Henry Johnson to complete the human act of which the mechanized, "black crowd" is also incapable. Dr. Trescott's relation to Henry Johnson is consistently that of liberal paternalism, but it is not the target of *Crane's* social criticism in "The Monster." Instead, Dr. Trescott's relation both to Jimmie and to Henry seems to reinstate what Crane assumes is the "proper" hierarchy of educated, responsible adults to less responsible children and African Americans. It is the failure of the citizens of Whilomville to recognize this "rational" social hierarchy and its civic virtues that is the primary object of Crane's social criticism.[31]

In other words, Crane uses Henry Johnson for the sake of exploring the unnatural consequences of a society that has traded its capacities for individual action for technologies that increasingly determine peoples' lives and actions. Like Hawthorne's Minister Hooper in "The Minister's Black Veil" (1836), the disfigured Henry Johnson becomes a screen on which images of Whilomville's new social psychology are cast.[32] The effects of the fire on Henry Johnson are both disfigurement and "insanity," so that forever after that heroic event Johnson merely figures in the narrative as an embodiment of the irrational and unnatural. In his analysis of how rumor, gossip, and fantasy contribute to the crowd psychology of scapegoating, Crane offers us a brilliant interpretation of the sorts of mass hysteria that would become perversely essential to modern urban experience and the objects of later analyses by theorists like Elias Canetti and Walter Benjamin.[33]

Henry Johnson's heroism is, then, the *agency* he displays while the majority of townspeople suffer from a "temporary insanity." Hannigan displays a similar ability to act in a crisis as an individual, but his behavior is not demonized by the citizens of Whilomville because he thereby "represents" them (even though he is in fact their "exception"). Dr. Trescott performs an heroic act that continues and completes Johnson's heroism when Dr. Trescott goes into the fiery house to find Jimmie wrapped in his blanket near the window (where Henry has placed him just before Henry passes out). By insisting throughout the rest of the narrative on Henry Johnson's heroism, Dr. Trescott risks his social and professional status by aligning himself with the socially and racially defined Other. Henry Johnson is an African-American servant marginalized by the dominant white culture, and therefore his act of heroism calls into stark relief the *absence of agency* among the white townspeople. Crane uses an African-American character to focus his narrative meanings not because Crane wishes to make any central statement about racism in America, but to call attention to white society's surrender of its authority to the technology and machinery of urban progress. Used as such a fictional "device," Henry Johnson differs little from the African-American "teamster" entertaining the Union troops in the opening scene of *The Red Badge of Courage*. In certain ways, his relation to Dr. Trescott is isomorphic with the relation between that teamster and the Union soldier waving his shirt to herald the news.[34]

Of course, I would prefer not to make this claim; I would much prefer to agree with Ralph Ellison, who found in "The Monster" a crucial understanding of the persistence of racism in postbellum America. Ellison's conclusion allows him to situate Crane in a great tradition of white American writers from Twain to Faulkner who addressed racism: "The important point is that between Twain and the emergence of the driving honesty and social responsibility of Faulkner, no artist of Crane's caliber looked so steadily at the wholeness of American life and discovered such far-reaching symbolic equivalents for its unceasing state of civil war."[35] Unfortunately, I think Ellison is wrong with respect to Crane's significance in the literary critique of American racism, but to make that case I will have to discuss at some length Crane's fitful response to Western imperialism and his general treatment of non-European peoples and cultures.

Stallman describes the story of a lost manuscript by Crane, "Vashti in the Dark," which Crane had written in February 1895, as the story of "a Methodist preacher" who "finds his wife has been raped by a Negro in a forest and kills himself. Acton Davies, who typed that tale for him, thought it marvellous, but Crane is said to have burnt it."[36] It is possible, of course, that Crane burned the story precisely because of its racist contents, but there is considerable evidence in Crane's nonfictional prose to confirm the thesis that he subscribed basically to the racialist rhetoric of his times. And the bare plot summary of the story seems to conform to the entanglement of race and gender that is explicit in "The Monster" and marginally operative in most of Crane's narratives. From his sketches in the West and Mexico (1895) to his reports of the Greco-Turkish War of 1897 to his writings about the peoples of Cuba, Haiti, and the Dominican Republic during his reporting of the Spanish-American War (1898), Crane is consistently anti-imperialist and just as consistently critical of the peoples of these very different regions as "backward," "primitive," and in need of "modernization." These attitudes are certainly contradictory, but they are by no means uncommon among educated European and U.S. travelers in the late nineteenth century; they are the contradictions of "liberal progressivism" as it confronts its own consequences in the far-flung corners of the various European and U.S. empires of the period.

In "Stephen Crane: Anti-Imperialist," Thomas Gullason argued in 1958 that Crane was an "ardent anti-imperialist," whose "serious, defiant, and sincere humanitarian" sentiments in this regard ought to link him with more familiar anti-imperialists of this period, such as Mark Twain and William Dean Howells.[37] Gullason has exaggerated the case for Crane as an anti-imperialist, in part by ignoring all of Crane's caricatures of native peoples as backward, often comical, and otherwise in need of Western enlightenment. In one of Crane's earliest journalist pieces, "The King's Favor," which he published in the *University Herald* in 1891 during his one semester at Syracuse University, he describes the visit of the New York tenor Albert G. Thies to "old King Cetewayo, the famous Zulu chief," who had been held under house arrest by the British since his military defeat in 1879. Gullason claims that "Crane championed the underdog whose 'dark-skinned impis had gone down . . . beneath the Enfield rifles of the scarlet-coated visitors from the sea,'" but Crane actually mocks King Cetewayo for his naïveté in inviting the tenor to "join him" in driving the British out of Africa and for his primitivism in offering Thies the "gift" of one of the chief's wives, Mursala.[38]

Of the native peoples he encountered in his travels in Mexico, Crane writes from Mexico City: "At first it seemed to me the most extraordinary thing that the lower classes of Indians in this country should insist upon existence at all. Their squalor, their ignorance, seemed so absolute that death—no matter what it has in store—would appear as freedom, joy." And although Crane goes on to what appears to be a comparison between Mexico's Indians and "the people of the slums of our own cities," he concludes that the American lower class's sense of oppression is "an appreciation that does not exist in the lower classes of Mexico."[39] Indeed, the Mexican Indian's lack of self-consciousness regarding his oppression fits Crane's view of other "primitive" peoples and the reason behind his insistence that they will either die out or be "saved" by modernization.

Crane is consistently critical of Great Britain, Germany, and Spain for imperialist ventures that are primarily commercial enterprises, defending as Twain would the rights to "free trade," which as we have seen was often a late nineteenth-century slogan of anti-imperialists.[40] Such a stance appears to put him in sympathy with the working classes and rural peasantry in colonized nations, and he expresses in his dispatches from Cuba his open contempt for the Spanish merchants in Havana who sided with Spain in the Spanish-American War. Yet, in his dispatches from Haiti and the Dominican Republic, Crane patronizes the native people, noting that the Haitian "natives, drooping about the dirty, sun-smitten streets, would have no basis of information upon which to form an opinion if it were not for the comings, goings, all the changes which take place amid a semi-maritime population," which is to say a population at the intersection of German, French, Spanish, British, and U.S. naval routes in the Caribbean.[41] Crane finds the people of the Dominican Republic to be improvements on their Haitian neighbors: "The citizen of San Domingo is a good deal of a man. He has not too much of the jealousy and suspicion that corrodes and perverts the Haytien; he is able to grasp modernity and apply it. He has distinctive ideas about sewage. There is not a town in a Spanish colony so clean, bright, cheering in every way. . . . And . . . as soon as a tropical town becomes clean its intelligence can be rated as of superior excellence." Concluding from this that "the more clean and modern the people the more they favor us," Crane reveals his own commitment to American expansion through the export of its technology.[42]

In many ways, Crane echoes in his journalism and war dispatches the basic principles of the U.S. foreign policy that John Hay developed at the same time.[43] In his 1899 interview in the London *Outlook*, "Mr. Stephen Crane on the New America," Crane distinguishes the United States from other imperial powers in ways remarkably similar to those of Hay and other government officials:

> The people of the United States consider themselves as a future Imperial Power only vaguely and with much wonder. The idea would probably never have occurred to them had it not been for foreign statements and definitions. The taking of Cuba was what they intended, and the taking of Porto Rico and the Philippines was a military necessity incumbent upon one country when it is engaged in war with another. . . . That is as far as the United States went in Imperialism. . . . As far as I see, there is no direct American sense of Imperialism. America stands on her land and she meets what she meets; she challenges whomsoever she challenges, and whomsoever comes may find her weak, but will never find her unwilling. I say this because I believe it.[44]

Crane endorses the popular belief of the time that U.S. annexation of the Philippines and Puerto Rico following the Spanish-American War was merely an "accident" of history, rather than compatible with the European powers' expansionist policies, as Mark Twain had criticized President McKinley in "To the Person Sitting in Darkness" (1901).[45]

Crane does criticize Great Britain, Germany, France, Spain, Italy, and Turkey for expansionist policies intended primarily to profit the home country, but he never comments on U.S. foreign policy as commercially motivated. He criticizes the British in such journalistic pieces as "A Foreign Policy in Three Glimpses" (1891) and "The Great Boer Trek" (1900); the Germans in China in his one-act satiric play "The Blood of the Martyr" (1898); the Spanish in virtually all of his dispatches for the New York *World* during the Spanish-American War, generally characterizing them as "evil"; the Russians in their contest with Great Britain over Afghanistan in "A Foreign Policy in Three Glimpses"; Italy as a purchaser of British "torpedo boats" for use in North Africa in his indictment of the British arms manufacturer Yarrow in "The Little Stilettos of the Modern Navy Which Stab in the Dark" (1898); and the Turks throughout his war dispatches from the Greco-Turkish War.[46] Consistent in all of these journalistic writings is Crane's patronizing attitude toward the native peoples of the colonized territories, especially when those native peoples are identifiable as people of color in Africa or the Caribbean. Throughout his dispatches from Cuba, he criticizes the "laziness," "cowardice," and "theft" of the Cuban insurgents, points he recalls in his 1899 interview for the London *Outlook*: "The Cubans will be given the independence . . . but they will be given it not until they have grown to manhood, so to speak. . . . The Cubans have not behaved well in the most prominent cases. . . . The Cuban says, 'We took San Juan Hill.' Any of us who were there know that there were no Cubans present within any other range than spent-shell range. . . . The Cubans back of the firing line stole his blanket-roll and his coat, and maybe his hat."[47]

In sum, Crane's anti-imperialist views are full of his contempt for peoples of color in Latin America, the Caribbean, and Africa. Although Mexican Indians, Afro-Cubans, and Africans are not African Americans, it is doubtful that Crane, who says so little of African Americans in his other writings, is making a case for Henry Johnson's salvation of Jimmie as a symbolic enactment of a revolution against the continuing racial injustice in post–Civil War America. Even Stallman's liberal claim for "The Monster" as "an appeal for brotherhood between white and black" may be open to question, although it is still possible that Crane expresses a sympathy for Henry Johnson's heroism and ritualized scapegoating that is equivalent to the compassion Crane expresses for such lower-class characters as Maggie Johnson in "Maggie: A Girl of the Streets" (1894) or George Kelcey, introduced to us as "a brown young man," in "George's Mother" (1896).[48]

These sympathies, however, are always qualified by Crane's characteristic narrative *distance* from his oppressed subjects; this narrative distance is epitomized by Crane's celebrated use of the "mock heroic," wonderfully illustrated by the opening scene from *The Red Badge of Courage*. Indeed, Crane uses the same disparity between his carefully constructed, often richly allusive narrative style and his characters' fractured dialects to represent Henry Johnson before he is disfigured and reduced to idiocy after the fire. The grandeur often parodically attributed to such characters, or at least their self-delusions, is actually Crane's style and authority, which allows him to rise above the otherwise deterministic world, made more so by modern technological progress, that turns the average citizen into a version of the native, the slave, the servant, or the "brown" working-class of the Bowery. Crane's use of the mock heroic also works within the established cultural codes of nineteenth-century gender hierarchies. The inflation of style involves a certain expansion of literary authority—the author "showing off" —that is part of the nineteenth-century masculine will-to-power.[49] Often identifiable by way of its explicit allusions or imitations of high-cultural works and styles (and those often classical), Crane's style displays "learning" of the sort identifiable in the period with the "educated *man*."[50] The common army shirt of the soldier in *The Red Badge of Courage* and the vulgar "lavender trousers" of Henry Johnson in "The Monster" become the showy trappings of Crane's style in both works, now transformed into the regal "red and gold" of this true "herald." As the moderns would make so explicit in their use of erotic rhetoric to represent their potent creative energies, *literary* authority can be made to appear richly phallic and thus sexually potent. For the sexually anxious Stephen Crane, the mock-heroic was merely one way he used literature to defend against such insecurities.

Among the various groups that help perpetuate Henry Johnson's "monstrosity" in "The Monster" is a group of women Crane uses to represent the everyday workings of gossip and its negative social consequences. Initially these women represent an alternative to the mechanism and determinism that appear to have invaded the masculine society of Whilomville, but Crane uses them ultimately to show how domestic space is structured according to the logic of the public sphere. Whereas the women of Whilomville ought to be sympathetic to Henry Johnson, whose heroism has saved one of their children, their gossip creates another, fantastic figure of Henry Johnson: a projection of the women's unconscious fears. Like the fire engines and factory sirens in the public sector, the women's gossip assumes a life of its own, independent of its different agents, until it utterly demonizes Johnson and contradicts what Crane leads us to believe are the maternal sensibilities of these women. By the end of the story, Crane argues that the domestic society maintained by women is as schizophrenic and mechanized as the masculine public world. Crane makes no effort in this regard to challenge the prevailing nineteenth-century hierarchy that subordinates feminine domesticity to masculine "civic virtue," even though much late nineteenth-century Anglo-American literature deals with the transgression of such gender boundaries.[51]

Most of these gossipy women are stock types, but Crane pays special attention to Martha Goodwin, whose Puritan tag-name complements her rigorous moral standards, which she applies in "adamantine" fashion to local and international problems:

> She was a woman of great mind. She had adamantine opinions upon the situation in Armenia, the condition of women in China, the flirtation between Mrs. Minster of Niagara Avenue and young Griscom, the conflict in the Bible class of the Baptist Sunday-school, the duty of the United States towards the Cuban insurgents, and many other colossal matters. Her fullest experience of violence was gained on an occasion when she had seen a hound clubbed, but in the plan which she had made for the reform of the world she advocated drastic measures. For instance, she contended that all the Turks should be pushed into the sea and drowned, and that Mrs. Minster and young Griscom should be hanged side by side on twin gallows. In fact, this woman of peace, who had seen only peace, argued constantly for a creed of illimitable ferocity. . . . Martha walked her kitchen with a stern brow, an invincible being like Napoleon. (M, 50)

Crane makes it clear that the violence of Martha Goodwin's moral judgment is an effect of her life's disappointments: "She lived with her married sister [and] performed nearly all the house work in exchange for the privilege of existence. Every one recognized her labor as a form of penance for the early end of her betrothed, who had died of smallpox, which he had not caught from her" (M, 49). Martha is what used to be called a "judgmental person," and Crane makes certain the reader understands that the consistency with which she condemns *everyone* is both ethically contradictory and secretly motivated by her personal disappointments.

What is genuinely *uncanny* about Martha Goodwin is that her foreign policy opinions agree with Crane's, except for the *violence* of drowning "all the Turks." Nevertheless, Crane certainly condemns the Turks for their massacre of at least 200,000 Armenians in 1894–1895, in reprisals for the organization of Armenians to protest the failure of the Turks to comply with the call for reforms in Turkish Armenia as provided by the Convention of Cyprus (June 4, 1878) and the Treaty of Berlin (July 13, 1878). In other respects, of course, Martha Goodwin's anti-Turkish views are conventionally Eurocentric, pitting as they do sympathies for Christian Armenians against Turkish Moslems.[52] Even her characterization as Napoleonic seems to agree with Crane's consistent admiration of Napoleon.[53] It is tempting to read these descriptions of Martha Goodwin as Crane's warning for the reader to take as seriously domestic policies of dominating and excluding minorities and women as the international stories of Turkish atrocities in Armenia or Spanish oppression of Cuban insurgents in the years prior to the Spanish-American War. Bill Brown notes that Martha Goodwin expresses "the nation's new imperialist internationality," specifically by linking "the local to the national and international."[54] Curiously, however, Crane trivializes just such an important connection between foreign and domestic affairs by identifying Martha Goodwin clearly with the mental schizophrenia he has earlier associated with the increasingly mechanized citizens of Whilomville: "Her dreams . . . were companioned in the kitchen curiously, Cuba, the hot-water kettle, Armenia, the washing of the dishes, and the whole thing being jumbled. . . . She was an engine, and the fact that she did not know that she was an engine contributed largely to the effect. . . . She remained a weak, innocent, and pig-headed creature, who alone would defy the universe if she thought the universe merited this proceeding" (M, 51).

A servant and victim of chance circumstance, Martha Goodwin ought to have sympathy for Henry Johnson, but her "character" is best expressed for Crane in her strangely equivocal judgments of "the monster." When she is told that Dr. Trescott is losing his patients because of his faithful support of the man who saved his son's life, she concludes: "'Serves him right if he was to lose all his patients,' she said suddenly, in blood-thirsty tones" (M, 52). But when she is told that Henry Johnson is responsible for making little Sadie Winter sick just from witnessing his "monstrosity," Martha disagrees, insisting that she has seen Sadie on her way to school many times since the girl's frightening encounter with Henry Johnson (M, 60). It is Sadie's father, Jake Winters, who is the first to reject Dr. Trescott's medical services, and it is Jake Winters's actions that cause Martha to say it will serve Dr. Trescott right if "he was to lose all his patients." Insisting that she "would try not to be afraid of" Henry Johnson, Martha nonetheless condemns Dr. Trescott for befriending the African American.

What Crane suggests with the character of Martha Goodwin is how moral standards in Whilomville have lost their proper reference in the face of the moral dilemma posed by the combination of Henry Johnson's subordinate racial identity, his heroism, and his deformity. In *Love and Death in the American Novel*, Leslie Fiedler considered "The Monster" yet another example of how American "literature defines so clearly the opposition between the demands of male loyalty and the claims of polite female society; and in none is the Negro more brutally portrayed at the limits of mindlessness and nauseating horror."[55] Connecting the representation of race and gender in Crane's narrative, Fiedler understands how the opposition between white male and female social spheres also affects the construction of racial boundaries. Whereas the domestic space controlled by women has been invaded by the mechanization and determinism of the masculine public sphere, so feminine "fickleness" and "irrationality"—both epitomized by women's gossip—have contaminated the civic space, where reason ought to rule. In short, both Henry Johnson and Martha Goodwin typify the *confusion* of realms that Crane considers symptomatic of modern decadence. "Heroic" African Americans and "political" women threaten the hierarchical order of Whilomville.

Martha's standard of justice exceeds the rigor of either the Old Testament or the Koran, but Crane seems intent on making his moral point that the problem in Whilomville has been caused by the failure of individuals to take responsibility for their actions. In so doing, he has made it impossible for us to judge the disfigured and brain-damaged Henry Johnson in any other way: he has "paid" for his salvation of Jimmie Trescott by losing his face, his mind, and his position as an African-American servant. Surrounded by citizens who have been subordinated to the machinery of the modern age and are thus incapable of thinking for themselves, consistently moral characters like Dr. Trescott are slowly driven mad by the fickleness of modern social behavior. Comforting his wife, Grace, who sadly sits alone in the dining room after she has been snubbed by the society women of Whilomville, Dr. Trescott consoles her in just the same way he had consoled Jimmie a few pages earlier: "'There, there. Don't cry, Jim'" and "'There, there,' he said. 'Don't cry, Grace. Don't cry'" (M, 57, 65). Whereas he makes an unfinished effort to explain to Jimmie the cruel consequences of Jimmie and his friends taunting Henry Johnson—"'Only I want to explain to you—'"—in his final encounter he makes no effort to explain, but merely counts the unused tea cups that represent the women who did not attend his wife's weekly reception: "As he sat holding her head on his shoulder, Trescott found himself occasionally trying to count the cups. There were fifteen of them" (M, 65). Like psychologically unbalanced patients trying desperately to gain some elementary grip on reality, Dr. Trescott is reduced to counting tea cups rather than explaining his moral philosophy.

Disempowered by his inability to comprehend what to do with Henry Johnson—that is, how to make Henry Johnson signify once again in normal society—Dr. Trescott begins to imitate the insanity of Martha Goodwin. Desperately trying to find in the pure formalism of the tea party's place settings the social significance of the feminine community from which Grace has now been excluded, Dr. Trescott is himself feminized according to the gender hierarchies of the nineteenth century. Earlier in the story, Crane represents Henry Johnson as parodying just such social forms and thereby intensifying his "monstrosity" even within the African-American community. Breaking out of the room he occupies in the "cabin" of Aleck and Mary Williams, where Judge Hagenthorpe has insisted Henry be segregated, Henry goes to his old girlfriend's house in "Watermelon Alley" and calmly invites her to a dance. As the family reacts in terror to his appearance, Henry mildly repeats his invitation: "I jes' drap in ter ax you if you won' do me the proud of acceptin' ma humble invitation to er daince, Miss Fa'gut" (M, 47).[56] Like the negro teamster on his "cracker box" in the opening of *The Red Badge of Courage*, Henry performs here the rhetorical act of prolepsis, anticipating the special "madness" of Dr. Trescott as he counts the tea cups. What continues to distinguish Henry Johnson from Dr. Trescott, however, is what weds Henry to the negro teamster: the performance of "race" that enables the dominant culture to commodify, control, and thereby "deface" African Americans. Blackface minstrelsy, theatrical performance, and "display" in museums and world's fairs become modernity's best means of maintaining fictions of race previously maintained by the violence of slavery.[57]

Because these acts by Dr. Trescott and Henry Johnson have been reduced to empty social "gestures," both characters have been feminized, but Crane's focus remains with Dr. Trescott, whose scientific and civic authority has been reduced by the end of the story to the level of his weeping wife and his monstrous servant. As he counts out the cups in the final sentence of the story, Dr. Trescott himself is reduced to a function of those numbers and statistics that characterize the mechanization of the self in the late nineteenth century. Seltzer uses the term "statistical persons" to describe the change from the nineteenth-century individual to the early modern subjectivity constructed by new industrial, market, and technological forces: "One of the new forms of life that the determinism/will polarity takes, in the later nineteenth century, is the statistical/anti-statistical polarity. And one form the statistical/anti-statistical polarity takes is the conflict between the logic of the market and possessive individualism and the logic of machine culture and disciplinary individualism. . . . Whereas the laissez-faire or atomistic conception of the individual protects an essential opposition between persons and cultures, the systemic conception of the individual understands persons as an effect or reflex of their culture."[58]

Reduced finally and quite pathetically to a "monster" propped on a "box" and veiled in "black crêpe," an object of entertainment for daring and taunting children, led by the very child he saved, Jimmie Trescott, Henry Johnson is an utterly commodified human being (M, 56). He is, however, only one step removed from the "dancing teamster," also on his "box," who performs for the Union troops in the opening paragraphs of *The Red Badge of Courage*. Indeed, commodification and spectacle are inextricably related in U.S. modernity.[59] They both "represent" for Crane, however, not the continuing racism in post–Civil War America, but the extreme commodification of the self that modernization threatens to effect in ordinary and decidedly *white* characters, like Henry Fleming and Dr. Trescott. Crane's argument in both literary works is, then, profoundly conservative as he reacts to what he brilliantly interprets as the emergence of a new kind of subjectivity shaped and determined by industrial culture and its technologies of the machine. To be sure, buried somewhere in this critique, there is the possibility of refunctioning Crane's argument to recall our attention to the African American, enslaved differently by the machinery of modern society than African Americans were by the rural practices of southern slavery, but enslaved nonetheless. Bill Brown makes this point effectively: "Crane's novel . . . specifies the maimed body of Henry Johnson as a literalization of the originary moment of American racism: a facelessness, the result of both literal and figurative maiming."[60] *Crane*, however, never provided us with the terms for such a critique, which depends upon our reinterpretation of literary naturalism as basic to the ideology of U.S. modernism. In his manipulation of lower-class "brown" people, African Americans, and other oppressed peoples of color to represent the frightening "wildness" our progress might strangely instill in us, he has contributed to the racial ideology of modernism in his very techniques of writing. In his use of nineteenth-century conventions of feminine domesticity and irrationality to represent the decadence of modern societies, he anticipates the characteristic modernist equation of woman with an otherness that variously threatens ideas of white male selfhood, national coherence, civic virtue, and sexual and racial identities.[61] In this way, Stephen Crane re-fought the Civil War not only in *The Red Badge of Courage* but also in works like "The Monster," and in so doing contributed to those ideological adjustments by which the United States adapted traditional hierarchies of race and gender to its pursuit of its destiny as a world power.

8

The Education of Henry Adams and the American Empire

He had nothing to do with Hay's politics at home or
abroad.[1]
> *The Education of Henry Adams*, chap. 24, 366.

With Hay's politics, at home or abroad, Adams had
nothing whatever to do.
> *The Education of Henry Adams*, chap. 24, 373.

The imperial power of the United States has traditionally relied
on its invisibility or what today might be termed its "deni-
ability." In "King Leopold's Soliloquy," Mark Twain claims that the invention of the Kodak may well be the means of exposing at long last the violence and cruelty of imperialism in the Belgian Congo.[2] Insofar as Twain
believes that photography's realism might really contribute to the down-
fall of European imperialism, then he betrays his naïveté regarding the ways
modern imperialism relies on cultural practices that shape our social psychologies and thus individual perceptions.[3] United States imperial power
may not be unique in the manifold ways it has disguised itself, but it has
certainly been notable for its ability to be accepted by another, nobler name,
such as national security, international responsibility, global policing, protection of free trade, or global diplomacy. Its apologists have also displayed
a perverse genius for feigning ignorance of its very existence and disbelief
that our foreign policies could ever be as brutal and immoral as those of
European imperialism. Just as the United States has claimed to be a class-
less society, so it has often declared itself to be anti-imperialist by virtue both
of its founding revolution and its democratic principles. We cannot, then,
simply point Twain's Kodak at U.S. imperialist ventures such as westward

expansion, the Mexican-American War, and the Spanish-American War and expect to expose the ideological means by which they were accepted quickly and easily by the majority of nineteenth-century Americans. We also have to direct our critical attention to those cultural texts where we might actually witness imperial ambition being disguised and denied. The ideological means by which a society refuses to accept responsibility for dominating and exploiting others must always be central to our cultural criticism, insofar as the ultimate aim of such criticism is an understanding that brings about social change.

From the many literary and cultural responses to the emergence of the United States as an imperial power from the end of the Spanish-American War to World War I, I have chosen *The Education of Henry Adams* for several reasons, not all of them compatible with each other. First, Adams writes almost nothing about U.S. and relatively little about European imperialism in his *Education*, despite his avowed purpose to represent the chief forces of "Twentieth-Century Multiplicity." His relative neglect of the political forces clearly reshaping the globe at the turn of the century might be considered merely a flaw in his general argument and thus a reason *not* to consider his book in this study, were it not that the *Education* works so hard to celebrate the life and character of Adams's close friend and Washington neighbor, John Hay, secretary of state in the McKinley and Roosevelt administrations and chief architect of the new American Empire.

Adams's *Education* is not, then, the obvious text to read to discover this elite American's judgments of "primitive" cultures and peoples in need of Western "civilization." In his letters from Tahiti and his "transcription" of the *Memoirs of Maura Taaroa, Last Queen of Tahiti* during his travels with John La Farge and La Farge's servant Awoki in the South Pacific, Adams more blatantly typifies the behavior of the privileged class of an imperial power surveying new territory. Much of this curious blend of tourism and political and economic will-to-power has been analyzed clearly in *Facing West*, written by Richard Drinnon, who early in his chapter on Adams in the South Seas quotes La Farge's version of "his friend's," Henry Adams's, "history lessons: 'The Pacific is our natural property. Our great coast borders it for a quarter of the world. We must either give up Hawaii, which will inevitably then go over to England, or take it willingly, if we need to keep the passage open to eastern Asia, the future battleground of commerce.'"[4] But Adams's snobbish letters from the South Pacific—from his colonial fascination with the apparently "opener" attitudes among the islanders toward sexual expression to his neo-Hegelian abhorrence of the backward "tribalism" of island politics—are not read today as *The Education of Henry Adams* is. Adams's letters and private "history lessons" to La Farge have to be ignored or conveniently forgotten in order for that curious classic of American literature to persist as the archetype of a certain skeptical modern American temper that has become fundamental to modernism.

In the interplay between what it says about the emergence of twentieth-century social and political forces and what it leaves strategically unsaid, *The Education of Henry Adams* exemplifies the subtle means by which American culture would help U.S. imperialism be accepted. My argument is not that this classic American work is actually crude propaganda, but that its very classic status—what causes it to be read by successive generations of serious readers—has much to do with the cultural work it continues to do on behalf of an imperialist ideology. More overtly propagandistic writings on both sides of the political fights over U.S. imperialism at the turn of the century read as dated and tendentious today; they may be of historical interest, but they tell us little about how this heritage has continued to shape our ideas of ourselves as "Americans" and our foreign policies in such late-modern conflicts as the Korean, Vietnam, and Persian Gulf wars.[5]

The Education of Henry Adams is directed at two audiences: the politically powerful Americans in whose company Henry Adams lived, and general American readers, probably white and middle-class, both male and female, in Adams's imagination. The private edition of *The Education* printed by Furst and Company at Adams's expense in 1907 was specifically directed to the power elite in the United States.[6] The public edition of 1918, published after Adams's death but planned by him in the instructions he left Henry Cabot Lodge, including the "Editor's Preface" that Adams wrote for Lodge's signature, was directed at middle-class readers confused by modernity and in need of explanatory theories ("A Dynamic Theory of History") and cultural role models (Henry Adams and John Hay). It is my contention that Henry Adams privately distributed those 100 copies of *The Education* because he wanted to make certain that what he had written would not offend his friends in the power elite by telling too much about how they maintained and wielded their considerable political, economic, and social power. Adams hoped the book would *not* offend his associates in this way, because he intended its public reception to be one in which such power would be acknowledged and accepted as necessary to rule the confusion of the modern age, especially as it was expressed in the changing international politics he analyzes in *The Education*. The protagonist of this narrative is, like the famous manikin of the "Preface," a fabrication that combines qualities of both Henry Adams and his politically powerful friend, John Hay. Unlike the manikin, however, this fabricated character is by no means intended to be a mere powerless effect of larger social and historical forces; the character constructed out of the historical Adams and Hay is intended to be twentieth-century America's "representative man."

In his biography of Adams, Ernest Samuels dates Adams's first plans for *The Education* in a variety of ways, including "the anniversary of Henry's wedding day in June 1904," with its reminder of the suicide of his wife, Marian, in 1885, and Adams's reading of his friend Henry James's *William Wetmore Story and His Friends* (1903), with its evocation of their New England generation and its fatal innocence of what history would bring (*Major Phase*, 318). As he wrote James on November 18, 1903: "So you have written not Story's life, but your own and mine,—pure autobiography,—the more keen for what is beneath, implied, intelligible only to me, and half a dozen other people still living."[7] Adams's mood of reminiscence, sometimes maudlin or excessively self-critical in the years 1903–1905, is mixed with his practical concerns to put the historical record in order regarding the significant lives of his powerful friends and relatives. From 1900 on, Adams's close friend and Washington neighbor, John Hay, had been in ill health made worse by the demands of his office as Theodore Roosevelt's secretary of state. A year and a half before John Hay died in July 1905, Adams wrote his friend from Paris in a jovial yet prophetic vein: "Please read Harry James's Life of Story! Also Morley's Gladstone! And reflect—wretched man!—that now you have knowingly forced yourself to be biographised! You cannot escape the biographer" (*Letters*, 5:526). Yet, it may well have been to escape becoming Hay's biographer that Adams wrote *The Education*, anticipating Hay's death and trying to find an alternative to what he described in that letter as the biographer's tendency to stick "pins" into historical figures, propped in their "cages," in the vain effort for them to "keep the lively attitude of nature" (*Letters*, 5:526).

In the aftermath of Hay's death, Adams would use *The Education* explicitly as his excuse for refusing the task of "biographising" his friend that Hay's widow and Adams's friends insisted he take on. As it turned out, Adams avoided the dreaded task only by agreeing to serve as "a kind of sub-editor" to Mrs. Hay's "artless" project of publishing *Letters of John Hay and Extracts from Diary*, which Ernest Samuels judges "one of the oddest memorials ever printed" (*Major Phase*, 397).[8] Typically ironic as Adams's claim was to have written *The Education* "'wholly due to piety on account of my father and John Hay (the rest being thrown in for mass),'" it nonetheless has a measure of truth in terms of what scholars have judged the pragmatic reasons for writing an autobiography so elusive and ironic (*Major Phase*, 397). Adams's *Education* reveals as it protects, explains as it mystifies, "confesses" as it represses some of the most significant personal and historical records of American modernity.

Adams had ended *Mont-Saint-Michel and Chartres* (1905) with the long chapter on "St. Thomas Aquinas," which was the part over which Adams had "worried" the most. St. Thomas both explained and thus hastened the transformation of Catholic religious authority in the Latin Middle Ages; what was a cultural "unity" for Adams under the authority of the Virgin Mary (the Cult of Mariolatry) was already multiplied in the rationalism of the Scholastics from Albertus Magnus to St. Thomas. In short, St. Thomas was a figure worthy of biography not for the sake of his personality, but by virtue of the historical transformation his work and life happened to identify and clarify. It has often been thought that Henry Adams is the modern equivalent of St. Thomas, and there is, of course, much to support this view.

Adams would have been pleased, indeed, to have been taken for a latter-day St. Thomas, figuring out the secrets of modern politics, history, and science with the same enthusiasm St. Thomas had theorized God's ways in the intricacies of scriptural hermeneutics.

The parallelism is both too neat and too exclusive, however, to tell the entire story of *The Education* as proper "companion text" to *Chartres*. St. Thomas is unthinkable without the Virgin, and I think that "Henry Adams," at least as this name figures in *The Education*, is unthinkable without John Hay. The medieval Virgin points to the unknowable Godhead of the Catholic church; the modern secretary of state points to the equally unfathomable authority of the nation state. St. Thomas ushers in modern "multiplicity" in his efforts to rationalize what the Virgin symbolically represents; Henry Adams carries that "multiplicity" a step further by attempting to explain and render intelligible the political authority that John Hay came to embody. Such analogies elevate, of course, the significance of both Henry Adams and John Hay to the level of cultural symbolism occupied by the Virgin and St. Thomas Aquinas, and it is precisely this symbolic apotheosis to which Henry Adams hoped his *Education* might contribute for both John Hay and him.

In the end, Adams did, then, write the biography of Hay that he tried desperately to elude, even as he did avoid "biographising" his friend, the statesman. He also wrote his "autobiography," despite his best efforts to keep such indulgence from the title page of a book he hoped would represent more than the mere vanity served by the many memoirs published by his powerful contemporaries. The lives and reputations of these two powerful men are deeply intertwined, and the circumspection of *The Education* regarding the personal secrets of one man usually applies as well to the other. Henry Adams imagined the two of them to constitute a single mythic figure—a new "representative American"—that he hoped to monumentalize in *The Education*; to achieve this end, however, Adams would have to avoid, if not deliberately bury, certain ugly facts about both of them.

The final 150 pages of Henry Adams's *Education*, from chapter 24, "Indian Summer," to chapter 35, "Nunc Age," confront the reader with the political and intellectual puzzles of Adams's contemporary world. This contemporary situation has been Adams's goal from the beginning of *The Education*; it is the troublesome product of the history he has analyzed with such care in the preceding chapters. Nowhere in *The Education* is Adams more deliberately confusing and evasive than in these concluding chapters. At the very moment that the reader expects Adams's preceding exposition to provide clarification of our contemporary situation, Adams plunges that reader into a chaos of names, dates, theories, competing disciplines, personal reminiscences. The world history Adams recounts from the Spanish-American War in 1898 to the Russo-Japanese War of 1904–1905 is, of course, enormously complicated in and of itself. With his penchant for finding chaos everywhere and ignorance in everyone, not least in himself, Adams seems to take pleasure in confusing the reader, as if to say, "There! You are as confused and powerless as I!" In a more generous vein, I might suggest that these chapters rhetorically simulate the kind of confusion experienced by a knowledgeable political observer faced with world events at the turn of the century. Confusing as those world events were, Adams makes them even more incomprehensible by digressing at crucial moments into philosophical speculations, tirades against the "New Woman," and sardonic judgments of the personalities of such major political figures as Teddy Roosevelt, Lord Pauncefote of Preston, Comte Cassini, John Hay, and the Kaiser. Scholars and critics have labored over these pages in efforts to do justice to the coherence of Adams's prose, often developing elaborate connections among "The Dynamo and the Virgin," "A Dynamic Theory of History," and the international politics described.[9]

Few critics, however, have been willing to read these pages in terms of their essentially digressive, discontinuous, and incoherent qualities, perhaps because there seems little profit in such work other than the conclusion that Henry Adams had lapsed already into his final nihilism. Instead, his world-weary pose in the last third of *The Education* is most often used to support the view of Henry Adams as radical skeptic and ironist, who has assumed a canonical place in American literature by displaying that contempt for politics so characteristic of the literary moderns.[10]

Like so many of these moderns, Henry Adams has been protected by his "literariness" from critiques of his political attitudes. In Henry Adams's case, there are practical reasons why such criticism might prove embarrassing. In his letters from 1890 to 1905, the year in which he wrote much of *The Education* and the Russo-Japanese War was settled by the Treaty of Portsmouth, Henry Adams repeatedly endorses the conservative political economy of his brother, Brooks Adams.[11] For both, U.S. economic expansion into new markets in the Far East, the Caribbean, Central America, and Africa is crucial to U.S. political stability as the powerful European colonial powers were either realigning their interests or losing their control of territories. Brooks favored the expansion of the domestic economy in accord with the development of new international trade routes and geopolitical commerce.

Timothy Paul Donovan acknowledges that "Henry Adams agreed to some extent with his brother's concern" but concludes that Henry "could never become quite as exercised. This was because Henry had resigned himself, at least intellectually, if not emotionally, to the fact of eventual degradation. Brooks' proposals would only delay the process; they would not avoid it."[12] Yet, Donovan's distinction of Henry's view from Brooks's depends primarily on Henry's literary writings, not on his correspondence in this period. The pose of world-weary, baffled, belated eighteenth-century observer of twentieth-century chaos is, as most literary critics have insisted, a highly stylized pose or narrative device. In his correspondence, Adams advises the most powerful leaders of his age to pursue policies that would consolidate the twentieth-century economic authority of the United States in international trade and serve as the basis for that special brand of U.S. neocolonialism understood in the era of the Vietnam War in the phrase "establishing spheres of influence."

Henry Adams's own contrived literary myth of the "manikin" on which the "education" of modern history would have to be draped has encouraged literary critics and even historians to forget the active role he played in U.S. foreign policy in the years of John Hay's service as secretary of state. Despite his insistence that he was simply an "eighteenth-century observer" of the monstrous birth of the twentieth-century world, Adams was an active participant in the crucial diplomatic negotiations that established the United States as the leading economic and political power from the end of the Spanish-American War and the annexation of the Philippines to the Russo-Japanese War of 1904–1905. These seven years, under the administrations of McKinley and Teddy Roosevelt, constitute the critical moment in which U.S. empire was developed.

Hay was ambassador to England—his reward for financially and politically supporting McKinley as the Republican candidate—when President McKinley invited him to become secretary of state in place of William R. Day, who was to head the peace commission in Paris at the close of the Spanish-American War.[13] In fact, Adams was with the Hays in Egypt when Hay's private secretary "Spencer Eddy brought them a telegram to announce the sinking of the *Maine* in Havana Harbor" (EHA, 360) and in England with the Hays at Surrenden Dering when "the order [came] summoning Hay to the State Department" (EHA, 364). When Adams returned to Washington at the end of 1898, "he bumped into Hay at his 'very doorstep,'" who immediately appealed to him for help (*Major Phase*, 192). Samuels recounts how the political patronage system made it impossible for Hay to offer Adams what Hay so needed: his friend as assistant secretary of state or something comparable. Adams himself had hoped to succeed Hay as ambassador to the Court of St. James (England), thus continuing the legacy of his father, in whose legation Adams served in London through the Civil War. Although Adams expressed great "relief" at having so alienated the McKinley administration that formal appointment was impossible, he understood clearly that he was to play the role of personal advisor to Hay: "The two friends fell into the habit of taking a walk at four o'clock each day 'through a triangle of back streets' reviewing the day's work and, as Hay put it, 'discoursing of the finances of the world, and the insolent prosperity of the United States'" (*Major Phase*, 193).

In *Authority and Alliance in the Letters of Henry Adams*, Joanne Jacobson describes Adams's keen interest in "offering counsel on political events" to Hay soon after Hay assumed "the ambassadorship to England."[14] Jacobson interprets Adams's correspondence as generally divided between the demands of the public sphere and his desire to maintain a private world restricted to a small circle of intimates. What is striking about his letters between 1898 and

1905, however, is their directness in treating foreign policy issues and the clear sense that Adams was acting as informal counsel to Hay. Jacobson also points out that as close friends and next door neighbors in Washington, Hay and Adams discussed U.S. foreign policy in even greater detail in conversation, making Adams's letter writing thereby serve as "an instrument of worldview—and of an alliance—within which private loyalty could viably compete with public power."[15]

Jacobson makes a good case for the literary qualities of Adams's epistolary mode—he was unquestionably one of the great letter writers in modern English, so her general thesis tends to stress the resemblances between the literary control of *The Education* and his correspondence.[16] Useful as her approach may be generally to the form and function of Adams's letters, it is still part of an aestheticizing of Adams to which he surely contributed and which has distracted us from political views quite forthrightly and consistently expressed in his correspondence with and about Hay between 1898 and 1905. It is the difference separating the irony, equivocation, and rhetorical ambiguity in *The Education* from the conviction and decisiveness of his correspondence that strikes me as curious and still largely ignored by both historians and literary critics.

In the midst of the many ambitious, self-serving, greedy, and jingoistic statesmen of this period, John Hay and Henry Adams appeared to uphold principles of rational diplomacy and to balance conflicting international interests in ways that would prevent world war. The popular reputation of Hay as a selfless statesman forced to compromise rational principles of diplomacy to the imperialist zeal of Teddy Roosevelt stretches from Adams's *Education* and William Roscoe Thayer's *The Life and Letters of John Hay* (1915) to Gore Vidal's historical novel *Empire* (1987), and it is obviously the sort of paradoxical position that is compatible with Adams's own views on the "degradation of the democratic dogma."[17] One of the last political survivors of the Abraham Lincoln administration, Hay suited well Adams's own self-image of the eighteenth-century rationalist struggling to cope with the madness of twentieth-century politics.

Richard Drinnon traces Hay's political lineage directly to Thomas Jefferson, John Quincy Adams, and William H. Seward. In the matter of Cuba's annexation, Jefferson helped motivate our long obsession with annexing the island by predicting in the 1820s its eventual acquisition by the United States.[18] As President James Monroe's secretary of state, John Quincy Adams had expanded our imperial vision to include "the West Indies . . . and Cuba," along with the North American continent as our "proper dominion."[19] As secretary of state under Lincoln and Andrew Johnson (1861–1869), Seward "purchased Alaska, . . . tried to buy the Danish Virgin Islands and the Spanish islands of Cuba and Puerto Rico, tried to annex Haiti or Santo Domingo or both, and advocated annexation of Hawaii."[20]

John Hay was more modern than his predecessors, in part because he envisioned American imperialism in the new century to be built upon commercial foundations. More than anyone else in the period 1898–1905, Hay helped popularize U.S. foreign policy, in part by skillfully manipulating the public image of the secretary of state. He was the Henry Kissinger of his own age, and he helped to promote the myth that American expansion in the Caribbean, Pacific, and Far East expressed the commercial interests and general "will" of the American people. Hay initiated the custom of regular press conferences, and he had remarkably strong support from the press in an otherwise turbulent period. In his speech "American Diplomacy," delivered at the New York Chamber of Commerce on November 19, 1901, shortly after McKinley died, Hay represents the United States as the world's peacekeeper, intent on preserving economic opportunities and the political autonomy of all nations: "We have striven, on the lines laid down by Washington, to cultivate friendly relations with all powers, but not to take part in the formation of groups or combinations among them. A position of complete independence is not incompatible with relations involving not friendship alone, but concurrent action as well in important emergencies."[21]

As secretary of state, Hay pursued aggressively the territorial ambitions of his predecessors by focusing on those regions most likely to contribute to U.S. commercial success. Negotiating the dispute with Canada "over Alaska's southeastern boundary" after gold was discovered in the Klondike, assuring Hawaii's annexation (July 7, 1898) even before he arrived in Washington to assume office, and partitioning Samoa with Germany to gain "U.S. sovereignty over several of the islands, including Tutuila and its harbor Pago Pago, destined to become a strategic naval base," Hay promoted mining and sugar interests, as well as establishing future commercial routes to Asia.[22] Hay's successes merely realized the imperial ambitions of what Richard Drinnon has called "the Adams-Seward-Hay empire" that virtually organizes U.S. foreign policy, as well as popular attitudes toward "foreign" peoples and cultures, throughout the nineteenth century.[23]

Yet, Hay's realization of earlier extraterritorial ambitions generally fits his more modern foreign policy of controlling global industry and commerce. No two policies better epitomize Hay's modernity than his negotiations of the treaties that would allow the United States to build the Panama Canal and his "Open Door Policy" in China. In his early diplomatic efforts to supersede the Clayton-Bulwer Treaty of 1850, which had prevented the United States from building a canal alone, Hay was intent on a Nicaraguan canal that would be politically neutral, like the Suez Canal, as its governance had been defined in the Convention of Constantinople (1888). The new canal would have to be kept open in times of war and peace to ships of all nations without discrimination, it could not be fortified, the territory around the canal could not be colonized, and other powers were invited to subscribe to these international guarantees. That treaty was signed with Lord Pauncefote on February 5, 1900, but Congress insisted on three amendments: specific abrogation of the Clayton-Bulwer Treaty of 1850, removal of the prohibition of fortification of the canal, and deletion of the clause requiring the concurrence of other powers. Teddy Roosevelt had argued vigorously that the original treaty created a canal that made the United States militarily vulnerable, rather than providing the sort of defense that Roosevelt insisted was necessary in the wake of the Spanish-American War. Although Hay resigned his position in response to these congressional amendments, President McKinley convinced him to try again, and the amended Hay-Pauncefote Treaty was signed on November 18, 1901, the day before Hay's speech "American Diplomacy."[24]

Whereas McKinley and Theodore Roosevelt still conceived of foreign policy in terms primarily of domestic defense, Hay viewed foreign policy in terms of the commercial interests he was convinced would replace military conquest as the focus of twentieth-century international politics. In "American Diplomacy" he equates our "peace-loving" character with "our normal activities . . . in the direction of trade and commerce; . . . the vast development of our industries imperatively demands that we shall not only retain and confirm our hold on our present markets, but seek constantly, by all honorable means, to extend our commercial interests in every practicable direction" (Hay, 122).

Hay's negotiations with Great Britain for a Central American canal were quite explicitly related to Hay's "Open Door Policy" in the Far East. His notes for the Open Door policy date from 1899–1900, and they are clearly motivated by his desire to keep China and the Far East open to U.S. commercial interests: "In the same spirit we have sought, successfully, to induce all the great powers to unite in a recognition of the general principle of equality of commercial access and opportunity in the markets of the Orient. We believe that 'a fair field and no favor' is all we require; and with less than that we can not be satisfied. If we accept the assurances we have received as honest and genuine, as I certainly do, that equality will not be denied us; and the result may be safely left to American genius and energy" (Hay, 122–23). In keeping with Drinnon's argument that Hay merely followed out the policies of nineteenth-century American imperial ambitions, we can conclude that Hay's "Open Door Policy" realized our long-held ambition to play a more central colonial role in the nineteenth-century European struggles to colonize Asia.[25] But there was also a certain timeliness to Hay's policies that allowed him to succeed where previous foreign policy architects, like John Quincy Adams and Seward, had failed. Hay's rapid consolidation of American imperial power depended, of course, on the work of his predecessors, but his "new empire" was achieved in large part because of Hay's understanding that it would be built on economic foundations and protected by U.S. cultural superiority. His posture in both the negotiations for the canal treaties and the settlement of European colonial claims in China in the aftermath of the Boxer Rebellion was that of the selfless statesman representing a government without imperial ambitions and committed only to world peace.

Self-evidently capable as U.S. commercial "genius and energy" might be of succeeding in "open competition" with the other commercial interests of the world, Hay was also working hard to guarantee such success. Having emerged from the Boxer Rebellion of 1900 both as a popular hero and as confirmed in the correctness of his "Open Door" policies, Hay negotiated the Canal Treaty with Great Britain in order to get Britain's assurances that it would withdraw from the Caribbean. In the press, Hay was simply defending the Monroe Doctrine, but in private negotiations Hay was trading the guarantee of U.S. dominance in the Caribbean and Central America for U.S. support of Britain's position in the Far East. Behind the apparently disinterested diplomacy on behalf of open commercial competition for increasingly global markets, Hay favored the Anglo-American imperial hegemony that would confirm their cultural and national superiority over "decadent" imperial powers and civilizations like China and Spain. In the racialist thinking of the nineteenth and early twentieth centuries, Hay's endorsement of Anglo-American coalition politics confused linguistic and historical ties between the two nations as *racial* filiation: "All in the family . . . were these bonds across the Atlantic, and in Hay's words, they had a near religious sanction. *Racism* bound kinspeople not only across space but across time, over the centuries binding together Puritan New Israelites with *fin de siècle* 'new' imperialists."[26]

The Hay-Pauncefote Treaty involved a number of other treaties with Colombia (Hay-Herrán Treaty of 1903) and with the new Republic of Panama. In the latter case, the Hay-Bunau-Varilla Treaty of November 18, 1903, granted the United States the Canal Zone in order to realize the Senate amendments requiring U.S. fortification and defense of the Panama Canal. Thus Hay's negotiations with Great Britain regarding the canal virtually guaranteed U.S. economic and political dominance in Central America, Colombia, and the Caribbean for the rest of the twentieth century. Hay considered these negotiations to be the beginning of a new coalition between the United States and Great Britain as the superpowers of the twentieth century. Hay was an enthusiastic Anglophile; his seventeen months as ambassador to Great Britain had been the happiest of his life. As Drinnon points out, Hay arrived "at his post in 1897, the year of Queen Victoria's Diamond Jubilee and, for all the imperial pomp and circumstance, the year her ministers searched more anxiously than ever for allies to protect the British Empire against the rise of Germany," as well as other competitors for her empire around the globe.[27]

In *The Education* and his correspondence from the 1890s to the end of his life, Henry Adams characterized himself as a dedicated Anglophobe. In *The Education*, he revels in what he takes to be the collapse of the British Empire, although he interprets the decline of British influence to be the sign of Russia's growing global dominance. Indeed, Adams's prediction that Russia would become the new "riddle" of historical forces for the historian to comprehend is often cited in support of his own ironic claims that "a dynamic theory of history" could be used to "predict" future events. Fear of Russia's "unpredictability" in global politics caused many of Adams's contemporaries, including vigorous anti-imperialists like Mark Twain and William Dean Howells, to advocate grudgingly alliances between the United States and Great Britain to "block" expansion by Russia and Germany, especially in Asia.[28]

In the years 1898–1905, one hardly needed the title of "scientific historian" to be able to predict the growing power of Russia and the Far East in international affairs or to anticipate the decline of the British imperium. Although he claimed not to share Hay's personal fondness for the British, Adams endorsed most of Hay's foreign policy decisions, most often on their shared understanding that the "new age" would depend upon commercial, rather than political, balances of power. In a letter to Brooks Adams of November 3, 1901, two weeks before the Hay-Pauncefote Treaty was signed and eight months after the U.S. annexation of the Philippines, Adams writes:

> All our interests are for political peace to enable us to wage economical war. Therefore I hold our Philippine excursion to be a false start in the wrong direction, and one that is more likely to blunt our energies than to guide them. It is a mere repetition of the errors of Spain and England. I wish we could have avoided it, or could escape it, and return to concentrating our efforts on the North Pacific. . . . Our true road leads to the support of Russia in the north—in both cases meaning our foothold in Asia. (*Letters*, 5:306)

Adams's reputation as historian and man of letters is built upon the scholarly account of his great powers of political prophecy: predicting in *The Education*, as well as in other writings, the new balance-of-power politics, the central role played by the United States in such politics, the emergence of the United States and Russia as "superpowers," and even the horrors of European fascism.[29] Part of this myth is that Adams foresaw also the terrible costs of the new foreign policies being adopted by the United States, including our eventual mistakes in the Cold War and Southeast Asia. Yet, most of what Adams "predicts" in *The Education* is the rise of the United States to global dominance, a future established rather clearly by the diplomatic work of his close and powerful friend, John Hay.[30]

My claim that Hay and Adams basically favored U.S. expansionism by way of developing commercial trade routes, opening foreign markets favorable to the United States, and controlling regions by way of "spheres of influence" is based on a rejection of the conventional accounts of both McKinley and Hay as "reluctant" advocates of imperialism, "forced" by historical events in the Spanish-American War to "pick up" that "white-man's burden" of which Kipling speaks in his odious little poem. By the same token, I do not wish to portray either Adams or Hay as a cynical manipulator of mass opinion working to consolidate the secret power of U.S. global dominance. A more nuanced historical account is needed of both figures, each of whom was a product of his historical moment and the good fortune that had positioned both men in situations of political power and social authority.

Hay and Adams's responses to the Spanish-American War and the Philippine-American War are crucial elements in my thesis, not only because Hay and Adams ostensibly differed over the future of U.S. involvement in the Philippines but also because of the curious part "the Spanish War" plays in *The Education*. "Indian Summer" (1898–1899) initiates the final movement of Adams's great work by invoking the complex historical questions raised by the Spanish-American and Philippine-American wars, only to sidestep the questions raised and both defer to Hay as political leader and distinguish Adams's from Hay's politics. The index to *The Education* lists one page number for "Philippines," p. 363, the second page of this chapter, and it is the invocation of the Philippines as a political issue and its repression in this chapter that renders Adams's political views so strange in this work.

The title for chapter 24, "Indian Summer," has rarely been taken to mean anything other than the idiom for "the final years of a person's life, regarded as being serene, tranquil, reminiscent, etc."[31] This is the principal way Adams will use the phrase throughout the rest of *The Education*, albeit with a certain sardonic twist about the incompatibility of his personal age with American modernity. But Adams's reference to the "summer of the Spanish War" that "began the Indian summer of life" suggests another, ironic connotation typical of his style. The irony of Henry Adams's "Indian summer" on reaching "sixty years of age" being one hardly tranquil when viewed in terms of international politics seems typical also of the general play between public chaos and private stoicism so characteristic of *The Education*. Yet, the other connotation of "Indian" summer is the suggestion that U.S. Manifest Destiny is finding a new project.

Adams could have easily put this irony to an anti-imperialist purpose, but he leaves it strangely undeveloped. Chapter 23 concludes with news of the sinking of the *Maine*, Hay's recall to the United States, and the Spanish-American War as the next proper topic of Adams's discussion. Instead, it is repressed or, perhaps more accurately, dismissed easily by Adams in the second and third paragraphs of chapter 24 (EHA, 363–64). Given Adams's strong views favoring Cuban independence from Spain, his apparent opposition to U.S. annexation of the Philippines, and his brother Charles Francis Adams's active role in these years as vice president of the Anti-Imperialist League, Adams's "silences" here are more worthy of interpretation than what he does say.[32] In his correspondence from late 1898 to 1899, Henry complains that "my brother Charles has once more made a fool of himself by talking . . . idiotically" against the annexation of the Philippines and condemns generally the "anti-imperialist crowd" as "one that I would rather have nothing to do with" (*Letters*, 4:633, 662).[33]

Defenders of Adams might reasonably object that his anti-imperialist views are well represented by his support of Cuban revolutionaries both in Cuba and in Washington, D.C., and that these activities are clearly represented in chapter 23 of *The Education*. Samuels recounts how Clarence King, who followed "the rebel General Gomez' masterly campaign across Santiago province" in 1895, enlisted Adams in active support of the Cuban insurgency, who in his turn urged Hay, "Come and revolute Cuba" (*Major Phase*, 161–62). In *The Education*, Adams recalls his visit to Cuba in January 1894 as a prelude to the coming revolution, a result of "the decaying fabric, which had never been solid" of Spanish colonial rule, which when it "fell on their heads . . . drew them with it into an ocean of mischief" (EHA, 349). Adams's metaphor of "an ocean of mischief" is deliberately obscure, even as it refers unavoidably to the Caribbean, thrown into upheaval in 1895 both by the Venezuela border dispute between the United States and Britain and the Cuban revolution. Both crises turned on the question of which nation would assume power in the Western Hemisphere for the next century. Spanish decadence and misrule, often for Adams replaying popular stereotypes of "Latin" inferiority, had clearly doomed its empire, especially in the Western Hemisphere; the only question was whether the United States or Great Britain would take its place and former colonies. In his second term (1893–1897), President Grover Cleveland rattled the Monroe Doctrine in the face of the British in the Venezuelan border dispute, but his proclamation of neutrality in June 1895 with regard to the Cuban revolution drove Adams and King into alliance with those who had long dreamt of annexing Cuba either as a formal territory or as a sphere of U.S. commercial and political influence. [34]

Delighted with his apparent radicalism of entertaining in his Washington home young Cuban revolutionaries, like Gonzalo de Quesada and Horatio Rubens, Adams also worked behind the scenes for formal governmental support of Cuban independence. Writing Senator James Donald Cameron's speech offering a "minority amendment" to the Senate Foreign Relations Committee's "joint resolution calling for recognition of Cuba" and providing Senator Henry Cabot Lodge with material for his speech condemning Spain and endorsing a free Cuba, Adams relished the role of radical friend to the revolutionaries (*Major Phase*, 164). In fact, it was a radicalism that drove Adams, as he confesses in chapter 23 of *The Education*, into the conservative camp of pro-imperialists who viewed the defeat of Spain and the exclusion of Great Britain from the Caribbean as two essential components in the foundation of U.S. hemispheric hegemony. In his speech in the Senate, Lodge argued: "Free Cuba would mean a great market to the United States; it would mean an opportunity for American capital, invited there by signal exemptions" (Lodge, as quoted in *Major Phase*, 164). [35]

Adams puts the matter more circumspectly in *The Education*, but the political consequence is to align him with pro-imperialist forces and, however reluctantly, with the hated trusts:

> The Cuban rebellion served to sever that last tie that attached Adams to a Democratic administration. He thought that President Cleveland could

have settled the Cuban question, without war, had he chosen to do his duty, and this feeling, generally held by the Democratic Party, joined with the stress of economical needs and the gold standard to break into bits the old organization and to leave no choice between parties. (EHA, 349)

Adams's suggestion that his criticisms of President Cleveland are shared by the Democratic party, which did not return Cleveland for the presidential nomination at the 1896 Democratic Convention, is very misleading. The Democrats nominated, of course, William Jennings Bryan to stand against McKinley, who would win the election, and Bryan's anti-imperialist stance is in direct disagreement with Adams's call for U.S. support of Cuban freedom. Just what Adams means by President Cleveland doing "his duty" on the "Cuban question" is left deliberately unclear, but the meanings range from mere political support of Cuba to annexation of the island. Reveling as usual in the signs of political and economic disorder, Adams complains to Brooks Adams in January 1896 that President Cleveland is driving the country to the breaking point, concerning the outcome of which "Lombard Street, Wall Street and State Street" "for once" "seem to agree with me," whose point after all is: "Of course I want [the country] to break. I see no hope of safety except in severing the ties that connect it with Europe, and in fortifying ourselves as an independent centre" (*Letters*, 4:362).

Perhaps Adams believed that the vigorous affirmation of the Monroe Doctrine would enable the United States not only to become the dominant power in the hemisphere but also break its lingering ties with European power, especially its old colonial master, Great Britain. But it is more likely that Adams understood our hemispheric policy as John Hay would formulate it publicly during his tenure as secretary of state. Great Britain would agree to withdraw from further colonial ventures in the Western Hemisphere, leaving the field to U.S. hegemony, as long as we supported British interests in the Pacific and Asia. Behind the talk of independence for the United States, Hay envisioned political cooperation between the United States and Great Britain as the imperial powers of the new century. Indeed, Great Britain not only supported the United States in the Spanish-American War but privately urged us to annex Cuba, as Hay wrote Senator Lodge from London in April 1898: "What I should have done, if the feeling here had been unfriendly instead of cordially sympathetic, it is hard to say. The commonest phrase is here: 'I wish you would take Cuba at once. We wouldn't have stood it this long.' And of course no power on earth would have shown such patience and such scrupulous regard for law."[36]

In his letters and *The Education*, Adams trivializes the Spanish-American War as an unfortunate consequence of an indecisive U.S. foreign policy in the Cleveland administration. A strong policy supporting Cuban independence in the years 1895–1896 might have averted the war, Adams argues, but his position in this regard seems less informed by his commitments to emancipatory movements and his antipathy to colonial oppression than by his desire for U.S. hegemony in the Western Hemisphere and the consolidation of the United States as a new economic and political "center" in the face of mounting evidence of the decay of older orders of "civilization," such as Spain and Great Britain, in the Caribbean, South America, South Africa, Manchuria, and the Philippines.[37] Far from being evidence that Henry Adams was a liberal advocate of anti-colonial struggle in Cuba, his support of the Cuban insurgency was from the beginning part of his sense that the United States must assume its role at the center of the new hemispheric, if not global, imperium.

Nevertheless, Adams's neglect of the Spanish-American and Philippine-American wars in chapter 24 cannot be completely explained simply on the grounds that he has anticipated their outbreak and outcomes by virtue of his involvement in the first stages of the Cuban revolution. The silences in chapter 24 speak volumes about Adams's tacit endorsement of Hay's foreign policy of U.S. expansionism in the Philippines, and they set the tone for the rest of *The Education*'s criticism of imperialism as primarily the work of European powers or Russia. In effect, the United States is exempted from such criticism, John Hay serving as its personification and thus legitimation. Instead, Adams criticizes the English and the Germans in the Boer War and China, and the Russians in Mongolia and Eastern Europe.[38] What Adams does write about the Spanish-American War suggests that his reservations about U.S. involvement in the Philippines have less to do with his criticism of imperialism and more to do with his endorsement of the white man's "burden" of colonial responsibilities:

> He knew that Porto Rico [sic] must be taken, but he would have been glad to escape the Philippines. Apart from too intimate an acquaintance with the value of islands in the South Seas, he knew the West Indies well enough to be assured that, whatever the American people might think or say about it, they would sooner or later have to police those islands, not against Europe, but for Europe, and America too. (EHA, 363–64)

In the only other reference he makes to the Philippines in this chapter and in *The Education* as a whole, Adams understands it as a way of realizing finally the Adamses' ambitions "of bringing England into an American system" (EHA, 362). What Samuels glosses in this context as Adams's "characteristic overstatement of the family policy" is in effect Adams's endorsement, despite his Anglophobia, of Hay's alliance with Great Britain (EHA, 644, n5). In fact, what the Philippines finally mean for Adams is just this Anglo-American alliance in the new balance-of-power politics necessitated by the decline of British imperial hegemony and the rise of multiple colonial powers: "As he sat at Hay's table, listening to any member of the British Cabinet, for all were alike now, discuss the Philippines as a question of balance of power in the East, he could see that the family work of a hundred and fifty years fell at once into the grand perspective of true empire-building, which Hay's work set off with artistic skill" (EHA, 363).

Richard Drinnon does not link Adams and Hay's attitudes toward the United States as an imperial power beyond their association as friends and members of the ruling elite, but his chapters on Adams and Hay in *Facing West* are companion pieces, joined by the passage quoted above from *The Education*, which Drinnon uses as the epigraph to "The Open Door of John Hay."[39] Drinnon fully comprehends, then, the common characteristics of wealth, privilege, and political connections that made Hay and Adams such fast friends. As a historian, he focuses understandably on the far more influential foreign policies carried out by John Hay, in keeping with imperial ambitions that stretch historically from Adams's grandfather John Quincy Adams to Hay and pays little attention to Adams's classic, *The Education*. But what *The Education of Henry Adams* highlights is the extent to which a modern statesman like John Hay would rely on a certain rhetorical artistry to sell his policies and thus find compatible the legitimation of literary work like Adams's autobiography, in which Hay becomes the new representative man.

It is the uncanny connection between Hay's empire-building and his artistic skill that prompts Adams to digress so obviously in the remainder of this chapter from the major issue on the minds of most Americans in 1898–1899: the future role of the United States in the Caribbean (Cuba, Puerto Rico, and Central America) and the Pacific (Hawaii and the Philippines). The evidence that some sort of repression is at work in the rest of this chapter is coded between the lines, in graceful rhetorical connections left undeveloped and too subtle for any but the professional reader. He is at Surrenden Dering with the Camerons and Hays when the "July 4, 1898" telegram arrives "announcing the destruction of the Spanish Armada, as it might have come to Queen Elizabeth in 1588; and there, later in the season, came the order summoning Hay to the State Department" (EHA, 364).

Of course, John Hay is Henry Adams's doppelgänger in these later chapters of *The Education*, with all the psychic ambivalences built into Rank's term.[40] On the one hand, Hay is the proper heir to the political ambitions of the Adamses for the United States, a legacy Henry had failed to carry on. On the other hand, Henry insists that he "had nothing to do with Hay's politics at home or abroad" and repeats this claim in a rhetorical chiasmus that I have reproduced in the epigraphs to this chapter and that forms the psychic knot of Adams's chapter 23. Having connected Hay with his family legacy by way of Hay's new foreign policy, Adams overtly rejects Hay's politics only to reclaim them covertly. Admiral George Dewey's destruction of the Spanish fleet in Manila Bay is the equivalent of Sir Francis Drake's destruction of the Spanish Armada in the Bay of Cadiz in 1587.

Adams dances away from the real issues for Americans in 1898–1899 by substituting discussions of his visit to Italy with the Lodges, recalling his study of medieval law at Harvard, and chatting about John La Farge's stained glass windows for Trinity Church in Boston. Amid these diversions, however, the Adams who "had nothing whatever to do" with "Hay's politics, at home or abroad," continues to justify Hay's policies. Whereas Twain and Howells, among other anti-imperialists, vilified President McKinley for his expansionist policies, Adams treats the president and his secretary of state as efficient managers: "Mr. McKinley . . . undertook to pool interests in a general trust into which every interest should be taken, more or less at its own valuation, and whose mass should, under his management, create efficiency. He achieved very remarkable results. . . . Himself a marvelous manager of men, McKinley found several manipulators to help him, almost as remarkable as himself, one of whom was Hay" (EHA, 373–74).[41]

Adams characterizes both statesmen with corporate rhetoric certainly intended to be ironic. True to his eighteenth-century heritage, Adams displays contempt in *The Education* for the capitalists, with their syndicates and monopolies, that he judged to be usurping political and social power from the older ruling elite from which he was descended. In his correspondence, he even sounds an anti-imperialist note when he hopes Congress will "save Cuba from the sugar-planters and syndicates whose cards McKinley will play, and who are worse than Spain" (*Letters*, 4:599). But what appears to be his anti-imperialist pose in such passages turns out merely to be his paranoia regarding "capitalists" pursuing private interests at the expense of the larger vision he shares with his brother Brooks for an American Empire: "I want peace. I want it quick. I want it at any reasonable sacrifice. I want it before we are obliged to annex Spain itself, in order to save our own heads. . . . I want it in order to recover our true American policy, which Congress has abandoned and McKinley has betrayed, but which must be the basis of every future extension towards Asia" (*Letters*, 4:599). Adams invokes in this letter to Brooks his ideal of American expansion across the Pacific to Asia (the so-called "Pacific Rim" in our contemporary idiom), rather than competition with England, whose empire is still vital, or with Spain, whose empire Adams judges to be finished: "The world has entered on a new phase of the most far-reaching revolution, and our only danger is lest the ruins of the old empires should tumble too quickly on America" (*Letters*, 4:599).

The United States must assume the role of leadership in this new and revolutionary phase, but Adams sees its destiny beset on all sides. He repeatedly identifies self-interested capitalists as "Jews," but he fears "the socialist—not the capitalist—who is going to swallow us next" even more. With Europe "in a parlous state," Adams sounds an apocalyptic warning that "If we do not take care, we shall drag the whole rotten fabric down on our heads," by which he means the ruins of the older European imperial systems epitomized by Spain's, now in the course of being replaced by the new economic orders—capitalist or socialist—of modern industrialism (*Letters*, 4:598–99). In the face of such real and imagined dangers, Adams appeals to the political order that Hay brings, even when he is burdened with leaders like McKinley or Theodore Roosevelt.

In *The Education*, Adams offers the Hay-Pauncefote Treaty as strong evidence supporting his thesis that McKinley and Hay were "efficient" managers and "manipulators" in the midst of such global disorder. Once again, the imperialist issues associated with the Philippines are side-stepped, but in a way that subtly justifies U.S. foreign policy in the South Pacific. Alliance with Great Britain is the United States' great destiny, Adams argues, and the British diplomats argue for us, as Kipling would in "The White-Man's Burden," that "the Philippines [is] a question of balance of power in the East." Working together, Anglo-American powers defeat Spain not only in military battle but also in treaties like the Hay-Pauncefote, with its consequences for U.S. hegemony in the Caribbean and British access to Asia.[42]

Little wonder, then, that the great theorist of twentieth-century multiplicity should conclude chapter 23 by insisting upon unity: "History has no use for multiplicity; it needed unity; it could study only motion, direction, attraction, relation. Everything must be made to move together; one must seek new worlds to measure; and so, like Rasselas, Adams set out once more, and found himself on May 12 settled in rooms at the very door of the Trocadero" (EHA, 377–78). This sentence is curious enough in its own grammatical right—clumsily periodic, as if imitating the very multiplicity of the times that the sentence itself argues "history has no use" for, it struggles to make something out of Adams's chronic tourism and dilettantism. Adams's identification with Samuel Johnson's Rasselas, prince of Abyssinia, invokes the skeptical rationality of his eighteenth-century heritage, as well as lends a certain seriousness to his otherwise idle travels. But this allusion is hardly sufficient to turn Henry Adams into a modern version of Johnson's fictional ruler. Adams must try to turn his idleness in Paris—he attended coin and art auctions, studied his French, and otherwise fiddled while global politics burned—into politically significant experience.

Adams's apparently casual reference to his locale in Paris has considerable significance for the careful reader. The "door of the Trocadero" refers overtly to his residence in "the Rue de Longchamps close to the Trocadéro, until Mrs. Cameron's apartment should again be lent to him," in the vicinity of the Place du Trocadero, which had been laid out in 1878 (*Major Phase*, 220). Originally, the general area was termed "the Trocadero," the name given to the area "in 1827 after a military tournament on the site had re-enacted the French capture four years previously of Fort Trocadero."[43] Indeed, the area is one devoted to imperial and military display, as well as national monuments. Beyond the Place du Trocadero is the Palais de Chaillot, built on the Chaillot Hill and commanding a view across the Seine of the Champ-de-Mars, which includes in the contemporary foreground the Tour d'Eiffel and, at the end of the prospect, L'École militaire (today flanked by UNESCO).

The military tournament in 1827 re-enacted the successful reinstallation of King Ferdinand VII (1784–1833) on the throne of Spain with the aid of the French army. King Louis XVIII had reaffirmed French support for the Spanish king that went back to Napoleon's re-establishment of Ferdinand as king of Spain in 1813. Fort Trocadero was the site, just outside of the Spanish city of Cadiz, of the military defeat of the Spanish troops resisting the French army in the Bourbon king's bid to reinstall the Spanish monarch. "Trocadero" refers, then, to the decline of Spanish authority in Europe and to the rise of French imperial power, both in the name of Napoleon and the Bourbon monarchy that sought to expand its early nineteenth-century European power by various military, political, and marital alliances. It is also, of course, a significant event in Spanish history, in large part because King Ferdinand reigned during the decline of Spain as a European and world power—a decline precipitated by the rebellion of its American colonies.[44]

In a chapter that promises to tell us something about the Spanish-American War, Adams evades the central political issues and ends up in Paris, gossiping about the sights. Yet, in this case, the site of the Place du Trocadero reminds the reader of an earlier shift in the European balance of imperial powers that is now being worked out again between the United States and Spain. Like other references in the chapter to Spain's waning power, this spare reference suggests that it is U.S. destiny to take over global responsibility from Spain. What was re-enacted in 1827 in Paris at the Trocadero is re-enacted a third time in Adams's 1907 *Education*, but now with the United States as the monumentalized power.

In the Parisian prospect Adams opens for the knowledgeable reader, there is much more than just this coded reference to "Trocadero" as the transfer of power from Spain to France and then from France to the United States in the seventy-four years separating the Battle of Fort Trocadero from the Spanish-American War. What Adams encompasses in his own cosmopolitan vista is also the Trocadero Palace built for the 1878 Paris Exposition and the Tour d'Eiffel, recently completed in 1889. Adams's next chapter in the *The Education*, "The Dynamo and the Virgin (1900)," opens with a reference to the Paris Exposition of 1900, the "Great Exposition" Adams claims to have "haunted, aching to absorb knowledge, and helpless to find it" (EHA, 379). I contend that Adams had already found the "knowledge" he needed but had no intention of sharing with the general reader. "The Dynamo and the Virgin" is Adams's own literary version of the great Paris *expositions universelles*, along with the other fairs and expositions in St. Louis, Chicago, and elsewhere that Adams views with loving skepticism in *The Education*. In short, Adams's global and cosmic speculations in *The Education* are his versions of the spectacle of new cultural authority staged in these early modern expositions and fairs.[45]

The Trocadero Palace is an excellent example of what Zeynep Çelik and Leila Kinney have called the "mechanisms of cultural production" that helped organize a new "global hierarchy of nations and races."[46] Built on the site of today's Palais de Chaillot, an uninspired but grand marble monument built in the early twentieth century, the Trocadero Palace was built in an eclectic style that "referred to the Islamic architecture of the [French] colonies, but its siting, size, and form as a whole created an image of France as a protective father/master with his arms encircling the colonial village."[47] The exoticism and exaggerated grandeur of the Trocadero Palace would not have been lost on Adams, who understood well the ideological purposes of such spectacular architecture. After all, his ostensible purpose in Paris was to complete the scholarship for his classic study of medieval art and architecture, *Mont-Saint-Michel and Chartres.*

Yet, this spectacle remains for Adams a token of an older imperial order committed to the occupation of territories and the material transformation of their cultures. The neoimperialist policies represented by John Hay's foreign policies and, I would argue, Henry Adams's grand historical theories and syntheses depended not on territorial or even spatial domination; they depended upon the command of "representational" power either in commercial markets or their equivalents in cultural productions. By chapter 25, Adams has "digressed" from the Spanish-American War in chapters 23–24 and the Paris Exposition of 1878 at the end of chapter 24 to the Chicago Exposition of 1893. What he discovers there is not so much the secret of the new technologies by which the United States would make good on its bid to become the new imperial power of the twentieth century, but his uncanny ability to harness the representational power of these new technologies. Adams's responses to the Chicago Exposition in *The Education* quite interestingly repeat with a certain exactitude his responses to the Paris Exposition in his correspondence from 1899 and 1900. Adams's condensation of the two expositions may merely indicate his sense of how similar all such world's fairs were, but it might also suggest his desire to appropriate for the United States the special technological authority that in Paris appears especially European.[48]

Admitting his ignorance of the technicalities regarding "electricity or force of any kind," Adams interprets the dynamo as "a symbol of infinity" and "began to feel the forty-foot dynamos as a moral force, much as the early Christians felt the Cross" (EHA, 380). This is a grand moment of rhetorical sublimity, often discussed by students of Henry Adams, but it is also typical of a certain rhetorical bombast, as grandiloquently empty as the Moorish architecture of the Trocadero Palace and as potentially dangerous. For Adams's rhetoric also organizes and hierarchizes the newly reordered "nations and races" soon to come under the sway of American economic and cultural authority. We have often enough understood this power to be based on American wealth or advanced technology, both of which other "nations and races" have needed with sufficient desperation to "pledge" themselves as shamelessly as King Ferdinand VII gave his allegiance to Napoleon and the French.

In a less complex manner, John Hay's public policy of respecting and even defending vigorously the rights of self-rule in the Third World often was merely rhetorical. Hay originally had favored a naval coaling-station in the

Philippines, rather than colonial rule, and this set him at apparent odds with the enthusiastic imperialist policies of the McKinley and Roosevelt administrations. But in diplomatic practice Hay supported as "inevitable" U.S. colonial rule of the Philippines following the Spanish-American War. As early as November 19, 1898, shortly after he had accepted his position as secretary of state, he wrote Whitelaw Reid to complain about the Anti-Imperialist League: "There is a wild and frantic attack now going on in the press against the whole Philippine transaction. Andrew Carnegie really seems to be off his head. . . . He says henceforth the entire labor vote of America will be cast against us. . . . He says the Administration will fall into irretrievable ruin the moment it shoots down one insurgent Filipino. . . . But all this confusion of tongues will go its way. The country will applaud the resolution that has been reached."[49]

The Philippine people did not, of course, "applaud" the Republican resolution that instituted U.S. rule of the country, and insurgents attacked Manila and declared war on the United States on February 4, 1899. Several months after Aguinaldo, the primary leader of the insurgents, was captured in March 1901, but the terms of peace between the United States and the Philippines were still to be worked out, Adams wrote Hay from Paris on November 2, 1901: "But I wish we were out of the Philippines. That is a false start in the wrong direction. . . . It leads us into a cul de sac in the tropics, and leads us away from our true line due west. Of course we are making mistake on mistake there, and drifting straight at the heels of England. The north Pacific is my line, not the south; our own race, and not the niggers, my instruments" (Letters, 5:304).

Adams had expressed similar sentiments in his correspondence from his travels with John La Farge in Polynesia, Ceylon, and the Middle East in 1890–1892. The anti-colonialism of Tahiti (1893) is directed at the British and French in Polynesia, but the cultural superiority of the dilettantish tourist endorses the general values of Western civilization over "primitive" cultures. Behind his scathing indictment of the British and French for the disease, corruption, and social chaos they brought to the South Seas, there is Adams's own profound fear of miscegenation and the dilution of the Anglo-Saxon race. Drinnon notes how Adams collapses Polynesians, African Americans, and Native Americans into the same racial "inferiority," betraying not only Adams's typical racism but also his appalling ignorance of the differences among their cultures and histories.[50]

Adams actually does make distinctions among the peoples he meets, but they are almost always informed by crude racial hierarchies. For example, Adams makes the following distinction between native Polynesians and Afro-Caribbeans: "Then comes the French Governor who is a Martinique negro. I am gratified to learn that some governments are stupider than our own. The French actually send here a full corps of West India negroes to govern a people almost as high-blooded as Greeks" (Letters, 3:403). The lineage of Tati Salmon is traceable to "a deceased London Jew named Salmon, who married the Teva heiress and created a princely house of Salmon" and to "Brander, a Scotchman of good family," and Adams finds the heirs "decidedly Polynesian, rather handsome" (*Letters*, 3:403). The five Brander sons, educated in England and accustomed to European habits and royal privileges, suffered financially when their mother took half of the estate and divided the rest among the nine children. The result is predictable: "The boys who were educated on the scale of a million apiece, were reduced practically to nothing, or just enough for a modest bachelor's establishment in Papeete" (*Letters*, 3:404).

Had she read her Anthony Trollope, of course, Mrs. Brander (Adams is careful to name the Polynesian women by their European married names) would have known the value of primogeniture, but this seems Adams's only complaint against intermarriage between these royal Polynesians and the European merchants, Salmon and Brander. On the other hand, Adams complains repeatedly of "the pervasive half-castitude that permeates everything; a sickly white-brown, or dirty-white complexion that suggests weakness, disease, and a combination of the least respectable qualities, both white and red" (*Letters*, 3:417).[51] Like other Euro-Americans in this period, Adams vaguely connects the tropical ambiance with racial miscegenation and cultural decadence. When he and La Farge visited Robert Louis and Frances Van de Grift Stevenson in Samoa, Adams describes Frances ("an American of Swedish and Dutch extraction") as wearing "the usual missionary nightgown which was no cleaner than her husband's shirt and drawers" and with a "complexion and eyes dark and strong, like a half-breed Mexican" (*Letters*, 3:296, 300n13).[52] Fascinated with physical differences in the native peoples he meets in Samoa, Adams takes their physical measurements, recording them neatly in his correspondence, anticipating the modernist scientific racism satirized so effectively in the character of schoolteacher in Toni Morrison's *Beloved* (1987) (*Letters*, 3:325, 327).[53]

Even as he condemns European imperialism in the South Seas, he endorses the values of European culture and the bourgeois family as "civilizing" influences. As I have pointed out elsewhere in this book, early modern Americans' critiques of global imperialism are often directed at the European powers without much awareness of U.S. complicity in territorial, commercial, and cultural forms of colonization; in this regard, Henry Adams follows the general pattern. Tahiti is full of analogies between the genealogical line of Tahitian royalty and European ruling classes from the Greeks and Romans to modern times.[54] What the European powers have ironically accomplished is the fracturing of a coherent class structure that might have endured as long as the islands themselves. Adams's "solution" is simply to dismiss the South Pacific as a political and intellectual "failure," turning instead to the more insidiously racist clichés of the "March of the Anglo-Saxon," shared by his friend, Hay, and prevalent in the late nineteenth-century United States and Europe:[55]

I am satisfied that America has no future in the Pacific. She can turn south, indeed, but after all, the west coast of South America offers very little field. Her best chance is Siberia. Russia will probably go to pieces; she is rotten and decrepit to the core, and must pass through bankruptcy, political and moral. If it can be delayed another twenty-five years, we could Americanise Siberia, and this is the only possible work that I can see still open on a scale equal to American means. (*Letters*, 3:519)

These "means" are apparently commercial, since a few lines above in this letter to Henry Cabot Lodge (August 4, 1891), Adams had dismissed the Pacific islands as "financial investments" hardly "worth touching. They are not worth the West Indies, if you lumped them all together" (*Letters*, 3:519).

By working to establish a powerful international coalition with Great Britain that guaranteed U.S. domination in Central America and the Caribbean and underwrote Great Britain's interests in the Far East, Hay helped accelerate Russia's own territorial claims in Manchuria and Korea. Adams might cheer perversely that U.S. diplomatic agreements had provoked Russia into the confrontation with Japan that resulted in the Russo-Japanese War (1904–1905), whose treaty was mediated by the Roosevelt administration at the peace conference in Portsmouth, New Hampshire. The settlement of the Russo-Japanese War to the advantage of U.S. interests in Asia would have been John Hay's last great triumph, but he did not survive the negotiations. As Samuels describes it: "The task of diplomacy . . . would have to be to deprive Japan of the more dangerous spoils of victory, control of the Asiatic mainland," while Japan was given sufficient power in Asia to be "an effective counterpoise" to Russia (*Major Phase*, 322, 321).

Although scandalized as always by the "methods" of Theodore Roosevelt, Adams essentially acknowledged the great power the Portsmouth Treaty virtually granted to the United States as international peacekeeper. But behind this noble purpose, there was the mission Adams shared with Hay to defuse military conflict for the sake of U.S. commerce. To his brother, Brooks, in 1901, Adams wrote: "We all agree that the old, uneconomical races, Boers, Chinese, Irish, Russians, Turks, and negroes, must somehow be brought to work into our system. The whole question is how to do it. Europe has always said: Buy or Fight! So the Irish, the Boers, and the Chinese are likely to remain unassimilated. We Americans ought to invent a new method" (*Letters*, 5:306). Such a new method seems clearly enough articulated in Adams's correspondence of this period to be dramatically at odds with the speculative, relativist, bombastic rhetoric of *The Education*. The "new method" appears to be just as deterministic as the history sketched by Brooks Adams in his *New Empire*: "The road of a true policy is always that of least resistance, but it is sometimes that of no resistance at all. In other words, every country held and administered by force is a danger, and therefore uneconomical. If it leads somewhere, the waste of energy may be necessary, but in itself it is a waste. It is resources—coal, iron, copper, wheat— that force markets, and will force them over all the navies and artilleries of the world" (*Letters*, 5:306). For Brooks Adams, the lines of force seemed to support the rise of the American Empire:

> The world seems agreed that the United States is likely to achieve, if indeed she has not already achieved, an economic supremacy. . . . And as the United States becomes an imperial market, she stretches out along the trade-routes which lead from foreign countries to her heart, as every empire has stretched out from the days of Sargon to our own. The West Indies drift toward us, the Republic of Mexico hardly longer has an independent life, and the city of Mexico is an American town. With the completion of the Panama Canal all Central America will become a part of our system. We have expanded into Asia, we have attracted the fragments of the Spanish dominions, and reaching out into China we have checked the advance of Russia and Germany, in territory which, until yesterday, had been supposed to be beyond our sphere. . . . [In fifty years] the United States will outweigh any single empire, if not all empires combined. The whole world will pay her tribute. Commerce will flow to her from both east and west, and the order which has existed from the dawn of time will be reversed.[56]

What Henry Adams could conclude from all this in *The Education*, beyond the familiar lesson that "a student nurtured in ideas of the eighteenth century had nothing to do" with this new "system," was that "this capitalistic scheme of combining governments, like railways or furnaces, was in effect precisely the socialist scheme of Jaurès and Bebel. That John Hay, of all men, should adopt a socialist policy seemed an idea more absurd than conservative Christian anarchy, but paradox had become the only orthodoxy. . . . Thus Bebel and Jaurès, McKinley and Hay, were partners" (EHA, 424–25). Often praised for his grudging acknowledgment of the inevitability of "state socialism," Adams actually embraced a much more conservative and, in our own age, utterly conventional notion: that the conflicts between capitalism and socialism were part of a larger narrative that would tell the ultimate story of the international corporation. Like his brother Brooks, Henry anticipated the subordination of self-interested capitalism to the "higher" purposes of U.S. national and expansionist interests, "governed" by statesmen like John Hay, proper heir of the Adamses.

The CEO for such commercial internationalism would hardly resemble the grasping Goulds or Fiskes of the Gilded Age, the competent but uninspired politician, like William McKinley, the brash and aggressive political leader, like Theodore Roosevelt; he would be a diplomat in the manner of John Hay:

> In his eight years of office he had solved nearly every old problem of American statesmanship, and had left little or nothing to annoy his successor. He had brought the great Atlantic powers into a working system, and even Russia seemed about to be dragged into a combine of intelli-

gent equilibrium based on an intelligent allotment of activities. For the first time in fifteen hundred years a true Roman pax was in sight, and would, if it succeeded, owe its virtues to him. Except for making peace in Manchuria, he could do no more; and if the worst should happen, setting continent against continent in arms—the only apparent alternative to his scheme—he need not repine at missing the catastrophe. (EHA, 503)

Those who admire Adams's prophetic powers ought to be reminded that this prediction has all the certainty of Jim's reading of the "Hair-Ball Oracle" in *Huckleberry Finn*. Peace or war, a new imperium would hold sway over the twentieth century. At its center would rule not simply the United States, but its best "representative man," the international diplomat capable of negotiating balances of power certain to be in the best interests of American genius and energy. Hay ended his speech, "American Diplomacy," with a quotation from Scripture, "which Franklin—the first and greatest of our diplomats—tells us passed through his mind when he was presented at the Court of Versailles. It was a text his father used to quote to him in the old candle shop in Boston, when he was a boy: 'Seest thou a man diligent in his business, he shall stand before kings.'"[57]

Adams's digressions at the end of *The Education* from the great and pressing historical issues of his day—that day in which the United States emerged as a new imperial power—are explained in part by his *fin-de-siècle* diffidence, his modernist ennui and skepticism. As each new international crisis "stumps" him, Adams turns apparently away to personal relations, philosophical speculations, nostalgic medievalism, scientific theorizing and prediction. Most of these topics have been used by previous critics to develop Adams's symbolic and literary responses to modern politics; that is, they have been read as the predicates of his literary modernism.

In another sense, they may be discursive efforts to legitimate international negotiations conducted by Hay (and the McKinley and Roosevelt administrations), the details of which Adams knew quite intimately, as his correspondence makes clear. His confusion and ignorance over such matters of foreign policy are literary poses to cover what he knew well were decisions made in the interests of a specific foreign policy intent on establishing a U.S. imperium—not only over lands, peoples, or even raw materials, but in the control of nations and, of course, their markets. At the end of 1913, Adams answered a letter from William Roscoe Thayer, who was writing *The Life and Letters of John Hay* (1915) as a public edition to replace Clara Hay's curious private volume, *Letters of John Hay and Extracts from Diary*: "The difficulties are chiefly political. You cannot possibly publish his private expressions about Russia, or Germany or Colombia, or the Senate, or perhaps others nearer to him—we'll say myself, to be cautious—yet without it, you can give no complete picture. I published all I dared" (*Letters*, 6:629). Adams seems here to refer to the final chapters of *The Education*, in which his literary and philosophical digressions now appear means of protecting the private side of John Hay's work of foreign policy—an achievement unparalleled by any secretary of state in U.S. history. Adams clearly mythologizes Hay in *The Education*, and yet he leaves his story deliberately unwritten, as if his life—the public and private man altogether—were some classified document. "Hay wrote little," Adams remarked, "he intentionally conducted his affairs by word of mouth" (*Letters*, 6:630).

The argument that the last third of *The Education* is a deliberate effort to distract readers from the new political power elite of men like Adams and Hay borders on a reductive, conspiratorial, even *paranoid* approach to literature's ideological function. My critics would be justified in pointing out that *The Education* was privately printed, circulated among friends, and not distributed beyond that inner circle until after Adams's death. A vulgar conspiracy thesis in this regard would depend, after all, on the widest possible readership for *The Education*. Adams devotes far too much effort to his theoretical speculations and his "dynamic theory of history," even if we grant that it remains a profoundly "anti-historical" theory of history, for us to interpret these pages as written simply to distract us from the historical facts.

Henry Adams's reputation as a major modern author depends in large part on his recognition of the fictional foundations of every mode of human action, and this knowledge accounts well for his fatalism and skepticism. Yet, even as Adams trivializes the human subject, he celebrates the new power of the modern author. Adams's modern recognition that every form of knowledge—mythic, political, historical, scientific—lacks any substantial foundation beyond its own rhetorical design effectively transforms the compositional method of modern artists into the hermeneutic foundation for every mode of knowing. Left only with the fragments of previous systems of interpretation and thus government wrecked by history, the modern author could sign his name with the technical virtuosity by which he recomposed these fragments and gave his temporary illusion the formal appearance of truth.

When such a theory of the "compositional method" is applied to Henry Adams, the author of *The Education*, the conclusions are quite predictably literary and allow Adams to join those other moderns who dismantled the illusion of the philosophical subject for the sake of those personae who only partially patch together the authors of *The Cantos, The Waste Land, Ulysses,* and *Absalom, Absalom!* What T. S. Eliot's Tiresias and Hieronymo, Ezra Pound's Odysseus and Confucius lack is supplemented by the formal properties of the works in which they appear with new, modern significances. When applied to John Hay's foreign policies, however, the "aesthetic" of the "compositional method" helps legitimate the authority of the new statesman. John Hay was called back into the center of international diplomacy for politically expedient reasons. Hay represented the solidity, integrity, and moderate politics the McKinley administration needed at the close of the

Spanish-American War. He skillfully worked with international diplomatic instabilities produced by the European colonialism so essential to capitalist expansion. For all his great accomplishments, he originated nothing, merely playing with the historical fragments he inherited. The authors of the recent past—Great Britain, France, Spain, Germany, China, and Russia—became his personae. In the balance-of-power politics that he played, Hay composed a new authority for the United States that bears comparison with that of the modern literary author's.

For the modern artist, the entropic drift of the West could be reversed by way of unexpected combinations, new compositions of old elements, intellectual and disciplinary transgressions that would open the "closed system" required for heat-death. For Adams, a "dynamic theory of history" depends on the assumption "that the rise of [man's] faculties from a lower power to a higher, or from a narrower to a wider field, may be due to the function of assimilating and storing outside force or forces" (EHA, 487). Throughout the final chapters of *The Education*, Adams stresses 1900 as the threshold of a new era characterized by the rapid acceleration of historical forces that could only appear to the citizen of the old order as confirmation of his own end. It is John Hay, however, who represents the transfer of historical energy from one epoch—1200–1900—to the next—1900–2000—in the final pages of *The Education*. The chapters "A Dynamic Theory of History" and "A Law of Acceleration" lead directly to Adams's extended elegy for Hay in the final chapter, "Nunc Age." Nowhere is Adams's irony better illustrated than in this portrait of the dying man, John Hay, exhausted by his diplomatic efforts, and his superhuman accomplishment: "One had seen scores of emperors and heroes fade into cheap obscurity even when alive; and now, at least, one had not that to fear for one's friend" (EHA, 504). Adams's historical theorizing at the end of *The Education* accomplishes a marvelous prosopopoeia, in which the dead John Hay speaks. Literally, of course, Hay speaks only of his own end, as Adams has him answer those who insisted he live long enough to complete the negotiations of the Portsmouth Treaty: "I've not time!" Literarily, Adams's theories have given credibility to Hay's diplomatic methods of balancing other world powers for the sake of an ultimate global authority for the United States. Drinnon has portrayed Henry Adams as a skeptical, indulged, and elitist tourist in Polynesia and Asia, establishing thereby the cultural ambiance for his friend John Hay's global restructuring in the interests of American imperial hegemony.[58]

Adams's *Education*, then, like his pseudo-scientific writings, is not just some literary diversion intended to distract us from the secret diplomatic negotiations that were consolidating a new power elite. Adams's theorizing is performed in all good faith as the intellectual complement to the imaginative work of the new foreign policy represented by Hay. There is a different sense in which we may understand Carolyn Porter's conclusion that "The narrative strategy of *The Education* . . . is designed primarily to deny what the act of writing it demonstrates—that Adams was a participant in the social process he presumed merely to observe."[59] The "contradiction" of observation and participation still belongs to a system of values in which thought and action, word and thing, are considered discrete categories. In the postindustrial era of the West that Hay and Adams helped define, such distinctions no longer have much relevance. Admittedly, both Adams and Hay still understand U.S. spheres of influence in terms of commercial markets, even raw materials; neither anticipated the economy in which no action can be distinguished from its mode of conceptual production, no thing escapes its discursive circulation.

Writing from Tahiti to Elizabeth Sherman Cameron in 1891, Adams notes: "La Farge has settled down to painting, varied by his usual mania for collecting photographs. I call it a mania because with me it has become a phobia; and he is almost afraid of telling me about his photographs because I detest them so much. Not that I blame him; for in my own line of manuscripts [in *The History of the United States*] I did the same thing, and had to collect ten times what I could ever make useful; but I hate photographs abstractly, because they have given me more ideas perversely and immoveably wrong, than I ever should get by imagination. They are almost as bad as an ordinary book of travels" (*Letters*, 3:408). Given Marian's suicide by ingesting photochemicals, Adams's phobia about photographs is understandable, but his hatred of them is clearly more than personal here.[60] Is the imagination a better representational tool in the "narrative" under way as early as 1891: the rewriting of world power in terms of U.S. interests? Would the "photograph" simply reveal what Twain insisted the Kodak did for King Leopold's Belgian Congo: expose the "facts" behind the story of ideology? In our own time, the Kodak is, alas, obsolete; the portrait of ideology is much more difficult to print. From positivist historian to literary modernist, Adams has often been celebrated for his searching critique of realisms and naturalisms of all sorts. But in light of his association with the new imperium of the United States, Adams's hatred of facts might anticipate the more ideological tasks that lay ahead for his beloved imagination.

9

W. E. B. Du Bois's Tropical Critique of U.S. Imperialism

In its larger aspects the style is tropical—African.
This needs no apology.
　　　Du Bois, "On *The Souls of Black Folk*" (1904)

I looked upon the Nile and raised the pyramids
　　above it,
I heard the singing on the Mississippi when Abe
　　Lincoln went down to New Orleans,
　　　and I've seen its muddy bosom turn all golden
　　　in the sunset.
　　Langston Hughes, "The Negro Speaks of Rivers,"
　　　　　　　　　　　　　　　　　　Crisis (1921)

Throughout his long career and its many different phases, W. E. B. Du Bois repeatedly criticized the United States for pursuing imperialist aims both at home and abroad. He also is one of the few modern American intellectuals to understand U.S. imperialism to differ from earlier forms of Eurocolonialism and to antedate considerably the Spanish-American War. For Du Bois, U.S. imperialism originates in slavery and depends on racism to legitimate colonial practices of territorial conquest, economic domination, and psychological subjugation. William Dean Howells and Mark Twain had criticized the United States for following the leads of England, Spain, and Germany in expansionist ventures around the globe, and Twain certainly understood slavery in the United States to be a colonial phenomenon. Nevertheless, slavery is for Twain a venerable example of human cruelty and just another reminder of how little we have progressed from our feudal past. On the contrary, Du Bois understands U.S. slavery to be especially modern, insofar as it is based on specific *racial distinctions* he argues were unknown in earlier forms of serfdom and enslavement. He may well agree with Twain about the persistence of human cruelty throughout history, but he sees it deployed differently in the modern period. In the modern work of colonial domination and its systematic, thus *imperial*, application to peoples defined thereby as "other," Du Bois judges the United States to have taken the lead.

Du Bois's theory of racial imperialism is profoundly modern, especially in his insistence from his earliest book, *The Suppression of the African Slave Trade* (1896), to his posthumously published *Autobiography* (1968), on the economic roots of all imperialisms. But Du Bois comes the closest of the American intellectuals critical of U.S. imperialism before World War II to understanding U.S. imperialism as a *neoimperialism* of the postmodern sort we now associate with the political control of spheres of influence, the corporate manipulation of foreign cultures to create new markets, and the exportation of American lifestyles by way of such cultural products as literature and film. Because Du Bois understood race and class to be the crucially related fictions by which modern nations justified the inequitable distribution of wealth and thus power, he viewed with special clarity the extent to which cultural work was indispensable to colonial hierarchies both at home and abroad. For this very reason, Du Bois also understood the power of culture to combat imperialism by challenging such hierarchies and building powerful coalitions of the oppressed to resist domination.

As Du Bois grew older and angrier about the unrecognized involvement of the United States in colonial ventures around the world, especially in Africa, Latin America, and at home, he endorsed an increasingly dogmatic economic thesis that is both vulgarly Marxist and curiously blind to the zealous imperialism of the Stalinism he espoused.[1] This turn in Du Bois's career has often distracted scholars from the subtlety of his earlier discussions of the United States as an imperial power and its novel use of culture to disguise and naturalize its practices of domination. Given the tendency of even America's most vigorous modern critics to localize its imperialism in such specific foreign ventures as the Spanish-American War and the general myopia of Americans until quite recently in regard to the imbrication of U.S. racism and imperialism, Du Bois is a forerunner of contemporary cultural and postcolonial criticisms of the role culture has played in disguising the imperialist practices of the United States. Wrong as Du Bois was about Stalinism and in his predictions of the inevitable triumph of socialism in the twentieth century, his insistence on connecting cultural analyses to their economic consequences also ought to be heard by contemporary cultural critics.[2] Especially in his writings before the mid-1930s, Du Bois also experimented with a combination of literary, historical, sociological, and political discourses (often within the same work) that might work together as a "counter-discourse" to the fantastic narrative of U.S. ideology.

The multigeneric qualities of *The Souls of Black Folk* and *Darkwater* are thoroughly modern in their respective challenges to conventional modes of representation, but both works also involve an implicit critique of the elite and deliberately inaccessible rhetoric of such high moderns as Henry Adams, Ezra Pound, T. S. Eliot, and Wallace Stevens. Adams employs a recognizably modernist aesthetic not only to disguise the bare facts of U.S. foreign policy, but also because he understands such literary style to be compatible with the public personae of the new power-elites, represented so well by John Hay. Determined to challenge hierarchies of race, class, and gender, Du Bois understood how powerfully social authority depended on forms of cultural capital traditionally unavailable to African Americans. Du Bois understood from his earliest works that African-American intellectuals and artists would have to provide alternative cultural resources to challenge such arbitrary but entrenched powers. The task of reconstructing the history of African-American culture and political activism was particularly urgent for Du Bois, because he saw it as crucial to resist myths of U.S. identity and culture that both excluded the contributions of women and people of color and played ever greater roles in the exportation of the "American Dream." Yet, Du Bois's critique of cultural capital's role in U.S. global expansion does not distract him from the fundamental economic and territorial purposes of this new imperium. Whereas Henry Adams develops a complex aesthetic modernism to disguise the more material and practical consequences of U.S. imperialism, Du Bois coordinates his conception of African-American culture with his critical analyses of the economics and racial politics of U.S. expansionism.

The history and development of African-American culture, then, are crucial parts of Du Bois's manifold plan for full emancipation, democratization, and decolonization. Education for the skeptical, modernist Henry Adams always ends in failure, in part because formal learning impresses him as so remote from the contradictory forces of modern politics and economics. Du Bois begins with this split between knowledge and reality, accepting it as part of the African-American heritage of double-consciousness, and then reaffirms the value of education in overcoming these disparities. The difference between Adams and Du Bois is not simply one of attitude—Adams's elitist irony set against Du Bois's optimism and ambition. Du Bois works out of his utopian sense that culture, economics, politics, and psychology are integral forces of social reality, each with a part to play for better or worse in the formation of human values. For all his claims to interdisciplinary knowledge, Adams merely plays with cultural representations, generally believing that the real work of society is being done on more basic economic and political levels.

I want to look again, then, at the role played by culture both in the legitimation of and the possible resistance to U.S. imperialism, especially in those earlier works by Du Bois in which he expressed hope in the utopian possibilities of culture. I shall focus my attention on *The Souls of Black Folk*

(1903) and *Darkwater: Voices from within the Veil* (1920), with some reference to *Black Reconstruction in America* (1935), each of which connects explicitly U.S. domestic policies toward African Americans with global imperialism and offers means of social emancipation for African Americans who will align themselves with other oppressed peoples of color around the globe. Because Du Bois treated culture, economics, and politics as related forces in social formation, then he overcame some of the limitations of approaches that celebrate African-American culture, economics, or politics as the best solution to marginalization by the dominant ideology.

Du Bois's often quoted prediction and recollection in *The Souls of Black Folk*: "The problem of the twentieth century is the problem of the color-line. . . . It was a phase of this problem that caused the Civil War" is obliquely elaborated in that work.[3] In particular, Du Bois never centrally works out the frequent hints linking slavery and racism in the United States with global imperialism, preferring instead to leave the reader to interpret such implications. Of course, such indirection is very much in keeping with the unique style of *Souls*, a work that Du Bois believed "conveyed" "a clear central message . . . but that around this center there has lain a penumbra of vagueness and half-veiled allusions."[4] Throughout the text, it is nonetheless clear that the "black folk" of the title are represented in a historically dramatic struggle to constitute themselves as a community against the many threats by white culture to destroy them as a people, ranging from the division of black families under slavery to the failure to deliver the economic, educational, and political promises of emancipation.

Du Bois's more explicitly Marxist perspective in *Black Reconstruction* is necessary for the reader to understand fully the anti-imperialist argument implicit in *Souls*. In *Black Reconstruction*, Du Bois makes clear that the *racialization* of labor conflicts in the United States is the foundation for a new imperialism, which he names in *Darkwater* "modern industrial imperialism."[5] Du Bois's Marxist reinterpretation of Reconstruction as the emergence of an African-American racial and class consciousness considers this awakening of collective action to herald an international movement of people of color similarly exploited by global capitalism: "Out of the exploitation of the dark proletariat comes the Surplus Value filched from human beasts which, in cultured lands, the Machine and harnessed Power veil and conceal. The emancipation of man is the emancipation of labor and the emancipation of labor is the freeing of that basic majority of workers who are yellow, brown and black."[6] In this volume, Eric Sundquist writes, Du Bois "codified his long-evolving characterization of slaves and ex-slaves as an industrial proletariat whose surplus labor was the cornerstone of global capitalism."[7] Du Bois interprets slavery in the United States as the economic and cultural system that rationalized its injustices in terms of racial hierarchies that would become the means for First World nations to justify economic and political involvement in underdeveloped communities around the world on the basis of First World racial and thus cultural superiority. Du Bois always understands U.S. slavery to be fundamental to industrial capitalism, which would merely replace rural bondage with factory feudalism in the developed nations and economic enslavement of colonized peoples of color in the Third World.

Instead of viewing antebellum slavery as an increasingly impractical agrarian practice swept away by northern industrial progress, Du Bois views it as a crucial stage in "modern industrial imperialism." In *The Souls of Black Folk*, he writes: "And now the golden fleece is found; not only found, but, in its birthplace, woven. For the hum of the cotton-mills is the newest and most significant thing in the New South today. All through the Carolinas and Georgia, away down to Mexico, rise these gaunt red buildings, bare and homely, and yet so busy and noisy withal that they scarce seem to belong to the slow and sleepy land. Perhaps they sprang from dragon's teeth" (*Souls*, 112). To be sure, the "slow and sleepy land" is Du Bois's invocation of the cliché about the old agrarian South, and the fantasy that the New South's cotton mills, whose "gaunt . . . bare and homely" buildings recall the slaves' quarters, must have sprung "from dragon's teeth," as in the myth of Cadmus, only underscores how little we have understood slavery's part in preparing for modern industrial exploitation.[8]

As Du Bois makes clear in *Black Reconstruction*, cotton was introduced as an antebellum agricultural product primarily because of its potential for the global market: "On free and fertile land Americans raised, not simply sugar as a cheap sweetening, rice for food and tobacco as a new and tickling luxury; but they began to grow a fiber that clothed the masses of a ragged world" (BR, 4). When the demand for cotton rapidly grew, as Du Bois carefully documents in the empirical manner of such earlier studies as *The Philadelphia Negro* (1899), "the black workers of America" found themselves "bent at the bottom of a growing pyramid of commerce and industry" whose growth "became the cause of new political demands and alignments, of new dreams of power and visions of empire . . . in Florida, in Louisiana, in Mexico" (BR, 5). As Rampersad points out, Du Bois consistently blames the industrial age for having "spawned slavery and the excesses of capitalism," even before Du Bois had developed the thoroughly Marxian analysis of the exploitation of labor and race in *Black Reconstruction*.[9] Rejecting the prevailing historical view in the 1920s and 1930s of nineteenth-century America as divided between "manufacturing and industry . . . in the North" and "agrarian feudalism . . . in the South," Du Bois insists that southern slavery was fundamental to the development of "a new slavery of the working class in the midst of a fateful experiment in democracy" (BR, 715).[10]

Despite Du Bois's gloomy assessment that southern slavery was finally abolished only to be promptly replaced by northern wage-slavery, his argument in *Black Reconstruction in America* is utopian in its effort to gain historical recognition for African Americans' contributions to their own emancipation and socioeconomic organization in Reconstruction. What African Americans attempted to achieve in the decades following the Civil War was nothing less than the first step of decolonization that Du Bois declares in the early twentieth century must be taken by people of color in Asia and Africa. During Reconstruction, Du Bois argues: "International and commercial imperialism began to get a vision. Within the very echo of that philanthropy which had abolished the slave trade, was beginning a new industrial slavery of black and brown and yellow workers in Africa and Asia" (BR, 632). When viewed from the perspective of the African Americans who attempted such a grand project, the failure of Reconstruction, sealed by the separate-but-equal ideology of the Supreme Court's 1896 *Plessy v. Ferguson* decision and the Jim Crow laws of turn-of-the-century America, can only be understood in mythic terms appropriate to this historical tragedy:

> The most magnificent drama in the last thousand years of human history is the transportation of ten million human beings out of the dark beauty of their mother continent into the new-found Eldorado of the West. They descended into Hell; and in the third century they arose from the dead, in the finest effort to achieve democracy for the working millions which this world had ever seen. It was a tragedy that beggared the Greek; it was an upheaval of humanity like the Reformation and the French Revolution. (BR, 727)

In this vision of an African-American *nekuia*, or descent to the Underworld, Du Bois offers a myth of African diaspora with its own history ("in the third century they arose from the dead"), but one that deliberately parallels the classical origins of Western civilization.

Du Bois's messianic style in this passage is familiar to readers of *The Souls of Black Folk*, *Darkwater*, and many of his other works, and it is itself part of Du Bois's strategy of decolonization both within the domestic United States and in more recognizable colonies around the world. By arguing that abolition and Reconstruction are original acts of revolution against modern industrial imperialism, Du Bois makes African-American history prophetic of what needs to be done elsewhere around the colonized globe, even as he acknowledges that without such decolonization the project of racial emancipation in the United States must be judged a failure. Indeed, the style itself contributes to the process of political and social reform Du Bois advocates, because it invokes the forgotten or deliberately neglected history of African-American self-emancipation during Reconstruction and revitalizes that history by connecting it with the utopian project of international decolonization. African America becomes the site of this crossing of past, present, and future, and thus it holds a privileged position as the *origin* of resistance to modern imperialism.[11]

Even when he is most critical of European imperialism in writings from *The African Slave Trade* to *Black Reconstruction in America*, Du Bois continues to connect the revolution of peoples of color against colonial domination with the Euro-American revolutionary heritage. The African-American revolt of abolition and reform of Reconstruction "beggars" Greek tragedy by its greater historical significance, and it is compared favorably with the Protestant Reformation and the French Revolution. Du Bois's point here is not simply that African Americans were persecuted under slavery on the basis of religion and class, as well as race, but also that the great emancipatory project of the European Enlightenment remains unfinished without the liberation of people of color, especially those non-Europeans colonially enslaved around the globe. Once again, the uniqueness of African Americans becomes apparent in Du Bois's argument, because they are in the enviable position of saving U.S. democracy from its corruption by the commercial interests that drive southern slavery, northern capitalism, and Euro-American imperialism.

In *The Souls of Black Folk*, Du Bois famously condemns vocational training for African Americans of the sort advocated by Booker T. Washington and practiced at his Tuskegee Institute on the grounds that it merely reinforces the commercialism of the modern age. Less commonly recognized is Du Bois's insistence that such practical training is integrally related to the "tendency . . . , born of slavery and quickened to renewed life by the crazy imperialism of the day, to regard human beings as among the material resources of a land to be trained with an eye single to future dividends" (*Souls*, 79). Equating the exploitative disciplining of the laborer's body with the colonial subjugation of foreign territory, Du Bois thus views liberal education of the student's spirit—the "soul" of the title—to be one means of resisting such colonization both of body and land. Attentive as Du Bois is in all of his writings to the importance of economic self-determination, he knows well the danger "of interpreting the world" exclusively "in dollars" (*Souls*, 67).

Racism is itself part of this process of commodifying the spirit, and it is thus not surprising that in *Darkwater* Du Bois makes "modern industrial imperialism" depend crucially on what he considers the "very modern" "discovery of personal whiteness among the world's peoples" (DW, 29–30). The claim to white superiority is "a nineteenth and twentieth century matter," Du Bois argues: "The Middle Age[s] regarded skin color with mild curiosity; and even up into the eighteenth century we were hammering our national manikins into one, great, Universal Man, with fine frenzy which ignored color and race, even more than birth" (DW, 30). Du Bois's very romantic notion that the Enlightenment was color-blind serves his polemical purpose of identifying racism with the "modern industrial imperialism" of the nineteenth and twentieth centuries; it also has the advantage of affirming a "purer" Enlightenment rationality whose salvation from capitalist degradation he makes one of the important goals of African-American solidarity in both *The Souls of Black Folk* and *Darkwater*.

Du Bois is wrong to claim that racism is a recent invention and that Enlightenment reason "ignored" race and class. In *The Invention of the White Race*, Theodore Allen documents convincingly the origins of "racial consciousness" in the economic practices of the seventeenth-century "continental plantation bourgeoisie," for whom the category of race was crucial "to achieve and to maintain the degree of social control necessary for proceeding with capital accumulation on the basis of chattel bond-labor."[12] Such historical errors may be the result of Du Bois's desire to understand the specific economic and cultural forces behind modern racism, which in other respects has led to important historical knowledge.[13] By refusing in *Darkwater* to universalize racial or class domination, Du Bois avoids Twain's despair and pessimism about the possibility of real social change. If little has changed in relations between masters and servants, except for the worse, from sixth-century feudalism to Hank Morgan's capitalist democracy, then Twain can offer little more than the final genocide in "The Battle of the Sand Belt," his own anticipation of Kurtz's scrawled madness, "Exterminate the brutes!" in Joseph Conrad's *Heart of Darkness*. In early essays on race, such as "The Conservation of Races" (1897), Du Bois subscribes to nineteenth-century conventions of "race" as constituted by essential characteristics distinguishing the "two, perhaps three, great families of human beings—the whites and Negroes, possibly the yellow race."[14] Even in these early statements, Du Bois equivocates regarding the biological determinants of race, including significant social and historical forces in the shaping of "race spirit" or "race consciousness": "What, then, is a race? It is a vast family of human beings, generally of common blood and language, always of common history, traditions and impulses, who are both voluntarily and involuntarily striving together for the accomplishment of certain more or less vividly conceived ideals of life."[15] In *Darkwater*, "whites" and "Negroes" are still represented as separate and distinct groups, but their racial division is far more explicitly the work of social, economic, and political history. Such "modern racism" has the advantage over more essentialized versions, such as those Du Bois invokes in his early essays, of being more amenable to historical transformation. Keeping alive the ideals of Enlightenment revolutions against tyrannies of various sorts—political, economic, racial, and intellectual, for example—Du Bois is thus able to offer his readers political theories and models to imitate in the pressing work of decolonization at home in the United States and around the colonized globe.[16]

Yet, the revolutionary spirit of the European Enlightenment has been replaced in the modern period with the imperialist "revolution" in social and national organization. In 1900 Du Bois seems uncertain about the role the United States should play in global affairs after the Spanish-American War. In "The Present Outlook for the Dark Races," he calls attention to the impact of recent foreign policies on racial and social relations within the United States: "The colored population of our land is, through the new imperial policy, about to be doubled by our own ownership of Porto [sic] Rico, and Hawaii, our protectorate of Cuba, and conquest of the Philippines."[17] Anticipating the global coalitions of peoples of color to which he would appeal in his subsequent writings, Du Bois also tacitly accepts the U.S. imperium as a possible means of extending democratic institutions and racial tolerance to other lands and thus overcoming the class and racial hierarchies of European imperialisms:

> What is to be our attitude toward these new lands and toward the masses of dark men and women who inhabit them? Manifestly it must be an attitude of deepest sympathy and strongest alliance. We must stand ready to guard and guide them with our vote and our earnings. . . . We must remember that the twentieth century will find nearly twenty millions of brown and black people under the protection of the American flag, a third of the nation, and that on the success and efficiency of the nine millions of our own number depends the ultimate destiny of Filipinos, Porto [sic] Ricans, Indians and Hawaiians, and that on us too depends in a large degree the attitude of Europe toward the teeming millions of Asia and Africa.[18]

The passage echoes the paternalistic rhetoric of U.S. imperialism in this epoch, as well as the idealism of many that twentieth-century U.S. foreign policies might differ drastically from the economic exploitation and institutional racism of the European imperial systems.

Such enthusiasm for U.S. democratic idealism realizing itself in our foreign policies toward new territories under our control is, however, quickly replaced by Du Bois's more critical view of U.S. imperialism. Nevertheless, he retains throughout his career the goal of international coalitions of people racially and economically oppressed as the best means of combating imperialist domination. In *The Souls of Black Folk*, *Darkwater*, and *Black Reconstruction in America*, Du Bois emphasizes the *failure* of the progressive spirit of the Enlightenment and the widening circle of human exploitation and misery. Du Bois places the United States at the vanguard of the "silent revolution that has gripped modern European culture in the later nineteenth and twentieth centuries," whose "zenith came in Boxer times: White supremacy was all but world-wide, Africa was dead, India conquered, Japan isolated, and China prostrate, while white America whetted her sword for mongrel Mexico and mulatto South America, lynching her own Negroes the while" (DW, 42).[19] Du Bois refers here to the development of U.S. imperialist policies from the Spanish-American War (1898) to the Russo-Japanese War (1905)—what we have come to recognize as the classical period of U.S. imperialism—and their consolidation during World War I. Echoing ironically hysterical appeals for "racial purity" made by apologists for the Mexican-American War ("mongrel Mexico") and advocates of U.S. superiority in the hemisphere ("mulatto South America"), he explicitly aligns the continuing persecution of African Americans at home—from their murder by white mobs in Atlanta and East St. Louis to southern lynchings—with the expansionist policies of the United States.[20] Sarcastically referring to the U.S. government's claims from Secretary of State John Hay to President Woodrow Wilson to negotiate peacefully the otherwise violent struggles for colonial territories by the European powers, Du Bois concludes: "It is curious to see . . . the United States looking on herself, first, as a sort of natural peace-maker, then as a moral protagonist in this terrible time. No nation is less fitted for this rôle. For two or more centuries America has marched proudly in the van of human hatred,—making . . . a great religion, a world war–cry: Up white, down black" (DW, 50).

Recognizing that "the using of men for the benefit of masters is no new invention of modern Europe," Du Bois nevertheless insists that modern colonialism is unique for its "imperial width" and goal of exploiting cheap labor (DW, 43). Eric Sundquist criticizes Du Bois's 1915 essay, "The African Roots of the War," for anticipating Lenin's mistaken conclusion in *Imperialism: The Highest Stage of Capitalism* (1916) "that colonialism was driven by the investment of surplus wealth."[21] But Sundquist acknowledges that when Du Bois revised this essay for inclusion in *Darkwater* as "The Hands of Ethiopia," he placed "less emphasis on economic statistics and [his] forecast of Lenin" in favor of advancing "a philosophy of 'Africa for Africans.'"[22] In fact, *Darkwater* does not abandon an economic explanation for modern imperialism; in place of Lenin's tenuous thesis, Du Bois offers his own theory of European and American imperialism as a solution to the growing labor problem in the First World nations:

> The scheme of Europe was no sudden invention, but a way out of long-pressing difficulties. It is plain to modern white civilization that the subjection of the white working classes cannot much longer be maintained. Education, political power, and increased knowledge of the technique and meaning of industrial process are destined to make a more and more equitable distribution of wealth in the near future. . . . But there is a loophole. There is a chance for exploitation on an immense scale for inordinate profit . . . of darker peoples. . . . Here are no labor unions or votes or questioning onlookers or inconvenient consciences. These men may be used down to the very bone, and shot and maimed in "punitive" expeditions when they revolt. In these dark lands "industrial development" may repeat in exaggerated form every horror of the industrial horror of Europe, from slavery and rape to disease and maiming, with only one test of success,—dividends! (DW, 43–44)

Far more effectively than Lenin's theory of exported surplus value, Du Bois's theory of modern colonialism anticipates our contemporary hierarchy of First and Third World nations, with their relative scales of economic "development" often being confused with their respective degrees of "civilization." By suggesting that these "dark lands" reflect imperialists' desires to hide their ugly exploitation from critics in the metropolitan centers, Du Bois also begins to counter the familiar Victorian racialization of colonial territories in such titles for Africa as "the Dark Continent."

Crucial to such an imperial hierarchy is a racial division that will align First World white workers with these imperial masters, in order to render invisible the exploitation of Third World workers of color. Once again, slavery and racism in the United States have played vanguard roles in such cultural mystification, insofar as the exclusion of African Americans from the American labor movement, first under slavery and then during Reconstruction, maintained within the United States just the sort of racial divisions of labor that would work so well in the twentieth-century exploitation of foreign colonies in Africa, the Middle East, the Pacific, and Asia. Crucial to maintaining this arbitrary distinction between "white" and "colored," "first" and "third," "superior" and "inferior" has been the work of human culture: "Everything great, good, efficient, fair, and honorable is 'white'; everything mean, bad, blundering, cheating, and dishonorable is 'yellow'; a bad taste is 'brown'; and the devil is 'black.' The changes of this theme are continually rung in picture and story, in newspaper heading and moving-picture, in sermon and school book" (DW, 44). Just as the industrialization of the South has led to the new peonage of African Americans, so the European development of Africa will "likely . . . be a hell" with "no voice or law or custom to protect labor, no trades unions, no eight-hour laws, no factory legislation" (DW, 63).

Du Bois suggests several ways to overcome the problem of "modern industrial imperialism" in *Darkwater*, and they range from armed revolution to political, economic, and cultural coalitions of exploited people of color around the world. Although most of these solutions are framed within the utopian prospect of an "industrial democracy" that for Du Bois means the socialization of the means of production, the postcolonial prospects in *Darkwater* are by no means dogmatically Marxian, especially when the role of culture is considered in this revolutionary project. Du Bois does, of course, stress the need for a basic economic transformation that is thoroughly Marxian: "We are rapidly approaching the day when we shall repudiate all private property in raw materials and tools and demand that distribution hinge, not on the power of those who monopolize the materials, but on the needs of the mass of men" (DW, 100). What Du Bois adds to the familiar slogan that the proletariat must seize the means of production is that "no real reorganization of industry could be permanently made with the majority of mankind left out. These disinherited darker peoples must either share in the future industrial democracy or overturn the world" (DW, 100).

Educating the white working class regarding its need to align itself with international workers of color is thus one of Du Bois's main tasks, and this is not simply a conventional Marxian project of awakening class-consciousness. True class consciousness can succeed only with the destruction of racial hierarchies and the concomitant exposure of the lies of cultural superiority on which imperialism is built:

There are no races, in the sense of great, separate, pure breeds of men, differing in attainment, development, and capacity. . . . The world today consists, not of races, but of the imperial commercial group of master capitalists, . . . predominantly white; the national middle classes of the several nations, white, yellow, and brown, with strong blood bonds, common languages, and common history; the international laboring classes of all colors; the backward, oppressed groups of nature-folk, predominantly yellow, brown, and black. (DW, 98)

Du Bois suggests potential coalitions among bourgeoisie, proletariat, and Third World native peoples that are already suggested in these modern class distinctions, but the actual work of forming such coalitions is clearly a complex task.[23] Fully aware of how deeply racist and isolationist many U.S. labor organizations were, Du Bois nonetheless imagines white American workers discovering their own self-interest in democratizing economic opportunities both within the United States and in the Third World nations dependent on its investment and trade.

Du Bois does not believe that labor organization alone can achieve the political and social coalitions that will transform the hierarchies of race, class, and nation on which capitalism depends. As he had argued in *The Souls of Black Folk*, so Du Bois insists in *Darkwater* that education is a crucial and continuing part of economic and political revolution. The fourth essay in *Darkwater*, "Of Work and Wealth," begins with Du Bois's meditation on his years teaching at Atlanta University. Du Bois's initial autobiographical reverie turns quickly into an historical analysis of the East St. Louis riots of 1917, when "the threat to white jobs from black newcomers" provoked "the worst urban violence yet experienced in the peacetime history of America."[24] Detailing a historical event that is still likely to be left out of the curriculum of modern U.S. history, Du Bois stresses not only the practical economic losses resulting from white attacks on African-American laborers, but also connects these riots with other pogroms against minorities throughout history: "It was the old world horror come to life again: all that Jews suffered in Spain and Poland; all that peasants suffered in France, and Indians in Calcutta; all that aroused human deviltry had accomplished in ages past they did in East St. Louis" (DW, 95). In so doing, Du Bois not only stresses the colonial situation under which African Americans continue to live in modern America, but he also calls attention to the internal colonialisms that have haunted European history.[25]

Du Bois wants the reader to understand in this chapter how the teacher "works," especially in the important task of forging the international awareness that will help bring about working-class and postcolonial consciousness. Du Bois had given special status to such intellectual labor in *The Souls of Black Folk* as belonging properly to that "talented tenth" that would provide leadership in the formation of a cohesive African-American community.[26] But in *Darkwater*, he rejects such elitism; the teacher is merely one among many who share the knowledge both of African-American exploitation and of its utopian promise:

> There must . . . persist in this future economics a certain minimum of machine-like work. . . . It must be accepted with the comforting thought that its routine need not demand twelve hours a day or even eight. With Work for All and All at Work probably from three to six hours would suffice, and leave abundant time for leisure, exercise, study, and avocations. . . . Who shall be Artists and who shall be Servants in the world to come? Or shall we all be artists and all serve? (*DW*, 104)

Throughout *Darkwater*, Du Bois advocates a postcolonial socialism built on a spiritual democracy that would encourage all peoples and classes to subordinate material production to the higher purpose of producing community. Among the many sins of modern imperialism, chief among them is its destruction of local communities and the suppression of native cultural traditions and languages. Du Bois works against imperialism by reviving such traditions, recalling minority history, and celebrating the widest and most diverse sorts of cultural representations:

> To tap this mighty reservoir of experience, knowledge, beauty, love, and deed we must appeal not to the few, not to some souls, but to all. The narrower the appeal, the poorer the culture; the wider the appeal the more magnificent are the possibilities. Infinite is human nature. We make it finite by choking back the mass of men, by attempting to speak for others, to interpret and act for them, and we end by acting for ourselves and using the world as our private property. (DW, 140)

This ideal and "infinite human nature" still resembles the Hegelian *Geist* that previous critics have noted plays such a central role in *The Souls of Black Folk*.[27] Indeed, Du Bois's continuing reliance on European literary and philosophical models, even when these are accompanied by African and African-American examples, is most pronounced in both *Souls* and *Darkwater* when he is trying to illustrate the highest reach of civilization, yet Europe serves in the latter work as a preeminent example of the selfishness and cruelty— the "barbarism," as he frequently terms it—of imperialism.

From *The Souls of Black Folk* to *Darkwater*, Du Bois expresses ambivalent attitudes toward European culture as either representative of liberating ideals or the tool of imperialism. In *Souls*, he would famously claim the inherent liberty and racial blindness of Europe's greatest writers and thinkers: "I sit with Shakespeare and he winces not. Across the color line I move arm in arm with Balzac and Dumas. . . . I summon Aristotle and Aurelius and what soul I will, and they come all graciously with no scorn or condescension" (*Souls*, 90). Du Bois's inclusion of Alexandre Dumas, who was of mixed-blood parentage, suggests to the careful reader that the great European cultural tradition has always been shaped by multicultural and multiracial influences.[28] It is difficult to reconcile this positive view of European culture, shaped in part by African and other non-European cultural traces, with what came to be the anti-imperialist vehemence typified by the following remarks in his 1915 essay, "Africa and the Slave-Trade":

> Such is the story of the Rape of Ethiopia—a sordid, pitiful, cruel tale. Raphael painted, Luther preached, Corneille wrote, and Milton sung; and through it all, for four hundred years, the dark captives wound to the sea amid the bleaching bones of the dead; for four hundred years the sharks followed the scurrying ships; for four hundred years America was strewn with the living and dying millions of a transplanted race; for four hundred years Ethiopia stretched forth her hands unto God.[29]

Du Bois's suggestion that the great artists and thinkers of early modern Europe contributed to the slave-trade of colonialism either because they neglected its reality or were supported by its profits could be extended to include Hegel's epic of the historical unfolding of *Weltgeist* as a philosophical legitimation of European expansionism. Indeed, it is just such a critique of Hegel that Frantz Fanon develops in *Black Skins, White Masks*, even as Fanon adapts the Hegelian model of self-consciousness to the anti-colonial struggles of non-European peoples.[30]

Some scholars solve this apparent contradiction in Du Bois's thought by arguing that Du Bois grew increasingly critical of the early European influences on his thought, especially such seminal figures as Hegel, Emerson, and Nietzsche. According to this argument, Du Bois's participation in the Pan-African Congresses of 1900, 1919, 1921, and 1923 focused his attention increasingly on African cultural sources, both as alternatives to Euro-American industrial capitalism and as foundations for African-American social solidarity. As Eric Sundquist writes: "However powerfully, Africa exists in [*The Souls of Black Folk*] for the most part in the register of cultural retentions. Within the next two decades, however, Du Bois more and more tied American slavery and European imperialism together in a net of exploitation that brought into sharp relief the meaning of Pan-African spirituality and the early modern political poetics of diaspora."[31] In his biography of Du Bois, however, David Levering Lewis suggests that Du Bois's Eurocentrism, especially when it came to European letters, was still a strong element in his thought as late as 1918–1919, when Du Bois visited France to witness the conclusion of World War I and to attend the 1919 Pan-African Congress. Thus Lewis can trace at least to the year before the completion of *Darkwater* the survival of what he terms "the eccentric Eurocentrism and radicalism-from-above that still resided in the marrow of the author of *The Souls of Black Folk*."[32]

Darkwater certainly shows the influence of African cultures in Du Bois's thought, but the persistence of European culture in this work argues against a consistent Afrocentrism or black nationalism. Instead, Du Bois argues that African and African-American cultures can *redeem* the best in Euro-

American culture by recalling its "spiritual" or democratic aims and rejecting its commercial and colonial applications. Du Bois does this in several strategic ways in *Darkwater* by invoking influential European ideas or intellectuals, identifying their limitations, and then *revising* them in terms of his knowledge of African and African-American history. From our contemporary perspective, we might understand this process of reinterpretation and adaptation to be deconstructive, but in the historical context of Du Bois's writings from *Souls* to *Darkwater*, it is probably more accurate to understand it as *dialectical* in the manner of modern revisions of Hegel.[33]

Decolonization thus involves economic reorganization, political coalitions among exploited peoples of color around the world, and cultural revision of those Enlightenment ideas that once promised universal freedom but have been corrupted to serve Eurocolonial mastery. The simultaneity of these different modes of revolt against global imperialism helps explain the formal complexity of texts like *Souls* and *Darkwater*, both of which mix empirical historical and economic analyses, rhetorical appeals for political solidarity, poetry and music, and prose allegories or fables. If we add to these differential forces Du Bois's persistent revision of prevailing European intellectual paradigms, we can begin to understand the innovative character of Du Bois's writing in both of these works.

Just how Du Bois achieves this cultural revision of the European intellectual tradition is well illustrated by his use of Hegel in *Darkwater*. As in *Souls*, Du Bois frequently invokes in *Darkwater* the Hegelian *Weltgeist* and its historical progress: "The history of the world is the history of the discovery of the common humanity of human beings among steadily-increasing circles of men" (DW, 148–49). Du Bois makes this Hegelian appeal, however, to conclude a paragraph in which he has discussed the need for exploited men to recognize their solidarity with women, who have for centuries been marginalized by patriarchy. Du Bois's argument in this regard is critical of Hegel's early nineteenth-century assignment of women to the domestic and men to the public spheres in his general social theory:

> None have more persistently and dogmatically insisted upon the inherent inferiority of women than the men with whom they come in closest contact. It is the husbands, brothers, and sons of women whom it has been most difficult to induce to consider women seriously or to acknowledge that women have rights which men are bound to respect. So, too, it is those people who live in closest contact with black folk who have most unhesitatingly asserted the utter impossibility of living beside Negroes who are not industrial or political slaves or social pariahs. (DW, 148).

While invoking the ways Hegel contributed to the nineteenth-century European ideology of the family and its gender hierarchies, Du Bois adapts Hegel's progressive *Weltgeist* to the emancipation of women and peoples of color otherwise subordinated in Hegel's philosophy.[34]

Writing on the eve of the passage of the nineteenth amendment, guaranteeing woman suffrage, Du Bois develops more fully in *Darkwater* his treatment of women in *The Souls of Black Folk*, especially African-American women, as a distinct political group with specific rights and issues. Nellie McKay reminds us that Du Bois supported "early feminist issues, especially the Suffrage Movement," not only in his books but "in many of the columns of the *Crisis.*"[35] In the African-American tradition he charts in *Souls*, Du Bois pays homage to many women who have influenced his life. Nellie McKay characterizes these women as "strong and resourceful, but . . . also generous of spirit, nurturing, and sensitive," empowering Du Bois "to cultivate both sets of qualities in himself."[36]

Josie, "a thin, homely girl of twenty," whom Du Bois meets while teaching in rural Tennessee, provides him with an object lesson in the limits of education unsupported by economic development, which Du Bois recognizes should include the domestic labor of women (*Souls*, 52). Although full of ambition and enthusiasm for learning when she first meets Du Bois, Josie is effectively worked to death by domestic labor in Nashville and her desperate efforts to help her own family survive. Du Bois honors Phillis Wheatley as the first published African-American poet, reserving for his "grandfather's grandmother" the distinction of being the mythic origin for the sorrow songs (*Souls*, 41, 207).[37] And in the parable "Of the Coming of John," in which the black John defends his sister against the white John's attempted rape, Du Bois characterizes black John's mother and sister as crucial figures motivating his ambitions to improve himself and contribute to the African-American heritage.[38] Nevertheless, women's rights are not addressed as distinct political and economic questions in *The Souls of Black Folk*, and the women he does discuss are stereotypes of victimization, like Josie; idealized motherhood, like his great-great grandmother; or aesthetic sensibility, like Phillis Wheatley, with little impact in the political sphere. Although sympathetically portrayed, the women in *The Souls of Black Folk* play more peripheral roles in society than his male predecessors and contemporaries.

Du Bois's inclusion of women's rights in *Darkwater* is by no means a mere gesture to political fashion. The passage discussed above occurs halfway through the sixth essay in *Darkwater*, "Of the Ruling of Men," which precedes "The Damnation of Women," an essay Du Bois wrote specifically for this volume. *Darkwater* is systematically organized into nine essays and one short story interwoven with eleven intertexts—poems and parables—that complement the essays. It is remarkable how many of these intertexts revolve around women's—black and white—struggles to transcend racism; taken together, they prefigure the allegory of the white woman, Julia, learning to recognize the humanity of the African-American man, Jim Davis, in "The Comet," the short story that is the final chapter in *Darkwater*.

The brief parable that connects "Of the Ruling of Men" with "The Damnation of Women" is entitled "The Call," the title referring to the "call" made by a "King, who sat upon the Great White Throne," for his "servants" (DW,

563). Exhausted from battle, the servants of the king do not respond to his call until "the third blast of the herald struck upon a woman's heart," and she "straightway left her baking and sweeping and the rattle of pans . . . and . . . her chatting and gossiping and the sewing of garments" to humble herself to the king: "The servant of thy servants, O Lord" (DW, 161). Despite her identification with domestic labor and because of her humility, the woman is commanded by the king to "Go, smite me mine enemies, that they cease to do evil in my sight" (DW, 162). Still not understanding the king, the woman repeats her inferiority, but the king turns this response into a ritual investiture of the woman with mythic power:

> "O King," she cried, "I am but a woman."
> And the King answered, "Go, then, Mother of Men."
> And the woman said, "Nay, King, but I am still a maid." Whereat the King cried: "O maid, made Man, thou shalt be Bride of God."
> And yet the third time the woman shrank at the thunder in her ears, and whispered: "Dear God, I am black!"
> The King spake not, but swept the veiling of his face aside and lifted up the light of his countenance upon her and lo! It was black. (DW, 162)

This sacred call of a black Madonna by a black god to go forth and battle what clearly is the racism and imperialism of the day "when the heathen raged and imagined a vain thing" complements Du Bois's more celebrated "Black Christ," who takes upon himself the history of violence toward black people and often expresses their rage, as does John in chapter 13, "Of the Coming of John," in *The Souls of Black Folk*.

In *Darkwater*, women of color are not, however, merely complements to the idealization of black male struggle in the "Black Christ." Not only does Du Bois represent mythically women of color in intertexts like "The Call" and "Children of the Moon," a poem narrated by Isis, he also elaborates an African-American feminine cultural heritage and addresses the specific political and economic issues of black women in the first decades of the century. In "The Damnation of Women," he links the rights of women of color with those of white women and the emancipation of both groups to that of men: "The future woman must have a life work and economic independence. She must have knowledge. She must have the right of motherhood at her own discretion. The present mincing horror at free womanhood must pass if we are ever to be rid of the bestiality of free manhood" (DW, 164–65). Tracing the "mother-idea" for social organization back to Africa, identifying "father and his worship" with Asia, and marginalizing Europe as "the precocious, self-centered, forward-striving child," Du Bois reminds us how patriarchal and paternalistic Western civilization has its origins in Africa and Asia.[39] He is also pointing out how African matrilineal societies may well offer alternatives to bourgeois capitalism and thus revivify Enlightenment ideals of universal democracy.

In just this spirit, Du Bois constructs an African-American feminine tradition of cultural and political resistance to slavery and patriarchy that includes artists like Phillis Wheatley and Kate Ferguson, children's rights' activists like Kate Ferguson and Louise De Mortie, and abolitionists and women's rights activists like Harriet Tubman and Sojourner Truth. Like the African-American male tradition he constructs in *The Souls of Black Folk*, this feminine cultural and political heritage is one with which he explicitly identifies himself, both by invoking the "four women of my boyhood" at the beginning of this essay and by mythologizing black womanhood as the "mother-ideal" of his African origins (DW, 163). Analyzing the economic causes for the high rate of single black working mothers, as well as the social consequences to black families when black men's earning power is so much lower than that of white men, Du Bois balances the cultural empowerment of women with specific accounts of their material circumstances and differences.

In an extraordinary conclusion to "The Damnation of Women," Du Bois indicts the cult of feminine beauty not only because it excludes so many women who do not happen to be "beautiful in face and form," but also because of its consequences for beautiful women who often endure the sort of commodification that differs little from domestic slavery: "A sister of a president of the United States declared: 'We Southern ladies are complimented with the names of wives, but we are only the mistresses of seraglios'" (DW, 170). Anticipating by fifty years feminist critiques of the fashion system as a means of interpellating women as subjects of a patriarchal ideology and objects of bourgeois consumption, Du Bois calls attention to our failure to realize the aesthetic ideals of the Enlightenment heritage. One of the foundations of Kantian aesthetics is an "ideal of beauty" that acknowledges physical differences among human beings by linking aesthetic pleasure to the "morally good." For Kant, "beauty" in its human representation has little to do with physical harmony or some generalization about how the "ideal" human being ought to appear, but crucially depends on "the visible expression of moral ideas that govern men inwardly."[40]

In view of Du Bois's effort to grant women their own terms of political critique, as well as civil and economic rights, it should not surprise the reader of *Darkwater* that Du Bois gives feminine characters special powers of speech and cultural representation. The intertext immediately following "The Damnation of Women" begins with a mythic woman speaking in her own voice, even if she does announce paradoxically, "I am dead" (DW, 187). Nevertheless, the Isis who utters the poem "Children of the Moon" combines both life and death in her mythic representation of Nature, just as Du Bois presents her as both an African origin of a revived "mother-ideal" for political action and social organization as well as an idealization of the African-American feminine tradition he has recovered in the preceding essay. Du Bois's Isis is a version of black feminine self-consciousness won from the struggle of black women to confront the bondage imposed on them by slavery and imperialism.[41] In short, Du Bois refigures the Hegelian model of self-consciousness in the master-servant dialectic as a struggle in which Hegel's *Knecht* may also be *ein Mädchen*: "The uplift of women is, next to the problem of the color line and the peace movement, our greatest modern cause. When, now, two of these movements—woman and color—combine in one, the combination has a deep meaning" (DW, 181).

In the political and cultural work of overturning the false hierarchy of mastery and servitude on which Western self-consciousness has been founded, Du Bois strives to replace it with a genuinely democratic "free rationality" of the sort never yet realized in the Euro-American tradition. In several of the intertexts in *Darkwater*, Du Bois offers parables of the recognition of the Black Christ by white women, notably in "Jesus Christ in Texas" and the concluding short story, "The Comet." In both of these stories, the black messiah is recognized only briefly before he is returned to his customary status as a "black convict" to be lynched (in "Jesus Christ in Texas") or as a servant to be paid and dismissed (in "The Comet"). But in these moments of recognition, each black mythic figure is identified by a white woman— the southern colonel's wife in "Jesus Christ in Texas" and the rich man's daughter, Julia, in "The Comet"—as a divine embodiment of human suffering that is imagined to encompass each woman's hitherto unrecognized bondage as a woman. "Jesus Christ in Texas" ends with a divine annunciation, in which the woman is told by "a voice . . . out of the winds of the night, . . . 'This day thou shalt be with me in Paradise'" (DW, 133). Even more explicitly, "The Comet" ends with a scene that mingles spiritual and sexual ecstasy "as the shackles seemed to rattle and fall" from the African American's "soul" and the white woman recognizes his divinity: "Their souls lay naked to the night. It was not lust; it was not love—it was some vaster, mightier thing that needed neither touch of body nor thrill of soul. It was a thought divine, splendid" (DW, 270).

Taken by themselves, such literary moments of ecstatic self-consciousness are merely melodramatic, hortatory gestures for the despairing victims of racism, sexism, and imperialism: a fantasy of a "new world 'beyond the veil,' where interracial union and Pan-African idealism are not contradictory."[42] The white, African, and African-American women in *Darkwater* do tend to be caricatures of various feminine ideals: maternity, self-sacrifice, spirituality, and moral purity. In his more thoroughly literary works, notably *The Quest of the Silver Fleece* (1911) and *Dark Princess* (1928), Du Bois often carries these male fantasies of the idealized feminine to extremes.[43] Nellie McKay has written eloquently about how Du Bois's heroine, Zora Cresswell, in *The Quest of the Silver Fleece* is the central focus of "a black female novel of development," unusual in its time.[44] And Zora's determination to take the initiative for "the social, political, and economic advancement of black people" also testifies to Du Bois's feminist commitments well before *Darkwater*, even if Zora's mythic achievements seem intended primarily for the education of Bles Alwyn, her childhood companion and black male protagonist in the novel.[45] The politically committed, incorruptible "Indian Goddess," Kautilya, in *Dark Princess* is quite simply unbelievable; the leftist orthodoxy that she teaches her lover and revolutionary aspirant, Matthew Towns, is often unintentionally comic in its extreme seriousness.[46] However, *The Quest of the Silver Fleece, Darkwater,* and *Dark Princess* are organized in terms of allusive and prophetic allegories, most of which are far more abstract and unrealistic than the autobiographical anecdotes Du Bois turns into homilies in *The Souls of Black Folk.*[47]

Read as parables that illuminate Du Bois's scholarly and historical arguments, however, such scenes of recognition not only call attention to the continuing racism of the age, but they contribute to the work of decolonization by constructing alternative myths of self-consciousness—and thus of individuality and reason—that cross the boundaries separating the imperial imagination of Western civilization and the early twentieth-century Afrocentrism known then by the names of Ethiopianism and Pan-Africanism. Some critics have interpreted Du Bois's parables of interracial recognition between black men and white women as unconscious expressions of his own desire to break through the veil of racial difference and his erotic fascination with light-skinned women.[48] Reinterpreted as prophetic allegories, the symbolic recognitions in *Darkwater* criticize the realities of racial and gender prejudices and uphold ideals of political coalitions among such oppressed groups. If racism and sexism are central to modern imperialism, then their common criticism becomes a powerful means of resisting such imperialism.

Often explicitly connected to folk and mythic traditions of storytelling, Du Bois's parables and allegories in *Darkwater* help prevent his ideas from being transformed into mere confessions or autobiography.[49] By invoking explicitly their folk roots in Africa and African-American oral traditions, Du Bois also attempts to connect his writing with popular literature.[50] In modernist terms, stories like "The Comet" and "Jesus Christ in Texas" and parables like "The Call" and "Children of the Moon" defamiliarize the "black experience," so often prized by white observers for its autobiographical truth. As radically as Bertholt Brecht, Du Bois creates unfamiliar and unrealistic literary moments that require the reader's active interpretation and reflective thought. Just as radically as Brecht, Du Bois combines popular folklore with scholarly and literary styles, often to create deliberately discordant, even subversive effects.

Beyond these merely literary strategies, important as they are for locating Du Bois in the traditions of modernist literary experimentation, the style of *Darkwater* is important for its deliberate grafting of European, African, African-American, and Euro-American authors, ideas, and cultures. By using Isis of "Children of the Moon" and Julia in "The Comet" to shape the heritage he endorses in *Darkwater*, Du Bois not only calls for but also helps *enact* the work of decolonization by transgressing the boundaries separating the metropolitan center from its far-flung colonies. From *The Souls of*

Black Folk through *Darkwater* to *Black Reconstruction in America*, Du Bois still imagined that the sins of "modern industrial imperialism" could be redeemed by concerted political organization, economic reforms, and cultural transcodings of African, African-American, and Euro-American traditions. By grafting European and African ideals to the continuing struggles of African Americans, Du Bois contributes to such cultural redemption and empowers his own people by transcoding the rhetoric of the dominant ideology.

Du Bois's later writings do not live up to this promise. Much as he would continue to cling to the notion that "the United States . . . is still a land of magnificent possibilities," he would insist that "democracy is for us to a large extent unworkable."[51] Rightly condemning U.S. imperialism around the globe and Cold War ideology, he would nevertheless rationalize stubbornly and blindly Stalinist oppression both within and outside the Soviet Union, ignoring the fact that state communism had been as corrupted in practice in the Soviet empire as democracy was corrupted by Western capitalism.[52] Du Bois himself should have listened to his own teachings in his earlier writings that the new forms of imperialism, especially as practiced by the United States, made the work of the anti-imperialist especially complex, necessarily cooperative, and ineluctably multicultural. In *The Souls of Black Folk* and *Darkwater*, Du Bois was one of the first U.S. intellectuals to challenge Euro-American imperialism's reliance on hierarchies of race, gender, and class.

In his effort to theorize new modes of self-consciousness that would attempt to overcome racial and gendered differences, Du Bois anticipated contemporary efforts to theorize postmodern subjectivity. He was also one of the few intellectuals of his generation to understand that modern imperialism had to be combated at a *cultural* level, because such imperialism relied as much on cultural as on economic and military forces. In imagining ways to transcode the cultural rhetoric of neoimperialism, especially as it perpetuated stereotypes of race, class, and gender, he anticipated contemporary cultural criticism and opened for us several paths to the elusive but still imaginable goal of global democracy. With his confidence in the emancipatory project of Enlightenment rationality—a project to which he subscribed consistently throughout a long and varied career—Du Bois made some of the same mistakes as many twentieth-century Marxists, who clung to modernist ideals of social revolution long after they had become irrelevant to the economic, political, and cultural hierarchies dictated by First World postindustrialism.

Nevertheless, Du Bois led the way for our understanding of how culture is employed by and potentially may be used to resist, perhaps even transvalue, U.S. imperialism. Never forgetting the economic factors involved in U.S. expansionism and cosistently linking domestic with foreign policies, Du Bois avoided a reductive economic analysis and a powerless celebration of "minority culture." Committed to historical study for the sake of uncovering the terms for political, economic, and cultural coalitions among peoples oppressed variously by class, gender, and race, Du Bois anticipated recent efforts to link the colonization of the body with territorial and commercial modes of imperialism. Understanding that new social injustices demanded new modes of criticism, Du Bois developed a modernist aesthetic that was also profoundly political, in large part because Du Bois understood his own forms of cultural expression to work in complementary ways with equally necessary forms of political activism and journalism. Whereas Henry Adams used literary expression to avoid and repress the ugly realities of the modern age and his ruling-class heritage, Du Bois developed his own modernist forms to demystify false authorities, recover his own history, and transvalue the cultural heritage of U.S. democracy for the sake of greater inclusiveness and thus justice.

10

The View from Rock Writing Bluff

The Nick Black Elk Narratives and
U.S. Cultural Imperialism

Medicine man, relent, restore—
Lie to us,—dance us back the tribal morn!
Hart Crane, "The Dance," *The Bridge* (1930)

Next we stopped at a sacred place where a big rock
bluff was. The Indians claim that before the Custer
fight the whole thing was pictured on it. No man
could possibly get up to where the picture is. Things
are foretold here always. When there was a man
hanging down headfirst, why something will
probably happen that year. And a year before [the]
Custer fight there was a bunch of soldiers with their
heads hanging down pictured on this bluff. Anything
important that will happen that year will be pictured
on this bluff. This rock is called Rock Writing Bluff.
This rock stands right next to the water on the
Rosebud. Here we camped and the drawing of the
Custer fight was still there and the other people also
saw it.[1]
Nick Black Elk, "Fleeing from the Soldiers" (1931), *The
Sixth Grandfather*, ed. Raymond J. DeMallie (1984)

The history of the Lakota Hehaka Sapa's, or Nicholas Black
Elk's, reception, celebrity, and complex mythologization by
Native American and Euro-American cultures represents effectively the possibilities and limitations of the colonized subject responding to U.S. imperialism in the modern period. The different and often contradictory ways in

which the Black Elk narratives represent Lakota culture and its relation to Euro-American culture do not fit conventional theoretical models either for assimilation to the dominant, colonizing society or for an ethnic or cultural traditionalism (or "nativism") that resists the constant pressures for assimilation and colonial subjugation. The Black Elk narratives represent the Lakota male subject struggling to adapt his social and religious views to changing colonial circumstances in ways that were neither strictly pragmatic nor idealistic, neither thoroughly co-opted by ideology nor free of neocolonial inflections. From the Dawes Act (1887) and the Massacre at Wounded Knee (1890) up to the Indian Reorganization Act (1934), U.S. myths about Native Americans, local conflicts between Native- and Euro-Americans, and federal Indian policies and laws produced a history of extraordinary contradictions and inconsistencies. The modern history of "Indian Affairs" developed in response to the impasse in earlier nineteenth-century U.S. policies, which Lucy Maddox characterizes as "the choice between civilization *and* extinction for the Indians."[2] In the assimilation and allotment period, Native Americans were expected to resolve this contradiction themselves by adopting the habits appropriate to U.S. citizens and therefore divesting themselves of their tribal and "racial" traits.[3] The Nick Black Elk narratives not only help focus the ideological irrationality of this history but also suggest several means of cultural resistance even when the dominant society's attitudes toward minority and subaltern communities are unsettled and thus prone to unpredictable and often sweeping changes.

This general characterization of the Lakota subject's relation to the dominant culture sounds much like the ideologically conflicted authority of John Rollin Ridge (Yellow Bird) in my interpretation of *The Life and Adventures of Joaquín Murieta* in Chapter 5, but my goal in this reading of the Black Elk narratives will be to distinguish between texts, like Ridge's, that *reflect* ideological conflicts of continuing historical interest to us and texts, like the Black Elk narratives, that challenge fundamental tenets of the dominant ideology while elsewhere falling prey to ideological traps. The distinction is important if we acknowledge that virtually every literary text is implicated in the ideological determinants of its historical period; the mere condition of "conflict" within a text should no more devalue its potential for social change than should the comparable situation of the human agent, who is himself or herself always caught within the web of larger sociohistorical forces and yet still capable of making choices that might challenge, even in some circumstances *transform*, those social forces. By the same token, unstable ideological circumstances do not necessarily provide opportunities for colonized peoples to assert their rights and reclaim cultural, political, and economic self-governance. Anti-colonial resistance is often particularly difficult when the terms of colonial domination are contradictory and ambiguous.

In Chapter 8 I suggested that Henry Adams disguised U.S. imperialism in the Western Hemisphere and in the Pacific simply by ignoring U.S. territorial and commercial expansion during the Spanish-American and Philippine-

American wars. In the case of Adams, then, the cultural critic need only question Adams's neglect of these topics in published works, like the *Education*, while calling attention to Adams's obsessive interest in these political events in his private correspondence, the speeches he wrote for Senator James Donald Cameron, and his idealization of Secretary of State John Hay, architect of U.S. foreign policy in this crucial period of our imperial ambitions. In Chapter 9 I argued that W. E. B. Du Bois performs just such a demystification of U.S. foreign and domestic policies as the example of Henry Adams seems to require. Interpreting racism as a crucial means of legitimating the imperial expansion of territory and markets, Du Bois helps us foreground the racism in Adams's writings, especially in his private correspondence, as an integral, rather than incidental, aspect of U.S. imperialism. Recovering and reconstituting African-American history and thus cultural identity is thus an obvious way for Du Bois to counter the racism he exposes at the heart of liberal progressivism.

In the study of both writers, then, U.S. imperialism emerges as a coherent and relatively stable set of foreign and domestic policies and social practices that become readable thanks to certain interpretive practices of demystification. In the case of the Black Elk narratives, however, the incoherence of the U.S. government's policies toward Native Americans from the reservation period (1863–1877) to the allotment and assimilation period (1871–1928) up to the period of Indian reorganization (1928–1945), during the early part of which John Neihardt interviewed Black Elk and his Lakota friends, poses a very different set of questions for the interpreter of culture's role in the critique or work of U.S. imperialism.[4] Anti-colonial and decolonizing efforts must take into account very different and often contradictory forms of colonization, responding to the question, "What is the source and character of colonial power?" Changing federal and local policies also have varied consequences for tribal identity, so that the warrior identity of Crazy Horse during the Plains Wars provides little guidance for a Lakota like Black Elk responding to the dual pressures of the Catholic Church to accept Christian values and the federal government to adapt to an economy based on private property and individual wealth. In this context, the critic of U.S. imperialism has to address the question, "Who speaks for the Lakota and with what voice?" The last question implies, of course, all the customary differences of language, hierarchies of social discourse, and different public spheres distinguishing most Native American from Euro-American societies. For a figure like Nick Black Elk, these differences also make explicit the troublesome question, "How do we speak to the dominant culture without accepting its terms—political, economic, legal, and rhetorical—and thus contributing to our own colonization?"

In what follows, I refer generally to the "Black Elk narratives," in order to focus on Nick Black Elk, the fictional Eagle Voice, and several other real and imaginary Lakota storytellers, as narrative voices and characters produced primarily by four discrete texts, all of which involve significant contributions from the biographical Black Elk, the most important textual and historical figure in these four narratives and their receptions. The poet and scholar John Neihardt interviewed Black Elk in 1931, near Manderson, South Dakota; Black Elk and several Lakota friends invited to the interviews spoke in Lakota, which was translated by Black Elk's son, Benjamin Black Elk, and transcribed in shorthand by Neihardt's daughter Enid. This collaborative project, in its own right an interesting example of anthropological work of cultural recovery and preservation done in rural areas in the 1930s, provided the material for Neihardt's organization and composition of *Black Elk Speaks: Being the Life Story of a Holy Man of the Oglala Sioux*, which was published in 1932 and is by far the most famous of the Black Elk narratives.[5]

Neihardt returned to the Pine Ridge Reservation in November and December 1944 to interview Black Elk and two other Sioux, Eagle Elk and Andrew Knife, who remembered pre-reservation ways of Lakota life; Ben Black Elk again provided translations, and this time Neihardt was assisted by his daughter Hilda, who transcribed directly on a typewriter the interviews that would be used to compose *When the Tree Flowered: An Authentic Tale of the Old Sioux World*, published in 1951.[6] Neihardt consciously composed *When the Tree Flowered* as a "fictional autobiography," including the courtship of Tashina Wanblee (Her Eagle Robe) by Eagle Voice but he insisted that "the adventures" narrated "are *all* authentic" (*Tree*, xx). The fictional character Eagle Voice is clearly a composite of Nick Black Elk, Eagle Elk, and Andrew Knife, as well as other Sioux Neihardt had known since he first interviewed Black Elk in 1931. Nevertheless, *When the Tree Flowered* deserves consideration as one of the "Black Elk narratives," because it includes substantial material from the new interviews that Neihardt conducted with Black Elk on December 5–8 and 11–13, 1944, and that are available in edited transcript form in *The Sixth Grandfather*.[7]

To this day, *Black Elk Speaks* and *When the Tree Flowered* are classified in libraries and by publishers as works by John G. Neihardt, even though any serious reader of these texts knows that they represent the collaborative efforts of Neihardt, Black Elk, and other Euro-American and Native Americans who contributed to the transcripts that Neihardt used to compose the final texts. In a similar manner, in the winter of 1947, the anthropologist Joseph Epes Brown interviewed Black Elk about Lakota religious rituals and beliefs, using those interviews as the basis for *The Sacred Pipe: Black Elk's Account of the Seven Rites of the Oglala Sioux*, published in 1953. Brown and Black Elk's scholarly account of the "Pipe Religion" of the Lakota has added considerably to Black Elk's stature as a Lakota holy man, revered both in Native American and Euro-American communities for his knowledge of spiritual values absent from modern industrial America. Brown and Black Elk's account of the Pipe Religion, given nearly half a century after Black Elk had converted to Catholicism, also prompted debates over *which* spiritual values Black Elk represented, adding thereby to the celebrity of this Lakota in both cultures.

Scholarly questions about Neihardt's degree of involvement in the composition of both *Black Elk Speaks* and *When the Tree Flowered* prompted Raymond J. DeMallie to edit, together with his scholarly commentary on both works, the transcripts of the 1931 and 1944 interviews in *The Sixth Grandfather: Black Elk's Teachings Given to John G. Neihardt* (1984).[8] In an effort to sort the "true" from the "fictional" Black Elk and to provide a scholarly guide to Neihardt's literary and editorial contributions to *Black Elk Speaks* and *When the Tree Flowered*, DeMallie also contributed to the myth that "Black Elk" is represented most authentically as a biographical person. Although this was by no means DeMallie's purpose, it is nonetheless one of the inevitable consequences of *The Sixth Grandfather*, especially when this text is read together with the three other Black Elk narratives and the scholarly, religious, and historical studies mentioned below. In what follows, I shall treat "Black Elk" always as the discursive effect—character or narrator—of one or more of these texts, including of course the texts of history and biography. I do so not because I wish to trivialize in any way the complex and very substantial reality of Hehaka Sapa, Nicholas Black Elk, as a living individual (b. 1858/1862?–d. 1950), who coped as well as anyone could have with the military, political, religious, and economic oppression he experienced in his long life, but because my interest in this chapter concerns what the Black Elk narratives continue to register for readers as critiques of or contributions to the imperial domination of the Lakota in the course of Manifest Destiny and its twentieth-century aftermath.

These are the four discrete texts to which I refer when I speak of the "Black Elk narratives," because Nick Black Elk played an active part in the composition of each work, even though scholarly debate continues over how to assess Black Elk's *authorial* share of each work. Obviously, each work poses its own special problems in regard to evaluating both Black Elk's actual contributions and the general authority of the collaborative efforts involved in that text's production. Although we can identify quite precisely which parts of *When the Tree Flowered* are based on Black Elk's interviews with Neihardt, thanks to DeMallie's work in *The Sixth Grandfather*, *When the Tree Flowered* includes materials gathered from at least two other Sioux. To refer to this work, then, as a "Black Elk narrative" in the same manner as *Black Elk Speaks* or *The Sacred Pipe* would be a factual mistake, but my purpose in so referring to these four narratives is to assess a narrative *effect*, which I can best describe as the rhetorical production of a recognizable "Indian personality," Nick Black Elk, who has gained a certain literary celebrity in both Native and Euro-American cultures.[9] Of the four narratives, the first three are those through which "Nick Black Elk, Holy Man of the Oglala Sioux" was culturally constructed and would achieve eventual celebrity.[10] DeMallie's indispensable work contributes to the scholarly debates and has an indirect, albeit extremely important, part to play in this culturally constructed "Black Elk."

There is a *fifth* cultural narrative that I do not include in my specific use of the "Black Elk narratives" but that has played a crucial role in the construction of this figure. I refer here to the various efforts to reconstruct the Christian Black Elk, who was required to convert to Episcopalianism in 1887, when he joined Buffalo Bill's Wild West Show in Europe, and who converted to Roman Catholicism in 1904, working as a Catholic catechist for twenty-seven years before being interviewed by John Neihardt and remaining a Catholic for the rest of his life (SG, 8–15). The narrative of the Christian Black Elk has obvious importance for anything that might be claimed by scholars and critics regarding the Lakota "Black Elk," the product of what I term the "Black Elk narratives," but unlike these the Christian narrative lacks the sort of substantial documentation of Black Elk's own statements provided by the transcripts of Neihardt and Brown's interviews with him. Instead, we have Michael F. Steltenkamp's biography, *Black Elk: Holy Man of the Oglala*, which he bases primarily on the memories of Lucy Looks Twice, Black Elk's daughter, especially her recollections of Black Elk's years as a Catholic catechist on the Pine Ridge Reservation.[11] This account of Nick Black Elk's Catholicism must be understood as the work of a Jesuit, Steltenkamp, and a Lakota Catholic, Lucy Looks Twice, raised in a primarily Christian environment (like many Lakota of her generation), both of whom represent "the later recriminations" by "the Jesuits who were so scandalized by *Black Elk Speaks*."[12] Both Steltenkamp and Lucy Looks Twice, for example, conclude that Nick's son, Ben Black Elk, had changed much of the content of what Nick said in Lakota as Ben translated into English during Neihardt's interviews in 1931, a conclusion that Steltenkamp claims to base rather vaguely on reports by "some Lakota," who "attribute much of the information" in *Black Elk Speaks* "to Ben."[13] Lacking its own direct testimony from Nick Black Elk, beyond his important and historically demonstrable work for the church as a catechist, the Christian narrative challenges the authority of the testimony by Nick Black Elk claimed in the "Black Elk narratives."

The Christian Black Elk may be divided into at least two different cultural figures: the Catholic Black Elk, who worked for the church and abandoned traditional Lakota religious practices, except as they are part of the history of the Christian conversion of many Lakota in the reservation period, and the Black Elk who represents that adaptation of traditional Native American spirituality either to Christianity or to the social ethos of a predominantly Christian culture, like the United States in the first half of the twentieth century. Steltenkamp's biography of Black Elk is the most important work in the first version of the Christian Black Elk, and Clyde Holler's recent *Black Elk's Religion: The Sun Dance and Lakota Catholicism* (1995) is the most important work in the second version. Advocates of the first version are "scandalized" by *Black Elk Speaks*, because it says nothing of Black Elk's conversion to Catholicism and work for the church and because Neihardt's narrative organization of *Black Elk Speaks* seems to follow the pattern of the *Protestant* fortunate fall and salvation in its version of the tragic history of the Lakota Sioux from the Plains Wars of the 1860s and 1870s to the Massacre at Wounded Knee on December 29, 1890.[14]

This latter interpretation of the Protestant subtext of *Black Elk Speaks* certainly finds sufficient evidence in the text itself, but it is complemented in most accounts by interpretations of Neihardt's poetic epic, *A Cycle of the West* (1915–1941), which concludes its poetic history of Manifest Destiny by representing the Massacre at Wounded Knee as a reenactment of the Crucifixion.[15] Thus the murder of 300 Lakota men, women, and children in December 1890 becomes a symbolic sacrifice that makes possible the poet's redemptive vision of Christian salvation and a secular dream of peace, love, and brotherhood:

> And then—as though the whole world, crucified
> Upon the heaped Golgotha of its years,
> For all its lonely silences of tears,
> Its countless hates and hurts and terrors, found
> A last composite voice—a hell of sound
> Assailed the brooding heavens. Once again
> The wild wind-roaring of the rage of men,
> The blent staccato thunders of the dream,
> The long-drawn, unresolving nightmare scream
> Of women and of children over all!
> Now—now at last—the peace of love would fall,
> And in a sudden stillness, very kind
> The blind would look astonished on the blind
> To lose their little dreams of fear and wrath!
> *(The Song of the Messiah, Cycle,* 108)

Of the several ironies involved in Neihardt's authorial roles in both the "Black Elk narratives" and in *A Cycle of the West*, perhaps the most important is the one noted by DeMallie: "It was in celebrating the white American conquest of the West that Neihardt came to appreciate the full cost of that conquest for the native peoples who had for so long before inhabited the plains and the mountains" (*Tree,* vii).

Yet, I think the Protestant themes of Neihardt's *A Cycle of the West* differ considerably from the more systematic efforts by Catholic missionaries to convert the Lakota and transform their lifeways, especially in the reservation and the allotment and assimilation periods. By placing too much stress on the Protestant eschatology in Neihardt's epic poem, the reader is prone to ignore his consistent criticism of westward expansion driven by Euro-American greed and ruthlessness. In *The Song of the Indian Wars* (1925), Neihardt anticipates the critique of U.S. imperialism in *Black Elk Speaks* by characterizing the pioneers as "hungry myriads," looking with "faded eyes [that] were icy" at "whatsoever pleased them, that they took" (*The Song of the Indian Wars, Cycle,* 4). Not only does Neihardt question the legal and moral validity of the U.S. government's appropriation of Native American lands, he provides a detailed account of the Plains Wars from the Treaty with Red Cloud in 1866 to George Armstrong Custer's defeat at the Little Big Horn (1876) and the murder of Crazy Horse at Fort Robinson in 1877.

Neihardt's account of the Sioux, Cheyenne, and Arapahoe's "last great fight for the bison pastures between the invading white race and the Plains Indians" still contributes to myths of the Noble Savage and the Vanishing America ("Introduction," *Cycle*, vii). Nevertheless, the concrete history Neihardt incorporates into his epic, especially in *The Song of the Indian Wars* and *The Song of the Messiah*, works against the dominant ideology by stressing the greed of Euro-American expansion and the legitimacy of Native American lifeways. Once again, it is important for readers to distinguish the limitations of an anti-imperialist cultural critique from the complicity of a text (or other cultural practice) in the work of imperial domination. The Protestant ethos of Neihardt's *A Cycle of the West*, like the later *Black Elk Speaks*, is certainly evident in Neihardt's tendency to distinguish tragic heroes, like Red Cloud, Sitting Bull, Crazy Horse, and Black Elk, thus subtly assimilating Lakota history and culture to the rhetoric of bourgeois individualism. But such ideological work is relatively minor when weighed against the anti-imperial consequences of Neihardt's history, in which the Plains Indians courageously resist the treachery and deceit of the U.S. government and settlers. Linking Custer, "Yellow Hair," with the Euro-American lust for gold in the Black Hills in "The Yellow God," Neihardt transforms Custer into a devil (*A Song of the Indian Wars, Cycle*, 106). Neihardt accurately represents the gathering of different tribes for the annual Sun Dance ceremony in 1876 as a cultural coalition that contributes to their military defeat of Custer ("The Sun Dance," *A Song of the Indian Wars, Cycle*, 121–35). Far from being an elegy for the Vanishing American, *A Cycle of the West* justifies twentieth-century pan-Indian coalitions that would begin to gain political and legal authority in the twentieth century, especially after the passage of the Indian Reorganization Act of 1934.[16] Neihardt locates the roots of modern pan-Indian organizations in the history of Native American resistance to U.S. imperialism from the Plains Wars to the Massacre at Wounded Knee, from the Sun Dance to the Ghost Dance.

The apparently specialized religious debates among the Protestant Neihardt, the Catholic Steltenkamp, and scholars interested in "comparative religions," like Clyde Holler, are part of the manifold process of appropriating the Lakota's residual lifeways and cultural practices, and otherwise accomplishing the work of cultural imperialism. I argue in this chapter that scholarly and religious disciplines, whose institutional specializations are often associated with the modern *technologizing* of knowledge, have contributed to the cultural domination of the Lakota, even when scholars in these disciplines have been consciously committed to resisting forms of cultural imperialism. Especially notable in this regard is the division of Black Elk's "religious" career from the political and social history of the Lakota (and Black Elk's family, of course) in the modern period. The debates over Black Elk's religious "identity" as Catholic, Protestant, Lakota, or hybrid are very important, but no more so than to the ways they have helped reinforce the political convention of the "separation of church and state" considered essential to U.S. democracy but quite alien to Lakota history. Lakota societies were, after all, traditionally theocratic, and the "conversion" of Native Americans by missionaries was often understood by the subjected people to be part of an overall political plan. Julian Rice argues effectively that Nick Black Elk was motivated primarily by his desire to resist cultural, religious, and political colonization, even if Black Elk was at times "ideologically inconsistent." For Rice, Black Elk "attempted to make survival conditions for Lakota consciousness and self esteem favorable in an overwhelmingly Christian world."[17] Black Elk did this work under extremely difficult historical and economic circumstances, sometimes subordinating his Lakota beliefs to Catholicism and at others endorsing "an ingenious, syncretic Lakota-Christian" position.[18]

Strictly literary approaches to the Black Elk narratives—and more generally to Native American symbolic rituals and practices—that interpret these narratives variously in terms of Euro-American literary genres and conventions (such as the novel and autobiography) or judge Native Americans to "lack" proper "literature" until they begin to imitate Euro-American forms also contribute to cultural imperialism. Often enough the scholarly claim that Native American "literature" is limited to folktales and sacred origin or creation stories ignores the complexly symbolic functions of many everyday social functions. Such misunderstandings of the interpenetration of the sacred and the quotidian, the symbolic and practical, also carries over to conclusions regarding the inferiority of the oral traditions of many Native Americans when compared with the print technologies of "advanced" Euro-American cultures. In particular, oral cultures tend to rely on multiple tellers, often empowering far more people to participate in their symbolic and spiritual activities than print societies.

Black Elk's several identities as Lakota holy man, Catholic catechist, and character in Neihardt's Protestant narrative cannot be understood apart from the history of U.S. federal policies toward the Plains Indians in his lifetime. Black Elk was born when the Homestead Law of 1862 opened the plains to settlers and put increased pressure on the federal government to consolidate existing reservations and force those tribes that had not accepted reservation life into such formal colonies. Prodded by settlers' demands for land, reformers' complaints about the inhumane treatment of Native Americans on reservations, fiscal mismanagement and outright corruption of many reservation agencies, and frontier violence, the post–Civil War federal government attempted to consolidate reservations and use them as sites of adapting Native Americans to Euro-American private property, yeoman farming, and capitalist economy (*Great Father*, 1:563–66). One of the principal aims of what came to be known as President Ulysses S. Grant's "Peace

Policy" was to prepare Native Americans for the allotment of private property and the break-up of tribal systems of government and communal economies (*Great Father*, 1:566). Another related motive for the consolidation of reservations was to adapt Native Americans to the geopolitical organization of the United States. The unrealized goal of consolidating smaller reservations into an Indian Territory that might eventually "become a State of the Union" represented the post–Civil War aim of making peace with Native Americans by fully incorporating their lands, institutions, and lifeways into the nation.[19]

The general policy of forcing Plains Indians onto reservations, where they would be taught to farm and subscribe to the work ethic of bourgeois America was undercut by the pervasive "graft and corruption of the Indian reservation agencies," which rarely delivered the farm animals, equipment, and seed to the reservation Indians that were required for mere subsistence.[20] Conditions on many reservations in the nineteenth century were *below* the subsistence level. In hopes of reforming this corrupt system, President Grant adopted another component of his Peace Policy: the distribution of reservation agencies to different church groups "for the civilization and Christianization of the Indian race."[21] Despite constitutional insistence on the separation of church and state, the United States distributed Indian "reservations . . . among the major religious denominations, which, in an unprecedented delegation of power by the American government to church bodies, were given the right to nominate new agents and direct educational and other activities on the reservations."[22]

Grant's Peace Policy ended when Rutherford B. Hayes was elected president in 1877, but it paved the way for policies of assimilation and privatization that would be formalized by the Dawes General Allotment Act of 1887. While Nick Black Elk traveled with Buffalo Bill Cody's "Wild West Show" in 1886, the Dawes Act was being debated in Congress. The provisions of the act allotted tribal lands to "individual Indians who were to be converted from hunters to farmers" and allowed the "'surplus' lands" to be "sold for non-Indian settlement" (*Federal Indian Law*, 168). The predictable result was that Native American lands were drastically reduced and "surplus lands . . . rapidly transferred to the whites."[23] Prucha points out that the Dawes Act was not simply another scheme to serve "western interests greedy for Indian lands," but was a proposal sponsored by "eastern humanitarians who deeply believed that communal landholding was an obstacle to the civilization they wanted the Indians to acquire" and who were convinced that "without individually owned parcels of land that could be defended in the courts, the Indians would soon lose everything" (*Great Father*, 2:669).

Although formal control of reservation agencies by the churches ended a decade before the Dawes Act was adopted, the idea of privatizing Native American lands complemented the assimilationist aims of the Christian reformers. Most of Black Elk's story occurs in the period of federal Indian policy generally termed "Allotments and Assimilation," dating from 1871 to 1928 (*Federal Indian Law*, 168). Yet when Neihardt transcribed Black Elk's story in 1931, federal Indian policy was undergoing changes that would effectively overturn the assimilationist philosophy of Grant's Peace Policy and the Dawes Act and lead to the Indian Reorganization (Wheeler-Howard) Act of 1934. The Meriam Report of 1928, commissioned by Secretary of the Interior Hubert Work and compiled by the independent Institute for Government Research, reported the "deplorable conditions in health, education, and economic welfare" of Native Americans and "incompetent and inefficient personnel" in the Bureau of Indian Affairs (*Great Father*, 2:810). Although the Meriam Report did not recommend overturning "existing policy," it was used by reformers to call attention to what many judged the utter failure of assimilation and allotment policies supported by the Dawes Act (*Great Father*, 2:810).

John Collier was one of those reformers who hoped that the Meriam Report might lead to dramatic changes in federal Indian policy. When he was named commissioner of Indian Affairs in 1933 (a position he held until 1945), Collier worked for a bill that would return government, cultural representation, education, and economic determination to Native Americans. Although the final bill was drastically revised before it became law in 1934, the original Wheeler-Howard bill provided for Indian self-government (Title I), special education for Indians (Title II), prohibition of further allotments of Indian lands (Title III), and a "special court of Indian affairs, to be conducted according to Indian traditions" (*Great Father*, 2:958). Although Prucha claims that Collier got only about "half" of what he wanted in the final bill, Collier did bring to an end the allotment system and began to reverse assimilationist policies by restoring to native peoples their rights to represent themselves politically, culturally, economically, and legally.

Neihardt's *A Cycle of the West* and the Black Elk narratives belong to this period in which federal Indian policy and law changed significantly from assimilation and allotment to Native American self-determination and self-representation. When Neihardt and his wife moved to Chicago during World War II to look for work, Neihardt met Collier, who in 1944 appointed him director of the Bureau of Indian Affairs's Bureau of Information, a position he held until the end of the war.[24] Although Collier and Neihardt did not meet until twelve years after *Black Elk Speaks* was published and then at the end of Collier's term as commissioner of Indian Affairs, Collier recognized in Neihardt a commitment to Native American political sovereignty and cultural autonomy that matched his own goals in the Indian Reorganization Act. DeMallie quotes from a letter Neihardt wrote to the secretary of the interior following his interviews with Black Elk, in which Neihardt pleads that the Lakota "be encouraged to revive and cherish their ancient culture to the end that they might develop a proud self-consciousness as a people and thus give them some incentive for striving."[25] DeMallie concludes that Neihardt's "suggestion may be interpreted to coincide with the philosophy

of the Indian Reorganization Act."[26] But Collier and Neihardt still represented government paternalism toward Native Americans, as both the policies of the bureau in Collier's administration (1933–1945) and Neihardt's
"editing" of *Black Elk Speaks* and *When the Tree Flowered* indicate.

We should also note that the damage done by Grant's Peace Policy and
the Dawes Act lasted well into the period of the Indian Reorganization Act
or the "Indian New Deal." The formal policies of assimilation and allotment
lasted more than sixty years and were supported by a complex network of
government institutions. Bureau of Indian Affairs and missionary schools
established on reservations to do the work of assimilation and religious conversion had succeeded in ways that could not be reversed simply by congressional fiat or even by the best intentions of the commissioner of Indian Affairs. Between 1871 and 1928 several generations of Native Americans had
to varying degrees adopted European cultural, spiritual, and economic
values. By the time the Indian Reorganization Act was adopted as law, many
Native Americans belonged to hybrid societies composed of traditional Native American and Euro-American practices and values. Any return to the
old lifeways was unthinkable, in large part because the economic foundations for most tribes, especially the Plains Indians, had been destroyed. And
although "traditional structures of tribal religious and political authority"
had managed to survive "by going underground, out of sight of the BIA
Indian agents and missionaries," such residual practices were often matched
by the effects of Eurocentric and often Christian education (*Federal Indian
Law*, 215). Even Native Americans claiming to resist allotment and assimilation by following tribal traditions and respecting kinship relations usually
had to acknowledge that other members of the tribe followed Euro-American
ways that changed the very meaning of tribal identity, political organization, and cultural coherence.

In traditional Lakota society, communal bonds are established by kinship relations of birth and marriage and by "gaining membership in what
the literature refers to as sodalities, warrior societies, or simply societies,"
the Lakota word for which is "*okolakiciyapi.*"[27] In addition, there is "a variety of shaman organizations . . . , along with women's guilds or groups,"
and all of these social organizations within the tribe contribute to the definition of tribal identity.[28] As Steltenkamp points out, "the early missionaries capitalized" on these existing social organizations by creating "comparable" Christian sodalities, such as the Catholic St. Joseph and St. Mary
societies, which gradually replaced the Lakota groups.[29] In 1891, the year
following the Wounded Knee Massacre, Jesuits initiated the first Catholic
Sioux Congress, a "three-day gathering of Catholic Sioux from all the reservations" that continued to be held annually for the next fifty years and
effectively served to create a larger communal identification for Catholic
Lakota in individual tribes and on specific reservations, as well as establish
foundations for the modern pan-Indian movement. These Catholic meetings
replaced earlier pan-tribal meetings arranged by different Sioux tribes for

political and religious purposes. Indeed, it was the Teton Council meeting of tribes on the Rosebud and Greasy Grass rivers, where tribal leaders met to discuss incursions of the U.S. military into the Black Hills as well as to perform the sacred rituals of the Sun Dance, that Custer attacked without provocation in the summer of 1876. Crucial to this Catholic appropriation of Lakota social and spiritual practices was the involvement of respected Lakota elders as "catechists," who "were the lifeblood for the societies (and the Catholic population as a whole)" and who laid the foundation for Catholic Lakota who "today serve as clergy among the people."[30]

Given status by the Catholic church in their Lakota communities and paid modestly for their services in times when Lakota earning power was desperately low, these catechists mediated between the priests and the far-flung communities of the Lakota reservations. In 1904 Nick Black Elk converted to Catholicism, explaining his decision to John Neihardt by saying simply, "My children had to live in this world."[31] Lucy Looks Twice recalls that her father "drew only ten dollars a month for his missionary work," but "we never went hungry."[32] Little as scholars know about Black Elk's actual work as a Catholic catechist, it would be a mistake to conclude that he converted simply for practical reasons. Lucy Looks Twice points out that "right after his conversion, . . . he gathered all his friends, called a meeting, and then asked his friends and relatives to help him build a place—a little house in which to have Mass when the father comes."[33] What Clyde Holler concludes from Black Elk's Catholic conversion and long service as a catechist is that Black Elk was attracted to Catholicism by his inveterate interest in religious practices and his desire to find some means of grafting traditional Lakota religion to the Catholicism he recognized as more powerful in a modern world dominated by Euro-Americans.[34]

As I wrote earlier, all of these Christian approaches to Black Elk and the related problems of interpretation posed by the "Black Elk narratives" belong to a complex but ineluctable narrative of U.S. cultural imperialism, even though there are many ways in which Catholics, Protestants, and scholars of comparative religions have attempted to help the Lakota and other native peoples resist colonization. There is no simple explanation or single theory that will allow us to distinguish Christian colonialism from Christian acts of charity, compassion, and understanding of native peoples, but one useful way to begin is to assess Christian approaches to non-Christian peoples in terms of the political and cultural authority Christians recognize as *necessary to* the social integrity of another people. Most often cultural colonialism manifests itself in acts that may respect individuals but trivialize or disregard the communal principles on which the very identity of such individuals is based. Nick Black Elk is by no means a passive victim of this narrative; he and his family members as well as other Lakota may be said to have contributed actively to the Christianizing of Lakota culture as part of the general U.S. effort at the time of Black Elk's conversion to eliminate migratory Indians from the Plains, control them physically and economically on reservations, and assimilate them to mainstream American culture. Crucial to this history of cultural imperialism is the process through which Lakota religion is separated from its traditional political and economic purposes in imitation of Catholicism's apparent detachment from secular affairs. As a "medicine man" (*pejuta wicasa*) whose spiritual experiences and abilities eventually qualified him as a "holy man" (*wicasa wakan*) in Lakota society, Nick Black Elk held positions of social, economic, military, and spiritual importance. By the end of his life, after retiring from "active church work," Black Elk "served as the 'medicine man' in the Duhamel Sioux Indian Pageant, a tourist attraction held each summer along the highway from Rapid City to Mount Rushmore," in which he "demonstrated the offering of the pipe, the Sun Dance, and the other rituals that he was to systematize in *The Sacred Pipe*."[35] Whether the elder Nick Black Elk followed Catholicism, traditional Lakota spiritual practices, or a hybridization of the two, he learned the disciplinary distinctions that separate religion and sociopolitical commitments in modern America.

In works like Brown's *The Sacred Pipe* and Steltenkamp's biography, *Black Elk, Holy Man of the Oglala*, Black Elk assumes the qualities of a "religious" figure, in whom memories of Lakota spiritualism survive along with his recognition of Catholic truth. Connected with this problem of rendering Lakota culture by way of its residual "spiritualism" as it is represented by a Lakota holy man is the more general issue of Nick Black Elk as a representative Lakota. Black Elk as a historical and biographical *person* is a crucial part of the narrative of cultural imperialism that I am tracing and that has been perpetuated, however unwittingly, by scholarly efforts to sort out the "true" Black Elk from such Euro-American interpreters as John Neihardt; Father Joseph Lindebner, the Catholic priest reputed to have converted Black Elk; and the Lakota friends and family, especially his children Ben and Lucy Looks Twice, who have shared the responsibility of telling Nick Black Elk's story. Like many other cultures in which oral and oral-formulaic methods are used to maintain communal, historical, and genealogical bonds, traditional Lakota culture lacks the concept of single authorship specific to Euro-American print cultures. Rendered often in modern scholarship as a "spiritual" and "literary" genius, Nick Black Elk takes on the identity of the Euro-American author, when in fact he is merely one conduit through which traditional Lakota culture represents itself in *Black Elk Speaks*, *When the Tree Flowered*, and *The Sacred Pipe*.

This tendency to personalize and even embody cultural authority as an individual also serves to *depoliticize* the culture represented, especially insofar as the reader's attention is shifted from large cultural issues to personal, psychological, and familial questions. The personal and cultural are, of course, always related, but they can be made to serve different purposes. Both *Black Elk Speaks* and *When the Tree Flowered* deal centrally with how the Lakota and other Plains Indians were driven from their traditional hunting grounds by settlers and miners, backed by the U.S. military, their primary food sources destroyed, and their very survival made dependent on a foreign government intent on changing their fundamental lifeways. Forced to accept reservation life and robbed of the basic means promised them for successful farming, Plains Indians were not only colonized but also driven to accept socioeconomic positions of utter dependency. As they were forcibly colonized by military and economic means, their tribal communalism was fractured by the adoption of Western housing, which stresses the nuclear family, and Christianity, with its emphasis on individual conversion and salvation. By substituting Catholic for Lakota sodalities and by drawing on respected tribal elders, like Nick Black Elk, to serve as catechists, the church helped achieve the social and psychological colonization of the Lakota that fit well with the allotment and assimilation policies of the federal government between 1871 and 1928.[36]

Of course, Western literary forms resemble Catholic and Protestant religious forms by reinforcing the social process of individuation. The basic narrative of *Bildung* so characteristic of the novel relies fundamentally on the concept of the unique philosophical subject undergoing a transformation that enables him or her to enter the social order. At least since Hegel and the romantic idealists, individual development and social history have maintained their manifest differences and yet shared infrastructural resemblances in the Euro-American imaginary. What binds individual and society together is often a religious or philosophical narrative whereby the discrete individual is brought to recognize his dependence on God, language, or truth.[37] In his efforts to formally organize the stories told by Nick Black Elk and his Lakota companions in 1931 and again in 1944, John Neihardt obviously adapts these stories to Western narrative teleology and its emphasis on the process of individuation. In *Black Elk Speaks*, Nick Black Elk's first vision leads systematically to his success as a "medicine man," then as a "holy man," capable of transforming Wovoka's "Ghost Dance" into the Sioux Ghost Dance, to his final appearance in the "Author's Postscript" as the sentimental figure on Harney Peak who ritually enacts the "Vanishing American."

Even more explicitly, the stories of old Sioux life and history gathered in *When the Tree Flowered* are organized around the fictional Eagle Voice's romantic pursuit of the Miniconjou woman, Tashina Wanblee, with the tragic history recorded from the Fetterman Fight on December 21, 1866 ("When the Hundred Died"), to the Massacre at Wounded Knee forming a convenient historical backdrop for the narrative. Only on the very last page does Eagle Voice find Tashina Wanblee, now "older and heavier, and . . . holding a child under her blanket," among the women and children who have survived the massacre (*Tree*, 247–48). Her husband has been killed in the battle, and she may thus join Eagle Voice on the "good road that we walked together" and that seems to keep intact some portion of the Lakota "sacred hoop" (248). Structuring this history in reference to particular individuals who have experienced it does, of course, help the reader imagine the human drama of Native Americans victimized during the Plains Wars. What cultural critics often term "voicing" the experience of the other includes representation of affective responses, sometimes of the most trivial sort, to major historical events, thereby providing emotional grounds for better historical understanding. Yet insofar as such *characterization* in the Black Elk narratives follows the sociological and psychological assumptions of Euro-American culture, then this process of individuation tends to contribute to cultural colonialism, rather than offer an alternative history from the Lakota perspective.

Such formal organization is usually the work of Neihardt, and it often works in conflict with the more communal, historical, and political aspects of the stories told by Black Elk and his Lakota companions in 1931 and 1944. Thanks to DeMallie's careful editing of the transcripts of those interviews, we can figure out with some exactness which parts of both narratives "belong" to the Lakota and which to Euro-American forms and ideological assumptions in these two narratives. Yet I want to suggest that to discriminate too precisely between "Lakota" and "Euro-American" aspects of these two narratives might commit another kind of error, because part of Black Elk and his companions' achievement was to have managed to get Neihardt to represent their stories in print in the first place. At a certain point, the Lakota ability to tell their story in a medium generally unavailable to them at the time must be qualified by Neihardt's tendency to translate that story into narrative elements familiar to the Euro-American reader. What occurs is a narrative conflict of wills, which, given the conflicted political interests of both Lakota tellers and Neihardt himself, can never be tidily sorted into emancipatory and neocolonial components. Instead, we must allow for a certain residual indeterminacy, a sort of liminal region of narrative in which the *contact* between different cultures and their relative *powers* are foregrounded. And yet such cultural undecidability by no means invalidates or neutralizes the different and often competing histories, often of the same events, told. What is remarkable is that history attains a certain *intelligibility* in these moments of cultural contact and conflict.[38]

DeMallie points out that among the important materials Neihardt added to *Black Elk Speaks* are historical accounts of "the Sioux wars with the U.S. Army," for which Neihardt "was forced to rely on published sources in order to fill in the background of Black Elk's story" (SG, 77). But the framework that compels Neihardt to "fill in" the history of the Plains Wars, including the U.S. government's violation of its treaty with Red Cloud (November 6, 1868) and its murder of Crazy Horse (September 5, 1877), is provided by the alternative history incorporated into the stories told in the 1931 interviews. In short, what Neihardt "added" as historical explanation is already motivated by the accounts of violence against the Lakota by the U.S. government and military provided by Lakota witnesses. Any reader of *The Song of the Indian Wars* and *The Song of the Messiah* in *A Cycle of the West* knows the extent of Neihardt's knowledge of this history, but Neihardt's narrative relationship with his Lakota storytellers in *Black Elk Speaks* appears to have changed his understanding of how the Lakota responded to the actual events.

In a previously published collection of Indian and frontier stories, *Indian Tales and Others*, which Neihardt based in part on folklore he had gathered from the Omaha, Native American characters and narratives are virtually stripped of contemporary political content.[39] "Indian" magic is represented in stories like "The Singer of the Ache" and "The White Wakunda," and primitive superstitions are retold for the amusement of Euro-American readers in "Vylin" and "Mignon." At the same time, conventional anxieties about the "dangers" of mixed marriages and the savagery of "half-breeds" are played upon in "Mignon" and "The Art of Hate." Despite the use of a dialogical narrative format in which many stories are told by a Native American to a Euro-American narrator, the "Indian" remains very much the curiosity or exhibit of similar nineteenth-century tales. In the Black Elk narratives, there are distinct Lakota voices that represent concrete historical events and make moral and political judgments of that history.

At the beginning of this chapter, I used as an epigraph Hart Crane's invocation in *The Bridge* of the Native American as a symbol of the pre-industrial, natural "magic" that the modernist poet proposes to revive. His modern version of the Pocahontas story substitutes the modern poetic imagination for the medicine man's "dance" that will lead us back to the "tribal morn," some atavistic version of Wallace Stevens's more classical "ring of men" in "Sunday Morning," who:

> Shall chant in orgy on a summer morn
> Their boisterous devotion to the sun,
> Not as a god, but as a god might be,
> Naked among them, like a savage source.[40]

For Crane, Powhatan's tribe, the Pamunkey, an Algonquian-speaking group, could just as well be Lakota, Pomo, or Navajo. But the storytelling of Black Elk and his Lakota companions encourage Neihardt to specify the history immediately relevant to the fate of Lakota peoples in forced transition from tribal to reservation lifeways. Already familiar with that history, as demonstrated by those parts of *A Cycle of the West* composed before the Black Elk interviews, Neihardt nevertheless adapts his knowledge to the Lakota efforts to tell their story in print. Hart Crane, like many other Euro-American writers, could easily appropriate the "Indian" as a metaphor for his own values; Neihardt has more difficulty doing this, even though there remains a colonial subtext in all the Black Elk narratives. The important point is that Lakota storytelling achieves communicative effects beyond the myth of the Vanishing American.

Often forgotten in the more specialized scholarly discussions of Neihardt's poetic license in composing *Black Elk Speaks* is the extraordinary achievement of Black Elk, Fire Thunder, Standing Bear, and Iron Hawk to represent in American English print culture their memories and criticisms of the dominant culture. Able to achieve such representation primarily as a consequence of Ben Black Elk's translations and what I would term the "familiarizing" rhetoric of Neihardt's narrative reorganization and contextualization, these Lakota storytellers nevertheless manage to offer a devastating critique of U.S. imperialism and a powerful reaffirmation of traditional tribal practices and values. *Black Elk Speaks* manages to communicate the vigor and utopian aims of traditional Lakota society while recounting the history of how it was attacked by the U.S. military, churches, and Indian policies and laws in the Allotment and Assimilation period.

It is tempting to judge *Black Elk Speaks* as a narrative that celebrates traditions and social practices no longer available to the Lakota; in this respect, the work is merely one more contribution to the myth of the Vanishing American. But this myth has also served as a kind of self-fulfilling prophecy, because every effort to recall the vitality of traditional tribal societies and every criticism of the injustices suffered by their peoples can be treated as nostalgia for a vanished past and as protests of the powerless. Few readers of *Black Elk Speaks* have missed the extraordinary sense of tribal responsibility each storyteller feels both in the telling of history and in his everyday conduct. In recalling the coherence and consensus of Lakota tribal societies and contrasting their communalism with the alienation and self-reliant individualism of modern Euro-American society, the storytellers in the Black Elk narratives establish a moral foundation and re-establish traditions for new Lakota communities. Throughout *Black Elk Speaks* and *When the Tree Flowered*, tribal collectivism is demonstrated in virtually every aspect of everyday life, including hunting, food preparation, war and defense, courting and marriage, spiritual rituals, education, and mourning. In this way, both texts resist the ideology of assimilation, including its emphasis on bourgeois individualism and private property, and call for a renewal of Lakota cultural identity at the very historical moment federal Indian policy endorsed Native American self-determination and expression.

Although *Wakan Tanka*, often translated as "Great Spirit," is the Lakota name given to the single spiritual force binding all natural, animal, and human forces together, it differs considerably from the Christian God, who so often appears in his singularity—or the "magic" of his trinitarian identity—as a patriarchal figure.[41] Black Elk's visions always involve multiple authorities and voices, generally combining Thunder Beings (or their representatives) with animal and natural divinities, as in this description of his "First Vision":

> This was not a dream—it actually happened. I saw two men coming out of a cloud with spears. As I was looking up to that, there was a kingbird sitting there and these two men were coming toward me singing the

sacred song and that bird told me to listen to the two men. The kingbird said: "[Look,] the clouds all over are one-sided, a voice is calling you." I looked up and the two men were coming down singing:

> Behold him, a sacred voice is calling you.
> All over the sky a sacred voice is calling you.

I stood gazing at them and they were coming from the north; then they started toward the west and were geese. (SG, 109)[42]

Various aspects of the natural and supernatural landscape "speak" with the "sacred voice" of *Wakan Tanka*.[43] DeMallie points out in his note that the "clouds" from which the Thunder Beings emerge are "one-sided," or *wasanica*, meaning "sacred" and "beneficial to mankind," and that these sacred clouds are identified as such by "a kingbird (flycatcher) who . . . for the Lakotas" is "*wasnasnaheca*, a word that may suggest *wasanica*, although it is not identical to it" (SG, 109n12).

Black Elk's visions typify the connected multiplicity of the sacred in Lakota culture. Within this visionary experience, various figures and voices carry out their designated responsibilities, and although everything has its place within the vision, as each space is carefully designated in such spiritual practices as the Sun Dance or the *Heyoka* ceremony, the rhetorical and metamorphic equivalences between bird and man, man and gods, gods and thunder suggest active relationships, rather than static religious conventions. In a similar fashion, the communalism of everyday tribal life follows this religious idea of relatedness, in which various groups within the tribe assume responsibilities that contribute to the completion of the overall task. Within this dynamic social structure, there is considerable flexibility and no absolute fixity in the social role achieved. In their descriptions in the 1931 interviews of a buffalo hunt, Standing Bear and Black Elk describe the delegation of responsibilities from the "crier" announcing the advisors' decision to break camp and follow the buffalo to the "soldier bands" (*akicita*) "in formation" leading the hunt "twenty abreast," followed by the "hunters . . . four or five abreast," the "people" bringing "meat to the counselors and the counselors all" saying, "'Hyya-a-a!' [*Haye*, 'Thanks!'']," and the "women" cutting the meat "to dry" "on the racks" and preparing the "hides of the buffalo" to be "tanned" (SG, 146–48).[44] The "akicita" exemplify this sense of Lakota relatedness as determined by social function. The Lakota "akicita" is not accurately translated either as "soldier bands" (as above), "rulers," or as "policemen," but refers to some combination of all these functions. Black Elk describes "akicita" as mediators between the Thunder-beings and the people: "When the medicine man had a vision the Thunder-beings said they and akichita [*sic*] would be relatives and the Thunder-beings would give their power to the people. The akichita saw to it that the laws made by the sub-chiefs were enforced. Just like the Thunder-beings, the akichita could not be stopped" (SG, 320). But "akicita" also means more generally, "if I tell you to do anything, it has to be done," thereby suggesting that the tribal representatives of the law—the *akicita* who lead the hunt—personify moral and juridical authority in general.[45]

In contrast, Euro-American life strikes Black Elk as unnatural, because it does not respect the communal ways of the Lakota and their responsibilities to their natural environment. The interview edited by DeMallie as "The Indians and the White People" records Black Elk's thoughts "just before telling about his trip with Buffalo Bill" to Omaha, Chicago, New York, and London (SG, 288). Neihardt adapts freely from this interview and places it at the end of Black Elk's stay in New York, as if to suggest he is judging urban life on the basis of his experiences in the city: "I could see that the Wasichus [white men] did not care for each other the way our people did before the nation's hoop was broken. They would take everything from each other if they could, and so there were some who had more of everything than they could use, while crowds of people had nothing at all and maybe were starving. They had forgotten that the earth was their mother" (BE, 217). In the actual interview, Black Elk is less concerned with urban materialism, selfishness, and the myth of progress; he is more concerned with the loss of relatedness among tribal peoples, animals, and the earth:

> The four-leggeds and the wings of the air and the mother earth were supposed to be relative-like and all three of us lived together on mother earth [*we all had a teamwork at that time*]. Because of living together like relatives, we were doing just fine. We roamed the wild countries and in them there was plenty and we were never in want. Of course at that time we did not know what money was and we got along just fine. We would get out just a little ways to bring home plenty of meat. . . . We got powers from the four-leggeds and the wings of the air. (SG, 288–89)

Using a metaphor of natural disaster, probably linked in his mind with creation stories, Black Elk compares the white man's westward expansion with "floods of water, covering every bit of land we had and probably someplace there is a little island where we were free to try to save our nation, but . . . we were always leaving our lands and the flood devours the four-leggeds as they flee. . . . Our relatives-like with the four-leggeds will vanish first because where they are there is no feed. The water just closes in on us continually" (SG, 289).

The condition of the Lakota and other Plains Indians in the face of Manifest Destiny is one of imprisonment and servitude, which Black Elk understands as the consequence of explicit warfare: "Now, when I look ahead, we are nothing but prisoners of war" (SG, 289). Indeed, the reservation system with its "square houses," rather than round tipis, and its undersupplied agrarian economy is frequently compared to the imprisonment and servitude Black Elk sees as the by-products of urban industrialism. In New York, he compares his people's situation to that of the prisoners he observes at the New York City penitentiary on Blackwell's Island in the East River: "There was a prisoner's house on an island where the big water came up to the town, and we saw that one day. Men pointed guns at the prisoners and made them move around like animals in a cage. This made me feel very sad, because my people too were penned up in islands, and maybe that was the way the Wasichus were going to treat them" (BE, 217).[46] Black Elk's comparison of reservation life with imprisonment on Blackwell's Island recalls how the Dawes Act matched the "square houses" of the reservation with the "squares" of allotted private property, usually "one quarter of a section (160 acres) . . . to each head of family" (Great Father, 2:667).

Nowhere in the Black Elk narratives do any of the Lakota storytellers explicitly connect their own colonization and eventual imprisonment on reservations with the domination of European settlers under British, French, and Spanish colonial rule. Although the storytellers miss thereby the opportunity to invoke the revolutionary and anti-colonial history of the United States, they nevertheless represent the military struggle of the Plains Indians against the U.S. Army as an anti-colonial struggle, however doomed they may know it to have been from the historical perspective of their interviews in 1931 and 1944. In describing the events leading up to the battles of the Rosebud and Little Big Horn in June 1876, the storytellers emphasize the consensus among the Sioux following the Black Hills Council of 1875 that they must make a last stand to defend the Black Hills from the U.S. government. Often represented in white historical accounts as valued by the Sioux for their religious significance, the Black Hills (He Sapa) gained this sacredness in part for their value as rich hunting grounds. In Black Elk Speaks, Neihardt relies primarily on Black Elk's account of the 1875 meeting between Sioux representatives and the U.S. government commission, appointed by "the secretary of the interior" and "headed by Sen. William B. Allison" (SG, 162n1). When his father tells him that the Sioux either must "lease the Black Hills to the Wasichus" to mine gold or else "the Wasichus would take that country anyway," Black Elk only concludes: "It made me sad to hear this. It was such a good place to play and the people were always happy in that country. Also I thought of my vision, and of how the spirits took me there to the center of the world" (BE, 81–82).[47] Standing Bear and Iron Hawk are much more explicit in their interviews in recalling Sitting Bull's claim "that the Black Hills was just like a food pack and therefore the Indians should stick to it. . . . I knew that the Black Hills were full of fish, animals, and lots of water, and I just felt that we Indians should stick to it" (SG, 163–64).[48]

The practical and the spiritual are inseparable in Lakota culture, but it is nevertheless important to amend Neihardt's version of the decision to make a last stand to defend the Black Hills to include economic as well as spiritual motives. From the Battle of the Rosebud to the Little Big Horn, the entire sequence of the military conflict between the Lakota and the U.S.

Army is represented by the Lakota storytellers as the defense of the large village composed of members of six different Sioux tribes that had camped on the Rosebud and Greasy Grass Creek (the Little Big Horn) in June 1876 for the Teton Council and Sun Dance ceremony. In their various accounts, Black Elk, Standing Bear, and Iron Hawk all stress the involvement of the entire tribe in these battles: women either singing the tremolo for fallen warriors or helping retrieve the wounded from the field of battle; boys too young to join in the real battles nonetheless doing what they can to wreak havoc on the enemy or simply gaining experience of military conflict; tribal elders urging warriors to protect the powerless in the tribe (SG, 180–95).

Unlike Hollywood representations of Indian "braves" encircling trapped soldiers in spatial arrangements amenable to wide-angle camera shots, the storytellers represent the Battle of the Little Big Horn as a confused series of events, taking place in a variety of locations, in which all members of the various Sioux tribes contributed to the defense of their community. Indeed, the Lakota narrative is far closer to the historical facts of the attacks by General Custer and Major Reno on the Sioux villages than popular Euro-American accounts of the U.S. cavalry "surrounded" by Indians. Quite the opposite, the Sioux found their homes invaded by troops ordered to exterminate them, and Custer's "last stand" was a direct consequence of the combined Sioux force that he had underestimated in size and ability to resist (SG, 180–85). The Lakota accounts combine the quotidian—"We got up late the morning of the fight. The women went out to dig turnips and two of my uncles went hunting" (BE, 113)—and epic drama—"Little Bear rode up to me on a pinto horse, and . . . said: 'Take courage, boy! The earth is all that lasts!'" (BE, 121). Practical needs repeatedly inform sacred purposes. On the one hand, Black Elk and Wooden Cup, among others, have spiritual anticipations of the Sioux defeat of U.S. troops at the battles of the Rosebud and Little Big Horn (SG, 123, 340). On the other hand, Iron Hawk's bare statement of fact seems to express well the sense of all the storytellers of the practical urgency of the military conflict: "Of course they came to fight us and we had to fight. I was there to fight. I went among them and met the soldiers, so I just took my bow and arrow and shot one of them straight through under the ribs and I heard him scream" (SG, 191–92).[49] Behind the warrior's stoicism, however, there is also a strong sense of indignation regarding the soldiers' invasion of the tribe's community: "These white men wanted it, they called for it and I let them have it. . . . Because they wanted it and called for it, I was very mad because the women and children had run away scared and I was thinking about this when I did this killing. I said: 'Hownh!' three times while hitting the man" (SG, 192).[50]

Black Elk Speaks is full of evidence of the communalism of Lakota tribal society, the Lakota individual's sense of obligation to communal ideals, and of numerous social, spiritual, economic, and military rituals designed to reinforce the relationship between the individual and the community. These communal ideals are well expressed in the collective modes of storytelling that are characteristic of Lakota culture and its oral-formulaic traditions.[51] Neihardt pays little attention to the fact that *Black Elk Speaks* translates Lakota historical and traditional stories both from Lakota into English and from oral into print forms. Communal forms of storytelling are reproduced in *Black Elk Speaks* by the occasional contributions of Black Elk's "long-hair friends" to the narrative, especially the accounts of battles, but Neihardt composes the narrative to reinforce the central authority of the "medicine man," Nick Black Elk, and the title finally selected for the volume, *Black Elk Speaks*.[52] DeMallie argues that "Neihardt chose the direct first-person narrative" form for the book because he wanted "to avoid the intrusion of himself as author (and the modern world at large) in order to bring a traditional Sioux perspective to the fore," but the effect of this narrative organization is to confuse the Lakota storytelling voice with the individualist authority of Euro-American print culture (*Tree*, xi). The Lakota qualities of storytelling that do survive, such as the terseness and repetition, tend to reinforce the romantic stereotypes of the solitary "Indian," who conveys an aura of exotic mystery.[53]

In the final chapters of *Black Elk Speaks*, Black Elk recounts his interest in the Ghost Dance Religion, his participation in several ghost dances, and the Massacre at Wounded Knee. These chapters (21–25) are followed by Neihardt's "Author's Postscript," in which Neihardt stages Black Elk's climb to the top of Harney Peak (the center of the Lakota world), where the thunder replies to Black Elk's appeal to Wakan Tanka for the salvation of his people. Framed as they are by Neihardt's effort to provide successful closure to the narrative by way of Black Elk's achievement of his identity as a holy man, these chapters are also overdetermined by Neihardt's use of Black Elk as the central character focusing the reader's understanding of the Ghost Dance Religion and the Massacre at Wounded Knee. Even so, Black Elk's commitment to traditional Lakota communalism and now to certain pan-Indian possibilities resists the narrative's construction of him as a discrete character or individual. By rehistoricizing Black Elk in this critical moment at the end of the Plains Wars, we can also recover a messianic impulse that belongs neither strictly to Lakota spiritual practice nor to Christianity. If we can read beyond Neihardt's well-intentioned "characterization" of Black Elk according to Euro-American conventions, then we might understand *Black Elk Speaks* as advocating a cultural hybridity that has pan-Indian, Euro-American, and Lakota aspects appropriate to the political circumstances of the Indian Reorganization Act.[54]

Chapter 21 opens with Black Elk concerned that he has lost his healing powers after returning in 1889 from England, where he had been touring with Cody's Wild West Show. Black Elk identifies himself with the abject, impoverished, and starving Teton Sioux, who had just faced the further humiliation of the "reduction and division of the Great Sioux Reservation" (SG, 256), which was part of the larger effort to force Native Americans "into an economic and social pattern acceptable to the whites" (*Great Father*,

2:632). Black Elk will recover his powers after he has danced the Ghost Dance, had several significant visionary experiences, and effectively performed ritual mourning for the death of his father and what it symbolizes: the destruction of traditional Lakota lifeways. But the Ghost Dance is itself a hybrid, pan-Indian spiritual practice of which Black Elk learns at first indirectly from reports of "some men named Good Thunder, Brave Bear, and Yellow Breast who had gone and seen the Messiah" (SG, 256).[55]

Black Elk never met Wovoka (Jack Wilson), the Paiute founder of the Ghost Dance Religion that was followed by many different tribal peoples in this period. The Ghost Dance posed a threat of pan-Indian solidarity that frightened officers of the Bureau of Indian Affairs sufficiently to cause them to ban or severely restrict its performance on the reservations.[56] DeMallie considers the Ghost Dance to have been "a cruel disappointment to the Lakota people, but to none more than Black Elk," because instead of "salvation, it brought death to as many as three hundred Lakotas at Wounded Knee, who were mowed down by gunfire in an unthinking, horrible slaughter," and continues to symbolize "an impenetrable barrier between themselves and the acceptance of white culture" (SG, 11). In these respects, DeMallie follows the "tragic" denouement of Neihardt's narrative in these final chapters of *Black Elk Speaks*, confirming the suspicions of many readers that the book concludes with a bittersweet affirmation of the myth of the Vanishing American. The Massacre at Wounded Knee thus seems to declare for Neihardt and DeMallie the failure of Wovoka's prophecy that the buffalo would return, Native American dead come back to life, and the whites vanish from the land.

Black Elk learns about the Ghost Dance by participating in it, not by going to consult its Messiah, Wovoka. He is attracted to the Dance, because he finds in its ritual and iconography certain elements of his own youthful vision given to him by the six grandfathers: "At first when I heard [about the Ghost Dance] I was bothered, because my vision was nearly like it and it looked as though my vision were really coming true and that if I helped, probably with my power that I had I could make the tree bloom and that I would get my people back into that sacred hoop again where they would prosper" (SG, 257).[57] To be sure, Black Elk does say that he "wanted to see this man personally and find out" whether they share the same vision, but the "Messiah" will appear to Black Elk only through Black Elk's participation in the Dance, which he travels to witness when "Kicking Bear held the first ghost dance" at the "head of Cheyenne Creek, north of Pine Ridge" (SG, 258).

What Black Elk witnesses at the Ghost Dance is "the sacred pole in the center" and "a circle in which they are dancing," red and yellow body paint and eagle feathers on the dancers, and the use of the sacred pipe, all of which convince Black Elk that "it was all from my vision" (SG, 258). In this moment, Black Elk is recalled to his vocation as holy man: "I was to be intercessor for my people and yet I was not doing my duty" (SG, 258). And in this same moment, Black Elk recalls "Harney Peak in the Black Hills" and what "the spirits had said to me: 'Boy, take courage, they shall take you to the center of the earth,'" where he would "behold all the universe, the good things of the earth" (SG, 258). Black Elk dances his first Ghost Dance as a way to communicate with "my father," who died the previous fall (1889), "about the other world" (SG, 259).[58] He describes that dance as ritual mourning not only for a family member, but also for his "people," who "were in despair," and thus about his responsibilities to help bring his people "back into the [sacred] hoop" (SG, 259).

By dancing the Ghost Dance, Black Elk recovers his power as medicine man and holy man. He begins to make Ghost Shirts for other dancers, and he has visions in the conventional manner of the Dance: after falling down in exhaustion at the end of a long period of dancing. What the visions reveal, however, are variations on the Lakota visions of his youth: of the dead tree flowering, of the sacred hoop reconstituted, of his people put back on the "red road" of prosperity and social coherence. The Thunder Beings again speak to Black Elk and his powers of prophecy return (SG, 265–66). In one of his visions, Black Elk does see the tree "in full bloom" and "against the tree I saw a man standing with outstretched arms." This is the visionary moment that has most often been cited to suggest Black Elk's vision is Christian and that the "Messiah" he mistakes for Wovoka is in fact Jesus Christ. In the transcript, however, Black Elk goes to some lengths to claim that "he did not resemble Christ," adding parenthetically "(At that time I had never had anything to do with white men's religion and I had never seen any picture of Christ)," both of which lines Neihardt deletes from *Black Elk Speaks* (SG, 263).[59]

DeMallie notes that Black Elk's claim "never" to have "seen any picture of Christ" is "not strictly true," since he was "familiar with Christianity while he was in Europe," and concludes that "he probably meant to indicate that at this time he had not yet accepted" Christianity (SG, 263). But Black Elk's denials and qualifications are not as simple to resolve as DeMallie claims. The episode is full of parallels between Lakota spirituality and Christianity, beginning with the figure's first appearance: "The man with outstretched arms looked at me and I didn't know whether he was a white or an Indian. He did not resemble Christ. He looked like an Indian, but I was not sure of it. He had long hair which was hanging down loose. On the left side of his head was an eagle father. His body was painted red" (SG, 263). In both what the figure says to Black Elk and its magical transformation, Lakota and Christian cultures are confused:

> "My life is such that all earthly beings that grow belong to me. My Father has said this. You must say this." I stood there gazing at him and tried to recognize him. I could not make him out. . . . As I looked at him his body began to transform. His body changed into all colors and it was very beautiful. All around him there was light. Then he disappeared all

at once. It seemed as though there were wounds in the palms of his hands. (SG, 263)

Neihardt deletes Black Elk's overt reference to Christ's stigmata, so that the transcript actually has more Christian overtones than the equivalent passage in *Black Elk Speaks*.[60] It is possible that Neihardt deleted such overt Christian links because he considered them heretical or simply vulgarizations of Christianity. Nevertheless, Wovoka's preaching was originally "compounded of Christian doctrines and Indian mysticism," promising a "new paradise if they would remain at peace, live honest and industrious lives, and perform a ghost dance that God had taught to the messiah" (*Great Father*, 2:726). The Lakota appropriation of the Ghost Dance Religion in 1890 may signal another political and cultural possibility for Black Elk and the Lakota serving as native informants for Neihardt in 1931. Both Wovoka and Black Elk failed in 1890 to graft Native American spiritualism to the Christian ethos of Euro-American culture, in part because the cultural attitudes of that period were shaped by the allotment and assimilation policies of the Dawes Act. But times were changing in 1931, renewing the possibility of a politics of cultural hybridization, which would combine pan-Indian organization with the insinuation of Native American spiritual and cultural practices into the dominant ideology.

Such a perspective changes significantly the ways we might understand the "tragic" conclusion of *Black Elk Speaks* and Black Elk's sentimental characterization as "Vanishing American." As activists of the American Indian Movement of the early 1970s recognized, Wounded Knee was not only the site of a "massacre" in 1890 but also of Native American resistance. Along with other warriors, Black Elk fights back, and the battle recalls the indignation and tribal pride of those who defeated Custer fourteen years earlier. Wearing a Ghost Shirt and bearing before him his "sacred bow," Black Elk invokes the heroism and spiritual aura of Crazy Horse (SG, 274). Wounded in battle, he combines qualities of Christ's sacrifice with the warrior-guardians' (*akicita*) social responsibility (SG, 278). When Red Cloud convinces them that "we cannot go on fighting because winter is hard on us," the warriors "make peace" rather than surrender, pass troops ordered "to present arms," and are greeted at the Pine Ridge Agency by officers who "saluted us" (SG, 281–82).

Neihardt's sentimental conclusion to chapter 25, "The End of the Dream," certainly emphasizes the tragic consequences of the events at Wounded Knee in 1890–1891: "I did not know then how much was ended . . . A people's dream died there. It was a beautiful dream. And I, to whom a great vision was given in my youth,—you see me now a pitiful old man who has done nothing" (BE, 270). In the transcripts, however, Black Elk concludes with the honorable arrival of the Lakota at the Pine Ridge Agency, adding simply: "Two years later I was married" (SG, 282). The differences in narrative intention seem clear in this instance: Neihardt stresses the defeat and humiliation of the Lakota at Wound Knee; Black Elk invokes traditions and responsibilities of the Lakota warrior and holy man to affirm tribal dignity. In the face of the genocidal policies of the U.S. government toward the Lakota, Black Elk and the other Lakota tellers argue that their people have resisted, adapted, and survived.

With the help of DeMallie's edition of the transcripts of the 1931 interviews, these different intentions are readable in *Black Elk Speaks*, but I should also point out that Neihardt's reliance on Euro-American narrative forms and techniques, especially those we associate with the "novel of education," overdetermine our reception of the work. Although knowledgeable of the different tribal cultures and histories of the Plains Indians from as early as *The Song of the Indian Wars* (1925), Neihardt does not seem to consider the importance of Lakota oral traditions of storytelling until he composed *When the Tree Flowered* (1951). In this later work, Neihardt replaces the first-person narrative of *Black Elk Speaks* with what DeMallie characterizes as "a dialogical format by which the author, who serves as unnamed recorder of Eagle Voice's story, stands between the narrator and the reader" (*Tree*, xiii). The "dialogical" narrative is more complicated and multiple than DeMallie suggests, because Neihardt includes frequent scenes in which several speakers reflect upon and employ traditional Lakota storytelling forms. There is, of course, some irony in the form of *When the Tree Flowered* representing more accurately the communal oral forms of Lakota telling, since the overall narrative structure of *When the Tree Flowered* is even more novelistic than *Black Elk Speaks*.

Nevertheless, *When the Tree Flowered* helps us understand the communal purposes of traditional Lakota storytelling more obliquely represented in *Black Elk Speaks*. As in many other predominantly oral cultures, Lakota society relies on storytelling to reinforce social bonds by reaffirming and transmitting traditional values. The role of the teller in most oral cultures differs significantly from that of the author in print cultures. In Lakota society, "Our history is handed down to us by our forefathers and we have to have it all in our heads," by which Black Elk means that adult membership in the tribe is in part constituted by knowledge of those historical, legendary, and spiritual stories that may be told on a variety of occasions, ranging from sacred rituals to everyday social exchanges (SG, 333). The telling of stories thus always involves several explicitly communal functions connecting present generations with the past, maintaining the existing social bond, and initiating the young into the community.

One of the subplots of *When the Tree Flowered* is how the fictional protagonist, Eagle Voice, was named. Eagle Voice's father is killed at the Wagon Box Fight on August 2, 1867, and Looks Twice becomes his new father. Looks Twice urges Eagle Voice to go on a "vision quest" and arranges for the holy man (*wicasa wakan*), Blue Spotted Horse, to instruct him (*Tree*, 43).[61] Before he will teach Eagle Voice, Blue Spotted Horse orders him to undergo the rite of purification (*inipi*) in the sweat lodge (*onikare*), which is prepared by two of Eagle Voice's friends.[62] Everything in this ritual is, of course, symbolically important: the water in the sweat lodge is "*Wakan-Tanka* [Great Spirit] who is always flowing, giving His power and life to everything"; the willows represent seasonal decay and regeneration; the rocks "represent Grandmother earth" (*Pipe*, 31–32). Once purified in this ritual, Eagle Voice is tutored by Blue Spotted Horse to cry for a vision (*hanblecheyapi*), a form of ritual "lamenting" that the initiated may perform at any time and is thus one indicator of their membership in that community. In his interviews with Joseph Epes Brown in *The Sacred Pipe*, Black Elk describes "many reasons for going to a lonely mountaintop to 'lament,'" including the desire to "understand . . . better" a vision already received, to be granted a vision, to "make ourselves brave" for the Sun Dance or "the warpath," or to ask for or give thanks for a favor or gift from *Wakan-Tanka* (*Pipe*, 45–46).

When Eagle Voice "cries" for his first "vision," he is reminded of the night he spent by his father's burial scaffold and then hears "a voice above and behind me," which when he turns "to see whose voice it was, it was an eagle soaring low and looking back at me until it was not there" (*Tree*, 52). This vision of what his spiritual teacher, Blue Spotted Horse, will explain "was your father talking through the eagle" follows Eagle Voice's vision of a "big whirling cloud of dust, . . . full of coup-sticks with scalps on them," which anticipates the successful, if Pyrrhic, battles the Sioux will wage against the U.S. Army in the 1870s (*Tree*, 54, 52). How Eagle Voice is "named" for the vision he has of his father, speaking to him from the spirit world through the eagle, is thus a complex process of symbolic narration that involves Eagle Voice, his natural father, his stepfather, Looks Twice, Eagle's Voice's two friends, and the holy man, Blue Spotted Horse. His narrative "naming" also situates him historically between his father's death at the Wagon Box Fight (1867) and his own desire to avenge that death, spiritually in the rituals of *Inipi* and *Hanblecheyapi*, and socially in the hierarchies of holy men (Blue Spotted Horse), fathers, and peers. The entire process of naming and thus of social initiation into adulthood involves Eagle Voice in a narrative process that includes representatives of his community as active participants in a process that virtually constitutes him as an individual. Although Western commentators often note the importance of individualism in Sioux society, it should not be confused with the radical individualism of bourgeois modernity. Deeply traditional, rooted in community responsibilities, the Sioux individual is unquestionably the work of distinct social processes.

The dialogical and communal aspects of such narration are typical of oral cultures, and *When the Tree Flowered* stresses that the function of storytelling in maintaining the social bond is not limited to highly formalized spiritual rituals, such as Eagle Voice undergoes in his initiation and naming. Formal tribal history was maintained in pictographic records of annual events, and these "winter-counts" served as mnemonic aids to professional storytellers, responsible for maintaining tribal tradition by connecting current events with the retelling of past achievements and troubles. The Lakota winter-counts date back to 1700–1701 (SG, 302). By the late nineteenth century, as traditional lifeways were increasingly threatened by Euro-American cultural and political incursions, such tribal histories were gradually forgotten: "In the case of the Teton Sioux we have a people who kept pictographic records or 'winter counts' to assist their memories; but when the counts were explained by their keepers soon after the year 1875 it became apparent that these tribal record-keepers had no better memories than the rest of the people. . . . when they got farther back than sixty years they were much in doubt as to what the pictographs really stood for."[63] Yet such professionally maintained histories were not the only ways the Lakota preserved their traditions. Everyday activities in Lakota culture are often accompanied by stories, such as those Eagle Voice describes young men "storytelling around the fire when we had feasted" or "when we were walking the horses slowly to rest them" (Tree, 57). Like the storytelling of rural African Americans in the South recounted in Zora Neale Hurston's Mules and Men and discussed in the next chapter, Lakota storytelling is often not restricted to a single teller: "Somebody would start a funny story, and others would crowd close to take it from him and go on with it" (Tree, 57). Listeners may fall asleep, as Eagle Voice does, during the telling of such stories, get bored and distracted, or take over the story and tell a different version. Generally, such open-ended stories are folktales, "called ohunkakan by the Lakotas," whereas sacred rites, prayers, and histories, such as winter-counts, follow certain formal rules of performance and are generally "handed down from one generation to the next as oral tradition by certain men who specialized in remembering and passing down these stories" (SG, 302).[64] Whether formally told by professional tellers or informally told and sung as part of everyday life, tribal stories exhibit their communal qualities and purposes in their contents and performances. Royal Hassrick divides Sioux stories about their "history and origin" into "factual, traditional, and mythical."[65] Whereas factual accounts, like the winter-counts, were preserved by elders designated as medicine men, traditional and mythical stories were frequently told around the fire after sunset and especially during the winter when hunting and migration had ended for the season.

In his narrative organization of When the Tree Flowered, Neihardt pays far more attention to these dialogical and communal aspects of Lakota oral traditions than he does in Black Elk Speaks. The general narrative situation of When the Tree Flowered is established by the Euro-American "I" narrator visiting Eagle Voice in his "teepee, with its rusty stovepipe thrust through its much-patched canvas," just "a hundred yards away" from a "one-room log cabin," both of which merely emphasize "the empty reservation landscape . . . hushed and bluing in the cold" (Tree, 1). Neihardt's narratorial "I" avoids the anthropologist's intrusive and paternal role, emulating instead the humility of a religious acolyte and the respectful curiosity of the ephebe. Stoking Eagle Voice's stove with chunks of cottonwood and performing other basic chores, the narrator soon earns Eagle Voice's title of "grandson" and the kinship of shared stories and traditions. Sentimental as this relationship between the Euro-American and his native informant may be in Neihardt's fictional representation, it nonetheless shifts the narrative logic away from the single authority of Euro-American print narrative and toward the dialogical oral traditions of the Lakota.

This is clearly a studied effect on Neihardt's part. Black Elk's story of "The Woman Four Times Widowed" has no narrative framing in the 1944 transcripts; Black Elk simply tells the story (SG, 352–57). Chapter 17 of *When the Tree Flowered* retells this folktale, but it is framed by Neihardt's fictional enactment of a feast, hosted by the narrator, which dramatizes the Lakota ritual of "thanking the food" described in the preceding chapter. Serving and feasting with Eagle Voice, No Water, and Moves Walking, the narrator is hailed by Eagle Voice as "grandson" and in his own actions imitates the Lakota warrior, as Black Elk describes this ritual in the 1944 transcripts: "Whenever they were going to give thanks to the food, the warriors that had been feeding the old and needy, they are the ones that make a feast. A warrior who had more than he needed would make a feast. He went around and invited the old and needy. . . . They would be coming and singing his praises. Usually the feast giver had done a great deed of some sort. . . . Maybe they would tell what he had done and say, 'It is great!'" (SG, 387–88). Having served these old Lakota "long-hairs" in the manner of the warrior, the narrator is praised by No Water "to the effect that I could not help being a Wasichu [white man] any more than he could be other than a Lakota. And, indeed, a little brown paint on my face and a blanket—'Could not tell the difference,' he said; 'could be Ta Shunka Witko [Crazy Horse]'. . . . 'Maybe Wakon Tonka gave him a Lakota heart,' Moves Walking added. 'Maybe if all Wasichus were so, things would be better'" (*Tree*, 138–39). No Water and then Moves Walking proceed to tell the folk story of "The Woman Four Times Widowed," which Neihardt had heard from Black Elk.

From this point on, the narrative of *When the Tree Flowered* relies even more centrally and explicitly on collaborative storytelling. Eagle Voice may begin a story, like the folk tale "Falling Star, the Savior" (chapter 18), only to turn it over to another storyteller to finish, as he does with No Water at the end of the chapter: "I think I will be a little boy now. I have raised Falling Star and made much *papa*. That is the hardest part. Now Moves Walking, my grandson here, and I will listen. No Water will be the grandfather and he will tell us all what happened next" (*Tree*, 167). In other places, the storyteller accompanies his story with gestures or performances, and in many cases he calls for similar enactments from his auditors, who are familiar with the oral-formulaic qualities of the story. Like the call-and-response of the African-American church and its adaptation to cultural forms as different as gospel songs and African-American lyric poetry and prose narrative, the storytelling situation presents itself in both *Black Elk Speaks* and *When the Tree Flowered* as an alternative to the conventional

Euro-American narrative protocol of the single author and individualized protagonist.

Although Neihardt's formal organization of *Black Elk Speaks* grafts elements of the novel of education with those of the anthropological and the conventional romance in *When the Tree Flowered* distracts us from that work's ideological critique, both texts establish a dialectical relationship in the encounter of Lakota and Euro-American cultures that respects the legitimacy of Lakota history and lifeways. DeMallie has repeatedly expressed his respect for Neihardt's knowledge of Lakota traditions, preservation of Black Elk's narrative authority, and use of *Black Elk Speaks* and *When the Tree Flowered* to reform our policies toward Native Americans.[66] Although Clyde Holler criticizes DeMallie and others for defending "Neihardt's faithfulness to Black Elk's message" by "unintentionally" deprecating "his art and . . . his true vocation as an artist," DeMallie is quite consistent in claiming that "Neihardt intended both of these volumes as contributions of American literature" and "interpretations of Lakota culture and history that would preserve what was good and beautiful and true in traditional lifeways" (SG, xx–xxi).[67]

Nevertheless, DeMallie himself relies on a conventional and very Euro-American theory of literature, as the work of a single author transforming real experiences into fictional or poetic expressions that may claim some special poetic authenticity or truth. Demonstrating in his own scholarship the extent to which both of Neihardt's texts rely on "primary material," DeMallie also concludes that such testimony survives as "American literature" thanks primarily to Neihardt's authorship:

> [Neihardt] served as a translator of the Sioux past whose audience has proved not to be limited by space or time. Through his writings, Black Elk, Eagle Elk, and other old men who were of that last generation of Sioux to have participated in the old buffalo-hunting life and the disorienting period of strife with the U.S. Army, found a literary voice. What they said chronicles a dramatic transition in the life of the Plains Indians; the record of their thoughts, interpreted by Neihardt . . . transcends the specifics of this one tragic case of cultural misunderstanding and conflict and speaks to universal human concerns. (*Tree*, xvii)

DeMallie's theory of literature is recognizably modern and Euro-American, arguing for the capacity of literature to transform the local and historical into the universal.

This is not the best way to describe the *literary function* of *Black Elk Speaks* and *When the Tree Flowered* from their first publication to the present. First, the "literariness" of these texts consists of the complex cultural encounter between Euro-Americans and Lakota, which is historically recounted in the U.S. government's genocidal policies toward Native Americans and the varieties of Native American resistance, adaptation, and survival. This complex history is represented best in the dialogical form of the narratives and their projection of a more dialectical historical relation between the two societies. In such an approach to the literariness of these texts, then, the rich symbolic and spiritual traditions of the Lakota would have to be included as constitutive elements, rather than merely "materials" composed into Western art by John Neihardt. In treating Lakota and Euro-American symbolic conventions in this manner, we also may overcome tendencies to link literary achievement with Euro-American civilization, trivializing the symbolic systems of Native American orality.[68] By the same token, Neihardt's "changes" in those materials have to be judged in terms of their two possible purposes either in service of the continuing work of cultural imperialism or as examples of how Lakota and Euro-American cultures might change each other in a more dynamic, productive, and decidedly less one-sided history. In short, we should assess Neihardt's changes in and additions to his Lakota collaborators' stories in terms of their contributions to an ideology of assimilation, nativism, or transcultural exchange.

When the Tree Flowered repeatedly stresses the communal work of telling the Lakota past that involves Eagle Voice, No Water, Moves Walking, and the Euro-American narrator, to whom the latter specifically refers as "collaborators" (Tree, 164). The myth of the Vanishing American contributes to the ideology of assimilation by pushing residual traces of Native American cultures into an ever-receding past and focusing on the tragic but inevitable powerlessness of the unassimilated remainder in the present.[69] Drawing on the stories of old Lakota men, Black Elk Speaks and When the Tree Flowered risk contributing to this destructive myth, but in affirming their powers as storytellers, critics of contemporary Euro-American culture, spiritual sages, and symbolic artists, the narrators of these two texts affirm the dynamism of Lakota culture and effectively interpret "old age" in the Lakota, rather than Euro-American, way: as a sign of tradition and wisdom deserving respect, rather than of a dead past.[70]

Produced in the period of crucial transition from the Dawes Act's ideology of assimilation to the Indian Reorganization Act's reaffirmation of Native Americans' rights to political sovereignty and cultural self-expression, Black Elk Speaks and When the Tree Flowered not only enable the Lakota to tell their own story but also thematize many of the epistemological problems confronted by Euro-Americans who are interested in hearing and understanding that story. Without learning some of the basic tenets of Lakota history, myth, religion, social organization, and storytelling, the Euro-American reader cannot understand the violence done to the Lakota in personal terms, equivalent to an injury that reader might experience. For example, the destruction of the great buffalo herds did more than deprive the Lakota of their primary food source and basic economy; it shattered ecological, social, and spiritual traditions tied to the buffalo and a hunting-gathering economy. Insofar as these two literary versions of the Black Elk narratives problematize the encounter of the different epistemologies of

Lakota and Euro-American cultures, then they go far beyond the traditional purpose of the anthropological text to acquire and classify "knowledge" of another culture, as an unproblematic commodity.

The historical information about the Plains Wars, Lakota spiritual practices, and the greed of both settlers and the U.S. government that Neihardt adds to the stories told by the Lakota in *Black Elk Speaks* should thus be understood to function often as part of the general project of cultural translation. Such translations are always flawed by their tendency to appropriate and thus totally displace the social text they are attempting to communicate, but it is a risk that Black Elk and his Lakota companions were willing to take when they agreed to be interviewed by John Neihardt. The damage to bodies in colonial conquest too often appears to the observer or reader as abstractly horrible, but lacks personal meaning and a sensible, affective dimension. Distancing and defamiliarizing such injury are often methods of neutralizing, even repressing, the violence of colonial domination. Personalizing such injury in universally "human" terms, without respecting specific histories and cultures, can often unwittingly do the same work of cultural repression. By dramatizing the epistemological, historical, and finally psychological difficulties involved in comprehending the military defeat, social containment, and eventual cultural and economic domination of the Lakota, the Black Elk narratives keep before the reader the suffering of particular individuals and historically specific tribal communities.

In dramatizing the encounter between cultures in terms of the problem of narrative authority, *Black Elk Speaks* and *When the Tree Flowered* encourage readers to consider how discursive and rhetorical practices, often of the most conventional and thus unconscious sort, can contribute to colonial domination and cultural misunderstanding. Each text in its own way reproduces some of these problems, even as each offers alternatives to conventional Euro-American modes of narration. *Black Elk Speaks* lends itself to anthropological conclusions, offering as it does each "native informant" in turn, including his testament for recording, translation, and archival classification. However much the communal ways of Lakota society speak through the different subjects of the 1931 interviews, *Black Elk Speaks* still constructs a central individual, Nick Black Elk, whose qualifications as medicine man and warrior-witness give him special authenticity for the anthropological inquiry undertaken by Neihardt. *When the Tree Flowered* subscribes to many of the conventions of the Euro-American novel, from its plot to its development of characters, and it thus allows readers to disregard its political criticism in favor of its aesthetic ideology. Operating at a second-remove from anthropological knowledge but derived unmistakably from it, Euro-American literary renderings of Native American lives and cultures have long served the purposes of cultural imperialism. *When the Tree Flowered* is not, however, simply another version of the many literary appropriations of "Indians" intended to celebrate the superiority of the Euro-American in the course of exploring the "curiosities" of savage customs.[71]

By encouraging communal modes of telling that are specifically Lakota and that run counter to the novelistic conventions of bourgeois individuation and education, the text offers alternative modes of knowing to those of the dominant culture.

As hybrid and at times contradictory texts, *Black Elk Speaks* and *When the Tree Flowered* are valuable literary performances that challenge ideas of Lakota authenticity, proper literary authority, and Euro-American knowledge production. To be understood in these ways, however, neither text can be considered the work of "John G. Neihardt." Similarly, our interests in these texts should not be governed primarily by discovering the "true" Nick Black Elk, who must forever remain a product of different symbolic systems. Scholarly work like DeMallie's reconstruction of the 1931 and 1944 interviews is invaluable in helping us assess the different and often incompatible literary purposes of Neihardt, Nick Black Elk, Ben Black Elk, and the other speakers and recorders who had discursive parts to play and thus rhetorical interests to serve in the interviews, the composition of the texts, and their popular and scholarly receptions. Yet insofar as the scholarly rendering of "Nick Black Elk" as a biographical and historical figure offers to substitute his person—and political and spiritual views—for the Lakota culture in conflict with Euro-American culture represented in *Black Elk Speaks* and *When the Tree Flowered*, then it is doing a disservice to two works of considerable historical and theoretical value in the critical account of modern U.S. imperialism.

I began this chapter with an epigraph from Black Elk's 1931 interviews, which would eventually be incorporated into *Black Elk Speaks* but without reference to the specific site on the Rosebud that Black Elk names in his interview, Rock Writing Bluff. Neihardt's rendering of Black Elk's account diminishes the "miracle" of this pictographic and prophetic writing on the rock, perhaps because Neihardt is embarrassed by Black Elk's confidence that such writings are truly miraculous and sacred.[72] "People said" this writing announces the defeat of Custer at the Battle of the Little Big Horn in 1876, Neihardt's Black Elk says, but "I do not know; but it was there then, and it did not seem that anybody could get up that high to make a picture" (BE, 132). Neihardt is perhaps also embarrassed by the fact that Black Elk claims such pictographic devices as "writing," so he omits the name of "Rock Writing Bluff" from this passage. But in his 1931 account, Black Elk speaks confidently of the appearance of these pictographs to anticipate the battle and to announce where the Lakota should camp. Euro-Americans are fond of thinking of Native American cultures as primarily oral, as if oral modes of cultural representation are inferior to the technology of writing, but Black Elk understands the "writing" on Rock Writing Bluff to be merely a mnemonic device, a reminder of what is already more truly graven in the hearts of the Lakota, thanks to their oral and communal modes of telling: that they will defend their lands and ways of life in *He Sapa* from the imperial power of the U.S. Army. Such pictographs often appear miraculous or prophetic to the reader unfamiliar with the oral traditions in which they function as markers of a narrative already known by each member of the tribe. Versions of the more formal historical records, the winter-counts, through which the Lakota maintained their tribal bonds, these prophetic writings on the cliff merely announce what ought to be well known to members of the tribe already. Like a political slogan, a poster, or mere graffiti ("Kick Custer's Ass!") posted or scrawled in a city's square, the pictographs on Rock Writing Bluff are instances of communal activism, the *writing* of the cultural unconscious. By enabling us to read this different kind of cultural narration in the Euro-American print narratives *Black Elk Speaks*, *When the Tree Flowered*, and *The Sixth Grandfather*, Neihardt, DeMallie, and their Lakota collaborators, even when they did not intend it, have helped expose and resist the colonization and eradication of Native American voices by making comprehensible the traditions of Lakota communalism. Put another way, they have enabled the Euro-American reader who questions U.S. policies toward Native Americans to view this history from the perspective of Rock Writing Bluff.

11

Opening the Gate to the Other America

The Afro-Caribbean Politics of Hurston's
Mules and Men *and* Tell My Horse

Afrique-Guinin Atibon Legba, ouvrir barriere
pour nous.
> Voodoo Chant to Papa Legba, quoted in Hurston,
> *Tell My Horse* (1938)

We were on a first-name basis, Stella and I, but I was
unhappy that she held that job [as librarian]. I was
unhappy because even though Stella was nice, she
was still a white woman. A white woman from a
place where there were only white Christians. To
her Shakespeare was a god. I didn't mind that, but
what did she know about the folk tales and riddles
and stories colored folks had been telling for
centuries? What did she know about the language we
spoke? . . . They often take the kindest white people
to colonize the colored community.
> Easy Rawlins in Walter Mosley, *White Butterfly* (1992)

Zora Neale Hurston's criticism of racial and gender hierarchies
in the United States and in our foreign policies toward other
nations, especially in the Caribbean, offers another variation on the cultural
response to U.S. imperialism. Unlike W. E. B. Du Bois, Hurston does not consistently and dogmatically condemn U.S. intervention in the economic,
political, and social spheres of other nations, even though she clearly connects domestic racism and sexism with neoimperialist foreign policies,
especially those directed at Third World countries. Also unlike Du Bois,
Hurston does not romanticize modern or historical Africa, even though she
argues consistently for the recognition of how African cultural influences

have contributed significantly to the artistic, intellectual, and social achievements of African-Americans. In a similar manner, Hurston refuses to idealize colonized peoples as exclusively victimized by their conquerors; she goes to considerable lengths to show how the process of decolonization, in Haiti, for example, has too often brought tyrants to power who have rationalized their injustices on grounds of national sovereignty and strident anti-colonialism. Du Bois put himself in an intellectual and political position where he finally had to choose between U.S. racism at home and imperialism abroad or Stalinist oppression and imperialism. Hurston criticizes all the tyrannies she witnesses, and she thus alienates herself from U.S. nationalists of various sorts, African nationalists (whom we would term today Afrocentrists), and Communist critics of U.S. imperialism.

At the same time, Hurston often seems to universalize the thesis that "power corrupts," in a way that trivializes concrete solutions to the problems she identifies in the United States and the Caribbean. In her autobiography, *Dust Tracks on a Road* (1942), Hurston criticizes Africans for having participated in the Euro-American slave trade and concludes that this history "impressed upon me the universal nature of greed and glory. Lack of power and opportunity passes off too often for virtue. If I were King, let us say, over the Western Hemisphere tomorrow, instead of who I am, what would I consider right and just? Would I put the cloak of Justice on my ambition and send her out a-whoring after conquests? It is something to ponder with fear."[1] In such moments, Hurston sounds like Mark Twain, universalizing imperialism and racism in ways that make resistance seem impossible or futile. Yet behind Hurston's scorn for arbitrary power, whether wielded by white or black tyrants, and her contempt for those who render virtuous their own victimization, there is Hurston's strong commitment to democratic rule and her conviction that solidarity among different victimized peoples will both empower them and effect appropriate social reforms. These reforms include for Hurston an end to racial and gender hierarchies and the extension of economic opportunities to underprivileged groups, both within the United States and internationally. The utopian model for such social reforms is a truly democratic society in the United States, despite Hurston's consistent criticism of social inequalities in the United States based on race and gender.

Whereas Du Bois would finally renounce the United States in despair over the persistence of its racism and its ever-expanding imperial ambitions, Hurston clings to her own version of American idealism even as she was alienated and finally silenced both by the white ruling class and African-American nationalist groups. Her notorious political conservatism in the 1950s reflects in part, I think, her long-standing commitment to the elimination of racism and sexism in the interests of a democratic United States that would be the *social model* for the rest of the world. As I shall argue, Hurston's social ideal depended on the assimilation and hybridization of different cultural and social traditions; it would not meet today's standards for "multiculturalism" in the United States, for example, and it would certainly be subject to criticism for endorsing "melting-pot" ideology. Hurston's social idealism also placed her in a potentially conservative political position in the 1930s and 1940s with regard to U.S. foreign policies in the Caribbean and Latin America, because she often endorsed in qualified ways foreign political, economic, and even military interventions by the United States that were in the interests of increasing democratic opportunities.

In short, Hurston did not reject categorically the idea of the United States as "global policeman" or the possibility of U.S. foreign policies, especially in the Caribbean, contributing to democratic ends. In this regard, she was by no means unusual among majority and minority U.S. intellectuals in the 1930s and 1940s. For example, Emily Greene Balch (1867–1961), who devoted her energies tirelessly to anti-imperialism and pacifism from World War I to the post–World War II era, noted in her "Social Values in Haiti," which she wrote in 1926 during her visit to Occupied Haiti: "The colonizing and imperialist countries have hitherto asked that we must either let 'backward peoples' alone or else take control of them. We have profited little by our evolving social experience if we cannot invent any ways of being useful to a country like Haiti that Haitians themselves would approve and welcome. . . . It is still possible for us to prove that a great power can be just, friendly, and respectful to a small one."[2] Arriving in Haiti to do research on Voodoo one year after the U.S. occupation had ended, Hurston concludes in *Tell My Horse*: "The occupation is ended and Haiti is left with a stable currency, the beginnings of a system of transportation, a modern capitol, the nucleus of a modern army. So Haiti, the black republic, and where does she go from here?"[3] In his biography of Hurston, Robert Hemenway perhaps exaggerates by claiming that in *Tell My Horse* Hurston "consistently praises the nineteen-year occupation of that country by American marines," but (with important exceptions I will address below) Hurston generally views the U.S. presence in Haiti as a necessary stabilizing influence in a supposedly "postcolonial" society that has had "fourteen revolutions [and] three out-and-out kingdoms" since it became independent (T, 74).[4]

By the same token, Hurston understood the continuing racism and sexism in the United States as forms of colonial domination, which required strategies of resistance that at times complement more explicit anti-colonial and post-colonial struggles around the world. Never did she confuse the reality of social stratifications by race, class, and gender with her ideals for democratic social, legal, and human practices. And it is the conflict between Hurston's strategies for revealing and resisting such oppression at home and abroad *and* her ideals for the spread of democratic institutions, especially as they are represented by the promise of U.S. democracy, that often contributes to the contradictory quality of her political judgments or the impression of her *apolitical* stance. Hurston's politics are often bound up with her own self-image as a progressive, "new Negro," embodying urban sophistication and specialized education, who sought to connect the rural and Afro-Caribbean heritage of African Americans with their modern future.

All of this is further complicated by Hurston's tendency to "code" messages into narratives she imagined were subject to the unofficial but still powerful censorship of the prevailing white social order, often represented for her by figures like her patron, Charlotte Osgood Mason, and Columbia mentor, Franz Boas.[5] On the one hand, Hurston believed that Euro-American culture, society, and psychology had much to learn from African-American forms of knowledge and experience; in her utopian moments, she imagines white America transformed and redeemed by such knowledge. On the other hand, she understood the prevalence of a white ideology that treated much of African-American knowledge as "backward," "superstitious," and "primitive," even as whites turned these very characteristics into aspects of an exoticized and fashionable "negritude." What some critics have referred to as Hurston's "coding" of her narratives should be understood as her primary mode of narration, whose purpose is to transform attitudes and feelings, together with preconceived ideas, rather than merely "hiding" her intentions to protect her patronage. Learning to read the "double consciousness" of Hurston's coded narratives is itself a way of transgressing the boundary separating African American from white American, even as it respects the social and historical differences of the racism that has yet to be overcome.[6]

Mules and Men (1935) and *Tell My Horse* (1938) are often treated together for generic reasons, because they are major examples of Hurston's work as folklorist and anthropologist.[7] They are also interpreted together by some critics as using literary techniques that anticipate Hurston's major fiction.[8] Still others distinguish sharply between *Mules and Men* and *Tell My Horse* as representing distinctly different stages in Hurston's anthropological methodology, transformed from the scientific ethnography of Boas and Ruth Benedict in *Mules and Men* to the more literary and comparative methods of *Tell My Horse*.[9]

Few have read the two works together, however, as related *narratives* with anthropological, literary, and *autobiographical* significance.[10] Interpreted in this way, the two works stage a drama in which the scientific and literary observer is reintroduced to her rural roots in the South, then initiated into her Afro-Caribbean heritage in New Orleans, Jamaica, and Haiti. Rather than treating this quest as an alternative to or escape from the urban experiences of African Americans in the North after the great migration of the post–World War I period, Hurston links urban and rural, northern and southern, U.S. and Caribbean cultural practices. She attempts to uncover the secret continuity of West African, Caribbean, rural U.S., and urban U.S. cultures for African Americans. Hurston's journey also retraces one of the principal routes traveled by Africans from West Africa to the Western Hemisphere. This is, of course, the path from capture by slave-traders in West Africa through the Middle Passage to slavery in the Caribbean and the

United States. Hurston's travels from her hometown of Eatonville, Florida, to New Orleans, Louisiana, in *Mules and Men*, then to Jamaica and Haiti in *Tell My Horse* put her back in touch with this history of the violent colonization of Africans. The journey also enables her to rediscover those modes of cultural self-expression used by Africans in the Americas to resist colonial domination, represent their own identities, and thereby establish their own communities.

In *Let Us Now Praise Famous Men* (1941), James Agee points out that the migrations of Africans enforced by slavery and then occasioned by revolution are also crossed and recrossed by migrations of Euro-Americans. Walker Evans and Agee meet the white landowner and "New Deal executive," Harmon in "the Coffee Shoppe," and he introduces them to an "other, whose name I forget, but which had a French sound." Agee continues: "It turned out that I had not been mistaken in the French sound of his name; ancestors of his had escaped an insurrection of negroes in Haiti. He himself, however, was entirely localized, a middling well-to-do landowner with a little more of the look of the direct farmer about him than average."[11] Whereas William Faulkner's Thomas Sutpen concludes his white migration consumed along with Sutpen's Hundred by apocalyptic flames, Agee and Evans's character has become an "entirely localized" southern farmer. Harmon and his friend with the French-sounding name introduce them to rural Alabama by summoning three young African-American men to "sing for Walker and for me," in a scene that is intended to be a narrative gateway to the South and an indictment of the anthropological voyeurism Agee and Evans hope to avoid. Describing music with the best modernist prose he can muster, Agee knows the words are inadequate: "It tore itself like a dance of sped plants out of three young men who stood sunk to their throats in land, and whose eyes were neither shut nor looking at anything." Agee and Evans are appropriately embarrassed to be party to the formal ceremony arranged by these white landowners, and yet they are dazzled by a music whose "nearest approach to its austerity" in "western music . . . is in the first two centuries of polyphony."[12]

Agee and Evans by no means retrace the sort of comprehensive journey back to the Afro-Caribbean and African roots of southern culture that Hurston enacts in *Mules and Men* and *Tell My Horse*. Nevertheless, they suggest the degree to which that pattern of cultural migration is marked all along its way by conflict and struggle with whites, who for very different reasons preceded and followed, contested and repressed, the forced and willed migrations of African Americans. It is the deliberate forgetting of this history of entangled fates and thus of cultural realities that Hurston condemns in the official histories of the United States and that we ought to class as an important aspect of U.S. cultural imperialism.

Most interpreters of *Mules and Men* discuss Hurston's complex narratorial relation to the African-American rural folklore she is encouraged by her mentor, Boas, to collect in her journey back home to Eatonville and then into Polk County, Florida. Often credited with anticipating the methods of the "New Ethnographic Movement of the 1950s and 1960s" and even the more recent poststructuralist anthropology of the "writing culture" group, Hurston incorporates into *Mules and Men* a metafolkloric dimension that focuses on her narrator's complex relation to her materials.[13] Hurston dramatizes in her double-consciousness of the educated, urban, sophisticated African-American anthropologist who is returning to her southern roots not only the potential problems facing African Americans divided between rural and urban influences; she also demonstrates the special advantages of this double-consciousness.[14] In order to gain access to the relatively closed communities she visits, Hurston's narrator must draw on her own powers of storytelling, "lying" in the idiom of the oral cultures she is visiting: "Them big old lies we tell when we're jus' sittin' around here on the store porch" (M, 8). Well-dressed, driving her Chevy coupe, Hurston's narrative delegate, "Zora," is suspected by folks in Polk County of being a revenuer or a detective of some kind until she poses as a bootlegger and is accepted (M, 60–61).[15]

Lying, woofing, and bookooing, among the many names given to storytelling in these oral cultures, are always rooted in the cultural sense that economic and social injustices require a certain *deception* at the economic and cultural levels in order for African Americans to survive their oppression. Unlike white Protestantism's reliance on strict moral divisions, for example, African-American folk culture gives special privilege to the trickster, who is embodied in characters like John and Jack, themselves avatars of the Devil. As Hemenway points out, "The devil in black folklore is not the terror he is in European folklore. Rather, he is a powerful trickster who often competes successfully with God."[16] In a story Mathilda tells early in the narrative about the origin of gender differences, Woman gets the keys to the kitchen, the bedroom, and the cradle from God, but only because the Devil tells her to ask for them and helps her interpret them. Of course, when Woman thanks the Devil—"If it wasn't for you, Lawd knows whut us po' women folks would do" (M, 33)—the unique patriarchy of the rural African-American community seems invoked, but in Mathilda's conclusion that African-American women rely on both God and the Devil she is expressing one of the secret truths—a "true lie" in the folklore (M, 171)—for both men and women of color.

The Devil in African-American folklore is generally treated as a counterforce to the deviltry practiced by whites on African Americans, but even the Devil himself can sometimes be outwitted by the folk hero. On her last night at the sawmill camp in Polk County, Zora hears "the last Loughman story around midnight" about "Jack and de Devil buckin' 'ginst one 'nother to see which one was de strongest" (M, 155). Cliffert's story celebrates finally not so much Jack's physical strength as his rhetorical powers. The Devil throws his hammer so high it takes two days to come down again; Jack never even throws the hammer, he just:

Walked 'round de hammer to de handle and took holt of it and throwed his head back and looked up at de sky: "Look out, Rayfield! Move over, Gabriel! You better stand 'way back, Jesus! Ah'm fixin' to throw." He meant Heaven.

Devil ran up to 'im, says, "Hold on dere a minute! Don't you throw mah damn hammer up dere! Ah left a whole lot uh mah tools up dere when dey put me out and Ah ain't got 'em back yet. Don't you *throw* mah hammer up dere!" (M, 156)

Jack's rhetorical power over the Devil derives in part from Jack's knowledge of Scripture and the Devil's history as a fallen angel. His familiarity with Jesus and the archangels also expresses his privilege and power, but it is clear in this and many other stories that both God and the Devil are equally capable of tricking African Americans. In this folk cosmology, good and evil are neither fixed nor exclusive categories; social and performative contexts shape moral consequences more than any recorded code of ethics.[17]

Retelling the traditional African-American folktale about the origins of the division of labor between African Americans and whites, Jim Presley seems to reinforce racial stereotypes about white superiority in reading, writing, and accounting and the African American's destiny as manual laborer: "When de nigger opened up his bundle he found a pick and shovel and a hoe and a plow and chop-axe and then de white man opened up his bundle and found a writin'-pen and ink. So ever since then de nigger been out in de hot sun, usin' his tools and de white man been sittin' up figgerin', ought's a ought, figger's a figger; all for de white man, none for de nigger" (M, 75). Elsewhere, I have interpreted this retelling of the folktale in *Mules and Men* as Hurston's way of subtly dramatizing the rhetorical superiority of the African-American folkteller over the white accountant.[18] *Mules and Men* offers repeated examples of the discursive complexity of African-American rural communities and of how the social bond is maintained by ceaseless and diverse oral practices. As Rosan Augusta Jordan argues, Hurston "keeps the focus . . . clearly on the community, dramatizing their performances . . . rather than letting the narrator give her own."[19] Whereas white culture is often criticized for its literal and strictly referential uses of language and nonverbal signs, the African-American communities Hurston visits self-consciously depend on the figurative qualities of language. Terms like "signifyin'," "woofin'," and "figgerin'" variously express the rhetorically and performatively flexible aspects of language. Larkins explains at one point: "There's a whole heap of them kinda by-words. . . . They all got a hidden meanin', jus' like de Bible. Everybody can't understand what they mean. Most people is thin-brained. They's born wid they feet under de moon. Some folks is born wid they feet on de sun and they kin seek out de inside meanin' of words" (M, 125). Whatever the etymology of "by-words," the term captures effectively the meaning of "parable":—to "throw" (*ballein*) "beside" (*para*) or to establish comparative, hence figurative, contexts for understanding. In so doing, the folkteller is always calling attention to the boundaries separating man from woman, good from evil, God from the Devil, white from black. Even when the stories repeat the stereotypes of patriarchy, racial superiority, or religious orthodoxy, they remind the listener of the socially constructed qualities of such meanings and thus the ability of the teller (and the listener) to *change* those meanings.[20]

Although richly allusive to Christian sources, especially the Bible, the folklore organized in part one of *Mules and Men* offers a very different representation of Christian spirituality than what we associate with Protestant or Catholic orthodoxy. Folk heroes and religious figures communicate easily; God, Jesus, the Devil, and archangels betray quite human inclinations to be tricked and to sin. In *Tell My Horse*, Hurston explicitly interprets the Voodoo gods as social and human constructs, claiming that "Gods always behave like the people who make them" (T, 219). In *Mules and Men*, she is not as overt, but the oral folk traditions of African Americans appear to imply as much. Commenting in the "Glossary" that "God never finds fault, never censures the Negro," Hurston notes that God "is lacking in bitterness as is the Negro story-teller himself in circumstances that ordinarily would call for pity," suggesting that such divine authority is just another persona or voice in which the storyteller speaks (M, 248). Indeed, the storyteller and God share the power of words to create and sustain worlds, and Hurston's affirmation, even exaggeration, of such discursive power is especially important for rural African Americans, many of whom were illiterate. As Beulah Hemmingway has written: "Functionally such folklore educated and inspired blacks while defending their humanity and preserving African culture."[21]

The African elements of the folklore in *Mules and Men* are prominent and help counter charges that Hurston's anthropology reinforces stereotypes of African-American rural primitivism. Using trickster tales, especially animal fabliaux, of West African derivation but adapted to the animals and natural landscape of Florida, Hurston's storytellers resist the white reader's temptation to stereotype them as uneducated naifs, charmingly expressing social conditions rapidly being replaced by modern industrial culture.[22] Rather than talking their ways into a kind of cultural provincialism, Hurston's *griots* repeatedly invoke folklore and mythic backgrounds unfamiliar in the usual mythic and religious traditions of Western civilization. Strong and intelligent folk heroes who beat the Devil and trick slavemasters and small, weak animals or people capable of talking their way out of life-threatening circumstances may have certain analogies, even occasional sources, in Euro-American folk stories and myths, but more often than not the stories Hurston collects, even when they are themselves obvious hybrids, challenge white conventions of self-reliant individualism, honesty rewarded, a just social order, and a world of equal opportunities. The folk heroes in these tales, sermons, songs, sayings, and games struggle with and in an unpredictable, often unjust world that more realistically represents the historical experiences of African Americans.[23]

The folktales organized and thus narrated by Hurston in part one of *Mules and Men* offer various forms of resistance to slavery; many of the stories focus on the ability of folk heroes, like John and High John de Conquer and Jack, to fool the slaveowner. But excessive emphasis on these folktales as principally rhetorical weapons of resistance to slavery and racism in the United States can distract us from Hurston's equally important point about the self-sufficient, oral-formulaic African-American cultures represented by such stories. Such folktales are not, in other words, exclusively driven by the need to resist dominant white rule and its system of values; taken collectively, this oral culture is not just the brave but finally sad expression of African-American victimization.[24]

Yet no matter how sympathetically Hurston attempts to assemble these stories or how often she appeals to her own childhood in Eatonville, as long as her narrative follows the ethnographic methods of Boas and Benedict she cannot overcome the impression that these folktales are either quaint mementos of a vanishing ruralism or the plaintive and compensatory tales of oppressed people. Even what Zora, her narrator, terms the narrative "between-story business" often contributes to the elaborate framing devices that suggest these folktales require anthropological forms and methods to *control* their unruliness. Only the sudden immersion of Zora into the social drama of the lives she had planned merely to observe enables Hurston to carry the narrative beyond intellectual classifications and sentimental autobiography. Crucial to this narrative shift is Zora's discovery at once of danger, passionate feelings, and the *existence* of her own body in the midst of a social conflict. As a consequence, she is virtually re-embodied, perhaps even *reincarnated*, in ways that will play ever more central roles in the recovery of her own African-American and African identity in part two of *Mules and Men*, "Hoodoo," and *Tell My Horse*.[25]

From her arrival at the African-American sawmill camp in Loughman, Florida, in Chapter 4 to the end of part one of *Mules and Men*, Zora's identity for the reader and the members of the community is shaped by her friendship with Big Sweet and Lucy's jealousy. At first best friends, Big Sweet and Lucy are jealous rivals for the same men and for Zora's friendship. Initially feared and then ignored by the sawmill residents, because of her outward signs of wealth (her car and store-bought clothes), Zora is clearly a stranger who provokes conflicting feelings of admiration, envy, and hatred (M, 63). The community's mixed emotions about Zora surface in Lucy and Big Sweet's conflict over her, culminating in the violent knife fight in the jook that ends part one. This is the climactic event that causes Zora to run for her life from Loughman, even though it is also the moment in which she ceases to be a stranger and achieves identity within the community. Hurston does not idealize the friendship between Big Sweet and Zora or the violence between Big Sweet and Lucy. Although Big Sweet's willingness to fight with

Lucy to defend Zora suggests friendship more strongly felt and thus more *real* than anything Zora might have known in New York or even Eatonville, it is a mistake to idealize this friendship, as some critics have, as a feminist alternative either to male-female relations or friendships between women in polite society.[26] The reality of the violence between Big Sweet and Lucy is meant to terrify the reader, reminding her or him that this is a rough community that should not be upheld as a viable alternative to modern urban life in the North or the South. Yet it is also one of the several kinds of rural southern communities from which many northern African Americans emigrated, and as such it is part of their cultural heritage, which Hurston is anxious not only to preserve but also to *retell* in connection with the modernization process in which she views African Americans integrally involved.

Loughman is neither a community to be despised nor idealized. Hurston tries to find within it those cultural forces, often connected with storytelling and folk-wisdom, that might help empower modern African Americans, but to do so she must immerse herself in a decidedly destructive element. Hurston suggests that Big Sweet uses her friendship with Zora in the same way she "figures" (shows off) with folktales or in cardgames. In general, the folktales told in Loughman are told in part to sublimate or, less subtly, momentarily defer the simmering violence of this community. Hurston implies that the source of this violence is the economic exploitation and social ostracism of African Americans by the dominant white culture, although she rarely makes explicit this social criticism, preferring instead to focus on the internal dynamics of the African-American community, just as she remains focused on the inner workings of Eatonville in earlier sections of the book. Except for the fact that people at the sawmill camp display an especially rich and diverse oral tradition of storytelling, there is little in this community that Hurston recommends to the modern urban reader.

Mules and Men does offer a sustained criticism of how patriarchy and racial hierarchies control African Americans in the rural South. Anticipating and influencing Alice Walker's *The Color Purple*, Hurston shows how violence within the African-American community often reflects the class, racial, and gender hierarchies of the wider social order.[27] In this respect, Meisenhelder is certainly right when she concludes:

> Gender inequality is not only grounded in racial inequality (the Black woman's burden can, after all, be traced back to the white man who originally orders the Black man to pick it up); it also operates in strikingly parallel ways in *Mules and Men*. . . . A world controlled by whites, one . . . in which Black men are economically oppressed and socially defined by them, is a world of mules and men. Tragically, for Hurston, when Black men draw their concepts from white people and make themselves feel like men by slipping their halters onto Black women, the Black community becomes another world of mules and men.[28]

The recognition that African-American women in the rural South and the urban North share a common heritage of racial and gender oppression may well be one important purpose of the dangerous conflicts among Big Sweet, Zora, and Lucy, thereby mitigating somewhat the aura of "primitive" violence surrounding this episode.

At crucial moments, Hurston clearly states that the violence between African Americans is often a displaced version of their rebellion against unjust social and economic circumstances. In her earlier confrontation with Lucy's friend, Ella Wall, Big Sweet vies with the Quarters Boss, who tells both women: "This place is for people that works on this job. . . . Gimme that knife you got dere, Big Sweet" (M, 152). But Big Sweet refuses, warning the Quarters Boss, "Don't you touch me, white folks!" and eliciting Joe Willard's admiration: "You wuz noble! . . . You wuz uh whole woman and half uh man. You made dat cracker stand off a *you*" (M, 152). When she rises above petty, local jealousies to challenge white authority, Big Sweet achieves the "oral heroic mode" that elevates her to status with mythic male folk heroes.[29] Such moments of open rebellion against white authority are, however, rare in *Mules and Men*; storytelling in which the African-American hero gets the better of the white man (or his mythic representative) seems a far more viable mode of resistance for Hurston, especially when the realities of rural and urban America in the 1930s are taken into account.

Zora's friendship with Big Sweet represents Zora's ties to a folk culture that is nevertheless threatening and still foreign to the very last moment of her contact with it. The tenuous connection she establishes with this culture depends crucially on her sense of her own body as constituted in and through the many discursive practices—folk tales, nicknames, songs and dances and music at the jooks, games, showing off (figurin') and flirting (woofin')—through which individuals attain social visibility in what appears initially to be a culturally as well as economically impoverished community. Lucy says as she bursts into the Pine Mill jook to attack Zora, who will be defended by Big Sweet, "Stop dat music. . . . Don't vip another vop till Ah say so! Ah means tuh turn dis place out right now. Ah got de law in mah mouf" (M, 179). Lucy's authority at this moment is more than just her commanding voice, more than just verbal language; it is a complex body-language—"So she started walking hippily straight at me"—and so is Zora's response: "I didn't move but I was running in my skin. I could hear the blade already crying in my flesh. I was sick and weak" (M, 179).

The celebration at Pine Mill is in honor of Cliff and Thelma's wedding, which would provide conventional narrative closure and social legitimation to end part one, were it not for the competing, disruptive claims of Lucy with her knife. Yet, a symbolic marriage does occur in the melee that follows at the jook-joint, because Zora finally enters into the community of the sawmill, however briefly, by experiencing physically and emotionally what she has hitherto tried primarily to describe and interpret in intellectual terms. In "How It Feels to Be Colored Me" (1928), Hurston distinguishes between her response to the jazz at the New World Cabaret and a white man's:

> This orchestra grows rambunctious, rears on its hind legs and attacks the tonal veil with primitive fury, rending it, clawing it until it breaks through to the jungle beyond. I follow those heathen—follow them exultingly. I dance wildly inside myself; I yell within, I whoop; I shake my assegai above my head, I hurl it true to the mark *yeeeeooww!* I am in the jungle and living in the jungle way. My face is painted red and yellow and my body is painted blue. My pulse is throbbing like a war drum. I want to slaughter something—give pain, give death to what, I do not know. But the piece ends . . . I creep back slowly to the veneer we call civilization with the last tone and find the white friend sitting motionless in his seat, smoking calmly.
>
> "Good music they have here," he remarks, drumming the table with his fingertips.
>
> Music. The great blobs of purple and red emotion have not touched him. He has only heard what I felt. . . . He is so pale with his whiteness then and I am *so* colored.[30]

Barbara Johnson notes how Hurston plays with white conventions of exotic primitivism and what Hurston criticizes elsewhere as the myth of the African-American "reversion to type."[31] The "color" that accompanies the music is not the same as the racist "color" the young Hurston unexpectedly discovers when she leaves home: "I left Eatonville, the town of oleanders, as Zora. When I disembarked from the river-boat at Jacksonville, she was no more. . . . I was not Zora of Orange County any more, I was now a little colored girl."[32] During the jazz performance, Hurston's "color" is, as Johnson notes, "skin *paint*, not skin complexion," another social mask that simply differs from the "veneer we call civilization."[33] Yet, if both African and Euro-American cultures are masks, the "jungle" Hurston experiences in the jazz performance "represents the experience of the body as such, the surge of bodily life external to conscious knowledge" that the white man, absent-mindedly "drumming the table with his fingertips," may need as much as Hurston and yet profoundly misses.[34]

In other words, Hurston's passionate experience of herself through the music is a racist "reversion to type" only if we conclude, as Hurston tempts us to do in this essay, that the music represents a pre-civilized release of instinctive passions that civilization is designed to repress and control.[35] Stylistically, figuratively, and narratively, however, the passage encourages us to identify with the African cultural vitality that is expressed in the music and the narrator's response and to distance ourselves from the comic figure of the white man, "so pale with his whiteness," for whom drumming is a nervous gesture rather than a part of social ritual. One civilization alienates us from ourselves; the other connects us to our natures in "the jungle beyond." In this context, Hurston's criticism of the alienation endemic to modern urban civilization and her suggestion of a potential cure are unremarkable conventions of the modernist avant-garde.[36]

The Pine Mill jook in Polk County, Florida, however, differs from "The New World Cabaret" in New York, because the connections among bodily sensation, affective experience, social signs, and Zora's consciousness—in this case, of *danger*—are far more immediately part of social reality. Indeed, the actual music stops on Lucy's command—"Stop dat music!"—and is replaced by the sounds of this social confrontation: "I could hear the blade already crying in my flesh," "a doubled back razor . . . whizzed past Big Sweet," "Slim stuck out the guitar to keep two struggling men from blocking my way," "Lucy was screaming," "curses, oaths, cries and the whole place was in motion" (M, 179). When she arrives in Eatonville, Zora attends a "toe-dance," where she feels foreign and alienated from her own hometown; at the end of part one, "Jim and Slim helped me throw my bags into the car," and she is, like so many other African-American women, on the run from violent husbands or lovers, jealous women, the law.

Of course, the heritage of being on the run is traceable back to slavery, and the violence that lingers in the African-American rural community is for Hurston never far from slavery's fundamental violence to the body and the spirit. When Zora lights out from that jook-joint, she has recovered some sense of the danger, risk, and violence that informs the everyday experience of southern African Americans; it is a heritage she wants to communicate to the more comfortable and secure urban intellectuals and artists of various backgrounds to whom the book is addressed. It is an experience that unsettles, destabilizes, even *terrifies* the reader far beyond the most sublime vision in romantic poetry or the most undecidable moment in Euro-American literature. Perhaps this is why Zora doesn't head north, but west to New Orleans, when she runs from Loughman. Even taking into account the great influence of the writers and artists of the Harlem Renaissance, New York remains primarily Euro-American; New Orleans is, however, "now and . . . ever . . . the Hoodoo capital of America," whose "great names in rites vie with those of Hayti in deeds that keep alive the powers of Africa" (M, 183). In part one of *Mules and Men*, Hurston uses the folktales and "in-between" narrative to criticize implicitly the economic and social racism in the United States, just as she calls attention to the residual Africanity of rural folk culture. Nevertheless, there is virtually no overt discussion of the internal colonization of African Americans by slavery and its Jim-Crow aftermath. The journey of spiritual rediscovery is incomplete at the end of part one, even if Zora "leaps" from the jook-joint with something like a new body and something like a new sensorium, in which the risks and violence of being African American are more than matters of polite discussion among the urban elite.

Although most of the material included in part two, "Hoodoo," comes from Hurston's 1931 essay, "Hoodoo in America," this part of *Mules and Men* is represented as a continuation of her narrative quest for Zora's cultural origins.[37] By turning from rural Florida to urban Louisiana, Hurston subverts a number of conventions about modern African-American experience and progress. Zora traces rural folk culture in Florida not to tribal village life in Africa but to the thriving cosmopolitanism of New Orleans, where the powers of figuring, signifying, and bookooing are more than just metaphoric—they possess the supernatural power of religious language, supported by religious forms and institutions. The "New World Cabaret" in New York, where black and white people recognize, however differently, Africanist influences on U.S. culture, is replaced in New Orleans by Hoodoo ceremonies, spells, and other sacred practices solicited both by white and black people. In New Orleans, the folk heroes of rural African-American communities—John, Jack, High John de Conquer—have their equivalents in those living celebrities, Hoodoo doctors like Luke Turner, Marie Leveau, Anatol Pierre, Father Watson (the "Frizzly Rooster"), and Kitty Brown. In the socially, racially, and culturally segregated North, the African heritage in the New World is primarily a source of entertainment; in New Orleans, that heritage has status as an organized religion that influences the overall cultural life of the city.

Hurston attempts to link together a wide variety of urban and rural folk practices of African Americans, both in the North and the South, into a coherent discourse of political resistance to what Hurston terms "the accepted theology of the Nation" (M, 185). The Voodoo cultural heritage follows a different path to the Western Hemisphere than Judeo-Christian traditions, and Hurston is one of the first theorists of a "black Atlantic" that constitutes not only African-American and Afro-Caribbean identities but also has had a demonstrable, although insufficiently recognized, influence in shaping the cultural varieties of the "New World."[38] Anticipating the more sustained argument of her novel *Moses, Man of the Mountain* (1939), Hurston begins the "Hoodoo" section of *Mules and Men* with an African origin story of Moses, "claiming that his true birthright is African and that his true constituency is Afro-American."[39] Today, we would conclude that Hurston's reinterpretation of Moses in *Mules and Men* and *Moses, Man of the Mountain* is decidedly Afrocentrist, but in *Mules and Men* her purpose seems more generously to establish a common figure linking Judeo-Christian and Afro-Christian heritages—a liminal Moses capable of speaking both to the European and African roots of the Americas. In both traditions, Moses is distinguished by his power of words, and it is precisely Hurston's goal to demonstrate that Voodoo, like European Christianity, draws much of its power from its command of signs:

> Moses was the first man who ever learned God's power-compelling words. . . . But Moses never would have stood before the Burning Bush, if he had not married Jethro's daughter. Jethro was a great hoodoo man. . . . He took Moses and taught him. So Moses passed on beyond Jethro with his rod. He lifted it up and tore a nation out of Pharaoh's

side, and Pharaoh couldn't help himself. Moses talked with the snake that lives in a hole right under God's foot-rest. Moses had fire in his head and a cloud in his mouth. The snake had told him God's making words. The words of doing and the words of obedience. Many a man thinks he is making something when he's only changing things around. But God let Moses make. . . . And ever since the days of Moses, kings have been toting rods for a sign of power. But it's mostly sham-polish because no king has ever had the power of even one of Moses' ten words. Because Moses made a nation and a book, a thousand million leaves of ordinary men's writing couldn't tell what Moses said. (M, 184–85)

Identified in Haitian Voodoo as "the father of Damballa, the king of the Rada gods," a figure often represented symbolically by the serpent (Damballa's living "rod of power"), Moses serves for Hurston as a figure of the African diaspora, especially as it was prompted by slavery: "Wherever the children of Africa have been scattered by slavery, there is the acceptance of Moses as the fountain of mystic powers."[40] Hurston continues by explaining her intention of using Moses as a mythic figure, however differently he is interpreted symbolically, for other peoples of diaspora, meaning virtually everyone who has come to live in the Western Hemisphere as a consequence of its modern colonization: "This is not confined to Negroes. In America there are countless people of other races depending upon mystic symbols and seals and syllables said to have been used by Moses to work his wonders. . . . So all across Africa, America, the West Indies, there are tales of the powers of Moses and great worship of him and his powers."[41]

Strongly influenced by Hurston's *Mules and Men* and *Tell My Horse*, Ishmael Reed would offer a similarly revisionary argument regarding the Africanity of Moses in *Mumbo Jumbo* (1972), but Reed pits the Judeo-Christian against the African Moses, reinforcing Afrocentrist arguments.[42] As Hemenway has observed, Hurston's aim is "not so much to debunk a Judeo-Christian prophet" as "to relocate him in Afro-American tradition."[43] My own view is that Hurston reinterprets Moses in an origin story about the magic of language that will link together the traditions of writing and orality that respectively organize Euro-American and African-American cultures. Moses is the common sacred figure who brings together different, but potentially complementary, modes of cultural expression, and who reminds the descendants of various diasporas that have ended in the Americas of a common element in their different histories. Paola Boi has aptly interpreted Hurston's use of Moses as "a man of power, a trickster, a mediator," connecting him thereby not only with Henry Louis Gates, Jr.'s African-American version of the "signifying monkey" but also with the Yoruban original.[44] In both the signifying monkey and Moses-Damballah, the mythic role played is that of cultural mediator, whose powers of language involve a "trickery" that we would today characterize as some combination of "critical" and "poetic" powers.[45]

Hurston undoubtedly uses Moses to introduce "Hoodoo," because she is aware of the white hysteria and paranoia surrounding African-American Hoodoo and Afro-Caribbean Voodoo. In *Moses, Man of the Mountain*, she explicitly declares Moses' magic powers—primarily those of language—as ancient sources of Hoodoo, as if trying to provide venerable (and thus more respectable) origins for Hoodoo/Voodoo.[46] Even today, popular films such as Wes Craven's *The Serpent and the Rainbow* (1987) exploit widespread fear and ignorance of Voodoo's history, basic purposes, and chief rituals.[47] Writing *Mules and Men* during the last years of the U.S. military occupation of Haiti (1915–1934) and visiting Haiti to do research for *Tell My Horse* in 1935, the year after the occupation ended, Hurston must have expected readers misinformed by sensationalist accounts of Voodoo as black paganism. As Dutton notes: "It was a time when books like *Cannibal Cousins* and *Black Baghdad* were being published, reinforcing the perception of Haitian peasants as primitive, or, more precisely, savage, largely through distortions of voodoo."[48] In this historical context, Hurston had to proceed carefully if she were to change the prevailing U.S. views about African-American social inferiority and cultural "primitivism."

Anticipating the stylistic methods she uses in *Tell My Horse*, Hurston primarily *describes* Hoodoo rituals, spells, potions, and feasts in New Orleans. Rarely does she make judgments regarding cause-and-effect relations between the magic practiced and the results reported to her; she merely describes and reports. Hurston's plain style in describing events extends to the active participation of Zora in several rites of initiation, ostensibly for the purpose of giving her greater access to the secret practices of Hoodoo doctors. Hurston describes in detail Luke Turner's formal initiation of Zora, which must have been a physical ordeal, but Zora's testimony is notable for its restraint: "I could have no food, but a pitcher of water was placed on a small table at the head of the couch, that my spirit might not waste time in search of water which should be spent in search of the Power-Giver. The spirit must have water, and if none had been provided it would wander in search of it. . . . For sixty-nine hours I lay there. I had five psychic experiences and awoke at last with no feeling of hunger, only one of exaltation" (M, 199).

Many scholars agree that Hurston obeyed the vows of secrecy she was required to take before being introduced to Hoodoo religious secrets; she herself writes that "in this book all of the works of any doctor cannot be given" (M, 202). There is also a sense that as a writer, delegate of Moses, Hurston is partaking in Hoodoo of a power that cannot be denotatively or scientifically explained, but would be understood in the Euro-American tradition as akin to "literary" or "sacred" genius.[49] Her experiences with Hoodoo practices bring together the oral traditions of rural folktales, the physical and sensory rituals of Catholicism and African religions, and the written texts of Euro-American literature in quite remarkable ways. Her mentor, Turner, asks Zora to bring "nine sheets of typing paper" to the swamp outside New Orleans, where they will sacrifice a sheep as part of her petition to the Great One to be admitted to the religion. The "nine sheets were blessed and my petition written nine times on each sheet," one "petition . . . thrust into" the sheep's slit "throat that he might cry it to the Great One," the sheep buried and then "covered with the nine sheets of paper bearing the petition and the earth heaped upon him" (M, 202). In other rituals, names are written on slips of paper and sewn inside animals' body parts, like the tongue and heart, so that body and text are made to assume reciprocal signifying functions. In Zora's initiation, the written petitions are just parts of an elaborate semiotic process—from sacrificing the sheep to sweeping the earth with a broom dipped in the sacrificial blood to the ritual of burying the sheep without touching it—that reconnects verbal signs to their performative and implicitly *natural* magic. We should recall here how Zora's rediscovery of her body's complex affective range in the fight between Big Sweet and Lucy prepares her for the Hoodoo emphasis on the body as a locus of cultural signification. Like the "face . . . painted red and yellow" and the "body . . . painted blue" in her imaginative response to the jazz in "How It Feels to Be Colored Me," Hurston now comprehends the body as a signifying system in Hoodoo.[50]

Zora's initiation by Luke Turner, who claimed to be the nephew of the celebrated Hoodoo mambo Marie Leveau, concludes with him inviting Hurston to "stay and work with him as a partner," claiming that "the spirit had spoken to him and told him that I was the last doctor he would make" (M, 205). Zora notes that it "has been a great sorrow to me that I could not say yes," and Hurston seems thereby to hint that the Hoodoo powers of New Orleans continue to circulate in her own writing, that she has somehow been "mounted" by the loa of Marie Leveau, celebrated by both whites and African Americans. In the beginning of "Hoodoo," Hurston hints that the results of the Hoodoo doctor's spells and rites are often successful because of the community's belief in the social efficacy of such religious practices; Hoodoo functions like Catholic morality as a sort of superego, scaring faithless lovers away from sin and luring wayward husbands back to their families. Toward the end of part two, however, Hurston seems no longer to know whether Hoodoo magic is a consequence of social conventions or the actual appearance of supernatural forces, long discounted by Euro-American society, except of course where its own religious beliefs are concerned. Fasting and purging herself for a day under the tutelage of Father Watson, the Frizzly Rooster, and his wife, Mary, Zora undergoes the ritual of "the Black Cat Bone," whose possession is supposed to make the bearer capable of invisibility. Boiling a live black cat, cursing him as he screams in agony, then tasting the "bones of the cat" to discover the one that "tasted bitter," Zora is momentarily transported in a way that Hurston describes with the passion and doubt she shares with her narrative representative: "Maybe I went off in a trance. Great beast-like creatures thundered up to the circle from all sides. Indescribable noises, sights, feelings. Death was at hand! Seemed unavoidable! I don't know. Many times I have thought and felt, but I always have to say the same thing. I don't know. I don't know" (M, 221).

In the Euro-American literary tradition, much is made of the poet's "negative capability," the capacity to remain open to new possibilities of knowledge and experience. In her "trance" during the ceremony of the Black Cat Bone, Zora abandons her confidence in Enlightenment rationality and her anthropological mission. Such doubt regarding her experience and the evidence of her senses is disturbing and yet potentially liberating, for it lures her to other epistemologies and their accompanying cultural contexts. There is a narrative line, then, that leads the reader from modern urban America, with its "accepted theology of the Nation," to the other Americas represented in the African retentions of rural southern folklore and in the semiotic magic of New Orleans's Hoodoo. There is a lure or perhaps just a narrative hook that draws the reader from New York to Florida, then from New Orleans to the Caribbean. In the course of creating such narrative interest (it also involves Hurston's own intellectual curiosity) in other cultural realities, she has gone a long way toward explaining to the white reader why "these voodoo ritualistic orgies of Broadway and popular fiction are so laughable" (M, 185). No, "Hoodoo is not drum beating and dancing"; it is the survival of an unrecognized American heritage that problematizes the conventional understanding of "America" as the "United States" and the "accepted theology of the Nation" as exclusively Judeo-Christian.

Read in this way, *Mules and Men* describes a process of narrative education for the fictive Zora that extends from New York to New Orleans and then beyond U.S. borders. *Mules and Men* drifts to an end, inconclusively reciting anecdotes of Hoodoo and conjure that lack the contextualizations of the earlier chapters. The unfinished quality of *Mules and Men* may reflect carelessness in composition or Hurston's awkward grafting of parts of her 1931 "Hoodoo in America" folklore essay to the rural "Folk Tales" of part one. But it might also be that Hurston built into *Mules and Men* a strategic incompletion, a kind of deliberate "negative capability," to argue that the answers to our questions about one significant part of American cultural reality—its African heritage—must be sought elsewhere, beyond the borders of this book and the United States.

Hemenway judges *Tell My Horse* to be "Hurston's poorest book, chiefly because of its form." In his view, Hurston's efforts to be "political analyst" and "traveloguist" conflict with her established abilities as "novelist and folklorist."[51] Subsequent literary critics and folklorists have also judged the book to be at worst a failure and at best a "compromise," which does not realize Hurston's goal of revising popular misconceptions in the United States about Jamaica and Haiti and the cultural significance of Voodoo.[52] These critics are undoubtedly right: *Tell My Horse* did not succeed as a popular work—it "did not sell well," Hemenway notes—and is a formal hybrid of literature, travelogue, folklore, and informal history. There are certain rhetorical subtleties in Hurston's deliberately plain-style approach that hasty judgments of the book's "failure" overlook, and I will try to call attention to some of Hurston's minor achievements in this regard. But the importance of *Tell My Horse*, especially when read in conjunction with *Mules and Men*, is its effort to reclaim Afro-Caribbean cultures as important for African-American and, more generally, U.S. cultural history. In redirecting our attention to Afro-Caribbean sources for U.S. culture, Hurston also can stress the importance of African cultural transmission in the Western Hemisphere and remind her readers how our unfamiliarity with these traditions is a consequence of the Euro-American privileging of Classical and Judeo-Christian influences. In short, *Mules and Men* and *Tell My Horse*, when read together as works that attempt to reconstruct the repressed African cultural heritage of the Western Hemisphere, constitute a sustained critique of the privileged status of Western civilization.[53]

Nevertheless, Hurston appears to endorse in *Tell My Horse* the United States as defender of political rights in the Western Hemisphere, and she appeals to the U.S. reader to acknowledge our responsibilities in the Caribbean by understanding our shared heritage of revolutionary struggle. "Part II: Politics and Personalities of Haiti" dwells on the political corruptions in Haiti since Toussaint L'Ouverture's successful revolution against French colonial rule and suggests that U.S. intervention and "stabilization" might be preferable to the excesses of post-colonial Haitian dictators. Visiting Haiti only the year after our nineteen-year military occupation had ended and aware of majority support in the United States for the occupation, Hurston may well be practicing her familiar method of coding more radical criticism in a narrative overtly sympathetic to popular views. But she may also be profoundly ambivalent about the best ways to achieve democratic self-rule in Caribbean nations, like Jamaica and Haiti, where the colonial heritage has been internalized in their class structures and political hierarchies, religious beliefs, and cultural practices. In the same paragraph, Hurston can include the "military occupation by a foreign white power which lasted for nineteen years" as the most recent in a long list of Haiti's failures to become a "black republic" and then conclude optimistically: "The occupation is ended and Haiti is left with a stable currency, the beginnings of a system of transportation, a modern capitol, the nucleus of a modern army" (T, 74).

For Hurston, the future of Haiti depends not on its continuing dependency on the United States, but on the "action of a group of intelligent young Haitians . . . who hold the hope of a new Haiti because they are vigorous thinkers who have abandoned the traditional political tricks" (T, 74). Appealing for Haitian intellectuals and political leaders to strive for a new democratic order, she can invoke "the American concept," even as she recognizes the degree to which the United States has failed to achieve its democratic promise *and* the historical fact that "Haiti is not now and never has been a democracy" (T, 75). Changes in political leadership, stabilization of the currency, and improvements in transportation will not by themselves democratize Haitian society without some equivalent transformation of the

"Haitian class consciousness and the universal acceptance of the divine right of the crust of the upper crust" (T, 75). Colonialism lingers in Haiti in its rigid class distinctions, which are glaringly evident in the succession of Haitian dictators who down to our own day "have lived to rob, oppress, and sail off to Jamaica on their way to Paris and the boulevards" (T, 75).

The familiar reasons given by critics for Hurston coding her ideas in works written for white audiences also apply to *Tell My Horse*, which certainly attempts to use such means to demystify white hysteria about the "primitive" and "savage" rites of Voodoo. In "Seeing the World As It Is," which, after the attack on Pearl Harbor, she did not feel she could use as the conclusion to her autobiography, *Dust Tracks on a Road*, Hurston clearly identifies the United States as a neoimperialist power, which along with the European imperial powers has substituted a new economic domination for older forms of colonial slavery: "But I know that the principle of human bondage has not yet vanished from the earth. I know that great nations are standing on it. . . . Already it has been agreed that the name of slavery is very bad. . . . Life will be on a loftier level by operating at a distance and calling it acquiring sources of raw material, and keeping the market open" (D, 248). Although *Tell My Horse* appears to endorse the U.S. "Good Neighbor" policy toward Latin America in the 1930s, supported by vague appeals to Pan-American unity and the Monroe Doctrine, in "Seeing the World As It Is" Hurston treats with withering sarcasm the United States as "the giant of the Western World," who "means to be a good neighbor" by teaching our "gay and fiesta-minded" neighbor to the south "right from wrong," which means learning "to share with big brother before big brother comes down and kicks his teeth in. A big *good* neighbor is a lovely thing to have" (D, 249). Referring explicitly to the "Good Neighbor" economic policies adopted by the United States and Mexico in 1933, Hurston reminds the reader of our long history of interfering with the economic, political, and cultural self-determination of Mexico.[54]

However, Hurston's anti-imperialism in works like "Seeing the World As It Is" and her post–World War II essay, "Crazy for This Democracy," in which she criticizes the United States for aiding the "French, Dutch and English to rivet these chains back on their former slaves" in Indochina, Indonesia, Burma, and Malaysia, is not conspicuous in *Tell My Horse*.[55] Instead, Hurston focuses on democratic idealism and the revolutionary struggles for democracy in both the United States and the Caribbean as sources of a shared history. She opens both her section on Jamaica and her first part on Haiti by reminding the reader that the mixed-blood peoples of both islands typify American racial hybridity: "Jamaica is two per cent white and the other ninety-eight per cent all degrees of mixture between white and black" (T, 6). Nevertheless, colonialism persists in the Jamaican tendency to imitate the English ruler, in a manner Hurston directly parallels with U.S. Anglophilia: "Being an English colony, it is very British. Colonies always do imitate the mother country more or less. For instance some Americans are still aping the English as best they can even though they have had one hundred and fifty years in which to recover" (T, 6).

The idea of Americans "aping" the English nicely subverts racist conventions of the colonial subject imitating the cultural "superiority" of the colonial master. In the place of this negative identification between Caribbean and U.S. "colonials," Hurston reminds the reader of the anti-colonial struggle against slavery that began in the Caribbean and then spread to the United States. Although the American Revolution antedates abolition by nearly a century, the fights against slavery and colonialism are inextricably connected in the Caribbean; Hurston celebrates the Maroon community at Accompong as "the oldest settlement of freedmen in the Western world" (T, 22).[56] The origins of Voodoo are traditionally traced to the Maroon communities established by slaves who had fled their colonial rulers and succeeded in establishing remote communities in the interior of Jamaica, Haiti, and the U.S. South. Hurston explicitly connects their rebellion against slavery with the revolutionary history of the United States:

> Men who had thrown off the bonds of slavery by their own courage and ingenuity. The courage of the Maroons strike like a purple beam across the history of Jamaica. And yet . . . I could not help remembering that a whole civilization and the mightiest nation on earth had grown up on the mainland since the first runaway slave had taken refuge in these mountains. They were here before the Pilgrims landed on the shores of Massachusetts. Now, Massachusetts stretched from Atlantic to the Pacific and Accompong had remained itself. (T, 22)

This is a curious passage, because it establishes the Maroon communities as the origins of rebellion in the Western Hemisphere against slavery and colonialism, links those communities with democratic aspirations in the United States, and yet equates the "Pilgrims's . . . Massachusetts," conventionally the symbolic locus of U.S. revolution, with the colonialism of Manifest Destiny.[57] If in this context Hurston seems to be subtly incorporating into the text a critique of U.S. colonialism, both on the North American continent and in the Caribbean, then she does so by way of an irony at worst lost on and at best confusing to her readers.

Hurston finds Colonel Rowe's contemporary Maroon community at Accompong to be "very primitive," despite Colonel Rowe's desire for progress, and its inhabitants to be utterly unaware of "what is going on in the world outside" (T, 23). Despite their isolation from the outward marks of progress—Colonel Rowe's pseudo-military rule of this community is for Hurston residually colonial—the 1,000 inhabitants are connected with other Africans and Americans, especially of color, by way of shared folk legends and characters, such as: "Brother Anansi, the Spider, that great cultural hero of West Africa who is personated in Haiti by Ti Malice and in the United States by Brer Rabbit" (T, 25). The isolation of the Maroons differs, of course, from the segregation of African Americans in the Jim-Crow South, because the Maroons have chosen and fiercely defend their independence. Nevertheless, the isolation of both groups is subtly transcended by the migration of stories and folk-practices, setting up an unrecognized consensus of shared cultural traditions that prepares the reader for Hurston's legitimation of Voodoo as a religious basis for community.

The folkloric purposes of Voodoo in Accompong are clearly meant to serve as positive contrasts with the use of Voodoo by Haitian dictators to consolidate their power. In Chapter 8, "The Black Joan of Arc," Hurston focuses on the ill-fated rule of Haitian president Francois Antoine Simon (1908–1911), also known as "Antoine Sam," whose daughter, Celestina Simon, was renowned for her Voodoo powers and her "marriage" to and divorce from her sacred goat, Simalo. One of Hurston's techniques in *Tell My Horse* is to establish comparisons between Euro-American and Caribbean religious practices, legendary figures, folk stories, and myths in order to help readers understand how socially symbolic purposes of Voodoo are analogous to more familiar cultural habits. Even as she indulges the reader's fascination with the exotic primitivism of a Voodoo mambo marrying her goat, Hurston also reminds the reader that the Catholic saint's marriage to Christ (a ghost, after all) might be just as perversely interpreted, if taken literally. Of course, Hurston relates Celestina Simon and Joan of Arc in terms of their peasant origins, their respective fights against colonial invaders, and their uses of sorcery. After all, it was sorcery of which Joan was convicted by her inquisitorial tribunal, a charge supported by the University of Paris, both groups pressured by the English, and for which she was burnt at the stake in Rouen on May 30, 1431.

Hurston opens Chapter 8 by noting the parallels between France's national hero and this "black daughter of France," whose martyrdom goes unrecognized by the French and Americans. The parallel between the two legendary women seems at first imperfect, because we remember Joan of Arc as victimized by the English invaders, not by internal dissension within feudal France, but Hurston reminds us: "The Duke of Burgundy burned Joan at the stake," just as the "conquering hordes of Michel Cincinnatus Leconte drove Celestina Simon from the Haitian palace" (T, 93). Colonial domination is not always achieved directly by the conquerors, but frequently works through the internal politics of a once colonized and nominally postcolonial people. Yet Celestina and Joan are both "sorcerers" in Hurston's judgment, because both failed to connect their "supernatural" powers with their folk roots. Celestina Simon's rise and fall, like that of her father, is told by Hurston as a monitory tale of what happens to leaders—like so many postcolonial Haitian rulers—who forget their obligations to the people and anti-colonial struggle in general. In the battlefield against Leconte, Simon discovers that "the most numerous and best directed bullets always win battles in spite of the gods," reinforcing Hurston's point throughout this book that Voodoo's "magic power" derives primarily from the social collective it symbolizes (T, 99).

Hurston's emphasis on the class and gender hierarchies of Haitian society has been criticized as part of her general condescension to Haiti as less advanced than the United States, but her criticism is also fundamental to her interpretation of how colonialism still affects many postcolonial societies.[58] Voodoo cuts across class lines in Haiti, which are also artificially maintained racial borders in the elaborately developed distinctions historically established to distinguish blacks, mulattos, and whites. The hybridized images and rites of Voodoo are reminders of how the modern societies of Haiti and the Dominican Republic are fundamentally mulatto, since the first Spanish invaders murdered the only native inhabitants when the Arawaks refused to become slaves. Hurston is careful, however, to deny the common misconception of Voodoo as simply a primitive interpretation of Catholicism. The central Voodoo gods, such as Erzulie, Damballah, Ogoun, and Papa Legba have West African pagan sources that inform their Afro-Caribbean religious meanings, even as they are often represented by available pictures of Catholic saints, such as the Virgin Mary for Erzulie and John the Baptist for Papa Legba. Like pre-Attic Greek and African gods of Nature, Voodoo gods represent natural powers of birth, seasonal regeneration, and sexual reproduction far more directly than Judeo-Christian gods.

Hurston regrets the absence of a study of "Haitian mysticism comparable to [Sir James] Frazer's *Golden Bough*," in part because she recognizes in the syncretic mythography of Voodoo possible alternatives to the colonial mentality of modern Haiti, especially its patriarchy and class stratifications (T, 131). The goddess Erzulie, for example, challenges conventions of the Catholic ideal of womanhood: "She has been identified as the Blessed Virgin, but this is far from true. . . . Erzulie is not the passive queen of heaven and mother of anybody. She is the ideal of the love bed." Erzulie is "the pagan goddess of love," who has "no children and her husband is all the men of Haiti. That is, anyone of them that she chooses for herself. But so far, no one in Haiti has formulated her" (T, 121). "Part III: Voodoo in Haiti" begins with a Voodoo mambo answering the question, "What is the truth?" by throwing "back her veil" to reveal "her sex organs," performing the answer: "There is no mystery beyond the mysterious source of life" (T, 113). A more recent cultural historian of Haiti, Joan Dayan, argues against any simple or reductive characterization of Erzulie in terms of other, especially Western, religions and mythologies, and her characterization of Erzulie's ("Ezili" in Dayan) "sexual ambiguity" has distinct resemblances with Hurston's in *Tell My Horse*: "In her many aspects, Ezili reveals a sexual ambiguity and a convertibility of class that is so pronounced that study of this goddess and her relations with other spirits and mortals—as well as her use in literary representations—would help articulate a phenomenology of eros in Haiti."[59]

Erzulie is also a "mulatto and so when she is impersonated by the blacks, they powder their faces with talcum," which may be one reason why Hurston argues she is as popular among the aristocratic Haitians as among the peasantry. Haitian peasants representing Erzulie in "white-face" call into question identities based on race, even if the Haitian aristocrat prefers Erzulie because "her perfect female attributes" are interpreted by them as resembling their mulatto identities. However, Haitian mulatto women were the particular targets of sexual abuse by white males from the period of slavery to modernity, often ending up as prostitutes or mistresses "kept" by white men.[60] Yet Erzulie's ability to transcend class and racial lines, as well as her representation of sexual and life forces that challenge Western conventions of femininity, gives her a special place in Hurston's account of Voodoo's potential for undoing the colonial heritage of Haiti. Joan Dayan contends that Erzulie is often represented in ways that perpetuate "masculine fantasies of women" as virgin and whore, and she specifically includes Hurston's *Tell My Horse* as contributing to this ideology.[61] But Hurston manages to distance herself from cultural rhetoric she knows may well carry patriarchal connotations. "Gods always behave like the people who make them," Hurston tells us several times in this book, insisting that these social constructions nevertheless have real, demonstrable powers that may be used for both good and evil.

Hurston's contention that Voodoo is popular among the Haitian aristocracy challenges the public image of Catholic and Europeanized respectability cultivated by most middle- and upper-class Haitians in this period. Maya Deren begins her popular book of the 1950s, *Divine Horsemen: The Living Gods of Haiti* (1953), by claiming that Voodoo marks a distinct division between classes in Haiti: "In the larger cities, and particularly in Port-au-Prince, the 'middle' and 'upper' classes, influenced, no doubt, by conventional criteria of 'civilized' cultures, as well as by pressure of the Catholic Church, have altogether abandoned Voudoun in favor of Christianity. The schism between these classes and the masses of the people is so great that the former are largely ignorant of Voudoun."[62] Hurston herself suggests that her discussion of Voodoo as practiced by the Haitian upper classes disturbs many of them, as if some ugly secret were being revealed, and it is just this ambivalence of the upper classes—drawn to the "cultivation" of their French and U.S. colonizers or to the local, anti-colonial folk-culture of their home—that Hurston believes must be resolved before Haitians can take charge of their own political future.

Hurston pays special attention to the communal purposes served by the feasts that are integral to so many Voodoo rituals. "Feeding the loas" is also a means of bringing the people together for native foods, special drinks, and the communal bonding of such occasions. Various cottage industries and small businesses flourish in conjunction with Voodoo and are independent of the Haitian macro-economy—the latter generally controlled and corrupted by colonial interests or their local delegates. Of course, the bocors, houngans, and mambos enjoy special powers within these communities that they may easily abuse; Voodoo is not a democratic religion, but one that relies on theocratic hierarchies. Nevertheless, describing the social and economic functions of Voodoo and by comparing it with Christian religions, Hurston goes a very long way toward legitimating social and religious practices that in the United States of the 1930s were identified with primitive rites ranging from erotic dancing and music to cannibalism and "black magic."

Hurston avoids the temptation, however, to develop a full-scale, inevitably U.S.–influenced interpretation of the social and political significance of Voodoo in modern Haiti. Just as she does not find in rural African-American folk culture in the South a romantic social utopia or the mere exemplification of social oppression, so she refuses either to romanticize or condemn Voodoo, preferring instead to view it "as a religion no more venal, no more impractical than any other" (T, 204). Much has been made of Hurston's anthropological method in *Tell My Horse* as an effort to combine careful observation by a professional anthropologist with the participation of a visitor in the social practices and rituals of the culture she is studying.[63] Crucial to her subject-position with respect to the Haitians who help her understand Voodoo and Haitian culture is Hurston's honesty regarding the problems in her own culture and her limited knowledge of Haitian culture. On several occasions, she restages for us how she made friends and thereby gained the confidence of her Haitian hosts. Although these scenes are meant in many cases to explain how she entered the inner circles of Voodoo, like her Hoodoo initiation by Father Watson in *Mules and Men*, they are also intended to typify how members of different cultures should communicate with each other. Describing her friendship with "a very intelligent young Haitian woman," Hurston writes: "We had gotten to the place where neither of us lied to each other about our respective countries. I freely admitted gangsters, corrupt political machines, race prejudice and lynching. She as frankly deplored bad politics, overemphasized class distinctions, lack of public schools and transportation. We neither of us apologized for Voodoo" (T, 204). A few pages later, she describes how a "well-known physician of Port-au-Prince" tells her how Haiti still suffers from the heritage of slavery and French colonialism, leaving Haiti "a nation continually disturbed by revolution and other features not helpful to advancement," and Hurston answers him: "But . . . with all the wealth of the United States and all the policing, we still have gangsters and the Ku Klux Klan. Older European nations still have their problems of crime" (T, 207–8).

Unlike most commentators on Voodoo, Hurston avoids definitive interpretations of the social significance of specific rituals or the origins of particular gods. In contrast, Maya Deren traces the Rada loas, generally identified with the "good" side of Voodoo, and the Petro gods, who represent its "evil" forces, to West African and American sources, respectively. For Deren, the Petro side of Voodoo was the specific result of the wrath of escaped African and Indian slaves, who in their *maroonage* "shared, as human beings, hatred of the white man, who had dislocated both races and from whose brutality both were fugitives."[64] Hurston avoids identifying Voodoo as a specific form of resistance to the enslavement of Carib Indians and Africans under Spanish and French colonial rule. Rather than viewing Voodoo as primarily a *reaction* to colonial pressures, Hurston stresses Voodoo as an independent religion, complete with its own hybridized gods, rituals, and myths. It is, of course, quite possible that Hurston was simply unfamiliar in the 1930s with the social psychological interpretations of Voodoo on which Deren and later anthropologists have based their theories of its origins. It does seem odd that Hurston would *not* take the opportunity to connect the injustices experienced by Indians and Africans enslaved by the Spanish, French, English, and Americans. In *Mumbo Jumbo*, Reed suggests that Native Americans and African Americans have long recognized common political causes, rooted in their shared experience of colonial slavery and genocide; his claim seems to be supported by the link contemporary anthropologists make between Haitian Voodoo and Brazilian Candomble and Cuban Santería.[65] Deren notes that "Spanish law permitted enslavement in the new world only of cannibals, others became serfs on their own land—Caribs (cannibals) were shipped about, carried by the thousand to Hispaniola [the modern island of Haiti and the Dominican Republic]."[66] In contrast, Hurston makes very few references to the Indians of Haiti, noting only that the reputedly cannibalistic secret societies, known variously as "Cochon Gris, Secte Rouge and the Vinbrindingue," may be "descended from the Mondongues and other cannibals who were brought to this Island in the Colonial days" (T, 208). But Hurston goes to considerable lengths to demonstrate that these violent secret societies are not properly part of Voodoo.

Hurston frequently does trace Voodoo back to its origins in slavery but unlike Deren avoids drawing categorical conclusions about the etiology of Voodoo gods, beliefs, and rituals. For example, Deren interprets the playful god, Guedé ("Ghede" in Deren), as "a Lord of the Dead of apparently African origin," whereas Hurston traces the god's origins to the Haitian border region of Miragoane, "where the Departments of the South and the West meet" and to the "Bossals who were once huddled on the waterfront in Port-au-Prince in the neighborhood of the place where all of the slaves were disembarked from the ships" (T, 223).[67] For Hurston, the "spirit of Guedé" is supposed to "expose and reveal," sometimes whimsically but often with "revelations" that are "startlingly accurate and very cruel" (T, 223). Whereas for Deren the heritage of slavery shapes the fantastic superstitions of "primitive" Africans and Indians responding violently to their cruel fates, for Hurston those who witnessed the early slave trade develop a loa whose commitment to the truth is the foundation for a strong class consciousness among exploited workers. This seems to be Hurston's motive in insisting upon Guedé's distinctly Haitian origins: "Guedé . . . is the one loa which is entirely Haitian. There is neither European nor African background for it.

It sprang up or was called up by some local need and now is firmly established among the blacks" (T, 219). Possibly avoiding interpretations of Voodoo that would allow its religious and political force to be restricted to a specific historical period, such as slavery, Hurston stresses the importance of Voodoo in modern Haiti for establishing coalitions across traditionally strict Haitian boundaries of class, color, and gender.[68] In Deren, Voodoo is the phantom of past resistance and the stimulus for a modernist aesthetic transcendence or cosmopolitan class-consciousness; for Hurston, Voodoo joins Hoodoo and rural African-American folklore as living forms of socially diverse communities.[69]

In her effort to represent Voodoo as a living religion, no better or worse than other religions of the world, Hurston stresses the social and pragmatic purposes of its gods and rituals and frequently compares Voodoo with European Christian practices. Although she was apparently unable to penetrate the inner circles of such secret societies as the Secte Rouge and Cochon Gris, Hurston is able to gather what she judges to be reliable testimony from Haitians who have witnessed their ceremonies, which she claims involve body-snatching and cannibalism, and to conclude decisively they have "nothing to do with Voodoo worship" and are more "like your American gangsters. They intimidate the common people" (T, 208). Frequently reminding her Haitian hosts and thus her readers that the United States has its own gangsters and Ku Klux Klan, lawless groups that cultivate mystic auras to heighten their powers of terror, Hurston carefully demystifies Voodoo of the superstitions commonly associated with it in the 1930s: wild erotic dances ("Congo dances"), cannibalistic rites, and grave robbery.[70]

In other contexts, Hurston appeals to science to explain Voodoo practices exoticized and thus sensationalized in Euro-American culture, especially zombification and Voodoo poisons. Opening Chapter 13, "Zombies," with her photograph "Felicia Felix-Mentor, the Zombie," Hurston claims, "I know that there are Zombies in Haiti. People have been called back from the dead" (T, 182). Proud of her photograph of Felix-Mentor, referring to it as the only documented photograph of a zombie ("I did what no one else had ever done, I photographed it" [T, 182]), Hurston also plays upon the Euro-American desire for empirical documentation of phenomena complexly entwined in religious and social practices. Acknowledging the existence of Zombies, Hurston discusses with Felix-Mentor's doctor possible causes for the state, concluding "that it is not a case of awakening the dead, but a matter of the semblance of death induced by some drug known to a few. Some secret probably brought from Africa and handed down from generation to generation. . . . It is evident that it destroys that part of the brain which governs speech and will power" (T, 196). In Chapter 16, "Graveyard Dirt and Other Poisons," Hurston will argue that the graveyard dirts, "called goofer dust" in the United States and commonly used in Voodoo potions, can be scientifically explained by authorities like Louis Pasteur, who argue for the long-term survival of disease-bearing organisms in cemeteries: "So it appears that instead of being a harmless superstition of the ignorant, the African men of magic found out the deadly qualities of graveyard dirt" (T, 238).

The ethnobiologist Wade Davis, who has pioneered research on Tetrodotoxin as the active ingredient in zombification, credits Hurston with providing him with "a critical clue" but also observes that Hurston's publication of such hypotheses "earned her the scorn of the intellectual community" in Haiti.[71] Davis claims that "Haitian social scientists trained in the modern tradition" and "anxious to promote the legitimacy of peasant institutions" connected Hurston's accounts of zombification, secret societies, and "goofer dust" with sensationalized misrepresentations of Haitian society in the United States and Europe that perpetuated the myth of Haitian primitivism and "rationalized the American occupation."[72] If this was the prevailing response in Haiti to *Tell My Horse*, then it is certainly opposite to Hurston's intention, which usually follows the advice of her Haitian hosts, especially middle-class intellectuals. As one "well-known physician in Port-au-Prince," urging Hurston to distinguish between Voodoo and secret societies, like the Secte Rouge, tells her: "Many white writers who have passed a short time here have heard these things mentioned, and knowing nothing of the Voodoo religion except the Congo dances, they conclude that the two things are the same. That gives a wrong impression to the world and makes Haiti a subject for slander" (T, 208–9). In her efforts to do comparative work on Haitian Voodoo; offer scientific speculations about sensationalized "superstitions," like Zombies and goofer dust; represent her own active participation in the social and economic practices sustained by Voodoo; and write in a plain style to describe most Voodoo practices, Hurston goes to considerable lengths to counter the "slander" of Haitian society that informed U.S. paternalism toward Haiti in the 1930s and helped legitimate the U.S. military occupation of Haiti from 1915 to 1934. As Dutton puts it, "Hurston sought to humanize voodoo."[73]

If this is, indeed, one of Hurston's purposes, then the relative absence of political commentary on the U.S. occupation in *Tell My Horse* is both striking and disturbing. When she does refer to our military occupation of Haiti, she seems to emphasize its political necessity, occasioned by the events of the revolutionary conflicts in Haiti from February 1914 to July 1915, when three different presidents (Oreste-Zamor, Davilmar Theodore, and Vilbrun Guillaume Sam) successively failed to hold power. And although she acknowledges the important roles played by the National Association for the Advancement of Colored People (NAACP) and journals like the *Nation* in lobbying for "the withdrawal of the Marines" from Haiti, she does so primarily to criticize Haitian president Sténio Vincent for claiming "a conqueror's role for himself" and for strutting as "the second deliverer of Haiti, thus ranking himself with L'Ouverture, Dessalines, and Christophe" (T, 86). Since Herbert J. Seligman's article, "The Conquest of Haiti," had been published in the *Nation* in July 1920, vigorous opposition to the U.S. occupation had been led in the United States by the NAACP and the *Nation*.[74] Much of this opposition at home, however, was supported by and relied on information provided by the Union Patriotique, which had been formed in Port-au-Prince in 1915 to organize opposition in Haiti to the U.S. occupation. The Union Patriotique included by 1920 virtually "every elite politician or intellectual" in Haiti opposed to the occupation, including Sténio Vincent, among other presidential aspirants.[75]

Hurston's oblique references to the political necessity of the U.S. occupation of Haiti, her apparently favorable endorsement of the NAACP and *Nation*'s vigorous opposition to the occupation, and her trivialization of President Sténio Vincent's claims to have liberated Haiti from the occupation are a strange amalgam of contradictory views on relations between the United States and Haiti at a crucial point in the history of our foreign policy in the Caribbean. Certainly Hurston writes *Tell My Horse* primarily for a white audience, and she thus avoids explicit identification of her own views with what were popularly understood as the radical politics of the NAACP and the *Nation* in their opposition to the U.S. occupation. Her brief acknowledgment that the "N.A.A.C.P., The Nation [*sic*] and certain other organizations had a great deal more to do with the withdrawal of the Marines than Vincent did and much more than they are given credit for" sounds like the sort of "coding" of political messages for the African-American reader in texts marketed primarily to white readers that other critics have found characteristic of Hurston's double-consciousness.[76]

There was also some motivation for Hurston to distance herself from President Sténio Vincent, already proving himself another Haitian dictator shortly after the withdrawal of Marines and his inauguration, and from the Union Patriotique, which had a popular reputation in the United States for having exaggerated the crimes of the U.S. occupation forces.[77] This popular view was probably supported in large part by the report of the Senate committee convened on August 5, 1921, chaired by Senator Joseph Medill and charged with investigating U.S. activities during the occupation, which concluded that most of the claims of atrocities by Marines during the U.S. occupation were "gossip or hearsay."[78] Hurston's effort to distance herself from discredited Haitian claims of U.S. atrocities during the occupation may also account in part for her notorious generalization about "the most striking phenomenon in Haiti to a visiting American. That habit of lying!" (T, 81). Concluding that Haiti's history is one of continuing colonialism, rather than the achievement of a modern republic, as its dictators so frequently have proclaimed, Hurston claims that "certain people in the early days . . . took to deceiving first themselves and then others to keep from looking at the dismal picture before them" (T, 81). What continues to be so "dismal" about Haitian history for Hurston is its failure to escape its colonial heritage; as a consequence, it survives as little more than the "wreck of a colony" (T, 81). Indeed, the exaggerations of Sténio Vincent and the Union Patriotique regarding U.S. atrocities in Haiti might well be just what Hurston has in mind in such passages, and in condemning Haitian "lying" as a national trait she may be commenting on the intellectual confusion and moral corruption of Haiti's postcolonial leaders.

None of these observations explains adequately Hurston's relative neglect in *Tell My Horse* of the U.S. occupation, especially for an interpreter of the book's anti-colonial themes.[79] A more likely explanation is that Hurston viewed the U.S. occupation as a necessary means of stabilizing Haitian politics and its economy as the first step toward the adoption of U.S. democratic institutions and ideals in Haiti. While recognizing the anti-colonial criticism by the NAACP and the *Nation* of our foreign policy in Haiti, Hurston does not fully embrace their condemnation of the United States as an imperialist power. Acknowledging throughout *Tell My Horse* that Haitians and African Americans are commonly victimized by racial and gender hierarchies, Hurston nonetheless endorses the democratic promise of the United States for Haiti. In some cases, she advocates very concrete reforms in Haiti based on U.S. precedents: "These new and vigorous young Haitian intellectuals . . . are advocating universal free grammar schools as in the United States and a common language" (T, 91). In other cases, she more generally invokes democratic opportunities by appealing for jobs, food, and clothing for a Haitian peasantry, whose members continue to live in economic servitude to corrupt governments. Seemingly dividing the anti-colonial Haitian elite from the peasantry, Hurston muses: "Why celebrate the leaving of the Marine Corps when nobody wanted the Marines to go anyway? Their [the peasants'] era of prosperity left with the Marines. If President Vincent had arranged for them to go, then he was no friend of the people. The man they wanted to honor was the one who could bring them back" (T, 87).

Hurston may well be writing in an ironic vein in such passages, but she reinforces the argument made throughout *Tell My Horse* that educational and economic opportunities, along with religious freedom, universal literacy, and monolingualism (at least, an "official" language), are U.S. ideals that might help liberate modern Haiti from the residual effects of European colonialism. We may be shocked by her apparent embrace of what we include today as part of U.S. "cultural imperialism," but Hurston still believed in the 1930s in the universality of U.S. democratic institutions. In this respect, she is a product of her times and was less sensitive than late twentieth-century cultural critics to the negative consequences of exporting "America." Although her general respect for and interest in Jamaican and Haitian cultures is a far cry from Stephen Crane's condescension toward the peoples of the Caribbean, she nevertheless comes close to endorsing similar foreign policies for the United States in its expanding global "responsibilities" in the World War II era. Insofar as she details carefully the sorts of internal social reforms Haiti must make in order to decolonize fully, she differs significantly from Crane.

We should also consider the possibility that Hurston was right and that Haiti might well have benefited more from U.S. economic assistance and even political cooperation than it has from the economic neglect and occasional military intervention we have directed toward this nation since the occupation ended in 1934. Today Haiti remains one of the poorest nations in the world, virtually ignored by First World corporations for significant development and thus exploited by a few for its unskilled and thus desperately underpaid workers. With a staggering rate of unemployment (70% in 1997), jobs paid at an immorally low rate ($ 0.29 per hour in 1997), and a history of governmental corruption that discourages serious economic assistance by other nations, Haiti is an example of what can happen to a small country when it is ignored by the economic and political leaders of its region.[80] Haiti has traditionally been overpopulated and thus its people inclined to immigrate, but the history of Haitian immigration in the Caribbean and to the United States has been crossed by violence and murder. Our equivocal responses to Haitian "boat-people" fleeing political persecution and starvation in the 1980s is only one recent example of how Haitian émigrés have been oppressed.[81] "Cultural imperialism" can also work by way of neglect and exclusion, as our quixotic embargo of Cuba demonstrates, and Haiti has suffered from U.S. neglect over the past six decades that has at times been clearly punitive. Although Hurston would later mock the "Good Neighbor" policies of the Herbert Hoover and Franklin D. Roosevelt administrations, which relied on a patriarchal understanding of the Monroe Doctrine, with the United States acting in the twentieth century as a "big brother" in Latin America and the Caribbean, in *Tell My Horse* she seems to endorse the U.S. occupation as a sort of benevolent political and economic intervention, which should be accompanied by qualified efforts to "win the hearts and minds" of the Haitian elite to democratic ideals and institutions. I am not so certain we can confidently claim she was wrong in this regard, especially given the sad consequences of our formal neglect of Haiti in the last half of the twentieth century.

What qualifies Hurston's tendency to minimize the colonial consequences of the U.S. occupation of Haiti is her confidence that a society with its own distinct cultural heritage can resist colonization and develop its own democratic institutions. Crucial for the consolidation of Haiti's cultural identity is the frank recognition of Voodoo as its primary religion and the rejection of Catholicism as a divisive, colonial religion: "Nominally Haiti is a Catholic country, but in reality it is deeply pagan. Some of the young men are ceasing to apologize for this. They feel that the foreign Catholic priests do the country much more harm than Voodoo does," both by collecting and exporting to Rome and France a portion of the gross national product and by maintaining "differences among the mulattoes and the blacks" fundamental to Haiti's class divisions (T, 91). By representing Voodoo as a cultural system that cuts across class and racial lines in Haiti and serves thereby as the foundation for a social consensus, Hurston hopes to contribute to the formation of an autochthonous Haitian heritage that can resist, even appropriate, the continuing influences of foreign powers.

Yet, Hurston should have known from her experiences in Eatonville, Polk County, and New Orleans that African-American folk cultures offered few means of countering the *economic* racism of the New South. Hurston finds in Voodoo ceremonies like "Tete l'eau," during which celebrants from all classes visit "the heads of streams, . . . the cascades, and the grottoes" and thus honor the natural powers of Haiti, potential models for national identification (T, 226). Thus she is particularly critical of the Catholic church's condemnation of such pagan rites: "I fail to see where it would have been more uplifting for them to have been inside a church listening to a man urging them to 'contemplate the sufferings of our Lord,' which is just another way of punishing one's self for nothing. It is very much better for them to climb the rocks in their bare clean feet and meet Him face to face in their search for the eternal in beauty" (T, 234–35). But Voodoo ceremonies, the authority of the local mambo and houngan, the genii loci of the local loas, and the small economies that are sustained by this uniquely Haitian culture offer few practical solutions to the macroeconomic problems of modern Haiti. Lacking Du Bois's Marxist appeal to the workers of the world to combat the racism and imperialism of capitalism, Hurston has few practical solutions to offer exploited peoples in the South and the Caribbean.

Internal political, racial, religious, and class conflicts divided Haiti in its first postcolonial era, stretching from the Haitian revolution against the French from 1791–1803 to the end of the U.S. occupation in 1934, and Hurston represents Voodoo as the basis for the national unity that will help Haitians achieve their own republican institutions in their second, genuinely postcolonial phase. Hurston knows that fuller employment and greater earning powers for the traditionally impoverished masses of Haitian peasants are essential for such democratic reforms to succeed, as are education and steady progress in literacy rates, but she pays little attention to just what sort of jobs and what kind of education will best suit modern Haitians. Religion, the arts, and other modes of cultural self-expression play central parts in Hurston's understanding of social progress, but they remain distinct from the realities of the economy and the market. Today, Voodoo still shapes the cultural lives of many Haitians; it has neither helped Haitians improve their socioeconomic conditions nor signified any particular "backwardness" on their part. Political instability and unemployment continue to go hand-in-hand, and Haiti is not considered a country of much interest even to those global corporations looking for the cheapest possible labor. Yet another U.S. occupation, aided this time by the United Nations, this time, has been needed to restore President Jean-Bertrand Aristide to power and to supervise new elections, which brought current president René Preval to power. Nevertheless, this is still not "democracy," despite the aura of free elections. Aristide certainly selected Preval as his successor, and the turnout at the Haitian polls is such a small fraction of the population as to leave government to the usual control of the urban elite. The once strategic military importance Haiti had, along with Cuba, for the United States in its zeal to control the Caribbean and thus access to the Panama Canal is today no longer vital to U.S. hegemony in the Western Hemisphere.[82] Insisting upon its own sovereignty, especially in its dealings with the United States during the years of its strategic importance in the Caribbean, Haiti has been marginalized and impoverished, not entirely unlike the ways the United States has "punished" Fidel Castro's Cuba.[83] In short, Haiti's cultural heritage and history of successful revolution against slavery have done little to protect it from the new forms of domination that have made it a dependent—and thus in the news media a "backward" and "primitive"—nation.

In *Tell My Horse*, Hurston appeals primarily for mutual respect between different cultures as an alternative to the racial and gender conflicts in the United States. Chapter 17, the penultimate chapter in *Tell My Horse*, followed only by her concluding Haitian folk tale, "God and the Pintards," is devoted to Dr. Reser, "the white man who is a houngan" and the "officer in charge of the state insane asylum at Pont Beudet" (T, 245–46). During her visit with Dr. Reser, Hurston learns of the Haitian peasants' love for the white man who claims that "all . . . I have ever done to earn their love is to return their unfailing courtesy" (T, 247). A humane scientist able to be "mounted" by a Haitian loa, who converses calmly with his patients in the asylum and who is "very intimate" with a Haitian woman of color, Dr. Reser tells Hurston that he comes originally from "Lapland," "where Missouri laps over on Arkansas" (T, 252–53). This southern doctor and scientist has clearly been transformed by his years in Haiti, and Hurston describes how Dr. Reser, "mounted" (spiritually possessed) by Damballa, "walked out of his Nordic body" and "throbbed and glowed" with the "soul of Haiti" and "the snake god of Dahomey hovering about him" (T, 257).[84]

Hurston probably included her portrait of a white man accepted by Haitians and initiated into Voodoo to counter legends of Faustin Wirkus, the U.S. Marine from Pennsylvania who was reputed to have been crowned by the Haitians as king of La Gonave. The story of how Wirkus was landed by U.S. Marine aircraft on the Île de la Gonâve in the harbor of Port-au-Prince was told by William Seabrook in his sensationalist and deeply racist *The Magic Island* (1929).[85] Indeed, Dutton argues that in *Tell My Horse* Hurston was explicitly responding to Seabrook's exoticized account of Haiti and Voodoo.[86] Seabrook's story of "King" Faustin Wirkus is a typical neocolonial version of the Great White Hunter, adopted by native peoples awed by his technological powers while he is attracted to their "simple" customs and affections. In Seabrook's popular version, Wirkus's "rule" of Île de la Gonâve is a synecdoche for the benevolent paternalism of U.S. occupational forces in Haiti.

In chapter 11 of *Tell My Horse*, Hurston makes her own visit to Île de la Gonâve and barely mentions King Faustin Wirkus, emphasizing instead the Voodoo legend that "La Gonave is a whale that lingered so long in Haitian waters that he became an island" (T, 133). Retelling the story of how the whale transported Damballa's woman, Cilla, to bring "a message" of peace from the god "to his beloved Haitians," Hurston also recalls the island's history as one of the original Maroon communities of escaped slaves (T, 133). And although she makes no mention of it in *Tell My Horse*, Hurston completed her second novel, *Their Eyes Were Watching God*, on the Île de la Gonâve in December, 1936.[87] Her deliberate refusal to replay legends of "King" Faustin Wirkus makes her reference to these stories in chapter 17 even more significant. In her conversation with Dr. Reser, Hurston herself brings up "King Faustin Wirkus," asking the good doctor: "Now in all the adventure tales I have ever read, the natives, finding a white man among them, always assume that he is a god, and at *least* make him a king. Here you have been in Haiti for eleven years. . . . You are on the most friendly terms with the Haitians of any white man in Haiti and still no kingly crown. How is that?" (T, 247).

Dr. Reser answers that the Haitians "just don't run to royalty," agreeing with Hurston's own hope for postcolonial Haiti as a society that can transcend colonial class distinctions. Pressed by Hurston that "on the island of La Gonave they made a king out of a sergeant of Marines," Dr. Reser answers decisively, "Oh, no, they didn't. . . . All I have to say about Wirkus and that white king business is that he had a good collaborator" (T, 247). The "collaborator" was, of course, William Seabrook; one task of *Tell My Horse* is to demystify such colonial "adventure tales" and the stereotypes of native peoples they sustain. But the consequences of her story of a white man adopted by the Haitians, now not as a king but simply as a man respectful of Haitian culture, has its own ideological significance.

Dr. Reser possessed by his loa provides Hurston with her own Voodoo epiphany, such that she may claim that "I knew how Moses felt when he beheld the burning bush," equating this white southerner in Voodoo possession with the divine power represented by Moses and thus the very liminal figure—white, Nordic, Haitian, African—that Hurston interprets as Moses in part two of *Mules and Men*. Dr. Reser is a man who "could break off a discussion of Aristotle to show me with child-like eagerness a stone he had found which contained a loa"—a man, in short, who is a sort of double for Hurston herself, with the significant difference that he is southern, white, and male. Hurston enjoys her visit to Dr. Reser's "comfortable house," where he "has three sets of bed springs suspended by chains with comfortable mattresses on this screened porch" (T, 246). Talking, drinking, lounging, and observing, the white houngan and his African-American guest offer a wonderful contrast to the conventional southern pastoral, also often set on the verandah, but testifying to the colonial authority of a white leisure class. Playing cards, swapping tales, and listening to the patients, Dr. Reser and Hurston compose the image of an ideal couple, who are themselves actors in a subtle parable. Transformed by Haitian culture, the white southern male and the African-American northern female represent two parts of the potential counterforce of Afro-Caribbean Voodoo and African-American Hoodoo acting on the larger culture of the United States. If this is a parable subtly staged by Hurston, then it is also one that marks the limitations of her very modernist critique of Euro-American imperialism. These two educated people, however respectful they may be of Haitian culture, still find themselves primarily in conversation with each other, listening a bit patronizingly to the patients in the state asylum.[88] Hurston intends her little parable to offer the white reader some chance of being affected as she has been by the cultural powers of Voodoo and thus understanding how another culture, when approached with respect and understanding, can help expand the horizons of the dominant culture.

Nevertheless, there is the unintended effect that Hurston's little story of intellectual, spiritual, even erotic contact between this white southern man and African-American woman is also a story of cultural imperialism, in which Voodoo exoticism and tropical Haiti serve as stage sets for a drama of U.S. racial and gender reconciliation. Much of her romantic parable depends on Hurston's idealized portrait of Dr. Reser, whom other visitors to Haiti have treated somewhat less favorably. The dancer and choreographer Katherine Dunham first visited Haiti in 1936 to "study primitive dance and ritual in the West Indies and Brazil" while she was a "graduate student in anthropology."[89] In *Island Possessed*, she gives a very different account of "Doc Reeser" than Hurston, challenging the popular notion that "he had at any time been chosen as a horse" mounted by Voodoo gods and claiming that he was more of a local "character," perhaps fonder of the clairin ("raw white rum") drunk at many Voodoo ceremonies than of the actual spiritual experiences. Dunham's "Doc Reeser" is a mildly comic figure, whose acceptance by Haitians is evidence for her of Papa Guedé's and Baron Samedi's decision to give the community of Pont-Beudet "some evidence of 'desegregation' and nonpreference" in the amiable figure of "the white Marine 'Doc.'"[90] Dunham's bibulous and garrulous "character" differs vastly from Hurston's idealized figure, especially when it comes to the latter's access to Voodoo spirituality. Although it is always possible that Hurston is coding any part of her text for different audiences, it seems more likely in this case that she romanticizes Dr. Reser for the specific purpose of offering readers some promise of improved social, racial, and gender relations in post-occupation Haiti as well as in the United States.[91]

There may even be a more historically concrete purpose served by Hurston's account of her visits with Dr. Reser. A southerner who came to Haiti eleven years before (1924) as "a pharmacist's mate, first class, retired U.S.N." to work "in the Public Health service at Port-de-Paix," Dr. Reser is the only fully developed portrait of a white American who has come to Haiti during the U.S. occupation (T, 247). Throughout the 1920s, American opponents of U.S. occupation charged repeatedly that the U.S. government deliberately sent a large percentage of Marines from southern backgrounds "on the theory that they would, from long acquaintance with Negroes, know how to 'handle' them."[92] Anti-imperialists like Emily Balch and Paul Douglas also argued in the 1920s that racial prejudices were rife among U.S.

occupational forces.[93] Even conservative military historians like Robert and Nancy Heinl, who attempt to refute these charges, admit "a question of what may be called atmospherics" with respect to the racial attitudes of the U.S. military force in Haiti and note that "Colonel Waller of Virginia was a conspicuous and very Southern figure of the occupation," as was General Russell, "a Georgian," who nevertheless was never "caught . . . in act or attitude suggesting racism."[94] Whatever the empirical evidence supporting or denying charges in the 1920s that racial prejudices dominated the U.S. occupational forces and treaty officers, certainly this was a publicly debated issue at the time Hurston was completing her fieldwork in Haiti and writing *Tell My Horse*. Her portrait of Dr. Reser should not be interpreted merely as an attempt to dispel this popular belief; I have suggested in the previous paragraphs some of the other narrative meanings Hurston gives Dr. Reser. Nevertheless, the possibility that a white southerner might be capable of a respectful and ultimately transformative understanding of the Haitian people is interestingly placed at the conclusion of her book.

In the second to the last paragraph of this chapter, Hurston offers one of her rare, typically oblique, comments on events during the U.S. occupation. Offering several kinds of evidence to support his "firm belief in the power of the Voodoo gods," Dr. Reser tells the story of the miraculous salvation of Prepti, "secretary to Charlemagne Peralt, one of the leaders of the Caco rebellion" (T, 256). Since the late 1860s, revolts and guerilla warfare mounted in the rugged North of Haiti had been termed "Caco" rebellions, the term deriving possibly from the Creole word, *caraco*, meaning "a kind of peasant clothing worn in the mountains of the North."[95] There were at least three distinct Caco rebellions against the U.S. occupational forces and the U.S.-backed president, Philippe Sudre Dartiguenave, and probably countless smaller insurrectionary activities in the course of our nineteen-year presence in Haiti. Charlemagne Masséna Péralte, "brother-in-law of [former president] Oreste Zamor and thus sworn foe of . . . Dartiguenave," led the major Caco Rebellion against the occupation. Between October 17, 1918, and October 30, 1919, when he was ambushed and killed by Marines disguised as Cacos, Charlemagne and his "Chief Minister of Revolution," Benoît Batraville, conducted a wide-ranging and surprisingly successful guerilla war against the Dartiguenave government and the U.S. occupation.[96] In *Mumbo Jumbo*, Ishmael Reed imagines "Benoit Battraville" arriving in New York harbor on board *The Black Plume* to teach (like Papa La Bas, he *lectures*) leaders of the Harlem Renaissance about the Caco Rebellion: "Charlemagne Peralte was hardly a bandit. Our leader was a member of the Haitian elite. He did not invite the American Marines to land in our country on July 28, 1915. The U.S.S. *Washington* landed uninvited. They came on their ships without an Act of your Kongress or consent of the American people."[97] For Reed, writing at the height of the antiwar and Black Nationalist movements, U.S. imperialism in Haiti anticipates our "undeclared" war in Vietnam and its racist subtext.

In Hurston's retelling of Dr. Reser's story, however, "Prepti . . . secretary to Charlemagne Peralt . . . had no desire to perform any such service . . . , but . . . was kidnapped by Peralt and tortured and forced to accompany Peralt during all of the fighting in the rebellion" (T, 256). Managing to escape from Péralte, "running away from an engagement with the Marines," Prepti "fell over a cliff into a crevice from which he could not extricate himself." Assuming he will die there of hunger or thirst, Prepti is instead "saved" by "a vision of Ogoun with his red robes and long white beard," who assures "Prepti that he would not die there," and is followed by "a vision of Erzulie, the goddess of love, who comforted him and also promised him that he would be rescued" (T, 256–57).

What can be the meaning of this story of the rescue of an unwilling Haitian participant in the Caco Rebellion at nearly the end of Hurston's narrative? Ishmael Reed's "VooDoo Generals" are represented by Hurston as vicious criminals, in keeping with popular representations of Péralte and Batraville in the United States in the aftermath of the Caco Rebellion. Even more tellingly, Hurston's story aligns the Voodoo gods of Ogoun and Erzulie with Haitian resistance to the rebellion and contextualizes the story as part of a white southerner's testimony of "his firm belief in the power of the Voodoo gods." Possibly, she is coding a double message in her rendition of Dr. Reser's story, suggesting for a white audience that some white people are capable, like Dr. Reser, of comprehending Voodoo while assuring her black readers that nothing could be farther from the truth. In this latter sense, Dr. Reser's use of Voodoo gods to legitimate the U.S. occupation and its suppression of the Caco rebellions would represent an extraordinarily flagrant instance of cultural imperialism. Perhaps Hurston is simply telling stories as she has heard and then recorded them, paying little attention to their ideological consequences in the overall narrative, as some have argued she composed much of *Mules and Men*. In this case, we might conclude with Hemenway that *Tell My Horse* is "Hurston's poorest book," not only for its formal incoherence but also for its author's failure to anticipate how the stories she recounts escape her narrative control.

Still another way to judge *Tell My Horse*, however, would be to conclude that this little story told by Dr. Reser does in fact draw together several common themes throughout the book with regard to Haitian history, the U.S. occupation of Haiti, and the possibility of democratic reforms in post-occupation Haiti. Distinguishing the U.S. occupation from the continuing effects of Spanish and French colonialism evident in the internal divisions by race, class, gender, and political power in nineteenth- and twentieth-century Haiti, Hurston endorses the potentially stabilizing influence of the United States, not only on the occasion of the political anarchy following the overthrow and assassination of President Vilbrun Guillaume Sam in 1915 but also in terms of the necessary modernization of Haitian transportation, economy, education, and political institutions. Unwilling to align her critique of U.S. racism with Marxism's anticapitalism, Hurston struggles to find the sort of democratic "foreign aid" that will not reproduce the usual sins of colonialism. *Tell My Horse* virtually invites the benign paternalism of the United States in Haiti, as long as Haitians commit themselves to the maintenance of a *cultural identity* that will allow them to assert a distinct national character hitherto confused and contradicted by residual elements of Spanish and French colonialism.

Voodoo as a religion, informal economy, source of local authority, and a cultural heritage connected intimately with Haiti's history as the site of the only successful slave-revolt provides this sort of cultural counterforce to the potential threats of U.S. modernization and its enduring social ills of racism, sexism, and economic stratification. To be sure, Hurston suggests some dialectical cultural exchange between Haiti and the United States in episodes like her visits with Dr. Reser that will result in positive influences on both nations and establish future relations of mutual respect. From our contemporary perspective, we must conclude that such idealism neglects the political and economic realities of U.S. interests in the Caribbean from the late nineteenth century to the present and places too much confidence in the powers of native culture to defend people from the effects of foreign intervention disguised as progressive efforts to "modernize" so-called "developing" nations. Cultural and anthropological analyses of foreign peoples that formally separate their subjects of study from the political and economic realities that inform their cultural practices and everyday lives are likely to become useful documents for neoimperialist domination, rather than critical tools in the struggle against imperial domination. Hurston's well-intentioned efforts to study and thereby respect African-American folk culture in the South and its sources in the Caribbean and West Africa are important lessons in how "folk culture" by itself is insufficient to resist the powerful forces of neoimperialist appropriation, transformation, and modernization.[98]

By the same token, Hurston's efforts to reconstruct and preserve African-American and Afro-Caribbean cultural traditions open the door to other Americas that still play too small a part in our understanding of the entwined histories of the United States and the other nations of the Western Hemisphere. While recognizing that Hurston's naiveté regarding U.S. "Good Neighbor" policies of the 1920s and 1930s is typical of the distinction many Americans would make between U.S. foreign policies and the overt imperialism of the European powers in this period, we can still recognize the importance of Hurston's concrete contributions in *Mules and Men* and *Tell My Horse* to a broader understanding of the cultural influences involved in the making of Americans. In later, vigorously anti-imperialist essays, like "Crazy for This Democracy" (1945), Hurston would express her disillusion with Franklin Roosevelt's "Arsenal of Democracy" by concluding that at the end of World War II, "The Ass-and-All of Democracy has shouldered the load of subjugating the dark world completely" by helping the Allied Powers reinstate their imperial power, even as global "decolonization" was announced as our official foreign policy.[99] In the 1930s Hurston still hoped that the

United States might learn from the revolutionary heritage of the Americas how to defend the rights of other nations to their own emancipatory struggles against colonial powers. A similar argument would be used much later by antiwar activists in the Vietnam era to condemn U.S. opposition to another struggle against colonialism. By 1945 she could only wonder: "How can we so admire the fire and determination of Toussaint Louverture to resist . . . Napoleon . . . , and be indifferent to these Asiatics for the same feelings under the same circumstances?"[100] *Mules and Men* and *Tell My Horse* are important books, not primarily because of their stylistic achievements or for their avant-garde anthropological methods—although these aspects deserve our attention—but because they struggle genuinely with the role *culture* should play in the construction of social identity and in the resistance to colonial domination. Because they overlook the ways in which U.S. neoimperialism combines economic, political, and cultural factors, they fail to comprehend the full reach and power of such imperialism, especially as it would develop in the post–World War II era. Their solid achievements belong to the social and cultural history of the 1930s; their intellectual limitations are important warnings to cultural critics of the present moment.

12

After America

Nota: his soil is man's intelligence.
That's better. That's worth crossing seas to find.
Crispin in one laconic phrase laid bare
His cloudy drift and planned a colony.
    Wallace Stevens, "The Comedian as the Letter C,"
                           Harmonium (1923)

Wallace Stevens understands that "America" begins in the imagination and that its geopolitical reality has always been an effect of the words it speaks. Stevens's substitution of Crispin, the bumbling poet, for such military and political colonizers as Columbus, Cortés, and Pizarro can be read in the two different ways relevant to my study of literature's relation to U.S. imperialism in the modern period. On the one hand, Crispin's America is a "world elsewhere," in which the borders between the United States, Mexico, the Caribbean, and South America, for example, are transgressed and their different cultural traditions meet. In such a poetic space where the "Maya sonneteers/Of the Caribbean ampitheatre" may sing along with Candide, "the Aztec almanacs," "dark Brazilians in their cafes," and Carolina farmers, the equation of "America" with the United States appears distinctly provincial and false.[1] "American literature," Stevens suggests, must transgress the traditional boundaries of U.S. culture and embrace the wider world of the Americas. By the same token, Crispin's imaginative gesture is itself an imperial act, as the narrative organization of the poem suggests in the metaphors of New World discovery and colonization it uses for section titles 3–6: "Approaching Carolina," "The Idea of a Colony," "A Nice Shady Home," and "And Daughters with Curls."

As a modernist, Stevens distinguishes between Crispin, who is "Fickle and fumbling, variable, obscure," and our customary portrait of the colonial conqueror, armed and armored, planting flags, speaking with delegated royal or presidential authority. Better, Stevens implies, to be the poet and philosopher, Crispin, whose hunger is primarily "gorged/ By apparition, plain and common things, . . . Making gulped potions from obstreperous drops," than the "Christopher Columbus," who opens C. L. R. James's *The Black Jacobins* by landing "first in the New World at the island of San Salvador, and after praising God enquired urgently for gold."[2] Stevens also knows, however, that the "idea of a colony" begins in the imagination and that the poet is thus deeply implicated in the ostensibly non-literary acts whereby "new worlds" are conquered and colonized. The ironic, allusive, playful, and connotatively suggestive language of his poetry is Stevens's defense against this expansionist imagination, but it is a fragile, ghostly world the poet inhabits and defends—a world of denial: "his polar planterdom" (40).

Because Crispin strives to reach "Beyond Bordeaux, beyond Havana, far/ Beyond carked Yucatan," he sees in other people and other cultures merely dim reflections of his own problem, his own face. The "Maya sonneteers" are French Symbolists influencing later moderns, like Crispin and Stevens, just as the Carolina or Georgian "yeoman" represents the poetic and philosophical pragmatism of U.S. culture that the "prickling realist" struggles to incorporate into his being (C, 40). When Stevens writes, "Sepulchral señors, bibbling pale mescal,/ Oblivious to the Aztec almanacs,/ Should make the intricate Sierra scan," we know he is referring generally to modern poetry, not to Mexican history, the colonial destruction of the Aztec, or even to the social function of Mexican men drinking Mescal together (C, 38).

Whether he knows it or not, Stevens provides in "The Comedian as the Letter C" a "disguised pronunciamento" regarding the poetic imagination's and figurative language's roles in modern colonialism. From the first words and symbolic acts by which colonial conquerors staked out territory for colonies to the literatures and other cultural practices by which nations have legitimated themselves, modern imperialism has relied centrally on discursive and symbolic means to exercise, disguise, and justify its force. By the same token, Stevens's poem reminds us that the colonial project is also vulnerable in its aesthetic and symbolic aspects. The poet, novelist, and critic may have no powers to combat the troops called up to secure territories for the empire, but they certainly do have the ability to question the rhetoric of imperialism and educate their readers regarding the cultures and peoples subjugated. As many of the writers discussed in the preceding chapters demonstrate, education regarding minority cultures cannot be accomplished without a complementary critique of the limiting ways in which those cultures are represented by the dominant culture. In other words, the histories of marginalized peoples are not represented adequately when they are simply added to the traditional curriculum. Some consideration of why and how they were first *excluded* is crucial. Criticism of that colonial rhetoric, the preservation and recovery of marginalized cultures, and the empowerment of peoples of those cultures to represent themselves are thus complementary, rather than discrete, tasks of social reform.

Insofar as neoimperialism works as much by cultural influence and the exportation of lifestyles and behaviors as by territorial control, then literary and intellectual challenges to the symbolic imperium may be especially powerful and effective. John Tomlinson argues in *Cultural Imperialism: A Critical Introduction* that since the 1960s "the distribution of global power" that we once understood in terms of "imperialism" is now commonly described as "globalisation."[3] Much of Tomlinson's study focuses on "cultural imperialism" as an effect of the modernization process, in which nationalist narratives of expansion were justified by claims for the economic and political "development" of other (usually Third World) countries. Tomlinson argues that most of the critiques of cultural imperialism in the modern period "could be thought of as . . . protests against the spread of (capitalist) modernity."[4] Whatever its economic, political, and cultural ambiguities, modern "imperialism contains, at least, the notion of a purposeful project: the *intended* spread of a social system from one centre of power across the globe."[5] Tomlinson seems to have in mind the British model of imperial expansion operating from a home country whose metropolitan centers, like London, control distant territories. What he describes as the postmodern "idea of 'globalisation'" seems to resemble much more closely the imperial practices of the United States, but not simply since "the 1960s" but in the period of modernity—that is, from the late eighteenth century to World War II:

> The idea of "globalisation" suggests interconnection and interdependency of all global areas which happens in a far less purposeful way . . . as the result of economic and cultural practices which do not, of themselves, aim at global integration, but which nonetheless produce it. More importantly, the effects of globalisation are to weaken the cultural coherence of *all* individual nation-states, including the economically powerful ones—the "imperialist powers" of a previous era.[6]

Tomlinson's relatively strict historical periodization of old "imperial" powers, like Great Britain, and the new "global" powers, like the United States and Japan, seems generally accurate, but it ignores the long history of the United States influencing international markets and local cultural practices in ways that were not overtly imperial but nonetheless helped produce the global hegemony of U.S. culture today. U.S. intellectuals may affect embarrassment that the internet is the result of Department of Defense technological initiatives and that it functions primarily by way of U.S. linguistic, scholarly, and economic protocols, but we still praise the internet for the access it offers to peoples in remote regions of the Third World and its potential for populist political and social organization. On the one hand, the internet is an obvious medium for increasing U.S. commercial and technological power in the postindustrial era; on the other hand, it seems available to many other peoples willing to compete for byte-space and web-time.

Technologically different from the free and open commercial development urged by John Hay at the turn of the last century, the internet nonetheless still carries the aura of his "Open Door" policies. In a similar sense, William McKinley and Theodore Roosevelt's postures of our "accidental" imperialism in Cuba and the Philippines anticipate the present role of the United States in the new postmodern economy with its promise of a "global village." The United States has been transformed significantly by the many twentieth-century diasporas, most occasioned by the economic sufferings and political and religious persecutions of different groups, some of whom have immigrated to the United States. By the "accidents" of crises in other parts of the world, we often claim we have become the political haven for many immigrants. Often forgetting or ignoring our responsibility for at least some of the crises that have produced such diasporas (Cambodia, Laos, Vietnam, Mexico, El Salvador, Guatemala, Chile, Haiti, and Indonesia are just some examples), we have "welcomed" new immigrants by insisting that they adapt quickly, quietly, and obediently to our cultural ways. Certainly the great tradition of U.S. democracy has been that the "cultural coherence" of the "nation" should be regularly *transformed* by the cultural influences of new peoples, but the more recent response to foreign immigration matches better Tomlinson's suggestion that globalization "weakens the cultural coherence" of the "nation-state." Indeed, the fervid defense of monolingualism by E. D. Hirsch, Jr., and the hysterical attack on "multiculturalism" by Arthur Schlesinger, Jr., otherwise reasonable intellectuals, suggest that what Tomlinson views as a positive development in the erosion of national boundaries—and with them the old claims to imperial authority—has been received by others as a call to defend the nation.[7]

Behind the "neo-nationalism" that some view merely as a momentary reaction by those fearful of a new, postnationalist era there is the heritage of a fervent U.S. nationalism built upon our own insecurities as a coherent "people." From the Alien and Sedition Acts and the anti-French, Catholic, and Irish xenophobia of postrevolutionary U.S. citizens discussed in Chapter 2 through the "Yankee" aggression toward "foreigners" in California following the Mexican-American War to the racial divisions of the United States in this century, "Americans" have been very unsure of themselves and thus quick to identify "others" as different according to such contrived categories as race, ethnicity, religion, region, lifestyle, and sexual preference. The destabilization of the category of the "nation," then, may well lead to some of the most violent and dangerous kinds of national self-assertion and affirmation, as we have witnessed in the terrible history of neonationalist revivals prompted by the breakup of the old Soviet empire. Such new nationalisms, even as they appeal to older national mythologies and symbols, certainly must be studied in their own historical contexts and should not be universalized under the category of "global neo-nationalism." In particular, the nationalism in the United States today does not signify a break with the past but an affirmation of what has traditionally been a defensive and unreflective "patriotism," rather than a critical and democratic "civic virtue."

This book is my way of reminding myself and the reader that the critical and historically informed citizen, who is able to discuss and debate important issues with other citizens, is our best defense of the civil and personal liberties fundamental to democracy. As a teacher, I hold before me the goal of enabling my students not simply to "think for themselves," but also to "think of others" without thinking *for* others. Good citizenship has always demanded this consideration and knowledge of other peoples and cultures. Thus it is by no means paradoxical or contradictory that I emphasize the pedagogical potential of the materials in this book to encourage students and readers to make their own decisions, even as I criticize American myths of "self-reliance" and "liberal individualism" in the preceding chapters. I have tried to suggest how we can organize our teaching of U.S. literature to communicate not only the artistic achievements of our literary writers but also our complex and often conflictual history. The texts treated in the preceding chapters do not constitute an aesthetic "tradition" of any sort or even a political movement or organization. They are works that have been organized according to a scholarly theme unavailable to most of their authors. Nevertheless, these works taken together do constitute a workable curriculum—a course of study that emphasizes how the interrelation of literature, other cultural practices, politics, and history has continuing interest and relevance for our daily lives.

My purpose has been to study the continuity of "cultural imperialism" in the United States, both as it has been challenged and advanced by some of our best intellectuals and verbal artists. By interpreting works that are overtly critical of U.S. foreign policies and others that contribute to an "American symbology," I argue that literature is neither inherently emancipatory nor ideological, neither our best means of dissent nor the subtlest form of propaganda. Literature is simply one among many different representational media available for the propagation of those myths and stories by which "Americans" have been made, just as it is one of the media available for the representation of minority cultures and for the critical questioning of accepted cultural values. Insofar as "literary culture" dominated the communicative practices of print culture in the United States from the eighteenth century through the first half of the twentieth century, literature was one of the most important *modern* means for both the propagation and criticism of cultural imperialism.

After World War II, however, we can no longer speak of "literary culture" as central to the formation of the dominant symbology or for those practices critical of that ideology. Although I recognize important continuities between modern U.S. cultural imperialism and our postmodern, openly neoimperialist economic, political, and cultural contributions to globalization, I also recognize that the new dominance of telecommunications, computer, film, television, and video in the communicative practices of differ-ent peoples and cultures has changed significantly our understanding of cultural imperialism. It may simply be a shift in degree, rather than kind, but there can be no question about the increase in the speed with which U.S. culture circulates globally as well as the concomitant demand for flexible, rapid, and sometimes contradictory modes of criticizing this circulation of global capital. Just how this flow, rather than accumulation, occurs is itself a topic of the greatest interest and importance for intellectuals interested in the relationship between cultural expression and political control. It is a question that lends itself to the sorts of hermeneutic procedures used in lit-erary and aesthetic criticism, at least when such interpretive practices are situated in relation to the larger political and social uses of cultural repre-sentations. Just how this cultural hermeneutics organizes the development and criticism of U.S. imperialism in the post–World War II era—a period notable for wars waged as much in the media as on the battlefield—is the subject for another study.[8]

Notes

Preface

1. Reginald Horsman, *Race and Manifest Destiny: The Origins of American Racial Anglo-Saxonism* (Cambridge: Harvard University Press, 1981), 231.

2. Amy Kaplan, "Manifest Domesticity," "No More Separate Spheres!" special issue, *American Literature* 70, no. 3 (September 1998): 581–606.

3. Edward W. Said, *Culture and Imperialism* (New York: Vintage, 1993), p. 8.

Chapter 1

1. Edward W. Said, *Culture and Imperialism* (New York: Vintage, 1993), 62–63.

2. Richard W. Van Alstyne, *The Rising American Empire* (New York: Oxford University Press, 1960), 7.

3. Ibid., 9.

4. Benedict Anderson, *Imagined Communities: Reflections on the Origin and Spread of Nationalism*, rev. ed. (London: Verso, 1991), 37–46.

5. I use this phrase "cultural symbology," which combines literary and religious symbolism with ideology, as Sacvan Bercovitch defines it in *The Rites of Assent: Transformations in the Symbolic Construction of America* (New York: Routledge, 1993), 15: "a configuration or tangle of patterns of expression common to all areas of society, including the aesthetic."

6. I disagree with Benedict Anderson's general treatment in *Imagined Communities*, pp. 47–65, of Spanish-American and Anglo-American nationalisms as in part motivated by "slave-owning agrarian magnates" wishing to *preserve* slavery as an economic practice in opposition to colonial rulers in Spain and England, because Anderson collapses important distinctions between nationalism in Latin America and the United States. Nevertheless, it is worth noting that had the original colonies remained under English rule, rather than becoming independent, then the legal process that resulted in British emancipation of slaves in the West Indies beginning in 1831 would likely have been extended to slaves in the American colonies, thirty-two years (a full generation) before the Emancipation Proclamation.

7. Reginald Horsman, *Race and Manifest Destiny: The Origins of American Racial Anglo-Saxonism* (Cambridge: Harvard University Press, 1981), 232.

8. My purpose here is not to offer a complete bibliography but merely to mention at the outset the names and titles of the most influential scholarly works in this mode. Citations are given as each work is used for specific historical and interpretive purposes.

9. In other words, the "internal colonization" thesis has contributed to the thesis of American Exceptionalism, which in and of itself should not be considered the target of recent critics of this idea, but rather the intellectual *provincialism* such American Exceptionalism has supported. The critique of American Exceptionalism is carried too far when *any claim* for "uniqueness" in the history of U.S. nationality is rejected automatically as "exceptionalist." Given the importance of "novelty" and "uniqueness" in U.S. discourse about nationalism and democracy, we would be foolish to ignore claims to such novelty and even occasional instances of it. The problem arises when "American Exceptionalism" is used to distinguish U.S. history and culture from international counterparts, thus provoking the intellectual's version of late nineteenth-century isolationism.

10. By "easily maintained," I mean conceptually understood, rather than regulated by political, economic, and social controls. As Anderson, *Imagined Communities*, pp. 50–53, points out, such strict divisions between "colonial" and "metropolitan" citizens of an imperial power often produce such resentments in the former group as to provoke national liberation movements, like those among the Creole communities in nineteenth-century Mexico and Venezuela.

11. Horsman, *Race and Manifest Destiny*, 271.

12. Walter Michaels, *Our America: Nativism, Modernism, and Pluralism* (Durham: Duke University Press, 1995), 16–23, stresses the conservatism and racism of anti-imperialism at the turn-of-the-century, but I do not agree that this political cast is characteristic of *all* U.S. anti-imperialism, which is another reason to broaden the historical scope of this subject.

13. Horsman, *Race and Manifest Destiny*, 250.

14. Said, *Culture and Imperialism*, xii–xiii.

15. Said is thinking primarily of contemporary struggles over territory in the Middle East, the area of European colonization and destabilization central to his general theory of imperialism in *Orientalism* (1978) and *Culture and Imperialism*.

16. Ken Burns, *Lewis and Clark: The Journey of the Corps of Discovery*, produced by Florentine Films, broadcast on the Public Broadcasting System (1997); Stephen Ambrose, *Undaunted Courage* (New York: Simon and Schuster, 1996); Thomas Jefferson, "Memoir of Meriwether Lewis," in Meriwether Lewis and William Clark, *The History of the Lewis and Clark Expedition*, ed. Elliott Coues, 3 vols. (1893; reprint, New York: Dover Publications), xv–xxxiii, which includes Jefferson's original instructions to Lewis, pp. xxiii–xxxiii. For a full account of the different editions of this *History*, see Chapter 3.

17. Jefferson, "Memoir of Meriwether Lewis," xxvi–xxvii.

18. I cannot resist a personal note about the current craze for Lewis and Clark—a fashion certainly fueled by politically conservative efforts to revive U.S. patriotism and bolster nationalism. Stephen Ambrose, coincidentally my academic advisor from 1966 to 1967 while I was a history major at Johns Hopkins University, introduces *Undaunted Courage* with a personal recollection of how

he came first to read the *History* of the expedition and then to share it with family and graduate students on canoeing and hiking trips in areas of Montana originally traversed by the expedition. It is a nostalgic account, laced with post–Vietnam War sadness about the decline of patriotism and "pride" in our heritage, and it centers on a real (I take it) but symbolically designed "reading" of the *History* Ambrose, his family, and select students did on July 4, 1976, at a campsite on the Snake River, which was originally touched by Lewis and Clark. I was listening to Ambrose's account as I drove my family to our usual summer retreat on the border of Idaho, Montana, and Wyoming, just outside Yellowstone Park, in a region also close to the passage of Lewis and Clark. Like Ambrose, I had never read Lewis and Clark's *History*, and I did so after listening to the audiotape of Ambrose's book, but with much more skepticism, even bemusement, than Ambrose. Not only do Lewis and Clark virtually ignore the sublimity of the North American continent and the great bounty of nature managed with considerable skill by the Native Americans they encounter, but they repeatedly interfere in Native American politics, exploit natural and human resources, and spread venereal disease at an alarming rate. As an athletic feat, the Lewis and Clark expedition may deserve some grudging recognition for sheer human endurance and luck; as an event mythologized for its patriotic value, it strikes me as vastly overrated.

19. Alvin M. Josephy, Jr., *The Indian Heritage of America*, rev. ed. (Boston: Houghton Mifflin, 1991), 334, describes Jefferson's plan to develop "government trading posts" across the Great Plains that "would encourage Indians to accumulate debts which they could pay off by ceding land. The government . . . would then settle the Indians benignly on agricultural reservations where they would learn to farm and become like their white neighbors."

20. See, for example, Fred A. Shannon's study of post–Civil War agriculture in the United States, *The Farmer's Last Frontier: Agriculture, 1860–1897*, vol. 5: *The Economic History of the United States* (New York: Farrar and Rinehart, 1945), 357: "For that matter, outside the cotton belt, the majority of the westward-moving population did not settle on farms. Farmers from farther east took up the Western lands, but they also swarmed to Western cities and towns."

21. See Ronald Takaki, *A Different Mirror: A History of Multicultural America* (Boston: Little, Brown, 1993), 234–38.

22. J. H. Parry, *The Age of Reconnaissance* (New York: New American Library, 1963), especially part 1, "The Conditions for Discovery," 33–145.

23. Tzvetan Todorov, *The Conquest of America: The Question of the Other*, trans. Richard Howard (New York: Harper and Row, 1984); Eric Cheyfitz, *The Poetics of Imperialism: Translation and Colonization from "The Tempest" to Tarzan* (New York: Oxford University Press, 1991); Stephen Greenblatt, *Marvelous Possessions: The Wonder of the New World* (Chicago: University of Chicago Press, 1992); and Mary Louise Pratt, *Imperial Eyes: Travel Writing and Transculturation* (New York: Routledge, 1992).

24. The rhetoric of the John F. Kennedy Administration's "New Frontier" was intended to promote the Cold War by way of such highly publicized competitions as "The Space Race" and has evolved into the justification of space travel and exploration on the grounds of national defense, as the "Star Wars" project initiated by the Ronald Reagan Administration does. Recent films, like *Independence Day* (1996), revive nationalism by extending the traditional boundaries of national competition to the solar system and outer space. These

ventures may appear relatively fantastic, part of the science-fiction imagination, even when transformed into formal domestic and foreign policies, but control of orbital routes for commercial satellites is already crucial in an economy defined significantly by telecommunications, information technology, and their collateral industries.

25. Richard Slotkin, *Regeneration through Violence: The Mythology of the American Frontier, 1600–1860* (Middletown, Conn.: Wesleyan University Press, 1973), 20.

26. Anderson, *Imagined Communities*, 40.

27. Ibid., 35.

28. I write "nearly impossible," because Francis Fukuyama's reading of Hegel in *The End of History and the Last Man* (New York: Avon Books, 1992) seems to do just that—ignore the imperialist implications of Hegel's thought by transforming them into a modern plan for global emancipation.

29. The Hegelian historical model is worked out in his *Phenomenology of Mind* (1807) and *Lectures in Fine Art* (1835), but it is systematized in *The Philosophy of History*, based on his lectures of the 1820s. Although scholars generally associate Hegel's historical plan with Eurocentrism, it should be noted that the goal in *The Philosophy of History* is more specifically the formation of "The German World," or German nationalism. See *The Philosophy of History*, trans. J. Sibree (New York: Dover Publications, 1956), 8–79, for Hegel's imperial history, and 341–438, for his invention of "the German World."

30. Raymond Williams, *Keywords: A Vocabulary of Culture and Society*, rev. ed. (New York: Oxford University Press, 1983), 87.

31. Said, *Culture and Imperialism*, xii–xiii.

32. Ibid., xii.

33. John Carlos Rowe, "A Future for American Studies: The Comparative U.S. Cultures Model," in *American Studies in Germany: European Contexts and Intercultural Relations*, ed. Günter Lenz and Klaus Milich (New York: St. Martin's Press, 1995), 262–78, and Rowe, "Post-Nationalism, Globalism, and the New American Studies," *Post-Nationalist American Studies*, ed. Rowe (Berkeley: University of California Press, 2000).

34. Philip Foner's *The Anti-Imperialist Reader: A Documentary History of Anti-Imperialism in the United States*, 2 vols. (New York: Holmes and Meier, 1984), is a good example of this tendency. In volume 2, *The Literary Anti-Imperialists*, Foner collects the usual texts, including William Vaughn Moody and William Lloyd Garrison's anti-imperialist poetry from the Spanish-American and Philippine-American wars and Mark Twain's satires and William Dean Howells's short fiction directed against U.S. expansion. There is no consideration of "internal colonization" in Foner's anthology, just as there is no representation of responses to U.S. neoimperialism in China, Japan, Korea, Southeast Asia, the Pacific, and the Caribbean.

35. Said, *Culture and Imperialism*, xii.

36. For a good account of how cultural studies differ from traditional literary study, which often tacitly supports an aesthetic ideology, see Cary Nelson, *Manifesto of a Tenured Radical* (New York: New York University Press, 1997), 13–28.

37. Our efforts to prop up President Diem's regime in South Vietnam are often criticized quite justly for our utter neglect of traditional Vietnamese culture and politics in our enthusiasm to "Americanize" South Vietnam as a defense against a Communist takeover. Thus our efforts to industrialize rapidly a

fundamentally agrarian society resulted in stockpiles of useless machinery—from hydroelectric generators to refrigerators many villagers had no electricity to operate—and the illusion of a centralized, urban, Catholic rule in the figure of President Diem that was nothing but an elaborately and expensively maintained fiction.

38. As Cary Nelson does in *Repression and Recovery: Modern American Poetry and the Politics of Cultural Memory, 1910–1945* (Madison: University of Wisconsin Press, 1989).

Chapter 2

1. The *Wallam Olum*, or *Red Record*, is the migration narrative of the Lenni-Lenape, or Delaware, people, and it recounts their migration from China across the land bridge to North America. The narrative was orally transmitted and recorded in mnemonic pictographs, probably on several "song-sticks." Translations of these pictographs are, of course, quite variable. Most modern scholars begin with Constantine S. Rafinesque's record and translation of 1833. Contemporary scholars also depend on the Indiana Historical Society's translation in the 1950s, *Walam Olum; or, Red Score: The Migration Legend of the Lenni Lenape or Delaware Indians. A New Translation Interpreted by Linguistic,Historical, Archaeological, Ethnological, and Physical Anthropological Studies*, trans. C. F. Vogelin, interpretation of pictographs Eli Lilly (Indianapolis: Indiana Historical Society, 1954). I rely on the more contemporary translation by David McCutchen, *The Red Record/The Wallam Olum: The Oldest Native North American History* (Garden City Park, N.Y.: Avery Publishing, 1993). Most authorities on the Lenni-Lenape agree that the original pictographs, now lost, were probably geometric in form; Rafinesque's manuscript includes freehand drawings of the pictographs. Red is the sacred color of the Lenni-Lenape and thus assumed to be the color of the pictographs. My purpose in so representing and explaining this epigraph to the chapter is to point out how impossible it is to "translate" oral Native American narratives without fundamentally violating the social, religious, and cultural practices in which such narratives functioned. The process of such "translation" is deeply involved in the cultural imperialism more explicitly represented by Charles Brockden Brown's use of the "Delaware" to work out the Gothic plot of *Edgar Huntly*.

2. "The Fragment" was included in the Rafinesque manuscript and written in English by "John Burns," who claims to have translated it from "the Linapi" and about whom little is known. It is clearly intended as an addendum, a sort of apocrypha, to the *Wallam Olum*, taking up the history of the people after their contact with the Europeans. See McCutchen, *The Red Record*, 148–63.

3. Leslie Fiedler, *Love and Death in the American Novel* (New York: Criterion, 1960), 130: "If Brown deserved no other credit, he should be remembered at least as the inventor of the American writer, for he not only lived that role but turned it into a myth, later developed by almost everyone who wrote about his career."

4. Jay Fliegelman, *Prodigals and Pilgrims: The American Revolution against Patriarchal Authority, 1750–1800* (Cambridge: Cambridge University Press, 1982), 237; Robert S. Levine, *Conspiracy and Romance: Studies in Brockden Brown, Cooper, Hawthorne, and Melville* (New York: Cambridge University

Press, 1989), 26; Jared Gardner, "Alien Nation: Edgar Huntly's Savage Awakening," *American Literature* 66, no. 3 (September 1994): 433–39.

5. Gardner, "Alien Nation," 436.

6. Michael T. Gilmore, "Charles Brockden Brown," *Cambridge History of American Literature*, vol. 1: 1590–1820, ed. Sacvan Bercovitch and Cyrus R. K. Patell (New York: Cambridge University Press, 1994), 648.

7. Cathy N. Davidson, *Revolution and the Word: The Rise of the Novel in America* (New York: Oxford University Press, 1986), 13.

8. Scott Bradfield, *Dreaming Revolution: Transgression in the Development of the American Romance* (Iowa City: University of Iowa Press, 1993), xi.

9. Fliegelman, *Prodigals and Pilgrims*, 239. Steven Watts, *The Romance of Real Life: Charles Brockden Brown and the Origins of American Culture* (Baltimore: Johns Hopkins University Press, 1994), 89, interprets Carwin as an expression of late eighteenth-century anxieties regarding "the 'serial self' of a liberalizing culture."

10. Brown, *Wieland; or, the Transformation: An American Tale*, vol. 2 of *The Novels and Related Works of Charles Brockden Brown*, ed. Sydney J. Krause, S. W. Reid, and Alexander Cowie, Bicentennial Edition (Kent, Ohio: Kent State University Press, 1977), 67. Further references in the text as W.

11. Julia A. Stern, *The Plight of Feeling: Sympathy and Dissent in the Early American Novel* (Chicago: University of Chicago Press, 1997), 159–60. Stern points to "two crucial scenes: the reader's introduction to . . . Carwin . . . in a Spanish amphitheater disguised as a Catholic peasant; and Theodore's massacre of his wife, children, and Louisa Conway, a tableau of horror that grotesquely rehearses (while it also makes impossible) their planned amateur performance of an imported German tragedy" (159). Although Stern makes no clear distinction between proper and improper drama for Brown, I would argue that Brown identifies Carwin's disguises and dissembling with immoral artifice—secret, selfish, and thus designed to deceive others—and formal plays with moral purpose—open artifice used by an author to instruct the audience. The latter aesthetic aim agrees with the general ethics Brown adapted from William Godwin's *Enquiry Concerning Political Justice*, discussed below.

12. See, for example, William J. Scheick's use of Derrida to interpret Brown's critique of origins in "The Problem of Origination in Brown's *Ormond*," in *Critical Essays on Charles Brockden Brown*, ed. Bernard Rosenthal (Boston: G. K. Hall, 1981), 127, or Watts, *The Romance of Real Life.*, 191, 193, who interprets Brown's fiction as an anticipation of Freud's depth psychology.

13. In 1799, the year after the publication of *Wieland* and the year *Edgar Huntly* was published, Brown also published "The Death of Cicero" and "Thessalonica," two examples of his "fictional portrayal of historical events," as Charles E. Bennett writes in "Charles Brockden Brown: Man of Letters," *Critical Essays on Charles Brockden Brown*, 219. Cicero was a popular classical author and thus a symbol of learning, especially for lawyers, in this period, as Christopher Looby, *Voicing America: Language, Literary Form, and the Origins of the United States* (Chicago: University of Chicago Press, 1997), 158–65, points out.

14. The French and Indian Wars refers to four different wars among England, France, and North American native peoples over Canada and the West: King William's War (1689–1697); Queen Anne's War (1702–1713), which corresponded to the War of the Spanish Succession in Europe; King George's War (1744–1748), which was part of the War of the Austrian Succession; and

the French and Indian War, which was part of the Seven Years' War. I use "French and Indian War" to refer to the last of these conflicts, "French and Indian Wars" to refer to the entire cycle of colonial wars in this period.

15. William Godwin, *Enquiry Concerning Political Justice* (1798; reprint, Harmondsworth: Penguin Books, 1976), Book V, "Of Legislative and Executive Power," rejects successively "hereditary monarchy," "virtuous despotism," "elective monarchy," "limited monarchy," "a president with regal power," and aristocracies of all sorts before turning to democracy and concluding: "The depriving men of their self-government is, in the first place, unjust, while, in the second, this self-government, imperfect as it is, will be found more salutary than anything that can be substituted in its place" (534). For a good discussion of Brown's uses of and departures from Godwin's political and moral philosophy, see Sydney J. Krause, "*Clara Howard* and *Jane Talbot*: Godwin on Trial," in *Critical Essays on Charles Brockden Brown*, 196–208, and Krause, "Historical Notes," in *Ormond; or, The Secret Witness*, vol. 2 of *The Novels and Related Works of Charles Brockden Brown*, Bicentennial Edition, (Kent, Ohio: Kent State University Press, 1982), 411–18.

16. Cathy N. Davidson's reading of Brown's tract on women's rights, *Alcuin, A Dialogue* (1798), in "The Matter and Manner of Charles Brockden Brown's *Alcuin*," *Critical Essays on Charles Brockden Brown*, 71–86, makes clear that Brown's position on women's rights is meliorist and by no means a radical critique of eighteenth-century English and American conventions regarding gender roles: "Brown apparently seeks some synthesis between the rhetorics of revolution and reaction," challenging thereby "the strengths and weaknesses of both radicalism and conservativism, rationality and sentimentalism, intellect and emotion—a debate he continued, in various forms, throughout all of his later major works" (83).

17. Shirley Samuels, *Romances of the Republic: Women, the Family, and Violence in the Literature of the Early American Nation* (New York: Oxford University Press, 1996), 54.

18. Stern, *The Plight of Feeling*, 28.

19. Krause, "*Clara Howard* and *Jane Talbot*: Godwin on Trial," 197. Godwin, *Enquiry*, 185, provides a clear definition of virtue in this respect: "I would define virtue to be any action or actions of an intelligent being proceeding from kind and benevolent intention and having a tendency to contribute to general happiness."

20. Pamela Clemit, *The Godwinian Novel: The Rational Fictions of Godwin, Brockden Brown, and Mary Shelley* (Oxford: Oxford University Press, 1993), 137.

21. On Brown's treatment of contradictory social values, especially in times of revolutionary change, see William Hedges, "Brown and the Culture of Contradictions," *Early American Literature* 9 (1974): 107–42.

22. Brown's diabolical protagonist in *Ormond*, pp. 263–64, goes through his manly initiation at eighteen as a "volunteer in the Russian army" in the Russo-Turkish wars by taking captive "a Tartar girl," killing his friend Sarsefield, when the latter claims her, then "having exercised brutality of one kind, upon the helpless victim, stabbed her to the heart" as an "offering" to his murdered friend. The next morning he attacks "a troop of Turkish foragers . . . and brought away five heads," which he tosses on the "grave of Sarsefield." Such bloody ventures on the Russian steppes seem apt preparations for Ormond's Gothic evil in America.

23. For an account of Brown's use in *Wieland* of the story of James Yates, see Alan Axelrod, *Charles Brockden Brown: An American Tale* (Austin: University of Texas Press, 1983), 53–58.

24. Alvin M. Josephy, Jr., *The Indian Heritage of America* (New York: Bantam Books, 1968), 311.

25. Clemit, *The Godwinian Novel*, 110, argues that Brown intends the distraction of the elder Wieland from missionary work among the Native Americans to farming as a criticism of "Jefferson's agrarian ideals."

26. Richard Slotkin, *Regeneration through Violence: The Mythology of the American Frontier, 1600–1860* (Middletown, Conn.: Wesleyan University Press, 1973), 487.

27. Joseph J. Kelley, Jr., *Pennsylvania: The Colonial Years, 1681–1776* (Garden City, N.Y.: Doubleday, 1980), 666.

28. Ibid.

29. Josephy, *The Indian Heritage of America*, 314–15.

30. C[linton] A[lfred] Weslager, *The Delaware Indians: A History* (New Brunswick, N.J.: Rutgers University Press, 1972), 247. Although the Paxton Boys' massacre occurred ten months after the Treaty of Paris (February 10, 1763), which concluded the Seven Years' War in Europe and the French and Indian War in North America, it was probably an aftereffect of English settlers' wartime animosity toward Native Americans.

31. Ibid.

32. Kelley, *Pennsylvania*, 488–92.

33. Slotkin, *Regeneration through Violence*, 250–51.

34. Weslager, *The Delaware Indians*, 315–17: "The militiamen held a council, and by majority vote decided to put all the Indians to death. . . . They were beaten to death with mallets and hatchets, and scalped. Williamson's men burned the buildings at Gnadenhütten to the ground, including the structures in which they heaped up the corpses of the victims. They also burned . . . the neighboring villagers of Schönbrunn and Salem and then loaded their horses with the spoils of the raid, which they divided and took home with them" (316–17).

35. In colonial Pennsylvania, the Militia Bill was passed by the legislature on November 25, 1755, as a consequence of raids by Native Americans on settlers in western Pennsylvania in the early years of the French and Indian War. See Kelley, *Pennsylvania*, 336–38.

36. Stern, *The Plight of Feeling*, 238, concludes that *Wieland* and *Ormond* are "protoliberal," but she does not take into account Brown's rhetorical use of Native Americans in *Wieland* and elsewhere explicitly cites *Edgar Huntly* as an "exception" (276n48) to Brown's characteristic narrative technique of creating an "edge of representation [that] marks the space in which the author's richest cultural observations unfold" (167), by which she means the liberal political observations that destabilize conventional hierarchies of race and gender.

37. Jane Tompkins, *Sensational Designs: The Cultural Work of American Fiction, 1790–1860* (New York: Oxford University Press, 1985), 57. Tompkins is one of the few critics of *Wieland* to notice the elder Wieland's attempts to convert Native Americans as important in the plot, but her treatment of it as Puritan allegory quickly transforms this literary datum as part of a familiar Puritan mythology, in which "Indians" have their typological parts to play.

38. I do not want to push this allegorical reading too far, but it does seem that the naked, burnt, and bruised Wieland, left only with his "slippers" and

"hair," resembles conventional images of the Native American with darkened skin, naked body, flowing hair, and moccasins.

39. Levine, *Conspiracy and Romance*, 17.

40. Ibid., 18–19.

41. Gilmore, "Charles Brockden Brown," 650.

42. Bradfield, *Dreaming Revolution*, 19.

43. Slotkin, *Regeneration through Violence*, 390.

44. Roy Harvey Pearce, *Savagism and Civilization: A Study of the Indian and the American Mind* (Baltimore: Johns Hopkins University Press, 1967), 199.

45. Ibid., 198.

46. Norman S. Grabo, *The Coincidental Art of Charles Brockden Brown* (Chapel Hill: University of North Carolina Press, 1981), 84.

47. In his reading of *Edgar Huntly* in *Regeneration through Violence*, Slotkin shows how Huntly imitates the psychology of the frontier "Indian-hater," who "has become the thing he hunts" by taking on the very "savagery" he abhors, but in demonstrating how Brown accomplishes this fictional work Slotkin reinscribes the "Indians" as phantoms of the Eurocolonial imaginary without cultural realities of their own (389). In his reading of *Wieland* in *Prodigals and Pilgrims*, Fliegelman reveals Brown's fears that the American Revolution may bring about a social "transformation" that will displace the stability of the family—and its figurative extension, the landed gentry—with the anarchy of the democratic mob, whose potential "savagery" must be controlled by new social categories, including the self-reliant man: "The necessary fall of man from familial security into a deceptive and competitive social world—the great story and history of the eighteenth century—created a new species of man: 'the man of the world' who superimposes onto his original familial identity a new self-made identity based on his relationship to society" (241). Fliegelman makes no reference to the admittedly spare use Brown makes of "Indians" in *Wieland*, but Fliegelman's reading tacitly endorses Brown's use of the Indian as the ideological horizon of "savagery."

48. Jared Gardner, "Alien Nation," 429–61; Sydney J. Krause, "Penn's Elm and *Edgar Huntly*: Dark 'Instruction to the Heart,'" *American Literature* 66 (September 1994): 463–84.

49. Krause, "Penn's Elm," 465.

50. Kelley, Jr., *Pennsylvania*, 358–59, points out how frequently the Lenni-Lenape cited the Walking Purchase as a source of their alienation from the English colonial government of Pennsylvania during the French and Indian War.

51. Norman S. Grabo, "Introduction," *Edgar Huntly; or, Memoirs of a Sleep-Walker* (New York: Penguin, 1988), xiii.

52. Brown, "Memorandum," part II (1801), as quoted in Krause, "Penn's Elm," 474.

53. Brown, *Edgar Huntly; or, Memoirs of a Sleep-Walker*, ed. Sydney J. Krause and S. W. Reid, vol. 4 of *The Novels and Related Works of Charles Brockden Brown*, Bicentennial Edition (Kent, Ohio: Kent State University Press, 1984), 173. Further references in the text as EH.

54. Krause, "Penn's Elm," 474.

55. In Krause's "Historical Essay" to the Bicentennial Edition of *Edgar Huntly*, published ten years before "Penn's Elm," Krause clearly aligns Brown with the prevalent "Indian-phobic tendencies" of his time and place, even

claiming that Brown went beyond these conventions "to blacken his native Americans with unmitigated brutality" and also "to make them objects of disgust" (EH, 365–67).

56. Krause, "Penn's Elm," 468.

57. Kelley, *Pennsylvania*, 202.

58. McCutchen, *The Red Record*, 20–21, provides a useful map of "the migration route of the Lenni Lenape," as he has reconstructed it from "the text of the Red Record as well as on the author's research" (21). The Indiana Historical Society's translation of and commentary on *Walam Olum* provides a somewhat different migration route in the inside front cover, "The Probable Route of Migration of the Delaware Indians," but it agrees with the general movement of the Lenni-Lenape from Asia across the Bering Strait, differing from McCutchen by tracing *two* different migratory paths across North America: one across Canada to Labrador and the other traversing the northern United States from Montana to Ohio, Pennsylvania, and Delaware.

59. Kelley, *Pennsylvania*, 202–3.

60. Ibid., 203.

61. Slotkin, *Regeneration through Violence*, 385; see also Robert Newman, "Indians and Indian-Hating in *Edgar Huntly* and *The Confidence-Man*," MELUS 15 (1988): 65–74.

62. Fiedler, *Love and Death*, 146: "For the corrupt Inquisitor and the lustful nobleman, he has substituted the Indian, who broods over the perils of Brown's fictional world in an absolute dumbness that intensifies his terror. . . . Brown's aboriginal shadows do not even speak."

63. Krause, "Penn's Elm," 469.

64. Mercutio's description of Queen Mab's influence on the soldier's dreams in *Romeo and Juliet* (2.4.82–88) has particular relevance for Old Deb/Queen Mab's violent characterization in *Edgar Huntly*:

> O, then, I see Queen Mab hath been with you. . . .
> Sometime she driveth o'er a soldier's neck,
> And then he dreams of cutting foreign throats,
> Of breaches, ambuscadoes, Spanish blades,
> Of healths five-fathom deep; and then anon
> Drums in his ear, at which he starts and wakes,
> And being thus frighted swears a prayer or two
> And sleeps again.

65. Tzvetan Todorov, *The Conquest of America: The Question of the Other*, trans. Richard Howard (New York: Harper and Row, 1984), 98–123, in the section of chapter 2 entitled "Cortés and Signs," makes this case at length, concluding his book with the controversial claim that the paradoxical "success" of "Western civilization" has derived in part from "Europeans' capacity to understand the other. Cortés affords us a splendid example of this, and he was conscious of the degree to which the art of adaptation and of improvisation governed his behavior. Schematically this behavior is organized into two phases. The first is that of interest in the other, at the cost of a certain empathy or temporary identification. . . . Then comes the second phase, during which he is not content to reassert his own identity (which he has never really abandoned), but proceeds to assimilate the Indians to his own world" (248). What is controversial is Todorov's generalization about the superiority of European languages' rhetorical powers over those of native languages, like Nahautl, and the latter's

relative powerlessness to resist such superior semiotic power. However we decide this controversy, Todorov's thesis about the primary role played by language in the process of colonization must be central to any consideration of colonialism in the Western Hemisphere and especially to the development of U.S. neoimperialist practices.

66. Scottish immigrants also helped subjugate Ireland in the seventeenth century, so that the Indians' persecution of this Scot and Irishman Clithero Edny's persecution of Huntly and his friends and relatives has a certain subtle parallelism that reinforces the linkage of Irish and Indian as "aliens" discussed by Gardner, "Alien Nation," 442–43. For a good historical account of the English construction of the Irish as a racialized minority in the eighteenth and nineteenth centuries, see Theodore Allen, *The Invention of the White Race*, vol. 1: *Racial Oppression and Social Control* (London: Verso, 1994), 29–31, which deals with analogies drawn between Native Americans and Irish in this period. On "Scotch-Irish, Ulster Presbyterians" in the eighteenth-century United States, see Looby, *Voicing America*, 253–56.

67. Slotkin, *Regeneration through Violence*, 387.

68. Ibid.

69. Krause, "Penn's Elm," 476.

70. Brown's prose landscapes of frontier Pennsylvania anticipate romantic representations of the American wilderness in Edgar Allan Poe's *The Narrative of Arthur Gordon Pym of Nantucket* (1838) and "Journal of Julius Rodman" (1840), as well as those by such visual artists as Baron von Egloffstein, artist and topographer with the Ives Expedition of 1857 into the Grand Canyon. Poe and von Egloffstein both stress the often-terrifying sublimity of narrow canyons, crevasses, and hidden recesses in the landscape of the West and the Western Hemisphere in general. For a good discussion of von Egloffstein in this regard, see Wallace Stegner, *Beyond the Hundredth Meridian: John Wesley Powell and the Second Opening of the West* (New York: Penguin Books, 1992), 189, as well as the first two plates between pp. 92–93. For a discussion of Poe in this regard, see Chapter 3.

71. Annette Kolodny, *The Land before Her: Fantasy and Experience of the American Frontiers, 1630–1860* (Chapel Hill: University of North Carolina Press, 1984), 3: "By the beginning of the eighteenth century, it was relatively commonplace for colonial promoters to promise prospective immigrants a '*Paradise* with all her Virgin beauties.' The psychosexual dynamic of a virginal paradise meant, however, that real flesh-and-blood women—at least metaphorically—were dispossessed of paradise." Watts, *The Romance of Real Life*, 120, claims that the "threatening world of hunters and hunted offered little room for women" in *Edgar Huntly*, in contrast with earlier novels like *Wieland* and *Ormond* or his dialogue on women's rights, *Alcuin*, suggesting thereby a change in Brown's attitudes toward women's rights in *Edgar Huntly*. But in all of these works, composed in a very short span, Brown confuses *feminine* and *libidinal* powers as threats to culture that need to be controlled by reason. Thus the development in Brown's fiction from Clara Wieland, who finds Carwin so sexually attractive and repulsive, to Anglicized Native American "witch" (as Watts calls her) Queen Mab/Old Deb does not represent a dramatic shift in Brown's moral universe, but merely a successive unfolding of the author's own reflection of the cultural unconscious.

72. As Shirley Samuels, *Romances of the Republic*, 52, concludes: "Yates's justifications [of his murder of his family] suggest that he has not so much in-

corporated the threat of the Indians as violently externalized the closely linked internal problems of belief and the family."

73. Clithero's name derives from the Greek *kleitoris, clitoris, kleiein*, meaning "to close or hide" and the root term for "clitoris." The explicit identification of Clithero's name with feminine sexuality reinforces his feminization.

74. Huntly actually kills *two* panthers, as if to reinforce the psychic themes of doubling and repetition by allotting one panther to represent Huntly and another to represent Edny. The second panther, which is the one Huntly eats raw, is presumed to be the "mate" of the first. The style of this episode, like many others in *Edgar Huntly*, is characterized by the metonymic displacements Paul de Man has interpreted as typical of romantic allegory in *Allegories of Reading: Figural Language in Rousseau, Rilke, Nietzsche, and Proust* (New Haven: Yale University Press, 1979), 205.

75. Fliegelman, *Prodigals and Pilgrims*, 140.

76. Ibid., 138.

77. Ibid., 141.

78. Gardner, "Alien Nation," 436. Slotkin, *Regeneration through Violence*, 42, 472, traces associations between "wild Irish" and "wild Indians" as far back as the seventeenth century. In the Victorian period, the "dark" appearance of the Irish often combines issues of class and race, since it is the working-class Irish who are most often so represented and the upper-class Irish Anglicized. Anthony Trollope's Irish novels, from *The Macdermonts of Ballycloran* (1847), *The Kellys and the O'Kellys* (1848), and *Castle Richmond* (1860) to *An Eye for an Eye* (1879) and *The Landleaguers* (1883), are examples of this racialization of the Irish peasant, whereas Trollope's Irish hero, Phineas Finn, in the Palliser novels, especially *Phineas Finn* (1869) and *Phineas Redux* (1874), epitomizes the appearance and eloquence of the English gentleman.

79. Fynes Moryson, *An Itinerary Written by Fynes Moryson Gent.* (1617; reprint, Glasgow: James MacLehose, 1907–1908), 203, as quoted in Kathleen Kane, "Nits Make Lice: Drogheda, Sand Creek, and the Poetics of Colonial Extermination," *Cultural Critique*, forthcoming.

80. Watts, *The Romance of Real Life*, 119.

81. It might be objected that Huntly's consumption of the "raw" panther he has just killed does not qualify as "cannibalism" but is merely an extreme representation of the carnivore's appetite. However, the "panther" gathers together the various human figurations of his name not only in the allusions to the story of Jane McCrea and the Wyandot, Panther, and to the subsequent "Abraham Panther" narrative, but also in the manner that Brown constantly switches beasts with "savage" people, so that a glimpse of Clithero Edny is followed by the appearance of the panther and the defeat of the panther is quickly replaced by the new threat of "four brawny and terrific" Lenni-Lenape braves guarding the entrance to the cave (EH, 132). In sum, Western anxieties about cannibalism often disguise the more compulsive desire to appropriate the foreign and the alien as part of what I term elsewhere in this book the "imperial imaginary."

82. Gardner, "Alien Nation," 430.

83. Krause, "Penn's Elm," 478.

84. The relation of Clithero Edny and Edgar Huntly as doppelgänger is established in many ways, but one of the most important and least recognized is the homophony between their names, confirmed by the "secret" "E-D-N-Y" encrypted in Edgar Huntly's name.

Chapter 3

1. See my argument regarding Poe's proslavery views and their impact on his aesthetics in John Carlos Rowe, *At Emerson's Tomb: The Politics of Classic American Literature* (New York: Columbia University Press, 1997), 42–62.

2. Reginald Horsman, *Race and Manifest Destiny: The Origins of American Racial Anglo-Saxonism* (Cambridge: Harvard University Press, 1981), 220.

3. Ibid., 221.

4. Ibid., 208–48. See Chapter 5 for a fuller discussion of the racialization of Mexicans, Californios, and Native Americans in the Mexican-American War.

5. Arthur Hobson Quinn, *Edgar Allan Poe: A Critical Biography* (New York: Appleton-Century-Crofts, 1941), 293.

6. Quinn, *Edgar Allan Poe*, 293. Eric Sundquist, "The Literature of Expansion and Race," *Cambridge History of American Literature*, vol. 2: *Prose Writing 1820–1865*, ed. Sacvan Bercovitch and Cyrus R. K. Patell (New York: Cambridge University Press, 1995), 145–46. Burton Pollin, in his "Introduction" to "The Journal of Julius Rodman," in *Collected Writings of Edgar Allan Poe*, ed. Burton R. Pollin (Boston: Twayne Publishers, 1981), 1:512, writes: "'Rodman' . . . more nearly resembles a verbal collage than any other work by Poe," but as I shall argue in this chapter Poe uses his sources to attain recognizably distinct Poe effects. In his "Notes and Comments" to "The Journal of Julius Rodman," Pollin provides an authoritative account of just which passages Poe used from these sources, and it is clear that the principal sources, in order of their frequency and length, are the 1814 *History* of the Lewis and Clark expedition, Irving's *Astoria*, and Irving's sequel, *The Adventures of Captain Bonneville*. See also Wayne Kime, "Poe's Use of Irving's *Astoria* in 'The Journal of Julius Rodman,'" *American Literature* 40 (May 1968): 215–22.

7. Pollin, in his "Introduction" to "The Journal of Julius Rodman," 508–9, points out that there were to be twelve chapters, and each chapter was equivalent to a monthly installment of *Burton's* for 1840. Only six chapters were published in the January through June 1840 issues of the magazine. The chapters were to follow a "predetermined route: to the West across the Rockies, up to the Yukon, and back to the starting point of Kentucky or Missouri" (509).

8. Kenneth Silverman, *Edgar A. Poe: Mournful and Never-Ending Remembrance* (New York: HarperCollins, 1991), 207. Silverman also points out that while "editing *SLM* [*Southern Literary Messenger*]—which published several defenses of slavery during his editorship—Poe several times commented incidentally on slavery, in one case praising the antiabolitionist strain in Robert Montgomery Bird's novel *Sheppard Lee*" (484n).

9. Sundquist, "The Literature of Expansion and Race," 146.

10. Poe, "The Journal of Julius Rodman," in *Poetry and Tales*, ed. Patrick F. Quinn (New York: Library of America, 1984), 1188. Further references in the text as JR. Pollin, "Notes and Comments," "The Journal of Julius Rodman," *Collected Writings*, 1:584–85n1.2A, points out that 1784 is exactly the date John Jacob Astor immigrated to the United States, as recounted in Irving's *Astoria*. For connections between Rodman and Astor, as well as between Poe's "The Journal of Julius Rodman" and Irving's *Astoria*, see below.

11. Pollin, "Notes and Comments," "The Journal of Julius Rodman," *Collected Writings*, 585–86n1.2B.

12. Ibid., 590n1.7–8A, argues plausibly that the "area which Poe designates [as unexplored] corresponds roughly to what is today the Yukon Territory,"

and the plan for the final chapters of "The Journal" included the extension of Rodman's travels all the way to the Yukon, improbable as this plan was in light of the fact that Poe hasn't managed to get Rodman and his party past the Rocky Mountains by the end of chapter 6. Nevertheless, it would be absurd to take Poe too literally in regard to what he means by "unexplored territory" in this work. Like his other imaginary voyages and literary hoaxes, "The Journal of Julius Rodman" merely plays with such historical "facts" for the sake of rhetorical and poetical effect. To be sure, the Yukon Territory would have served Poe reasonably well to pit U.S. and British interests against each other, but the Oregon, or Northwest, Territory, mentioned frequently in the "Journal," is far more relevant to the actual struggles for British or U.S. hegemony in Poe's 1830s.

13. Thomas Jefferson, "Memoir of Meriwether Lewis," in Meriwether Lewis and William Clark, *The History of the Lewis and Clark Expedition*, ed. Elliott Coues (1893; reprint, New York Dover Publications n.d.), 1:xxvi–xxvii.

14. The Oregon Territory was not established formally until President James K. Polk signed a bill to organize the vast territory between the 42d and 49th parallels, the Rockies and the Pacific, on August 14, 1848, two years after the border dispute had been settled with Canada.

15. Pollin, "Notes and Comments," "The Journal of Julius Rodman," *Collected Writings*, 599n2.1C, notes that Poe "appears to be forgetful or heedless of the Spanish hegemony in the 1790s over . . . Louisiana, which was trying to divert all trade, including that in furs, to New Orleans." It is hard to imagine that Poe would "forget" something so obvious to U.S. citizens in the first decades of the nineteenth century as Spanish colonial influence in Louisiana up to 1800 and in the other areas of the Western Hemisphere. I think Poe is simply *ignoring* the Spanish, much in the manner that other Americans between 1830 and 1850 would judge Spanish colonialism in the Americas to be "decadent"—as Herman Melville does in *Benito Cereno* (1855)—and thus doomed to be overtaken by the English and the United States, with the French playing a supporting role. For a fuller account of this demonization of Spanish colonial rule in the Western Hemisphere in this period, see Horsman, *Race and Manifest Destiny*, 229–48.

16. Pollin, "Notes and Comments," "Journal of Julius Rodman," *Collected Writings*, 583n1.1F.

17. Washington Irving, *Astoria* (1836; reprint, Portland, Oreg.: Binfords and Mort, 1967), 23. Further references in the text as A.

18. The term "free-trade imperialism" was developed by Ronald Robinson and John Gallagher in "The Imperialism of Free Trade," *Economic History Review*, second series, 6 (1953), 1–25, and is discussed at length as "the theory of free-trade imperialism" in Wolfgang J. Mommsen's *Theories of Imperialism*, trans. P. J. Falla (Chicago: University of Chicago Press, 1980), 86–93. See Chapter 6.

19. Irving mentions this plan in *Astoria*, although he trivializes it: "It was a part of the wide and comprehensive plan of Mr. Astor to establish a friendly intercourse between these islands [Hawaiian Islands] and his intended colony [Astoria], which might, for a time, have occasion to draw supplies thence; and he even had a vague idea of, some time or other, getting possession of one of their islands as a rendezvous for his ships, and a link in the chain of his commercial establishments" (A, 47).

20. Elliott Coues expanded the 1814 Biddle edition of Lewis and Clark's jour-

nals, relying on many sources unavailable to Biddle, but Coues included in brackets the original pagination of the Biddle edition and termed his own version "A New Edition" of Biddle's *History of the Expedition under the Command of Lewis and Clark to the Sources of the Missouri River, Thence across the Rocky Mountains and down the Columbia River to the Pacific Ocean, Performed during the Years 1804–5–6, by Order of the Government of the United States*, 2 vols. (Philadelphia: Bradford and Inskeep, 1814). Like a character in a Poe story, Meriwether Lewis died in 1809 under mysterious circumstances, either murdered or a suicide, while on his way to Washington, D.C., having done little since his return from the West to prepare his much-awaited journals of the expedition for publication. Rodman's "melancholic hypochondria" may be modeled after Lewis's manic-depressive personality.

21. Jefferson, "Memoir of Meriwether Lewis," 1:xix. Interestingly, Jefferson first proposes the expedition by Michaux and Lewis to "the American Philosophical Society" as a "subscription," rather than a publicly funded enterprise. Pollin, "Notes and Comments," "The Journal of Julius Rodman," *Collected Writings*, 587–88n1.3A, points out that Michaux was prevented from accepting Jefferson's mission, not because of what Jefferson terms "'botanical inquiries' pursued 'elsewhere,'" but because he was "given (with Stephen Drayton) charge of the filibustering expedition organized by 'Citizen' Genêt, minister of France, in 1793, against the Spanish government of Louisiana." Unfortunately for my argument, Poe seems utterly ignorant of Michaux's paramilitary, colonial ventures in Louisiana territory.

22. The references to Jonathan Carver, André Michaux, and Washington Irving are part of Poe's effort to transform the physical journey into a literary voyage. Carver's exploration of the old Northwest Territory was less important than his popular *Travels through the Interior Parts of North America in the Years 1766, 1767, and 1768*, which was published in London in 1778 and went through four translations and more than thirty editions. Michaux's botanical works were also well known in the early nineteenth century: *Histoire des chenes . . . de l'Amerique septentrionale* (1801) and *Flora borealiamericana . . .* (1803).

23. Pollin, "Notes and Comments," "The Journal of Julius Rodman," *Collected Writings*, 604n2.9A, suggests rather improbably that Laurence Sterne's "Uncle Toby" influences Poe's choice of name, but Pollin acknowledges that Toby's "grotesque appearance and whimsical behavior" are typical of what Poe "usually associated with blacks and even with the 'hybrid' Dirk Peters" in *Pym*. Pollin also notes Poe's use of the name for "Toby Dammit," the foolish character who loses his head in Poe's satire of transcendentalism, "Never Bet the Devil Your Head" (1841), but this seems less probable as an affinity with the African-American Toby, despite Poe's racialization of Toby Dammit's response to violent abuse as a child: "He grew so black in the face that one might have mistaken him for a little African" (*Poetry and Tales*, 459).

24. Poe, *Narrative of Arthur Gordon Pym*, in *Poetry and Tales*, 1043. Further references in the text as *Pym*.

25. The People, Respondent, v. George W. Hall, Appellant, Supreme Court of California, 4 Cal. 399 (1854); Cal. LEXIS 137. I am citing the text of this decision from the electronic legal archive: Lexis (http://lexis-nexis.com). I am grateful to Kay Collins, U.S. government information librarian at the University of California, Irvine Library, for helping me obtain a transcript of this 1854 decision.

26. Ibid. It should not be forgotten that the irrational and contradictory racist arguments of the Supreme Court of California were used to reverse the judgment of murder against George Wells on the grounds that the Chinese witnesses' testimony could not be admitted in a "white" court and Wells's "cause remanded."

27. In a long footnote to the 1893 edition, Coues connects York and his gossip back in St. Louis after the expedition, when he was freed, with the "famous old hoax of a nation of bearded, blue-eyed, and red-haired Indians on the Upper Missouri," which is traceable at least back to the 1760s (Coues, 1:159n31). Poe gives no indication he was familiar with such myths, but it is unlikely he would have introduced them in his narrative in any connection with the obviously degraded African-American character of Toby.

28. Pollin, "Notes and Comments," "The Journal of Julius Rodman," *Collected Writings*, 639n5.17C.

29. Rodman describes their travel through a country "infested with Indian tribes, of whom we knew nothing except by vague report, and whom we had every reason to believe ferocious and treacherous" (JR, 1204). For a useful discussion of the colonial rhetoric of "disease" and "infection" applied to Native Americans, see Kathleen Kane, "Nits Make Lice: Drogheda, Sand Creek, and the Poetics of Colonial Extermination," *Cultural Critique*, forthcoming.

30. Sergeant Patrick Gass kept his own journal of the Lewis and Clark expedition, which he published in 1807. Coues characterizes Gass as "an intelligent and observant person of very limited education," and his journal as "a plain, straightforward, and connected account" (Coues, "Bibliographical Introduction," 1: cxvii).

31. John Wesley Powell's chief geologist, Clarence Edward Dutton, for example, in the 1880s lavished Oriental names on significant landmarks in the Grand Canyon, as Wallace Stegner points out in *Beyond the Hundredth Meridian: John Wesley Powell and the Second Opening of the West* (New York: Penguin Books, 1992), 196: "The fixed binoculars at the lookout points will, for a dime, bring you close up to the Hindoo Amphitheater, the Ottoman Amphitheater, Vishnu's Temple, Shiva's Temple, the Temples of Isis and Osiris. . . . the Tower of Set, named by Moran on Dutton's example, . . . and Krishna Shrine and Rama Shrine."

32. Silverman, *Edgar A. Poe*, 207.

33. "A Tale of the Ragged Mountains," *Poetry and Tales*, 657–58. Further references in the text as RM.

34. For a complementary reading of Poe's Orientalism in his poetry, see Betsy Erkkila's essay in *Exorcizing the Shadow: Race and Edgar Allan Poe*, ed. J. Gerald Kennedy and Lilliane Weissberg (New York: Oxford University Press, forthcoming). The locus classicus in Western thought for such Orientalism is Hegel, whose interpretation of Hinduism and its social and artistic representations stresses the essential anarchy and failure of abstract thinking in Hinduism's pantheist chaos of gods. See Hegel, *Aesthetics: Lectures on Fine Art*, trans. T. M. Knox, 2 vols. (Oxford: Oxford University Press, 1975), 1:332–70.

35. The rhetoric of "The Journal of Julius Rodman" is replete with references to Sioux "infesting" the landscape and other terms suggestive of disease and natural deterioration, as in the passage quoted earlier regarding the "foul-smelling" waters in the vicinity of the Sioux. To be sure, the Teton tribe lived in the vicinity of the geothermal marvels of Yellowstone, but Poe's purpose here seems hardly to be to take notice of such natural wonders but instead to pro-

vide a psychic landscape for these demonic, warlike, and dangerous "freebooters." Irving also treats the native peoples of the West as thieves and "pirates," commenting that the "Sioux Tetons were at that time a sort of pirates of the Missouri, who considered the well freighted bark of the American trader fair game" (A, 141). Irving also repeatedly refers to the Plains in oceanic metaphors to reinforce the reader's impression that the frontier resembles the oceans by which modern America will pursue "free trade."

36. Rowe, *At Emerson's Tomb*, 48–62.

37. Hastings was eventually acquitted on April 23, 1795, although he had been financially ruined by the long-running trial. He was, however, given an annuity by the East India Company that allowed him to live comfortably for the rest of his life.

38. Horsman, *Race and Manifest Destiny*, 227.

39. Now known as "Liberty Island," where Frederick Barthold's Statue of Liberty was placed in 1885.

40. Loisa Nygaard, "Winning the Game: Inductive Reasoning in Poe's 'Murders in the Rue Morgue,'" *Studies in Romanticism* 33 (Summer 1994): 223, makes this same point at the beginning of her essay: "But the problem with Poe's works goes beyond the unreliable narrator to the unreliable *author*. Poe as a writer was fascinated by what he called 'mystification,' by duplicity, obfuscation, manipulation."

41. Quinn, *Edgar Allan Poe*, 401.

42. Kim F. Hall, "'Troubling Doubles': Apes, Africans and Blackface in *Mr. Moore's Revels*," in *Race, Ethnicity and Power in the Renaissance*, ed. Joyce Green MacDonald (Cranbury, N.J.: Associated University Presses, 1997), 120–44. I am grateful to Kim Hall for discussing her research with me during her lecture on this topic at Irvine.

43. Ibid., 125.

44. Edward Topsell, *The Historie of Foure-footed Beastes* (London: William Iaggard, 1607), 4.

45. Ibid., 13.

46. Ibid., 4. Elsewhere, describing the baboon, Topsell writes: "They cannot speake, and yet they understand the *Indian* language" (11).

47. Nygaard, "Winning the Game," 251.

48. Ibid. Nygaard footnotes here the infamous review of James Kirk Paulding's *Slavery in the United States* and *The South Vindicated from the Treason and Fanaticism of the Northern Abolitionists* (*Southern Literary Messenger* [April 1836]), as if this review were indisputably the work of Poe. For my discussion of this controversy and its relevance to the discussion of race and imperialism in Poe's writings, see *At Emerson's Tomb*, 42–51.

49. Shawn Rosenheim, *The Cryptographic Imagination: Secret Writing from Edgar Poe to the Internet* (Baltimore: Johns Hopkins University Press, 1997), 83.

50. Louis A. Renza, *A Poetics of American Privacy: Edgar Allan Poe and Wallace Stevens* (Unpublished ms; Ms, 44), argues that Poe *identifies* with the orangutan, because of the verbal pun in acrostic: a p e = e a p. Such paronomasias are typical of Poe and in this instance demonstrate how far Poe's poetic "ape" is from the murderous brute in his story.

51. "The Murders in the Rue Morgue," *Poetry and Tales*, 416. Further references in the text as M.

52. Nygaard, "Winning the Game," 254.

53. Rosenheim, *Crytographic Imagination*, 74.

54. Baron Georges Cuvier, *Cuvier's Animal Kingdom*, ed. and trans. H. McMurtrie (London: Orr and Smith, 1834), 44.

55. Ibid.

56. Ibid.

57. Rosenheim, *Cryptographic Imagination*, 73.

58. Horsman, *Race and Manifest Destiny*, 47–48, claims that Johann Friedrich Blumenbach's "fivefold division" of the human species was "the basis of the work of most influential writers on race in the first half of the nineteenth century" but notes that Cuvier's "threefold division" also had "great importance" and influence.

59. Cuvier's classification is hierarchical, and "The First Order of Mammalians" is "Bimana, or Man," which he organizes in order of the "three races . . . very distinct—the *Caucasian* or white, the *Mongolian* or yellow, and *Ethiopian* or negro" (*Cuvier's Animal Kingdom*, 40). The Caucasian has given rise to "the most highly civilised nations, and those which have generally held all others in subjection," whereas "great empires have been established by" the Mongolian, but its "civilisation . . . has always remained stationary" (40). For Cuvier, the "Negro race" is composed of "hordes" that "have always remained in the most complete state of utter barbarism" (40). In his reading of Poe's tale, Rosenheim in no way connects Poe's uses of Cuvier's natural science with their ideological consequences for nineteenth-century European and U.S. conventions regarding race.

60. "Hop-Frog," in *Poetry and Tales*, 904. Further references in the text as HF.

61. Cuvier, *Cuvier's Animal Kingdom*, 40.

62. The McMurtrie edition and abridgment of 1834, cited above, does not include the passage regarding Chimpanzees' tendencies to "abduct" women. I am citing here from Baron Georges Cuvier, *The Animal Kingdom, Arranged after Its Organization; Forming a Natural History of Animals and an Introduction to Comparative Anatomy*, trans. and adapted to the present state of science by W. B. Carpenter and J. O. Westwood (London: Henry G. Bohn, 1863), 44.

63. On antebellum southern hysteria regarding slave insurrections around the world, see Eric Sundquist, *To Wake the Nations: Race in the Making of American Literature* (Cambridge: Harvard University Press, 1993), 146–51, 210–20.

64. On the relation between gender and racial hierarchies in Poe, see Joan Dayan, "Amorous Bondage: Poe, Ladies, and Slaves," in *Subjects and Citizens: Nation, Race, and Gender from "Oronooko" to Anita Hill*, ed. Michael Moon and Cathy N. Davidson (Durham: Duke University Press, 1995), 109–43. On Poe's biographical and literary fantasies of dismembered women, see Silverman, *Edgar A. Poe*, 515n.

Chapter 4

1. Carolyn Karcher, *Shadow over the Promised Land: Slavery, Race, and Violence in Melville's America* (Baton Rouge: Louisiana State University Press, 1980), 2–3.

2. Wai-Chee Dimock, *Empire for Liberty: Melville and the Poetics of Individualism* (Princeton: Princeton University Press, 1989), 10.

3. Ibid., 7. Recent interpretations of Melville's complicity with antebellum

U.S. ideology also depend on Michael Paul Rogin's *Subversive Genealogy: The Politics and Art of Herman Melville* (Berkeley: University of California Press, 1985), which adapts depth psychology to the reading of Melville's thought as symptomatic of conflicts in antebellum U.S. culture and politics.

4. T. Walter Herbert, Jr., *Marquesan Encounters: Melville and the Meaning of Civilization* (Cambridge: Harvard University Press, 1980), 178.

5. Ibid., 179.

6. See, for example, James Clifford and George Marcus, eds., *Writing Culture: The Poetics and Politics of Ethnography* (Berkeley: University of California Press, 1986); and Wolfgang Iser, *Prospecting: From Reader Response to Literary Anthropology* (Baltimore: Johns Hopkins University Press, 1989), 262–84, and *The Fictive and the Imaginary: Charting Literary Anthropology* (Baltimore: Johns Hopkins University Press, 1993), 281–303.

7. Kaori O'Connor, "Introduction," *Typee: Four Months' Residence in the Marquesas* (London: KPI, 1985), viii.

8. Herbert, *Marquesan Encounters*, 19.

9. David F. Long, *Nothing Too Daring: A Biography of Commodore David Porter, 1780–1843* (Annapolis: U.S. Naval Institute, 1970), 110.

10. See my discussion of *Pierre* in *At Emerson's Tomb: The Politics of Classic American Literature* (New York: Columbia University Press, 1997), 63–95.

11. Long, *Nothing Too Daring*, 109, discusses the discovery of the Marquesas by Ivaro de Mendaña y Castro in 1596, naming the islands for the wife of the viceroy of Peru, "Las Islas Marquesas de Don Garcia Hurtado de Mendoza de Cañate," and the visit by Captain James Cook on April 8, 1774.

12. Charles R. Anderson, *Melville in the South Seas* (1939; reprint, New York: Dover Publications, 1966), 96–98.

13. Herman Melville, *Typee: A Peep at Polynesian Life*, vol. 1, *The Writings of Herman Melville*, ed. Harrison Hayford, Hershel Parker, and G. Thomas Tanselle, Northwestern-Newberry Edition (Evanston, Ill.: Northwestern University Press, 1968), 11. Further references in the text as T.

14. Edmund Fanning, who visited the islands in the spring of 1798, refers to "The Marquesas and Washington Islands" in his *Voyages and Discoveries in the South Seas: 1792–1832* (1833; reprint, New York: Dover Publications, 1989), 99.

15. See James Kavanagh, "That Hive of Subtlety: 'Benito Cereno' and the Liberal Hero," in *Ideology and Classic American Literature*, ed. Sacvan Bercovitch and Myra Jehlen (New York: Cambridge University Press, 1986), 352–83.

16. Brook Thomas, *Cross-Examinations of Law and Literature: Cooper, Hawthorne, Stowe, and Melville* (Cambridge: Cambridge University Press, 1987), 137.

17. Long, *Nothing Too Daring*, 109.

18. Ibid., 124.

19. Ibid.

20. David Porter, *Journal of a Cruise Made to the Pacific Ocean, in the U.S. Frigate "Essex," in the Years 1812, 1813, and 1814*, 2 vols. (Philadelphia: Bradford and Inskeep, 1815), 2:14. By the early nineteenth century, the attribution of an inherent lasciviousness to women of Africa, Polynesia, the Middle East, and Asia was a convention of the pervasive Orientalism of Euro-American societies. See Sander L. Gilman, *Difference and Pathology: Stereotypes of Sexuality, Race, and Madness* (Ithaca, N.Y.: Cornell University Press, 1985), 76–108.

As I point out in Chapters 3, 5, and 10, Euro-Americans interpreted Native American women in similar ways, often projecting their own erotic desires onto these women in utterly fantastic ways.

21. Long, *Nothing Too Daring*, 126.

22. Anderson, *Melville in the South Seas*, 96.

23. Herbert, *Marquesan Encounters*, 82–83. Herbert is quoting from Allan B. Cole's edition of "Captain David Porter's Proposed Expedition to the Pacific and Japan, 1815," *Pacific Historical Review* 9 (1940): 63ff.

24. Ibid., 83.

25. Dimock, *Empire for Liberty*, 75.

26. Herbert, *Marquesan Encounters*, 167.

27. Ibid., 158. Herbert's reading here agrees basically with D. H. Lawrence's judgment more than fifty years earlier in *Studies in Classic American Literature* (New York: Viking Press, 1923), 141: "In his soul he was proud and savage. But in his mind and will he wanted the perfect fulfillment of love; he wanted the lovey-doveyness of perfect mutual understanding. A proud savage-soul man doesn't really want any perfect lovey-dovey fulfillment in love; no such nonsense. A mountain lion doesn't mate with a Persian cat; and when a grizzly bear roars after a mate, it is a she-grizzly he roars after—not after a silky sheep."

28. Jay Leyda, *The Melville Log: A Documentary Life of Herman Melville: 1819–1891*, 2 vols. (New York: Harcourt, Brace, 1951), 2:515.

29. Mitchell Breitwieser, *American Puritanism and the Defense of Mourning: Religion, Grief, and Ethnology in Mary White Rowlandson's Captivity Narrative* (Madison: University of Wisconsin Press, 1990), 150, views the disparities in Rowlandson's narrative as part of a process whereby she discards Puritan values and comprehends Algonquian society: "The practice of exchange, the disaffection with Puritan values, and the burgeoning capacity to recognize Indian society as such, then, culminate in representations of the Algonquians that markedly depart from moral symbolization after the initial pages of the narrative, perhaps because in the course of writing she discovers layers of significance in experience that she is reluctant to cover over."

30. H. Bruce Franklin, "Animal Farm Unbound; or, What the *Narrative of the Life of Frederick Douglass, An American Slave* Reveals about American Literature," *New Letters* 53 (Spring 1977): 46, concludes by neatly connecting Douglass's 1845 *Narrative* with Melville's *Typee*: "Douglass, writing as a nonwhite slave in white America, had to veil some of his message in imagery. Melville, writing as a white American who had lived in a non-white society under the shadow of imperialism, spoke more bluntly when he distinguished 'the white civilized man as the most ferocious animal on the face of the earth.' . . . When Melville's *Narrative* was published in America as *Typee*, these words, along with many other crucial passages, were deleted. When Douglass' *Narrative* was published in America, he had to flee his native land."

31. For more detailed discussions of how Douglass and Jacobs deconstruct the boundary between southern slavery and northern freedom, see my *At Emerson's Tomb*, chapters 5 and 6. *Our Nig* is set in the North, so it does not as explicitly challenge regional boundaries, focusing primarily on northern racial prejudices.

32. Karcher, *Shadow over the Promised Land*, 7.

33. For example, see Edgar A. Dryden, *Melville's Thematics of Form: The Great Art of Telling the Truth* (Baltimore: Johns Hopkins University Press,

1968), 42, who comments on Tommo's flight and wounded leg in terms of motifs of symbolic castration and the Puritan *felix culpa*.

34. In "'Made in the Marquesas': *Typee*, Tattooing and Melville's Critique of the Literary Marketplace," *Arizona Quarterly* 48 (Winter 1992): 19–45, John Evelev connects tattooing in Typee society with the problem of artistic representation for Melville in nineteenth-century America: "Tattooing is . . . used by Melville as a tool to critique colonial practices and the binary opposition of 'civilized' and 'savage'" (25).

35. Melville's sardonic comparison of the queen's tattooed legs with Trajan's Column, that venerable tourist destination, recalls the double significance of Trajan for the modern reader of *Typee*. Not only does his column declare his victory over the ancient Dacians, in what is now Germany, and thus the Roman conquest of Europe, but he himself was converted to Christianity and one of only two pagan emperors admitted to heaven, according to the early church.

36. Melville repeatedly satirizes such classicism, especially in *Pierre*, whereas Poe relies on classical references and style to establish his narrative superiority over "primitive" peoples, Crane relies on the mock epic for similar purposes, and Henry Adams establishes classical ideals for the Tahitians in his *Tahiti*. See Chapters 3, 7, and 8.

37. Stephen Greenblatt, *Marvelous Possessions: The Wonder of the New World* (Chicago: University of Chicago Press, 1992), 122.

38. Ibid., 150.

39. Ibid.

Chapter 5

1. Shelley Streeby, "Joaquín Murrieta, the U.S.–Mexican War, and the Migration of Popular Cultures," in *Post-Nationalist American Studies*, ed. John Carlos Rowe (Berkeley: University of California Press, 2000), 206.

2. Douglas Monroy, *Thrown among Strangers: The Making of Mexican Culture in Frontier California* (Berkeley: University of California Press, 1990), 173.

3. Leonard Pitt, *The Decline of the Californios: A Social History of the Spanish-Speaking Californians, 1846–1890* (Berkeley: University of California Press, 1966), 52–53, estimates 100,000 newcomers to the gold fields in 1849: "80,000 Yankees, 8,000 Mexicans, 5,000 South Americans, and several thousand miscellaneous Europeans—and with numbers that swelled to a quarter million by 1852."

4. Monroy, *Thrown among Strangers*, 203–4: "The Land Act of 1851 wreaked havoc on the rancheros' claims. It created a three-person commission to which all titles of the Spanish and Mexican eras had to be submitted for validation. . . . [It] effectively dispossessed Californios of approximately 40 percent of their lands held before 1846."

5. For President James K. Polk (1845–1849), his campaign slogan of "54°40' or Fight," by which he referred to settlement of the Oregon boundary question with Great Britain, and his campaign promise to acquire California were related foreign policy questions. In his campaign, Polk played on traditional U.S. antagonism to Great Britain as anticolonial struggle.

6. Monroy, *Thrown among Strangers*, 44.

7. Ibid., 185–86. Article 6 forbade Indian testimony against a white person. Article 14 allowed a white person to pay the fine of a convicted Indian and then

use that Indian for labor in payment of the fine. And Article 20 imposed such strict rules forbidding Indian "vagrancy" that virtually all Indians displaced from their lands could be subjected to the law at any given moment, making them subject to conviction, payment of the fine by a white person, and indentured labor.

8. Pitt, *The Decline of the Californios*, 49.

9. Monroy, *Thrown among Strangers*, 198, points out that even when Californian Native Americans were moved to reservations, they were not given adequate food or other supplies in the 1850s. As I point out in Chapter 10, this was also the way the Lakota and other Plains' tribes were treated on the reservations in the Midwest.

10. Reginald Horsman, *Race and Manifest Destiny: The Origins of American Racial Anglo-Saxonism* (Cambridge: Harvard University Press, 1981), 260.

11. Pitt, *The Decline of the Californios*, 49–50. Pitt points out that the success of the Californios in the mines was short-lived, because by 1849 they had been forcibly driven from the gold fields by Yankee aggressors, anticipating the gang of Yankees who drive Joaquín from his claim and rape his wife, Rosita, at the beginning of Ridge's novel.

12. James W. Parins, *John Rollin Ridge: His Life and Works* (Lincoln: University of Nebraska Press, 1991), 61.

13. John Rollin Ridge, "Oppression of the Digger Indians," *Daily Bee*, 12 July 1857, collected in *A Trumpet of Our Own: Yellow Bird's Essays on the North American Indian, Selections from the Writings of the Noted Cherokee Author John Rollin Ridge*, ed. David Farmer and Rennard Strickland (San Francisco: Book Club of California, 1981), 69. Further references in the text as *Trumpet*, but first reference to specific journalism, with citations of first publication, in the Notes.

14. Parins, *John Rollin Ridge*, 13–31; Cheryl Walker, *Indian Nation: Native American Literature and Nineteenth-century Nationalisms* (Durham: Duke University Press, 1997), 230–31n3.

15. Walker, *Indian Nation*, 116.

16. Ibid., 116–17. Parins, *John Rollin Ridge*, 28, estimates "four thousand Cherokee died, a fifth of the Nation" and points out that the majority of the victims were "women, children, and the aged," including "John Ross's wife, Quatie."

17. Parins, *John Rollin Ridge*, 29.

18. Ibid., 29–30.

19. Ibid., 35–37, 50–55.

20. Ibid., 55.

21. Louis Owens, *Other Destinies: Understanding the American Indian Novel* (Norman: University of Oklahoma Press, 1992), 32, 33.

22. Eric Sundquist, "The Literature of Expansion and Race," *Cambridge History of American Literature*, vol. 2: *Prose Writing 1820–1865*, ed. Sacvan Bercovitch and Cyrus R. K. Patell (New York: Cambridge University Press, 1995), 211.

23. Parins, *John Rollin Ridge*, 184–221.

24. Ibid., 188.

25. Ridge complains of making no money from "my life of Joaquín Murieta," because "my publishers, after selling 7,000 copies and putting the money in their pockets, fled, bursted up, tee totally smashed, and left me, with a hundred others, to whistle for our money," in a letter to Stand Watie of October 9, 1854,

as quoted in Joseph Henry Jackson, "Introduction," *The Life and Adventures of Joaquín Murieta: The Celebrated California Bandit* (Norman: University of Oklahoma Press, 1955), xxxii. Further references to this edition of Ridge's novel in the text as JM.

26. Jackson, "Introduction," xxxii; Parins, *John Rollin Ridge*, 95. Pitt, *The Decline of the Californios*, 81, argues that Ridge's condemnation of racism in *Joaquín Murieta* was "too strong a homily for the 1850's, and the book sank out of sight until the gringos could swallow it more readily," but Pitt doesn't explain his reasons for believing the novel to have been "unpopular," other than Ridge's equivocal letter to Stand Watie. Given the hysteria about *bandidos* in California from 1850 to 1856, it is far more likely that Ridge's slight moralizing about the negative consequences of racial prejudice would have been ignored and readers' interest in the graphic violence, ruthless robberies, and conspiracy to rebellion gratified. The incorporation of liberal political sentiments in contemporary mass-cultural texts with conservative political aims is today a conventional practice, visible in a wide range of post–Vietnam era films, from the *Rambo* series to *Lethal Weapon* and *The Terminator* series.

27. Pitt, *The Decline of the Californios*, 75.

28. Robert W. Johannsen, *To the Halls of the Montezumas: The Mexican War in the American Imagination* (New York: Oxford University Press, 1985), 189–91.

29. Horsman, *Race and Manifest Destiny*, 208.

30. Ibid., 210, 231.

31. Pitt, *The Decline of the Californios*, 60. Green had proposed initially a monthly tax of $20, but reduced that to $16. In fact, the tax was "collected" in such erratic ways and by so many unauthorized collectors that it would be impossible to determine just what the average monthly tax was for those who paid it. Sometimes, the tax amounted simply to what the foreign miner could afford. Chinese miners often paid $3–$5.

32. Ibid., 64: Mexican, Latin American, and Chinese miners "knew that they alone of all foreign miners were being subjected to the tax: when they taunted the collectors to tax Irishmen, Frenchmen, and other Europeans they received no satisfactory reply."

33. Josiah Royce, *California from the Conquest in 1846 to the Second Vigilance Committee in San Francisco: A Study of American Character* (Boston: Houghton, Mifflin, 1886), 358–59. The Harvard philosopher's late nineteenth-century history of California indicts squarely the "sinful" and "unmoral" conduct of Americans in the gold fields toward foreigners and each other, and it is a distinct contrast with the exploitation of frontier anarchy and racism in more celebrated works, including Mark Twain's *Roughing It* (1872) and Bret Harte's racist ballad "Plain Language from Truthful James" (1870), which led to the pirated broadside, *The Heathen Chinee*, and Harte and Twain's stage adaptation, *Ah Sin* (1877).

34. Monroy, *Thrown among Strangers*, 203.

35. Pitt, *The Decline of the Californios*, 50–52.

36. Ibid., 56–57.

37. Monroy, *Thrown among Strangers*, 208–10.

38. Louise Amelia Knapp Smith Clappe's letters from "Rich and Indian bars on the North Fork of the Feather River in California's gold diggings" were written in 1851 and 1852, signed "Dame Shirley," and "first published serially in *The Pioneer Magazine* of San Francisco during 1854 and 1855," as Carl I. Wheat

notes in his edition of *The Shirley Letters from the California Mines: 1851–1852* (New York: Knopf, 1949), v. In her "Nineteenth Letter," dated August 4, 1852, p. 167, Clappe describes the whipping of a "Spaniard," who "implored for death in the most moving terms," rather than be whipped and dishonored. When refused, "he swore a most solemn oath, that he would murder every American that he should chance to meet alone." This episode is often cited as a possible source for Ridge's account of Joaquín's whipping and vow of vengeance at the beginning of the novel.

39. One of the modernizations of the legend of Joaquín Murieta is Walter Noble Burns, *The Robin Hood of El Dorado: The Saga of Joaquin Murrieta, Famous Outlaw of California's Age of Gold* (New York: Grosset and Dunlap, 1932), 6–8, in which Joaquín and Rosita come from "old pioneer stock and boasted pure Castilian descent" with just a "drop or two of Yaqui or ancient Aztec blood," but must elope from Sonora because Rosita is affianced by her father, Ramon Féliz, to an elderly Hidalgo, Don José Gonzales, whom she does not love. Ridge does not include such details, but Burns's later version does seem to work out the logic of Joaquín and Rosita's desire for the liberty of the United States over the European class determinants governing nineteenth-century Mexico.

40. Walker, *Indian Nation*, 123–25, 138.

41. See, for example, Immanuel Kant, *The Critique of Judgement*, trans. James Creed Meredith (Oxford: Oxford University Press, 1952), 181: "Genius . . . is the exemplary originality of the natural endowments of an individual in the *free* employment of his cognitive faculties." As Parins, *John Rollin Ridge*, 87, points out, "Mount Shasta, Seen from a Distance" "closely follows Shelley's 'Mont Blanc' in theme, natural description, diction, and even meter." Both Kant and Shelley's romantic conceptions of genius are fundamental to Enlightenment notions of middle-class individualism.

42. Ibid., 122, 136.

43. Pitt, *The Decline of the Californios*, 70–74.

44. Frank Latta, *Joaquín Murrieta and His Horse Gangs* (Santa Cruz, Calif.: Bear State Books, 1980), 101–5, 279, provides biographical background for "Three-Fingered Jack," also known as "Tres Dedos," who was born Manuel Duarte in the state of Sonora and often called "Garcia" or "Jack." According to Catarina (Aunt Kate) Duarte de Wilson, granddaughter of Antonio Duarte, Three-Fingered Jack's brother, he was not given this nickname until *after* his death and legends of his three-fingered hand circulated with other stories about the Murieta gang. He was reputedly known for his "violent nature" from his earliest years. According to Juan Joaquín Murrieta's testimony, "When Jack had his forefinger injured Grandfather cut it off so he couldn't shoot a gun to do any good anymore" (279). Of course, Ridge plays upon the "inherent" violence of the character, which suggests some of these stories must have been in circulation during the gang's brief reign of terror. I am grateful to Jesse Luna, who produces reenactments of the Murrieta legend, for directing me to the oral history contained in Latta's book.

45. Although Harry Love and his rangers probably turned in someone else's head other than that of the *real* Joaquín Murieta, should he have actually existed, primarily for the bounty offered by the California State Legislature (Love's allotted time was, after all, running out), our contemporary skepticism regarding Love's "heroism" should not distract us from recognizing that Ridge consistently portrays Harry Love, who earned his military title in the

Mexican-American War, as "a leader . . . whose soul was as rugged and severe as the discipline through which it has passed, whose brain was as strong and clear in the midst of dangers as that of the daring robber against whom he was sent, and who possessed a glance as quick and a hand as sudden in the execution of a deadly purpose" (JM, 146). Harry Love is never ironized by Ridge.

46. Americo Paredes, *Folklore and Culture on the Texas-Mexican Border*, ed. Richard Bauman (Austin: Center for Mexican American Studies and University of Texas at Austin Press, 1993), 135. According to Robert Selph Henry, *The Story of the Mexican War* (New York: Ungar, 1961), 373, Padre Cenobio Jarauta, "best known of the guerilla leaders," was "so active" in guerilla activities that "he appears in most of the contemporary American accounts as two persons—'Cenobio' or sometime 'Colonel Zenobia,' and 'Jarauta.'" His legendary qualities and multiple identities resemble characteristics of Joaquín Murieta stressed by Ridge in his novel.

47. Monroy, *Thrown among Strangers*, 206, notes that the Los Angeles *barrio*, where Mexican immigrants lived, was named "Sonoratown," in reference to the large percentage of Mexican immigrants from the state of Sonora. Once again, Ridge's views in this regard seem to fit neatly with the dominant U.S. ideology. In the *Career of Tiburcio Vasquez, the Bandit of Soledad, Salinas and Tres Pinos, with Some Account of His Capture by Sheriff Rowland of Los Angeles*, a pulp thriller "compiled from newspaper accounts" of the later California bandit, Vasquez, and published in a single volume with the "third edition" (1871), supposedly revised by Ridge before his death, of *Life and Adventures of Joaquín Murieta*, under the collective title, *The Lives of Joaquin Murieta and Tiburcio Vasquez: The California Highwaymen* (San Francisco: Frederick MacCrellish, 1874), 1, the anonymous editor notes: "One thing, however, was greatly in [Vasquez's] favor, as was also the case with Murietta [*sic*]: in all those counties where he operated, he had the moral and physical aid of his countrymen, and especially his countrywomen, the native Californians. There seems to be an ever present hostility of these later remnants of the early mixed Indian and Mexican stock that roamed the hills, cañons, and all the valleys of California; who owned the mighty bands of wealth-producing cattle, and whose hospitality was ever generous to the stranger knocking at the gates of their haciendas." The original of this 1874 edition of the two narratives bound together is in the Huntington Library in San Marino, Calif., and is the basis for a 1927 edition, issued in Hollister, Calif.

48. Ridge may anticipate here his anti-Lincoln, anti-abolitionist journalism in the Civil War, in which he consistently attacked the Republican administration as war-mongering and anti-Union while defending the Confederacy as *upholding*, however improbably, the Union by seceding. See Parins, *John Rollin Ridge*, 184–85.

49. Johannsen, *To the Halls of the Montezumas*, 170.

50. Horsman, *Race and Manifest Destiny*, 234.

51. Parins, *John Rollin Ridge*, 84–91, discusses the influence of "the works of English and American romantic poets of the early nineteenth century, poets that Ridge read at school" on his love and nature poetry and his familiarity with "major British and American romantics such as Byron, Shelley, Keats, Poe, and Bryant" (84, 91). My suggestion here is that Ridge works more in the vein of American transcendentalism than has hitherto been acknowledged and that *Joaquín Murieta*, as well as Ridge's poetry, is organized in large part around

transcendentalist concepts of radical individualism, regulated and directed by social law.

52. Ronald Takaki, *Iron Cages: Race and Culture in Nineteenth-century America* (New York: Knopf, 1979), 220.

53. Ronald Takaki, *A Different Mirror: A History of Multicultural America* (Boston: Little, Brown, 1993), 191.

54. Ridge makes no reference to African Americans in the novel, ignoring the important debate surrounding the use of slaves by southerners in the gold fields. My guess is that Ridge omits such cases of organized labor to avoid the contradiction between his condemnation of the use of *péons* by *rancheros* in the gold fields and his continuing advocacy of slavery in the United States and in California. For the history of slave labor in the gold fields, see Pitt, *The Decline of the Californios*, 57–58.

55. Pitt, *The Decline of the Californios*, 77.

56. At one point, Ridge describes the "industrious Chinese" miners as "innumerable ants, picking up the small but precious grains" of gold, thus reinforcing popular anxieties about "foreigners" taking gold from "Americans" (JM, 83). Elsewhere Ridge describes the "miserable Chinamen" killed by the gang, who leave their bodies "along the highways like so many sheep with their throats cut by the wolves" (97).

57. Ridge, as quoted in Parins, *John Rollin Ridge*, pp. 141–42.

58. In Ridge, "A True Sketch of 'Si Bolla,' a Digger Indian," *Sacramento Bee*, 24 June 1857, collected in *A Trumpet of Our Own*, 58, "old Si Bolla," the Native American Ridge describes, sends Ridge a written invitation that resembles the style of the Yankee miners in their writings in *Joaquín Murieta*: "Mr. _____deer sur: _F you want enny bar mete cum to my camp." Compare with examples of Americans' bad grammar in the novel: JM, 131–32.

59. Owens, *Other Destinies*, 39.

60. Walker, *Indian Nation*, 131–32.

61. Ridge's letter to the New Orleans *True Delta*, 1 November 1851, collected in *A Trumpet of Our Own*, 62.

62. "Woh Le," the name given a Chinese traveler spared from Jack's violence by Joaquín's mercy, may well be a tag-name, as in "Woe Le," an Orientalist "Woe-is-me."

63. Walker, *Indian Nation*, 119, specifically refers to Ridge himself "as an example of the metropolitan postmodern."

64. Ridge's letter to the New Orleans *True Delta* and "Oppression of the Digger Indians," *Daily Bee* 12 July 1857, collected in *A Trumpet of Our Own*, 62, 64.

65. O. Henry popularized "The Cisco Kid," who "killed for the love of it—because he was quick-tempered—to avoid arrest—for his own amusement—any reason that came to his mind would suffice," in "The Caballero's Way," in *Heart of the West* (New York: Doubleday, Page, 1904), 187. Like Joaquín, Cisco represents frontier anarchy—the Spanish word *cisco* means colloquially "a noisy brawl" or "to smash something to bits," as in *hacer cisco*. O. Henry's "Cisco Kid" combines the ruthlessness of Three-Fingered Jack with the courtliness of Joaquín, but the Kid plays a deadly game of romance, arranging a plot in which his lover, Tonia Perez, will be mistakenly killed by Lieutenant Sandridge, the man to whom she has betrayed the Kid. Of course, later Hollywood and television versions of *The Cisco Kid* would thoroughly sanitize this potent brew of colonialist evils. Johnston McCulley (b. 1883) wrote the origi-

nal story for the *Zorro* films, made first for Douglas Fairbanks, whose production company made the first films in the 1920s (such as *The Mark of Zorro* [1920] and *Don Q., Son of Zorro* [1925], both silent films), and the 1940 remake, *The Mark of Zorro* (directed by Rouben Mamoulian and starring Tyrone Power as Zorro), whose popularity led to the 1950s Disney television series. McCulley's book, *The Mark of Zorro* (New York: Grosset and Dunlap, 1952), is an early version of the "made-from-movies" books now so popular. Sony Pictures' recent *The Mask of Zorro* (1998), starring Antonio Banderas, has revived the exotic and romantic "Spanish/Mexican outlaw" for this generation of Americans. The Zorro films are set, of course, in "Spanish California" and much more explicitly play upon the "Robin Hood" themes than *Joaquín Murieta*. Yet, both Zorro (Spanish for "fox") and Joaquín rely on the respectability and cultivation of the Californio's Hidalgo heritage—Zorro is the Los Angeles Hidalgo, Don Diego de la Vega, fighting the corrupt Alcalde of Los Angeles, Luis Quintero, in a symbolic enactment of the Mexican Revolution against Spain. Such are the wayward routes of popular culture!

66. Joaquin Miller [Cincinnatus Hiner Miller], "Joaquin Murietta," in *The Complete Poetical Works of Joaquin Miller* (New York: Arno Press, 1972), 36. Like Ridge and Nahl, Miller identifies Joaquin Murieta with romantic sublimity. Miller was derogatorily referred to as "Joaquin" in the press for this poem, and he defiantly took the nickname as his poetic name (40). See also James F. Varley, *The Legend of Joaquín Murrieta: California's Gold Rush Bandit* (Twin Falls, Idaho: Big Lost River Press, 1995), 1.

67. Walker, *Indian Nation*, 136.

68. Varley, *The Legend of Joaquín Murrieta*, 129–55, gives a good sample of the persistence of the myth of Murieta in the state and abroad. As reported the *Los Angeles Times*, 9 January 1998, B1, recent restoration of the Greystone Church at Mission San Juan Capistrano has revealed numerous inscriptions on the interior stones, including the neatly incised and mysteriously dated:

JOAQUIN MURRIETA
1865

69. Walker, *Indian Nation*, 119.

70. James Monaghan, *Chile, Peru, and the California Gold Rush of 1849* (Berkeley: University of California Press, 1973), 214, notes that Quillota, Chile, "religious and extraordinarily conservative, was an odd background for the outlaw revered by Chileans." The legend of Joaquín as Chilean probably derives from Roberto Hyenne's translation back into Spanish of a French edition of the pirated "second edition" of *Joaquín Murieta*, published by the *California Police Gazette* in San Francisco from September 3 to November 5, 1859, in "ten installments of an anonymously-written Murrieta story," as Varley, *The Legend of Joaquín Murrieta*, 141, describes the pirated work. According to Monaghan, *Chile, Peru*, 216, Hyenne's new translation of the story from French into Spanish (again) "was published in Santiago, Chile, under his name as author and with the title *El Bandido Chileño*," in which Hyenne "moved Joaquín's birthplace from Mexico to Quillota and made him a national figure who avenged the persecutors of his fellow countrymen in California."

71. Monaghan, *Chile, Peru*, 217.

72. Jackson, "Introduction," xxxviii.

73. Don Hutchinson, *The Great Pulp Heroes* (Oakville, Ontario: Mosaic Press, 1996), 5, traces "'pulp' fiction" back to "as early as the 1840's when publishers decided that one way to lower costs, and thus price, was to use newspaper presses and cheap newsprint paper." The first edition of Ridge's novel was printed in this pamphlet format, which may be why only one known copy has survived.

Chapter 6

1. Wolfgang Mommsen, *Theories of Imperialism*, trans. P. S. Falla (Chicago: University of Chicago Press, 1980), 4: "It was Disraeli's opponents, especially Gladstone, who used the opprobrious term 'imperialism' to describe his policy of external aggression inspired by domestic motives," in response to the British foreign policies announced in Disraeli's famous Crystal Palace Speech of 1872.

2. Richard Bridgman, *Traveling in Mark Twain* (Berkeley: University of California Press, 1987), 143. Bridgman goes on to acknowledge that if "these hopeful sentiments . . . represented Mark Twain's best judgment as he came to the end of his last extensive journey, in fact he would shortly be obliged to repudiate them, and did, with unparalleled indignation, in a series of critiques of imperialist policy" (143–44).

3. Forrest G. Robinson, "The Innocent at Large: Mark Twain's Travel Writing," in *The Cambridge Companion to Twain*, ed. Forrest G. Robinson (New York: Cambridge University Press, 1995), 43.

4. William Gibson, "Mark Twain and Howells: Anti-Imperialists," *New England Quarterly* 20 (December 1947): 470, tries to reconcile Twain's anti-imperialism with his general criticism of America's failure to realize its democratic and republican promise: "Throughout the Gilded Age, Twain and Howells were aware of the problems implicit in democratic government in the United States, and critical of what they held its shortcomings to be, but at no time were they more jealous of its preservation than at the end. At the turn of the century they attacked imperialism as Emerson and Thoreau had attacked slavery. Like Emerson and Thoreau before them, they also wrote in a major tradition in American letters." David R. Sewell, "Hank Morgan and the Colonization of Utopia," *American Transcendentalist Quarterly*, n.s., 3 (March 1989): 32, argues that two of Twain's literary projects in the 1880s—his "abandoned novel about Hawaiian colonization and the longer fragment 'Huck Finn and Tom Sawyer among the Indians'"—are evidence of his anti-imperialist sentiments in the period he wrote *Connecticut Yankee*.

5. Robinson, "The Innocent at Large," 34, characterizes the narrative voice of *Roughing It* as that of "an increasingly bitter cynic."

6. Eric Sundquist, "Introduction," *Mark Twain: A Collection of Critical Essays*, ed. Eric Sundquist, New Century Views (Englewood Cliffs, N.J.: Prentice Hall, 1994), 6.

7. Mark Twain, *Roughing It*, ed. Harriet Elinor Smith et al., vol. 2 of *The Works of Mark Twain*, ed. Robert H. Hirst (Berkeley: University of California Press, 1993), 126–27.

8. Ibid., 127.

9. Joseph Conrad, *Heart of Darkness*, ed. Robert Kimbrough, Norton Critical Edition (New York: Norton, 1971), 5–6.

10. Yeats, Pound, and Eliot helped revive classical traditions in the early modern period, even as they ironized their sources, blasted traditionalists, and

claimed avant-garde status for their new "classicism." There is nevertheless a certain cultural narrative linking Victorian "medievalism" with early modern "classicism" that becomes more readable if we understand its function to be the reconsolidation of the cultural resources of the European and American nation-states as they shifted from political to economic and cultural modes of colonial domination in the same historical period.

11. See Chapter 4.

12. Rudyard Kipling, "The White Man's Burden: The United States and The Philippine Islands," *Rudyard Kipling's Verse* (Garden City, N.Y.: Doubleday, 1940), 321–23.

13. At the beginning of the Spanish-American War, McKinley claimed not to have known the location of the Philippines within 2,000 miles. To this day, standard reference books, like the *Encyclopedia Americana*, treat our annexation of the Philippines as an "accident" of history, thus thrusting us unwillingly and unexpectedly into the role of imperial power. McKinley assumed this role quite well, but Twain makes clear in "To the Person Sitting in Darkness" (1901) that McKinley was following quite consciously the European plan.

14. As quoted in Gibson, "Mark Twain and Howells, 446.

15. See Chapter 8.

16. Robinson, "The Innocent at Large," 47.

17. Ibid., 43–45.

18. Mark Twain, *Following the Equator: A Journey around the World*, 2 vols., in *The Writings of Mark Twain*, Author's National Edition (New York: P. F. Collier and Son, 1899), 16:298–99.

19. Mommsen, *Theories of Imperialism*, 4.

20. Mark Twain, "To the Person Sitting in Darkness," *Selected Shorter Writings of Mark Twain*, ed. Walter Blair (Boston: Houghton Mifflin, 1962), 295. Further references in the text as "Person."

21. Twain, *Following the Equator*, 16:299. Western political analysts had worried about the unpredictable role Russia would play in the struggles for territory among the European imperial powers since the Russo-Turkish War of 1877–1878, during which Russian troops had driven as far as Constantinople in their support of the Serbs and Bulgarians. The new threat posed by Russia to the established nineteenth-century European empires, especially in Asia Minor and the Far East, does explain in part Twain's begrudging endorsement of British law and order elsewhere in *Following the Equator*. Like other Westerners, Twain tended to demonize the colonial and expansionist policies of non–Euro-American powers, as his reference to Czar Nicholas II's descent from "an obscure tribe of Muscovite savages" indicates.

22. See Blair's discussion of Twain's use of Western sources in *Hannibal, Huck, and Tom*, ed. Walter Blair (Berkeley: University of California Press, 1960); Richard Slotkin, *The Fatal Environment: The Myth of the Frontier in the Age of Industrialization, 1800–1890* (New York: Atheneum, 1985), 516–32; and Ronald T. Takaki, *Iron Cages: Race and Culture in Nineteenth-century America* (New York: Knopf, 1979), 167–69.

23. Interpreting the concluding "Battle of the Sand Belt," for example, as a commentary on the Custer myth and an anticipation of the tragic consequences of European expansionism in genocide and even world war, Slotkin writes in *The Fatal Environment*, 529–30: "It is a horrible vision, prophetic in many of its details of the causes and tactics of the Great War, and of the revolutions that grew out of the exhaustion of society's military frenzy. But it is also a brilliant

and complex development of the implications of the Custer myth and the ideology of class struggle that it contained—one in which the Last Stand becomes a metaphor for the fate of both savages and cavalrymen, peasants and aristocrats, proletarians and elites; and the 'Instinct of Progress' itself willingly calls upon the 'Spirit of Massacre.'"

24. Like Slotkin, David Sewell, "Hank Morgan," 28, understands Twain's "fable of progress" in *Connecticut Yankee* to involve a general commentary on "the historical confrontation between Europe and the noncivilized world."

25. Robert Hirst, "Note on the Text," *A Connecticut Yankee in King Arthur's Court*, the Mark Twain Library (Berkeley: University of California Press, 1983), 477.

26. Lytton Strachey, *Eminent Victorians* (New York: Weidenfeld and Nicolson, 1988), 149. Further references in the text as EV.

27. Jen Yu-wen, *The Taiping Revolutionary Movement* (New Haven: Yale University Press, 1973), 443–44, 494–510.

28. The Taiping Rebellion provides a historical backdrop for the contemporary action in Amy Tan's novel *The Hundred Secret Senses* (New York: G. P. Putnam's Sons, 1995), in part to remind her readers of the long history of imperial involvement by the United States in the history of China and, of course, in the formation of Chinese-American culture.

29. There are many parallels between Hank Morgan and "Chinese" Gordon. Although he died representing the British government, Gordon was a new kind of foreign adventurer and diplomat, who served other rulers than Victoria but always (it would appear) with the larger interests of the British Empire in mind. He had served the Khedive Ismail of Egypt before returning to Africa, and he had been invited by King Leopold II to serve as his representative in the Congo Free State (an assignment Gordon declined). In a similar fashion, Hank Morgan serves Arthur, even as the Boss knows that his best interests lie in serving the higher authority of modern U.S. interests—both commercial and political. Gordon's disdain for British bureaucracy and his insistence on accomplishing tasks on his own is another quality he shares with Hank (as well as with later figures, like T. E. Lawrence, who modeled themselves after his overtly anti-imperialist cosmopolitanism). In the final siege of Khartoum, Gordon ordered the cellar of the palace to be loaded with gunpowder, so "that the whole building might, at a moment's notice, be blown in the air," anticipating the Boss and Clarence's plans to blow up their factories should they fall into the hands of the church and the Boss's earlier "demonstration" of his power by blowing up Merlin's Tower (EV, 188). Finally, Gordon's one constant in all his adventures was a curious sense of missionary zeal, that he was doing "God's" work. One of Hank Morgan's major projects—and differences from Mark Twain—is his plan to begin the Reformation "early," substituting the Protestant church for Catholicism. For a good recent account of Gordon's adventures and historical significance, see John H. Waller, *Gordon of Khartoum: The Saga of a Victorian Hero* (New York: Atheneum, 1988).

30. Slotkin, *The Fatal Environment*, 526, points out that Hank Morgan, the Connecticut Yankee, aka "the Boss" is related by these three names to the northern carpetbagger, the confidence man, Boss Tweed, "the famous pirate Henry Morgan," and "the great financier and Robber Baron J. P. Morgan."

31. Twain's "The Dervish and the Offensive Stranger" (1902), reprinted in *Mark Twain's Weapons of Satire: Anti-Imperialist Writings of the Philippine-American War*, ed. Jim Zwick (Syracuse: Syracuse University Press, 1992), 147–

50, uses a "Dervish" as the dialogic foil for a later version of the "mysterious stranger," who indicts global imperialism, links federal policies toward the Utes and other Native Americans in Utah to such imperialism, and condemns Columbus while reluctantly granting the progress achieved by the French Revolution, despite the Reign of Terror (148–49).

32. V. I. Lenin, *Imperialism, the Highest Stage of Capitalism*, vol. 22 of *Collected Works* (London: International Publishers, 1964), 185ff.

33. Mark Twain, *A Connecticut Yankee in King Arthur's Court*, ed. Allison R. Ensor, Norton Critical Edition (New York: W. W. Norton, 1982), p. 184. Further references in the text as: CY.

34. Twain, "The New Dynasty" (March 22, 1886), in CY, 285.

35. Henry Nash Smith, *Mark Twain's Fable of Progress: Political and Economic Ideas in "A Connecticut Yankee"* (New Brunswick, N.J.: Rutgers University Press, 1964), 100. Further references in the text as Smith.

36. Adam Smith, *Inquiry into the Nature and Causes of the Wealth of Nations* (1776; reprint, New York: Random House, 1937), 440–65, for the classic discussion of the advantages of free trade and the division of international labor (Book 4, "Of Systems of Political Economy," chapter 3).

37. Slotkin, *The Fatal Environment*, 523.

38. Walter Benn Michaels, "An American Tragedy; or, The Promise of American Life," *Representations* 25 (Winter 1989): 71–98, argues that Bellamy's "industrial army"—the state organized economy that "provides equal work, equal pay, and equal rights to all citizens" (80) and thus the basis for the citizen-worker's identity—expresses aptly (if unintentionally) the degree to which the incorporation of individuals into the capitalist economy would also *require* the organized and mechanized warfare of the modern period. In other words, Michaels interprets Bellamy's "socialism" as a rationalization of capitalist incorporation and mechanization, as well as their complementary legitimation in political and economic *expansion* (i.e., imperialism). The contradictoriness at the heart of Bellamy's utopian writing helps explain the contradictions in the thought of sympathetic anti-imperialists, like Twain and Howells.

39. Ronald Robinson and John Gallagher, "The Imperialism of Free Trade," *Economic History Review*, 2d ser., 6 (1953): 1–25. See Mommsen's discussion of Robinson and Gallagher, *Theories of Imperialism*, 87–90.

40. Mommsen, *Theories of Imperialism*, 88.

41. Ronald Robinson and John Gallagher, with Alice Denny, *Africa and the Victorians: The Official Mind of Imperialism* (London: Macmillan, 1961).

42. In his "Explanation" to the second edition of *Africa and the Victorians: The Official Mind of Imperialism* (London: Macmillan, 1981), xix, Robinson points out that subsequent scholars have taken the "hypothesis regarding informal empire, or 'the imperialism of free trade' . . . too narrowly," and he expands the term to include "the many ways in which dependence on British loans or British markets influenced foreign states in favor of commercial and political alliance with Britain"; "the effects of that dependence in bringing their economic growth into complementarity with the expansive needs of the British economy"; and finally "the Anglophile effects of economic dependence on their domestic politics and policies." In this last quality of "informal imperialism," I find the undeveloped elements of a theory of "cultural imperialism" that might be adapted to U.S. practices in the nineteenth and twentieth centuries.

43. Ibid., 6–8.

44. Mark Twain, *Fables of Man*, ed. John S. Tuckey, vol. 7, of *The Mark Twain Papers*, ed. Frederick Anderson, 15 vols. (Berkeley: University of California Press, 1972), 428–29.

45. Ronald Robinson, "The Conference in Berlin and the Future of Africa, 1884–1885," in *Bismarck, Europe, and Africa: The Berlin Conference 1884–1885 and the Onset of Partition* (Oxford: German Historical Institute of London and Oxford University Press, 1988), 1.

46. Ibid., 3.

47. In particular, Twain stresses in "King Leopold's Soliloquy" (1905), in *Mark Twain: Life as I Find It*, ed. Charles Neider (New York: Harper and Row, 1977), 275–76, the fact that the Belgian Congo was the king's private possession, not a colony administered in the traditional way as an extension of the "home" government, specifically tracing this colonial anomaly to the "convention in Berlin," where Leopold was made "Head Foreman and Superintendent of the Congo State."

48. As I point out in Chapter 12, the argument of John Tomlinson, *Cultural Imperialism: A Critical Introduction* (London: Pinter Publishers, 1991), typifies this sort of approach to neoimperialism, although Tomlinson does not focus exclusively on U.S. neoimperialism.

49. Michaels, "An American Tragedy," 82–83, argues that *Connecticut Yankee* exemplifies the ways in which late nineteenth-century concepts of individuality were being subordinated to the defining qualities of capitalism—incorporation, for example—and its technology—mechanization, for example. Mark Seltzer, *Bodies and Machines* (New York: Routledge, 1992), 94–95, views *Connecticut Yankee* as especially expressive of the late nineteenth-century contradiction between "the artificial" and the "natural" foundations for individuality: "On the one side, 'training, training is everything . . . ; but, on the other side, and set against this Taylorite disciplinary scenario, . . . 'a man is a man at bottom' . . . or, most basically, that 'there is no accounting for human beings'" (95).

50. Slotkin, *The Fatal Environment*, 526, brilliantly reads this "Connecticut Yankee" as a version of the carpetbagger of Reconstruction and thus of Twain's criticism of Reconstruction's moral failure but economic success in shifting the southern economy from agrarian to urban slavery. See also Sewell, "Hank Morgan," 29, who understands the commentary on slavery to be integral to the form of *Connecticut Yankee*: "Among the narrative forms that are incorporated, parodied, or even partially invented are Arthurian romance, science fiction, lost-race tales, travelogue, exploration accounts, adventure stories, slave narratives, dime novels, and ethnographic and sociological reportage." Howard Baetzhold, *Mark Twain and John Bull: The British Connection* (Bloomington: Indiana University Press, 1970), 151–52, analyzes Twain's adaptation of the slave narrative.

51. Susan Gillman, "Mark Twain's Travels in the Racial Occult," in *The Cambridge Companion to Twain*, 206.

52. See Chapter 9.

53. The failure of Hank Morgan's revolution is anticipated in Twain's "The Great Revolution in Pitcairn," which was first published in *Atlantic Monthly* 43 (1879): 295–302, and included by Ensor as one of the "Backgrounds and Sources" in his Norton Critical Edition of *Connecticut Yankee*. Not only does "The Great Revolution in Pitcairn" suggest that Americans, like Hank Morgan and Butterworth Stavely, are just as prone to imperial power as the Brit-

ish and the Europeans, it also establishes the continuity of Twain's anti-imperialist thinking from the 1870s to the early twentieth century. It is, however, yet another instance of what I can only term the *bathos* that Twain uses to represent his fictional revolutions. Focusing on the tiny rock of Pitcairn to burlesque larger imperial practices, Twain extends his anti-imperialist criticism but trivializes his suggestions for overturning European and U.S. imperialisms.

54. I should point out that Robinson and Gallagher are economic historians, so they can't really be blamed for ignoring the role of culture in modern imperialism in either its "free-trade" or political-military manifestations. In his 1968 essay, "The Case for Economic Aid," in *Developing the Third World: The Experience of the Nineteen-Sixties*, ed. Ronald Robinson (Cambridge: Cambridge University Press, 1971), 270, Robinson can conclude that late-modern, postcolonial economic assistance from the First World should be given to the Third World more in the form of "economic" development than "military and political aid," as if reinforcing the benign aspect of colonialism's beginnings in "free-trade imperialism." I can hardly argue with this conclusion, given the available choices between military-political "aid" or "helping recipients achieve the highest rate of balanced economic growth," but the U.S. foreign policy in Southeast Asia during our war with Vietnam in the period of Robinson's essay suggests that economic "assistance" in achieving "balanced economic growth" is not so easily distinguished from "military and political aid," unless the latter is taken exclusively in terms of overt military and political intervention.

55. See my discussion of Twain's critique of American higher education in *The Gilded Age* in *At Emerson's Tomb: The Politics of Classic American Literature* (New York: Columbia University Press, 1997), 162–65.

56. Takaki, *Iron Cages*, 169.

57. Twain, "The Dervish and the Stranger," 148.

58. Mommsen, *Theories of Imperialism*, 89.

59. Bernard Nietschmann, "The Third World War," *Cultural Survival Quarterly* 6 (1989): 6.

60. Twain, "King Leopold's Soliloquy," 294.

61. Nietschmann, "The Third World War," 3, provides a helpful definition of "Fourth World Nations" as "the nation peoples and their countries that exist beneath the imposed states. . . . Fourth World nations may be surrounded, divided or dismembered by one or more international states. The Fourth World encompasses most of the world's distinct peoples, about a third of the world's population and approximately 50 percent of the land area." These "nation peoples" are notoriously "invisible," because of their relation to "one or more international states."

62. Sewell, "Hank Morgan," 29, observes that the "most radical implication of *A Connecticut Yankee* . . . is that utopian narrative is a variety of literary imperialism—that Utopia is always a colony."

63. Takaki, *Iron Cages*, 170, concludes by summarizing how Twain's critique of nineteenth-century entrepreneurs focused on their employment of "technology as a mode of production as well as an instrument for the domination and reinforcement of social relations," including the creation of "centralized bureaucracies" and the control of society by "professionals and scientific managers." What I argue here is that we should link this scientific and instrumental "modernity" to *aesthetic* modernism, including Twain as one of its important precursors.

Chapter 7

1. Stephen Crane, *The Red Badge of Courage*, ed. Sculley Bradley et al., Norton Critical Edition, 2d ed. (New York: Norton, 1976), 5. Further references in the text as RBC.

2. Ralph Ellison, "Stephen Crane and the Mainstream of American Fiction," first published as the introduction to the Dell edition of *The Red Badge of Courage* (New York: Dell, 1960), reprinted in *Shadow and Act* (New York: Random House, 1964), 81: "For all the complex use of the symbolic connotations of blackness, only one Negro, a dancing teamster, appears throughout the novel." Ellison suggests that Crane does this intentionally, in order to leave "the reader . . . to fill in the understated background, to recreate those matters of which the hero, Henry Fleming, is too young, too self-centered and too concerned with the more immediate problems of courage, honor and self-preservation to be aware." Colonel Robert Gould Shaw organized the predominantly African-American Massachusetts regiment that endured heavy losses while attempting to take Fort Wagner in South Carolina on July 18, 1863.

3. R. W. Stallman, *Stephen Crane: A Biography* (New York: George Braziller, 1968), 18; Stephen Crane, *Great Battles of the World* (Philadelphia: J. B. Lippincott, 1900).

4. Crane, *Great Battles*. "Skobeleff said, 'Osman the Victorious he will remain, in spite of his surrender'" (78), "Peace had been signed at Ghent on December 24, 1814. The real battle of New Orleans was fought on January 8, 1815" (240).

5. In the midst of the Civil War, the usually moderate Emerson could write the following inflammatory lines in his 1862 essay "American Civilization," *The Works of Ralph Waldo Emerson*, ed. Edward W. Emerson, 14 vols. (Boston: Houghton, Mifflin, 1883), 11:282–83: "Better the war should more dangerously threaten us,—should threaten fracture in what is still whole, and punish us with burned capitals and slaughtered regiments, and so exasperate the people to energy, exasperate our nationality. There are Scriptures written invisibly on men's hearts, whose letters do not come out until they are enraged. They can be read by war-fires, and by eyes in the last peril."

6. See Eric Sundquist, *To Wake the Nations: Race in the Making of American Literature* (Cambridge: Harvard University Press, 1993), 225–70, for an excellent account of the relation between Twain's fiction and the Supreme Court decision of 1896 in *Plessy v. Ferguson*.

7. According to Stallman, *Stephen Crane: A Biography*, 311, Crane wrote his brother Edmund from Ireland in early September 1897 "that he had finished a novelette of 20,000 words—'The Monster.'" The story was rejected by *Century* magazine in 1897, published by *Harper's Magazine* in August 1898, and collected with other stories in *The Monster and Other Stories* (New York: Harper and Brothers, 1899).

8. Ibid., 333.

9. Stephen Crane, "The Monster," in *Tales of Whilomville*, *The Works of Stephen Crane*, ed. Fredson Bowers (Charlottesville: University of Virginia Press, 1969), 7:11. Further references in the text as M.

10. Like Twain in *Pudd'nhead Wilson* (1894), Crane deliberately and utterly confounds the biological and social determinants of the concept of "race." See Susan Gillman, "'Sure Identifiers': Race, Science, and the Law in *Pudd'nhead Wilson*," in *Mark Twain's "Pudd'nhead Wilson": Race, Conflict, and Culture*, ed.

Susan Gillman and Forrest G. Robinson (Durham, N.C.: Duke University Press, 1990), 102–3: "[*Pudd'nhead Wilson*] confirms in an American context what Twain's later anti-imperialist essays would conclude globally: that in spite of the Fourteenth and Fifteenth Amendments [to the Constitution], the law had not only failed to solve the 'Negro Question,' but worse still had been positively enlisted in the service of reconstituting white supremacy, both in the United States and abroad." This does not mean for either Twain or Crane, however, that "race" is therefore an utter social construction. Appealing as this conclusion is, because it aligns Twain and Crane with our modern understanding of the fiction of race, it may also be an ambiguity that is merely *played with* by Twain and Crane for the sake of literary effect. In this sense, *Pudd'nhead Wilson* and "The Monster" would merely express late nineteenth-century U.S. anxieties regarding the de-stabilization of familiar conventions regarding "racial identity"—a destabiliza-tion prompted in part by growing demands by African-American intellectuals for equal rights in the social and economic domains.

11. Mark Seltzer, *Bodies and Machines* (New York: Routledge, 1992), 112.

12. Ibid., 163.

13. Ibid., 163, 164; Klaus Theweleit, *Male Fantasies*, trans. Stephen Conway, 2 vols. (Minneapolis: University of Minnesota Press, 1987).

14. Theweleit is obviously concerned with the elaboration of the demon-ized "feminine other" in the writings of the German Freikorps between World War I and World War II into a "racial other" in the fascist racialization of Jew-ish and Slavic peoples, and even of political groups, such as Communists, in the hysteria of National Socialism. See Theweleit, *Male Fantasies*, 1:79.

15. Stallman, *Stephen Crane: A Biography*, 334, claims that "Crane's so-cial irony is that the white man's face is also disfigured—by white society's cruelty to the Negro." Such a conclusion assumes, of course, that Crane's irony extricates *Crane* from complicity in the system of producing "body-machines" (and thus demonizing "natural" bodies) I have been describing with the help of Seltzer and Theweleit. I certainly share Stallman's liberal sentiments, but I am not certain that they apply with exactness to the moral conclusion we must draw from the racial logic of Crane's writing in "The Monster" and *The Red Badge of Courage*.

16. John Berryman, *Stephen Crane* (Cleveland: World Publishing, 1950), 192–93.

17. Norman Mailer, "The White Negro," in *Advertisements for Myself* (New York: Putnam, 1959).

18. Christopher Benfey, *The Double Life of Stephen Crane* (New York: Knopf, 1992), 260.

19. Benfey's approach is organized around his observation that "Crane's double life was not so much duplicitous as strangely *duplicate*. His fictions were not retrospective; they were eerily predictive. The question is why he felt it necessary to try to live what he had already so masterfully imagined" (Ibid., 12).

20. And therefore did not arrive with either Fire Company Number Six or Five, which arrives somewhat later.

21. Crane, "Maggie: A Girl of the Streets," in *The Red Badge of Courage and Other Writings*, ed. Richard Chase (Boston: Houghton Mifflin, 1960), 15. Jimmie Johnson's love of fire engines also anticipates themes and images in "The Mon-ster." There is a curious doubling between "Maggie" and "The Monster" that deserves closer critical attention.

22. Crane uses the Tuscarora in conventional ways for the 1890s. Driven out of North Carolina by white settlers, the Tuscarora joined the Iroquois Confederacy, remained friendly to Americans during the Revolution, and were thus attacked and dispersed by the British. Crane may be trading on the popular cliché that the Tuscarora were "friendly" and "patriotic" in so naming this fire company, but the suggestion of their "savagism" linked with the machinery of the fire company is probably the main connotation here. In other respects, "The Monster" focuses racial "primitivism" on the representation of African Americans.

23. Stallman, *Stephen Crane: A Biography*, 334.

24. I am grateful to Professor Rosella Mamoli Zorzi (Università di Venezia) for suggesting Harriet Beecher Stowe's *Dred: A Tale of the Great Dismal Swamp*, 2 vols. (Boston: Phillips, Sampson, 1856), as a work by a nineteenth-century white American author that represents the heroic actions of African Americans. For the character Dred's naming and genealogy, see *Dred*, 1:253. Dred's heroic physical qualities are complemented by his extraordinary voice, powers of rhetoric, and his nearly supernatural abilities to communicate with animals. Of course, the promised 'revolution" never arrives, Stowe cannily substituting southern white, proslavery vigilantism for the violence the reader has been carefully prepared to fear and anticipate through this monumentally long novel. Sundquist, *To Wake the Nations*, 194, interprets the novel as a failed effort to engage the question of African-American revolution in the antebellum period. Yet the novel manages to keep the *idea* and *threat* of African-American rebellion before the reader for more than 600 pages without indulging conservative fantasies of the "brutality" and "violence" of rebellious slaves. Instead, Stowe offers the reader the pastoral charms of the maroon community Dred leads in the Great Dismal Swamp of North Carolina. *Dred* is a remarkable literary and political achievement that deserves more critical attention.

25. Toni Morrison, *Playing in the Dark: Whiteness and the Literary Imagination* (New York: Random House, 1992), 44.

26. See Sundquist, *To Wake the Nations*, 68–83, for an account of how these slave insurrections struck fear into the antebellum South.

27. *The Signing of the Declaration of Independence* was painted by John Trumbull (1756–1843) for the Rotunda of the U.S. Capitol in Washington, D.C. Like Gilbert Stuart's unfinished portrait of George Washington, this painting was a common testament to patriotism in nineteenth-century U.S. homes. Crane may have been referring obliquely here to his Revolutionary War namesake, the Stephen Crane who signed the Declaration. Crane might also have had in mind Trumbull's active life in the period of the Revolution, which very much anticipated Crane's. Trumbull suspended his art studies to fight in the Continental army, and he later studied with the expatriate painter Benjamin West in London. *Phaidon Encyclopedia of Art and Artists* (Oxford: Phaidon Press, 1978), 663–64.

28. Benfey, *The Double Life of Stephen Crane*, 167, notes that "Crane successfully applied in April of 1896 . . . for membership in the Sons of the American Revolution." This is hardly the personal identification for a firebrand revolutionary intent upon following the radical path of William Lloyd Garrison in burning a copy of the Constitution.

29. I am grateful to Giorgio Mariani (Università di Salerno) for pointing out to me Crane's complex representation of the actual "salvation" of both Jimmie

and Henry Johnson. By turning the African-American "hero" into an unconscious victim who also needs to be saved, Crane puts Johnson on the same plane as Jimmie, effectively infantilizing the African-American male while rendering ambiguous the consequences of his heroism.

30. Household laboratories were commonplace among medical practitioners and scientists in the period. Nathaniel Hawthorne's "mad" scientists—Rappaccini, Owen Warland, for example—and Gustave Flaubert's merely clumsy medical doctor, Charles Bovary, all have them.

31. Benfey, *The Double Life of Stephen Crane*, 167, notes how concerned Crane was with "being 'properly-born,'" especially in the period when he began to gain recognition for *The Red Badge of Courage* and while he was writing "The Monster."

32. Milne Holton, *Cylinder of Vision: The Fiction and Journalistic Writings of Stephen Crane* (Baton Rouge: Louisiana State University Press, 1972), 305n32, comments on other possible allusions to Hawthorne in Crane's writings, even though Holton warns us that "Crane, even in his own time, was annoyed by source hunters." There is, however, a good deal of internal evidence connecting "The Monster" with Hawthorne's "The Minister's Black Veil," including the eventual "veiling" of Henry Johnson in chapter 20: "The monster on the box had turned its black crêpe countenance toward the sky, and was waving its arms in time to a religious chant" (M, 370).

33. See Elias Canetti, *Crowds and Power*, trans. Carol Stewart (New York: Viking Press, 1966), 50: "The baiting crowd is very old. It goes back to the most primitive dynamic unit known among men: the hunting pack. . . . Among the death penalties which a horde or a people can inflict upon an individual, two main forms can be distinguished. The first is *expulsion*." Walter Benjamin, "The Work of Art in the Age of Mechanical Reproduction," in *Illuminations*, ed. Hannah Arendt, trans. Harry Zohn (New York: Shocken Books, 1969).

34. This analogy is by no means complete, because Dr. Trescott is clearly superior to the white soldier ironized in *The Red Badge of Courage*. One way we know this is by means of the contrast between Dr. Trescott's educated speech and the soldier's dialect, with its many elisions and verbal corruptions.

35. Ralph Ellison, "Stephen Crane and the Mainstream of American Fiction," 88. Ellison's unqualified judgment of Faulkner's "driving honesty and social responsibility" is also by now a little dated. Faulkner was concerned centrally with racial issues in his writings, but he is often complicit with southern ideology in both his politics (he favored the "Go Slow" political philosophy of southern moderates reacting to civil rights' activism in the 1950s and 1960s) and in his aesthetic desire to "speak for" African Americans in his fiction. In the latter regard, see my treatment of Faulkner in *At Emerson's Tomb: The Politics of Classic American Literature* (New York: Columbia University Press, 1997), 222–46.

36. Stallman, *Stephen Crane: A Biography*, 426.

37. Thomas Arthur Gullason, "Stephen Crane: Anti-Imperialist," *American Literature* 30 (1958): 237.

38. Crane, "The King's Favor," in *Stephen Crane: Uncollected Writings*, ed. Olov W. Fryckstedt, Studia Anglistica Upsaliensia (Uppsala, Sweden: Acta Universitatis Upsaliensis, 1963), 1:5, 6.

39. Stephen Crane, *Stephen Crane in the West and Mexico*, ed. Joseph Katz (Kent, Ohio: Kent State University Press, 1970), 75.

40. On Crane's criticism of the British, Germans, and Spaniards, see Gullason, "Stephen Crane: Anti-Imperialist," 239–41. On the connection between "free-trade" and "anti-imperialism," see Chapter 6. Crane described himself as "a Free-Trader" in an interview with him published in the London *Outlook* on February 4, 1899, reprinted as "Mr. Stephen Crane on the New America," in *The War Dispatches of Stephen Crane*, ed. R. W. Stallman and E. R. Hagemann (New York: New York University Press, 1964), 243.

41. Crane, *The War Dispatches of Stephen Crane*, 132.

42. Ibid., 133.

43. See Chapter 8.

44. "Mr. Stephen Crane on the New America," *The War Dispatches of Stephen Crane*, 243.

45. Mark Twain, "To the Person Sitting in Darkness," *Selected Shorter Writings of Mark Twain*, ed. Walter Blair (Boston: Houghton Mifflin, 1962), 295.

46. All the journalism mentioned, except for "A Foreign Policy in Three Glimpses," is collected in *The War Dispatches of Stephen Crane*. See Gullason, "Stephen Crane: Anti-Imperialist," 238–39, for discussion of these pieces, and Stallman, *Stephen Crane: A Biography*, esp. 346–347, for a complementary discussion of Crane's comments on European imperialism.

47. "Mr. Stephen Crane on the New America," *The War Dispatches of Stephen Crane*, 242.

48. Stallman, *Stephen Crane: A Biography*, 334. "George's Mother," in *The Red Badge of Courage and Other Writings*, 62, 63. Before he is named in the narrative, George has been referred to twice as "a brown young man" and "the brown youth," referring of course to the presumed "darker" color of the working class—a nineteenth-century cultural convention.

49. I am grateful to Elizabeth Young of Mount Holyoke College for this suggestion.

50. The Latinate, deliberately learned styles of Margaret Fuller in *Woman in the Nineteenth Century* (1845) and George Eliot in *Romola* (1863) are two examples of how nineteenth-century women writers explicitly responded to masculine rhetoric by attempting to appropriate it for feminine personae, like Fuller's "Miranda" (a self-portrait) and Eliot's Romola.

51. Henry James's *The Tragic Muse* (1890) and *What Maisie Knew* (1897), Kate Chopin's *The Awakening* (1899), Theodore Dreiser's *Sister Carrie* (1900), and Edith Wharton's *The House of Mirth* (1905) are familiar examples from turn-of-the-century U.S. literature. For my discussion of these two novels by James in this context, see *The Other Henry James* (Durham: Duke University Press, 1998), chapters 4 and 6; for my discussion of Chopin in this respect, see *At Emerson's Tomb*, 200–221.

52. This is not intended in any way to trivialize the historical reality of the genocide of Armenians by the Turks in this period, but the massacres, which the European colonial powers did nothing to suppress, were popularly viewed in such Orientalist terms in the West and the national conflict over an independent Armenia represented as a holy war between Christians and "infidels."

53. See Crane, *Great Battles*, 62, in regard to the "Battle of Vittoria," for example, where Crane writes: "Perhaps it was lucky for Wellington that the worthless make-trouble, Joseph Bonaparte, had been in the place of his tremendous brother." In discussing the significance of the "Battle of Solferino" in the eventual unification of Italy, Crane credits Napoleon with initiating such

unification: "a beneficent counter-irritant—a wholesome, cleansing force throughout" Italy, in large part because Napoleon got rid of the Hapsburgs and Bourbons (242).

54. Bill Brown, *The Material Unconscious: American Amusement, Stephen Crane, and the Economies of Play* (Cambridge: Harvard University Press, 1996), 212.

55. Leslie Fiedler, *Love and Death in the American Novel* (New York: Criterion, 1960), 367.

56. Crane indulges in apparent racial humor by giving Henry's girlfriend Bella the family name of "Farragut," the same surname as Admiral David Glasgow Farragut (1801–1870), the Union naval hero of the Civil War. Admiral Farragut was a southerner who was devoted to the Union. Naming Bella's family "Farragut" connotes both their social aspirations within the African-American community of "Watermelon Alley" and the continuing postbellum dependency of African Americans on white American culture. In keeping with the main themes of the story, such naming suggests how the African-American community anticipates the dehumanization and mechanization of the white community.

57. Bill Brown, *The Material Unconscious*, 214–15.

58. Seltzer, *Bodies and Machines*, 83–84.

59. Bill Brown, *The Material Unconscious*, 208, points out: "By staging the monstrous sight, Jimmie organizes the perception of Henry and contains all excess within the boundaries of amusement."

60. Ibid., 229.

61. Andreas Huyssen, *After the Great Divide: Modernism, Mass Culture, Postmodernism* (Bloomington: Indiana University Press, 1986), 44–62.

Chapter 8

1. Henry Adams, *The Education of Henry Adams*, ed. Ernest Samuels and Jayne N. Samuels (Boston, Mass.: Houghton Mifflin, 1973), p. 366. Further references in the text as EHA.

2. Mark Twain, "King Leopold's Soliloquy," in *Mark Twain: Life as I Find It*, ed. Charles Neider (New York: Harper and Row, 1977), 294: "Then all of a sudden came the crash! That is to say, the incorruptible *kodak*—and all the harmony went to hell! The only witness I have encountered in my long experience that I couldn't bribe."

3. There are many reasons to believe that Twain was being ironic in his appeal to the "realism" of photography in exposing King Leopold's crimes in the Belgian Congo, but Twain did subscribe to a historically universal and culturally transnational theory of imperialism. See Chapter 6.

4. Richard Drinnon, *Facing West: The Metaphysics of Indian-Hating and Empire-Building* (Minneapolis: University of Minnesota Press, 1980), 249. Drinnon is quoting from John La Farge's *Reminiscences of the South Seas* (Garden City, N.Y.: Doubleday Page, 1912).

5. Amy Kaplan, "Black and Blue on San Juan Hill," *Cultures of United States Imperialism*, ed. Amy Kaplan and Donald Pease (Durham: Duke University Press, 1993), 219–36, for example, shows how Richard Harding Davis's reporting in *The Cuban and Porto Rican Campaigns* (1898) reflects the "more overtly violent form of post-Reconstruction politics" and their racial hierarchies in Theodore Roosevelt's *The Rough Riders: A History of the First United States*

Volunteer Cavalry (1899). In effect, Kaplan argues that Davis and Roosevelt contributed to the racial propaganda of the dominant ideology in the United States at a time when domestic policies were informing foreign policies. Without diminishing the importance of Kaplan's work for our historical understanding of U.S. imperialism, I do want to suggest that there is a certain self-evidence to her interpretation of texts by Davis and Roosevelt that are predictably racist and jingoistic. In a similar manner, Walter Benn Michaels in *Our America: Nativism, Modernism, and Pluralism* (Durham: Duke University Press, 1995), 16–23, bases his arguments regarding the fundamentally "conservative" politics of turn-of-the-century "anti-imperialists" on politically reactionary and overtly racist southern novels like Thomas Nelson Page's *Red Rock* (1898) and Thomas Dixon's *The Leopard's Spots* (1902) and *The Clansman* (1905). Once again, Michaels does useful historical work in helping explain how U.S. imperialism and anti-imperialism drew upon racial and national stereotypes, but the overt propaganda of Page and Dixon, like that of Davis and Roosevelt, had little enduring impact in the developing imperial imagination of twentieth-century U.S. culture. To be sure, the entanglement of racism and nationalism (and aristocratic pretense) that Michaels emphasizes in Dixon's novels continues in twentieth-century culture in other popular forms. But what is interesting about *The Education* is the extent to which it *continues to be read* and thus influences readers, even if its interpretations may have changed from one generation to the next.

6. According to Ernest Samuels, *Henry Adams: The Major Phase* (Cambridge: Harvard University Press, 1964), 332, Adams used the index to the *Education*, "asking the imprimatur of 'every friend drawn by name into the narrative'" and thus appealing to these early readers for something very much like formal permission to mention their names in such contexts. As Samuels points out, "The 'permissions' came in with gratifying speed—and submissiveness," because Adams "had of course written with considerable restraint and self-censorship" (333). Further references in the text as *Major Phase*.

7. *The Letters of Henry Adams*, ed. J. C. Levenson et al., 6 vols. (Cambridge: Harvard University Press, 1982 and 1988), vol. 5 (1899–1905), 524. Further references to this collection of Adams's *Letters* in the text as *Letters*, 5:524.

8. To solve the problem of her husband's private correspondence giving possible offense to the many public figures mentioned in his letters and diaries, Mrs. Hay adopted the simple but disastrous solution of reducing "all proper names to an initial and a dash and, by doing so, made the volumes almost unreadable" (*Letters*, 6:40). Such volumes would be "almost unreadable" by the general public, but for those familiar with Hay and his world, such "initials" would be in most cases perfectly legible. It is this doubleness, if not duplicity, that more subtly structures Adams's *Education*.

9. Ernest Samuels's interpretation of *The Education* in chapter 9 of *The Major Phase* remains one of the most comprehensive and historically specific readings we have had. Yet, even Samuels is distracted from the historical issues in the second part of *The Education* by Adams's complex scientific and philosophical speculations. Samuels even finds an implicit division in the book: "To a large degree the first—and longer—part of *The Education*, divided from the second part by the hiatus of 'Twenty Years After,' is shown as the drama of the potential participator whereas that of the second part is more markedly the drama of the detached observer" (382). It is a distinction that subsequent scholars have generally reaffirmed, including Samuels's identification of the point

of narrative division: "The succession of chapters beginning with 'Indian Summer' dramatizes the overthrow of the certainties of scientific theory and the abandonment of the assumption of the unity of the sciences" (384). The "relativism" of the last half of *The Education* thus appears to give warrant to all sorts of wild theories and half-baked speculations, even as this happens to be the period of history in which the most important political events were occurring when the time of writing *The Education* is considered.

10. It is just a step, then, from Samuels's division of *The Education* to a claim for Henry Adams's "divided persona," which has been one of his hallmarks for critics who have made him central to literary modernism. With his detachment, irony, and skepticism regarding history and technology, and his commitment to radical relativism, he provided an excellent complement to the values and aesthetics of such high moderns as Yeats, Pound, Eliot, Stevens, Joyce, and Stein, many of whom cite his work as uniquely influential. This was my argument regarding Adams in *Henry Adams and Henry James: The Emergence of a Modern Consciousness* (Ithaca, N.Y.: Cornell University Press, 1976).

11. David R. Contosta, "Henry Adams and the American Century," in *Henry Adams and His World*, Transactions of the American Philosophical Society, ed. Contosta and Robert Muccigrosso (Philadelphia: American Philosophical Society, 1993), 83, pt. 4:40–41, qualifies this by arguing: "Henry did not accept every detail of Brooks's theory. . . . According to Henry's version of [Brooks's] law, 'All Civilization is Centralization. All Centralization is Economy. Therefore all Civilization is the survival of the most economical (cheapest).'" Nevertheless, Henry shares enough of Brooks's historical theory to warrant the conclusion that Henry was a political conservative in this period.

12. Timothy Paul Donovan, *Henry Adams and Brooks Adams: The Education of Two American Historians* (Norman: University of Oklahoma Press, 1961), 154.

13. Drinnon, *Facing West*, 266–67, notes that Hay, made a millionaire by his father-in-law's suicide, gave "about $ 10,000 for McKinley," who "paid off by naming Hay minister to the Court of St. James," the ambassadorial post held by Henry Adams's father during the Civil War.

14. Joanne Jacobson, *Authority and Alliance in the Letters of Henry Adams* (Madison: University of Wisconsin Press, 1992), 64.

15. Ibid., 67.

16. Jacobson writes of the "interpenetration between Adams's letters and his imaginative works" to the degree that "a convincing case might be made for calling all these [imaginative] works 'letters,' both because they so aggressively privatized their original audiences and because they built so much mutuality into the process of reading" (113).

17. William Roscoe Thayer, *The Life and Letters of John Hay*, 2 vols. (Boston: Houghton Mifflin, 1915), 2:199–201, for example, discusses Hay's role in U.S. imperialism in terms of the familiar thesis that our annexations of "the Hawaiian Islands, then Porto Rico, and then the Philippines" were the results of "a fateful change" in history and foreign policy that "occurred so casually that Americans scarcely perceived its far-reaching consequences" (200). Under these new historical circumstances, Thayer argues, "John Hay was among the few who understood the significance of the change from the very first moment; and he accepted it without looking back, or, so far as appears, without feeling regrets. Seeing its significance he shaped all his work as Secretary of State with reference to it. To place this country as speedily as possible in such relations

with the rest of the world as became its character, was henceforth his control-ling purpose" (201).

18. Drinnon, *Facing West*, 268.

19. Ibid., 270.

20. Ibid., 272.

21. John Hay, "American Diplomacy," *Addresses of John Hay* (New York: Century, 1907), 121–22. Further references in the text as Hay.

22. Drinnon, *Facing West*, 272–74, provides a list of Hay's colonial achieve-ments during his term as secretary of state.

23. Ibid., 275.

24. Thayer, *The Life and Letters of John Hay*, 2:260–61.

25. For a discussion of the U.S. role in the Taiping and subsequent Boxer rebellions in China, see Chapter 6.

26. Drinnon, *Facing West*, 268.

27. Ibid., 267.

28. See Chapter 6.

29. See, for example, Contosta, "Henry Adams and the American Century," 47: "Despite exaggerations and downright mistakes in judgment, Adams an-ticipated nearly every major shift in the international balance of power during the twentieth century, including those that transpired long after his death."

30. The other part of this myth is that such prophecy is possible by virtue of Adams's poetic imagination, rather than his extraordinary access to the sources of political and social power.

31. *Webster's New World Dictionary*.

32. See Samuels, *The Major Phase*, 185–86. Charles Francis Adams, Jr.'s participation in the anti-imperialist movement was admittedly short-lived, last-ing only from the onset of the Spanish-American War in the spring of 1898 to May 18, 1899, when he published in the *Springfield Daily Republican* his let-ter declining Thomas Wentworth Higginson's invitation "to an anti-imperial-ist rally at Cambridgeport, Massachusetts," explaining his growing opposition to the anti-imperialists' positions, as Robert L. Beisner describes his change of mind in *Twelve against Empire: The Anti-Imperialists, 1898–1900* (New York: McGraw Hill, 1968), 113–17.

33. It is possible, of course, that some of Henry Adams's contempt for the Anti-Imperialist League and anti-imperialism in general stems from his accu-rate interpretation of its politically conservative interests. As he writes Eliza-beth Sherman Cameron on January 15, 1899: "A party made up of cranks like Carnegie, mugwumps like my brother Charles, malcontents like Eugene Hale and Tom Reed, scoundrels like John McLean, blatherskites like Bryan, and rank-and-file of southern democrats, is mighty amusing, but my representative in it is my brother Brooks. I am a pure and simple anarchist, and run a machine of my own" (*Letters*, 4:662).

34. Samuels, *The Major Phase*, 162–63: "The budding imperialists among his intimates rejoiced in his quixotic support and quickly adopted King's ideal-istic program for Cuba with their own private modifications. Roosevelt, then police commissioner in New York, took heart at the Venezuela message and wired Secretary [of State] Olney, 'I only wish you would take the same attitude as regards Cuba.'"

35. John C. Orr, "Beneath the Manikin's Clothes: Displacement and Engage-ment in the Biography of Henry Adams," *Genre* 31:1 (Spring 1998), 33–54, points out, Adams's role as Senator Cameron's occasional speechwriter dates

back at least to September 25, 1893, when Adams wrote the latter's speech "arguing against repeal of the Sherman Silver Purchase Act of 1890" (33). I want to thank John Orr for discussing with me Adams's position on Cuban independence and Adams's tendency to keep private his political lobbying efforts.

36. Thayer, *The Life and Letters of John Hay*, 2:166–67.

37. In adopting this tone of an old civilization passing and a new working for centralization, Adams is consciously echoing his brother Brooks's arguments in *The Law of Civilization and Decay*, which Henry had just read and had just been published in 1895.

38. Even in his criticism of British, German, and Russian imperialism, however, Adams often sounds insincere or unconcerned, as if his long historical view enables him to understand the apparent triviality of such local events as the defeat of the Boers or the invasion of Manchuria. In "Indian Summer," Adams describes the dinner at which he and John La Farge meet the painter James Whistler, a vocal critic of Britain's conduct in the Boer War. Adams comments on Whistler's political "raging" that "in substance what he said was not merely commonplace—it was true!" (EHA, 370, 371). But Adams's agreement with Whistler's political position is condescending in tone, as if to say that everyone knows that the British are wrong, and he quickly changes the subject from politics to art, suggesting that as Whistler's artistic career declines so La Farge's career is on the rise. Such digressions at crucial moments in the discussion of political issues are characteristic of Adams's style in the last third of *The Education*.

39. Drinnon, *Facing West*, 255.

40. For the classic account of how Rank's doppelgänger became the modern psychological and literary concept, see Sigmund Freud, "The 'Uncanny'" (1919), in *On Creativity and the Unconscious: Papers on the Psychology of Art, Literature, Love, Religion*, ed. Benjamin Nelson, trans. under the supervision of Joan Riviere (New York: Harper and Row, 1958), 129ff.

41. Even in his correspondence with Elizabeth Sherman Cameron, who had reason to hate William McKinley for the way he had manipulated her uncle, John Sherman, out of national politics for the sake of promoting Mark Hanna for the Senate, Adams defends McKinley in a backhanded sort of way: "On the whole, McKinley has done my work well, both in Cuba, in Hawaii and here. I believe the field is swept clean of our old opponents. My brother Charles and Edward Atkinson [vice presidents of the Anti-Imperialist League] alone watch their tattered shadows in the wave, and hourly droop" (*Letters*, 4:632).

42. Adams seems to have changed his mind regarding Anglo-American cooperation since the Spanish-American War. In the letter to Brooks Adams of June 11, 1898, quoted above, Henry worries about the consequences of a "premature English alliance" drawing the United States into the shifting-balance-of-politics in Europe: "The worst is this premature English alliance with which we are threatened, and which will probably become inevitable if we occupy Manila and are driven to attack the Canaries. The appearance of our forces in European waters can hardly fail to upset the balance of the world" (*Letters*, 4:599). Although Henry sounds paranoid in such correspondence, thanks to his anti-semitic, anti-capitalist, and anti-socialist cant, he nonetheless does predict with some accuracy the destabilization of European empires and thus global "order" that would play a significant part in causing World War I.

43. *Michelin Guide to Paris* (Summer 1972), 44.

44. I am indebted to my friend Lillian Manzor-Coats for much of the historical information about Fort Trocadero.

45. In his letter of November 7, 1900, to John Hay, Adams begins by discussing McKinley's reelection and the current negotiations for the European and Russian "joint military occupation" of China at the end of the Boxer Rebellion. Adams's exaggeration of what turned out merely to be the temporary placement of foreign troops in Beijing to protect their legations (objects of attack by the Boxers) and payment by China of "damages" as part of the treaty signed in 1901 is indicative of Adams's imperial ambitions for the United States. He concludes this letter with a discussion of the importance of the Paris Exposition for him, indicating clearly how the Exposition is another example of the West's modern right to rule: "The period from 1870 to 1900 is closed. I see that much in the machine-gallery of the Champ de Mars. The period from 1900 to 1930 is in full swing, and, gee-whacky! how it is going! I . . . go down to the Champ de Mars and sit by the hour over the great dynamos, watching them run as noiselessly and as smoothly as the planets, and asking them—with infinite courtesy—where in Hell they are going" (*Letters*, 5:169).

46. Zeynep Çelik and Leila Kinney, "Ethnography and Exhibitionism at the Expositions Universelles," *Assemblage* 13 (December 1990): 35, 37. I am grateful to my friend Susan Jeffords for calling my attention to this essay.

47. Ibid., 37.

48. In his November 7, 1900, letter to John Hay, Adams concludes that the "dynamos . . . are marvelous. The Gods are not in it. Chiefly the Germans!" (*Letters*, 5:169).

49. Thayer, *The Life and Letters of John Hay*, 2:199.

50. Drinnon, *Facing West*, 248. As a historian, Drinnon is rightly appalled by a fellow historian's ignorance: "For a historian of his stature to generalize so wildly from a foundation of almost total ignorance was in itself significant. . . . He had readied himself for Samoa hardly beyond reading novels and travelers' narratives—largely because he had not known what to expect."

51. This is not to dismiss or trivialize Henry Adams's anti-semitism, but Adams speaks of "Jews" most often in economic, rather than racial, terms. Intermarriage of Polynesians with Scots and Jews does not trouble Adams, but intermarriage between Polynesians and Africans does.

52. Adams's nasty banter about the "dirty" conditions in which the Stevensons were living establishes the ambiance for his generally patronizing attitude toward Stevenson himself, which displays little gratitude for the Stevensons' hospitality and the fact that Stevenson provided Adams with "letters of introduction to Ori a Ori and Tati Salmon" in Tahiti, effectively giving Adams the social access he would need there to do the interviews that would result in *Tahiti*. Edward Chalfant, *Better in Darkness: A Biography of Henry Adams, His Second Life: 1862–1891* (Hamden, Conn.: Archon Books, 1994), 600.

53. Edward Chalfant, *Better in Darkness*, 599, tries to suggest that Adams was just getting to know the people better when he "measured many young Samoan women, studied their characters, and tried persistently to sound their feelings," but the correspondence makes clear that Adams took special interest in "measuring" young women and particular satisfaction in their commodification within Samoan society as a consequence of its marriage-dowry practices. In his letter of November 22, 1890, to Elizabeth Sherman Cameron, he seems to be trying to shock her by noting dryly: "In pigs and

mats, she [a Samoan wife] would come higher, in apparent price, than in coin. Cash-down, in Chilian [*sic*] silver dollars, Samasoni thinks that a hundred dollars would be sufficient. This is about seventy dollars in gold. Dog-cheap, as far as the gift is concerned." Needless to say, this is the rhetoric of a slave-economy, and, despite Adams's attribution of it to the Samoans (and thus their "primitivism"), he takes pleasure in casting such phrases before the elegant Elizabeth Sherman Cameron.

54. See my "Henry Adams," *Columbia Literary History of the United States,* ed. Emory Elliott (New York: Columbia University Press, 1987), 645–67.

55. Drinnon, *Facing West,* 276–77.

56. Brooks Adams, *The New Empire* (Cleveland: Frontier Press, 1967), 194–95.

57. Hay, *Addresses of John Hay,* 125.

58. Drinnon, *Facing West,* 249, imagines La Farge and Adams's ethnocentrism as they head for the South Seas: "What they brought in their heads and hearts, their 'education,' shaped how they saw and what they felt about native peoples of the South Seas. Their intellectual and emotional baggage had predisposed them to see those peoples as infantile, and that seeing had larger implications."

59. Carolyn Porter, *Seeing and Being: The Plight of the Participant Observer in Emerson, James, Adams, and Faulkner* (Middletown, Conn.: Wesleyan University Press, 1981), 209–10.

60. As Otto Friedrich, *Clover* (New York: Simon and Schuster, 1979), 318, recreates the event of December 6, 1885, Adams found his wife, Marian ("Clover") Hooper Adams "lying on the rug" in her room; she had eaten "Potassium cyanide," "one of the chemicals that she used for her photography."

Chapter 9

1. For a good summary of the several scholarly explanations for Du Bois's stubborn adherence to the "Stalinist violation of his democratic principles in the 1940s and 1950s," see William E. Cain, "From Liberalism to Communism: The Political Thought of W. E. B. Du Bois," in *The Cultures of United States Imperialism,* ed. Donald Pease and Amy Kaplan (Durham: Duke University Press, 1993), 456–71.

2. In her October 1996 inaugural address as the new president of the American Studies Association, "Insiders and Outsiders—The Borders of the Nation and the Limits of the ASA," Patricia Nelson Limerick warns contemporary scholars to be careful not to stress cultural factors at the expense of economic forces in understanding minority and marginalized groups. As she points out, a rich cultural heritage can often be seen as a sort of consolation prize for a group repeatedly exploited by the prevailing forces of production and the market. Du Bois's increasingly strident insistence that we focus on economic factors in the shaping or deformation of minority cultures may thus be explained in part by his frustration with other American intellectuals, especially after the Stalinist purges and show trials of the late 1930s and 1940s, who abandoned economic explanations for injustices and retreated to safer and more exclusive analyses of culture. For contemporary cultural critics, the question is not how to choose between "cultural" or "economic" forces in the determination of social values, but rather how to understand the relationship between such powerful social forces.

3. W. E. B. Du Bois, *The Souls of Black Folk* (New York: Penguin Books, 1989), 13. Further references in the text as *Souls*.

4. Du Bois, "On *The Souls of Black Folk*," first published in *The Independent*, 17 November 1904, collected in *The Oxford W. E. B. Du Bois Reader*, ed. Eric Sundquist (New York: Oxford University Press, 1996), 305.

5. W. E. B. Du Bois, *Darkwater: Voices from within the Veil* (1920; reprint, New York: AMS Press, 1969), 138. Further references in the text as DW.

6. W. E. B. Du Bois, *Black Reconstruction in America: 1860–1880* (New York: Atheneum, 1992), 16. Further references in the text as BR.

7. Eric Sundquist, *To Wake the Nations: Race in the Making of American Literature* (Cambridge: Harvard University Press, 1993), 542.

8. Du Bois's use of the Greek myth of Cadmus seems to be intended as an ironic commentary on both the speed of industrial development in the New South but also its future end in the sort of industrial "suicide" Du Bois often predicted for capitalism, much in keeping with Marxist dogma. In the myth, Cadmus sows the teeth of the dragon, sacred to Ares, that he has killed, and armed men spring up from the ground. Flinging a stone among them, Cadmus causes them to kill each other, except for five survivors who become his allies. Du Bois seems to have in mind the conflict between white and African-American workers in the industrialized South and North after the Civil War. For Du Bois, the survivors will be those workers who not only seize the means of production, but also establish political and cultural coalitions across racial lines.

9. Arnold Rampersad, *The Art and Imagination of W. E. B. Du Bois* (Cambridge: Harvard University Press, 1976), 183.

10. In this passage, Du Bois is criticizing Charles and Mary Beard's *Rise of American Civilization* not only for its neglect of the contributions of African Americans to "American Civilization" but also for its "sweeping mechanistic interpretation" of northern industrial progress in the post–Civil War era.

11. As Sundquist puts the matter in *To Wake the Nations*, 548: "Du Bois tended to view African retentions, such as those he found evident in the African American church and the spirituals, to be as much a set of theoretical ideals as a set of concrete practices that had left their stamp on post–Civil War black culture. The study of black history therefore became an act of recovery that could itself rekindle latent African sources of spiritual belief in African America."

12. Theodore Allen, *The Invention of the White Race*, vol. 2: *The Origin of Racial Oppression in Anglo-America* (London: Verso, 1997), 240. Allen details these seventeenth-century origins in vol. 1: *Racial Oppression and Social Control*.

13. Ibid., 2:148: "W. E. B. Du Bois, in his 1909 address to the American Historical Association on post-Civil War Reconstruction in the South, broke the silence regarding the role of bond-laborers as a self-activating social and political force in American history."

14. Du Bois, "The Conservation of Races," first published in *American Negro Academy Occasional Papers*, no. 2 (1897), collected in *The Oxford W. E. B. Du Bois Reader*, 39.

15. Ibid., 40.

16. Sundquist, *The Oxford W. E. B. Du Bois Reader*, 37, points out that "'The Conservation of Races' is steeped in the argument that nations are primarily formed and driven by the 'race spirit,'" which is the sort of nineteenth-century liberal progressive idealism that Du Bois borrows from Hegel and uses heavily

in *The Souls of Black Folk*. I don't want to revise the conventional interpretation of Du Bois's early writings as heavily imitative of European Enlightenment and Idealist models, thereby repeating many of the ideological limitations of these Eurocentric thinkers, but I do want to suggest how Du Bois puts modern European thought of this sort to a very different purpose than most Euro-American modernists.

17. "The Present Outlook for the Dark Races of Mankind," first published in *Church Review* 17 (1900), collected in *The Oxford W. E. B. Du Bois Reader*, 53.

18. Ibid.

19. The change in Du Bois's views since "The Present Outlook for the Dark Races of Mankind" (1900) is especially noticeable in this indictment of U.S. imperialism in *Darkwater*. In the former, he could speak hopefully of Japan's "recent admission to the ranks of modern civilized nations" and of "English India," where "a fairly honest attempt to make in some degree the welfare of the lowest classes of an alien race a distinct object of government," reflected in the "cordial sympathy shown toward Queen Victoria's black and brown subjects at the late jubilee" for the Queen (*The Oxford W. E. B. Du Bois Reader*, 49).

20. Du Bois appears to be referring here to specific events in the classic period of U.S. imperialist foreign policy, including U.S. negotiations for the Panama Canal and the Canal Zone (1903), Hay's formulation of the "Open Door Policy" in China (1899–1900) in response to the Boxer Rebellion, Hay's negotiation of the conclusion of the Russo-Japanese War in the Portsmouth Treaty (1905), and U.S. military intervention in the Mexican Revolution in 1914 (the year U.S. Marines landed in Vera Cruz). Given Du Bois's clear purpose of identifying U.S. slavery and racism with the origins of nineteenth- and twentieth-century "modern industrial imperialism," it seems odd that Du Bois does not take into account earlier extraterritorial ventures by the United States, such as the Mexican-American War of 1846–1848. In regard to Hay's "Open Door" policy in China, Du Bois writes: "Where sections could not be owned by one dominant nation there came a policy of 'open door,' but the 'door' was open to 'white people only'" (DW, 48). On the popular rhetoric of "racial purity" in the nineteenth-century United States, especially during the Mexican-American War, see Chapter 5.

21. Sundquist, *To Wake the Nations*, 546.

22. Sundquist, "Introduction," *The Oxford W. E. B. Du Bois Reader*, 27.

23. In his "Introduction" to *The Oxford W. E. B. Du Bois Reader*, 17–18, Sundquist argues that "as early as *The Philadelphia Negro*, economic and environmental factors played a large role in Du Bois's view of the constructedness of race. . . . But in his cultural and historical works at least through *Darkwater* and *The Gift of Black Folk* (1924), he clung to distinct modes of racialism." Passages of the sort I just quoted from *Darkwater* challenge the idea that Du Bois's racialism dominates this work.

24. David Levering Lewis, *W. E. B. Du Bois, Biography of a Race: 1868–1919* (New York: Henry Holt, 1993), 536.

25. Du Bois's acknowledgment in *Darkwater* of the persecution suffered by Jews corrects his more anti-semitic discussions of the "Jew [as] the heir of the slave-baron" in *The Souls of Black Folk*, 103. By treating the exploitation of Jews and African Americans as colonial, Du Bois tacitly imagines anti-imperialist coalitions between them.

26. Although he clearly intends for the reader of *The Souls of Black Folk* to understand "the talented tenth" to refer to African-American leaders,

Du Bois puns on the concept in later works by reminding his readers that African Americans constitute 10 percent of the U.S. population. If the revival of the progressive revolutionary spirit of the Enlightenment is to be initiated by African Americans challenging internal and external colonialisms, then they would constitute all together the "talented tenth" of a population otherwise divided and deluded by classism and racism.

27. Lewis, *Biography of a Race*, 139–40, traces Du Bois's interest in Hegel back to his graduate work at Harvard with William James and at the University of Berlin. Joel Williamson, *The Crucible of Race: Black-White Relations in the South since Emancipation* (New York: Oxford University Press, 1984), 402–13, stresses Du Bois's use of Hegel's notion of the *Volkgeist* to theorize African-American solidarity in *Souls*, although Arnold Rampersad, *Art and Imagination*, 74–75, traces Du Bois's concept of "black folk" to Americanized versions of Johann Gottfried von Herder's writings.

28. Alexandre Dumas (1802–1870) was the grandson of Antoine Alexandre Davy, marquis de La Pailleterie, and Marie Cessette Dumas, an African-Haitian; his father, Alexandre Dumas (1762–1806), was their natural son and took his mother's name after his break with his father, the marquis. In *Darkwater*, 199, in his eulogy for the Anglo-African composer Samuel Coleridge-Taylor, Du Bois writes: "He was one with that great company of mixed-blood men: Pushkin and Dumas, Hamilton and Douglass, Browning and many others," but he goes on to conclude about Coleridge-Taylor, "but he more than most of these men knew the call of the blood when it came and listened and answered."

29. "Africa and the Slave Trade" is part of Du Bois, *The Negro* (1915), and it is quoted here from *The Oxford W. E. B. Du Bois Reader*, 637.

30. Frantz Fanon, "The Negro and Hegel," in *Black Skin White Masks*, trans. Charles Lamm Markmann (New York: Grove Press, 1967), 216–22; Shamoon Zamir, *Dark Voices: W. E. B. Du Bois and American Thought, 1888–1903* (Chicago: University of Chicago Press, 1995), 208–10.

31. Sundquist, *To Wake the Nations*, 547–48.

32. Lewis, *Biography of a Race*, 566.

33. Zamir's *Dark Voices*, especially chapters 4 and 5, is a sustained interpretation of Du Bois's revision of Hegelian thought in accord with "Marx's, Sartre's, and Alexandre Kojève's existentialist and materialist commentaries on Hegel" (14). My argument here is much indebted to Zamir's argument, although I wish to call attention to Du Bois's crucial use of black *women* and thus gender issues in his revision of Hegel.

34. See Hegel, *The Phenomenology of Mind*, trans. J. B. Baillie (New York: Harper and Row, 1967), 478–79, for a typical example of how he analyzes the "distinction of the sexes" and their very different "ethical content." For a more developed discussion of Hegel's contribution to the nineteenth-century ideology of the family, see my discussion in *At Emerson's Tomb: The Politics of Classic American Literature* (New York: Columbia University Press, 1997), 70–72.

35. Nellie McKay, "W. E. B. Du Bois: The Black Women in His Writings—Selected Fictional and Autobiographical Portraits," *Critical Essays on W. E. B. Du Bois*, ed. William L. Andrews (Boston: G. K. Hall, 1985), 232. See also Irene Diggs, "Du Bois and Women—A Short Story of Black Women 1910–1934," *Current Bibliography on African Affairs* 7 (Summer 1974): 260–63, for a bibliography of Du Bois's extensive writings on women in this period.

36. Ibid., 235.

37. Josie appears in chapter 4, "Of the Meaning of Progress," Phillis Wheatley in chapter 3, "Of Mr. Booker T. Washington and Others," and his paternal great-great grandmother in chapter 14, "The Sorrow Songs."

38. McKay, "W. E. B. Du Bois: The Black Women in His Writings," 238.

39. In making such generalizations about vast areas of the earth, Du Bois imitates the racialist rhetoric of the nineteenth century, which often equated "race" and "nation." Du Bois does not appear to be using an ironic style in such passages, but he also does not seem to be using such rhetoric in an un-self-conscious manner. I think he employs such persistent rhetoric for his own purposes in the hopes of transcoding it—making it serve the interests of emancipation rather than further subjugation. Such rhetorical play is risky, and it may well have backfired on Du Bois, who often appears to substitute his own stereotypes—of white culture, of capitalism, of "Europe," of "yellow people," even of "Negroes"—for those of the dominant culture.

40. Immanuel Kant, *The Critique of Judgement*, trans. James Creed Meredith (Oxford: Oxford University Press, 1952), 80. Kant begins this distinction between the *"normal idea"* of beauty and his "aesthetic ideal" with an explicit discussion of how the physical differences among human beings cannot be used as the philosophical bases for the "beauty" of the human form: "If, again, for our average man we seek on similar lines for the average head, and for this the average nose, and so on, then we get the figure that underlies the normal idea of a beautiful man in the country where the comparison is instituted. For this reason a negro must necessarily (under these empirical conditions) have a different normal idea of the beauty of forms from what a white man has, and the Chinaman one different from the European. . . . But the normal idea is far from giving the complete *archetype* of *beauty* in the genus. It only gives the form that constitutes the indispensable condition of all beauty, and, consequently, only *correctness* in the presentation of the genus" (78–79). The philosopher must concern himself with determining the moral ideal lying behind such empirical manifestations, each of which remains trapped with the historical and geographical limitations of the specific "genus."

41. Wilson Moses, *The Golden Age of Black Nationalism, 1850–1925* (New York: Oxford University Press, 1978), 162–67, reads "Children of the Moon" as a combination of Western and African myths.

42. Sundquist, *To Wake the Nations*, 618. In the symbolic encounters between black messiahs and white women in *Darkwater*, Du Bois is also attempting to transcode white fantasies of the rape of white women by black men used to rationalize the continuing violence toward African Americans from Reconstruction onward.

43. Du Bois, *Dark Princess: A Romance* (New York: Harcourt Brace, 1928), 8, describes the first appearance of Kautilya, the Indian princess, to the hero, Matthew Towns, in the following idealized terms: "First and above all came that sense of color: into this world of pale yellowish . . . , that absence or negation of color, came, suddenly, a glow of golden brown skin. . . . It was a living, glowing crimson, veiled beneath brown flesh. . . . Then came the sense of the woman herself: she was young and tall even when seated, and she bore herself above all with a singularly regal air. She was slim and lithe, gracefully curved . . . with eyes that were pools of night—liquid, translucent, haunting depths."

44. McKay, "W. E. B. Du Bois: The Black Women in His Writings," 239.

45. Ibid.

46. Ibid., 291, for example, where Kautilya instructs Matthew to abandon Christianity as the opiate of the people for the true religion of historical materialism: "I know, I know, heart's-ease, but that is not enough: back of it all, back of the flesh, the mold, the dust, there must be Reality; it must be there; and what can reality be but Life, Life Everlasting? If we, we our very selves, do not live forever, Life is a cruel joke." Claudia Tate, *Psychoanalysis and Black Novels: Desire and the Protocols of Race* (New York: Oxford University Press, 1998), 47–85, interprets *Dark Princess* as divided between its overt propaganda and erotic themes that reveal Du Bois's unresolved attitudes toward his mother, femininity, and racial difference. Acknowledging the internal contradictions of the narrative, Tate interprets them as "manifestations . . . of Du Bois's unconscious fantasmatic template" and thus the sources of his "imaginary discourses" (59). Princess Kautilya is for Tate "hardly a real woman" but a "feminized emblem of racial loyalty [who] fails to remain a fully political object but becomes instead an erotic object" (67).

47. For example, the story in chapter 4 of *The Souls of Black Folk* about Josie in the hills of Tennessee is drawn from Du Bois's own experiences teaching in rural Tennessee during his summer break from undergraduate work at Fisk University, and the moving chapter 11 ("Of the Passing of the First Born") is based on the death of the Du Boises' infant son in Atlanta. These and many other autobiographical stories in *Souls* serve homiletic purposes, but the anecdotes still retain their historical realism.

48. Tate, *Psychoanalysis and Black Novels*, 71–73, notes how Du Bois's contemporary George Schuyler satirized Du Bois for this apparent contradiction of his commitment to black uplift in *Black No More* (1931).

49. Although Tate repeatedly claims that her interpretation of Du Bois's *Dark Princess* in *Psychoanalysis and Black Novels* is not intended to "pscyhoanalyze Du Bois," her psychoanalytic approach tends toward just this sort of conclusion, marginalizing the more strategic purposes served by Du Bois's erotic themes, folkloric retentions and refigurations, and interracial or international coalitions (59).

50. Hanna Wallinger, "Secret Societies and Dark Empires: Sutton E. Griggs's *Imperium in Imperio* and W. E. B. Du Bois's *Dark Princess*," *Empire: American Studies*, ed. John G. Blair and Reinhold Wagnleitner, vol. 10 of *Swiss Papers in English Language and Literature* (Tübingen: Gunter Narr Verlag, 1997), 208.

51. Du Bois, *The Autobiography of W. E. B. Du Bois* (New York: International Publishers, 1968), 418–19.

52. William Cain, "From Liberalism to Communism," 471: "Du Bois was one of the great pioneers of anti-imperialist scholarship, yet even as he exposed and corrected one form of bad history—the whitewashing of what imperialism had wrought—he transcribed another himself. He saw what he wished and needed to see, and thus he replicated the hard, domineering consciousness he condemned." Du Bois's 1953 essay on "Joseph Stalin" eulogizes and idealizes Stalin and ignores what was by that late date the certain evidence of Stalinist terror, repression, and genocide ("Joseph Stalin," in *The Oxford W. E. B. Du Bois Reader*, 287–89).

Chapter 10

1. In Neihardt's narrative organization of *Black Elk Speaks: Being the Life Story of a Holy Man of the Oglala Sioux* (1932; reprint, Lincoln: University of

Nebraska Press, 1988), 132: "Then we moved on down stream to a sacred place where there is a big rock bluff right beside the water, and high up on this bluff pictures used to appear, foretelling something important that was going to happen soon. There was a picture on it then, the Lakota perspective of many soldiers hanging head downward; and the people said it was there before the rubbing out of Long Hair. I do not know; but it was there then, and it did not seem that anybody could get up that high to make a picture." Further references in the text as BE.

2. Lucy Maddox, *Removals: Nineteenth-century American Literature and the Politics of Indian Affairs* (New York: Oxford University Press, 1991), 8, my emphasis.

3. Ibid., 9.

4. David H. Getches, Charles F. Wilkinson, and Robert A. Williams, Jr., *Cases and Materials on Federal Indian Law*, 3d ed. (St. Paul, Minn.: West Publishing, 1993), 167–228, provides the periodization of federal Indian policies I am employing here. Further references in the text as *Federal Indian Law*.

5. Other familiar examples of such anthropological work in the 1930s include the efforts by musicians and musicologists to record the folk music in rural areas—work that contributed significantly to the folk music revival of the 1950s and 1960s, as well as subsequent hybridizations of folk music with rock and country; documentary and docudramatic accounts of rural life, such as Walker Evans and James Agee's *Let Us Now Praise Famous Men* (commissioned in 1936 by *Fortune* and published in 1941) and Margaret Bourke-White and Erskine Caldwell's *You Have Seen Their Faces* (1937); and collections of folklore and folkways, the most famous of which is probably Zora Neale Hurston's account of southern African-American folkways and Afro-Caribbean influences in *Mules and Men* (1935), discussed in chapter 11.

6. Raymond J. DeMallie, "Introduction to the New Edition," *When the Tree Flowered: The Story of Eagle Voice, a Sioux Indian*, new ed. (Lincoln: University of Nebraska Press, 1991), ix. Further references in the text as *Tree*. The first edition published by Macmillan in 1951 carried the subtitle *An Authentic Tale of the Old Sioux World*, and the first edition published by the University of Nebraska Press carried the subtitle *The Fictional Autobiography of Eagle Voice, a Sioux Indian.*

7. *The Sixth Grandfather: Black Elk's Teachings Given to John G. Neihardt*, ed. Raymond J. DeMallie (Lincoln: University of Nebraska Press, 1984), 307–409; further references in the text as SG.

8. *The Sacred Pipe: Black Elk's Account of the Seven Rites of the Oglala Sioux*, recorded and edited by Joseph Epes Brown (Norman: University of Oklahoma Press, 1953); further references in the text as *Pipe*.

9. I use the phrase "Indian personality" here in keeping with ideologically driven generalizations that ignore the historical and cultural particularities of different American Indian tribes. Indeed, it is just the construction of this ideological category—the "Indian"—with which the Black Elk narratives must contend if they are to transform successfully the ways in which Native Americans are represented by the dominant culture.

10. Nick Black Elk's celebrity in popular American culture had to wait until the late 1960s, when he became a cultural icon of the counterculture, which was inspired in part by the revival of interest in Native American cultures as part of the civil rights movement (including the American Indian movement) and its reaction to late industrial capitalism, the Vietnam War, and the per-

sistence of social and economic racism and sexism. In his "Introduction to the New Edition" of *When the Tree Flowered*, DeMallie points out that "although *Black Elk Speaks* met with acclaim from the critics, it was not a popular success. Sales were not strong, and eventually the book was remaindered and allowed to go out of print. It was a stark contrast to Neihardt's volumes of the epic poem [*A Cycle of the West*], all of which remained in print throughout his lifetime" (*Tree*, viii).

11. Michael F. Steltenkamp, *Black Elk: Holy Man of the Oglala* (Norman: University of Oklahoma Press, 1993).

12. Clyde Holler, *Black Elk's Religion: The Sun Dance and Lakota Catholicism* (Syracuse: Syracuse University Press, 1995), 13. Julian Rice, *Black Elk's Story: Distinguishing Its Lakota Purpose* (Albuquerque: University of New Mexico Press, 1991), 23–24, points out that "Holler has been more forthright than DeMallie in setting down fundamental differences between Neihardt and Black Elk" and "develops his conception of Black Elk's purpose in terms of the anthropological record, comparing his metaphors to other Lakota sacred men (Fools Crow, Plenty Wolf, and Lame Deer)."

13. Steltenkamp, *Holy Man of the Oglala*, 87.

14. Julian Rice, *Black Elk's Story*, 48–64, criticizes *Black Elk Speaks* for using the Protestant mythology in Neihardt's *The Song of the Messiah*, published in 1935, four years after *Black Elk Speaks*.

15. John G. Neihardt, *A Cycle of the West* (Lincoln: University of Nebraska Press, 1961). Further references in the text as *Cycle*. Rice, *Black Elk's Story*, 48, argues that "Neihardt's portrayals of the Ghost Dance and especially of Wounded Knee are persuasively Christian" for the ideological purpose of "redeeming" the suffering of Native Americans by rendering it a significant stage in the "eschatological promise" of Christianity.

16. Francis Paul Prucha, *The Great Father*, 2 vols. (Lincoln: University of Nebraska Press, 1984), 2:1011–12, explicitly credits the reforms of the Indian Reorganization Act with stimulating "pan-Indian developments," which Prucha traces to the tribal congresses the Indian commissioner John Collier "held to promote the Wheeler-Howard bill" that later became the Indian Reorganization Act. Further references in the text as *Great Father*.

17. Rice, *Black Elk's Story*, 12.

18. Ibid., 8. Rice identifies "three Black Elks from the biographical record and from the text edited by Brown," *The Sacred Pipe*: "1) a Black Elk who was a sincere Catholic but who returned to Lakota religion after the Neihardt interviews; 2) a consistently active and committed Catholic who never turned back; and 3) an ingenious, syncretic Lakota-Christian." Rice suggests that "it may be that all three images are equally true."

19. *Report of the Board of Indian Commissioners* (1869), as quoted in Prucha, *The Great Father*, 1:563.

20. Alvin M. Josephy, Jr., *The Indian Heritage of America* (New York: Knopf, 1968), 339.

21. Commissioner of Indian Affairs Ely S. Parker (himself a Seneca) in 1870, as quoted in Prucha, *The Great Father*, 1:516.

22. Josephy, *The Indian Heritage of America*, 339.

23. Prucha, *The Great Father*, 2:671, who notes: "The Indians held 155,632,312 acres in 1881; by 1890 they had 104,314,349; and by 1900 only 77,865,373, of which 5,409,530 had been allotted."

24. Lucile F. Aly, *John G. Neihardt: A Critical Biography* (Amsterdam: Rodopi, 1977), 227–44.

25. Raymond J. DeMallie, "John G. Neihardt's Lakota Legacy," in *A Sender of Words: Essays in Memory of John G. Neihardt*, ed. Vine Deloria, Jr. (Salt Lake City: Howe Brothers, 1984), 123.

26. Ibid.

27. Steltenkamp, *Holy Man of the Oglala*, 13.

28. Ibid.

29. Ibid., 44. See also *The Sixth Grandfather*, 15: "Such men's and women's sodalities as the Roman Catholic St. Joseph and St. Mary societies could function as replacements for traditional men's and women's societies that had been fundamental social building blocks in earlier times."

30. Ibid., 48.

31. Hilda Neihardt's report of Black Elk's explanation, as quoted in *The Sixth Grandfather*, 47.

32. Steltenkamp, *Holy Man of the Oglala*, 49.

33. Ibid.

34. Holler, *Black Elk's Religion*, 12–13.

35. Ibid., 11.

36. Lakota sodalities had developed as *akicita* societies that trained future warriors as defenders of the tribe, as Royal B. Hassrick, in collaboration with Dorothy Maxwell and Cile M. Bach, *The Sioux: Life and Customs of a Warrior Society* (Norman: University of Oklahoma Press, 1964), 20–24, points out, tracing the origins of these *akicita* societies often to "someone's dream," in which he is "directed by supernatural beings to form an organization which would promote the best interests of the tribe" (20). There is thus a direct political and military gesture in substituting Catholic religious sodalities for Lakota societies dedicated to preserving ways of military defense.

37. Hegel's secularization of the Christian narrative of salvation also serves the purpose of legitimating the progressive scheme of Enlightenment and thus is one of the most effective and resilient philosophical rationalizations of imperialism.

38. I am borrowing here from Mary Louise Pratt's notion of the "contact zone" between cultures and the rhetorical and linguistic undecidability that occurs in such moments of contact and their historical representations. See Mary Louise Pratt, "Arts of the Contact Zone," *Profession 91*, 33–41, and my discussion of Pratt in "A Future for 'American Studies': The Comparative U.S. Cultures Model," *American Studies in Germany: European Contexts and Intercultural Relations*, ed. Günter H. Lenz and Klaus J. Milich (New York: St. Martin's, 1995), 262–78.

39. John G. Neihardt, *Indian Tales and Others* (1926; reprint, Lincoln: University of Nebraska Press, 1988).

40. Wallace Stevens, "Sunday Morning," *The Collected Poems of Wallace Stevens* (New York: Knopf, 1972), 69–70.

41. DeMallie points out that the "concept of *Wakan Tanka* was amorphous. *Wakan Tanka* was never born and so will never die. *Wakan Tanka* created the universe and at the same time was embodied in the universe. One Lakota explained: 'The *Wakan Tanka* are those which made everything. They are *Wakanpi*. *Wakanpi* are all things that are above mankind. . . . *Wakan Tanka* are many. But they are all the same as one'" (SG, 81). DeMallie is quoting the

Lakota Little Wound, whose description of the plurality of *Wakan Tanka* even more effectively conveys their spiritual difference from the Christian godhead than DeMallie's description. Of course, medieval theological conceptions of Catholic divinity, such as one finds in St. Thomas Aquinas's *Summa Theologiae*, stress its "unity-in-multiplicity," but Catholics would not refer, as Little Wound does above, to their "gods," perhaps for fear of recalling the pantheon of Greek and Roman gods.

42. In my effort to reassess the abilities of the Black Elk narratives to speak beyond Neihardt's composition of the interviews in Euro-American ways, I have decided to cite, whenever possible, the original transcript, collected in *The Sixth Grandfather*, of the corresponding passage in *Black Elk Speaks* or *When the Tree Flowered*, noting differences between the two versions parenthetically in the text or in the notes. I acknowledge that this procedure in certain ways falsifies the integrity and even "literariness" of Neihardt's composed narratives, but only in this manner can we hope to distinguish Lakota historical and political aims from Neihardt's. This is by no means a foolproof procedure, but it is worth trying in the interests of allowing us to focus on those qualities of Lakota history, religion, and tribal organization that the Lakota interviewed most hoped to communicate to Euro-American readers. My ultimate aim is not to fracture the texts composed by Neihardt but to make them once again "readable" as part of a larger critical account of U.S. imperialism. I also hope in this way to gain greater recognition for the Lakota authority of the various tellers on whom Neihardt relied for both *Black Elk Speaks* and *When the Tree Flowered*. In this particular passage, Neihardt retains the essence of Black Elk's account of his first vision, but Neihardt narrativizes it so that the reader knows that the "two men coming out of a cloud" are "thunder beings" associated with rain and thunder—"two men were coming there, headfirst like arrows slanting down" and "then they were gone, and the rain came with a big wind and a roaring." In a similar manner, Neihardt must add specific actions to the thunder beings to account for their metamorphoses into geese: "they *wheeled about* toward where the sun goes down, and suddenly they were geese" (emphasis mine; BE, 19).

43. Holler, *Black Elk's Religion*, 48–49, cites the writings of the nineteenth-century Congregational missionary Gideon H. Pond as "excellent" introductions to "the concept of *wakan*" as a "foundational Sioux religious concept," and points out that Pond "argues that the idea of a supreme being is of missionary origin, claiming that alongside the great struggle between Christianity and heathenism is 'a strife between the old system of worship rendered to the *Taku-Wakan*, and the new, which is rendered to the *Wakan-Tanka*.' According to Pond, all Dakota gods and *wakans* are mortal, being eternal only in the sense that they succeed themselves" (49).

44. Neihardt attributes part of Standing Bear's remarks from the transcripts about the Buffalo Hunt to Black Elk and, as usual, provides more narrative connections than in the transcripts, but he retains the collective telling of this event by both Standing Bear and Black Elk, thus reinforcing in the actual storytelling the communal qualities of the hunt itself (BE, 48–60).

45. James R. Walker, *Lakota Belief and Ritual*, ed. Raymond J. DeMallie and Elaine A. Jahner (Lincoln: University of Nebraska Press, 1980), 81, offers the following description by George Sword of *akicita*'s tribal responsibilities: "In former times the Lakotas had customs and ceremonies that governed almost everything they did. The shamans governed the ceremonies. The *akicita* gov-

erned the other customs. The council appointed the *akicita* and considered all matters concerning the band."

46. I quote Neihardt's version here, because the transcript is somewhat difficult to understand out of context, although the basic sense of both seems quite similar: "There was something here at the prisoners' house that made me feel very bad. Men pointed guns at them and ordered them around and I thought maybe my people would probably be treated this way some day" (SG, 247).

47. Once again, I cite *Black Elk Speaks* here for clarity; the transcript edited by DeMallie reads: "Black Elk thinks that the highest peak in the Black Hills—Harney Peak—is the one to which the spirits took him in the vision to see the whole earth. The Spirits had told him that the people would prosper there" (SG, 163).

48. This is Standing Bear's recollection. Iron Hawk also quotes Sitting Bull as saying to One Horn, leader of the Minneconjous: "'these hills are a treasure to us Indians. That is the food pack of the people and when the poor have nothing to eat we can all go there and have something to eat" (SG, 171–72).

49. Neihardt omits this matter-of-fact statement, although he tries to express it differently by writing: "I met a soldier on horseback, and I let him have it" (BE, 123). DeMallie's edition of the transcript suggests a more stoic attitude toward the inevitability of battle with the white soldiers, rather than merely the directness of individual violence stressed in Neihardt's version.

50. DeMallie glosses "Hownh!" also used in Neihardt's account, as "the sound of an angry grizzly bear, used by Lakota warriors in battle" (SG, 192n37). Neihardt reorganizes the syntax slightly, but the connotations are roughly the same: "I kept on beating him awhile after he was dead, and every time I hit him I said 'Hownh!' I was mad, because I was thinking of the women and little children running down there, all scared and out of breath" (BE, 123).

51. Oral modes of narration tend to be more explicitly communal than print forms, even when the specific responsibilities for the oral narration are relegated to an individual storyteller, as was the case with the "winter counts" of the Sioux. Jean-François Lyotard in *The Postmodern Condition: A Report on Knowledge*, trans. Geoff Bennington and Brian Massumi (Minneapolis: University of Minnesota Press, 1984), 20–21, distinguishes between "traditional knowledge" and "developed knowledge," such as scientific knowledge, by noting how "traditional knowledge," no matter who may transmit it, relies on a "pragmatics of transmission" that involves both narrator and narratees in the overall storytelling process. They are, in short, all authors. Lyotard's examples for "traditional knowledge" are taken in this context from the Amazonian Cashinahua Indians, whose specific traditions and cultural values should not be equated with those of the Oglala Sioux, but nonetheless both tribal peoples appear to rely on oral modes of cultural narration and knowledge production that, as Lyotard puts it, constitute "the social bond" in their very performance and are thus distinct from scientific knowledge production and transmission in Euro-American societies.

52. DeMallie, "Introduction to the New Edition," *When the Tree Flowered*, viii, points out that Neihardt's original title for *Black Elk Speaks* had been "The Tree That Never Bloomed," but the "perplexed publisher objected to the title, and the simpler and more direct 'Black Elk Speaks' was a compromise suggested to Neihardt by his wife, Mona."

53. For a fuller discussion of these romantic stereotypes of North American Indians, see Robert A. Berkhofer, Jr., *The White Man's Indian: Images of the*

American Indian from Columbus to the Present (New York: Knopf, 1978), 23–31.

54. The Indian Reorganization Act was criticized by many groups, including such Native American political organizations as the American Indian Federation. Native American objections to the act and to Collier as commissioner focused on the central role for the Bureau of Indian Affairs in the realization of "Indian sovereignty." In short, Collier's plan for Native American cultural, political, and economic independence was still designed by white men for Native Americans and administered through the white man's government. See Prucha, *The Great Father*, 2:995–96.

55. BE, 232. Neihardt connects Black Elk's absence in England with the fact he did not go to visit Wovoka (Jack Wilson) himself, but the transcript does not suggest this, noting: "I did not go over there, I just heard of it, that's all" (SG, 257).

56. James Mooney, *The Ghost-Dance Religion and the Sioux Outbreak of 1890* (1896; reprint, Chicago: University of Chicago Press, 1965), 90–92. Although the agents on the Sioux reservations did not initially consider the Ghost Dance dangerous, they increasingly viewed it as a symbolic protest by the Sioux to reduced food supplies from the government, further cessions of land, and demands to accept U.S. customs. When Agent Wright on the Rosebud reservation forbade the Ghost Dance, he did so "on account of its physical and mental effect on the participants and its tendency to draw them from their homes" (92). The fact that the dancers believed that the ghost shirt protected them from bullets may have led some agents to think the Ghost Dance was preparation for war.

57. BE, 21:234: "I had had a great vision that was to bring the people back into the nation's hoop, and maybe this sacred man had had the same vision, and it was going to come true, so that the people would get back on the red road."

58. In the transcript, Black Elk reports his father's death in the same paragraphs he describes his experience dancing in his first Ghost Dance, clearly connecting that performance with ritual mourning for his father's death. Neihardt separates the two events, having Black Elk report that "my father died in the first part of the winter" three pages from the end of chapter 21 and describe his participation in his first Ghost Dance at the beginning of chapter 22, "Visions of the Other World."

59. BE, 22:245.

60. Ibid.

61. In the following discussion of Eagle Voice's vision (chapters 7–8) in *When the Tree Flowered*, I refer to the text as composed by Neihardt, because DeMallie includes only the transcripts of Neihardt's 1944 interviews with Black Elk in *The Sixth Grandfather*. DeMallie's decision not to include the transcripts of the interviews with Eagle Elk and Andrew Knife is both curious and symptomatic of the ease with which Euro-American assumptions about the "author" can reshape Lakota oral traditions and subjectivity as communally defined. The exclusions are curious, because DeMallie includes the 1931 interviews with Fire Thunder, Standing Bear, Black Tail Deer, and Iron Hawk that resulted in *Black Elk Speaks* and because DeMallie acknowledges that "a significant portion of the material in" *When the Tree Flowered* "came from Neihardt's interviews with Eagle Elk, also recorded in 1944," including "many biographical details of the fictional narrator Eagle Voice" (SG, 304). DeMallie's decision is symp-

tomatic of basic Euro-American assumptions about individuality, because DeMallie refers repeatedly to the importance of "Black Elk's 1944 teachings" in providing "new insights into Black Elk and his perceptions of his people," implying that the value of the 1944 transcripts lies in the insights they offer us into the character of the discrete individual, Nicholas Black Elk (304).

62. See "*Inipi*: The Rite of Purification," in *Pipe*, 31–44.

63. George E. Hyde, *Red Cloud's Folk: A History of the Oglala Sioux Indians* (Norman: University of Oklahoma Press, 1937), ix.

64. DeMallie defines the Lakota "winter-count" as "an annual calendar depicting a significant event for each 'winter' (the Lakota year, measured from first snow to first snow), beginning in 1700–1701" (SG, 302). Hassrick, *The Sioux*, 8, adds to this definition: "Factual knowledge of the past was recorded in the winter counts. These records were kept by important individuals, apparently the headman of each band. They were painted on deerskins, usually in spiral form with the first record at the vortex. Each picture served as a reminder of the most important event of each year. The years were titled, not numbered. . . . named for one outstanding event, such as the death of a famous man or some startling and unusual phenomenon." DeMallie restricts those Lakota qualified to represent tribal history and religion by adding, "Only a few of them recorded their stories and knowledge in such a way that they could be preserved in books for future generations. Among those who did, we can see strong parallels with Black Elk's teachings" (SG, 302).

65. Hassrick, *The Sioux*, 8.

66. Holler, *Black Elk's Religion*, 4–8, summarizes the critical revaluation of Neihardt's relation to Black Elk and DeMallie's contribution to and position with respect to these critical revaluations. For DeMallie's defenses of Neihardt against recent critics, see *The Sixth Grandfather*, xx–xxii, 51–57.

67. Holler, *Black Elk's Religion*, 8.

68. Maddox, *Removals*, 36–37.

69. Such historical distancing is characteristic of Charles Brockden Brown and James Fenimore Cooper's representations of Native Americans. Cooper's Chingachgook, for example, is "last of the Mohicans" in the French and Indian War (1755–1763), long before contemporary readers of *Last of the Mohicans* (1826) can do anything about the problem. For a discussion of such historical distancing as a strategy of the myth of the Vanishing American in Brown's writings, see Chapter 2.

70. In traditional Lakota societies, the Euro-American idea of the aesthetic or cultural "avant-garde," intent always on trivializing the past to create space for new styles and expression, is alien; instead, individual expression gains validity by its appeal to tradition and its invocation of ancestral sources and spirits.

71. There are, of course, numerous examples of such literary imperialism in the history of U.S. destruction of Native American peoples and cultures, but consider as a representative example James Hall's stories in *The Wilderness and the Warpath* (New York: Garrett Press, 1969), first published in 1846. Hall opens the collection by noting that "the simple structure of their communities, and the sameness of their occupations, limit the Savage within a narrow sphere of thought and action" and that "beyond his own tribe, his intercourse extends only to savages as ignorant as himself" (2). Clearly the literary experience is for Hall a broadening of the reader that distinguishes that reader from this "Savage," thus implicating literature both in the philosophical (and literary) project

of enlightenment and the anthropological classification of "civilized" and "savage" peoples. Herman Melville satirizes Judge Hall and his frontier fiction in the character of Colonel Moredock in *The Confidence-Man: His Masquerade* (New York: Dix, Edwards, 1857), 224–36 (chapters 26–28). For a recent treatment of Melville's satire of Hall, see Maddox, *Removals*, pp. 83–87.

72. On the other hand, Neihardt experiences no scruple in "staging" Black Elk's "vision" on Harney Peak at the end of *Black Elk Speaks*—a vision that we now know Neihardt fabricated to achieve literary closure to the work. It is, as many critics have pointed out, a formal closure that reaffirms the myth of the Vanishing American, in this case by staging an "End of the Trail" scene, and the *felix culpa* of Neihardt's Protestant spiritualism in the final volume of *A Cycle of the West: The Song of the Messiah*.

Chapter II

1. Zora Neale Hurston, *Dust Tracks on a Road: An Autobiography* (New York: Harper and Row, 1991), 145–46. Further references in the text as D.

2. Emily Greene Balch, "Social Values in Haiti," in *Beyond Nationalism: The Social Thought of Emily Greene Balch*, ed. Mercedes M. Randall (New York: Twayne Publishers, 1972), 147. Randall, "Introduction," to the reprint of *Occupied Haiti*, ed. Emily Greene Balch (1927; reprint, New York: Garland Publishing, 1972), 9, describes how Balch led a "committee of six disinterested Americans," including two African-American women, sponsored by the Women's International League for Peace and Freedom, who visited Haiti in 1926, favored "restoration of the Independence of the Negro Republic," and submitted their findings to the Hoover Commission, formed to review our military occupation of Haiti from 1915 to 1934. As Randall notes: "The American policy for Haiti adopted by President Hoover on March 20, 1930, was very much along the lines recommended by the unofficial group of the Women's International League for Peace and Freedom" (9).

3. Hurston, *Tell My Horse: Voodoo and Life in Haiti and Jamaica* (New York: Harper and Row, 1990), 74. Further references in the text as T.

4. Robert E. Hemenway, *Zora Neale Hurston: A Literary Biography* (Urbana: University of Illinois Press, 1977), 249.

5. Susan Meisenhelder, "Conflict and Resistance in Zora Neale Hurston's *Mules and Men*," *Journal of American Folklore* 109, no. 433 (Summer 1996): 268, argues that Hurston had to take "an indirect approach" because of her white supporters, like Charlotte Osgood Mason, who "literally owned Hurston's material and consistently pushed Hurston to express only the 'primitivism' she saw in Black culture."

6. Barbara Johnson, "Thresholds of Difference: Structures of Address in Zora Neale Hurston," *Critical Inquiry* 12 (Autumn 1985): 289, concludes that Hurston's narrative strategies constitute a general deconstructive practice that destabilizes the socially constructed boundaries separating people by race and gender and that finally is describable as a trickster tale (both African-American and deconstructive): "To turn one's own life into a trickster tale of which even the teller herself might be the dupe certainly goes far in deconstructing the possibility of representing the truth of identity." While acknowledging the helpfulness of this formulation, I will interpret Hurston's rhetorical "double-consciousness" as designed for historically concrete and demonstrably referential effects for the reader.

7. Hurston, *Mules and Men* (New York: Harper and Row, 1990). Further reference in the text as M.

8. Sandra Dolby-Stahl, "Literary Objectives: Hurston's Use of Personal Narratives in *Mules and Men*," *Western Folklore* 51, no. 1 (January 1992): 62–63.

9. Gwendolyn Mikell, "When Horses Talk: Reflections on Zora Neale Hurston's Haitian Anthropology," *Phylon* 43, no. 3 (September 1982): 222.

10. Hazel Carby, "The Politics of Fiction, Anthropology, and the Folk: Zora Neale Hurston," in *History and Memory in African-American Culture*, ed. Geneviève Fabre and Robert O'Meally (New York: Oxford University Press, 1994), 40–41, is a notable exception, including *Their Eyes Were Watching God* with *Mules and Men* and *Tell My Horse* in her brief reading of the migratory journey sketched variously by African Americans, characters in these books, and Hurston herself in search of cultural origins and "for an appropriate vehicle for the expression of black culture" (40).

11. James Agee and Walker Evans, *Let Us Now Praise Famous Men: Three Tenant Families* (Boston, Mass.: Houghton Mifflin, 1960), 25–26.

12. Ibid., 29. Agee's description of the singers' style as "jagged, tortured, stony, accented as if by hammers and cold-chisels, full of a nearly paralyzing vitality and iteration of rhythm, the harmonies constantly splitting the nerves" is one of his most extraordinary verbal descriptions of music in a book notable for Agee's extraordinarily musical style, influenced clearly by the rhythms of jazz and the blues.

13. Mikell, "When Horses Talk," 219, discusses *Tell My Horse* as an anticipation of the New Ethnography of the 1950s and 1960s, although Mikell distinguishes its anthropology from that of the earlier *Mules and Men*. Dolby-Stahl, "Literary Objectives," 57, uses Alan Dundes's notion of "metafolklore" to describe Hurston's narrative method in *Mules and Men*. The "writing culture" movement is generally identified with James Clifford and George E. Marcus, eds., *Writing Culture: The Poetics and Politics of Ethnography* (Berkeley: University of California Press, 1986).

14. I am thinking here, of course, of the negative and positive connotations of "double consciousness" that Du Bois famously discusses in *The Souls of Black Folk* and are developed further in Chapter 9.

15. For rhetorical convenience, I will follow Hurston's own method in identifying the narratorial persona as "Zora."

16. Hemenway, *Zora Neale Hurston*, 223–24.

17. Mack Ford tells the story of "unh hunh," the "one word de Devil made up," later in *Mules and Men*, in which a man on earth tricks the Devil into letting the angels he has kidnapped from heaven escape (M, 160–61). Although a variation on "beating the Devil" in the first story, this one more conventionally respects the sacredness of heaven and the evil of the Devil.

18. John Carlos Rowe, *At Emerson's Tomb: The Politics of Classic American Literature* (New York: Columbia University Press, 1997), 226–28.

19. Rosan Augusta Jordan, "Not into Cold Space: Zora Neale Hurston and J. Frank Dobie as Holistic Folklorists," *Southern Folklore* 49, no. 2 (1992): 126.

20. Although my point here is primarily literary, I also think it helps to change our thinking about *Mules and Men* as more strictly ethnographic in the scientific manner developed by Boas and Benedict, as Mikell, "When Horses Talk," 221, has argued. Boas and Benedict both believed comparative ethnography was likely to reproduce the values of the ethnographer's dominant cultural viewpoint. Benedict in particular advocated an ethnography that focused

with scientific rigor on the formal logic of the culture studied and avoided comparative generalizations. Mikell and others have argued that the more subjective qualities of travelogue in *Tell My Horse* reflect Hurston's conscious shift from the scientific ethnography of Boas and Benedict to her own, more literary method. But *Mules and Men* is always comparative in its approach, because the tales she collects and then narratively arranges always depend upon some reflection, usually critical, regarding the ruling white culture.

21. Beulah S. Hemmingway, "Through the Prism of Africanity: A Preliminary Investigation of Zora Neale Hurston's *Mules and Men*," *Zora in Florida*, ed. Steve Glassman and Kathryn Lee Seidel (Orlando: University of Central Florida Press, 1991), 39.

22. Ibid., 40.

23. Deborah G. Plant, *Every Tub Must Sit on Its Own Bottom: The Philosophy and Politics of Zora Neale Hurston* (Urbana: University of Illinois Press, 1995), 45: "From the cultural heroes of African American folktales, African Americans imbibed a tenacity of mind and spirit and the paradigms of behavior needed to negotiate a hostile environment."

24. Fifteen years later, in "What White Publishers Won't Print," *I Love Myself When I Am Laughing . . . And Then Again When I Am Looking Mean and Impressive: A Zora Neale Hurston Reader*, ed. Alice Walker (Old Westbury, N.Y.: Feminist Press, 1979), 170–71, Hurston describes "The American Negro exhibit" in her imaginary "AMERICAN MUSEUM OF UNNATURAL HISTORY" as consisting of "a group of two. . . . One is seated on a stump picking away on his banjo and singing and laughing. The other is a most amoral character before a share-cropper's shack mumbling about injustice. Doing this makes him out to be a Negro 'intellectual.' It is as simple as all that."

25. Although she does not discuss *Mules and Men* or *Tell My Horse* in her interpretation of Hurston's autobiography, *Dust Tracks on a Road*, Sidonie Smith, *Subjectivity, Identity, and the Body* (Bloomington: Indiana University Press, 1993), 103–25, shows how Hurston develops an idea of a "diasporan 'I'" that is "strategic as well as incorporative," insofar as Smith's Hurston "hails the individual as a way of circumventing the essentializing agenda of identity politics, be it that of professional anthropology, of the dominant culture . . . , and of indigenous folk proverbs, three cultures to which she has access as both insider and outsider and three cultures which fix identities along racial, gender, class, and national lines" (124). Smith's postmodern Hurston is, like Barbara Johnson's, an important version, but one that tends to dehistoricize Hurston and, in this case, trivialize the importance of the body and the affective-emotive bases for meaning that she rediscovers in *Mules and Men* and *Tell My Horse*.

26. Meisenhelder, "Conflict and Resistance in Zora Neale Hurston's *Mules and Men*," 283, treats Big Sweet as a feminine idealization of virtually mythic proportions, who necessarily makes Zora appear inadequate: "For women of less titanic proportions the strategies necessary to battle sexual inequality are often more indirect ones."

27. Shug Avery and Celie's friendship in *The Color Purple* has certain echoes of Big Sweet's friendship with Zora in *Mules and Men*, although Walker develops Shug and Celie's friendship in ways integral to her plot. The influence of Hurston on Alice Walker's life and writings is best expressed in Walker's "Afterword: Looking for Zora," in *A Zora Neale Hurston Reader*, 296–313. Most critics have focused on the influence of Hurston's Janie in *Their Eyes Were Watch-*

ing God on Walker's Celie in *The Color Purple*. See, for example, Michael Awkward, *Inspiriting Influences: Tradition, Revision, and Afro-American Women's Novels* (New York: Columbia University Press, 1989), 135, 138–39, and the essays collected in Lillie P. Howard, ed., *Alice Walker and Zora Neale Hurston: The Common Bond* (Westport, Conn.: Greenwood Press, 1993), most of which focus on *Their Eyes Were Watching God* and *The Color Purple*.

28. Meisenhelder, "Conflict and Resistance in Zora Neale Hurston's *Mules and Men*," 284.

29. Dana McKinnon Preu, "A Literary Reading of *Mules and Men*, Part I," *Zora in Florida*, 59–60.

30. "How It Feels to Be Colored Me," *A Zora Neale Hurston Reader*, 154.

31. Johnson, "Thresholds of Difference," 283. Hurston, "What White Publishers Won't Print," *A Zora Neale Hurston Reader*, 172: "That brings us to the folklore of 'reversion to type.' . . . No matter how high we may *seem* to climb, put us under strain and we revert to type, that is, to the bush. Under a superficial layer of western culture, the jungle drums throb in our veins."

32. "How It Feels to Be Colored Me," *A Zora Neale Hurston Reader*, 153.

33. Johnson, "Thresholds of Difference," 283.

34. Ibid.

35. Johnson, "Thresholds of Difference," 283–84, distinguishes between Hurston's intentions in "How It Feels to Be Colored Me" (1928) and "What White Publishers Won't Print" (1950) by arguing that in the earlier essay Hurston plays upon the "exotic primitive . . . in vogue in 1928" only to "disavow" "this 'jungle' stereotype" in the 1950 essay. My suggestion here is that Hurston expresses the same view in both essays, clarifying in the later essay's discussion of the "folklore of the reversion to type" that her endorsement of the African passions of jazz, for example, differs from the racist "exotic primitivism" that appealed to many whites during the Harlem Renaissance by asserting the recovery of feelings and the body so integral to Africanist survivals as a cure for modern, urban, and white civilization's ills.

36. Hurston's abandonment to the jazz energies could be compared with the Dionysian passions Nietzsche complains we have lost in *The Birth of Tragedy*, Eliot's critique of our alienation from our basic feelings and bodily functions throughout *The Waste Land*, Pound's appeal to "lost" African cultures in *The Cantos*, and Williams's invocation of African "fertility" in *Paterson*. Of course, the "African presence" in the writings of these high moderns is often used as a kind of "neo-primitivism," whose recovery depends upon the white author's incorporation of its energies into the Western tradition, itself a kind of Eurocentric elitism analyzed at length by Marianna Torgovnick, *Gone Primitive: Savage Intellects, Modern Lives* (Chicago: University of Chicago Press, 1990). In this regard, Hurston's effort to reclaim Africanity as a means of African-American cultural representation is a radical, self-conscious departure from the traditions of Euro-American modernism.

37. Hurston, "Hoodoo in America," *Journal of American Folklore* 44 (October–December 1931): 317–418. Wendy Dutton, "The Problem of Invisibility: Voodoo and Zora Neale Hurston," *Frontiers: A Journal of Women's Studies* 13, no. 2 (1993): 136–37, notes of "Hoodoo in America": "More than one hundred pages long, the article represented the first study of voodoo by a black folklorist. It also was one of the first studies to treat voodoo in a nonracist way."

38. Paul Gilroy, *The Black Atlantic: Modernity and Double Consciousness* (London: Verso, 1993).

39. Hemenway, *Zora Neale Hurston*, 257. Hemenway is referring to what Hurston does with the Moses story in *Moses, Man of the Mountain*, but it seems equally applicable to her use of Moses at the beginning of "Hoodoo."

40. Hurston, *Moses, Man of the Mountain* (Chatham, N.J.: Chatham Bookseller, 1967), 8.

41. Ibid.

42. Reed, *Mumbo Jumbo* (New York: Bantam Books, 1973), 192–214, which includes Reed's two-part "Chapter 52," in which he reinterprets Moses as an African-Egyptian. Reed risks criticism for anti-semitism in his use of the Hebraic Moses as a Western "sell-out"—a risk Hurston quite consciously avoids in *Mules and Men* and *Moses, Man of the Mountain* by interpreting Moses as an inclusive, rather than exclusive, religious archetype. Nevertheless, much of Reed's novel follows Hurston's lead, including the nominal plot in *Mumbo Jumbo* to recover the lost sacred text of Africanity, the "Book of Thoth," which Moses in Hurston's novel also seeks. See, for example, *Moses, Man of the Mountain*, 73.

43. Hemenway, *Zora Neale Hurston*, 258.

44. Paola Boi, "Moses, Man of Power, Man of Knowledge: A 'Signifying' Reading of Zora Neale Hurston (Between a Laugh and a Song)," in *Women and War: The Changing Status of American Women from the 1930s to the 1950s*, ed. Maria Diedrich and Dorothea Fischer-Hornung (New York: Berg Publishers, 1990), 115.

45. Henry Louis Gates, Jr., *The Signifying Monkey: A Theory of African-American Literary Criticism* (New York: Oxford University Press, 1988), 8–9, compares the Yoruban trickster figure with the Greek Hermes, although Gates is aware that the connection between the powers of the two figures is inexact, a mere approximation across cultural borders for Gates's own purposes of analogy.

46. See Hurston, *Moses, Man of the Mountain*, 150, 154, 179, for example. Paola Boi, "Moses," 119, interprets Moses' complex rites of initiation by his tutor, Prince Mentu, and his father-in-law, Jethro, into sacred mysteries as explicitly designed by Hurston to resemble "a hoodoo rite of initiation."

47. Craven connects the evils of the Haitian dictatorships of François "Papa Doc" and Jean-Claude "Baby Doc" Duvalier with the superstitions of Voodoo, and he loosely links together "secret practices" of Amazonian Indians and Haitian houngans in a Hollywood pastiche of the legitimate historical connections between Haitian Voodoo and Brazilian Candomble. Craven's film has only the flimsiest connection with Wade Davis's book, *The Serpent and the Rainbow*, in which Davis visits Haiti to do scientific research on Tetrodotoxin, the active ingredient Davis speculates causes the catatonia of Zombies. Davis was inspired in part by Hurston's speculation in *Tell My Horse* that Zombies' states were caused by some natural poison. See Wade Davis, *The Serpent and the Rainbow* (New York: Simon and Schuster, 1985), 206–11, 213–15.

48. Dutton, "The Problem of Invisibility," 139–40.

49. Mikell, "When Horses Talk," 219, considers Hurston's anthropological method to rely on a double-consciousness, anticipating the distinction made by the New Ethnography movement of the 1950s and 1960s between the "emic"—"the logical patterns inherent within a culture and reflected in their culture"—and the "etic"—and the "outsider's viewpoint"—views of a culture.

50. "How It Feels to Be Colored Me," *A Zora Neale Hurston Reader*, 154.

51. Hemenway, *Zora Neale Hurston*, 249–50.

52. Dutton, "The Problem of Invisibility," 133: "She wanted to change the popular perception of voodoo. She wanted to tell the story so anyone could understand it. Although *Tell My Horse* fails as serious anthropology, it doesn't fly as fiction either. Hurston's voodoo work dwells in the murky middle ground between fiction and anthropology, not fully aligned with either."

53. Including, of course, the educational methods and institutions through which this Western civilization is generationally transmitted. Hurston's *Mules and Men* and *Tell My Horse* anticipate the critique of that tradition and the alternative pedagogy claimed by many contemporary U.S. writers from Reed to Morrison, Erdrich, Kingston, Tan, and Silko, among others.

54. "The Good Neighbor" policy was first adopted between the United States and Mexico to assure Mexico that the United States would no longer discourage, as it had in the 1920s, Mexico from attracting foreign investment capital.

55. "Crazy for This Democracy," *A Zora Neale Hurston Reader*, 166; the essay was first published in *Negro Digest* 4 (December 1945): 45–48.

56. Ann Douglas, *Terrible Honesty: Mongrel Manhattan in the 1920s* (New York: Farrar, Straus and Giroux, 1995), 309, notes that Du Bois's interest "in rewriting genealogies" to make "the Negro . . . the first, the ur-American . . . became the credo of the New Negro of the 1920s." The deliberate confusion of the avant-garde "original" with the historical "origin" is also characteristic of a wide variety of ideas of "America," ranging from Emerson to the Moderns.

57. Hurston has in mind Jamaica's (or the "West Indies'") importance for antebellum abolitionists, especially in Massachusetts, who cited frequently the British abolition of slavery there more than three decades before abolition in the United States. See my discussion of Emerson's "Emancipation in the British West Indies," in *At Emerson's Tomb*, 25–29.

58. Mikell, "When Horses Talk," 222: "She made the cross-cultural comparisons, bluntly pointing out that her vantage point is that of a female born in the more technologically advanced society of the United States. While we may wish to accuse her of patronization, the skill with which she unmasked these social sensitivities remind us that, as an intellectual, she was the contradictory product of the class- and race-conscious American society of the 1930s."

59. Joan Dayan, *Haiti, History, and the Gods* (Berkeley: University of California Press, 1995), 63.

60. Ibid., 57. Dayan is quoting C. L. R. James's *The Black Jacobins: Toussaint L'Ouverture and the San Domingo Revolution*, 2d ed. (New York: Random House, 1963), 32, where James describes the general degeneracy of white planters and Catholic priests in eighteenth-century Santo Domingo.

61. Ibid., 59.

62. Maya Deren, *Divine Horsemen: The Living Gods of Haiti* (London: Thames and Hudson, 1953), 15. As a socialist writer and filmmaker, Deren stressed the seemingly insuperable class conflicts in Haiti as part of its colonial and capitalist legacies.

63. Whatever mistakes he made in this regard, John Neihardt was attempting to become just this sort of participant-observer in his recording and then narration of *Black Elk Speaks* and *When the Tree Flowered*, discussed in Chapter 10.

64. Deren, *Divine Horsemen*, 64–65.

65. Reed, *Mumbo Jumbo*, 189, for example. On the relations among Voodoo (Vodun), Candomble, and Santería, see Gerdès Fleurant, *Dancing Spirits:*

Rhythms and Rituals of Haitian Vodun, the Rada Rite (Westport, Conn.: Greenwood Press, 1996), 9.

66. Ibid., 67.

67. Ibid., 70.

68. Dutton, "The Problem of Invisibility," 148, is typical of several feminist readings of *Tell My Horse* that praise Hurston in the book as an independent woman, "a woman on her own, moving amid magic with ease. She served as a kind of bridge for an imaginative matrilineage extending from the tradition of conjure to the literary genius of black women writers in the last two decades." It should be pointed out, however, that Hurston's feminism is restricted to straight women in *Tell My Horse*; she tells a pointed anecdote about a lesbian possessed ("mounted") by Guedé who kills herself while so possessed out of guilt for her behavior (T, 222).

69. In the 1950s Deren uses Haitian Voodoo explicitly for purposes we associate today with the stylized "primitivism" of modern aestheticism. Deren, *Divine Horsemen*, 8, writes in her preface: "In a modern industrial culture, the artists constitute, in fact, an 'ethnic group,' subject to the full 'native' treatment. . . . We too are misrepresented by professional appreciators and subjected to spiritual imperialism, our most sacred efforts are plagiarized for yard goods, our histories are traced, our psyches analyzed, and when everyone has taken his pleasure of us in his own fashion, we are driven from our native haunts, our modest dwellings are condemned and replaced by a chromium skyscraper. Of all persons from a modern culture, it is the artist who, looking at a native looking at a 'white' man . . . would mutter the heart-felt phrase: 'Brother, I sure know what you're thinking and you can think that thought again!'" In her sympathy with the colonial oppression of Haitians, Deren also betrays the condescension of urban Left intellectuals toward Third-World peoples that alienated many African Americans from the CPUSA (Communist Party USA) in the 1930s and 1940s.

70. Hurston's claim that these secret societies have nothing to do with Voodoo seems contradicted by Wade Davis's conclusion in *The Serpent and the Rainbow*, 211, that Hurston's description of their methods of "killing" their enemies was "what she could not have realized was the primary method of zombification."

71. Davis, *The Serpent and the Rainbow*, 213–14.

72. Ibid., 214.

73. Dutton, "The Problem of Invisibility," 148.

74. Robert Debs Heinl, Jr., and Nancy Gordon Heinl, *Written in Blood: The Story of the Haitian People 1492–1971* (Boston: Houghton Mifflin, 1978), 468.

75. Ibid., 425, 468.

76. As Meisenhelder, "Conflict and Resistance in Zora Neale Hurston's *Mules and Men*," 268, argues of *Mules and Men*.

77. James G. Leyburn, *The Haitian People* (New Haven: Yale University Press, 1941), 230, paints a different picture of President Vincent as "an able man to whose credit much can be said," but acknowledges that his "régime rested upon his alliance with the efficient Garde d'Haïti" and that there "were few signs of democracy or of respect for civil liberties, as Americans understand those terms, in Vincent's eleven years."

78. Heinl and Heinl, *Written in Blood*, 471–72. The Senate committee, a forerunner of the Hoover Commission that finally recommended U.S. with-

drawal from Haiti in 1934, invited representatives from the NAACP and the Union Patriotique to testify before it.

79. Mikell, "When Horses Talk," 221: "Hurston saw colonial domination as a major causal factor in shaping the cultural forces within Haiti's history. . . . This nascent element of causation, while abruptly developed and heavy-handedly and unevenly applied, separates Hurston's approach from the straight cultural configurationism of Benedict."

80. Stanley Meisler, *Los Angeles Times*, (18 October 1997, A6.

81. Leyburn, *The Haitian People*, 271, pointed out in the 1940s that overpopulation and little money for travel restricted most émigrés to "seasonal migration from Haiti" to "near-by countries," like Cuba and the Dominican Republic, but that in 1937 Batista "expelled thousands of Haitians" from Cuba, and the Dominican Republic "butchered or drowned" as many as 20,000 Haitians (of the 60,000 living in the Dominican Republic in 1937). The recent migrations of the Haitian "boat-people," then, should be understood in this larger historical context.

82. Another strange omission from Hurston's consideration of Haiti's colonial past and republican ambitions is the history of U.S. efforts from the late nineteenth century to the period of U.S. occupation to secure a naval base on Haiti. How the U.S. government failed to get the northwestern harbor of Môle St. Nicholas ceded or, at the very least, leased to it, as Guantanamo was leased by Cuba to the United States, is a chapter in U.S. neoimperialism in the Caribbean of particular importance to African American intellectuals for three reasons: 1) Haiti's consistent refusal to grant the United States this naval base testifies to the importance of Haitian national sovereignty through many different Haitian governments; 2) Frederick Douglass was U.S. minister to Haiti from 1889 to 1891, when U.S. Navy rear admiral Bancroft Gherardi botched negotiations with the Hyppolite government for the naval base, implicating Douglass to a degree that would compel him to resign his post and clarify his role (in an essay in the *North American Review* of October 1891); 3) Haiti's strategic importance in the Caribbean to the United States in preparation for the opening of the Panama Canal. For a succinct account of this history in relation to Frederick Douglass, see William S. McFeely, *Frederick Douglass* (New York: Norton, 1991), 334–58.

83. UN sanctions against the military rulers of Haiti from 1991 to 1994 did little to topple those rulers, who finally had to be removed by U.S. military intervention, but the sanctions did result in destroying Haiti's already fragile economic independence.

84. As I noted earlier, Hurston interprets Damballa as a West African version of Moses, giving Dr. Reser special authority in linking Judeo-Christian and Afro-Caribbean, as well as white and black, religious traditions. In this same passage, Hurston identifies herself with Moses, thereby expanding the social bond between her and Dr. Reser to include religion, as well as transgress gender boundaries.

85. William B. Seabrook, *The Magic Island* (New York: Literary Guild of America, 1929), 171–93. Seabrook's text is illustrated by Alexander King's drawings, which are highly stylized neoprimitivist images of Haitians and Voodoo rites that are obviously racist caricatures. Seabrook, 174, practices a little superstitious magic of his own by arguing that the Catholic priest in Pittston, Pennsylvania, baptized the baby Wirkus "Faustin," recalling Faustin Souloque,

who became president of Haiti in 1847, then proclaimed himself Emperor Faustin I and ruled until 1859, even though Faustin Wirkus's German-American and Polish-French parents knew nothing of Haitian history.

86. Dutton, "The Problem of Invisibility," 141. Unfortunately, Hurston was not entirely successful in distinguishing her work from Seabrook's. Harold Courlander's review of *Tell My Horse* in the *Saturday Review*, 15 October 1938, 6, considers "the sensationalism reminiscent of Seabrook and the anthropology a melange of misinterpretation and exceedingly good folklore."

87. Hemenway, *Zora Neale Hurston*, 230.

88. As if sensitive to this possible allegorization of the insane asylum at Pont Beudet as representing Haitian culture in general, Hurston focuses on a Syrian patient who speaks with Dr. Reser in apparent riddles.

89. Katherine Dunham, *Island Possessed* (Garden City, N.Y.: Doubleday, 1969), vii.

90. Ibid., 20. Dunham goes as far as to suggest that "Doc Reeser" "really hoped to emulate, the creator of the myth of the Magic Island, William Seabrook" (20), taking the opposite tack to Hurston's explicit effort to distinguish Dr. Reser from Seabrook's myth of Faustin Wirkus.

91. Claudia Tate, *Psychoanalysis and Black Novels: Desire and the Protocols of Race* (New York: Oxford University Press, 1998), 148–77, interprets Hurston's *Seraph on the Suwanee* (1948) as a novel about southern whites who speak in African-American dialect, thereby deconstructing racial distinctions maintained by the dominant ideology (and at the same time writing a novel Hurston hoped would sell). In Tate's view, Hurston's celebrated "coding" is often used to subvert "modern racial binary classifications" (169), which is very much what I understand Hurston to be doing with the account of Zora's relations with Dr. Reser and the latter's acceptance by Haitians.

92. Leyburn, *The Haitian People*, 103n4.

93. See Emily Greene Balch, "Memorandum on Haiti," *Beyond Nationalism*, 152. Balch points out that Haitians' "ideas and ways of thinking . . . are French. . . . their attitude is worlds asunder from that of the United States Negroes. They too often think Americans boors, brutal, ignorant and uncaring of literature and ideas, interested only in practical things" (150). Of course, Balch's sharp distinction between French Haitian identity and African-American identity is contrary to Hurston's arguments in *Mules and Men* and *Tell My Horse*.

94. Heinl and Heinl, *Written in Blood*, 487–89. In their efforts to defend the U.S. Marines from the charge of racism, Heinl and Heinl point out that "several treaty civilians (Wilson appointees under a Southern Democratic administration) were Southern" (489).

95. Ibid., 239. Leyburn, *The Haitian People*, 226: "In the North these professional guerilla warriors were known as *cacos*, in the South as *piquets*. . . . They were a constant menace to the peace, and their suppression was one of the announced purposes of the American Occupation, for every revolutionary chief felt it necessary to hire their services."

96. Ibid., 449–63. Not surprisingly, Heinl and Heinl treat the Caco Rebellion as primarily a self-serving insurrection of two local warlords out to make quick profits from the unstable political situation.

97. Reed, *Mumbo Jumbo*, 132. Reed relies heavily on Hurston's *Tell My Horse* (although he uses the English edition, titled *Voodoo Gods: An Inquiry into the Native Myths and Magic in Jamaica and Haiti*, published one year later, in 1939) but seems unaware of the potentially conservative implications of

Hurston's treatment of the U.S. occupation. For Reed, Charlemagne Péralte and Benoît Batraville are clearly heroes of an anti-imperialist rebellion, "VooDoo Generals," in one of his headlines, who continue the heritage of Haitian anti-colonialism that begins with Touissaint L'Ouverture, Dessalines, Christophe, and Rigaud (125). In this latter regard, see *Mumbo Jumbo*, 155.

98. The mistaken confidence that cultural solidarity in and by itself can effect lasting political and social change continues to be made by those who study Haitian society and Voodoo. Thus Fleurant, *Dancing Spirits*, 23, can argue in 1996: "Because of the debilitating context of the social justice system—the peasantry and the urban proletariat have little recourse before the courts—Vodun has emerged as one of the means to tackle sociopolitical oppression. . . . Vodun has become one of the few forces capable of dealing with the country's predicaments. It is a philosophy and way of life that allow for appropriate responses to a historically oppressive and debilitating situation."

99. Hurston, "Crazy for This Democracy," in *A Zora Neale Hurston Reader*, 165–66.

100. Ibid., 166.

Chapter 12

1. Wallace Stevens, "The Comedian as the Letter C," *The Collected Poems of Wallace Stevens* (New York: Knopf, 1972), 30–32, 38, 42. Further references to this poem in the text as C.

2. C. L. R. James, *The Black Jacobins: Toussaint L'Ouverture and the San Domingo Revolution*, 2d ed. (New York: Random House, 1963), 3.

3. John Tomlinson, *Cultural Imperialism: A Critical Introduction* (London: Pinter Publishers, 1991), 175.

4. Ibid., 173.

5. Ibid., 175.

6. Ibid.

7. E. D. Hirsch, Jr., *Cultural Literacy: What Every American Needs to Know* (Boston: Houghton Mifflin, 1987), 70–93; Arthur Schlesinger, Jr., *The Disuniting of America* (New York: Norton, 1992).

8. The political fixer (Robert De Niro) in Barry Levinson's film *Wag the Dog* (1998) says several times in the film, "So what did you *see* day after day of the Gulf War? The one smart bomb falling down a chimney? We shot it in Falls Church, Virginia, a 1/10 scale model." Then he pauses, "At least I *think* we did!" In March 1999 the film was aired on Yugoslavian television as President Milosevic's criticism of the NATO bombardment of Yugoslavian military positions.

Index

Absaroka, 61
Act of Union (1707), 4
Adams, Brooks, 170, 176, 179, 182, 188–189
Adams, Charles Francis, 177, 340n32
Adams, Henry Brooks, x, 19–20, 79, 124, 198, 216, 218–219
   Education, 19–20, 165–193, 219
   Mont-Saint-Michel and Chartres, 168–169, 185
   Tahiti, 166, 186–187, 319n36, 342n52
Adams, John, 20, 83
Adams, John Quincy, 20, 172, 174, 181
Adams, Marion Hooper, 167, 193
Africa, 200, 203, 205, 211, 253–254, 256–257, 260, 265–268, 270, 273, 290
Afrocentrism, 214, 254, 266
Agee, James (with Evans, Walker), *Let Us Now Praise Famous Men*, 21, 257, 349n5
Aguinaldo, Emilio, 124, 186
Ahmed, Mohammed, 127
Alaska, 6, 173
Alien and Sedition Acts (1798), 16, 26, 29, 40, 49, 50, 103, 296
Allen, Theodore, 202, 309n66
Allison, William B., 237

Ambrose, Stephen, 9, 300n18
American Indian Movement, 242, 349n10
American Revolution, 5, 22, 32, 34, 39, 48, 68–69, 78, 81, 103, 125, 151–152, 273, 291, 296
Anderson, Benedict, 4, 12
Anderson, Charles, 82, 84
Anti-Imperialist League, 8, 177, 340nn32–33. *See also* Adams, Charles Francis
Aquinas, St. Thomas, 168–169
Arapahoe, 224
Arawak, 275, 278
Arikara, 60, 62, 63
Aristide, Jean-Bertrand, 284
Aristotle, 207
Armenia, 159–160, 336n52
Assiniboin, 61, 63
Astor, John Jacob, 58–59, 66, 69
Aurelius, Marcus, 207
Axelrod, Alan, 306n23

Balch, Emily Greene, 255, 287
Balzac, Honoré de, 207
Bancroft, Herbert Howe, 119
Batraville, Benoît, 288–289
Bebel, Ferdinand August, 189
Bellamy, Edward, 131, 329n38
Benedict, Ruth, 256, 261
Benfey, Christopher, 148

Benjamin, Walter, 154
Bercovitch, Sacvan, 299n5
Berkhofer, Robert, ix, 6
Berlant, Lauren, xii
Berlin Conference (1884–1885), 132
Berlin, Treaty of (1878), 160
Berryman, John, 147–148
Biddle, Nicholas, 55, 60
Black Elk, Benjamin, 220, 222, 230
Black Elk, Nick, x, 15, 21, 24, 79,
    217–251, 349n10. *See also*
    Neihardt, John G.
Black Hills, 229, 237
Black Hills Council (1875), 237
Blair, Walter, 127
Boas, Franz, 256–258, 261
Boer War, 122, 126, 180
Boi, Paola, 267
Boudinot, Elias, 101
Boxer Rebellion, 86, 122, 174–175,
    203
Braddock, General Edward, 33
Bradfield, Scott, 27, 38–39
Brecht, Bertholt, 214
Bridgman, Richard, 122
Brown, Bill, 160, 163
Brown, Charles Brockden, x, 11–12,
    14, 15, 16–17, 25–51, 79, 103,
    303n1
    "Death of Cicero," 304n13
    Edgar Huntly, 16, 26–28, 31, 34,
    38–51, 310n74
    Memoirs of Carwin, 28
    "Memorandums," 41
    Ormond, 32, 38, 305n22
    "Thessalonica," 304n13
    "Walstein's School of History," 41
    Wieland, 16, 26–40, 44–46,
    306nn36–38
Brown, Gillian, xii
Brown, Joseph Epes, 21
    Sacred Pipe, 220–221, 230, 244
Brown, Kitty, 266. *See also* Hoodoo
Bryan, William Jennings, 124, 179
Buffalo Bill's Wild West Show. *See*
    Cody, William F[rederick]
Burns, Ken, 9, 300n16
Burns, Walter Noble, 118
Byron, Lord George Gordon, 112

Caco Rebellion, 288–289
Californios, 99, 103, 107, 109, 112
Cameron, Elizabeth Sherman, 181,
    183, 193
Cameron, James Donald, 178, 181,
    219
Candomble, 278
Canetti, Elias, 154
Captivity narratives, 45, 48, 78, 87–
    89, 94
Caribbean, 253–257, 267, 270–291,
    293, 302n34
Carnegie, Andrew, 186
Carver, Jonathan, 59
Cassini, Comte, 170
Castle, Terry, xii
Catholicism, 29, 30, 49, 79, 296
    Haitian, 268, 269, 275–276, 283–
    284
    Lakota, 219–220, 222, 228–231,
    351n36
Çelik, Zeynep, 184–185
Cetewayo, king, 156
Chamberlain, Neville, 126
Charles V (Holy Roman Emperor),
    124
Cherokee, 98, 100–103, 106, 109
    Trail of Tears, 22, 101–102
Cheyenne, 224
Cheyfitz, Eric, 10
Chicago Exposition (1893), 185
China, 105, 113–115, 159, 302n34
Chinese Exclusion Acts, 119
Cicero, Marcus Tullius, 30
Cisco Kid, the. *See* Henry, O.
Civil War (American), 18, 19, 20,
    22, 134, 141–146, 151, 155,
    163, 171, 198, 200
Clark, Dora, 147
Clark, William, 9–10, 60, 300n16
Clayton-Bulwer Treaty (1850), 173
Clemit, Pamela, 32
Cleveland, President Grover, 178–
    180
Cody, William F[rederick], 222, 226,
    236, 239
Collier, John, 227–228
Columbus, Christopher, 293–294
Compromise of 1850, 142

Congo Free State. *See* Imperialism, Belgian

Conrad, Joseph, 123–124, 129, 202

Constantinople, Convention of (1888), 173

Cooper, James Fenimore, 34, 355n69

Coues, Elliott, 60

Crane, Dora Taylor, 147

Crane, H[arold] Hart, 233

Crane, Rev. Jonathan Townley, 147

Crane, Stephen, x, 19, 20, 79, 141–163, 282

  "The Blood of the Martyr," 157

  "The Blue Hotel," 148

  "The Bride Comes to Yellow Sky," 148

  "A Foreign Policy in Three Glimpses," 157

  "George's Mother," 150, 157

  Great Battles of the World, 142

  "The Great Boer Trek," 157

  "The King's Favor," 156

  "The Little Stilettos of the Modern Navy," 157

  "Maggie," 150, 157

  "The Monster," 15, 19, 144–163, 337n56

  The Red Badge of Courage, 15, 19, 141–147, 155, 157, 162–163

  "Vashti in the Dark," 155

Craven, Wes, 268

Crazy Horse, 219, 224, 232, 242, 246

Cuba, 124, 135, 139, 147, 155–157, 160, 172, 177–182, 203, 283–285, 296, 363n82

Custer, George Armstrong, 22, 127, 129, 224, 229, 237–238, 242, 250–251

Cuvier, Baron Georges, 62, 70, 72–73, 316n59

Cyprus, Convention of (1878), 160

Damballa. *See* Voodoo, Damballa

Dartiguenave, Philippe Sudre, 288

Davidson, Cathy N., 27

Davies, Acton, 155

Davis, Richard Harding, 146

Davis, Wade, 280

Dawes General Allotment Act (1887), 10, 21, 218, 226–227, 237, 242, 248

Day, William R., 171

Dayan, Joan, 275

Delaware. *See* Lenni-Lenape

DeMallie, Raymond J., 21, 223, 227–228, 247

  Sixth Grandfather, 220–221, 232, 235–236, 239, 241, 243, 250–251

De Mortie, Louise, 212

Deren, Maya, 276–278

Derrick, Scott, xii

Dewey, George, 181

"Diggers," 99–100, 114, 116, 123

Dimock, Wai-Chee, 78–79, 87, 95

Dominican Republic, 155–157, 172, 275, 278

Donovan, Timothy Paul, 170

Dos Passos, John, 21

Douglas, Ann, xii

Douglas, Paul, 287

Douglass, Frederick, 88, 363n82

Drake, Sir Francis, 181

Dreiser, Theodore, 146, 149

Drinnon, Richard, ix, 6, 166, 172, 174–175, 181, 186, 192

Du Bois, W. E. B., x, 15, 20–21, 79, 102, 134, 195–216, 219, 253–254, 284, 345n20, 347n39

  "Africa and the Slave-Trade," 208

  "African Roots of War," 204

  Autobiography, 196

  Black Reconstruction in America, 20, 131, 197–201, 203

  "Conservation of Races," 202

  Dark Princess, 213–214

  Darkwater, 20, 197–198, 200–215

  "Joseph Stalin," 348n52

  Philadelphia Negro, 199

  "Present Outlook for the Dark Races," 202–203

  Quest of the Silver Fleece, 213–214

  The Souls of Black Folk, 15, 20, 131, 197–201, 206–215

  Suppression of the African Slave Trade, 196, 201

Dumas, Alexandre, 207–208, 346n28
Dunham, Katherine, 287
Dutton, Wendy, 268, 280, 285

Eagle Elk, 220, 247
East India Company, 67–69. *See also* Hastings, Warren
Eddy, Spencer, 171
Eliot, T. S., 21, 191, 198, 326n10, 359n36
Elizabeth I, queen (England), 181
Ellison, Ralph, 141, 147, 155
Elm Treaty (1682), 40. *See also* Penn, William
Emerson, Ralph Waldo, 113, 142, 208
Ethiopianism. *See* Afrocentrism
Eugenics. *See* Galton, Francis
Evans, Walker. *See* Agee, James

Fanning, Edmund, 85
Fanon, Frantz, 208
Faulkner, William, 155, 191, 257, 335n35
Ferdinand VII, king (Spain), 183–185
Ferguson, Kate, 212
Fetterman Fight (1866), 231
Fiedler, Leslie, 43, 161
Fire Thunder, 234
Fiske, John, 189
Fliegelman, Jay, 26, 29, 48, 307n47
Fontainebleau, Treaty of (1762), 57
Foreign Miners' Tax (1850), 104–105, 321n31
Foucault, Michel, 11
Franciscans, 99
Franklin, Benjamin, 35–36, 83, 190
Frazer, Sir James George, 275
Frederick II, king (Prussia), 30–32
Free Masons, 16
French and Indian Wars, 22, 30, 32, 41, 57, 304n14
French Revolution, 125, 201

Freud, Sigmund, 147
Fugitive Slave Law, 142
Fugitive slave narrative, 78, 88–89, 94, 153–154

Gallagher, John. *See* Imperialism, free-trade
Galton, Francis, 153
Gardner, Jared, 26, 39, 40, 49–50
Garrison, William Lloyd, 152
Gates, Henry Louis, Jr., 267
Gherardi, Bancroft, 363n82
Ghost Dance, 224, 231, 239–242, 354n56
Gibson, William, 124
Gillman, Susan, 134
Gilman, Sander, 317n20
Gilmore, Michael, 27
Gnadenhütten, Ohio, 34–36
Godwin, William, 31–33, 36, 46, 304n11
Gold Rush, California, 98–100, 102–105, 109–110
Good Neighbor policies. *See* Pan-Americanism
Gordon, Charles George ("Chinese"), 127–129, 132, 328n29
Gould, Jay, 189
Grabo, Norman, 40–41
Grant, President Ulysses S., 225–228
Greco-Turkish War (1897), 142, 155, 157
Green, Thomas Jefferson, 104
Greenblatt, Stephen, 10, 94–95
Guadalupe Hidalgo, Treaty of (1848), 6, 18, 99, 109–110. *See also* Mexican-American War
Gullason, Thomas, 155–156

Haiti, 155–157, 172, 255–256, 268, 274–291, 296, 363n82
classes, 271–272, 275–276
U.S. Occupation (1915–1934), 22, 255, 268, 271, 280–290
See also Voodoo
Hall, James, 355n71
Hall, Kim, 70–71

Hancock, John, 83
Hannibal, 29
Haralson, Eric, xii
Harlem Renaissance, 265, 288. *See also specific artists*
Hassrick, Royal, 245
Hastings, Warren, 67–69, 315n37
Hawaii, 6, 123, 172–173, 181, 203
Hawthorne, Nathaniel, 153–154, 335n30n32
Hay, Clara Stone, 168, 190, 338n8
Hay, John, 9, 19–20, 81, 86, 139, 157, 166–183, 184–185, 187–193, 198, 204, 219, 296, 345n20
Hay-Bunau-Varilla Treaty (1903), 175
Hayes, President Rutherford B., 226
Hay-Herrán Treaty (1903), 175
Hay-Pauncefote Treaty (1901), 174–176, 182–183
Hedges, William, 305n21
Hegel, Georg Wilhelm Friedrich, 12–13, 166, 207–209, 213, 231, 302n28, 313n34, 351n37
Hemenway, Robert, 255, 267, 270, 289
Hemmingway, Beulah, 260
Henry, O. [Porter, William Sydney], 117, 324n65
Herbert, Thomas, 70
Herbert, T. Walter, 79–82, 85–87
Hicks, William, 127
Hirsch, E. D., Jr., 296
Hitell, Theodore, 119
Holler, Clyde, 222, 224, 229, 247
Homestead Law (1862), 225
Hoodoo, African-American, 261, 265–270, 279, 286
Hoover, President Herbert, 283
Horace [Quintus Horatius Flaccus], 30
Horsman, Reginald, ix, x, 6, 7, 8, 54, 69, 104
Howells, William Dean, 18, 131, 139, 156, 176, 182, 195
Hudson's Bay Company, 58

Hume, Levi, 144
Hung Hisu-ch'üan, 128
Hurston, Zora Neale, x, 15, 21–22, 24, 79, 253–291
"Crazy for This Democracy," 272, 290–291
Dust Tracks, 254, 358n25
"How It Feels to Be Colored Me," 263–265, 269
Moses, 266–268
Mules and Men, 15, 21–22, 245, 256–271, 286, 289–291
"Seeing the World as It Is," 272
Seraph on the Suwanee, 364n91
Tell My Horse, 15, 21–22, 255–257, 260–261, 268, 270–291
Their Eyes Were Watching God, 286
"What White Publishers Won't Print," 358n24

Illuminati, 26, 38
Imperialism, Belgian, 138, 165, 193
Imperialism, British, 54–55, 58–59, 65, 74, 157, 180, 183, 195, 237, 273, 295
in Africa, 127–129, 132–133, 156–157, 180
in Asia and South Pacific, 175–176, 179–180, 183, 186, 188, 272
in Caribbean, 174–175, 178–180, 278
in India, 67–70, 122, 203
Imperialism, Dutch, 157, 272
Imperialism, free-trade, xi, 58–60, 74, 131–133, 136
Imperialism, French, 157, 184–186, 237, 272, 276, 278, 290
Imperialism, German, 156–157, 173, 175–176, 180, 189, 195
Imperialism, Russian, 175–176, 180, 188–189
Imperialism, Spanish, 99, 124, 156–157, 160, 175, 178, 182–184, 195, 237, 275, 278, 290, 312n15

Indian laws and policies, federal, 225
   allotment and assimilation period (1871–1928), 219, 226–227, 231, 234, 248
   Indian reorganization period (1928–1945), 219, 227–228, 248
   reservation period (1863–1877), 219, 225–226, 236–237
Indians, praying, 34
Indian Reorganization Act (1934), 21, 218, 224, 227–228, 239, 354n54. *See also* Indian laws and policies, federal
Ingraham, Joseph, 82–83, 85
Irish, 26, 49, 63, 100, 296, 309n66
Iron Hawk, 234, 237–238
Iroquois, 38
Irving, Washington, 17, 55, 58–59, 64, 81

Jacobs, Harriet, 88
Jacobson, Joanne, 171–172
Jamaica, 256–257, 271–274
James, C. L. R., 294
James, Henry, 167–168
Japan, 203, 295, 302n34
Jarauta, Padre Cenobio, 110
Jaurès, Jean Léon, 189
Jefferson, Thomas, 9, 57–60, 172
Joan of Arc, 274
Johannsen, Robert, 111
Johnson, Barbara, 264
Johnson, Samuel, 183
Jordan, Rosan Augusta, 259
Joyce, James, 191

Kant, Immanuel, 95, 108, 212, 347n40
Kaplan, Amy, xii, 337n5
Karcher, Carolyn, 78–80, 89
Kavanagh, James, 82–83
Kell, David, 102
Kelley, Joseph J., Jr., 42–43
King, Clarence, 178
King Philip's War (1675–1676), 88
Kinney, Leila, 184–185
Kipling, Rudyard, 124, 176, 183

Kissinger, Henry, 86, 139, 173
Knife, Andrew, 220
Knox, Henry, 83
Kolodny, Annette, ix, 6
Korean War, 167
Krause, Sydney J., 40–42, 45
Krusenstern, Ivan Federovich, 81

La Farge, John, 166, 181, 186, 193
Lakota, 63, 138, 219, 224–225, 229–231, 233–235, 238–243, 245–251, 355n70
   akicita, 235–236, 242, 351n36
   Heyoka, 235
   ohunkakan, 245
   Sun Dance, 224, 229–230, 244
   Teton, 62–67, 72, 239, 245, 314, 314n35
   Teton Council, 229, 238
   Wakan Tanka, 234–235, 239, 244, 246
   winter-counts, 244–245, 251, 353n51
Land Act of 1851 (California), 99
Leconte, Michel Cincinnatus, 274
Lenin, Nikolai [Vladimir Ilyich Ulyanov], 129, 204
Lenni-Lenape, 8, 9, 16, 17, 39–47, 49–50
Leveau, Marie, 266, 269. *See also* Hoodoo
Levine, Robert, 26, 38–39
Lewis and Clark expedition, xi, 9–10, 17, 55, 57–66, 301n18. *See also* Lewis, Meriwether and Clark, William
Lewis, David Levering, 208
Lewis, Meriwether, 9–10, 57–58, 60, 65, 313n20
Limerick, Patricia Nelson, 6, 343n2
Lindebner, Father Joseph, 230
Little Big Horn, Battle of (1876). *See* Custer, George Armstrong
Lodge, Henry Cabot, 167, 178–179, 188
Long, David, 81, 83–84
Looks Twice, Lucy, 222, 229–230
Louis XVIII, king (France), 183–184

Louisiana Purchase, 6, 9–10, 17, 22, 49, 57–58, 312n15
L'Ouverture, Toussaint, 271, 280, 291
Love, Harry, 109–110, 322n45
Lucian, 30
Lyotard, Jean-François, 353n51

McCrea, Jane, 48
McCulley, Johnston, 117, 324–325n65
McKay, Nellie, 210, 213
McKinley, President William, 124, 126, 157, 166, 171, 174, 176, 179, 182, 189–192, 296, 341n41
Mackenzie, Sir Alexander, 55
Maddox, Lucy, 218
Madison, James, 83–85
Mailer, Norman, 148
maroonage, 273–274, 277–278, 286
Marquesas, 78, 80–85, 90–95
Marshall, Edward, 43
Marxism, 134, 146, 196, 198, 205, 215, 284, 289
Mason, Charlotte Osgood, 256
Mather, Cotton, 87
Medill, Joseph, 281
Meisenhelder, Susan, 262
Melville, Herman, x, 17–18, 24
    "Bartleby," 95
    Benito Cereno, 82–83, 95, 124
    Billy Budd, 88
    Confidence-Man, 355n71
    Mardi, 87
    Omoo, 87–89, 95
    Pierre, 81, 95
    Typee, 15, 17, 77–96, 124
Mendaña y Castro, Alvaro de, 82
Meriam Report, 227. See also Indian Reorganization Act.
Mexican-American War, 5, 14, 18, 22, 55, 98–99, 103–106, 113, 203, 296, 345n20
Mexico, 100, 104–107, 111, 117, 158, 187, 272, 293, 296, 300n10, 345n20
Michaux, André, 59–60, 313n21
Miller, Joaquin, 117

Mommsen, Wolfgang, 131
Monroe Doctrine, 4, 11, 178–179, 272, 283
Monroe, James, 83, 172
Montaigne, Michel [Eyquem] de, 95
Moravians, 34, 35
Morrison, Toni, 151, 187
Moses, 266–268, 286. See also "Hurston, Moses" and "Voodoo, Damballa"
Murieta, Joaquín, 118–119

Nahl, Charles C., 116–117
Napoleon Bonaparte, 57, 160, 184–185, 291
Narragansett, 88
Nation, 280–282
National Association for the Advancement of Colored People (NAACP), 280–282
Native Americans. See specific tribe or group
Navajo, 233
Neihardt, Enid, 220
Neihardt, Hilda, 220
Neihardt, John G., x, 21, 24, 79, 220–251
    Black Elk Speaks, 220–251
    A Cyle of the West, 223–224, 227, 232–233, 243
    Indian Tales, 233
    When the Tree Flowered, 220–221, 228, 230–231, 234, 243–251
    See also Black Elk, Nick
Nelson, Cary, 302n36, 303n38
Neruda, Pablo, 118
New Echota Treaty (1835), 101
New Orleans, Battle of, (1815)
New Orleans, city of, 256, 265, 268–269, 270
Nietzsche, Friedrich, 208, 359n36
Norris, Frank, 149
North, Oliver, 139
Northwest Territory, 59
Nygaard, Loisa, 71–72

Oklahoma Territory. See Cherokee
Omaha, 233

Open Door policy, x, 4, 11, 81, 86, 173–175, 181, 296, 345n20. *See also* Hay, John
Oregon Territory, 17, 22, 54, 57–59, 69, 312n14, 319n5
Owens, Louis, 102, 115

Pai Shang-ti Hui, 128
Paiute, 240
Pamunkey, 233
Pan-African congresses, 208
Panama Canal, 86, 173–175, 189, 285
Pan-Americanism, 22, 272, 290
Pan-Indian movement, 239, 242
Panther (Wyandot), 48
Panther, Abraham, 48
Paredes, Americo, 110
Parins, James, 101–102
Paris expositions, 184–185
Parry, J[ohn] H[orace], 10
Pasteur, Louis, 279
Pauncefote [of Preston], Sir Julian P., 170, 173
Paxton Boys, 35–36, 38
Payne, Howard, 101
Peace Policy. *See* Grant, President Ulysses S.
Pearce, Roy Harvey, ix, 39
Penn, John, 17, 41–42, 45, 50
Penn, Thomas, 17, 41–42, 45, 50
Penn, William, 40–42, 45, 50
Péralte, Charlemagne Masséna, 288–289
Persian Gulf War, 138, 167
Philippine-American War, 6, 9, 22, 86, 124–126, 128, 177, 180–181, 186, 218–219, 302n34
Philippines, 121–122, 124, 135, 138–139, 147, 157, 176–177, 181, 183, 186, 203, 296, 327n13
Pierre, Anatol, 266. *See also* Hoodoo
Pitt, Leonard, 105
Plains Wars, 219, 223, 232, 239, 244, 249
Plessy v. Ferguson (1896), 142, 147, 200
Pocahontas, 233

Poe, Edgar Allan, x, 14, 17, 50–51, 53–75, 79, 95
"The Gold-Bug," 56
"Hop-Frog," 17, 70, 73–74
"The Journal of Julius Rodman," 17, 55–67, 69–70, 74, 309n70
"The Man of the Crowd," 70
"The Murders in the Rue Morgue," 17, 69–74
Narrative of Arthur Gordon Pym, 55, 61–62, 65–66, 69, 74, 309n70
"Never Bet the Devil Your Head," 313n23
"The Purloined Letter," 70, 73
"A Tale of the Ragged Mountains," 17, 55, 67–70
Pollin, Burton, 57, 58, 63
Pomo, 233
Porter, Carolyn, 192
Porter, David, 9, 17, 78, 80, 82–87, 89
Portsmouth Treaty (1905), 86, 170, 188, 192, 345n20
Post-structuralism, 74–75, 258
Pound, Ezra, 21, 191, 198, 326n10
Pratt, Mary Louise, 10, 14, 351n38
Preval, René, 284
Prosser, Gabriel, 151
Prucha, Francis Paul, 226, 228, 239–240
Puerto Rico, 157, 180–181, 203
Puritanism (American), 12, 89, 159, 273

Quesada, Gonzalo de, 178
Quinn, Patrick, 66

Rampersad, Arnold, 199
Red Cloud, 224, 232, 242
Reed, Ishmael, 267, 288–289
Reid, Whitelaw, 186
Ricardou, Jean, 66
Rice, Julian, 225
Ridge, Elizabeth Wilson, 102
Ridge, John, 101
Ridge, John Rollin (Yellow Bird), x, 14, 79, 323n48, 324n54
Joaquín Murieta, 15, 18, 97–119, 218

Ridge, Major (The Ridge), 101
Robinson, Forrest, 122, 125
Robinson, Ronald. *See* Imperialism, free-trade
Rogin, Michael Paul, 6
Roman Empire, 92, 124, 187
Roosevelt, President Franklin D., 283, 290
Roosevelt, President Theodore, 166, 168, 170–172, 174, 182, 186, 188–190, 296
Rosebud, Battle of (1876), 237–238
Rosenheim, Shawn, 71–72
Ross, John, 101–102, 111
Rowe, John Carlos, 70, 259, 302n33
Rowlandson, Mary, 48, 87–88
Royce, Josiah, 105
Rubens, Horatio, 178
Russo-Japanese War (1904–1905), 86, 122, 169–171, 188, 203, 345n20
Russo-Turkish wars (1768–1774; 1787–1792), 32, 305n22, 327n21

Said, Edward, 3–4, 8–9, 13–14, 15
St. Louis, riots in (1917), 206
Sam, Vilbrun Guillaume, 280,289
Samuels, Ernest, 167–168, 171
Samuels, Shirley, 31
San Ildefonso, treaty of (1800), 57
Santería, 278
Schlesinger, Arthur, Jr., 296
Scott, Winfield, 110
Seabrook, William, 285–286, 363n85
Sedgwick, Eve Kosofsky, xii
Seligman, Herbert J., 280
Seltzer, Mark, 145–146, 162
Seven Years' War (1756–1763), 30, 32. *See also* French and Indian Wars
Seward, William H., 172–174
Shakespeare, William, 44, 207
Shoshone, 61
Silverman, Kenneth, 56
Simon, Celestina, 274
Simon, Francois Antoine, 274
Singh, Chait, 67–68

Sioux. *See* Lakota.
Sitting Bull, 224, 237
Slotkin, Richard, ix, 6, 11, 15, 38–39, 43, 45, 48, 127, 131, 134, 307n47
Smith, Adam, 131
Smith, Henry Nash, 130, 135–136
Smith, Sidonie, 358n25
Spanish-American War, 6, 9, 19, 22, 86, 122, 124, 128, 155–158, 160, 169, 171, 176–177, 179–181, 184, 186, 192, 195–196, 202–203, 218–219, 302n34
Stalinism, 20, 196, 215
Stallman, R[obert] W[ooster], 144, 151, 155
Standing Bear, 234–235, 237–238
Steltenkamp, Michael F., 222, 224, 228, 230
Stern, Julia, xii, 29, 31
Stevens, Wallace, 197, 233, 293–294
Stevenson, Frances Van de Grift, 187, 342n52
Stevenson, Robert Louis, 187, 342n52
Stewart, Reverend Charles, 80, 84
Story, William Wetmore, 167–168
Stowe, Harriet Beecher, 151, 334n24
Strachey, Lytton, 128–129
Streeby, Shelley, 99
Sudan, 127–129, 132
Suez Canal, 173
Suffrage, women's, 210
Sundquist, Eric, 56, 102, 123, 198, 204, 208

Taiping Rebellion, 22, 86, 128
Takaki, Ronald, xii, 6, 113, 127, 137, 301n21
Tejon, 114–115
Teton Council. *See* Lakota
Texas, 104–105
Thayer, William Roscoe, 172, 190
Theweleit, Klaus, 146
Thies, Albert G., 156
Thomas, Brook, 83
Todorov, Tzvetan, 10, 44

Tomlinson, John, 295–296

Tompkins, Jane, xii, 37–38

Topsell, Edward, 70–71

Townsend, John K., 55

Trajan [Marcus Ulpius Trajanus], 92, 319n35

Trocadero, Fort (Spain), 183–184

Trocadero, Place du (Paris), 183–185

Trollope, Anthony, 187, 310n78

Trumbull, John, 151–152, 334n27

Truth, Sojourner, 212

Tubman, Harriet, 212

Turkey, 157, 159–160

Turner, Luke, 266, 268–269. *See also* Hoodoo

Turner, Nat, 151

Tuscarora, 150, 334n22

Tuskegee Institute. *See* Washington, Booker T.

Twain, Mark, 15, 18–19, 24, 79, 156, 182, 195–196, 254, 302n34

(with Bret Harte) *Ah Sin*, 321n33

A Connecticut Yankee, 18–19, 121–139, 202

"The Czar's Soliloquy," 122

"A Defense of General Funston," 122

"The Dervish and the Offensive Stranger," 328n31

"The Fable of the Yellow Terror," 132

Following the Equator, 122, 125–126, 134

(with Warner, Charles Dudley), *The Gilded Age*, 136

"The Great Revolution in Pitcairn," 330n53

Huckleberry Finn, 135, 142, 151, 190

"King Leopold's Soliloquy," 122, 133, 165–166, 193

"To the Person Sitting in Darkness," 122, 126, 137

Pudd'nhead Wilson, 135, 332n10

Roughing It, 123, 321n33

Tom Sawyer, 138

Union Patriotique, 281

Valenzuela, Joaquín, 110

Van Alstyne, Richard, 4, 5

Varley, James, 118

Vasquez, Tiburcio, 323n47

Vesey, Denmark, 151

Victoria, queen (England), 175

Vidal, Gore, 172

Vietnam war, ix, xi, 118, 138, 167, 171, 176, 288, 291, 296, 301n18, 302n34, 331n54, 349n10

Vincent, Sténio, 280–281

Voodoo, Caribbean, 266, 270, 272–291

bocor, 276

Damballa, 267, 275, 285

Erzulie, 275–276, 289

Guedé, 278, 287

houngan, 276

loas, 276–277, 286

mambo, 274–276

Ogoun, 275, 289

Papa Legba, 275

Petro (gods), 277

Rada (gods), 267, 277

Zombies, 279–280

See also "Haiti," "Hoodoo, African-American," and "Jamaica"

Wagon Box Fight (1867), 243–244

Wakan Tanka. See Lakota

Walker, Alice, 262

Walker, Cheryl, 108, 115, 117

Walking Purchase (1737), 9, 17, 41–43, 50. *See also* Lenni-Lenape

Wallam Olum, 42, 303n1, 308n58

War of 1812, 22, 78, 82–85, 142

Washington, Booker T., 201

Watie, Stand, 101

Watson, Father ("Frizzly Rooster"), 266, 269, 277. *See also* Hoodoo

Watts, Steven, 49

Wheatley, Phillis, 210, 212

Wieland, Christoph Martin, 30

Williams, Raymond, 13

Williams, William Carlos, 359n36
Wilson, Harriet, 88
Wilson, Jack. *See* Wovoka
Wilson, President Woodrow, 204
Wirkus, Faustin, 285–286, 363–364n85
Work, Hubert, 227
World War I, 166, 341n42
World War II, 132, 282, 290–291, 297–298
Wounded Knee, Massacre at (1890), 22, 139, 218, 223, 228, 231, 239–240

Wovoka, 231, 240–242. *See also* Ghost Dance
Wyalusing, Pennsylvania, 34, 36, 38
Wyandot, 48

XYZ Affair, 22

Yates, James, 33, 46, 306n23
Yellow Bird. *See* Ridge, John Rollin
Yoruba, 267

Zamor, Oreste, 280, 288
Zorro. *See* McCulley, Johnston